ESTEEM ENLIVENED BY DESIRE

Esteem Enlivened by Desire

THE COUPLE FROM HOMER TO SHAKESPEARE

JEAN H. HAGSTRUM

THE UNIVERSITY OF CHICAGO PRESS
Chicago & London

JEAN HAGSTRUM is the author of *Sex and Sensibility: Ideal and Erotic Love from Milton to Mozart,* published by the University of Chicago Press.

This book was published with the generous assistance of Samuel R. Rosenthal.

ISBN (cloth): 0-226-31287-9

Library of Congress Cataloging-in-Publication Data

Hagstrum, Jean H.
    Esteem enlivened by desire : the couple from Homer to Shakespeare
/ Jean H. Hagstrum.
        p.   cm.
    Includes bibliographical references and index.
    ISBN 0-226-31287-9
    1. Marriage in literature.   2. Love in literature.   3. Sex in
literature.   4. Marriage in art.   5. Love in art.   6. Sex in art.
I. Title.
PN56.M28H34   1992
809'.93354—dc20   91-43353
                                                           CIP

⊛ The paper used in this publication meets the minimum requirements of the American National Standard for Information Sciences—Permanence of Paper for Printed Library Materials, ANSI Z39.48-1984.

To my brothers: Homer, Vincent, and the memory of Paul

But happy they! the happiest of their kind! . . .
Attuning all their passions into love; . . .
Where friendship full-exerts her softest power,
Perfect esteem enlivened by desire.

James Thomson, "Spring" in *The Seasons* (1728)

CONTENTS

ILLUSTRATIONS

*The sciences have been much hurt by pusillanimity,
and the slenderness of the tasks men have proposed
themselves.*

Francis Bacon

y intention in the book that follows is to study the couple in the art and literature of Western antiquity, the
Middle Ages, and the Renaissance, periods more hierarchical than any I have hitherto investigated intensively. I have already written about the eighteenth century (in *Sex and
Sensibility: Ideal and Erotic Love from Milton to Mozart,* 1980, and in
Eros and Vision: The Restoration to Romanticism, 1989)—a period of
great change, of secularization, and of a kind of founding modernism. I
have also explored the matter of sexuality among major Romantic poets
in England (in *The Romantic Body,* 1985), a literature of great intensity,
subtlety, and originality with respect to love, and also one with a striking
and perhaps surprising affinity for the values behind marriage, at least for
what the ideal embodies. That work has been done—at least as well as I
am capable of doing it. The great contributions of the nineteenth and
twentieth centuries to my theme will have to be studied by others, who
are already approaching the subject in strength and in numbers.

To some the present project will seem to possess an ambition that is
excessive and unseemly. In defense I can only say that I have not been
able for the past decade or so to shake off my preoccupation with the
theme in the earlier periods. One reason is that I remain curious about
whether these periods were indeed as cold and calculating about long-
term coupling as commentators on later periods (including myself) have
said or implied. Another is that belles lettres must now be seen in relation
to an impressive body of mid and late twentieth-century social history
concerned with love and the family, to new formulations in intellectual
history, and to recent approaches to myth, ritual, and religion. Finally, the
question has continued to nag: Should not contemporary social science

and movements like feminism take full and detailed—if not necessarily respectful—cognizance of the Western heritage regarding unions of esteem and desire, even though much of it resides less in actual achievement than in artistic imaginings?

I hope my readers will bear in mind the large historical and intellectual contexts to which I have just alluded, but I hope they will also remember the limitations, distinctions, and exclusions I shall now make, admittedly somewhat too categorically and dogmatically. The primary emphasis of this study will be on the heterosexual couple, but this by no means implies that I exclude value and pleasure from other modes of sexuality. Though drawing upon history, I am concerned primarily with literature and art—that is, with a highly structured and already edited form of reality. And finally I am fundamentally concerned with expression not in its social or political aspects—that is, with political oratory and rhetoric—but in its most energetic, influential, lasting, and humanly revealing forms. These are the product of mind-altering imaginations that have had the power to transcend the culture of their origins and to influence women and men in vastly different venues and environments.

In introducing imagination, I remind the reader of the Greek critical category of the *plastic,* or *plasmatic,* as distinguished from the *true* and the *false,* the *plasmatic* presenting things as they conceivably could be.[1] I shall have a good deal more to say later about this topic, which is important enough to be given this introductory illustration. It comes from Montaigne, writing in the late sixteenth century and commenting on *his* intellectual heritage from antiquity. In his famous essay on friendship he makes a sharp distinction between it and love, separating both from marriage, and he alludes teasingly and suggestively to centuries of thought and practice concerning intersexual relationships. For him marriage is primarily a bargain ordinarily made for ends other than love. Purposes like money, political alliance, and the rewarding stability of success in life tend to dominate. Moreover, marriage "is a bargain to which only the entrance is free—its continuance being constrained and forced, depending otherwise than on our will." But then Montaigne goes on to *imagine* an ideal of love and friendship combined: "If such a relationship, free and voluntary, could be built up in which not only would the souls have this complete enjoyment but the bodies would also share in the alliance, so that the entire man would be engaged, it is certain that the resulting friendship would be fuller and more complete. But [the female] sex in no instance has yet succeeded in attaining [such friendship] and by the common agreement of the ancient schools is excluded from it." If Montaigne is only fractionally right in summarizing the Western tradition, feminists and their sympathizers have their work cut out for them in destroying age-old stereotypes.[2]

But had the witty Frenchman followed his own implicit lead and examined thoroughly the *imagined* possibilities of body-soul friendship that appear in literature and art, he might have reached a different or at least a somewhat modified conclusion about the past. Whatever the truth about Montaigne himself, his offhand comment raises serious concerns for the modern scholar, who must disclose the energy and the effectual emotional workings of what he studies in order to demonstrate how it structures desire, how it mythologizes reality, how it challenges whatever status quo surrounds it, and how it piques the mind into dreaming dreams and seeing visions. For such mythologized reality takes its place in the landscape of our antecedent cultures and influences us as much as historically authenticated events, leaders, and movements; it therefore deserves a place in our contemporary literary and artistic canons. The rationale of my study lies precisely here.

The ordering of chapters in this study mostly follows a chronological scheme, and there consequently lurks the danger of allowing history to compromise the coherence or even the visibility of theme. I therefore call attention to the following thematic treatments, which often fuse with each other and undergo change in and of themselves but each of which should nevertheless be regarded as a kind of continuity.

1. The first and most important is signaled by the title of this book, the *union of esteem and sexual desire,* an amazing collocation if one thinks about it. I believe that its imaginative renditions along with its intellectual formulations constitute one of the great achievements of Western culture. But that union did not come easily. Esteem had to be divorced from an all-male context, and sexuality from the stigma of sin or excess. The latter task was sometimes thwarted but sometimes aided by religion itself—by pagan and Hebrew myth and legend, by a powerful tradition of *Christian naturalism* or even *sensualism.*

2. Integrally related to uniting esteem and desire is the notion (sometimes only an intuitive sense) that marriage or other long-term relationship represents a *pacification* after earlier, sometimes only implied, struggle— what Bacon in "Of Friendship" called "peace in the affections," an emotional settlement, as it were.

3. Such a settlement is vastly different from the usual one of dowry, gift, or material endowment, and the reader must be alert to the fact that *marriage of choice* often struggles against political, dynastic, or other forms of *arranged partnership.*

4. Historically, the nuclear marriage of individual choice had little

chance of success until *romantic or love marriage,* often based on a sudden, overwhelming attraction that was believed to establish unshakable bonds, came to be greatly valorized and privileged.

5. Such love, such unions, had to compete with other forms of amorous satisfaction, prostitution, to name but one. *Love vs. lust* was indeed a deep and wide obsession. But in traditional Western culture the most persistent contrast may well be the one drawn between *friendship and love,* perhaps because it was early associated with a less abstract antithesis, the contrast between *heterosexual and homosexual love.* This comparison was often strenuously and formally drawn, and it sometimes, as in Shakespeare, warrants being called a contest, or *paragone.* One reason for the importance of this theme is that when esteem united with desire in marriage, the new fusion could easily challenge other arrangements (like all-male friendship, for example) that had traditionally been accorded the highest privilege.

6. Some of the topics summarized above suggest illuminating parallels or antitheses to my main topic, long-term amorous commitment, which usually implies physical consummation. One cluster of these related but different kinds of love requires special mention: long-term relations that remain *unconsummated,* valorizing delayed or obviated climax, prolonged *foreplay,* ascetic discipline, traditional *Platonic* or *Petrarchan love,* or various forms of *sublimation.* This last, in at least some of its forms, is dialectically and psychologically tied to my main theme: it is one kind of long-term love relationship with often more than a tinge of the erotic, as Augustine's *Confessions* powerfully demonstrates, a filament in the life-strand of my theme that I have found it impossible to separate out. Thus works of one or another kind of denial remain prominent and permanent features of our cultural landscape.

Placed in juxtaposition with my texts of fulfillment in love, all of the above six topics are mutually illuminating aspects of long-term affectionate commitment. Thus I regularly explore not only marriage per se but motifs that stand, as it were, in its penumbra and enrich its significance.

I hope my intellectual debts will be acknowledged in text and notes. By all odds the two most fruitful academic years during the production of this book were those spent at the National Humanities Center in Research Triangle Park, North Carolina, where I read, wrote, conversed, and delivered four lectures on subjects much more fully treated in the ensuing pages. I am deeply grateful to the stimulation provided by fellows, staff, and visitors to the Center, particularly those who edited (David Halperin, Robert Edwards, Stepher Spector, James Turner) and contributed to the three books on antiquity, the Middle Ages, and the Renaissance that have grown out of the conferences I arranged. I also benefited from a later conference at the center on the aesthetic and philosophical theory relevant to my topic, and from my five-week stay at the Villa Serbelloni, the Rockefeller Foundation's center in Bellagio on Lake Como, Italy, where I wrote the preface and rewrote the introduction and had a chance to have my ideas discussed. The many audiences I have addressed on versions of this topic, partly as a visiting Phi Beta Kappa scholar, provided stimulating responses. I acknowledge with pleasure the intellectual stimulation and the financial research support provided by the English Department and the College of Arts and Sciences, of Northwestern University. The chairman during seven of the years that went into the making of this book, Martin Mueller, has been highly supportive, as has the friendly and skillful staff, particularly Mary Cameron and Kathleen Daniels, who have helped me in computer-related problems. I am also grateful to the library of the Garrett Evangelical Theological Seminary in Evanston. As always, I have been well served by the Northwestern University Library, particularly by Rolf Erickson, Charles Fineman, Russell Maylone, Mette Shayne, and Ya'aquov Ziso (who has helped me with Hebrew biblical texts). I gave courses on love in the Western world at both the Folger Shakespeare Library and the University of Delhi, receiving "organized" stimulation in the form of papers and discussion from my students and colleagues. Not only libraries but art museums and galleries the world over have displayed their usual courtesy as well as their precious wares, and their help is acknowledged in the notes and in the figure captions. The following have contributed valuable kinds of intellectual aid, each different from the others: Alfred Appel, Annette Baier, Christelle L. Baskins, Elizabeth Clark, Marcia Colish, Loring Danforth, C. J. Dyck, Paul Elmen, Victor Fuchs, Darryl Gless, Gerald Graff, Cyrus Hamlin, Herbert Hrachovek, Thorkild Jacobsen, Constance Jordan, Eva Keuls, Richard Kieckhefer, Christopher Kleinhenz, Heinz Kuehn, Maynard Mack, Rebecca Martin, Gary Saul Morson, the Reverend David L. Myers, Dr. S. Nakos, John O'Connor, Shalom Perlman, Naomi Quinn, Mary Beth Rose, David Sanford, George A. Sheets and the computer program at the University of Minnesota known as IBYCUS, James Sledd, Lawrence Stone, Joan Thirsk, Ali Töre (an undergraduate in the Humanities College of Northwestern, who helped in securing illustrations from Turkey), A. D. Trendall, Raymond Van Dam, Wendy Wall, Aubrey Williams. I make special mention of Moody Prior, who has been my earliest and best reader; he has generously responded to everything I have previously published on this subject and specifically to the lectures and papers that have been expanded into the present book, and he has given me valuable help on the Shakespeare sections. How can one sufficiently thank fellow scholars who have taken the time to read the entire manuscript—or substantial portions of it—in draft form and give it their best scholarly and literary attention? I can only say that Rupin Desai, Lawrence Lipking, Victor Matthews, Martin Mueller, Barbara Newman, and Stuart Small deserve vastly more than the conventional exoneration from remaining errors and infelicities, for which I alone must stand at the bar of judgment. Since much in this book testifies to influences springing ultimately from my parental home, I think it is fitting that I dedicate this book to my brothers, who have always given me staunch support in my work even though they themselves took other paths.

ESTEEM ENLIVENED BY DESIRE

The unentranced vision of the flesh and the heart—
the dying tremulous flesh, the secretive divided
heart—need not destroy [the highest] love.

Roberto Unger, *Passion: An Essay on*
Personality (1984)

ONE

Introduction

*T*his is a book largely but by no means exclusively about marriage, still an established institution for millions. The very subject may therefore strike many as running counter to contemporary sensibility, which tends to favor dark over well-lighted places, "sin" over "virtue." Shelby Foote, the distinguished narrator of the American Civil War, confesses to gratitude for the presence in his story of the somewhat less than noble Stanton, Lincoln's secretary of war: "I was absolutely delighted every time he walked into the book, because of what he could lend the book in the way of narrative drive."[1] There will be abundant opportunity for the "delights" of realistic complication and tragic outcomes in the pages that follow. But I cannot resist saying that in addition to being grateful that men sin that the grace of fiction and poetry may abound, we should also be aware that colorful evil would lose much of its appeal without colorless good. T. S. Eliot saw clearly how much blasphemy depended upon orthodoxy, and surely adultery would long since have lost its poignancy had it not been for the ideal of marital fidelity. We demystify ideals at the risk of impoverishing art—and of course much else in our culture. I flatter myself that there has to be my kind of book on the scholarly landscape; others of a different kidney will provide other perspectives, and welcome ones, for the subject is vast and complex.

Though it is sought by fewer than formerly and terminated by more, marriage is still the commonest outward and visible sign of some kind of inward erotic grace, now largely secularized. Attitudes within our culture toward this venerable, almost universally known, and still widely respected institution range from sentimental overevaluation to harsh denigration and also to both ad hoc and systematized hostility. Perhaps most contemporary Americans, at least those in their earlier years, believe—or strongly want to believe—that intense, involuntary love, with powerful propulsions toward exclusive intimacy and with hearty expectations that such love can fully meet mutual needs, will be unending. Why such high hopes and intense expectations should attend what George Bernard Shaw called union for life with a half-stranger I shall not inquire here. But the prevalence and power of love marriage over various traditional forms is attested by what is happening in the church, notoriously slow to change but ultimately reflective of powerful or irresistible forces. Of religious redefinitions of the marital I give but one example. In a stunning change of emphasis the Anglican *Book of Common Prayer* seems to have embraced the ideal of amorous friendship in marriage. The version of 1662 (I could have chosen virtually any version from the late sixteenth century on to almost the present) says marriage is "for the procreation of children" and "for a remedy against sin and to avoid fornication, that such persons as have not the gift of continency might marry and keep themselves undefiled members of Christ's body." But in the 1980 edition men and women are said to marry "that with delight and tenderness [dare we say "sex and sensibility"?] they may know each other in love, and through the joy of their bodily union, may strengthen the union of their hearts and lives."

On the other hand, our own age is by no means solely animated by sentimental overevaluation. Influenced by powerful tendencies in the nineteenth century, it has mounted fierce and unrelenting attacks on the institution of marriage and produced countertendencies with power to compel. I give but two examples, one of an organized intellectual movement, the other of a sensibility. Marx and Engels, following many earlier nineteenth-century leads, initiated what has come to be an organized or systematic attack on romance and marriage. Monogamy embodied the earliest type of class oppression known to history. "Monogamous marriage," said Engels, "comes on the scene as the subjugation of one sex by the other," a condition of domestic slavery that he thought had continued up to his own day. Some feminists have adopted an aggressive form of Marxism in approaching this subject, though there are of course many varying points of view.[2]

Marxist and feminist thought seems often to have sought an accommodation with the values that underlie traditional marriage, but some modern sensibility turns away in disgust from man-woman intimacy as it has been institutionalized and internalized. Edmund Leach finds the family, "with its narrow privacy and tawdry secrets," to be "the source of all our discontent."[3] And Roland Barthes says that he has always regarded the domestic scene as "a pure experience of violence. . . . The retorts engender one another, without any possible conclusion, save that of murder." The home is constituted of "an essential violence which delights in sustaining itself."[4] Such statements express less thought than sensibility. They represent a neat, almost exquisite, reversal of what we find in a Dickens or in a Tolstoy at their most optimistically or conventionally idealistic. They may do more to chill amorous expectations than even the attacks of the reformatory movements and of course may in part either underlie or reinforce the programs of systematic hostility. But even when there is little programmatic or dogmatic hostility, and when the countertendencies to marriage do not seem compelling, many sophisticated contemporary mates who wish and need to dance "the olde daunce" do so to different pipers.[5]

Obviously if my analysis of the present scene has been even partially correct, contemporary society is in a state of deep division about the romantic legacy. Any attempt to revitalize or even study it sympathetically is bound to be met with tension and dismay on the one side (perhaps especially among the sophisticated), while on the other the satisfied or the complacent may want to ignore paradoxes and contradictions that do not soothe ears itching to hear stable truths told with flattering assurances. The present division and unrest may seem to call for a rhetoric and a method of proceeding that favors antithesis and paradox, if not outright deconstruction of aesthetic order and the demystification of idealism. I hope this book will faithfully represent the contradictory and the inconsistent when they appear overtly or implicitly in the texts analyzed and will dig deep into ambiguity and ambivalence. For our heritage has not always come to us in Spenserian stanzas or celebratory epithalamia. Earlier artists and critics have found the oxymoron, sometimes bitterly constructed, an almost inevitable literary and rhetorical device in treating the subject of love and even—or perhaps especially—marriage.

Our Heritage and How It Can Be Described

I shall be concerned in this book with the Western literary and artistic heritage regarding the loving couple. But what specifically is a heritage? Of what does it consist?

First, I certainly include what actually happened, to the extent that this can be determined, and I have drawn heavily on relevant *social history,* which in recent years has made love and marriage a major concern. Art is of course never a replication of external, factual reality, which is, however, its matrix and so inevitably one of the chief preoccupations of its creators. "Do I have it right?" is their obsessive question even when they know they can never get it right. Nor do they really wish to. As Donald Barthelme says in a brilliant essay, "art thinks ever of the world, cannot not think of the world, could not turn its back on the world even if it wished to." But as he also says, "art is always a meditation upon external reality rather than a representation of external reality or a jackleg attempt to 'be' external reality."[6]

But many social historians do wish, desperately, to discover the social facts that concern intimacy, and some of them have, it seems to me, succeeded beyond their predecessors of any previous generation. To these impressive achievements I have paid respectful heed and given much devoted attention. But for the literary critic, using history is not merely adapting the insights of historians to given works of art but sensing how deeply fused are historical data and imaginative insights. I have often turned away from obviously illustrative texts to more complex works, where my theme is obscured, even dirtied, by the soil of historical and personal experience out of which living literature grows. Thus I choose for extended analysis Ovid's *Metamorphoses* over his *Heroides,* Boccaccio's comedy of life over his allegories, the Wife of Bath's Tale over the Franklin's, or Shakespeare's portrayals of love under extreme stress in the tragedies and tragicomedies as well as his treatment of courtship in the comedies.

Second, *intellectual codifications*—statements by and about philosophers and theologians—are certainly easier than historical data to come by and apply, though by no means easier to understand or interpret, and I have benefited by the comprehensive and impressive analyses of Irving Singer on thinkers and writers from antiquity to the present.[7] Such codifications are of the utmost interest even when they did not, or do not now, possess regulative force. In our own day we know by statistics how indifferently and independently even the religiously committed respond to decrees about birth control and abortion. And the past, though in some epochs more accustomed to obedience than in the present, must have seen to it—quite often enough to complicate matters!—that practice differed from precept. Even so, both exploratory and regulative thought are of the highest relevance, not least theology. For although I shall exclude *agapē* (God's love of man) and man's love of God from direct study, religion is everywhere implicated in intimate human relationships, and therefore what was thought and felt to be God's rule for purely human love is of central interest. For the purposes of this study, I am close to Ludwig Feuerbach's position that in essence "theology is anthropology"—that theosophy (in its etymological sense) is the "deified essence of man," that religion can be viewed as fundamentally the history of man. Thus the basic difference between a pagan god and the Jewish or Christian God is the difference between a pagan individual and a Jew or a Christian.[8]

Third, and perhaps even more important but also certainly more elusive than philosophical or theological codifications, are the *mythological tales and orderings* revealed in sacred writ, in early epic, in even the unwritten sagas of a people's identity. These reflect practice more than precept, although in their written forms they can of course become codes and commands. For such mythic texts, and others too, structural and social anthropology opens up suggestive modes of interpretation and can reveal ideology and its confrontation with reality, especially in early periods. P. N. Medvedev and M. M. Bakhtin are particularly helpful in suggesting to literary scholarship a formal method that grows out of twentieth-century anthropological concerns and also out of contemporary revolutionary impetuses of more than one kind: "Nor do philosophical views, beliefs, or even shifting ideological moods exist within man, in his heart or in his 'soul.' They become ideological reality only by being realized in words, actions, clothing, manners and organizations of people and things—in a word: in some definite semiotic material. Through this material they become a practical part of the reality surrounding man."[9] Some of the literature and art I shall study I recognize as belonging to this kind of "semiotic material," even when I do not or cannot make connections with other materials these thinkers mention.

Fourth, the chief emphasis of this study falls on *consciously and individually created art and literature.* I hope to achieve for each of the stories I shall try to elucidate in the body of my text what Clifford Geertz calls a "thick description"—one that will take account of the ideology (as just defined), the social milieu, and the established intellectual formulations that each "complex specific" has gathered unto itself.[10] But the "thickness" of my descriptions will, I hope, also arise from acculturated nature, the nature that in human beings creates something resembling the unrepeatable particulars that biology studies but also something resembling the "laws" that govern physics, astronomy, and mathematics. Later in this chapter I shall state the view that the formation of the loving couple is a long-range, fully human, body-psyche enterprise. As such it does not escape history, ideas, and ideology, but it can rise above these to the kind of universality that Aristotle and Samuel Johnson found embodied in art (Johnson called it "general nature"). In our day Roberto Unger finds that art can go beyond "all the societies that exist or have existed," and that such large visions are a part of our heritage because our gifted and gift-giving ancestors were "context-transcending and insatiable beings."[11]

Michel Foucault has argued that Freud differs from Galileo in one fundamental respect: if you reexamine the texts of Galileo and come up with new insights, you may change perceptions about the history of mechanics but you will never be able to change mechanics itself. But if you come up with radically new and compelling insights into the Freudian texts, you will modify psychoanalysis itself.[12] I do not know that this is true, since I do not know how to place or categorize the enormous achievement of Freud—within science primarily, within a philosophical-mythological matrix, or within both. But it is conceivable to me that one day, in the next century, say, a towering imagination might arise and wish to produce a historical novel on our epoch and its mentality, specifically on Freud and the part of this century that he especially helped to form. The author might well choose to tell this epic story in the form of a long-range heterosexual love affair in the modern manner—its beginnings, its initial union, its conflicts, its separations, its appeasements, its recurring crises, and its final equilibrium—for I choose to imagine a novelist sympathetic to the achievements of depth psychology. I could have postulated an important, even awe-inspiring work of historical scholarship on such a topic. But I chose fiction since I want to introduce a work about literature and art by suggesting possibilities for human nature that fidelity to history as such might miss.

Since we have imagined thus much, let us imagine more. My novelist is a woman, who wishes to incorporate into her tale the twentieth-century experience as a woman knew it who was affected by psychoanalysis and who in turn influenced it. Part of the conflict I just alluded to between the hero and the heroine concerns clashing careers but it also involves clashing views of female and male nature.

What could such a work of fiction accomplish that historical analysis, however brilliant and comprehensive, might not? It could in its conversations (for I imagine a situation not unlike that in Thomas Mann's *Magic Mountain,* where there is abundant opportunity for good talk) delineate conditions and events unknown to history that might be truer than literal truth, deeper and more transformative of our insights than what actually happened. The female experience could be brought into the sharpest kind of focus by imagining that the Freudian consultation room had originally contained not only a male doctor, a couch, and a patient, but a female nurse, or a sister of Freud, or a female practitioner present as well. Or indeed it might even be imagined that a woman founded a psychoanalytic movement. With what results? Much the same? Different? Vastly or subversively different?

It is unlikely that such a novel will ever be written, for novels are seldom produced in response to prescriptions by scholars or critics. And the talent required would be staggering—perhaps the combined powers of a Thomas Mann and a Marcel Proust. I have allowed my imagination to play over such possibilities in order to tease readers into allowing theirs to wander similarly over these materials as they confront my stories from the past: the unconscious, the conception of woman, the place of sex, the concept of sexuality, the relation of love to aggression, all more or less familiar but profoundly interesting nonetheless. I have also tried to provoke such imaginative play because it is inevitable that we moderns bring some version of these concepts into our responses to the fictions of the past. And it is perhaps not outrageous to say that my imaginary but fact-respecting and at the same time fact-modifying and fact-transcending novel might be essentially close to the very condition of our literary heritage from the past, which is surely a fiction, but one growing out of reality and experience that we can now only partially reconstruct. Our heritage can be said to be in part fictional because it was created by imaginers, not copiers, and also because the sober scholar, the reconstructor, is himself a human being influenced by the thoughts and prejudices of his own milieu.[13]

I wish now to consider the theoretical dimensions of long-term intimacy in Western culture, asking what are its essential and dynamic constituents, and what can logically be said about its prospects for success. But why Western? And why *culture* in the singular? The longer I have examined the body of Western imaginative creation the more I have felt its unifying ligatures and organizing musculature. It is an organic body with many parts, not a collection of disparate entities. One need only think of the vital presence of Greece in Rome and of Rome in Christianity, of the Hebrew Bible in the Christian, and all of the aforementioned in the Renaissance to see the justification of my synoptic treatment of the heterosexual couple from Homer to Shakespeare. The past need not have come to us in this way, but it did. And I am convinced that its striking and welcome diversities, so brilliantly brought to the fore in our day, can best be appreciated against the background—perhaps the fiction—of a persistent though not a compulsively regulating unity. That very unity—perhaps it might better be called an outline—was a culturally imposed one, arising from revolutions in thought, taste, manners, and economic, social, and political life, and also from a good deal of cultural and intellectual colonizing. If we bear this last point in mind, we will see that acknowledgment of some kind of unity need not be an evasion of a scholar's responsibility to confront difference; it can instead be a recognition of the powerful forces that have made us what we are even when they attacked and modified diversity but never extinguished it. In short, there is always an obligation to confront both *e pluribus unum* and *ex uno plurimum*.

Taxonomy

Aristotle divided friendship into three kinds: that of utility (as between business partners), or of pleasure (as between those who enjoy wit or sex), or of noble virtue (as when esteem unites with the normal human desire for companionship and benevolence). Ever since, it has become customary to divide the complex, multilayered concept of love into constituents. Samuel Johnson required thirteen categories in his *Dictionary*, C. S. Lewis and Stendhal four apiece, Herbert Spencer nine.[14] Even though I do not follow my taxonomy closely or sequentially and usually keep it implicit, I think I need to define the following five categories: (*a*) libido, (*b*) affection, (*c*) eros, (*d*) friendship, (*e*) agapē. In addition, there is a floating category which I call, for want of a single term, the egocentric context. This I postulate as an inescapable presence in all the other categories.

Libido. That human sexuality begins authentically, decisively, even fatally in early childhood, as Freud taught, I suspect to be true. But I really do not know. Nor do I know whether pair bonding in adolescence is a new or a continued experience, and I am not able to verify from history and culture whether, as Robert Sternberg believes, romantic love in adulthood is essentially the same kind of experience as the child's love of its parents.[15] My studies do not tell me where the greatest moment of sexual satisfaction lies—whether in the orgasm (so much solicited today), in the moment of entry (as Rollo May insisted), or in the foreplay (as Rousseau, Sterne, and others at that cultural moment seemed to imply).[16] But the following beliefs I am willing to be categorical about: that sexuality is basic, pervasive, long-lasting; that it influences and can insinuate itself into all the forms of love I shall subsequently discuss; that though it possesses constant elements, it can be greatly modified by culture; that it is not necessarily fixed to a single or hitherto accepted form of expression, such as the heterosexual; and that it can be controlled, diverted, and even aborted, not always with disastrous, and sometimes, indeed, with salutary, results. Whatever its paradoxes, libido is powerful and awe inspiring. Even that great Platonist, George Santayana, referred to the "glory of animal love" and called friendship "vital and biological." Love was for him a "brilliant illustration" of a universal tendency, "turning the friction of material forces into the light of ideal goods."[17] Libido can make a human being a creator like God and has been well called a tree of knowledge. Even in adultery, as a dominant strain in the novel enforces upon us, one can see something awesome as well as adventurous, dangerous and, yes, dignified (the very ingredients of the Burkean sublime). As a contemporary poet, T. R. Hummer, has put it:

> He touches her with the absolute authority
> The body, revealed, reveals. History, mythology,
> Biology, the art of the family
>
> Suspend as the man and woman move together.[18]

It is important to realize that nature studiously perceived usually becomes culture but that culture can sometimes recede, if only for a while, when nature reveals itself in dignity and force as a pristine presence. This brief discussion of libido is as good a place as any to express my layman's belief in the independent existence of external nature, which supports the enterprise not only of science but of all culture. Existence is a condition of actual objects in space-time and also of other entities like the cube root of 27, as W. V. Quine has said. Almost everyone agrees that observation of nature is relevant to determining the existence of objects. But, as Quine also says, observation of nature is relevant to cultural inquiries as well, for example, " 'the ratio of the number of centaurs to the number of unicorns.' If there were such a ratio, it would be an abstract entity, viz. a number. Yet it is only by studying nature that we conclude that the number of centaurs and the number of unicorns are both 0 and hence that there is no such ratio."[19] Thus, to get back to literature, nature is relevant to Pegasus after all, and in love it is surely present in such highly different acculturated and psychologized entities as purely pleasurable sex or the *vagina dentata.*

Affection. I realize that this word and its cognates have had strong and broad meanings in the past, but here I associate it with tender feelings. Cicero's *affectio* meant an abrupt mental seizure; the King James Version modified *affection* with *inordinate* and associated it with vileness (Romans 1:26) and with "fornication, uncleanness, . . . evil concupiscence" (Colossians 3:5). For Shakespeare it meant sexual passion, lust peculiar to each man, in contrast to desires, which, like passions, are universal forces.[20]

The *Oxford English Dictionary* in its third definition of *affection* calls it "passion, lust," classifying it as obsolete and giving 1736 as the date of its last usage. During the eighteenth century it was made a separate category in the complex of ideas called *sensibility,* and earlier in Christianity it had been hypostasized as *caritas,* the central attribute of the Godhead. Tender affection must surely have a sexual component, otherwise how could we explain the highly libidinous dreams and visions of some Christian believers and saints and their artistic representations, notably Bernini's wonderfully sensual portrayal of Saint Teresa and the visitation of the angel with the flame-tipped spear? But I myself have no way of knowing from my materials whether Freud is right in holding that the tender is older than the sexual and primitively directed to those who care for the child and who thus become the first sexual objects or whether Theodor Reik is correct to maintain that the sexual is the older drive and that tender affections come later.[21] J. J. Bachofen, Robert Briffault, Philip Slater, and recently Adrienne Rich and Marilyn French have urged that the mother-child relationship is the essential one and that the maternal predates the mating sentiment, making tender affection the primary human emotion in both individual and social life (see chapter 2). These thinkers tend to believe that either a historical matriarchy or, if not matriarchy itself, various forms of matriliny and matrilocality in which woman was central or at least prominent preceded the later and almost universally dominant patriarchy. Neglecting for the moment which has priority, libido or affection, I am greatly impressed by Freud's view that there is a split in male loving between the Virgin Mother, whom one can love but never enjoy, and the whore, whom one can enjoy but never love. Who can fail to be impressed by the millennial coexistence in pagan and Christian centuries alike of two such powerful sexual institutions as marriage and prostitution, both receiving abundant husbandly patronage? But if the virgin-whore split is defined literally and is regarded as fatal, inevitable, and permanent, then much in Western literary culture will have to be considered purely fanciful—that esteem can be enlivened by desire (and not debased by it), and that desire can be enlivened by esteem (and not chilled by it into fruitless frigidity). Freud himself believed—at least at times—and apparently Shakespeare as well that the lesion between sexual love and tender affection could be healed in a successful marriage.

Eros. Thomas Hobbes disclosed the hollowness of the claim that Platonism and Neoplatonism were essentially pure in spirit: "But why . . . should the wise . . . be more charitable toward the beautiful than to others? . . . The *continent* have the passion they *contain,* as *much* and more than they that *satiate* the appetite; which maketh one suspect this *platonic* love for merely sensual; but with an honourable pretence for the old to haunt the company of the young and beautiful."[22] In other words, libido lurked in the hearts of philosophers questing for beauty.

What the Platonists called beauty and Hobbes suspected was libido I wish to call *eros,* my term for the decoration of sexual impulse by art and thought or, more deeply, for the absorption of sexual impulse into art and thought. I shall of course display the term in its historical senses as we confront its use in literature. But the meaning that I am now adopting lies at the center of my enterprise—the appropriation of the libido into art and philosophy. This can of course happen in life, in which case sex becomes sexuality, instinct becomes a personality trait or a style of life.

Let me explain my intention by invoking Hume. He found that love consists of three parts: bodily desire for generation; a pleasing sensation of beauty; and kindness (good will or generosity). He also believed that love most commonly arises from beauty—observe to which element he gives priority—"and afterwards diffuses itself into kindness and into the bodily appetites."[23] Hume's *beauty* is, I suggest, better served by my term *eros,* with its combined association of desire and culture, particularly aesthetic culture. The point is that eros is a deeply acculturated condition.

I realize that when I come to the analysis of literature my words may sound as though in the erotic the cultural has taken over completely from the sexual—perhaps inevitably so, since what has survived is experience already shaped into art. But I would be unhappy if that impression should obscure what all art to a greater or lesser degree bears as one of its distinguishing marks: signs of conflict in the artist and his work, signs of a tension between the claims of the natural body and those of culture.

I am trying to avoid two unhappy extremes. One completely separates libido from eros, nature from art, sometimes conceiving of art as arising only or mostly from other art, only or mostly from the necessities imposed by grammar and language. The other extreme, like Krafft-Ebing's formulation, finds no other foundation for art and poetry than sexuality; he seems to hold with Freud that the "libido of our sexual instincts would coincide with the Eros of the poets and philosophers which holds all living things together."[24] Perhaps Nietzsche, taken as a whole, comes fairly close to what I am requiring of eros. There can be no doubt of his favoring hearty, untrammeled sexuality, if for no other reason than to produce the Superman. But at the same time, in *The Will to Power,* he sees art as "an indirect demand for the ecstasies of sexuality," love itself providing an "imaginative 'transposition' of values," the lover being the supreme artist of the senses. Irving Singer regards this spiritualization of love through the aesthetic as ultimately defining the nature of love in Nietzsche.[25]

Placing eros in culture—particularly literary culture—does not weaken it and may, in fact, strengthen it. Surely in days when the sexes could not mingle freely and when satisfactions were postponed, the song, the sonnet, the letter, the drawing were powerful substitutes for experience itself, and from that association and sublimation these forms of artistic expression draw much of their power even today. C. S. Lewis and Denis de Rougemont can conceive of erotic power even without what the former calls the "fuel" of "plain animal desire." Lewis described an apparently cultivated but weakly libidinized adulterer who breaks hearts and betrays friends as being under the sway of "a soaring and iridescent Eros," one who has, however, very little sexuality. When such separation occurs, de Rougemont fears the idolatrous and that kind of sexless mysticism that ferments without a sense of social obligation or even without fruitful fulfillment in Tristan and Isolde and in the popular arts of our own day. So it has often been and is. But it need not be so, and Western art and culture provide many examples of an assertive and healthy eros, an eros that through art has refined libido without losing it. Besides, our tradition is varied and rich enough for an acculturated libido to take many forms and so give us multiple choices. C. S. Lewis has said, "We are under no obligation at all to sing all our love-duets in the throbbing, world-without-end, heart-breaking manner of Tristan and Isolde; let us often sing like Papageno and Papagena instead."[26]

Friendship. Friendship is wishing another well for his or her own sake, desiring to do good things for my friend, wanting him or her to flourish, and placing my friend's welfare on a par with or even above my own. It must build on esteem, as the purely libidinous cannot and as even erotic love need not. Esteem is induced by virtue, intelligence, ability, or all three and is capable of being deepened and enforced by gratitude for shared pleasure and responsibility. I shall be much concerned in the pages that follow with friendship, which can of course exist without libido but need not be destroyed by it. In fact, libido-become-eros is, I believe, one of the best ways of instituting and deepening friendship, though I know that both Montaigne in his essay on friendship and Shaw in his preface to *Getting Married* have sharp things to say about such dreams. Both the pleasures and pains of love can plow up the rocky surface of the ego and prepare the soil of the personality for the plantation of benevolence and altruism.

I am partly led to this faith by the force of literary examples but also by evolutions in linguistic usage. An example, mediately from the Latin, immediately from the Italian, is relevant. *Voglio bene* literally meant "I wish well," and was easily extended to mean "I feel good will." But it came to have loving and perhaps erotic connotations, so that even today a young man alone with a young Italian woman on a moonlit night would do well to think twice and examine his intentions before the whispering in her ear, "I wish you well" (*ti voglio bene*).[27] Kant's separation of the cupidinous from the benevolent inclinations, denying that the latter have anything to do with love and placing them under moral law and reason, will not stand up under pressures from our linguistic and artistic past. His sharp division of moral love and goodwill from beauty of the sensuous order and from tender sentiment puts asunder what people in their richest imaginative insights have joined together.[28]

We need to ask an important question, though I shall not be able to answer it fully here: Is friendship possible between unequals? Definitely yes, thought Aristotle, who defined woman as inferior by nature (*Politics* 1254a). Holding the most exalted view of friendship, he readily granted its possibility between husbands and wives, parents and children, though he did think the distance between a god and a man unbridgeable. We should phrase the question more pertinently to our own sensibility: Has the notorious, millennial, *de jure* subjugation of women always and necessarily put its fetters on the *de facto* situations in which the life of the past was lived and the creative imagination did its work? The answer has to be a categorical no, if one has a supple and realistic view of history, and if one has respect for human creativity. Even, Juno, Venus, Helen, Penelope, Alcestis, Andromache, Phaedra, Mary, Dido, Heloise, the Wife of Bath, Elizabeth I, Rosalind, Desdemona, and the Duchess of Malfi simply do not come from the world we moderns tend sometimes to extrapolate from restrictive precept or oppressive practice. To deny these women and their many sisters full humanity, full spiritual equality with and sometimes superiority to men, is to insult our perception of worth and dignity, even in sinners and workers of evil, and mischievously to distort the story of intersexual friendship in our heritage.

Agapē. The New Testament word for divine love of a fallen and needy humanity, *agapē,* constitutes so important a category of Western experience that no student can fail to take it into account. It is not my immediate subject, but in subtle and indirect ways it enters my primary concern, which is interpersonal human love. *Agapē* and *caritas* have by no means driven out eros or libido, nor is the reverse true. In our tradition, with its love of paradox and antithesis, extremes—the spiritual and the physical above all others—implicate and even recommend each other. And value is bestowed up and down (to use old-fashioned spatial metaphors) our scale of categories. Define God's being as Love, and you will send erotic impulses all through the chain of being. Let Jesus and John establish a law of love, and you will encourage a spirituality that can be boldly sensual in its manifestation, a physically suggestive form of devotional expression that even Augustine did not escape. The point about the bishop of Hippo should and will be made more strongly: his great personal effusion of prayer and praise, vitally unified as it is by what can only be called a religious eroticism, is the most vivid expression of the insinuation of *agapē* into the individual's nerves and senses. Thus my fifth category would seem to be as inescapable in its way as sex.[29]

Ego Context. It is no difficult descent from religious love to my floating category, the ego context, a category that attaches itself to all others, even the most exalted. The ego (broadly conceived to include most of the meanings that Amélie Rorty has displayed in her brilliant taxonomy of the self)[30] enters into all lovemakings and love doings, quite as much as do the libidinal and the transcendent. Irving Singer has seen that self-confidence or self-affirmation, as distinct from mere selfishness, is basic to Aristotle's magnanimous man. It also underlies the loving self in Spinoza, Rousseau, and Nietzsche, and is present in both psychiatry and Hasidic law.[31] I add the most important example of all for Western culture since pagan antiquity, the Golden Rule: "And as ye would that men should do to you, do ye also to them likewise" (Luke 6:31), a rule essentially rooted in what *pleases us*.

This fact about the famous ethical command makes it intellectually cogent and often workable: it is self-referential, though of course not self-regarding, to use C. D. Broad's distinction.[32] Thus we did not have to wait for realism about love until modern social science introduced "the instrumental theory" of sexual affection, welcome though that is. We may not wish to embrace fully the belief that the basic element in bonding is "the reciprocal need gratification of lovers" or that in forming couples men and women "seek to use each other as instruments." Still, men and women in love ignore the self and its needs to their own peril— and quite pointlessly, since a civilized and mutual instrumentality in love need not reduce lovers to objects but can in fact support affective values and rewarding intimacy, to preserve which an unyielding respect for the ego may indeed be required. Another way of putting this is that love requires more than emotion, titillation, or sentimental overevaluation. Though a major strain of romance would deny this, love requires a context outside itself, a context conceived realistically enough to minister to the needs of the whole personality for economic security, emotional support, familial love, work gratification, creature comforts other than the libidinous, and the general flourishing of the self. It was an acute awareness of my present floating category that led Samuel Johnson, who had the most exalted view of love, marriage, and friendship, to say, "It is com-

monly a weak man who marries for love." When Boswell pressed him,
"Pray, Sir, do you not suppose that there are fifty women in the world,
with any one of whom a man may be as happy, as with one woman in
particular," Johnson replied, "Ay, Sir, fifty thousand"; and he went on to
say that marriages would be just as happy, often more so, if they were
made by the lord chancellor without giving the parties any choice. But he
laid this qualification upon the lord chancellor's choice: it must be made
"upon a due consideration of characters and circumstances." Johnson
was here not defining love but most dramatically illustrating the absolute
importance of the ego context.[33]

What Is Love and Is It Possible?

It should be clear that my conception of love requires that it be seen as a
complex entity. Space does not permit a separate consideration of those
who have influenced me, though it would have been a pleasure to accord
each of the following—and others too—a separate analysis: Roberto
Unger, Michel Foucault, Irving Singer, Annette Baier, Robert C. Solomon, Roger Scruton, Martha Nussbaum, Stanley Cavell, David
Halperin, John J. Winkler, Martin Buber. But I do wish, very briefly, to
say a few words about those thinkers in our tradition who have also led
me to the following summarily stated beliefs about love.

1. Love is of the body, for the psyche is of the body.

2. Love thus requires the embodiment of the self but of the Other
   too, in whose incarnated consciousness the original self is always challenged and can be realized anew in a different and
   more comprehensive configuration.

3. Love can exist in an enterprise which the lovers create and pur-
   sue thoughtfully and contextually and which, perhaps paradoxically, implies freedom.

4. Concurrently, love is a deeply mutual emotion that can, though
   it is steeped in contingency, bring distinct and separate identities together for their mutual flourishing.

5. As implied by all of the above, pair bonding that leads to a long-
   term relationship (the central focus of my study) not only permits but requires the reciprocal enlivening of desire and esteem.

This five-tiered structure of ideal love—phenomenologists might refer to it as "intentional love"—I do not regard as the potential habitat of
heterosexual couples only. Surely the spice of *human* difference (implicit

in number four above) is not confined to *sexual* difference. The tension between personal autonomy and benevolent regard for the other must most certainly arise whenever two individuals embark on the project of making lasting love. And I see no logical reason for denying the presence of creatively fermenting similitude-dissimilitude in relations between women and women, between men and men, between formally unattached men and women (like the Greek man and his hetaira or like the potentially serious but institutionally unblessed relationships so often called for in the personal advertisements of *The New York Review of Books*). I for one am not willing to confine the possibility of *amitiés amoureuses* of long and deepening companionship to married couples.

But "esteem enlivened by desire" cannot be said to point to a self-evident truth. On the face of it, esteem seems to belong to a moral order that has traditionally separated itself from sexual desire. But that this *need not be* so is attested by the fact that it *has not been* so even in the history of thought itself. The reverse of Thomson's phrase ought also to be considered seriously: if desire can enliven esteem, why cannot esteem enliven desire? Awaken it, establish it, mix with it, dignify it? But let there be no *temporal* priority, for esteem, desire, and also considerations of utility ferment together. Who could disentangle these strands in the heroines of Jane Austen, for example? The Austen page vibrates with libidinally charged esteem and also with desire tempered by prudence and dignified by respect. The threads cannot be separated but they energetically produce a pattern.

Let us now consider some philosophical approaches that discourage or encourage the coexistence or interaction of the qualities we have been considering. Kant insists on their separation and can be used to set up a point of contrast with most of the systems we shall confront. He was not a total ascetic in his thought: The "strength, vigour, liveliness, and courage" of the body must be cultivated by care, and from the management of *Hang* (propensity) and *Neigung* (inclination or habitual sensible desire) could come important practical precepts. But moral law transcended the world of common sense and prudence, and Kant feared *vaga libido* (unfocused desire) so much (for it could transform persons into objects to be devoured) that he set up high walls between the two worlds he acknowledged to exist, the world of sense and that of moral reason. His system is scarcely congenial to a union of desire and esteem.[34]

Spinoza believed man was a social animal, who united with his fellows for both safety and pleasure. Spinoza established his kind of realism by fully accepting the ego context of love, but his *Ethics* envisions a relationship of flesh and spirit that is vastly more sympathetic to uniting esteem and desire than Kant's and that leaves room for human beings acting as independent agents to enhance their welfare and foster their flourishing through conscious intention. Spinoza breaches the barrier between mind and body: "Whatsoever increases or diminishes, helps or hinders the power of activity in our body, the idea thereof increases or diminishes, helps or hinders the power of thought in our minds." Spinoza leaves room for agency and for distinctly external personal relations: "love is nothing but pleasure accompanied by the idea of an external cause." Love and pleasure, both parts of a conscious enterprise, are related, and both are linked to external causation: "We endeavour . . . to bring about . . . that what we love should be affected with pleasure accompanied by the idea of ourself as causes."[35]

In Spinoza the chief actors are present though perhaps only implied. Sartre provides a precise delineation of the psychological situation that exists in love. The Other comes to me as an immediate presence with a separate consciousness and a palpable body. That body is not a machine in which a soul acts as driver or guide. I *am* my body. It is a permanent structure of my being. When it feels and acts, *I* feel and act. The Other exists for me in her/his body, and this fact means, with dramatic force, that I have a body-for-me and also a body-for-the-Other. To refine further, I also have a body-seen-by-the-Other, which is my body as the object of another's perception. Here we enter the heart of the matter: "the structures of my being-for-the-Other are identical with the Other's being-for-me." I come to apprehend her in her body; in such knowledge I come to realize that she apprehends me in my body. She knows and uses my body as I know and use hers. I am her object as she is mine; she becomes revealed to me as a subject for whom I am an object. All this begins in the look, the glance; and the fact that her nakedness and my nakedness are, as it were, uncovered before we meet in actual union sets up a lively drama, partly intentional, that is filled with shy tensions and blushing conflicts. Sartre is surely right up to this point. There has been much sentiment and much poetry about the exchange of hearts—about my heart being in another's body and another's heart in mine, about my being reflected in the eye of the Other and she in mine. Paradoxically, barriers are challenged just when I am most acutely aware of my own body and being and precisely when my Other is also most acutely aware of hers.[36]

But the very Sartre who so brilliantly described the psychodrama of love and its chief actors—the self alone, the self in the world, the self making another the object of *his* consciousness, that Other in turn making the original self the object of *her* consciousness—later aborts the working of the machinery of relationship he has created. "The Other cannot, by principle, be appropriated; he escapes me when I seek him, and he possesses me when I flee him." Love cannot last, reality inevitably disappoints. Why? The lover wants to be "the unique and privileged" possessor of the Other's freedom, which he intends to "glue down." The "facticity" of my own being challenges the mutual demand to be one's own and the Other's "absolute choice" and "unique end," making love ultimately impossible. "The more I am loved, the more I lose my *being*." It is not only that the Other turns out to be an alienated and an alienating reality but that she possesses the secret of my being and penetrates to its very roots. My autonomy and my commitment to the Other—and more especially her commitment to me—are incompatible, and the whole enterprise, which Sartre had so successfully analyzed into its component parts, inevitably breaks down. In creating myself as being-for-the-Other, I am taken away from myself.[37]

It is not apparent to me that Sartre has by argument or cogent example proved his pessimistic case. It is useless to try to isolate the reasons, personal or philosophical, for this deep pessimism, but *Being and Nothingness* remains a central text, even though Sartre himself disowned its nihilism and later professed to see the positive side of love. For he never himself answered it logically and dialectically, and it remains a Slough of Despond which every investigator of love must cross.

If there exists a cogent argument to answer Sartre I have not found it nor been able to create one. I should perhaps fall back on the old logical axiom that a single counterexample refutes the claim that "X does not exist" or on Martin Buber's religion-derived insight, formulated during the trauma of World War I, that the basic truth in human life is dialogic, "Man becomes an I through a You."[38] In general, I have only matched other intuitions, truer to my own experiences both as human being and scholar, against Sartre's. But I remain certain that there is a refutation and that it lies embedded in the literary and artistic tradition which is the subject of this book. That tradition now and then appears compellingly on the current scene, with many resonances of what we shall confront in this book though with new complexities and ironies, whose pressures one can encounter in contemporary American poetic English, as in these lines from John Ashbery:

> The love that comes after will be richly satisfying,
> Like rain on the desert, calling unimaginable diplomacy into
>   being
> Until you thought you should get off here, maybe this stop

Was yours. And then it all happens blindingly, over and over
In a continuous vivid present that wasn't there before.
No need to make up stories at this juncture, everybody
Likes a joke and they find yours funny. And then it's just
Two giant steps down to the big needing and feeling
That is yours to grow in. Not grow old, the
Magic present still insists on being itself,
But to play in. To live and be lived by
And in this way bring all things to the sensible conclusion
Dreamed into their beginnings, and so arrive at the end.[39]

Two cities in the spacious shield he built, with
    goodly state
Of divers-languaged men. The one did nuptials
    celebrate,
Observing at them solemn feasts, the brides from
    forth their bowers
With torches ushered through the streets, a world of
    paramours
Excited by them; youths and maids in lovely circles
    danced,
To whom the merry pipe and harp the spritely
    sounds advanced,
The matrons standing in the doors admiring.
    Otherwhere
A court of law was kept, where throngs of people
    were. . . .
The other city other wars employed as busily: . . .
        They . . . armed themslves by stealth,
Left all their old men, wives, and boys behind to
    man their walls,
And stole out to their enemy's town. The queen of
    martïals
And Mars himself conducted them,— . . .

    Chapman's Homer, *Iliad* 18 (1611)

TWO

Early Western Antiquity: The Archaic Periods

as prehistoric society a matriarchy? The answer is probably no, but it should not be given dogmatically. Evidence in the form of archeological and anthropological
traces is still coming in, and humanistic speculation remains lively. Without the benefit of mathematics it cannot be expected to
do what cosmology in astrophysics is likely to accomplish and reconstruct a compelling history. Still, it may well open up new approaches to
the texts we do possess and continually feel the need of reinterpreting.
The "Lunar Sphere" in Pope's *Rape of the Lock* contained the wits of
beaux and heroes, broken vows, lovers' hearts, and harlots' smiles,
among other things, "Since all things lost in Earth, are treasur'd there"
(5.113). The empty spaces of our own Western prehistory, though allowed to remain pretty much free of social frippery, constitute a vast
screen on which we have projected the world we have lost—and our
desires and fears, especially in thinking about the relations of the sexes
in love, marriage, and the family. It will be helpful to analyze a few influential speculations about earliest history in approaching our literary
heritage, partly because they are instructive in themselves and partly because, under the influence of some of my texts from diverse cultures, I
intend to do a little projecting of my own and so keep us alert to a persistent Western mythical-literary theme, that of male-female pacification
after deeply embedded recollections of former conflicts (see chapter 12).

Freud, in his philosophical as distinct from his scientific writings,
thought there once existed a primal horde of brothers out to destroy a
father who was determined to preempt all the females including the
mother, thus entailing sexual conflict upon the children of men—a notion that reveals much more about Freudian dynamics than about our
ancestors. Ralph Linton, the anthropologist, writing during a period (the
thirties, forties, and fifties of this century) when faith in marriage was

strong and when optimism about both our forebears and ourselves was fashionable, would have no truck with the primal horde, regarding it as a nineteenth-century fantasy, pure and simple. For it—and indeed for virtually all primal promiscuity—he substituted marriage, extending it not only to the early history of human beings but to primates as well, where it existed as both monogamy and polygamy.[1] I use the two contrasting examples of Freud and Linton to show the projecting machinery of historical speculation at work, but it will be more relevant to my own subject, the heterosexual couple, to concentrate on some of the theories regarding matriarchy.

The influential nineteenth-century thinker, J. J. Bachofen, did populate what he called a primitive hetairist-aphrodisiac horde with a male tyrant in charge who chose any woman he wished. But Bachofen's main business was to set forth "the moving principle of the matriarchal age," a product of a maternal tellurian but not of a paternal uranian attitude toward existence. In other words, the presiding force was the Magna Mater, Gē, not the male patriarch, Zeus. Indeed, in our earliest moral darkness the only light there was came from the love between the mother and her offspring, the originating relationship of all culture, making the woman the repository of love, value, and faith. With woman as prophet and keeper of religion, matriarchal people, more strongly than any other, felt the unity of all life, the harmony of the universe, the importance of agriculture, the sanctity of the body, and the consequent pain of separation and death.[2]

Bachofen has been very influential in our century as well as the last; Engels, Wagner, Nietzsche, Karen Horney, and Mao Zedong seem to have adopted his belief in matriarchy;[3] and in the work of Robert Briffault, an anthropologist, he may have achieved his most learned monument. The three stout volumes entitled *The Mothers: A Study of the Origins of Sentiments and Institutions,* each containing some 800 to 900 pages, with 200 pages of bibliography, appeared in 1927 and is closely related to the concerns of the American and English 1920s. This master of virtually all anthropological learning to date and of cultural history from Babylon to the Iroquois firmly believed that matriarchal rule had been corroborated as existent in Lycia; that all later patriarchal societies had had their matriarchal phases; and that there is no room for ambiguity about the love of primitive mothers for their offspring, though there is about intersexual love and emotion-laden sexuality. Finding no trace of patriarchal organization in the animal world, he early came to the conclusion that "the social characters of the human mind are, one and all, traceable to the operations of instincts that are related to the functions of the female and not those of the male."[4] In other words, our whole emotional life ultimately springs from a primitive matriarchy, which has enormous implications for the future, since apparently the future of relations between the sexes and of marriage lies with women.

A current polemical determination has attacked the myth of matriarchy—even among the Iroquois, that last holdout for believers in its literal existence—as exalting a "mystical, pure, and uncorrupted Mother Goddess," a myth that has become a tool to keep woman in subjection.[5] Bachofen has therefore been strongly opposed and Briffault forgotten or ignored. Until very recently, that is. For in the seventies and eighties there has been a decided shift in reconstructive and projective belief. A literary and cultural critic, Julia Kristeva, finds the earliest Chinese family to have been matrilinear and believes that the mother was the most respected member of earlier communities. Under her benign influence the soil was perceived as maternal and feminine, the imagination was oriented to the genital act, there were no sinful erogenous zones—and there appear traces of this Great Ancestress, the tribal mother, in many subsequent religious and theological formulations, though of course Confucianism was a total and unfortunate reversal. The poet Adrienne Rich goes even further for Western culture and, although she evades the question of the existence of a universal matriarchy, opts for a woman-centered set of beliefs and for a "gynocentric" period, approving of Philip Slater's belief that some kind of matriarchal culture was supplanted by a later patriarchy. But the novelist Marilyn French, in an enormously learned, passionate, and stimulating reconstruction of our earliest past that extends its worldwide scope into the present, returns us to the Bachofen-Briffault orientation: "In the beginning was the Mother; the Word began a later age." And that Word was the Fall, that is, the establishment of the patriarchy, when the concept of "power over" became firmly entrenched.[6]

What was society like before that life-limiting Word was spoken? Among the hominids, who looked like chimpanzees and gorillas though they walked upright and who lived some three and a half million years ago, it was close and affectionate, centered on women and infants, the hominid female entering into relations with her male according to her desire. Society was anything but Freud's primal horde, and this successful society lasted over a million years. *Homo sapiens,* who began no earlier than 200,000 years ago and perhaps as recently as 35,000 years ago, may never have known a matriarchy, but its society was matrilinear. Marriage was matrilocal, informal, and casual, while the religious life at least of the Aegean world was dominated by the great Earth Mother, who presided over a gentle and kindly agricultural economy. All the ills we know so well arose when men came to dominate nature—and men began to assume such colonizing power when the male role in procreation came to be known.

Into such monumental vessels to contain primitive life and love have the dreams of our own cultural present been poured. Are the Bachofen-Briffault-Rich-French reconstructions as fanciful as most dreams of the Golden Age? They are certainly in large part illusory projections upon vast stretches of the historically unknown, since they are unaccompanied by material data and lack the cogency of compelling argument. They appear to be excessively accommodating to the best hopes and wishes of our own era and therefore may be completely unthinkable for what must have been the greatly different codes of primitive humanity. The gentler, kindlier female Eden envisaged is surely a sentimental fairy tale, partly because it ignores or underplays endemic aggressivity, universal selfishness, and the preponderance of male power in most of the pantheons known to us. But we cannot dismiss the female-oriented reconstructions summarily, since women and their sensibilities are so integral a part of humanity and may in the best moments of our own dawning contemporary consciousness provide a useful perspective on what preceded our earliest literary past. And it should be borne in mind that our imaginings in this study about the grandly expansive early domain constitute a preface to a literary, not a historical, study and that visions of the earliest past were also indulged in by many of the writers we shall later encounter.

The Amazons

The ancients themselves provide no such revolutionary perspective, but since they are closer in time and feeling to primitive myth than we are, their imaginative histories possess a peculiar pertinence. And one of their most telling and insistent myths about the male-female past can scarcely be said to invoke an irenic, female-guided Utopia. It is that of the Amazons. We do well not to dismiss this myth as minor and secondary, though some distinguished classicists have. Despite much Voltairean skepticism about it even in antiquity, it persisted for well over a thousand years in learned commentary, travel literature, geography, history, oratory, poetry, and art. Several great heroes fought against these female warriors, whose right breast was supposed to have been cauterized to enable them to shoot with the bow: Bellerophontes on Pegasus; the young Priam, who enlisted the aid of Penthesilea at Troy (Achilles later slew her and was touched by the beauty of her dying body); Herakles, one of whose labors was to bring back the girdle of the Amazonian queen; and of course

FIGURE 1   Eretria Painter, *Battle of Greeks and Amazons,* c. 430 B.C., Attic red-figure squat lethykos. (Catharine Page Perkins Fund. Courtesy, Museum of Fine Arts, Boston.)

Theseus. The Theseum contained representations of an Amazonomachy, perhaps created by Polygnotus.[7] The Painted Stoa (Stoa Poikile) also promulgated the myth of such conflict, and metopes on the Parthenon probably represent the Amazon attack on the Athens of Theseus (here as elsewhere in visual representation the women always possessing two un-mutilated breasts). Phidias portrayed another Greek-Amazon encounter on the outside of the shield held by Athene Parthenos in his colossal statue, and many Greek vases inscribe the conflict, often with intense individual concentration on its leaders and their sexual members (fig. 1). The great orators Isocrates and Lysias found these female warriors proud and worthy foes whose defeat redounded to the glory of Greek arms—they took their place among the most highly respected barbarians as the foes of civilization and decency. Nor were their exploits confined to the historical imaginings of the mainland Greece of Attic classicism: Alexander met an Amazonian queen, and the Roman-British conflict produced Boadicea.

Bachofen, as we would expect, believed in the existence of Amazons. He associated them with the hetairism he despised and which he thought a benign matriarchy had supplanted, but even so he conceded that they

did represent an appreciable rise in the level of human culture. Few today accept their historical reality, and it is the conclusion of one of the
most careful students of Amazonian myth that "there is no single instance in which what the Greeks called the rule of women, in Greece or
outside it, can be identified as a matrilinear system, and independent evidence is needed, in every case, for the society in question to be identified
at all."[8]

What, then, might the persistent myth reveal? Can the imaginings of
the Greeks be said to constitute part of our heritage? One clear answer to
the first question is that the Greek stories about fierce warrior-women
were cautionary tales directed to their own society: any female who
breaks the established familial role is an enemy to society as much as the
Medes or the Persians and must be defeated. The classical Greek woman
was supposed to be subservient to her husband, respect monogamous
marriage, stay in the home, rear children, remain outside the mainstream
of social life, and tend to her tasks of weaving and domestic management.
The Amazons were the exquisitely exact reverse: they engaged in the
hunt, they were warriors, they disfigured themselves in their most maternal and nourishing parts, they dismissed men from their societies and
used them only for procreation, and they threatened to cross the frontiers into civilized society. They were immodest, aggressive, disobedient,
disillusioned about men, and in almost all accounts were capable of mur-
dering them singly or in groups. They thus represented a direct threat to
one of the most important of Greek institutions, hierarchical, patriarchal, monogamous marriage; and they had to be destroyed in art and
rhetoric time and time again. They undoubtedly represented deep fears,
perhaps arising from childhood, that the woman, with all her vigor and
sexual charm, could indeed be a threat that must, at least rhetorically and
artistically, be recurringly repelled. Thus the stories about the Amazons
had the perennial appeal of the forbidden and the feared, even as they
stretched outward from the innermost recesses of the individual being to
express his widest communal concerns.

But even with the concession that these tales possessed intimate
psychological fascination for the men who told and heard them, the explanation that they starkly inverted a present desirable reality for homiletical and cautionary purposes and so served a conservative function still
seems much too simple and one-dimensional. It has been well said that
the Amazons were triply the other: they were women, they were anti-
male, and they were the enemy (often the equals of and sometimes the
superiors to men). But that otherness may have lain less in the nervous
fears of dominant males in fifth- and fourth-century Athens than deep in

the Greek—or indeed the entire European—past and hence, lingering on in racial memory, may not have been all that alien. Although the Amazons seem to have entered Attic history only after 575 B.C., they may yet have recalled a much older heritage that remains not far beneath the surface of sacred and epic story and also of what looks like sober history and observation. First history, then story.

Herodotus's account involving Amazonian females (*Histories* 4.110–17) is worth retelling because it lacks the fear, hostility, and even nationalistic pride often seen as a motive for such stories and also because it suggests that an accommodation between the sexes might well have existed even up to his own day. (Of course one cannot expect historical accuracy from Herodotus, who frequently judged earlier periods and other cultures by his own classical values; but like good art his work can bear suggestive implications.) After conquering the Amazons at the battle of Thermodon, the Greeks sailed away with three shiploads of them, all they could capture alive. At sea these women cut down their captors, but not being acquainted with sailing (usually considered another sign of their barbarity but here passed over in silence) they drifted to an area possessed by free Scythians, who fought with them thinking they were men. But when the Scythians learned their foes were women, they sent young men to breed with them. The first men went back to bring other men, who then met the Amazonian women singly. Ultimately the camps were combined, each man keeping the woman he had lain with first. The women were linguistically superior to the men and learned their language, and when a fair degree of understanding was achieved all around, the men invited the women back to their original homes as wives. The Amazons refused, protesting that the Scythian women stayed in wagons and did women's work only and never went out even to hunt. Not prepared to join women like that, the Amazons invited the men to join them, shrewdly instructing the men to possess their rightful property first. They all agreed to put some distance between them and the old community, and so they crossed a river and settled on the far side of the Tanaïs, a six-day journey from the former home of the men. There they created a society and were known as the Sauromatians, where the wives in part followed their old ways of riding horseback, hunting both with and without men, wearing the same dress as the men, and sometimes going to war with them. One warlike custom persisted—no woman could marry until she had killed one of the enemy, and some died old maids for failing to fulfill that demand.[9]

In his story Herodotus is coolly neutral—neither hostile nor admiring—and shows very little of the emotional tension and prejudice which on other occasions he could display abundantly. Why did not a society so sharply and basically different from that of classical Greece shock the historian's orthodox sensibilities? Perhaps because the society he describes is unlike other Greek imaginings about the Amazons, such as those of the much later Strabo and Diodorus Siculus, by whose time, of course, new concepts may have evolved. In the one recorded by Strabo the women live among themselves and have relations with men from neighboring peoples in order to reproduce, the Amazons retaining only the female children. Diodorus Siculus conceives of the Libyan Amazonian society as one in which men stay at home, tend the children, and do as they are told. But the Sauromatians, whom Herodotus describes, provide a more subtle type of inversion, one in which Greek values have a greater stake and in which men and women share and share alike in war and government, while Herodotus apparently remains silent about who actually does the housework.

But the inversion of Greek norms in this society remains stark and doubtless illustrates one feature of the mentality of a historian given to the coincidence of opposites, though apparently not to stylistic antithesis. Herodotus loved to dwell on Greeks vs. Persians, Athenians vs. Spartans, large cities vs. small; on contradictions within the individual person, and on such matters as permanence and change, order and hidden irregularity, law and custom. Men vs. women constitutes a similar polarity, and the ultimate settlement the historian recounts is surely not unrelated to his view of history as both an opposition of forces and ultimate reconciliations within historical time.[10]

One must, however, continue to speculate about Herodotus's unwonted calm. Was he somewhat reconciled to a society in which he saw a most unconventional sharing of power and work, because it honored monogamous marriage?[11] Did this widely read and traveled and shrewdly observant student of human mores and myths also sense that behind the Sauromatians lay centuries of female-oriented beliefs and customs to which the established Olympian hierarchy with its regnant father did scant justice? He may have asked himself why the Scythian men so willingly left their society for one in which not only the bed was shared but usually male-controlled power and pursuits as well, and he may possibly have concluded that they were guided, albeit unconsciously, by an ancient and alternative tradition.[12]

Love and Sexuality in Prehistory: A Reconstruction

The projections upon prehistory I have so far discussed, those from antiquity and from our own day, including my own, reveal more about the projectors than about the projected. In an attempt to imagine an earlier context for the literature we shall soon confront, I shall continue to make a few speculations that will, I hope, be guided by the implications about the past provided by the texts of the archaic world we shall soon confront.

The following summary conclusions may not be unreasonable. Fear of the earth around and beneath and of the heavens above must surely have provoked suspicion and superstition and led early to placatory rituals. The desire and respect for fecundity in natural and human life multiplied gods and incantatory practices. Even after the disappearance of the estrus, the act of copulation itself must have gradually come to provide a form of recurring pleasure—if not the later "civilized" pleasure of asserting power or of achieving mutuality, at least that of the excitements of chafing and the ejaculatory relief of physical pressures. But surely also more and other than these last, as time passed and consciousness grew. The adoption of frontal intercourse contained the seeds of mutuality and further humanization as well as the possibility of new fears and pains, as Elizabeth Marshall Thomas seems to reveal fictionally in *The Animal Wife.* The mother's role in birth was necessarily known as soon as full self-contemplating consciousness dawned, but we cannot be sure about how or when knowledge of the father's role and resultant responsibilities developed or how they were mythologized. (We shall consider this last at greater length when we come to discuss the creation and fall in Genesis.) Nor do we know much about what I have defined as eros in chapter 1— that is, the decoration of sexual desire with beauty and charm. But nature suggests that preening in courtship may have developed with the species itself, and archeology contains early records of the adornment and enhancement of natural beauty by combs, mirrors, brushes, cosmetic jars, unguents, beads, necklaces, belts, and all kind of jewelry. To this preliminary and summary list I shall add topics and details as the recorded literature seems to reveal or imply them.

Joseph Campbell comments on the patriarchal view of goddesses: "In this masculine dream world, the excellence of the female is supposed to reside in: a) her beauty of form (Aphrodite), b) her constancy and respect for the marriage bed (Hera), and c) her ability to inspire excellent males to excellent patriarchal deeds (Athene)."[13] This smooth statement needs to be "roughened up" a bit even for the Olympian period, to say nothing of the earlier antiquity that is now our concern. Can anything be said about the Great Mother—Gē (Gaia) or Rhea or Cybele—relevant to the earthly couple in love? Perhaps not much, but the facts that Marilyn French and her sources record are impressive: that between 7000 and

6000 B.C. most of the figurines dug up from the Mediterranean world or early European cultures near it are female and must in some way be related to worship of the Great Mother. There are four times as many Neolithic female figurines as male, and in Minoan frescoes the females dominate.[14]

The following "earthy" beliefs, which arise from considering the Mother Goddess, are peculiarly relevant since they will enter our story with frequency. The Earth is feminine—a virgin to be fertilized and then a productive mother. Nevertheless, Titans and Giants were produced from the Earth. The serpent is an earth creature par excellence, and it, like other animals, has entered many important founding myths not least in relation to women and marriage. All agricultural and even nomadic people are necessarily close to the Earth. Women are not naturally farther from animals than men, and early women may, like many female animals, have joined the hunt and its rituals. It is woman who produces children and nurtures them, and she might well seem to possess magical and creative powers not vouchsafed to man. For all these reasons it is not hard to believe that early man felt the attractions of a powerful female orientation and that his beliefs and practices were guided and shaped by earthy and even chthonic influence. In any event one can assert, somewhat categorically, that throughout antiquity, from as far back as the Paleolithic, the Mediterranean and Middle Eastern world regarded the Earth as a goddess and worshipped her as such, grateful to her for such gifts as drink, bread, and milk. Later familiar—and familial—goddesses like Aphrodite, Artemis, Hera, Persephone, and Demeter bear some relation to her, if they are not literally her avatars. She undoubtedly possessed a personality and shape of her own, fully identifiable and iconically related to her fertility functions.[15] This is strikingly illustrated in what may be the earliest known surviving figure of the Mother Goddess of the Middle Eastern world, one discovered in Turkey. She is squat, fat, coarse, fertile, determined, all her reproductive parts vulgarly emphasized, a totally ungracious and unsentimentalized woman, sitting on a stone between two leopards, whom she has tamed and dominates, and giving birth to a child (fig. 2). Two impressions are strongest: she unmistakably stands for something specific—and that is generative productivity—and she is badly in need of the graceful and erotic modifications that come later. But the essential features are prototypical and, when this goddess was invoked, they remained the same until the fall of Rome.[16]

Amazonism always involves conflict, and that aspect too seems not at all out of line with what can reasonably be hypothesized of prehistory. Males come into adolescence and adulthood, and wish to assert them-

FIGURE 2 *Mother Goddess,* c. 6000 B.C., terracotta, from Çatal Hüyük, Turkey. (Museum of Anatolian Civilization. Courtesy, Administration of Culture, Ankara.)

selves when they tire of and leave the nest. Both the division and the over-lapping of labor possess built-in tensions, and male physical strength in obvious places and ways can be expected to assert itself. And if strife arose, it was followed by some kind of pacification, general, local, re-peated, which prevailed until strife once more shattered the calm. Ag-gression in sexuality probably asserted itself more often than pacific enjoyment and mutuality, and recorded history would suggest that toler-ance and respect were culturally induced and hard won.

In summary, there is too much in myth that refers to struggle and pacification between Titan and Olympian, man and woman, satyr and maenad for this element to be ignored. Such alternations seem to point to antecedent reality kept stored in human memory, like the recollections of a great flood. The vases of early Greek art show the waxing and waning of hostility between maenads and their satyr companions, whose relations can be cool and cruel or playful and inconsequential. Strife there often is; figure 3 shows a dramatically violent bit of concentrated sexual hostility. But even bitter struggle is sometimes fully reconciled in energetic dances, which themselves can be either wild or tender.[17] One can suppose that this kind of male-female oscillation existed for centuries before the fifth century; it may indeed show tensions and reconciliations between the female and the male residing in human nature itself. One need not be-lieve in long periods of female rule followed by long periods of male dominance, each formally established or codified and changed only cataclysmically. One need only believe that there lingered on into patri-archal cultures ineradicable memories of alternative arrangements. Such memories were the seedbeds of myth, art, and literature, with their often contradictory but always revealing layers and palimpsests, subplots and subtexts.

The Great Mother and her equivalents may not be available for much comment relevant to this study, but the familiar goddesses of the Greco-Roman pantheon are, and we shall encounter them again and again. A contextual word needs to be said about the great ones associated with love and the family. Even a familiar, established goddess like Aphrodite had an exotic past—Phoenician, Syrian, Semitic, Chaldean—and ver-sions of her appear in the epic of Gilgamesh and the Old Testament. Al-though she bears many resemblances to Asiatic goddesses, she, unlike the earthy Gē, is of the sky skyey, a queen of heaven—originally perhaps a hypostasis of Dawn and the gold-pink-red of presunrise. The sophis-tication of her epithets in epic poetry suggests a long development. And her functional range is impressively board and at times ambiguous and contradictory. She is of course the goddess of sexual love, and the Greek

FIGURE 3 Makron, *Maenad vs. Satyr,* 500–470 B.C., red figure cup. (Courtesy, Staatliche Antikensammlungen und Glyptothek, Munich.)

common noun *aphrodite* can mean, simply, sexual intercourse. She is the patroness of the passionate wife, but also of the adulterous wife; she herself achieves the pride of motherhood with a mortal and produces Aeneas; but she is also beloved of prostitutes, and at Corinth her worship required ritual prostitution. She is associated with grace and the Graces, with all the embellishments of life and art, with fine stuffs, embroidery, perfumes, with beauty, smiling, pleasure. She is never far separated from flowers, amorous animals, fertility, mating dances, and the rites of Spring. All Olympus is subject to her charms, save only Athene as goddess of war (a realm not congenial to Aphrodite, as we know from the *Iliad*), Artemis, the virgin-huntress, and Hestia, the queenly maiden, guardian of the hearth fire. These three are related in some way to the hunting, roasting, and eating of animals and to the killing of men. But the goddess of love is the patroness of human and animal generation—and the enjoyment that attends the process. Her own liaisons are also varied and somewhat contradictory when viewed together: she is the wife of the lame and dwarfed Hephaistos, the smithy god, but also unites with Ares, the handsome god of war; and on her own initiative she seeks the bed of Anchises, a mortal, woos him as a shy nubile virgin might; but in the end bows to the will of Zeus and enforces his decrees about the separation of deities and mortals, the while establishing her terrible-admirable status as goddess.[18]

From all these traits and acts, complexly developed over a long period of time and in many places and drawn from literature as late as the Homeric *Hymn to Aphrodite,* what shall we select as central and primitive? Not, I believe, the radiance of the early morning sky, nor the beauty and value of the royal metal, gold, nor the grace of physical movement— though these beauties are her signs and seem close to her essence. But it is surely the Aphrodite who stimulates and sanctions the sex act, who fosters the instinct of reproduction, and who presides over the cycle of birth, childhood, adolescence, marriage, and then birth again that constitutes the central Venereal heritage of the archaic writers from the dim antiquity that preceded them.[19] This is the goddess who should be regarded as a single field of related forces and not separated, as she later was in dialectical or moral division, into the heavenly and the earthly Aphrodite.[20] As the inspirer of sexual love she is *pandemos,* belonging to all the people; and as the fosterer of erotic and reproductive love she is also heavenly but not remote from the concerns of human beings or conventionally religious or life-denying. She is an affirmation of the most universal, understandable, and obvious creativity people at any time have ever known, one fully and joyously supported by the Greek heaven, though of course with sensible reservations. She is mediated to us forcefully by sculptured marble, which moves, like almost everything else in surviving Greek art, from the stiff, even slightly grotesque, hierarchical, and iconic representations to expressions of lofty sensual dignity and beauty in classical art and then to the more overtly sexual, superficial, but sometimes breathtakingly lovely figures of the Hellenistic period. The earlier figurations, most relevant to us in this chapter, can be suggestive and sophisticated, requiring no apology for age or remoteness. A terracotta from Rhodes of about 540 B.C. presents a clothed and hierarchical figure, holding her iconic sign, the dove, but the face, though partly eroded, shows a limpid, tender, and slightly ambiguous beauty (fig. 4).

FIGURE 4 *Aphrodite with Dove,* c. 540 B.C., terracotta, from Kameiros, Rhodes. (Reproduced by courtesy of the Trustees of the British Museum, London.)

The myth of Demeter and Persephone (or Korē) is one of the oldest, most solemn, most pervasive, and longest lasting to come out of the ancient Greek world. Bearing striking similarities to Christianity—and indeed, because of its absorption by the Eleusinian mysteries with its dark secret, of special interest to the Christian fathers—this divine story is almost inevitably related both to our broad subject and to our immediate concern with the prehistorical heritage with respect to love and marriage. It seems generally agreed that the three most important institutions of classical Greece were Olympian worship, agriculture, and marriage, all three of which are important in this myth of the mother-daughter goddesses. Since Olympian worship will be an important concern of later pages, let us consider the other two here.

If there was ever an agricultural myth, this can be said to be it. Hades springs forth from his chariot, seizes the girl Persephone as she is gathering flowers with her nymphs, the earth gapes, the girl screams. She is not located for a considerable time by her distraught mother, the stately, powerful, rich-haired, queenly, and "awful" Demeter. All nature is in disorder at her loss and grief—even human life on earth is threatened—and it is not until Zeus intervenes that the girl is found, now the bride of Hades in the underworld and bound to him by her having eaten that symbol of fertility, the fruit with the many seeds, the pomegranate. She is restored to her mother and Olympus for two-thirds of the year, but for one-third (the season in which the ground is dead either during the Greek winter or parched summer) she remains underworld and unproductive. Fertility is closely and fundamentally related to agriculture, but also to love and human sexual relations, and it is these that are of paramount interest here.

Modern psychoanalytical readings of the Homeric hymn to Demeter (the oldest version of her story that has come down to us) have stressed the mother-daughter relations in this myth, and Persephone's coming of age and arriving finally, even after violation, at joyful selfhood. But the most original implications for human intimacy—many other myths, including those that feature Aphrodite and Hera, also enforce fertility—arise from the mother-daughter relationship. *Relationship* is not a strong enough word, for mother and daughter attain a kind of fusion and are regularly referred to as the twin goddesses, the Twain, obviously aspects of the same and single reality, surely womanhood itself. Both maid and woman were simultaneously attributes of the Eleusinian goddess, a duality engraved on the sacred stone at the place of worship. This duality bears little resemblance to the Freudian split between virgin and whore in man's perception of woman, referred to in my first chapter, or indeed to

the very familiar division in female nature between innocence and experience. Both mother and daughter are sexually experienced and are
mothers; both are fertile, and their rites are combined with *aischrologia*
(ritual jesting), which may be a verbal replacement of bodily exposure
but still remains related to it. They are bonded with strongly erotic
mother-daughter ties. And both are necessary to human life—they are
twins, so to speak, and duplicate one another. Their closeness typifies
one of the most essential features of the family in its internal structure,
mother-daughter bonding. This alone, because of its universality, would
explain the enormous popularity of the two goddesses.[21]

This quality of close relationship is brought out strikingly in a lovely
and dignified sculpture in low relief found at Eleusis and now in the National Archaeological Museum of Athens, dating from the second half of
the fifth century B.C. (fig. 5). Triptolemos, the Eleusinian youth who was
one of Demeter's pupils and first initiates and whom she sent forth to
instruct mankind, stands between Demeter, who holds a scepter and
hands him divinely viable seeds, and Persephone, who holds a long torch
in her left hand and touches the youth's head, as though in blessing, with
her right. (The blessing may, in fact, be a gift of wealth.) Shorter by a head
than both goddesses, the youth, in profile, is fully human, frontally nude
though his back is draped, his penis visible though not tumescent.

The goddesses dominate. They can certainly be differentiated,
clothes, posture, and coiffure being iconically characteristic of each.
Demeter is clothed in a garment that drapes itself, while Persephone's
clings a bit more. But similarities seem to transcend the differences. Both
have stylized, wavy hair, both have prominent breasts, both are reverent
and dignified, their heads slightly bowed, though Demeter's may be
slightly less so. Both are open-eyed, the daughter's eyes softer and tenderer. Persephone's torch bears delicate hints of sexuality: it is certainly a
scepter suggesting her queenly status in the underworld, lined and
grooved like a column. But it may also have signs of penile suggestiveness
toward the top, apart from one obvious meaning of fire and flame. A divine myth but clearly and beautifully realized on the human plane, love
and agriculture here meet and give to heterosexual relationships the context of the divinely sanctioned productive society that is so prominent in
Homer.[22]

This work of art is late, but I see no reason why, if one subtracts some
of its smooth and softly idealized human realism and adds a bit of ritual
and hierarchical density and even archaic awkwardness, at least some of
its values may not be posited of the preliterate past. We might wish to
give a bit more emphasis to some elements of the story were we to create

FIGURE 5 *Triptolemos Between the Two Goddesses,* second half of fifth century B.C., marble relief. (National Archaeological Museum, Athens/Art Resource, NY.)

an icon for earlier days. Persephone the girl might lead in ritual dance the nymphs of the bubbling spring, who are associated with birth, growth, marriage. More could be made of the dancing that accompanied some festivals, like those at Orchomeneus, and of the return of spring flowers associated with marriage and birth—further details that characterize the maiden daughter and her marriage. The more terrible aspects of Demeter, with her threats of extinguishing humanity by famine and her burning of the human babe in a peasant fireplace to give it immortality, would not only darken the myth but show its solemn importance to ongoing life and thus increase its intensity and its ultimate joy. This last is beautifully brought out in Hilda Doolittle's translation, where Demeter is made to symbolize a hope of transcendence and where the pagan grain, vine, and branches are made to hint at sacramental bread and wine.

It may at first seem to be a descent to move from Demeter, the most powerful and dignified version of the Great Mother available to us, to Hera, often thought of as the nagging or seducing housewife of Olympus.[23] But the wife of Zeus, perhaps older and longer reverenced even than the father of gods and men, should not be patronized or stereotyped: her husband may in fact have come as an outside intruder into her already established and maternally and uxorially oriented realm. Visual evidence exists that she was sometimes thought of as young and alluring, and she may in fact not have needed the amorous aid that she gets in Homer from Aphrodite in order to arouse and satisfy her Olympian lord. She was widely honored with the invocation of *parthenos* (young virgin). She was cow-eyed—as in the case of other deities her animal epithet may recall a theriomorphic state—but cows were loved and revered not only in India, and for obvious reasons. Though she was not polygamous and certainly never faithless or adulterous in the great period of the established pantheon, she did recall the periodicity if not the inconstancy of the moon and may thus have been tied to her own sex through menstruation. But, more romantically though not more humanly, her lunar nature may be related to what C. Kerenyi has called "the spellbinding moonlight of Greece," and in Sparta at least Hera was frequently paired with Aphrodite.[24] Still bearing the dignified and potent Demeter in mind, we can see a parallel between her and Hera, for both were associated with marriage, though the former with its procreative purposes primarily.

Zeus and Hera became the Olympian paradigm of conjugality; they were invoked at weddings and betrothals and remained sponsors and supporters of the marital state.[25] But there are recollections of the earlier Hera's relationship to the pre-Olympians in the late archaic period. The Homeric *Hymn to Apollo* tells the following story arising from Hera's anger at being ignored and having the marital bed dishonored, when Zeus conceives and bears Athene cephalically. She complains to the gods in assembly about the slight, saying that she would have been more than glad to bear the child and calling her powerful husband stubborn and wily as well as thoughtless. Her revenge will be carefully parallel: she will bear a child independently of the marital chamber though not in such a way as to disgrace the holy wedlock. Leaving Olympus and coming to earth, she prays, then strikes the ground with her mighty hand, and addresses Earth, Sky, and the Titans, ancestors of men and gods alike, who dwell under the earth and around the great Tartaros. She asks for a child who will be as much stronger than Zeus as he is stronger than Kronos. For over a year she did not visit her husband's bed but frequented her own temples, delighting in the sacrifices. Then she bore the "dreadful and baneful" Typhon, who turned out to be a scourge to mortals, though resembling neither them nor the gods, and who had to be confined to the care and service of a she-dragon, thus multiplying evil until Apollo's bow dispatched the female beast at Pytho. This act may have rendered Typhon powerless, and the story is surely a cautionary one about defying the will of the husband-ruler. But it does show the primitive spirit and original affiliations of Hera, who at a moment of marital crisis goes to her own people for help, advice, succor—and mischief. She had undoubtedly once been chthonic herself, and a striking relief on the neck of a pithos from Thebes, dating back to the seventh century B.C., shows her seated, like the Earth Mother herself in many representations, between two rampant lions positioned somewhat like those on the lion gate at Mycenae, her eyes staring down, her mouth open and somewhat fiercely showing her upper teeth.[26] In pre-Olympian periods she must have brought her considerable powers to serve the fruitfulness and perhaps also to sanction the private ecstasies of dynastic marriage.

Her most dignified and familiar role—verifiable because late and recorded—is that of Hera Teleia (Hera the Fulfilled, the Mature), which was never totally divorced from the Hera Parthenos (the young virgin), showing a cyclical range no more limited than that of Aphrodite—from birth to growth to adolescence to marriage to maternity. But it is as a marriage goddess that Hera achieves her full *telos* (purpose). She then matches closely the Zeus of the fructifying moistures of the sky and especially the friendly father, the son of Philia, the popular Zeus Philios, who often presided over dinners of several courses. But Zeus, even in his most endearing side, never sent Hera into eclipse. Pausanias says that in the Hera temple at Olympia (dedicated in the later seventh century B.C., following an even earlier one dating from about 1000) a statue showed that the queen of heaven had chosen a young husband who shared but did not shadow her beauty. And in Paestum in Italy, where there still stand the handsome ruins of a sixth-century temple to Hera and where Zeus was also worshipped, the remains of a house that belonged to Hera alone suggest human warmth and charm: there she had a couch, which was surrounded by nine jars, hydrias, and amphoras of bronze, which must certainly have contained honey and wine. Pictures portray Herakles's journey to the underworld and the dance of maenads and satyrs around Dionysos. Everything points to jollity, sweetness, intoxication in this endearing monument to Hera Teleia.[27]

I have called my comments on preliterate Western antiquity a reconstruction, and so they must inevitably be speculative but, I hope, not unreasonable. No one believes that Homeric song, meter, and form sprang up suddenly, nor should we think that in the relations of the sexes, human or divine, there was not a slow, rich, and sophisticated evolution to the still inspiring human intimacies of the *Iliad* and the *Odyssey*. That evolution seems to have moved slowly away from maternal and female-oriented phases or periods of shared and alternating power to what we now call patriarchy. In the maternal and feminine phases, Aphrodite, Demeter-Persephone, and Hera stimulated and sanctioned sexuality, fertility, family. And it would stretch credulity and also churlishly underestimate centuries of human development to deny that grace, ornament, and beauty in life and art (what in my earlier taxonomy I called eros) failed to accompany the large human ends these goddesses promoted even in very early days of strife and the arduous formation of civilized identity.

Nor must we ever, in concentrating on community and general culture, lose sight of individual human needs. I close this section with two examples. The stimulating French structuralists of our day have shown how Adonis was celebrated in the classical period as an embodiment of erotic power and also as a god of hot spices and of an excessive and ultimately destructive sexuality that leads to quick growth and early blight. Adonis begins in frankincense, myrrh, and heady, seductive perfumes, ignores the cereals and grains that sustain life, and ends ironically in wet, cold, antaphrodisiac lettuce.[28]

Does this collective, cautionary ritual myth of fifth- and fourth-century Athens about the value of stable marriage and the danger of a brief and ill-fated blaze of unsanctioned lust necessarily tell the whole truth about *individual* life even in that period of high Attic classicism, to say nothing of the preliterate centuries? Contrast it with a personal and passionate Sumerian poem, where lettuce is also an important image and where it and wool stand for pubic hair and the *dubdub* bird for the clitoris. The poem is a love song addressed to Inanna, the Mesopotamian Aphrodite, but secularly it refers to the love life of the royal couple in the Third Dynasty of Ur, particularly to the passion of the queen, which apparently a court poetess was capable of imagining as her own.

> My 'wool' being lettuce he will water it,
> it being box (-grown) lettuce he will water it
> and touch the *dubdub* bird in its hole!
>
> My nurse has worked at me mightily,
> has done my 'wool' up in a 'stag,'*
> has gently combed it,
> and is straightening my 'May He Come!'†
>
> Let him come! Into my 'wool,' it being
>   the most pleasing of lettuces,
> I shall with arousing glances
>   Induce the brother‡ to enter. . . .²⁹

*A kind of arrangement at present unknown.
†Breast-shields.
‡Like *sister,* a term of endearment that did not necessarily show kinship.

The "lettuce" of the Adonis myth is collectively oriented and of course warns about impotence after excessive indulgence. The Sumerian song is individually passionate, a cry that the "lettuce" of innermost female physical space be pleasurably fertilized. But this private experience is also seen against the empyrean, and the goddess Inanna is invoked without loss of realistic intensity. The short poem amazingly epitomizes the Sapphic mood and manner, though with a frankness unknown in the fragmentary art of the later poet. Her inspiration must have extended far back into the earlier antiquity we have here been thinking about and whose lingering structures will be exemplified in the canonical texts of the next section.

Established Patriarchy and Alternative Voices

A late twentieth-century elite has opened many eyes to these suggestive points of view about patriarchy: that it is not an inevitability of either nature or culture, that it began historically and can end historically, that it competed with and overcame other forms of male-female relationship, and that it was not a single, monolithic entity but existed in different times and places with striking degrees of variation. It does seem to have been in place in the Mesopotamian world, with many familiar features firmly established and finally institutionalized in the Code of Hammurabi; these included premarital chastity for the girl, monogamous marriage, a high degree of social control over woman's social behavior— and also assurance of the legal and economic rights of women in marriage. Still, as Sumerian myth and literature reveal, woman was highly regarded and even romantically wooed and wed, though Ishtar- and Inanna-love could be dangerously ambiguous. Besides, it sometimes had to compete with a male friendship and an active heroic partnership that were as committed and emotionally overwhelming as that between Gilgamesh, the beautiful godlike hero, and Enkidu, the powerful natural man, who is, however, tamed and made ready for friendship and civilizing exploits by a harlot.[30]

The Hebrew Bible everywhere reveals an established patriarchy and authoritatively sets out the ideals of family life, virginity before marriage, and fidelity afterwards, vesting authority in the husband-father. It also recalls matrilocality (as in the Jacob and Laban stories) and sometimes even matrilinearity, and it brings into view in Genesis 6 a brisk sexual commerce between generative sons of God and procreative daughters of men that must be a relic of earlier times. Biblical image, precept, and practice over a long period of development show that within patriarchy the father also had a tender and sympathetic role, including care and fostering of the children; the concept of the Godhead as emotional participant in the sufferings of humanity strongly suggests some influence from female sensibility.[31]

The turbulence of the Greek Olympus can both reflect and influence the always grimmer conditions on earth. But Zeus, father of gods and men, as Homer calls him, does preside over affairs both above and below and enforces the keeping of covenants and the laws of hospitality, though of course he imposes no rigorous ascetic standards. In the great epics we shall shortly consider, divine and human patriarchy is firmly in place, but the paternal reins are not always held tightly. Thus, though Hera and Athene are constantly impatient that authority is not generous enough toward the Greeks during the Trojan War, Zeus ruthlessly thwarts his family as he redeems his promise to Thetis, the mother of Achilles, and allows the Trojans to drive the Greeks back to their ships. Humorously reflecting what may have been the actual domestic situation in the great houses of the Greek rulers, Zeus has come, however grudgingly, to respect Hera's will and would rather face Athene's disappointment than his wife's rage. Humor and wryness there may be, but no easy sentimentality. The epics show that war increases though it can also jeopardize wealth, and women are bartered and exchanged along with goods, though female captives and slaves sometimes attain virtually the status of wives and often that of an enjoyed and honored concubinage.

The force of patriarchal authority appears on Ithaca at the very outset of the epic, before Odysseus's return and virtually as a theme. Book 1 of the *Odyssey* establishes the home as central, male succession as regulative, and the rule of the male, even a young and untried male, as undisputed. Rebuking his mother for her complaints, Telemachus declares categorically the rule of men and bids his mother go to her chamber and there mind her household tasks with her handmaidens. Speech in assembly is for men only, especially for the lord of the house, a role Telemachus now assumes gladly and authoritatively, though only after Athene has given him strength and courage. He becomes a worthy son of a worthy father. But, as in the case of Mesopotamia and among the children of Israel, patriarchy is sometimes beautifully and energetically mitigated—and at greater length in the Greek epics than in what survives from Semitic antiquity.

For the softening of male power within patriarchy and the civilizing limitations laid upon it great credit must surely be owing to women. To the women celebrated in literature, who are often strong and attractive, as subsequent pages will show. But to historical women as well, not only for their natural and domestic roles but also for the more aggressive traits developed out of capture, exchange, and the indignities of loveless political marriage. Out of hard experience women learned to be resourceful; as mediators they saw more than one culture from the inside as it were; they strengthened their wills and their dedication to themselves and their offspring by being uprooted; and they were sometimes capable of hardening themselves to deeds of revenge and crime. Such schools of raw experience could create decisive wills and also deep dedication to the values of tenderness and stability that had been known, desired, imagined, and then disastrously interrupted. The sufferings of war are gender blind; they can produce female heroes as well as male.

Since there is always something to be said for order, patriarchy must be thought of as sometimes establishing stable forms and pacific conditions, which, though admittedly mischievous and unjust in their own ways, did minister to human development. For the imagination remains active in controlled, orderly, even oppressive environments. William Gass has said in discussing Nietzsche that "only an Apollonian could have invented Dionysus, because the Dionysian is too deep in the wallow ever to wonder."[32] Creative minds are seldom at their best in bacchic wallow, but within and beside if not directly out of patriarchy came the alternative voices and visions to which we now turn.

Hesiod belongs to the late archaic period, perhaps between the second half of the eighth and the first quarter of the seventh century B.C. Whatever his exact dates, this combination of poetic theologian (the author of *Theogony*) and practical agricultural adviser (the author of the *Works and Days*) looked backwards to myths that he consolidated and also around him and ahead to the labors of real men struggling to make a living from a harsh soil.³³

I hear him as an alternative voice, along with Sappho, but alternative to what? Certainly not to the patriarchy, for one of his aims in his Greek Book of Genesis is precisely to tell the story of Zeus—of male dominance; of the first hierarchical families; of the establishment of order; of the birth by Themis, his second wife, of Law, Justice, and Peace.³⁴ Furthermore, Hesiod in the *Theogony* is doing what we have seen the classical Greek mind doing in creating the myth of the Amazons and the modern feminist mind doing in postulating an irenic matricentric society in earliest antiquity, but here more boldly projecting upon even the pre-human past the kind of sexual love the poet desired for monogamous human unions. That projection does not occur at once. First, the primal powers (Chaos, Gaia, Tartaros, and Erōs) appear without normal generation. But then, once Gaia has given birth to tall mountains and the raging sea without mating in sweet love (ater philotētos ephimerou, line 132), sexual coupling of a recognizably human kind appears. It can sometimes be cruel and repulsive, as when Gaia lures Ouranos to lie with her, and Kronos his son hacks off his genitals, which he tosses behind him while Gaia keeps the bloody drops and produces furies and giants. Kronos in the meantime throws his father's genitals into the sea, and from the white foam that froths up Aphrodite is born. From then on, *himeros* (desire) and *philotēs* (that untranslatable *philos* word meaning "reciprocal sexual love, friendship, mutual goodwill") unite and produce the pantheon of gods and powers who keep the universe in place and make it productive. And the words Hesiod uses to characterize human heterosexual love at its best are those also used by Homer and other archaic writers—words, in fact, that cling to sexual union all through Greek classical antiquity.

So far, then, Hesiod's, far from being an alternative voice, is an establishing and epitomizing one, and the question must be raised whether those codal and legislative qualities also attend his less emphatically placed presentation of Erōs alone and then of the pair, Erōs-Eris (sexual desire and strife). In Homer *eros* (spelled with an omicron, not an omega) is never personified and means simply desire for food or drink, for woman, or even for lamentation. Centuries later in classical Greece the Erōs of Euripides is a child of Zeus and is "all men's lord," casting a sweet spell (charis); shooting fleet, hot, and speedy shafts; poisoning the home (oikos); and, along with Aphrodite, fostering the wild, lawless, incestuous love felt by Phaedra for Hippolytos.

Between Homer and Euripides stands Hesiod's influential formulation. His Erōs, as Jean-Pierre Vernant has demonstrated, assumes two forms. The first is one of the four primordial powers already described, the last named in the line of Chaos, Earth, and Tartaros, the most beautiful among the immortals and one of the most powerful. A force acting within fertile, overflowing unity, he forces it to produce individual beings and so serves both the homogeneous cosmos and its power of progressive individuation. The other Erōs, the child of Aphrodite, whose ministrations we have also noted, serves "an already established sexual dimorphism" and inspires two to unite to create a third.[35] This is the Erōs we know well, he who unstrings the limbs and subdues both reflective and sensual thought in gods and men. Such epithets as these clung to him for centuries, and even when he lost his fierceness and became something of a teasing and mischievous pre-adolescent, he still possessed a considerable degree of indomitable might. And although he is not often mentioned in the genealogy that follows his great first appearance, he must surely be thought of as being present implicitly as a generative and propulsive force. To have so succinctly and influentially portrayed the ambiguous but unmistakable power of Erōs is no small achievement, and the often underpraised and sometimes ridiculed Hesiod should be given due credit for a simple and formative insight.

But we can go further and praise Hesiod for a subtlety that paralleled or influenced pre-Socratic and post-Aristotelian thought. He liked to move by antithesis, no doubt partly because the powers he describes have contrary effects and need to be presented oxymoronically. His juxtaposition of Erōs and Eris is at once normative and philosophically suggestive.[36] Eris, the second and usually underprivileged member of the antithesis, is also associated with *philotēs* (the more orthodox and sometimes uxorial term for love); both are children of Night, that is, equal siblings, like all the issue of Night. But both are subordinate to Aphrodite and to Erōs, the primordial force from whom all things began, and are thus contingent and derivative beings, apparently associated with human institutions like marriage and war but unable to operate without the inspiration or sanction of mightier powers.

All this gives dignity and force to what men on earth do in both their most creative and their most destructive moments. The speculation that has clustered around the Erōs-Eris antithesis or its variants has been voluminous and influential: *discordia concors, concordia discors, coincidentia oppositorum* have resonated from Empedocles, Plato, Aristotle, Cicero, Horace, and Seneca at least to Johnson, Coleridge, Blake, and Hegel. Speculation has oscillated among several beliefs: that both contrarieties must exist in effectual counteraction, or that a *tertium quid* can eventuate, or that one (usually desire, the drive toward unity) predominates and swallows up the other. Here I wish to state—in the spirit not of dialectically solving an age-old dilemma but of enforcing what I have come to believe are the lessons of literature, art, and practical experience—that the truest paradigm for what we are studying is one of continuing and fructifying contrariety. Since the *Theogony* is about origins, one may be permitted to speculate further and say that the view that the universe came into being as a conflict between love and strife may itself be a projection upon cosmology of the usually ambiguous and conflict-ridden human experience of sexuality and not the other way around. In other words, abstract concepts did not in and of themselves logo-centrically create the universe, but men, gradually learning during eons of ignorance how they themselves produced life and inevitably observant of the pleasures and pains that accompanied generation, imposed their experiences onto a myth of origins that itself became intellectually powerful, mostly because it seemed to reflect human experience.

To a stable and authoritarian patriarchy, Hesiod presents an available alternative of mutually energizing contrarieties, although he was himself largely patriarchal in his own learned and even quirkish way. By contrast Sappho seems all delicacy, living in a land where the Dawn comes on little golden feet. But what can she be said to be an alternative to? Need we ask, since she was a woman and a homosexually oriented woman at that? It is one of the sad turns of history that almost the entire corpus of this talented and eccentric woman (in the literal and far from pejorative sense) was shredded and fragmented by the depredations of both slow time and swift religious zeal.

Ancient Lesbos, where Sappho lived—its closest point only about eight miles from Asia Minor—possessed a delightful climate; great cities; wealth in the form of gold, olives, wine, and grain; and beauty in its blue skies, flowers, and embroidered cloth imported from Sardis and Persia. Competition and patriotic pride ensured the presence of soldiers and archers, long ships, sleek horses, and chariots and charioteers. Its free women were courted, and they themselves sang in choruses under dancing stars and a rose-red moon.

Much of this lavendered vision may of course be only a projection from the verse that remains: without the structures of plot or logic, isolated and disparate sensuous images give us our first dominant impressions. The Sapphic landscape is the violet-colored and rose-scented Lesbos intensified, a place of beautiful boys but especially of delicate girls with the forearms of the Graces paler than any light tea rose, their sleeves tucked back at the elbow. Here the slender, trim, and violet-breasted Aphrodite reigns, attended by a subtly sad Erōs and by sweet persuasion, the goddess Peithō, muse of gentle seduction. The Sapphic scene is also urgent—above all, the place of the headlong heart, freed of cold inhibition and stern masculine prohibition, and thus congenial to the likes of the Victorian critic John Addington Symonds.[37]

It does not require a long acquaintance with the poet to know that she presents much more and other than an attar-drenched idyl. Her Erōs can be snake sly, is a limb loosener, like Homer's, can stalk like a beast; the love he induces can be gall and honey, salt and sweetness (130). Erōs is also the bringer of pain, who can shatter one's being like a powerful wind (47), and is powerless to overcome withering and death. His very essence is to be *glukupikros,* that is, bitter sweet.[38]

How much of these frustrating and complicating qualities belong to the homoerotic orientation of the love? Or to the environment that surrounded Sappho? (Did she run a school for training in charm and manners and in the arts of dancing and singing?) It is difficult to answer these questions, since all human love knows the ambiguous and tension-filled qualities I have mentioned, giving Sappho's poetry a wide resonance whatever its immediate orientation in her psyche or society. Without suggesting that Sappho hated men or that her Aphrodite was exclusively lesbian or that her many wedding songs did not celebrate conjugality, I emphasize the appeal of girl to girl and girl to woman, in case there still exist pressures that it be ignored or allowed to go unnoticed, as it seems to have been in antiquity until Hellenistic times, or suppressed, as it has been in Christian centuries. It should now be seen as an integral part of our long-term erotic heritage from Greece. The uniqueness of hymning female homosexual attraction even in antiquity gives it an honored place, and certainly no interpreter can escape the impression that the real Sappho (or, if one prefers, the persona of the poetry, the Aeolic *Psappho*) is perhaps at her most intense in comforting Atthis separated from her beautiful beloved female friend or in longing herself for Anaktoria or in wishing for death, as she does in Fragment 94, where a mutually loving same-sex relationship is being broken by separation. It is important for a properly attuned history of love that exclusively female experience be perceived as receiving in this body of poetry the tribute not only of such words as *himeros* (desire) and *pothos* (longing for what is absent) but also of the complex and dignified *philotēs* (1). Female lovers are called *philai* (142), once again that comprehensive and complex word that encompasses both erotic love and friendship.

The famous Fragment 31 leads us deep into the nature of the Sapphic *erōs*:

> He seems to me equal to gods that man
> who opposite you
> sits and listens close
> to your sweet speaking
>
> and lovely laughing—oh it
> puts the heart in my chest on wings
> for when I look at you, a moment, then no speaking
> is left in me
>
> no: tongue breaks, and thin
> fire is racing under skin
> and in eyes no sight and drumming
> fills ears
>
> and cold sweat holds me and shaking
> grips me all, greener than grass
> I am and dead—or almost
> I seem to me.

The triangle here—man, girl, woman—introduces the whole matter of erotic triangulation in Sappho and far beyond. In a brilliant interpretation Anne Carson sees in the threesome a "geometrical figure formed by their perception of one another"—and, more importantly, by their perception of the space between them, for the most sophisticated Greek *erōs* requires absence, an emptiness that needs to be filled. Finally and climactically, what the solitary poet perceives is her own mind contemplating what *erōs* in and of itself is and means, a contemplation that activates both lover and beloved and also that uncrossable space that comes between them and so almost destroys the speaker.[39]

In another brilliant interpretation, Lawrence Lipking finds the poem physically immediate and shattering in its passion, but he reduces the man to an abstraction: " '*anyone* able to sit close to you seems like a god to me.' " The leading authority on abandoned women regards this poem as less illustrative of his theme than expressive of a "manless, woman-to-woman" love, almost unendurable because it affects us like a divine intimation of our mortality.[40] To Kenneth Dover, however, the situation is less subjective and more overtly dramatic: the imminent occasion is the marriage of the girl to the man, who to the loving female speaker seems to be a god since it is impossible to compete with him. And the poet is left to envy and to her own solitary and frustrated affection.[41]

All three interpretations are suggestive, each in a different way, and more needs to be said about the broader implications of each. The triangulation of two plus *erōs*-as-absence is just and imaginative, but it needs psychological, social, and perhaps even religious broadening. In virtually all known societies, some form of *nomos* (law, custom, practice) inevitably interposes itself between lovers. In Plato's *Phaedrus* it is a god who is present, a god who is a disposition either individually inherent or socially and politically induced, so that if the god is Ares one kind of relation ensues, if Hermes, another. During centuries of Christian ritual and commandment, religious norms and prohibitions have governed and organized the practice of love even in the bedroom. For Freud the mother is almost inevitably present between the lovers; for Jung the presence is that of the archetypal wise old man, a father figure. Against all these third-party interventions, the loving two must shape their destinies— sometimes simply and even crudely, as when commandments are blunt and decisive; sometimes complexly, as when the intervening *nomos* is as sophisticated as the subtle and changing Greek pantheon or as shifting and intricate as is implied in the phrase *poikilos nomos* (law that is riddlingly ambiguous [lit. dappled]). Some form of triangulation, it seems, must be the obsessive concern of anyone trying to understand Western love.

Lipking's interpretation lends support to my plea that Sappho be acknowledged as a supreme celebrant of lesbian love, but Kenneth Dover's suggestion that a future marriage is envisaged in Fragment 31 also bears important implications for not only Sapphic but all serious or long-lasting amorous engagement. There are many male presences in Sappho, but there is no need to hypothesize an intense heterosexual longing for the fair boatman Phaon, as Ovid did in *Heroides* 15, or to imagine a suicidal leaping into the Aegean waters because of frustrated love for a male. There are hints that the poet did not want to marry a younger man, that she could be stirred by youthful male beauty, and that farewell to a male beloved could cause pain. But it appears that the chief function of the male is to carry off a girl in wedlock and so break a tender bond set up in whatever female *thiasos,* or company, it was that attended Sappho. If so, *nomos* is very important indeed in the Sapphic triangle. It can cruelly elide already existing love in the interest of state or family. But it can also exemplify and intensify a natural longing for permanence and mature fulfillment in the amorous life—a longing that *need* not have been, but usually *was,* associated exclusively with marriage.

Many of Sappho's fragments are thought to be parts of epithalamia, and if in fact it was her practice to write hymeneal songs for what inevitably meant the painful separation from herself of the girls she knew and loved, a deep and moving irony exists. Sappho was impelled by the very exercise of her talent to contemplate ritualized unions supported by society, sanctioned by the gods, beautified by grace and the Graces. These unions were intended to eventuate in procreation, the establishment of a society even more intimate and surely longer lasting than any she had experienced, and the kind of prosperity and permanence that from the outside at least seemed to provide a hedge against the shattering separations she knew all too well. In such unions—or so it must surely have been believed on Lesbos as elsewhere—love could be supported by shared tasks and predictable recurrences of pleasure and opportunity. This, not violet sunsets and perfumed breezes, may constitute the Sapphic idyl, and it does not weaken—in fact, it may strengthen—the force of the poetry if we must regard the idyl as only a dream.

If Sappho presided over a school, its purpose may have been, as Claude Calamé has suggested, to lead the girl from Artemis to Aphrodite, more likely than not the Aphrodite of the wedding bed.[42] If so, the fulfillment of her pedagogical goal was, tragically and ironically, the death of a lasting *erōs* for her. My suggestion of the matrix for her frustration may of course be no more than fanciful. But reality is here less important than the realization that Sapphic verse expresses with great beauty the loss that seems regularly if not inevitably to attend the Aphrodite love of real life—a loss as poignant as the attraction is compelling. Such loss inevitably turns us to the embodiment in art of our consuming hopes and tenderest and intensest desires. What libido and affection lose is reborn in the *erōs* of art and beauty. Thus the allure of the Lesbian and Sapphic landscape which I invoked in opening my discussion of a poet who has haunted the imagination for centuries may not be entirely irrelevant after all, since it is to a union with a Swinburnian and not a Platonic beauty that the poet so insistently summons us. Even, perhaps especially, institutionalized long-term relations have their share of bittersweet eros, and Sappho has a poignant, though indirect, relation to our theme, which I am content to leave implicit.

Homer

If Sappho ends with longing for the permanent and the fulfilling, Homer ends with its embodiment, beautifully, authoritatively, influentially. The *Odyssey* has taught and entertained not only Greece but the whole world, and the archaic period has thus, at the very earliest part of my historical inquiry, provided a climax. For Homer is indeed one of the greatest love poets of the Western tradition, if love is not defined as romantic rapture. He has achieved this inside patriarchy, as we have said, not outside it as an alternative voice. Nevertheless, like all richly layered authors, Homer is the inheritor and exploiter, not the victim of socioeconomic and political conditions, historical developments, and religio-artistic traditions and so is fully capable of creating subtexts, if not subcultures—subtexts pregnant with human possibility, rich in imaginative fulfillments not present in the status quo that pressed upon him. These appear with force if we respond to his centrally powerful and abundant antitheses, doing what he piques us into doing by his humanity and his art—giving privilege to the often underprivileged member, to dying humanity over immortal gods, peace over war, love over violence, gain over loss, and women over men. All this interests someone who is not primarily in search of the actual conditions of Mycenean Greece but of an available heritage concerning the loving couple.

That heritage would surely be richer if we still possessed intact the great epic cycle of narratives from the beginning of the world to the end of the heroic age, including five books, not merely one, of homecomings from Troy; the *Aethiopis,* concerned as it was with the Amazons and the deaths of Achilles and Penthesilea; epics of Thebes, Herakles, and Theseus. But the *Iliad* and the *Odyssey* are far from insubstantial, and whatever one believes about single, double, diverse, or multiple authorship, the two epics can still be profitably regarded as complementary— the fulfilling pluses of the latter fully anticipated even in the life-denying negatives of the former. My intention is to resist a contemporary view that finds power the central "value" of the *Iliad,* a power that corrodes beauty, pleasure, and love in a story portraying man as predominantly a killer.[43] Power there surely is, but more than anything else it serves to heighten what men in war miss and what the civilized king of the Phaeacians and husband of an even more civilized wife lists in the *Odyssey* as

the climax of his people's achievements in sport, commerce, and art—
"the warm bath, and love, and sleep." Love is thus perceived as something that can be enhanced by good, earthy, homey things (Book 8). I also
resist the view that the *Odyssey* presents a culture in which nature is the
enemy and that man escapes from a female-dominated world to come
home to male domination pure and simple. Nature is of course present
and can persecute people cruelly, but the restored Ithaca at the very end
presents—not without sentimentality in view of the bitterness of the
climactic slaughter of the suitors—man and nature in collaboration,
women and men as partners, and a vision of formerly warring men as
potential brothers in friendship and wealth, all admittedly within the matrix of a patriarchy, but one humanized by experience and the artistic
imagination. The vision is a compelling one precisely because it is realistic, springing from a lively sense of what is possible as well as just and
always cognizant of what I have called the necessary ego context of all
value.

That context appears if we consider some of the great Homeric
words for love between the sexes and within families. We begin with
philos, a word that enters into a plethora of verbal structures, some of
them complex, culturally as well as grammatically polysyllabic. The
philos words we have encountered earlier, noting that they encompass
both ardent love and friendship, here possess an even broader range than
we have so far considered, one that keeps the ego very much alive in love
and shows that what is dear is also what is mine and is dear precisely
because it is mine. Thus my hands, arms, throat, or knees can be dear
(*Il.*19.209; *Od.*21.55). All my organs are dear, as well as my bedclothes,
my decisions to undertake something, my guests; indeed hospitality itself
is dear ("a whole month he loves [*philei*] me" [*Od.* 10.14]), showing that
philos can be applied to that on which or those on whom my safety and
survival depend. Such origins in selfishness do not by any means demean
love and friendship but rather enforce them, in the most satisfying
and even ecstatic intimacies. When Odysseus and Penelope approach
their stable and immovable marriage bed in the climactic moments of
the reunion, a *philos* word joins an *erōs* word (philotētos, erasteinēs,
*Od.*23.300); the first of these appears again at the very end of the epic
(24.476, and see "allēlous phileontōn," 485) when Athene requests and
Zeus decrees pacification and friendship between the victors and the
vanquished after the bitter survivors of the suitors take up arms.[44]

Grace (charis) is another great love word in Homer. It is closely related to what in my taxonomy of terms and values I called eros, the embellishment of love and sexuality by beauty and charm in art and life,

precisely what those delightful and perennial personifications, the Three Graces, were intended to embody. Grace attends Aphrodite, and it also attends the woman's gift of herself to the man, as when the goddess herself woos Anchises in the beautiful Homeric hymn and impels the man to accept her. Nausicaa, a maiden, possesses *charis,* and the grizzled veteran Odysseus frequently has it poured over his head and shoulders by Athene to give him irresistible heroic charm. It too has a practical resonance, for it attends the judgments of the intelligent and capable Queen Arētē when she administers justice in Phaeacia and bestows great favors among her people, and it can refer to the simple bestowing of favor, to anything in fact that produces gratitude and obligation. It thus possesses ego roots almost as deep as those of *philos.* It is unpretentious and realistic but is also fundamental in Greek religion and the Greek psyche, and Homer is engaged in a traditional and very substantial act when he applies it to the giving of the self in marriage.[45]

The great New Testament word, *agapē,* is anticipated when Hector's baby son is called *agapēton* in the famous *Iliad* scene at the gates of Troy (6.401); the word is also used of Telemachus, another son well beloved of both his father and mother. Plutarch, centuries later, joined the word *charis* with *philophrosunē* (wise love) and applied them both to marriage. Homer's word is *homophrosunē* (compatibility). It appears in Odysseus's wish for Nausicaa, that she may soon find a husband, a home, and *homophrosunē* (*Od.*6.181–84).[46]

Nausicaa must take her place in the gallery of attractive, clever, and practical Homeric women; she is only a nubile maiden, but one on her way to wifehood in a civilized society that stands in contrast to the wild and ugly societies of the likes of Polyphemus and to the attractive but unhuman isles of Calpyso and Circe. In the company of these immortal, even ravishing beauties, Odysseus shows himself to be a pleasure-loving natural man who seizes the sensual day, but he is protected from the sloth or bestiality on Circe's island by his wit and decisiveness. His longing for home and humanity never seems forced or out of character, and when he rejects the blandishments of immortality with eternal youth and joy, he remains peculiarly and poignantly himself however much idealized. The Odysseus of Hesiod had children by both Circe and Calypso and so contributed to mythic and sacred genealogy. Not so the insistently human Homeric hero, who may accept temporary enjoyment when it lies in his way but confines the serious matters of offspring and dynasty to humanity alone.

It is after some nine years in the company of beautiful goddesses that he is vouchsafed the company of the civilized Phaeacians.[47] In their society Nausicaa and her future are big with promise, not least because of her queenly mother, Arētē, who is superior even to the humane, gifted, and adoring king her husband. Her female subjects, who possess skill in the domestic arts, resemble their queen in the maturity of their wit and intelligence. Even a brief stay in this society further ripens the hero's manhood and also the artistry of his storytelling, which here comes to possess all the narrative energy and skill that Homer and the tradition can give it.

For such leisure the *Iliad* had little time, but in brief vignettes of telling beauty and pathos and in epic similes of dignified recollection and contrast, the civilized ways of home and hearth are always kept before us, not least when tragically lost or pathetically delayed. I have already called attention to the cluster of words relating to love and family that appear when Andromache and the child meet Hector at the Skaian gates of Troy. The tragic conclusion of their separation is told with force and dignity, and much has been made of Hector's rejecting love and family for war and honor. But the context in Troy is sometimes forgotten, unfortunately so since it heightens the pathos of the scene. Even though the family Priam presides over is far from nuclear or conventional even for Homer's day (showing us that monogamy and polygamy are categories too imprecise to be fully valuable), he is a loving and fruitful sire, respecting one capable wife above all others, and his many sons and daughters sleep in the palace (Paris and Hector have palaces of their own) with their chosen partners. (The architecture seems to have achieved both the privacy and the communication that some architectural historians have attributed to the coming of romantic love in post-Renaissance Western culture.) Homer, who is never exclusively uxorial, emphasizes the strong bond between Hector and his mother during the battles, as he does that between father and dead son at the close of the epic. Homer saturates the terrible Trojan scene with domesticity, familial affection, and fruitfulness. To all this the flighty though attractive Paris provides a cautionary contrast, while the unhappy and regretful Helen is herself an effective counterpoint to him. Of such antitheses is woven the tragic sense of keen and almost unbearable loss that we find in the *Iliad*.

But both the threatened domesticity of Troy and the utopia of Phaeacia are subordinate in aesthetic energy to the realistic and hard-won Ithaca, and Andromache, Hecuba, and Arētē must yield as wifely paragons to the clever, steadfast, and capable Penelope, whose presence invokes both the modest Artemis and the sensual Aphrodite. She is linked to Odysseus not only in sexual attractiveness and shared character traits like prudence, wisdom, and qualities of leadership, but also in that indefinable unity of spirit Homer wishes for Nausicaa, *homophrosunē,* which here receives its fullest elaboration. The story of the reunion—the careful preparation in part set up by Penelope; the prudent caution; the grim, realistic, but just action; the long-delayed sexual meeting on the im- movable bed, its tree-bedpost so firmly rooted in the earth and nature;[48] the mutual storytelling after the sexual climaxes (she too apparently being a narrative artist)—is well known and need not be retold here, ex- cept to give emphasis to the climactic quality of the nuptial relationship, sometimes obscured, slighted, or perhaps even regretted.

What needs emphasis is that Penelope, though a paragon, is not a goddess. Odysseus has had quite enough of goddesses, and now he needs what he gets: a tried, experienced, tortured woman, who even close to final triumph prays to Artemis for death. Threatened by evil men, always afraid of intervention by a deceiving or malicious immortal, Penelope is entitled to a good *nostos* (homecoming) of her own after many spiritual wanderings and trials. And she gets it. Hers and her husband's tears mingle, her knees melt (that sure sign of Aphrodite's presence), she learns of his gentle future death, and she proceeds formally to their bed with him, led by a maid with torches, as though to renew the days of their beginnings. Emphasizing the sanctioned dignity of the ecstasies they have now come to, the virgin goddess Athene releases the dawn only when she is sure the two have had their fill of love and sleep.

Against such satisfying and emotionally charged normality Homer places not only the relatively shallow or dangerous blisses of Calypso and Circe, but also the crimes against marriage, the family, the household, and all society that attended Agamemnon's homecoming. Clytemnestra is the evil wife, her lord the most unfortunate of mortals, and their story is retold or alluded to all the way through the *Odyssey* with almost com- pulsive force and regularity—both in this world and in the underworld, initially, centrally, and climactically after the victory of Odysseus at home. This is surely one of Homer's greatest and starkest antitheses.

But there is another, more nuanced, full of light and shadow, and both like and unlike the story of Odysseus and Penelope. It is that of Helen, and she is kept before us through both the epics. Both her pre- and post-Homeric story is instructive. She may have been venerated in several places long before Homer wrote, as a fertility goddess with Indo- European forebears or as one possessing some kind of association with both the sun and the moon. In Homer she shares a rare and powerful epithet with Athene, Artemis, and Aphrodite but with no one else—*dios kourē* (daughter of Zeus).[49] Sappho's Helen is one who acts, who creates her own destiny in pursuing what she loves and desires, and is therefore

something of a model for the poet who persists in loving Anactoria. Alcaeus makes her a victim of madness. Herodotus pursues her story first to
Egypt where he talks with Egyptian priests about her and is convinced
that she was not in Troy during the holocaust but in Memphis, where she
is worshipped as the foreign Aphrodite. He also finds that in Sparta
Helen, properly supplicated, could endow an ugly child with beauty. For
Isocrates, she embodies charm and beauty, without which everything, including virtue itself, is useless, and for Theocritus she is the rosy, shining
Helen, skillful in weaving and making patterns, the embodiment of
grace, virtually the goddess of mutual love.

Homer's portrait of this venerable and powerful figure of lust and
divinity is, by the necessity of his inheritance from the past, ambiguous,
providing an interesting and richly textured comparison-contrast with
his figures of normative love. He never calls her a goddess, and she must
play her role on a human level, though she is given great powers, powers
that the local and isolated Penelope (who, however, knows of her and
finds her a fatally god-driven woman) does not achieve. It is through her
observations that we and the Trojans meet the great Greek heroes, and
her terrible and godlike beauty and power are attested when the elders at
the gates see the living person about whom such enormous and prolonged fuss is being made—and they understand why. It is she who,
appropriately, leads the lamentation for Hector, since this good man,
whom she admires and who never spoke a bad word to her, died seeking
honor in a conflict she caused. As a seer she interprets the bird-sign as
Telemachus is about to leave Sparta, and like other mythical women
of great sexual power she is given the gift of prophecy as well as divi-
nation—showing, one takes it, the high regard with which sensual drive
was regarded even when feared.

One very striking feature emerges in Homer's treatment of the
several appearances of Helen: she transcends the traditional role that
Penelope and tradition assigned her of being a fated, Aphrodite-drunk
sensualist. She is destined, it is true, to be intimate with Paris, and at
the direct intervention of Aphrodite goes to bed with him in *Iliad 3*,
where she shows her intelligence by penetrating at once the disguise of
Aphrodite as an old woman. Her boldness in resisting the impulse is de-
terred only when an angry Aphrodite threatens her: I terribly love you
but I could also terribly hate you. But even with Aphrodite in the chamber Helen proceeds to deride Paris, wishing he had been slain and revealing her abiding admiration for Menelaos as both man and warrior. When
Telemachus meets Helen in her Spartan home after the return of her husband, he meets in the gleaming palace not an Aphrodite but a gracious

wife and hostess calling herself, as she has and will elsewhere, a shameless wanton and the cause even of Telemachus's dilemma (*Od*.4). A Restoration wit would say that she has dwindled into a wife, but not so Homer. His values are different, and they never appear more strongly than when he coopts the greatly sinning sensualist for monogamy. She ends up not only as a dutiful wife (though still capable of a marital quarrel) unusually skilled in cloth making and the weaving of pictures into her patterns, but also as seer and prophetess while remaining fully human as she interprets the heavenly omens. In other words, after some censure from others but considerably more from herself, Helen takes her place as one of Homer's great uxorial women, superior alike to Paris and Menelaos.

It is time to ask precisely where long-term sexual commitment stands contextually in Homer. The wedding ceremony appears centrally on the shield of Achilles created by Hephaistos, suggesting that it belong with the goods of the city at peace (*Il*.18). In the moving contrast between the ways of war and the ways of peace, male-female coupling is of course on the side of peace, though war in Homer is not without its own terrible eroticism when men spill their blood on the thirsty earth. Homeric commitment between the sexes contrasts with the unions of Olympus, which are bitchy and angry, leading to recriminations and demeaning punishments (like the threatened hanging of Hera by a chain for her deceptions). One must admit that these can achieve verve and humor, as in the celebrated seduction of Zeus by Hera, followed by an abrupt and angry awakening. But there is no human tragedy, pathos, deep love, or great faithfulness on high, and we must look to Phaeacia and Ithaca for the mutual energizing of respect and eros.

Not being sentimental in the later, weak sense of the term, Homer shows that human commitments at best mix good and evil. For that reason he surrounds and sanctions them with other goods, such as property, children, inheritance, and love of country; if evil, greedy, and selfish men threaten that order, they are put to the sword and their women allies are hanged by the neck until dead. Concubinage and the prizes of war and exchange are not scorned, and a concubine or captive could achieve a loved and honored place, with sometimes a promise of true marriage. There must have been tensions between wife and concubine, as the story of old Phoenix and the days of his youth reveals, when because of such conflict he was forced to flee from his home to save his life. But Odysseus is never *portrayed* with a concubine or a human war prize during the Trojan War (although *Il*.1.138 passingly *refers* to a prize, which Agamemnon threatens to take away from Odysseus; but it is by no means certain that this is a girl). And if immortality with Calypso could not shake Odysseus's dedication to hearth and home, what else could? The couple—not just the loving and desiring couple but the generative, propertied, managing, cooperating, intelligent, and resourceful couple—is one of the highest values Homer knows. And Homer was the teacher of all Greece, and all the world.[50]

Le plus grand plaisir qui soit après amour, c'est d'en parler.

    Louise Labé, *Le Débat de Folie et d'Amour* (1555)

*Il y a une histoire des attitudes et des discours amoureux, qui est sans doute le dépot le plus exquis de l'*âme *occidentale.*

    Julia Kristeva, *Histoires d'amour* (1983)

THREE

Classical Greece

s early as 1925 a distinguished Greek scholar quarreled with a commonplace modern opinion concerning classical Athens—that its women occupied an ignoble position. Since that date, the indictment has become codified—more specific, more sophisticated, more intense. The following *sententiae* are not untypical: ancient Athens was "an exclusive men's club"; a beautiful and cultivated woman on the Athenian scene was almost always a stranger; the polis was in effect ruled by the phallus; marriage guaranteed the death of individuality, so that only celibate, divorced, or childless women were individual persons. In his comprehensive study of Western sexuality, Michel Foucault expresses more discriminating and nuanced views: he quite rightly discerns in later antiquity (that is, in Hellenistic Greece and Rome) a new ethos within married love, which he believes requires virtually a new Aphrodite, one who can create not only sexual desire but amity as well. And that synthesis of *gamos* (marriage) and *erōs* (sexual desire) seems to the philosopher so powerful that he is sure it must rest on the deep philosophical foundations of nature, reason, and indeed essential humanity. But for earlier Attic culture Foucault adds his voice to the consensus: the relations of the sexes were stiflingly hierarchical, and cognitive value could appear only when the male happened to be benevolent and wise, having submitted himself to a dietary and spiritual regimen of rigorous exercise and self-control. Foucault concedes that in earlier Athenian thought there is "nothing . . . that would rule out personal feelings of attachment, affection and concern," saying that the classical way of thinking about marital relations did not in the least exclude the kind of intensity that was acknowledged in the relations of friendship. Such concessions—and they are made by others as well—may reveal no more than scholarly caution or defensiveness. But they may also reveal a sense that much has been left out of the regnant opinion, and indeed much has: religion, mythology, literature, and art, matters that dietetics, medical advice, and ethical formulation, important though these are, are not equipped to consider or even imagine as being relevant. It is my intention in this chapter to supply what has been left out, mostly by consulting the creative imagination and expressions of religious feeling; these will, I believe, disclose a heritage of organized and organizing energy still available to us—a heritage to which ad hoc and concessive waves of the hand do scant justice. In my analysis it has been difficult to escape A. W. Gomme's categorical conclusion that there is no literature or art of any country where woman is more prominent, more important, more assiduously studied than in the drama, sculpture, and painting of fifth-century Athens. When philosophers denigrate her, they place her in relations crucial to society: Aristotle, for example, finds the *philia* that is within the family (the Greek word, difficult to translate, signifies both friendship and love, often in combination) to be the cement of the state, its greatest blessing. Plato and many others privilege marriage politically and socially, exalting it as one of the three most important Greek institutions, the other two being established religion and the polis itself.[1]

The philosophers may politically recommend and dialectically analyze the complex emotions of love and bonding; art displays them as being internalized and compulsively operative. They appear even when amorous situations are depleted or perverted and murderously divisive, or for other reasons become tragic in issue. Consider Iphigenia's outcry in the land of the Taurians, when she bewails her outcast state in the laconic privatives Euripides gives her (line 220), calling it *agamos* (marriageless), *ateknos* (childless), *apolis* (stateless), and *aphilos* (loveless, friendless). Or consider how in that grimly powerful portrayal of deprivation and loss, Euripides's great *Trojan Women,* the beauties of family love and sentiment rise over the smoke, fire, and ruins of recently fallen Troy and appear with force even in so grim an inversion of civilized marital and erotic values as the scene in which the wild Cassandra appears brandishing her "marital" torch, parodying the epithalamion, and swirling in a mad dance to which she summons her aging, crippled, and grieving mother Hecuba, whom she urges even now to call upon Hymenaios. The prophetic virgin—quondam priestess of Apollo, but now deprived of her religious calling as she is being led into an unwanted liaison with the enemy commander-in-chief—is made by dramatic art to remember, even in her inverted moment of hideous parody, the familial values she had cherished.

Values and desires can of course appear directly and simply, and redfigure cups of the sixth and early fifth centuries B.C. portray amorous or courting scenes showing that in classical Greece marital, heterosexual love had to compete with rival forms of erotic expression. In a pederastic scene by the Burgos painter, for example, a man teases a boy's genitalia as the lad seems to respond eagerly, and Peithinos displays a scene of heterosexual courting that is beautiful, dignified, aristocratic.[2] Additional introductory examples might well be given to alert us to the fact that the values we seek may appear in contexts of parody, reversal, satire, tragedy, or comedy, as well as in direct discursive statement, in moments of pathos and sentiment, and in both single and juxtaposed pictorial images.

Words are revelatory as well as constitutive—that is, they portray life and at the same time constitute a fiction—and so they are relevant to the historian or anthropologist in the process of recovering historical structures and facts.[3] They are of course especially important when we interrogate literature and art and ask them to reveal their secrets. I have chosen four words and their cognates, all of them important in Attic Greece, some among the most value-laden words in its language and all of them intimately associated with love and the family, constituting, as it were, zones of intersexual amorous energy: *oikos* (the house, household), *erōs* (sexual desire), *charis* (benefit and grace), and *philos* (lover and friend). All these words are rooted in the practical, even the selfish, but they broaden out to embrace intense affective relationships. Each will require separate analysis and exemplification.

Oikos (the House, Household)

In cultures that provide imposing public space, notably perhaps in those near or bordering the Aegean and Mediterranean seas, the house need not be prepossessing in order to be important and even solemn. It was here that the sacred fire burned constantly, tended by the master of the house as a religious obligation. Although it is hard to believe that the home provided either the inducement or the appointments for the richest kinds of family entertainment and companionship, meanings like intimacy, affection, and even friendship seem to be involved, almost from the beginning, in the notion of the homey adjective *oikeios,* humanizing and dignifying the more basic meanings of house, dwelling, kindred, and the state of living or belonging together. Modern research has shown that the *gunaikon* may have been exactly the same size as the men's quarters, though on the second floor, and when the wife produced a child, the husband moved upstairs and she came down to be nearer facilities for washing the baby.[4]

It has been said that the separated quarters for women can be regarded as symbolic not only of segregated space but also of the unseen and the hidden, like the woman's sexual parts. I would add, further, that this inner and intimate *oikos* space also implied mystery, pleasure, and preindustrial productiveness and must have been accorded the respect and love quite naturally felt for the seedbed of life, fortune, family, prestige, and the ongoing state, to say nothing of the sexual pleasure that Greece always found to be legitimate and natural, however much a good economy of health and usefulness might wish to regulate it.

Such a domestic vision lies beyond the reach of Xenophon in the *Oeconomicus,* which many regard as setting the norm by which classical Greece regulated conjugal relations. Ischomacus one day talks to Socrates about his wife and their domestic relations. She, not quite fifteen when he married her, had up to that time remained in leading-strings, seeing and hearing little and saying less. But she had been trained in the control of her appetites—the most important training of all. The couple sacrificed and prayed together, and he constantly enforced upon the girl the purposes her parents had in mind in arranging the marriage—the production of children and the prudent management of the house. Sex is inevitably implied in the desire for children, but the marital bed the husband might well have shared with anyone who was healthy and strong. The greatest value of the wife lay in the cooperative management of the house, fields, and possessions—he outside, she inside. There is no mention whatever of sexual joy, and though there is a considerable degree of complementarity, there appears to be no union of spirit: the divided managerial functions are themselves allowed to form the psyche and control the emotions.[5]

The most famous sentence in pseudo-Demosthenes oration, *In Neaeram*—that we keep mistresses (hetairai) for pleasure, concubines (pallakai) for the daily care of our bodies, and wives (gunaikes) to bear legitimate children and guard the household—seems to support the Xenophontic model. But though the story told in the oration presents a fascinating portrait of how prostitution could press on legitimate marriage, the orator's tripartite classification of women was certainly not intended to *exclude* the wife from providing and sharing in sexual pleasure or intimacy any more than it was to keep her from administering care for the body, the taxonomic list being cumulative and climactic: the wife can and does assume *all* the functions, though not always or necessarily with exclusive privilege.[6]

My subject is not historical reality as such, but our literary and artistic heritage from antiquity, and for the latter the household of Xenophon is excessively stark and limited, though one cannot escape the force of its exemplary power, since the common Western household has resembled it virtually up to our own day. The first departure from the norm we have just laid out comes from philosophy, notably from Plato, who in his relatively unknown and often underrated *Lysis* addresses the meaning of *oikeion* (the proper, the domestic, the intimate) and its central place in the psyche, a brilliant discussion that can be easily extended to include the more creative aspects of domesticity, which the philosopher does not address directly. In the beginning situation of the dialogue, Plato sets out to show that man's love of what is his own has to be realistically conceived. What is called the *prōton philon* (that which organizes a lover's wants into a coherent pattern) is not so much a conscious lofty purpose, as it is that which suits *my* nature, *my* interests. This at least is where you begin. Hans-Georg Gadamer leads us into Plato's expansion of this realistic concept—that is, into what remains when the lack or privation that longing consists of is replaced by a presence, the presence of another. The house then becomes tension-laden, paradoxical. It is an economic unit, to be sure, as Xenophon shows so determinedly, but it is also a place where you feel at home. The presence of the other gives you self-knowledge and self-confidence, and so *to oikeion* can be seen as a semantic field where what is mine becomes *dear,* as wine unlike water, is dear even after the thirst is slaked. The dear one then becomes a permanent possession, which expands the boundaries of the self without destroying its integrity. It is the power of great thought to extend its insights beyond the immediate context, and Plato leads us to the insight that the *oikos*—or perhaps more strictly and primarily the *oikeion*—in its conjugal as well as its filial relationships was conceived of as potentially life enhancing as well as life producing.[7]

It would be instructive to move from philosophy to literature by way of a peculiarly Athenian marital myth, but only a woefully deficient and contradictory one exists—that concerning the legendary king Cecrops, half serpent, half man, who was regarded as the establisher of monogamous marriage.[8] It would be mistaken to regard the marginal importance of this myth as itself a commentary on a putative lowly estate for matrimony, if for no other reason than that we have the monumental *Oresteia* of Aeschylus, which grandly inscribes heroic legend for the primary purpose of idealizing marriage and the *oikos* and of locating them in a newly reconceived, humane, and democratic state.[9] My own special purpose is to discuss this great work not as an essentially historical document or a tract for our times but as an imaginative and socially reflective creation that allows several points of view and sensibilities to clash dramatically in the full working out of its final resolution. In my retelling I hope we will see that the great shift from Earth Goddess to Athene, from *oikos* to *domos,* from a hideously tortured traditional house to a firmly stable and potentially life-enhancing one is a movement recalling but by no means reproducing the enormously influential return of Odysseus to Penelope, Telemachus, and the estate in Ithaca. At the end of the *Odyssey* (24.191–202), Agamemnon's bitterly disillusioned ghost calls for two great songs, one to immortalize the faithful Penelope and another to portray the treacherous Clytemnestra. Homer has given us the first, Aeschylus the second.

Homer's Agamemnon, however, might not have been fully pleased in the event, for Aeschylus's Clytemnestra is surely one of the great characters of world literature, surpassing Penelope in dramatic interest. Still, the wife of Agamemnon and mistress of Aegisthus strikes deeper than a *coup de théâtre,* however stunning, for she is primarily a compelling human figure, clothed in antique but perennial power, representing a long tradition. Euripides's Clytemnestra in *Iphigenia in Aulis* inverts Aeschylus's by being essentially good, but this august, multilayered, loving-grieving mother, who is vastly superior to the conventional men she dominates, is not unrelated to the Aeschylean prototype.[10]

Few dramatic beginnings can compare with Aeschylus's early presentation of Clytemnestra. Her brilliant speech describing the victory signal zigzagging its fiery way through the expectant Greek world, along with the thrilling geography of its progress, unveils a leader as well as a poet: "my commands, . . . my law, my fire. . . . I ordained it all" (p. 118). But the dramatic work also reveals her as a murderess after having been an adulteress, and in so attacking the *oikos* at its foundation she fully deserves the death she will receive in the sequel play. But she will not die until she has enforced herself upon our attention as a deeply aggrieved and surprisingly sympathetic mother, mourning the loss for political and military reasons not of a son but of a daughter, standing in an old theological tradition (recalling Demeter and Korē), and calling upon Earth and the ancient laws of blood and family ties to vindicate her.

At the end of *The Libation Bearers* the final lines sung by the Chorus seem to indict Zeus, at least in part, as it calls for a solution to murderous hate, for a breaking of the endless chain of terror and counterterror. It introduces the Father-God in one of his greatest roles, the "saving Zeus" (Zeus Sōtēr), but then it immediately asks, "Or should we call him death?" (p. 249). That kind of boldness, perhaps even impiety, toward the Olympian establishment can be relevantly uttered by otherwise conventional voices, in part because of the commanding presence of Clytemnestra, who by her greatness compels alternative opinions into view and so does not permit us to accept too easily or optimistically the virtues of the patriarchy being established.

Clytemnestra's death at the hands of a son summons up all the energies of the chthonian world, and these are, despite their terror and hideousness, forces that like the queen herself command respect, even awe, not just as existential realities but also as reasoners guided by the greatly admired and recurringly invoked Greek ideal of *peithō,* a fact that simply does not allow us to see these dramas as documents of Greek misogyny. The Furies are of course repulsive enough—both literally with their oozing rheumy eyes and their emitting bodily orifices and also symbolically as old virgins, children without children, everlastingly unproductive and never philoprogenitive. In their own way they are unforgettable, even though they lack the solemn and dignified beauty of Blake's Har and Heva, arrested in innocence forever. They are endowed with approximately the same theological dimensions as Clytemnestra, and it is not by chance that Gē is recurringly invoked all through the trilogy. The Furies are anticipated in the plays long before they make their repellent appearance. At the very outset of the *Agamemnon* there is real fear of Fury because it is child avenging and so lies deep in the womb of memory. The mad prophetess Cassandra, revealing in herself more than a little of ancient mantic frenzy, sees as her enemy the old blood decrees of Mother Earth, and as if to tell us that things are not susceptible to easy generalization, Electra the good, uncompromisingly patriarchal in her orientation, also invokes the ancient Mother, partly of course because the Earth first drinks any libation offered to the dead. Even Orestes invokes the Earth twice, while Pythia the priestess of Apollo, recapitulating history, honors the Earth first and does not neglect the feminine Moon.

It is the Furies themselves, however, who are the most totally Earth oriented, but it is not only because of the venerability and persistence of their functions that they, amazingly enough, compel respect. They avenge matricide in a cause difficult to regard as in itself unworthy or reprehensible, and with some justification they regard themselves as the deterrents of crime. They claim to have forced upon men that great Greek virtue of restraint and moderation; without them a lethal tide would long since have rolled over the earth. Their two highest values appear to be honor of parents first and then of the stranger within the gate; they hate both extremes of anarchy and tyranny; they abhor violence and hope for prosperity and peace.

How can we fail to give them a hearing as we read Aeschylus? They boldly attack the "whelp" Apollo, apparently not without some sanction from the dramatist himself, who makes the god something of a prig capable of an inconsistent and dogmatic logic that does scant honor to the great verbal ideals of Greece, tolerant rhetoric and patient dialectic. These ugly women, supported by Fate, have the not totally unattractive audacity to challenge even divine erotic and marital power, the great trio of Zeus Teleos, Hera Teleia, and Aphrodite, the creator of *philotēs* (line 216). And they do so in principled adherence to the ancient doctrine that blood ties are profounder than marital vows and arrangements, which, as we know, were so often made tyrannically for the crassest of reasons.

In the final play Athene is presented as clearly superior to Apollo, and surely this is one reason why she is able to coopt the Furies and transform them into the Eumenides, who in the single greatest conversion of the entire play and perhaps of the ancient world, now rank marital ties as being on a par with blood ties and who, now accorded a place in the most sacred spot of Athenian earth, will receive worship and homage and be awarded the ancient earthy rewards of grain and wine. Thus they become a part of the final synthesis of *philotēs* and *sōphrosunē* (lines 999–1001). But the lowly spot of earth given them at the base of the Areopagus cannot contain them. They will rise, indeed they have already risen. And by virtue of that resurrection we are not permitted to regard Night, Earth, and long generations of aggrieved women merely as the displaced members of an old antithesis that has now become outmoded by a new and smoothly satisfying synthesis. A modern reading of Aeschylus's great work must leave us with that kind of comprehension, for he has given us an untidy play whose energies do not move obediently at the command of patriarchal authority. This is not to say that the *Oresteia* remains unstructured in its values—its architecture is all too obvious. But against it the energies of the innovating imagination and of old humanity are allowed boil and beat, and no satisfactory reading can arise from simple political agenda, old or new.

It is time to reenter the house, if only to introduce an alternative perspective to that provided by the essentially rural vision of Xenophon and by the heroic-mythical canvas painted by Aeschylus. In *The Clouds* Aristophanes's Strepsiades, who tries to get his son out of bed, is answered only by a snore. He then proceeds to give us a glimpse into a Greek marriage that has united a town "mouse" and a country "mouse":

> By god,
> I hope that meddling matchmaker who prodded me on
> to marry your mother dies a nasty death!
> I used to be a farmer—the sweetest life on earth,
> a lovely moldy, unspruce, litter-jumbled life,

bursting with honeybees, bloated with sheep and olives.
And then, poor hick, what did I do but marry
your mother, a city girl, and a niece of that Megakles
who was son and heir to old Blueblood Megakles himself?
She was a pretty piece: Miss Megakles-de-luxe.
Well, so we got married and we clambered into bed—
me, a stink of wine-lees, fig-boxes, and wool fat;
she, the whiff of spices, pure saffron, tongue kisses,
Luxury, High Prices, gourmandizing, goddess Lechery,
and every little elf, imp, and sprite of Intercourse.
But I'll say this for your mother: she was a worker.
Nothing slow about *her.* All day long she'd sit there
working away at her loom and shoving in the wool,
and then in bed at night she'd work on me
for more.
     Expense meant nothing.
      Clipped?
       I was *shorn.*
"Madam," I said, "what do you think I am? A man
or a goat?"[11]

That kind of Hogarthian interior realism, brought out idiomatically in William Arrowsmith's translation, brings us down from idealistic heights, but it does not fully prepare us for what takes place in the three comedies in which "women are on top." There they occupy public, not private, space, even the Acropolis and the Agora; men and women confront and threaten each other; and the solutions advanced by the women seem at first extreme and ludicrous. And so they are, in large measure. But it is significant that these inversions were in fact not only imagined but publicly presented, and they do imply much about both what the status quo would tolerate and what was imagined as alternative to regnant orthodoxies. Lysistrata is young and beautiful, she grieves over the grief of all womankind, and her aim is no less than to save the state. She will use feminine allure (cambric robes, saffron silks, small shoes, paints, perfumes, and gauzy garments) to achieve her ends, and so she differs from the feminist stereotype imposed by later ages. She had not read Freud and hence in her marvelously naughty concentration has no idea that what she wants women to forego (peos) is what they have all along envied but never really enjoyed. Aristophanes, however, does endow her with the ability to lead open-air confrontation: she meets the magistrate head on and even in anti-Amazon Athens stages a battle of men versus women, male fire versus female water, in which the men are routed. As for the final antiwar victory, it would have been unthinkable, as would the marital strike in the first place, had not the *oikos* been a place much desired by both men and women—especially in what Froma Zeitlin has called its "female-female" part, its innermost recesses, the *muchoi* of the women's quarters. Sir Kenneth Dover has said that "when every allowance is made for . . . comic convention, the central idea of the play, that a sex-strike by citizens' wives against their husbands can be imagined as having so devastating an effect, implies that the marital relationship was much more important in people's actual lives than we would have inferred simply from our knowledge of the law and our acquaintance with litigation about property and inheritance; more important, too, than could ever be inferred from a comprehensive survey of the varieties of sexual experience and attitudes which were possible for the Greeks."[12]

We can go beyond the historical moment even in comedy and say that the women in this play express a great cry for sexual gratification partly because womanhood, like manhood, fleets so soon away. But pleasure is not all, though, as we have seen, it is here highly concentrated and even phallic: comfort, peace, children, normality, and the supportive domestic order are also goods the women long for and are willing to use the temporary denial of sexual pleasure to rewin and maintain.

In the *Thesmophoriazusae* the claims on behalf of women go far beyond the (largely unjustified) rebuke of Euripides that in this play Aristophanes had insulted the female sex and violated the integrity of the household and all it stands for. Near the end of this strange and rollicking play the chorus of women, addressing Athene, claim for their sex the honor of being the founders of home and the sustainers of city. It is for this reason that the women are presented in the opening of the *Ecclesiazusae* as being wiser than men, keepers of that most conservative of institutions, the family. But the family can, when threatened, also be seen as subversive—subversive, that is, of remoter and less immediate values than those it embodies. What the family usually tends to subvert, perhaps even demystify, is idealism and ill-considered change, and so Jesus, Paul, Marx, and Freud are not its most notable friends, whatever accommodations their followers might later make. Aristophanes exploits to the hilt the irony that members of the conservative sex should in this play end up as experimenters and social engineers, treating young and old, the beautiful and the ugly, men and women, as equally privileged, the hearth becoming a soup-kitchen and love being made, and quickly unmade, on the streets—a frightful immodesty. The *oikos* has dissolved into thin air.

But has it? All these comedies show that human nature will win out in the end, both against man-made wars and woman-made schemes. One reason for this is that it contains the capacity for both esteem and desire, which in the end hold the *oikos* together. This was not at all apparent in Xenophon, or even Aeschylus, who makes the virgin Athene preside over the establishment of marital right over mother right. But the great realist and comedian chose not to ignore this human endowment, and one can guess that in the end the couple from *The Clouds* whom I introduced at the beginning of this discussion, the country-smelling husband and the perfumed wife, had a better chance of achieving rapport in the home than anywhere else, despite having produced a lazy and pseudo-intellectual son.

At least that would be the Greek view even at its most realistic. The Greek home of this period will make some of us uncomfortable, since as Marylin Arthur has suggested, it can be said to embody inequality. To some of us it may even awaken the stench of kinder, küche, and kirche. But I am not writing now as a postrevolutionary modern, nor do I suggest that the Greek house is exemplary for us. I do suggest that on its own culture it had a powerful imaginative hold—and that it is emotion-laden and replete with energetic paradoxes and with many potential unions of opposites. The canon of literary, artistic, and philosophical responses to the classical Greek home is in need of a more comprehensive scrutiny than it has hitherto received.[13]

Erōs (Sexual Desire)

Erōs the god may not have come into the world of Attic Greece from the archaic period with the full majesty and variety of Aphrodite, but he had been understood as both a primordial, creative force in cosmology and a desirable and necessary but also a subtle and paradoxical component of human intimacy. Did the art and thought of classical Greece associate him with marriage? It did, contrary to some modern views. Phaedrus in Plato's *Symposium* is not the raisonneur of the dialogue but his view may be taken as typical. Gregory Vlastos clarifies the meaning of the example from the heroic age that the Platonic Aristophanes uses: "Alcestis had *philia* for her husband, Admetus, and so did his parents; but 'because of her *erōs* for him she so surpassed them in *philia*' that she was willing to die in his place, while they were not." David Halperin agrees, saying that a strong and militant love, energized by erotic passion, motivated Alcestis to self-sacrifice, but he then goes on to argue, persuasively and fully, that Plato chooses in the ensuing masterpiece to discuss desire not love, *erōs* not *philia*.[14] And it is precisely in his concept of desire that the greatest philosopher of *erōs* who ever lived sets up obstacles to uniting it with *gamos* (marriage) or, for that matter, with any long-term relationship in which appetitive, recreational, and/or procreative sexuality is a continuing ingredient.

Why should this be so? First, because Plato separates Erōs (not a god but a *daimōn,* who is defined as a lack, an absence, a longing for what is not yet possessed) from the appetitive and generative libido. A beautiful body arouses *erōs* but that body does not drive the lover (erastēs) to "consume" it as an object in a sexual liaison (inevitably a terminal gratification). No, the lover seeks the general, eternal, pervasive beauty that the beloved's body instantiates; stimulated by such *erōs* the lover becomes endowed with the power of climbing the philosophical ladder until he attains a unifying vision of beauty and truth combined and achieves a godlike immortality of happiness and virtue. Such a quest transcends physical consummations, and it is creative, though not procreative. For the aim of *erōs,* as Diotima in the *Symposium* says, is to give birth in beauty; and poetry, art, science, laws, the constitution of a state can all be viewed as the ultimate products of the *erōs* that sees in a single beautiful body the gleam of a divine Form or Idea. But marriage finds no place on that ladder, in that quest: unlike other objects of desire, a wife or a husband is usually present and therefore seldom lacked. The centrality of the libido and physical birth, the omnipresence of the appetitive *erōs,* and the concentration upon a single beloved body give little opportunity for the broader data base that leads to generality, abstraction, and a growing transcendental kind of contemplation.

It is beguilingly easy to make Plato Platonic, but the temptation should be resisted. Even though uncongenial to orgasms and climaxes, Plato gives great scope to arousal in the presence of beauty, though I do not pretend to know how far up the dialectical ladder sexual longing goes. And even though Plato ultimately does not recognize cognitive value in marriage or long-term sexual liaisons, he gives to Socrates's great teacher in erotics, Diotima, spiritual and intellectual insights beautifully and climactically energized by physically erotic, obviously intersexual, and insistently and inescapably procreative metaphors. (Perhaps Plato only allows his Diotima to *retain* insights derived from traditional sources, but even such vivid repetition of them would be significant.) It is worth saying that a verbal artist of Plato's stature is not likely to have used tropic language incidentally or neutrally.

In the *Phaedrus* Socrates comes to recognize the powerful intellectual as well as religious values of *mania,* which must surely modify, if it does not invert, the obsessive Greek concern with *sōphrosunē* (moderation, control, measure). The *Phaedrus* tells the erotic story rhetorically and mythically and not dialectically, as in the *Symposium,* but the concern with *erōs* remains as obsessive as ever: the whole chariot group, including the charioteer (who symbolizes the soul driving the body while questing for beauty and truth), feel the Platonic kind of desire induced by the beautiful body. How close to sexual arousal the language of the myth makes that desire seem! The white (or good) horse does not rear, kick, and poise itself to pounce as the libidinal black horse does, but it too shows symptoms. The growing of wings in response to the godlike beauty of human form produces shudderings, heat, irritation, tickling, swelling—all of these taking place from the root upward and suggesting penile excitation as well as religious awe.[15]

The Platonic philosophy of *erōs* is original, stimulating, human, if not always humane. It exalts the heavenly Aphrodite without liquidating the earthly. By insisting upon erotic reciprocity it radically revises standard Greek pederasty, which hierarchically kept the young beloved (erōmenos) from enjoying and participating in the attractions of desire and friendship. Plato's synthesis associates beauty, truth, and physical desire for a beautiful body with creative intellectual achievement and with what David Halperin has called "an ongoing and eternal urge to make what is best in us a perpetually living force."[16] And although he may not have intended to do so, Plato invites us to think hard about whether we can transfer from all-male realms to intersexual relationships the values explored and organized in male friendship. He even makes us wonder if the power structure of pederasty itself might not be reconceived to embody reciprocity.

But problems remain, and one wishes that Plato had gone further in resolving them. Are there no cognitive or generally human possibilities in commitment to one body or to one friend, comparable to the generalizing search through many physical particulars for the ideal? Although the object of desire is continually present in an ideal marriage, are there no possibilities of renewal of erotic interest through mutual examinations of pleasure, through considerations of health and bodily betterment, through imaginative reconstitutions or even fetishes? Is not confinement of *erōs* to those possessing beautiful bodies exclusive, elitist, discriminatory, limiting? Can the soul clap its wings and sing only when stimulated by the fair and shapely? Without consummations, is not an *erōs* induced by a beautiful body in danger of the frustration and tension that could come from a kind of perpetually changing and repeated foreplay (as in Keats's romantic fantasy: "To lie forever on my fair love's ripening breast") or from a coitus, if not interruptus, certainly forever dilatus?[17]

Nor is there in this great master of erotics any searching analysis of the intellectual differences or the emotional tensions that may exist between matrimony and homoerotic attractions and couplings. There seems to be a beginning of such thought in our day. Harold Beaver, in a subtle exploration of "homosexual signs" and ecstasies, says of married love: here there is fulfillment, for children reveal "the inner truth that predetermined their existence." But homosexual couplings "lack that promised plenitude of seedbed and core, of an ultimate mystery that reveals the hidden principles of truth, value, life, of 'reality' itself."[18] For that mystery Plato's Diotima substitutes the birth in beauty of mental and imaginative offspring. Are the two realms irreconcilable? Blake seems to have thought so, or he would not have separated his Eden (the place of intellectual achievement) from his Beulah (the place of sexual refreshment and rest and of marital affection), though he did believe that the sexual, even consummated sexuality, could energize and fructify the intellectual and imaginative. Plato gives us no such comparative analysis of the domestic and the heavenly Aphrodite.[19]

The subtle Platonic *erōs* does not figure in Greek art or literature, and perhaps by its very nature it could not have. What kind of *erōs* does? That question will lead us to a brief consideration of a few erotically charged dramas, but first a word about what the vases reveal. The red-figure vases sometimes show a cynical corruption, bribery, lust, and much else that makes them unsentimental, but they also show affectionate, mutual offerings by both sexes. Erōs himself appears prominently after 440 or thereabouts, and in marriage scenes the bride demonstrates a range of emotions from demureness to eager willingness and acceptance, shyness being more frequently portrayed. Glances deepen into the fully romantic and the maritally reciprocal by the third quarter of the fifth century, as revealed beautifully, for example, in a loutrophoros in Boston (c. 430–20) and in a pyxis in Athens.[20]

In the dramas it soon becomes apparent that a more popular and pervasive *erōs* than Plato's cannot be effectually separated, as it is in his redefinition, from Aphrodite. Still, two of Euripides's greatest plays are not unrelated to the *Phaedrus* since they enforce the view that some kind of reason-transcending *mania* (that of Dionysos in *The Bacchae* and that of Aphrodite in *Hippolytos*) is, however dangerous, necessary to life, culture, and at least by implication to matrimony and the family. The intellectual pivot of both plays is found in the wisdom of Tiresias and of the accompanying Chorus, expressed in the first: that the new invasive outsider-god of wine, liquids, and ecstasy must be respected as Demeter of the grains is respected; that sexuality, which the gods have placed deep within nature, need not destroy the Apollonian and the Delphic but if ignored can bring disaster. The political puritan of this play, Pentheus, who insults the god of wine and attacks the women in their ecstatic worship, and the religious puritan of the second, Hippolytos, a worshipper of Artemis and a scorner of Aphrodite, are or become antifeminists and are destroyed by divine power attacking them at those points where they are most vulnerable, in the family itself. Pentheus is decapitated by his mother in her ecstasy, the mother who had loved him and whom he loved; but when he attacks the primitive, the feminine, even that Earth Mother whom we have seen lingering on in Attic consciousness, he ignores what the Chorus preaches, that even the grape of Dionysos has its own *charis* (or grace). And he pays a hideous price for his proud, self-satisfied neglect.[21]

The revenge of Hippolytos comes when physical *erōs* toward him is aroused in the breast of his stepmother, Phaedra, which impels her to level a lying charge that incriminates her innocent stepson in incest and rivalry with his father, a sin of which he was actually incapable and to which he was totally disinclined. The son, however, is blameworthy precisely because of his larger, impious innocence (even though it has the religious cloaking of Artemis), his innocence of that which creates families and dynasties and legacies, innocence, too, of what is more private but also truly admirable, namely *sōphrōn erōs* (wise desire). It is strikingly ironic, therefore, that an incestuous perversion and an unseemly *erōs* directed by his father's wife against her stepson and mediated by the insulted and neglected Aphrodite, should in the end destroy this young, high-minded, antaphrodisiac virgin. Euripides has thus placed in the home not the sophisticated Platonic *erōs* but that erōs which if wisely moderated and controlled can be a domestic blessing, but if ignored or despised on whatever grounds can strike with ferocious force. The grounds for divine punishment in these two plays are in the second (*Hippolytos*) an unnaturally prolonged dedication to an ideal of personal virginity and in the first (*Bacchae*) a life-denying and proud political ideal of rationality and a tyrannical control over emotionality. It surely qualifies some modern ideas of the strength and pervasiveness of Greek misogyny that both these hideously punished characters are outspokenly antifeminine.[22]

Sophocles in the *Trachiniae* shows us that ferocious punishment can overtake other than virgins and puritans. Here it is visited upon Herakles, the greatest Greek hero, who, though he protects his wife from monsters, is himself frequently monstrous. In the home, united in matrimony with a dignified and yet desiring woman, the tone is lowered from heroic adventure to allow the action, whatever its hideous outcome, at least to arise in the domain of the domestic. Disaster strikes not for Herakles's continuing peccadilloes of unfaithfulness away from home, but only when his *erōs* threatens Deianeira's carefully and proudly constructed spiritual *oikos.* Herakles's wife, surely one of the many great women of classical Greek literature and like many others of her sex greatly transcending her husband and the men she encounters, might have grown into the likes of Pentheus and Hippolytos, for she commenced adulthood in virginal ice. She approached marriage with the kind of sexually fearsome imaginings that attended young Psyche on her way to meet her divine husband, Erōs, in the later legend. But it is soon clear that Deianeira now desperately loves her husband, misses him grievously when he is out on his adventures, and, in this respect at least, may well be called "la femme moyenne sensuelle et pathétique." But when she discovers that one of the captives her husband brings back from his last exploit, the princess Iole, whom the humane and sensitive wife at first pities even more than other captives, is the object of Herakles's *erōs* (a "monos erōs" at that!), she feels that she has been fatally stabbed, sensing a threat to her house and to monogamy itself. She now becomes not only an impersonal instrument of a kind of marital *dikē* (governing order) but also an even more fully human being than before—jealous, protective, insulted, ready to take risky action. One of her most vividly presented earlier traits had been her tolerance of Herakles's sexual waywardness (balm no doubt for itching male ears), which, she used to aver, was human enough and never a threat to the stability of her life. Does she protest too much in proclaiming her forgiving ways? Is she like some of Doris Lessing's proudly modern, liberated heroines who, despite their bravura, are inwardly repelled all along by the extramarital liaisons with which their husbands console their absences from home?

In any case, neither she nor the somewhat mentally, morally, and emotionally inferior Herakles deserves the fate the Nessos shirt brings on both of them: she had sent it to him only because she was under the misapprehension that it was an aphrodisiac that would bind the man she loved to her. She suffers perhaps more than he does, for his agony is in his proud flesh, hers in her deeply sensitive spirit, going to her death by her own hand, open-eyed about the truth. She makes her end in the bedroom, the *thalamos* of Herakles, addressing the bed, that unmistakable symbol of matrimony itself.

This searing play, its language so plastic to the meanings and emotions evoked, demonstrates that a great woman can also be a good wife, fully human, endowed with a rich sexuality, capable of anger and jealousy, married to the greatest man in the world who is not worthy of her. It suggests, as *Othello* does, what might have been in a more nearly perfect union in a more accommodating world. But again no tragic pity would have arisen from the loss and hideous suffering had not the author—and the culture that honored him and also the *Trachiniae*—shown us how much there was to lose and how much might have been gained in more humane circumstances. In fact, the play may be said to show what happens when desire and esteem break apart.[23]

Erōs, which also existed in many other places, may seem to reside uncomfortably in the *oikos,* but the Greeks put it there anyhow, hoping that it would be wise and controlled while knowing all too well that very often it was not. Their purely philosophical vision seldom overtly emphasized the "interinanimating" combination of esteem and desire in heterosexual love that later cultures tried to make normative, but some of their most memorable tragedies live on because they valorize the union of sex and respect and place it at the heart of human intimacy.

Charis (Benefit and Grace)

Erōs may not always have lived at ease in the Greek household any more than it did for centuries in the Christian. But *charis* did, from the epics of Homer to the fictions of Tolstoy. The Christians exalted the concept philosophically and religiously, even in its domestic setting, believing that the word signified a great salvific continuity, relating it to the Hebrew *ḥesed,* or seeing it as part of the *preparatio evangelica;* the Greeks of course did not. There is no *Symposium* or *Phaedrus* that analyzes or mythologizes grace. Nevertheless, it is an important word, crucial to understanding how the Greeks could feel about long-term love commitments, particularly heterosexual ones. *Charis* is not fully translatable, since its range is broad: it moves back and forth between inanimate objects and the hearts of men. Thus it can lie in objects as a quality for which we are grateful; Aeschylus refers to the grace of untouched or holy things ("athiktōn charis," *Ag.*371), and Euripides endows the vine of Dionysos with *charis.* Its free bestowal always awakens pleasure and gratitude in both bestower and recipient, and Plato elevates it to the level of critical or aesthetic response to music or art. The Athenian Stranger in the *Laws* (667B) announces three criteria for judgment: correctness or fidelity of the copy to the original, moral effect or utility, and charm or pleasure (that is, *charis*).[24]

Our interest lies in its erotic and amorous associations, and these turn out to be abundant and unexpectedly varied. In the *Agamemnon charis* can be a powerful, even violent term: the *charis daimonōn* (182) brought down Troy. Helen's beauty is called *charis* even when its absence pains her husband, and the Chorus in Euripides's *Hippolytos* (526–27) gives the word an unambiguously sexual meaning when it calls *erōs* a sweet or even bewitching grace (glukeia charis). Plato in the *Symposium* frequently uses the verb *charizesthai* to denote the gratification a boy (erōmenos) can provide his *erastēs,* or lover. Of the three leading *Charites* (Graces)—clarity or brilliance, liveliness or spirit, and flowering or verdancy—the last two bear some relation to the erotic and the generative.[25]

It is perhaps Pindar who, more than any one else, embodies both the range and force of *charis* in high classical Greece. In the fourteenth *Olympian,* he defined and discriminated among the Graces.[26] Concentrating on his association of grace with love, desire, and closely related matters, I note, miscellaneously, that *charis* brings all things to fulfillment for the delight of men; that a bride's consent is a form of grace; that the cultivated garden is a secret close of the Graces; that the way of friends to settle matters is the way of grace; that the Graces, who mediate all delight ("ta terpna," *Ol.*14.5–6) and all that is sweet ("ta gluké" ibid.), can also be associated with Dionysos; that grace is peculiarly associated with Apollo and Aphrodite but its opposite, gracelessness, with Ixion and the Centaurs; that Aphrodite, when associated with the Graces, can shed a kind of winsome shyness over the bed of lovers and that by extension grace can mediate the shyness and modesty that precede and accompany the first encounters in love. We can even say that it is the genius of Pindar to endow virtually all value with *charis,* silken bonds that may be too light and frail to tie together the broader society with its sweat and strife but can sweeten love and procreation with what they badly need—the delicate and gentle in life, art, and even social customs and folkways.

Pindar's complex aristocratic magic should not, however, be allowed to blind us to what in fact he himself recognized: that *charis* also possesses a decidedly practical and unglamorous side, since the term always retained the sense of a practical or useful favor bestowed or received. But the Greeks had their own way of exalting it without deserting the healthy practicality many of its meanings conveyed, an exaltation that may be related to the Indo-European root of the word, *gher* (to desire, to be pleased), and its consequent association with *chairō* (rejoice) and *chara* (joy).[27] So the semantic alternations between practical benefit and self-validating joy in *charis* is not unlike the play in *oikos* between what is mine and what is dear for its own sake. *Charis* comes to have a richer coloring than the Greek word for house, surely in part because it was often associated with women and girls in their deepest needs, as even the Septuagint and Philo Judaeus show, and also in their most alluring moments, as Greek religion abundantly demonstrates.[28]

Because of its association with generative sexuality, *charis* belongs in the *oikos*. Charis in Homer is the wife of Hephaistos, her name possibly in part ironical, since a good deal of charitable favor would be required to be the female consort of so unpromising a physical specimen.[29] And one bell krater reeks of unattractive domesticity (perhaps illustrating a fourth-century comic scene): a husband and wife snack together; he looks well fed and complacent and she (named "Charis" in letters over her head) has a cavernous mouth and a large wart on her nose (fig. 6). *Charis* could obviously be domesticated in the comfortable sort of way that shows that the Greeks could, if they wished, parody or in other ways make light of a usually honorific term.

But *charis* gets much of its glamor outside the home. I do not refer to the frontier beyond cultural boundaries where Dionysos so powerfully and violently stimulated women to frenzy, as in the *Bacchae,* places where "the wild things are." I refer to another frontier, that between innocence and experience, between the virginal and the connubial state, invoked when girls in dance and song honored Artemis, Hera, Demeter, Aphrodite, and even Athene—all patronesses in one way or another of marriage and fecundity. The ritual movements accompanying initiation may be the purest embodiments of high *charis* the Western world has known; because they were solemnly religious as well as beautiful, their power is only partially recalled by classical ballet, which achieved during the eighteenth and nineteenth centuries a place in aesthetic thought under the term *grace,* that is, beauty in motion.

Pertinent to our discussion of marital love are these considerations: (1) that the music and movement of girls in chorus and dance signifying the attainment of nubility constitute a clear embodiment of grace (as Pindar says in the fourteenth *Olympian,* even the gods cannot order their dance without the Graces); (2) that such rituals both express and help create the charm and glory of *all* human life—again, a Pindaric point— and love and marriage benefit by association; (3) that therefore grace and also the Graces could not possibly have ritually expired at the consummation of marriage, an institution which, as we have seen, all Greece honored greatly and one which as we have also seen, did accommodate *erōs,* though the requirement was that it be wise and disciplined (sōphrōn).

But could this institution fulfill its chief purposes only by regulation

FIGURE 6 *Husband and Wife (Charis) Eating,* fourth century B.C., Apulian bell krater. (Museo Civico Archeologico [ex Moretti and Caputi collections], Milan.)

and moderation? Did it not need also to honor and encourage sexuality? Greece accomplished just that by giving to the institution it honored what in any culture matrimony badly needs, a strong infusion of *charis.* Marriage was of course seen under many other aspects: it was regarded as work (ergon) as opposed to play (paidia, or pleasure outside the house with recreational partners); it was the ploughing of land with the woman as the furrow and the man as laborer (not an insult, surely, because of the importance of agriculture and of those goddesses called the Twain, Demeter and Korē, whom we contemplated in the previous chapter).[30] Marriage was also for the Greeks a form of domestication, even taming:

as a wild animal is tamed, so woman with her powerful natural impulses, more primitive than a man's, is in peculiar need of socialization. But marriage was also and supremely a state of grace, both secular and divine, in the sense of both benefaction, where woman is implicitly honored as the bestower of favor, and grace, by which the energies and arousals of puberty are transposed to adult sexual obligations. Those adolescent arousals were doubtless regarded as delicate, attractive, and ambiguous, with touches of homoerotic feeling (see any of Sappho's works, and think of Mozart, who conceives Cherubino ambiguously, "non so cosa son, cosa faccio"). Such arousals were doubtless mostly innocent, coming before Time coughs from the shadows, to recall Auden's memorable phrase. One can become sentimental and project too much early joy on later sorrow, when Time coughs all too frequently. No doubt we should always remember the human condition, but it would be unfair to a great period of human cultural history not to notice that like a shaft of diagonal baroque light, *charis* shines down on the marital couch, the *lektron,* a word that in its plural form could stand for marriage itself.

Charis added its sexual charge to the *oikos,* and concurrently to virginity, premarital modesty, and postmarital chastity, a charge that had not spent itself in the century of Wordsworth, Coleridge, Keats, Tennyson, and Browning. That electrification of the house was fully in place in Homer and Semonides, and James Redfield finds early Greek sexual *charis* to be both feminine and marital, at once charming and powerful. "Sex," he says, "is one of the things that makes the [Greek] marriage work, and sex is largely the responsibility of the woman. . . . Marriage is something more than a merely sexual relationship, but (paradoxically) it is the sexual relationship which makes the marriage more than mere social arrangement."[31]

All sexuality is paradoxical and oxymoronic, including the Greek, early and notably expressed in the bittersweet love in Sappho. It was no small or uncomplicated task that a young bride faced in undertaking life with a man and in producing children—tasks much richer and more challenging than the economic duties laid upon her by Xenophon. One aspect of these difficulties appears in Euripides's *Medea,* where in her opening speech the title character movingly shows the difficulty of defining herself as a woman against the character and work of men. Another arises from the fact that, as Jean-Pierre Vernant has seen, the girl was psychologically situated between Artemis and Aphrodite, the first a virgin huntress, the mistress of wild beasts and uncultivated fields, the peremptory and sometimes savage repulser of male intrusion or male proposal. To this goddess the girl was related by nature and cultural heritage. But on the other side stood equal and opposite temptations, Aphrodite Pandemos, who could create excess even within marriage, and the hetaira with her unbridled seductiveness, to which the Greeks thought the woman was also peculiarly attracted. Small wonder that she might fail or that the task of finding the median between reluctance and indulgence should be safeguarded by restrictions but also by providing ritual outlets! Small wonder too that if she managed to escape the fate of the Adonis of the hot spices and luxuriant summer growth, she might at last yield to Dionysos and, as apparently Aristophanes thought, become bibulous. Her task was not easy, but her position as one who could and surely often did unite nature and culture was too close to the achievement of art itself to have been neglected by it, too close to elemental reality not to have been built into ritualized religion, and of too much consequence to the future not to have been honored by society. It is for these reasons that Plato, no great friend of physical consummation but, as we have seen, a sponsor of *charis* as a fundamental element of literary and artistic judgment, speaks with such solemnity when he addresses the subject of marriage and offspring in the *Laws:* Marriage "is the way by which the human race, by nature's ordinance, shares in immortality, a thing for which nature has implanted in everyone a keen desire. . . . Thus mankind is by nature coeval with the whole of time, in that it accompanies it continually both now and in the future; and the means by which it is immortal is this:—by leaving behind it children's children and continuing ever one and the same, it thus by reproduction shares in immortality."[32]

Philos (Lover and Friend)

One of the great charms of Xenophon's *Symposium* (8.21–22; 9.3–7) is its sense of realism and the alternatives it suggest even to the disciplined Socrates or to the Uranian Aphrodite. Nor does the author allow quotidian and ordinary concerns to stand without divine inspiration, as is beguilingly evident at the end when the serious discussion is over. Ariadne is announced. Dionysos, a little flushed with the wine of a celestial banquet, joins her. They play merrily together—the verb being *paizein*—and their adolescent play parodies (or perhaps expresses without irony) a lovemaking (*paidia* again as including recreational sex) in which the male leads and the female, though modest, reciprocates fully. It is a love play in which *epithumia* (the normal word for desire) and *philia* (friendship, love) fully combine. The effect on the male spectators is immediate—

they are rendered *philountes* (a *philos* word again) as they watch. Then they ride off home, as fast as they can to their marital couches, while Socrates and a friend go out for a walk and a talk.

The scene I have just delineated is suffused with *philia,* which Nathan M. Pusey has somewhere called the strongest form of commitment in Greek life. This great word has a political aspect: the Chorus in Euripides's *Suppliant Women,* in pleading with Theseus to rescue the fallen and impiously unburied bodies outside Thebes, addresses him "Ō philos" (278), and the Chorus later hopes for a *philia* based on *charis* between the two cities (374–75). The word and its cognates also had religious meanings, for a Greek could address his god as *philos,* perhaps with obvious intentions and hopes, but the word tends to be insistently and essentially human. It does not usually gleam, as *charis* does, with an empyrean shine, but like the other words we are discussing, even *charis,* its primary involvement is with the practical, the possessive, the selfish. Without a clear Indo-European link, it may be related to the Lydian pronominal possessive adjective, *bilis;* if so, the meaning "intrinsically proper to" or "belonging to" attached itself to *philos* from the beginning. But, as for *oikos,* the sense moved from ownership to meanings of "dear, beloved," even "dearest, most precious." We have already commented on this semantic range in earlier Greek antiquity. Arthur Adkins makes much of the original self-directed referentiality in the word—the Homeric hero regards his own bedclothes, the parts of his own body, and the functions of his psyche as *philoi.* But "mine own" soon becomes "dear," and Adkins may be right in saying that the "mine" and the "dear" are so closely intertwined in Homer that they cannot be separated. The Homeric hero needed friends as he needed limbs, tools, and weapons in order to survive, so that *philos* is "quite untranslatable, for it is locked firmly into the Homeric situation."[33] And Aristotle speaks of voluntary action as that which one does oneself or does through one's *philoi,* that is, as instrumental extensions of the self. Ties to the self that provide satisfaction, power, or dignity do not in either the short or long run require apology. They do not make the beloved any less dear, and we do not insult or weaken a human relationship by seeing its psychologically egoistic roots.

But what about our subject, men and women in long-term relationship? Does *philia* apply here? The answer is strongly affirmative. Though, as Gregory Vlastos has said, *philein* is never used in Greek prose to refer to sexual intercourse, the word suffuses the Greek household with its richness; and Kenneth Dover regards one of its several instantiations as being "the relationship between a man and a woman accustomed to mutual enjoyment of intercourse." In other words, *philia* can be "esteem enlivened by desire."[34]

Philia (as friendship) summons up Aristotle as surely as *erōs* invokes Plato.[35] His essays on friendship have been exemplary and influential through the centuries—at least to just shortly before our own time[36]—and it is well to recall the famous taxonomy of the *Nicomachean Ethics*. As we remember from my own taxonomy (see chapter 1), Aristotelian friendship, a broadly practical and an idealistic term, is defined as including a relationship of (1) utility (as between business partners) and (2) pleasure (as between people who mutually enjoy wit, sex, or haute cuisine). But its highest version (3) is the relationship of men equal in lofty virtue, who can indeed become one mind in two bodies. To these heights Aristotle did not require that all men should desire to climb—nor did he imagine that they could even if they wished. Perhaps only a few choice spirits might be expected to attain disinterested, equal, and reciprocal goodness. He found that excessive inequality—between a man and a god, say—might well make friendship impossible. But he did assert emphatically that it could and did exist between parents and their children and between men and women in marriage, and such spiritual and physical liaisons he encouraged. Friendship means mutuality (a friend is one who loves and is loved in return), and, as we have seen, it is *philos* that makes the family the bonding cement of the state. I do not claim a modern spirit or emotional warmth for Aristotle (who has?), the kind that led Plato to poetry and myth. Moderns are properly chilled by what he says in defining woman as exemplifying a natural deformity or in insisting that the inferior must render to the superior the love and respect which he always deserves in greater quantity—as though such matters of the heart could be rationally regulated. The great philosopher can at times suggest, as many other Greeks did, that some of us can be as depersonalized as fish or wine, and he does not seem to give to the individual human being the kind of glowing and unassailable existential integrity that drives our separate parts to seek unity or at least fructifying inner antitheses—such, for example, as the uniting of *erōs* and esteem. But his brilliant taxonomies are thought provoking precisely because he does leave one grasping for alternatives to his syllogisms or for extensions and new applications of his insights. We reach out from Aristotelian analyses because we wish friendship to be the birthright of all sorts and conditions of men and women, remembering that Aristotle regarded it as making life worth the living.[37]

If we turn to Greek drama we see that it too bristles with *philos*, with possibilities for long-term human relationships, but without the Aristotelian chill, often in a context of denial and loss. It is a deep and tender *philia* that binds brother and sister in Sophocles's *Electra* and *Antigone,* but, typically, we must turn to Euripides for the intensest applications and instances, and also for the most compelling and suggestive inversions of *philos* values.[38] It is he who brings love, marriage, and the family to their Attic climax, and there would seem to roll from him the wave of the future in his situations of intense individualism and realism, where ideals must either flourish or be destroyed. Euripides creates circumstances that challenge and disrupt marital love but that in the end do not alter its essential lineaments. In other words, an ideal remains intact through much tragic buffeting, and this makes it possible to say that a great playwright sensitive to his audience and its needs and presuppositions has produced a vision of marital love in and for a culture that has long been thought to be without it. That said, it must be reemphasized that no one has put marital love under greater stress than he or made it eventuate in more unnatural violence. The marvelous, hideous poetry of his *Medea* makes *erōs* clash clamorously with *philos* (871, 1071–72), which, rejected, turns to hatred, raw revenge, and tragic waste—all within the bosom of the family. The heroine's sufferings and retaliations take on preternatural power, with invocations to Gē and other hints that she belongs or has reverted to the older, pre-Olympian revenge ethos, which the impressive domestic settlement of Aeschylus had not been able fully to quiet or quell.

Before we analyze the *Andromache* we must consider the heroine's Trojan past as seen by Euripides in *The Trojan Women.* There, as the wife of Hector she incarnated the Greek ideal of womanly and wifely discretion, though with plenty of latitude, for at times her will had its way over her husband's. Now another tragic day has dawned, and Hecuba, her mother-in-law, another in the succession of great women in Greek art and the wisest person in this play, urges the young widow to give up her disinclination to a second marriage, to try to forget Hector, whom of course Hecuba also dearly loved, to live on resolutely in a vastly different future, and even to use the ways of a woman to make her new man love and cherish her. Such is the practical marital ideal that survives the hideousness and loss outside the ruined walls and the smoking city.

In the *Andromache* the union that Hecuba desiderated has now survived for several years, an unsentimental but productive one (there is a beloved son) that by the strictest Greek standards would have to be called irregular.[39] But this relationship between the late Hector's wife and the son of Achilles, Neoptolemus, is "valorized" nonetheless.

Though the *oikos* may not have been all that it should have been, *philia* existed between the pair and also between the mother and the son, along with more than a gleam of *charis*. (We learn in the course of the play that Andromache in Hector's day had become a seasoned wife, like Deianeira, and if he was ever tripped up by Aphrodite-Kupris, the wife had the good *charis* to forgive him and even take the bastards to her bosom.) The relationship between a Trojan captive of war who still honors her slain husband and the son of the greatest Greek hero, who slew him, has now after ten years been succeeded by the fully regular marriage of Neoptolemus to the daughter of Menelaos and Helen, Hermione, who, however, remains barren, leading her to harbor lethal jealousy toward the fruitful mother, Andromache. The earlier relationship, though it did not and could not achieve the full status of a Greek marriage, is handsomely sanctioned at the end by Peleus. He has the humanity to perceive the value of his grandson's liaison just as he perceives the lack of grace in the mean-spirited, cruel, but superficially conventional Spartan alternatives. (Sparta, he says, does not produce "gunaikas sōphronas" [wise women].) So it is dramatically appropriate that at the end Thetis (herself the epitome of grace) should confer immortality on her old consort, Peleus, and allow a good line ultimately to spring from the pleasures of a mortal bed, which, according to Homer, she had at the time sorely disliked.

Andromache shows that marital values could survive tragedy, loss of hero-sons and hero-husbands, threats of villainy, and even technical irregularity in the relationship, *if* the man and woman were linked in bonds of *philia;* if they were decent, sensible, and humane; and if the woman was loyal, brave, decently selfish, loved her man and her son, and was a reasonably good logician to boot.

In Euripides's *Alcestis* the dynamics are entirely different: a good and perfectly valid marriage is threatened by a divine decree, not directly aimed at the husband Admetus, to be sure, but providing the dilemma that leads to the wifely sacrifice of her life for his. For the Fates in a decree delivered by Apollo, who loves the husband and who by implication gives his high sanction to this mutually loving marriage, say that he must surely die unless another dies in his place. The situation becomes poignant when the wife (other potential candidates having refused) accepts the challenge and brings to the household a depth of sentiment and symbol that Hestia, the Lares, and the Penates combined could scarcely have achieved. The almost superhuman self-sacrifice should not obscure the genuinely human reality of the uxorial relationship, so movingly tender that it stirs to the depths of his giant being the earthy and experienced

Herakles, who defeats Death in hand-to-hand combat and so provides a resurrection for this saintly wife, who died for her husband when no one else would. It is not only the ancient giant who was stirred by this story; Philippe Ariès in our own day has found the play "one of the most beautiful texts celebrating conjugal love," with anticipations of the romantic view of unique and irreplaceable love that was to come only after a thousand years or so.[40]

Not all moderns can be counted on to feel this way. Admetus is something of a prig; some will disapprove of his summary dismissal of his father at the end, whom he can no longer hold *en philoisi* (630), dismissing him from the family love entirely for what many would have regarded as an entirely natural reluctance to sacrifice his life. Many are sure to feel that we have had quite enough of female sacrifice. And still others in our day, who exalt the pre-Olympian feminine world, will not like the heroine's apparent acceptance of the *Eumenides* settlement, that has decreed once and for all that the marriage vow is superior to and totally supersedes the ties of blood and family.

And yet it is fair to point out that if symmetry between the sexes is not fully realized in this play, it is because the wife is superior to the husband, not only in heroic capabilities (William Arrowsmith has pointed out the radical and pervasive parallels between Alcestis and the great male cultural heroes who confront death and give up their lives for others), but also in humanity and love. This exaltation of the woman may be a piece of affirmative action on the part of Euripides, who knew how to manage inversions for dramatic effect and for vivid explorations of value. In any case, the playwright, addressing a culture not exactly poor in excellence of many kinds, does present a heroine who is, quite simply, the *best*—the "aristē gunaikōn" (see lines 83–84), the best character in the play regardless of sex, and certainly one of the best in the gallery of ancient women. It is significant that in both the eighteenth and nineteenth centuries, when marital love was exalted as never before or since, Alcestis took her place in the imaginative achievements of Gluck and Browning. This moving exemplum of the good wife is thus an important legacy from classical Athens. She takes her place on the landscape of the Western world as a paradigm of sacrifice, but she is as far from the patient Griselda as she is close to Beethoven's Leonora in *Fidelio* or Wordsworth's Laodamia.

We cannot let *Alcestis* stand as our final example of the classical Greek heritage, powerful though its influence has been. Even though there are, as we have said, major inversions in this play, mostly in favor of the woman, it is perhaps truer to Greek mentality to bring back into final view the modern, ironic, revisionary spirit of Euripides. We do so by turning to Euripides's strange and relatively underdiscussed *Helen*. Helen herself has not been neglected in these pages. We have seen how Homer makes his great heroes and even the exemplary Andromache, Hecuba, and Penelope share the stage with Helen, not only as the greatest *causa causans* in history but as a woman who was wickedly sensual and faithless but also, before the whole story has been unfurled, a wise and humane wife and prophet. Aeschylus's treatment is more one-sided, the Chorus of the *Agamemnon* blaming Helen, the half-sister of Clytemnestra, for the fate of the hero. Euripides likewise—and perhaps with more insistent bitterness than anyone else—recurringly has Helen reviled, often by other women, as a sensualist, an adulteress, a destroyer of family, city, and the lives of men and women. Thus the good Andromache in the *Troades* expresses her hatred of the vile Helen; Menelaos decides to have her murdered; the common soldiers taunt and mishandle her; and the playwright, when he puts her on the stage, gives her what his liberated religious spirit must surely have regarded as a lame and shallow theology, conventionally though not piously blaming the gods for everything.

Helen can scarcely be expected to win the fame accorded the *Alcestis,* though in the summer of 1987 it had a Chicago run of at least a month in an outdoor presentation. The play takes place in Egypt, on one side of the tomb of King Proteus, where Helen, the real, living Helen, had taken sanctuary, led by Hermes. She is of course not to be confused with her likeness, the *eidōlon,* which Hera, disgruntled at the judgment of Paris that chose Aphrodite, had conjured out of air and sent to Troy as the consort of Paris. Despite being sexually importuned in Egypt by the new king Theoklymenos, the real Helen continues to keep herself untouched and chaste, loyal to and longing for her husband, Menelaos. Her shame is increased when the hero Teucer arrives, reporting that Helen's reputation killed her mother and may have led to the suicide of her two brothers. These additional indictments Helen had not needed to cause her to repent, for glancing at her unnatural though divine birth, she breaks completely with the murderous goddess of love, Aphrodite, in favor of Hera. Her soliloquy embodies many of the values of Attic Greece: love of home, country, family, children—and husband. He arrives shortly, in rags, the marks of his suffering upon him; and when the phantom Helen, who has accompanied him from Troy, disappears into air, he comes back to embrace his flesh-and-blood wife, who calls him dearest of men and proclaims that their joys are now fresh and bright. The rapturous embrace is modern, sentimental, natural, and not overdone, anticipating (though Wagner may not have been conscious of this) the famous love duet of Tristan and Isolde, "Ich bin dein, du bist mein." In the truly exciting dēnouement Menelaos reveals himself as conventionally manly, possessing *andreia* perhaps, but not what Euripides has elsewhere praised as *euandria.* Menelaos is inferior to Helen in every respect, mostly in his boastful impracticality and especially in the practical matter of their escape from Egypt and from a hostile antifeminine king. Helen embodies Greek wit and resourcefulness at their best. Perhaps the only blot for a modern on her otherwise shining escutcheon is her excessive and even bloodthirsty rejoicing at the slaughter of the Egyptians. But she is not a paragon—not a Christian or an eighteenth-century sentimentalist—but a long-suffering Greek woman, not above using ruses to return with her husband, to home and country.[41]

Euripides has thus given us another play in which men are more decent than gods, and women (including Theonoe, who enshrines justice in her heart) are regularly superior to boastful, murderous, or incompetent men. It is a play that embodies both marital and romantic values, with not much *erōs* but a good deal of *charis* and *philos,* though not in the *oikos,* for it has been deserted for some seventeen years in the holocaust of a foolish and unnecessary war. *Helen* was parodied at length by Aristophanes in the *Thesmophoriazusae,* but some of its values lived on to enter specifically into New Comedy, Menander, and Plautus, more generally into Hellenistic Greece and Rome, Christianity, and ultimately Shakespeare.

Thus in or near the Greek *oikos,* often humble and confining in reality and, when palatial and shining, often stained or emptied by murder, warfare, blood revenge, cannibalism, incest, and adultery, there even today abide *erōs, charis,* and *philia.* And the greatest of these is *philia.*

The birth of Psyche is a critical event in human history, as is shown by the radical transformation of man's relation to Aphrodite. It corresponds exactly to the cry 'Great Pan is dead!' that rang out at the end of antiquity.

Erich Neumann, *Amor and Psyche* (1956)

The entire sexual life between husbands and wives was to give rise, in the Christian pastoral ministry, to a codification that was often quite detailed; but already before this, Plutarch had broached questions concerning not only the form of sexual relations between spouses but their affective significance as well; he had underscored the importance of reciprocal pleasures for the mutual attachment of husband and wife. This new ethic would be characterized, not simply by the fact that man and wife would be restricted to one sexual partner, the spouse, but also by the fact that their sexual activity would be problematized as an essential, decisive, and especially delicate component of their personal conjugal relation.

Michel Foucault, *The History of Sexuality* (1978)

Hellenistic-Roman Culture (I)

*s it possible to treat Hellenistic-Roman culture as a unit? Most assuredly, at least for the topic of this book, since a few vitally organizing ligatures seem to tie together the works to be discussed, ranging in time roughly from the death of Alexander the Great in 323 B.C. to the last of the Greek romances, some time in the third or fourth century of our era. No one, least of all a critic intent upon disclosing unique artistic energies, could possibly deny profound differences within so long a span of mind-altering time. But Aphrodite *did* with considerable ease become Venus, and Erōs Cupid, without ever forgetting that he had once been Erōs; and it is now virtually a commonplace that Roman culture not only was influenced by Hellenism but in the minds of some creators of Latin art actually *was* Hellenism.

Sappho's brilliant description of infatuation was as memorable to Hellenistic Greeks and to Romans as it was to post-Renaissance Europe even up to the present, and philosophical filiations emanated from Plato and Aristotle. No modern student of culture can avoid pausing before the fact that the events in Bethlehem and on Calvary occurred in about the middle of this temporal frame and that the last genre I will discuss for this period was contemporaneous with the creation of primitive Christianity, to which the Greek romances sometimes bear haunting resemblances (some of these doubtless being our own anachronistic impositions). Some church fathers placed the child of Virgil's fourth eclogue in the prophetic network that foretold the coming of Jesus Christ, virtually canonizing the Roman poet, and it is difficult not to sense considerable resonance for our theme in that famous pastoral. At its climax Virgil creates a Mother and Child: "Begin to know your mother through a smile, o little child." Virgil does not stop there: let the baby smile first, let the parents smile too—without that smile there will be no divine honor for table or bed. As is so often the case in reading this poet, our minds begin to leap—first back to the famous civilizing smile

of archaic Greek sculpture and then ahead to the Voltairean smile of Enlightenment portraits or to the infant smiles of Blakean innocence or to
the therapeutic smiles of Eric Ericson's psychology.

More relevant to the institutional and legal aspects of long-term
Christian love ideally realized in marriage are the celebratory lines of
Horace, written in a time when divorce was rampant and erotic degen-
eracy legendary:

> They are happy three times over,
> > who are held by a tie that remains unbroken,
> > whose love no bitter words divide
> > > and who are never parted before their last day
> > > *Odes* 1.13[1]

These parallels—additional ones will be mentioned later—are not meant
to be understood as part of a *preparatio evangelica* or as evidence that
a gentler world was being created. But they do suggest that a cultural
force, not unlike that of sensibility in the eighteenth century, was pacify-
ing and softening the erotic relations of the sexes, thus creating a soil
congenial to seeds of loving, mutual trust, and even an esteem that could
be quickened by desire. Such could turn out to be the most important,
far-reaching, and unifying achievement of Hellenistic-Roman culture,
but it needs to be studied skeptically and at length, and its claims should
not be overstated.

A few randomly ordered examples may illustrate the field of cultural
force I have just introduced.

Paul Veyne believes that between Cicero and the century of the
Antonines a largely unnoticed revolution took place that made the
end of antiquity closely resemble, without a trace of influence from
the Gospel, the Christian marital morality that was to follow—a
large claim that a widespread cultural mutation took place, which
moved relations between men and women from spiritual inequality
and misunderstanding to mutual service.[2]

Early Republican Rome may have featured an all-male cast, but
monuments and statuary in neighboring Etruria obsessively epitomized family life in nude, heroically equal, and sometimes radiantly
smiling heterosexual pairs.[3]

At least one medical writer of great renown anticipated centuries of Christian asceticism by enforcing the healthfulness of retaining perpetual virginity in both sexes, though most gynecologies
took a more conventional line by valorizing fertility.[4]

Mental acts for Stoics are simultaneously rational and emotional, a consideration that often opened the way for love to become an important presence in Stoical ethics.

For the Cynics, self-sufficiency and a desire for isolation were countered by the human urge to sexuality, which provides an opportunity for free, mutual, and beneficial relations.[5]

Antipater of Tarsus regarded marital affection as providing genuine interpenetration of essences, like the mixing of wine and water— a view of marital union that greatly transcended Xenophontic comradeship and cooperation in the labor of the household and also transcended the traditional triple duty toward morality, religion, and the state that many Peripatetics envisioned as the obligation of marriage. Antipater's model might even seem to invoke the total love fusion of Romanticism.[6]

Some Relevant Cultural Paradigms

We can surely say that by the third century B.C. in both the Greek and Roman worlds the ideal of tender and lasting conjugal love had taken firm root, though it had to exist within the context of the family patriarchate, fiercely authoritarian in Rome for centuries, somewhat more relaxed and flexible in the later Greek world. But such strictly bounded love had its own polarities, contrasts that persisted for centuries; these can still be illustrated in paradigmatic myth and heroic legend even though growing naturalism, realism, and individualism spreading through all art and thought gave privilege to lifelike plays and novels of broad and sentimental appeal.

The extreme of sexual austerity and heroic faithfulness even unto death is revealed in the archetypal story of Lucretia.[7] In about 509 B.C., some Roman noblemen were boasting of their wives' faithfulness. That of Collatinus's wife was almost at once put to the test by the lustful son of the Roman king, who entered the lady's bedchamber at night, armed. He tried to seduce her, first by promising to make her his queen and then by threatening her life. She remained firm. But when he came back to swear that he would kill her and his slave and place the slave's naked body next to hers and that he would vouch he had found them together and had killed them both in righteous anger, as he would have had every right to do, Lucretia submitted. The next day before both her father and her husband and their two most trusted friends (the party included the formidable Lucius Junius Brutus) she told her story, and when she had secured their solemn pledges to avenge her rape, she stabbed herself in the breast.

The story awakened clashing resonances well into Christian times: both Jerome and Tertullian praised her, listing her among the most admirable of women, but Saint Augustine vilified her as a suicide. The immediate effect of the original event in Rome was to drive out the monarchy, and its long-run influence sustained the ideal of the unshakably and heroically virtuous Roman matron. Plenty of esteem here and an absolute centering of erotic affection exactly where it belonged—if indeed much sexual passion can be said to have existed in so stern a breast. The story put iron in the Roman marital spine and added a domestic dimension to the Roman *gravitas* which we see clearly in Cato, Cicero, Seneca, Pliny the Younger, and many others.

But the secular advance within marriage, though it did not ever bury and forget the bare bones of Lucretia's virtue, was propelled by a different dynamic during the centuries we are here concerned with, and that dynamic animates the well-known story of Amor (Cupid) and Psyche, which need not be retold here.[8] Erōs, we remember, had been made primal and primary in Hesiod's theogony, and Psyche as the soul had been individualized in mythology during the fifth or fourth century B.C. Beautiful bronze reliefs from Asia Minor portray the god and the maiden together in serene harmony—reliefs contemporary with Plato, who in his myth of the soul as a chariot brings out a close connection between desire and the psyche. But the Amor-Psyche myth had to await *The Golden Ass* in about 180 A.D. for its definitive human telling. Its major refigurings in the arts of post-Renaissance Europe display the growing union of sex and sensibility and give further evidence of Hellas-Rome as an important fountainhead of the maritally erotic. What Apuleius inserts into his novel may be a fairytale, a story of universal wish fulfillment in which romantic love overcomes even the formidable obstacles imposed on human beings by the gods themselves; but it has many mundane, human meanings fully localizable in real time and place. Still, a myth whose heroine is named "Soul" is itself already allegorical or on the verge of becoming so. It early entered the Neoplatonic world of flesh-spirit conflict, and no great effort was needed virtually to Christianize the fable and almost to bring it into the canon. And yet its carnal, human, and even institutional meanings are insistently present, and it is beautifully typical of Hellenistic-Roman realities and imaginings about the good estate of marriage.

Even Plotinus recognized the physical basis of Erōs,[9] and the Roman statue *Amor and Psyche* (fig. 7) points up the truly human and physical aspects that Apuleius's retelling conveys. Cupid is wingless, nude, and robust even as he points reassuringly upward. Psyche, modestly draped

FIGURE 7 *Amor and Psyche,* late Roman antiquity. (Collezione Ludovisi, Museo Nazionale delle Terme, Rome.)

below the waist but still full-bodied and full-breasted, is a potential mother, with the air of a future Roman *matrona* about her clothes, coiffure, and face (though it shows considerable worry or curiosity here). If that statue suggests the marital, the marble statue *Amor and Psyche Kissing* (fig. 8) more directly introduces the erotic without, however, losing the uxorial. Cupid is wingless and completely nude, his genitalia fully developed and prominent, though not in a state of excitement. Psyche is nude except for one leg and the genital area, and her belly is round and prominent as if to suggest pregnancy. The kiss and the embrace bring together two lusty and committed human beings, giving to the male a slightly more aggressive sexual role. The fact that it is the girl who is tested in this story and that the husband is himself already a god does of course suggest that for late antiquity preparation for marriage was thought to require more of the female than the male, as the many marriage rites going back to archaic Greece would also suggest. There is admittedly notable movement in this later period toward equalizing the sexes, but the male-oriented bias of the Amor-Psyche legend remains in most of the literature and art. At the same time the humanization of Erōs himself is steadily taking place. The personified god, with his attendant *erōtes,* could ornament the splendor and power of the Alexandrian court, and, as we shall see, virtually every Hellenistic narrative and many a Roman elegy made him a motive or organizing power, either inside or outside marriage. Wherever he is located, it is his role to enter human life and to create heterosexual couples that irresistibly implicate the human psyche either in playful or serious action, at whatever cost to his quondam philosophical and religious dignity.

If the legend of Amor and Psyche is suggestively prototypical, one work by Plutarch, who died about 125 A.D., can be said decisively to epitomize the marital theme for late antiquity.[10] I do not refer to the *Advice to Bride and Groom,* which invokes lifelong partnership and states the need for uniting reason and pleasure and creating emotions that are gentle and amiable. The *Advice* possesses too many strains deriving from the *Oeconomicus* of Xenophon (it is suggested, for example, that the wife remain invisible except in the presence of the husband) to make it fully typical of dominant Hellenistic-Roman taste. Nor does Plutarch's collection *Apothegms of Spartan Women* fully achieve the late classical ideal, though he stresses the bravery of women, seeks to feminize argument and poetry alike by adding *charis* (grace), and asserts flatly that the *aretē* (virtue) of man and woman is one and the same (242F, 243A–C). It is not the purpose of any of the famous *Lives* to discuss marital and sexual relations directly, though the author is capable of treating, with sympathy and

FIGURE 8 *Amor and Psyche Kissing,* late Roman antiquity. (Capitoline Museum, Rome; Alinari/Art Resource, NY.)

good humor, both the irregular but alluring relationship of Pericles and Aspasia and also the austerely but beautifully traditional marriage of the sober, simple, and dignified Phocion.

It is rather in the readable and highly dramatic *Dialogue on Love* in the *Moralia* (the *Amatorius,* or *Erōticos*) that Plutarch embodies the thought and artistic practice, though perhaps not the broadest quotidian realities, of late antiquity. He does so without showing in any way that he shares the modern scholarly sense that late antiquity introduced a totally new episteme, which effectually divided it from the Attic and the archaic. He is surely aware, however, that in his dramatic confrontation of love for boys with love for women and in his tolerant and undogmatic but unmistakable preference for the latter he is breaking with Platonic tradition. That great synthesis, as we have argued, had an essentially homo-erotic eros (though without consummation) as its matrix. It was that which provided cognitive value and could initiate the ascent of the dialectical ladder to permanent Forms. Plutarch, however, is not merely diversifying the lovers' physical sex but is producing an institutional revision as well. That is, he is privileging not just heterosexual eros in general but the marital in particular. The latter he regards as natural, while man-man and man-boy relations are contrary to nature—a commonplace by the time he wrote (one of his speakers climaxes a list of pejorative adjectives by calling boy love "anaphroditos" [751E], an insult to the goddess of love herself). But more positively he is also imbuing the uxorial with two of the greatest of Greek concepts, *charis* (grace) and *philia* (friendship). In finding grace in marital love he fulfills what we have already seen as an achievement of Attic Athens, where the Greek *oikos* could accommodate and encourage the presence of *philos. Charis* appeared in a marital context even earlier, for Plutarch reminds us that Sappho described a girl not yet ripe for marriage as being "acharis" (graceless, 751D). But the *Amatorius* gives greater emphasis to friendship and not only places it in the house generally as a lurking possibility but specifically locates it between husband and wife as an opportunity for spiritual development. More than that, Plutarch sees a dynamic relationship between grace and friendship, for it is by the instrumentality of grace (an eminently female quality) that woman is exalted, and it is grace that leads the couple into friendship ("eis philian dia charitos," 751D).

The Plutarchan *philia* possesses a fourfold ingredient, and its full verbal panoply is by the very logic of the constituent terms themselves extended to the married household: kinship, hospitality, comradeship, and love (here called significantly "to erōticon," 758D; see also 759C). This last ingredient of friendship logically calls for the continued (or perhaps renewed) deification of Erōs, a contribution that the priestly Plutarch either creates himself or derives out of erotic narrative. It measures his reverence if we note that even the life-giving Aphrodite is in need of Erōs, for without him her fruit can be *aphilon* (that is, lacking one of the greatest of all goods, *philos*).

Though its ingredients have all been anticipated, Plutarch provides the clearest synthesis in antiquity of what enters into the marital ideal of esteem and desire mutually interacting. Its authenticity and consequent force can be verified, at least partially, in literature and art from New Comedy to the latest of the Greek romances. And if we knew more about lives as they were actually lived by subaristocratic and even sub-bourgeois classes than the papyri and the tomb monuments have as yet revealed, its paradigmatic force might be even more compelling. Scholars since the nineteenth century have tended to exaggerate the change that overtook Greek mentality in this period ("the greatest change perhaps that has ever come over art").[11] Our earlier discussions have suggested that the contrasts between the Attic and the Hellenistic-Roman world with respect to love and marriage are not as stark as has sometimes been thought, but they are certainly striking. And literary evidences of gentler sensibility and more individually concentrated and dedicated eroticism spring up all over the Mediterranean world.

Transitional and Harbinger Texts

From social or intellectual history alone—even texts as dramatic as Plutarch's—we would never appreciate fully the products of changing *mentalité,* and we must turn to artistic expression to feel on our twentieth-century pulses what was happening to the imaginations of men and to discover what may be still available to the modern spirit.

Theocritus is an important begetter of pastoralism, one of the most self-flattering and perdurable mental escapes ever dreamed up by Westerners.[12] This great poet once vowed never to desert the Graces and expressed a longing to "dwell with them forever." They could of course invoke a special kind of Theocritean Erōs, the one located in the Golden Age, when lovers were equal and love reciprocal, and this golden god specialized in inducing climaxes which, if not fusions of the melting Romantic kind, did achieve simultaneity and presumably mutuality ("kai es pothon ēnthomes ampho," 2.143). The god could create soft and tender hearts (13.48), at times even lending his name to cute and diminutive terms of endearment; Theocritus enforced these characteristics by recalling a minor myth that the god was born of Iris and Zephyrus. At the same time Erōs (or Aphrodite or their equivalents) can be grievously cruel, vengeful, irresistible, even blind, although this last quality was not often ascribed to him in antiquity (1.97, 2.15, 4.59).

It is this torturing god who presides over one of the greatest poems of antiquity, the second Idyll, a poem that gives its author a high place among those who made the intimate handling of love themes the "most important legacy of the Alexandrian to European poetry."[13] The lover, Delphis, is apparently of a fairly high social level, perhaps something of a dandy, familiar with merrymaking (lines 118, 153), typically capable with either sex, and a frequenter of the gymnasium. The girl, Simaetha, is well below him in social rank, a fact that gives a kind of class edge to her stinging rebukes and laments as well as to the hopes he had aroused in her. What were these hopes? They may well be close to those expressed in the twenty-seventh Idyll, one surely not written by Theocritus, though inspired by him. The girl's fears about marriage (it is filled with vexation, wives fear their husbands, love leads to the pangs of childbirth and loss of beauty) are answered, one by one, by the goatherd lover in the stichomythy (marriage brings not pain but dancing, wives rule their husbands, Artemis lightens the birth pangs, children will assure recovery of beauty). Conversation ceases when he touches her breast, causing her almost to swoon. The two reach a climax. She says, "A maiden came I here, but go home a wife"; he says, "Wife, mother, and nurse of children, girl no more," and promises offerings to Erōs and Aphrodite.

Such fulfillment after her violation Simaetha of the second Idyll has cogent reasons to fear will never take place, for it is now eleven days and her lover has not returned. Into the hands of this determined, now grieving, and sexually aggressive girl (it was she who in their sexual encounter pulled Delphis down onto her couch), Theocritus places the magic wheel with or without the wryneck (iunx) spread-eagled on it. From her mouth issues a series of brilliantly phrased curses uttered singly with each revolution of the wheel. These curses are also accompanied by a contemplated symbolic act and an implied wish for the lover's return despite her imprecatory prayers: she burns barley and hopes his bones will be strewn; she burns bay leaves and hopes his flesh will likewise waste in flames; she burns bran and beseeches Artemis to turn loose her dogs on him; she melts wax and hopes that he will melt and waste in love as she has, that he will be as neglected by a woman (or indeed a man: see line 44) as she is now, and that she will get a chance to knead his bones. All this because he has not made her a wife (gunē) but a wretched being (kakan) who is no longer a maiden ("aparthenon," 41), all of these being powerful and solemn words, especially the last with its forceful privative *a*.

The refrains now change as Simaetha addresses the moon—not the moon of the Romantics' delight, but rather the moon of Hecate and the chthonic—and tells how her love began (such beginnings, greatly expanded and decorated, were later to become the hallmark of the Greek romance, though rarely told in the first person by a lover). Madness seizes the girl when she sees the blond-bearded Delphis walking with a friend, their breasts shining more brightly than the moon, apparently because of the oils that had been applied for their wrestling. (The hint of the homoerotic here is also an anticipation of much that is to follow, in the dialectical comparisons not only of Plutarch already discussed but also of rhetorical passages in the Greek novels—and more besides after antiquity.) Simaetha now ventriloquizes her lover's speech, and he makes the kind of learned theological allusions that continue all through the later love elegies. She invokes magic, he myth, a sign of class differentiation. It is she, perhaps ominously, who now recounts the consummation of her blisses (his apparently remain dubious and can only be partially deduced from the rhetoric of his seduction) and ends this fierce and passionate poem by turning again to magic and, if necessary, to evil drugs. She becomes a subaristocratic Medea.

Theocritus has created his art not out of sexual experience and sensual fulfillment, though that has often been done and though the smooth and perhaps experienced Delphis and the hungry Simaetha would have given abundant opportunity for drama. It cannot be proved that Theocritus himself here drew directly on the marital myth we saw prominent in some Theocritean verse. But it seems to me highly likely that Simaetha's murderous cries spring not from the abortion of a carnal "affair" but of her hopes of a very good marriage with a social superior. Cries of abandonment have remained in the erotic literature of the West as an enduring source of continuing poetic energy. Such energy is inconceivable without the enormously strong valorization of the married state that has been characteristic of the West from Homer to at least Dickens and Tolstoy. Let its putative benefits be denied the woman and she turns to dark and blasphemous ways. Scenes as remote as fifteenth-century Venice, when the holy wafer and holy water became in the hands of abandoned or prostituted or merely unsuccessful woman an instrument of the blackest magic, can be thought of as a gloss on Simaetha and her magic wheel. That wheel had had an impressive history before Theocritus, for it is said to have been invented by Aphrodite and named after that bird, the *iunx,* formerly a nymph, who had captured the affections of Zeus and been turned into a wryneck for exercising her charms.

In the Christian heaven there may be neither marriage nor giving in

marriage, but in the Theocritean pastoral there is, or wants to be. What
was true of that prolific, witty, seemingly detached, highly polished, and
mythologically learned poet Callimachus or of the school that may have
clustered about his name we shall perhaps never know, since not much
more than fragments remain.[14] Propertius called himself the Roman
Callimachus, and the Greek poet, who was born about 310 B.C. and who
may have gone to Alexandria during the reign of Ptolemy II between 285
and 247, might well have been an important link between the Homeric
hymns and the Roman world. Although there does not seem to be much
of love or sexuality in the literary remains of Callimachus, one story, that
of Acontius and Cydippe, is teasingly suggestive. Erōs himself taught
Acontius, not a very clever lad in his own right, the art of love and made
him blaze at the sight of the beautiful and marriageable Cydippe. He had
already had many lovers, presumably boys, at school and at his bath,
but now he is in the hands of one whose supernatural force is to bond
couples. Every time the highly nubile girl, Cydippe, approaches nuptials
to someone selected for her by her father she becomes grievously ill of,
in succession, the holy disease (epilepsy), the quartan fever (for seven
months), a deadly chill. By the fourth attempt the father has become distraught enough to consult Apollo, who says that Artemis is frustrating his
marital arrangements, advising that the girl be allowed to unite with
Acontius, a boy of good lineage. The girl agrees for she now feels bound
and tells how the commitment came about: in the temple of Artemis,
Acontius had thrown in her direction an apple (a frequent symbol of
love in Greece) bearing the inscription, "I swear by Artemis to marry
Acontius." When she read these words, she knew she had uninten-
tionally bound herself even though she threw the apple away. To us the
scruple may seem silly, but it was taken seriously in a superstitious society
constantly alert for signs. The wedding now ensues, and a bridal night of
true rapture, and since all knew the power of the stern god Erōs, no one
was either surprised or discountenanced at the outcome.

So subtle an artist as Callimachus reputedly was may have wanted
us to sense that the illnesses were psychosomatic, that the girl loved
Acontius all along, and that the divine merely ratified the irresistible human tendency to form lasting bonds. The fragment (75) from the *Aetia*
(*Causes,* book 3), an elegiac poem in four books containing legends from
Greek history and custom, that contains this story may seem to us neither
memorable (though Ovid remembered it) nor typical. But it does celebrate the power of the maritally oriented Erōs in a way that continued for
centuries. And that power is shown to be antipatriarchal in the sense that
parental arrangement mischievously frustrates human desires (Apollo

approves of the boy and not the paternal choices and overrules Artemis, who apparently wished to hold the virgin in her keep). The love begins on sight—that itself being a sign of natural sympathy or supernatural approval—and it moves to consummation by what looks like the sheerest accident, all of this constituting an erotic situation that possessed viability as late as Shakespeare.

Menander and the New Comedy: Ancient Sense and Sensibility

Modern critical opinion of Menander and the New Comedy may have been excessively excited by the thrilling discovery in the dry, favoring sands of Egypt of one complete play by the ancient master and intelligible fragments of some six others.[15] This may not be much preservation out of a total of some 108 dramas, of which about 96 titles are still known, but it has been sufficient to give a glow to professional criticism that modern lay readers do not always share when they read what survives.

Antiquity itself provides the best orientation for the modern student. Propertius, poetically deciding to abandon Cynthia and light poetry, turns to high intellectual pursuits in learned Athens, where he will encounter the successors of Plato, admire statues and paintings, and study Demosthenes—and Menander! (3.21.23–30). We do not today often put the playwright in such company. We are somewhat closer perhaps to the combination of morality and pleasure that Plutarch finds in Menander and his colleagues of the New Comedy: they provide good company for men relaxing with their wine, and their eroticism is appropriate for husbands who after their wine will go to bed with their wives. Besides, Plutarch believes, Menander's polished charm, apparent in his unaffected sentiments, helps to elevate morality, for in all these plays no one is enamored of a boy, affairs with casual women are cut short as the male sinner repents or is otherwise chastened, good but unprivileged girls who return love for love find a father and attain legitimate status, and when a virgin is seduced a marriage ensues.

Perhaps our best introduction to Menander comes from even later antiquity, from the imaginary sophistic letters of Alciphron in the second or third century A.D. He dramatizes and embroiders the famous story of Menander and his mistress Glycera. "Menander" writes first, saying that he will reject the rich offer of King Ptolemy to come to Egypt and write at court for rich rewards, for what is the Nile worth without his Glycera, no royal diadem could possibly replace her presence in his audience (she being his Areopagus council, his judgment ["gnōmē," 18.6–7]), and how can he desert Athenian rewards and opportunities in order to sing to

Dionysos? The letter is moving, and we should notice that the passion is placed in an impressive and clamant sociopolitical context. The emotion that obviates his accepting royal rewards is surely erotic esteem, as is "Glycera's" response. She uses *erōs* words of her love for him and their joint feelings, but she also calls her lover *erastēs* and *philotēs* (19.18–19) and describes her own *erōta* as being *sophos* (19.20). In earlier days his love was passionate and ardent—it combined *pathos* and *erōs*—but could be regarded as fleeting and insecure. Now it embraces reason and judgment (krisis), which is much better than affection based on passion alone. Pleasure (hēdonē) still exists, but it is without fret and worry (19.12–13). It is not recorded that this long relationship was ever "regularized"—but no matter. Graham Anderson has said truly that Glycera's letter sums up the Alexandrian dream, adding wittily that this hetaira is "all but offering to be the first editrix of the *Dyskolos!*" (Menander's one fully surviving play, which we are about to consider).[16]

Glycera in a sweeping survey characterizes his plays as accurately portraying all forms of life and character: the superstitious, covetous, faithless; fathers, sons, servants; and *the enamored.* The portrayal of this last category she surely knew how to judge from her own experience, but her full critical judgment she would have gladly admitted came from Menander's tutelage, since a beloved, she says, can be wise and learn from her lover. In any event her critical judgment as reported by Alciphron is very close to that of Paul Veyne, who says that Menander "depicts ordinary humanity without illusion, but does so with a rightness, a truth, a quality of detail sometimes so great that he might justly be compared to Tolstoy."[17] This is high praise indeed, especially if we remember that the contemporary classicist Veyne can take no refuge in what was available to Glycera, the old and lasting human tendency made famous by Freud to overevaluate the beloved object.

What does a modern student of love in Western culture see in the greatly depleted Menander available to us? For one thing, an important difference between what we have just been considering (an "irregular" love relationship imagined some centuries after Menander's death) and the public attitude of the playwright, who, though he might occasionally end a play by uniting hero and hetaira, made marriage or the reunion of a divided married pair his favorite dramatic resolution by far. And the marriage he prized was by no means the traditional matrimony of the patriarchy, Greek or Roman, but rather one characterized by tender sentiment and a forgiving ethic, by little class consciousness and dynastic ambition, by much higher respect for the woman (who is never coquettish but often courageous and independent and occasionally well read), and by a desire to suffuse virtually all heterosexual relations with this kind of marital glow.

Thus in the fragment *Misumenos,* a soldier on a cold, rainy night makes himself a voluntary *exclusus amator* as he stands outside the house in which remains a female companion of several years whom he took in as a girl; whom he expects to call him back since he has treated her as a wife; and for whom he feels a deep affection which he describes by using the prestigious *philos* words, adding to them a derivative of the word made famous by the New Testament, *agapē.*

In another fragment (this one virtually a complete play), *The Samia,* two relationships overlap, that between an older man and a hetaira and that between a young man, the son of the older man, and the girl he has raped, a union that has produced a child. The "irregular" relationship (such relationships are usually precarious in Menander) does almost collapse when the father mistakenly believes the child has been produced by his mistress impregnated by his son, a distasteful, quasi-incestuous liaison that has to be wiped off the slate. When it is, the resolution can be reached quickly: the father, almost oppressively repentant and charging himself with having a filthy, suspicious mind, forgives the son his peccadillo of producing an illegitimate child since it is not by the father's hetaira. What is important in the resolution is the quality of love that unites the young people: to him she is *philtatē* (line 630) and *Erōs* remains the master of his will (a strikingly different combination of *philos, erōs,* and *gamos* from what we find in much classical tragedy). When he accepts her father's offer of the girl, he uses three verbs that suggest the modern ritualistic phrase, "to have and to hold," and that are surely more progressive than the former "love, cherish, and obey" of the Book of Common Prayer: he says, "I hold, I take, I cherish," ("echō, lambanō, stergō," lines 728–29, the last being a highly honorific word used mostly of mutual family love, especially between parents and children).

In the one surviving complete play (an early one), *The Dyskolos* (translatable "grouch, curmudgeon, scrooge"), the setting is rural though near Athens, and the eros, which flares up suddenly, mysteriously, is mediated by Pan, to whom the heroine, Myrrhine, dressed humbly but a radiant beauty nonetheless, has been devoted for years. She has been brought up in a grimly avaricious and quarrelsome house by Grouch and an old servant, but at least she has escaped being spoiled by silly women. Sostratus, the lover, is the son of a rich farmer and has lived stylishly in Athens for some years, where he absorbed some city ways but not to his ultimate detriment, leaving him willing to do a hard day's work in the country, making him a pleasing contrast to the true dandy who is his friend, and so partly closing the social space between him and his beloved. Sturdy country values appear in the heroine's half-brother, and the youth turns out to be as humane as he is intelligent. His initial, suspicious resistance to the lover's suit as setting up too much distinction of class and wealth between the pair disappears when he knows all the facts, and it is arguable that he, not the lover, is the raisonneur of the play. The father of the lover is generous and kind, in the end fully acquiescent in his son's desire to have him use his money to make life easier for as many as he possibly can.

Against these good characters stand the roistering, mischievous servants, who can be crude but are good-hearted, and of course the title character himself, a misanthropic old man, whose bark is worse than his bite and who almost comes around to decent courtesy as the festivities begin. If the worst evil we know in life is his kind of isolation, stinginess, and irascibility that can be largely mitigated by rescue from an inopportune fall into a well, we are clearly not in either Ovid's Age of Iron (of this more in the next chapter) nor in the Paulinian or Augustinian world of original sin (of that more in ensuing chapters). Few would argue that this play is an erotic masterpiece, but it is precious in its rarity and also in its typicality of Greco-Roman antiquity and of what is to come for centuries in the West—the notion that suddenly and mysteriously induced erotic love, more or less within class boundaries, brings long satisfactions to the couple and also to most of those who witness its formation and wish it well.

Remains are too fragmentary to permit us to do justice to the genius of Menander. His influence in antiquity was great; the educator Quintilian names him, with some reservations, after Homer as a poet to be read in the schools. And he and some sixty-odd other comic dramatists in Greek active in this period established a notably ground-breaking literary genre, to say nothing of what Plautus's and Terence's use of him did for Roman antiquity and also for Western culture from the Renaissance on. Too little survives for us to say who was Menander's authentic sentimental predecessor. Was the dream embodied in the once famous and now lost *Lyde* by Antimachus of Colophon, a contemporary of Plato? Certainly in the comedies that survive (an early version of the Hollywood dream machine) an economic base for the union remains intact, nor is all prudential caution thrown to the winds. And though we do not find the emphasis upon fate or fortune or chance or the inescapable norm of nature or way of the world as prominent as it was to become in the later romances, *tuchē* (what men receive from the gods) is clearly present and can sometimes be much stronger than love itself. Nor should we denigrate or downplay the persistent respect for women and the female principle that seems to animate much of this work, particularly in consistent resolutions in their favor. Fathers may not have been freed en-entirely of cantankerous suspicion of the young, but they are for the most part surprisingly tolerant and generous. We remember that Theocritus even in an idyllic setting and genre denied to his Simaetha the fulfillment of permanent love and liaison that she craves. What now happened in the changing cultural ambience to obviate or silence her bitter curses?

Modern curiosity trained by the social sciences reaches out for causes of the new marital ethos. Why does a dominant realistic trend suddenly turn optimistic? What relations can the New Comic endings bear to the voluntary limitation of children through contraceptives, abortion, or abandonment and exposure of the child, often the initial situation of a literary plot? What weight should be given to the extension of celibacy or to threats to marriage by concubinage, and to counter these, the populationist propaganda of the second century? And what are the causes of these potential causes? The enormous extension of travel, the increase in the size of the reading public, the transformation of the classical polis into the great Hellenistic metropolis, the accumulation of enormous wealth—all these are subjects worthy of social and economic analysis. But for an exploitable literary heritage we must use what we have and hope that dry sands and isolated desert caves may yet yield up additional texts. In the meantime genres like the Roman elegy and the Greek romance can still produce erotic-marital harvests for our own canonical bins.[18]

Myth, Law, Paradigm

If Hellenistic remains seem sparse, the Roman heritage is full and de-tailed.[19] The long-loving and committed couple does indeed exist in Latin art and expression, though often by implication only, but the student again and again encounters a strange but powerful taboo about discussing or portraying family life, even its innocent or commonplace details. It is that taboo in part that may make Roman erotic literature subtle, indirect, arch, witty, often with undecidable resolutions. The Romans seemed to have obeyed Emily Dickinson's injunction to "tell all the truth but tell it slant." And yet we need only recall the Lucretia story to remember that Roman mythic and traditional stereotypes could also be clear and forceful. All cultures, of course, have their inconsistencies, but it does seem peculiarly appropriate in approaching Rome to think in oxymorons. The evil but heroically resisted and politically atoned rape of

Lucretia is countered by the equally paradigmatic rape of the Sabine women, who unresistingly become good Roman wives in Romulus's (and Livy's) bland vision, where love and friendship follow injury and injustice, but who in Ovid's bitter vision are grabbed by lustful hands and "cower like a flock of timid doves / beneath an eagle," attaining no chaste home (domus casta) in a rape that can be seen as being staged by Romulus.[20] Both monarchical and republican times were patriarchal with a fierce austerity known to few cultures, offering little or no chance for divorce, harshly punishing female adultery, and threatening capital punishment even for female drunkenness (the law is so worded as to suggest that a drunken wife was easily susceptible of becoming an adulterous wife). But there was no time when prostitution was unknown or even concubinage in the household, and women could escape some of the rigors of established marriage by marrying not *in manu* but *sine manu,* thus becoming able to acquire property, seek a divorce, and even attain wealth and independence. Late republican tombs praised faithful, loving wives, and the most famous encomium of them all, the *Laudatio Turiae,* praised the wife's natural qualities—modesty, deference, affability, amiability, faithful attendance to household duties, enlightened religion, unassuming elegance, modest simplicity of attire, preservation of the patrimony, and heroic risk taking during the husband's exile—and in that order. It hailed some forty-one years of unclouded happiness, but quickly added that such a marital life was uncommon, since marriages of long duration terminated only by death and not by divorce are now very rare indeed. The imperial period soon tried to remedy such degeneracy by draconian marital laws that tried to reinstitute earlier traditions of monogamous faithfulness and fruitfulness, leading Horace to proclaim the return of "Faith and Peace and Honor and ancient Decency" (Fides et Pax et Honos Pudorque / priscus). But almost simultaneously both the daughter, Julia, and the granddaughter, also Julia, of the reforming Augustus had to be relegated (the term is a technical one) to separate islands as a punishment for immorality and licentiousness. And society and art slipped into the priapia of domestic wall paintings, Fescennine verses, the grossest varieties of gourmandise, weird forms of homosexuality, and scenes that made the *Satyricon* seem realistic and led one scholar to conclude that Fellini's lurid scenes were not after all very far off base.[21]

To represent such cultural paradoxes, continuing all through Roman history, what texts should be selected as prototypical? Obviously no one text will do, or even several. But there are two that will bring out the contrasts that made high imperial Rome complex and interesting. The first is Juvenal's brilliant and widely imitated sixth satire; the second,

Pliny the Younger's letters to his wife. Juvenal savagely attacks upper-class Roman wives for their cruelty, drunkenness, artificiality, lusts, and adulteries, and he makes death a quite attractive alternative to marriage. A less dramatic alternative might be a young boy, who will never wrangle with you at night, never ask for presents when in bed, never complain when you take your ease or ignore his solicitations: "Won't it be better when a young boy sleeps with you?" ("nonne putas melius, quod tecum pusio dormit?" line 34). Juvenal's usually grave tone may lighten a bit in these words, but the juxtaposition is typical: Homosexuality (here apparently of the pederastic variety) is often placed alongside love and marriage in the rhetorical sections of the romances, as it was in the *Amatorius* of Plutarch, which we have already analyzed.

We find a considerable contrast in the letters of Pliny the Younger, written to his third wife Calpurnia before and after 100 A.D. Michel Foucault sees in them a clear sign that attention has shifted from the stern economy of the house to the couple that occupies it; there is now a new conjugal individuality, highly romantic, intense, affective, personal, constituting an emotional and passionate fusion and reciprocity, the man recognizing and submitting to this new reality.[22]

The comment is welcome but needs to be made more nuanced, critically and historically. The putative fusion does not turn out to be quite that if we think ahead to nineteenth-century Romantic unions, but the intensity of the monogamy does seem revolutionary if we lay it alongside Xenophon's domestic economy of some four centuries earlier. It seems less so if we place it in the context of this study, viewing it not only in terms of its own time but also in light of earlier antiquity. Besides, Pliny, though writing personal letters, is still a sophisticated writer, publicly and politically conscious, involved with his class, a partner in a recognizably Roman marriage. My qualifications of Foucault's view are not intended to deny that we have here a remarkable example of eroticized friendship, but merely to say that it becomes more compellingly prototypical if given a broader, earlier, and more evolutionary context. Mental history is not usually divided by the sharply divisive, watershedlike epistemes that excited the distinguished French scholar.

The letters have doubtless been carefully selected and are artfully arranged for publication. Pliny mentions Callimachus, and very naturally and without strain refers to Hellenistic literary culture (4.3). He everywhere reflects and sometimes lightly revises literary stereotypes and commonplaces about love: Amor can be the best of masters (nothing about the fateful or cruel Erōs here) when Calpurnia is setting her husband's verses to music, since her study of literature also comes from her love for him (ex mei caritate). Love is as firmly associated with chastity as in the Greek romances: "she loves me, which is an indication of chastity" (amat me, quod castitatis indicium est). When she is away from him, her image is present and he repeats the word *desiderium* of his longing condition. He goes to her room, finding it empty leaves it, and departing feels like a rejected lover—an *amator exclusus* like the soldier in Menander's play, for he uses the technical love word *exclusus* about his own condition at the moment (4.19, 6.7, 7.5).

At the same time that he is being somewhat literary and formal, he remains keenly aware of his status and his class. He apparently accepts as necessary the full penalty of Augustus's Julian law sentencing an adulterous wife to forfeiture of half her dowry and a third of her property as she is banished to an island (10.120). He settles a handsome sum on the bride-to-be of a man of public distinction so that she can dress as befits the career of her husband (6.32). It goes almost without saying that he associates family matters with piety; and when he is called upon by fathers and friends to recommend husbands for nubile daughters, he is careful, intelligent, class conscious, and prudential (1.14; 6.26, 31). He applies such standards as the following to the candidates for a worthy aristocratic hand: a native place that is characterized by honest simplicity and ancient rusticity (he evidently participates in the widespread wish that older virtues could animate present-day Rome); male beauty of a dignified sort and worthy of a senator or a noble (though here he is somewhat apologetic, saying that handsomeness is after all a good reward for the virginity and chastity of the girl). And finally money and status are requisite—though here again he can be a bit defensive, in one case perhaps fearing to insult an already rich father while venturing to point out the importance of inheritance for future generations.

The presence of some of these public and prudential qualities in his letters makes him seem somewhat arrogant and self-regarding to a modern. Need he make so much of his tutelage or her devotion to his fame as a legal orator? Need he try to allocate blame for his wife's miscarriage, unchivalrously thinking her youth and inexperience partly to blame? But *we* need to heed a caution to be historical, and the fact that he is unmistakably a Roman of his class does not deny that we have here an ardent love, even though my earlier chapters should qualify the view that this love in marriage reveals a notably *new* ethos. Pliny esteems Calpurnia, no doubt of that (her *acumen* is *summum*, 4.19); he misses her when she is gone; he grieves over her illness and suffering; he longs to have a child by her; he loves her *ardentisssime* (though he puts the accompanying subjunctive verb *diligas* in the second person [6.4], attributing the love either to her or to a general and impersonal "you" rather than to himself); as we have seen, he confesses to desire and longs that their *concordia* will be *perpetua* (4.19). His was of course not a modern marriage—the wife is too submissive, the arrangements have been too careful. But it apparently succeeded—in one sense, how could it have failed?—as did others in Roman society, and it must have brought considerable mutual satisfaction. It would be blind and churlish to think otherwise. The impressive tradition embodied in this marriage explains why Augustus felt he had to act as he did about threats to the institution, why the *Satyricon* must have seemed unspeakably shocking to many, and why Ovid's earlier adulterous poetry contributed to his banishment.

The Roman Elegy

Why should so artificial a genre as the Roman elegy interest a student of marital love, since its aristocratic speaker seeks pleasure in a sexually permissive demimonde as he cultivates an *otium* frowned on by his class, a dangerous kind of leisure that leads him to passion and adultery, which at once attack his own autarchic self and the institution that putatively cements the state?[23] What can this relatively short-lived form (flourishing for about sixty years or so shortly before the birth of Christ), noted for its insincerity and cynicism, possibly contribute to a marital ideal?

Opposites attract but they also create one another, and the austere Roman ideal, especially in or shortly before the time that its austerities were being revived and enforced, might well wish to imagine relief in freedom and naughtiness. But illicit love in the elegy, except for important stretches in Ovid, produces less joy than deep pain and the inglorious feeling that passion entails servitude—and this surely provides little relief from the bonds of matrimony. In fact, *miser* is a kind of code word for the condition of amorous passion, and to fall in love was sometimes idiomatically expressed as "to be miserable" or "to live miserably" (see the *miser vive* of Catullus, 8.10). The female objects of desire in these poems are surely not prostitutes (no moneyed transaction requires this degree of learned expenditure) but rather freedwomen or intelligent hetairai capable of witty companionship. One might therefore expect a celebration of heterosexual friendship that could suggest values for marriage or liaisons more permanent than a series of one-night stands. But there is very little that celebrates friendship, although one glimpses moments of high spirits. One can scarcely give to these relations what Plato thought homoerotic eros possessed but that marriage lacked, cognitive value in a search for basic philosophical meaning. Indeed, the furtive illicit love of the elegies would surely have been regarded by him as a quicker means of falling off the dialectical ladder than any marital consummation. The lady is seldom an *amica* in the nobler sense (the word was sometimes used simply as a synonym for mistress); and although she is often a *domina,* this address implies not the mistress-ship of the house for the female but servitude for the male. And it does not seem to say very much about the exaltation of woman for her own sake, however useful such verbal flattery may have been in a flirtation or in the persuasions of a seduction.

But what one does find in the elegies of relevance to the notion of long-term heterosexual friendship lit up by desire and sexual consummation are some moments of intense longing for permanence that structurally or imagistically if not discursively find in the married state a succoring parallel. These moments may be fleeting in Tibullus, Propertius, and the early Ovid; but they do exist—and they are dynamically exploited by Catullus, of whom more later.

Tibullus beautifully realizes a pastoral setting in hard, severe, simple solitude, which is not sentimentalized but represents his chosen venue of inaction ("mea paupertas" [1.1.5], referring not to hard, grinding poverty but escape into the *deliciae* of love and sensuality from aristocratic, military, and state responsibilities).[24] A warm fire on the hearth, a sufficient supply in the agricultural bins, a mistress in a tender embrace— these are enough to compensate for glory, which no longer has charms since he has no fear now of being called lax and unsuccessful. Yet he wants permanence with the lovely girl—the fact that she has fettered and conquered him does not matter—and he wants to meet inert age ("iners aetas," 1.1.71) and even death in a relationship of mutual love ("iungemus amores," 1.1.69). When he dies, she will surely shed tears, but now it is time for the blithe, insouciant Venus ("nunc levis est tractanda venus," 1.1.73), which gives this pastoral its focus. The poem is effective, because unpretentious and understated. It is a *coniugium* of sorts, expressing a modestly stated desire for more of the same or a continuing renewal of the same. It is somewhat in the spirit of Keats's "Bright Star," though it does not eternalize sensual foreplay but takes age and death, tears and separation into account as well as the playful joys of the light Venus.

Tibullus is in the country; Propertius is in town and gives us a night scene (2.15), in which he expresses desires closer to Keats's longing for immortality pillowed upon his fair love's ripening breasts.[25] He apostrophizes the night, then the bed of pleasure, then the lovers' mutual assaults—reversals are the stock in trade of the elegies, and here the girl is the aggressor in initiating the love play while he, sensing godlike powers, demands her total nudity, contrary to some respectable Roman custom. The scene is tempestuous, but these wars hurt no one: would that the whole world might settle for this kind of conflict! The poetic "I" wants lovemaking eternalized into a permanent tableau of love and then of intertwined bodies asleep after drinking (it may heighten the ironic contrasts present in this "immortality" if we recall that a drinking woman could be regarded as capitally offensive according to some statutes). The longing here assumes greater intensity than in either Tibullus's or Keats's dream, and the poetic speaker feels he must appeal for his sanctions, conventionally to nature (doves mate permanently) or audaciously to a reversal of nature (let the sun drive night-black horses). Before we conclude that such passions as these are not usually thought of as marital, we should bear in mind that literature and experience often encourage us to believe that many have approached the altar with longings for permanently passionate coupling not unlike the dreams in these elegies. Propertius cannot be called sentimental or romantic, since he does not tie his longings to any institutional form, and his poem ends with a one-line vision of imminent death. But he does make memorable one of the traditional uxorial ingredients, as indeed did Sappho.

And as does Ovid, in a subtly realized daytime scene (*Amores* 1.5), with the Italian-type shutters half closed, producing a crepuscular light like that between darkness and dawn, which serves as a kind of soft cloak for the intimate action. In steals Corinna with rustling summer skirts, like a fabled Eastern queen approaching her bridal chamber, but the tone is soon lowered and Semiramis becomes Lais, loved by many. As in Propertius, the poet tears off her clothes, and a lovely description of the girl's body and a chastely brief and general reference to consummation follow. The longing for immortality comes in the beautifully understated last line, a simple wish for many more such mid-days (proveniant medii sic mihi saepe dies). A sensitive contemporary critic has noted the domestic details of this lovely poem—*she* comes to his room during the day—and the whole has a relaxed air of domesticity about it. Peter Green uses this poem to support his thesis that Corinna is a poetic version of Ovid's very youthful first wife.[26] There is no need to take so biographical an approach, but the marital dream is surely not devoid of such daytime encounters and the desire for their repetition or prolongation.

Catullus, the earliest and much the most intense of the elegists—"I am tormented" (excrucior), the poet speaker exclaims—also intensifies, expands, and even virtually institutionalizes the desire for permanence we have noticed in the others.[27] The author of the strangely violent and barbaric Attis poem (*Carmina* 63); of the finely, hungrily excessive kissing poem (5) that makes Leporello's list in Mozart look skimpy; of bisexual and homosexual songs (see 15 and 25); of bitter and even mad laments over his beloved's unfaithfulness, calling his rivals adulterers (using the Greek-derived word *moechi* at 11.17); and of a searing description of the fall of Lesbia into a frequenter of crossroads and alleys as she now serves filthy lusts (58)—the author of such verse has also written some of the greatest marriage hymns in any literature. These often contain haunting and inescapable ambiguities (see 99), making us realize that if the elegiac world of free love was precarious, so was the more stable world of marital love. One of the longest and noblest of the hymeneal songs brings Peleus and Thetis to the bed that will produce Achilles, but on the coverlet of that bed is represented Theseus's desertion of Ariadne, realized by Catullus in a brilliant *ekphrasis* (64.50–250).

Quite apart from ironical paradoxes, Catullus made a direct contribution to the erotics of long-term relations. He brings together the great Latin verbs, *amare* and *velle bene* (72, 109), and in one song (109) he enshrines the perpetuity of both *fides* and *amicitia* in marriage. Here he lets the woman lead off: she proposes a love that is at once pleasant and perpetual ("iucundus" and "perpetuus"). He replies, in a religious mood, that he hopes she is sincere and can keep the promise and that it will be their joint lot to realize all through their lives this eternal pact of sacred friendship (aeternum hoc sanctae foedus amicitiae). The words are solemn, *amicitia* usually bearing all-male human privileges but also political implications, and *foedus* being a word of high politics and international relations. The line might well have been baptized and taken into Christian ritual—with this qualification, that it took centuries of Christian thought and practice before such an ideal did in fact become canonized. From *iucundus* to *foedus* we run the gamut from desire to esteem, and are not far from the eighteenth-century synthesis of sex and sensibility as marital qualities or from the nineteenth-century ideal of the angel in the house. In his dream of pastoral permanence in love, Tibullus did, we remember, invoke the "levis venus" (the trifling Venus). Catullus in his despairs and conflicts (61) allowed his mind to turn to the "bona Venus" and "bonus amor" (61.44–45); to Penelope (61.226); to the venerable emblem of marriage, female vine and male tree (61.102–5); and to the stability of the household in which love and desire need not be hidden (61.228–31).

Catullus on love, with the energetic richness and organized complexity of his thought and art (encompassing love and hatred, joy and pain, life and death, health and disease), brings to mind that persistent oxymoron for natural creation, *concordia discors* and *discordia concors*, which was applied to love and friendship by the pre-Socratics, as we have seen, and also, strikingly, by Dr. Johnson. We are told that Callicratidas in our period defined marriage itself as a harmony of opposites.[28] And surely the young and vibrant Catullus in part achieves his impressively chaotic unity because he was haunted by and admired a marital ideal.[29] Against that steady norm both his consonant and contradictory erotic experiences and values struggle to achieve their focus and form. No other ancient lyrist quite achieves that effect of boiling rationality.

We have come to expect from so volatile a subject as love abundant paradoxical antitheses in the literary expression it has inspired and indeed in entire cultural epochs it has dominated. Nothing is more striking in a period already hyphenated by history—the Hellenistic-Roman world—than that the marital ideal we have studied so far should include both the brilliantly indirect, tortured, and naughty inwardness of the sophisticated Roman elegy and the open, sentimental, popular declarations and resolutions of the New Comedy. A similarly striking antithesis awaits us in the next chapter, which continues the exploration of late pagan antiquity.

*Entre l'époque de Cicéron et le siècle des Antonins,
il s'est passé un grand événement ignoré: une
métamorphose des relations sexuelles et conjugales;
au sortir de cette métamorphose, la morale sexuelle
païenne se retrouve identique à la future morale
chrétienne du mariage. Or cette transformation s'est
faite indépendamment de toute influence
chrétienne. . . .*

Paul Veyne, *Annales* (1978)

FIVE

Hellenistic-Roman Culture (II)

*A*n antithesis parallel in structure and contrasting in content to the one we have confronted in the previous chapter between the Latin elegy and the Greek New Comedy awaits us now. We shall first consider the wry, ambiguously poised Ovid, vastly different from his immediate Roman predecessors but nonetheless a continuer of their erotic achievements, and then study a phenomenon that both recalls and stunningly develops the sentimental-romantic ethos of Menander—the Greek novel, which in spirit as well as in date brings us virtually into the Christian world.

Ovid

Ovid was the most interesting and the most productive love poet of antiquity, as Catullus at his most intense may have been the greatest. It may strain credulity to say that in some ways Ovid resembles our paradigmatic Pliny: each was married three times, each was deeply in love with his third wife, both were deeply though differently involved with the government of Rome, which honored Pliny with great rewards and which both applauded and exiled Ovid.

We may never, to be sure, arrive at the erotic center of so ironic and varied a poet as Ovid, but no interpretation is worth much without considering his long and dramatically varied career. We must juxtapose the latest poetry (usually serious and often highly personal) with his earliest (delightfully light and wittily inversive). Hermann Fränkel has said, "It is axiomatic for Ovid that the woman should be on an equal footing with the man and should be looking for the same kind of benefits from their association"—an important insight without which one can make little sense of the poet's strivings and triumphs.[1] In fact, the aim of this section is not so much to study marriage in Ovid—if it were we should make the *Heroides* central—as to test the validity of this book's title and learn whether one of the greatest of love poets ever implies or expresses erotic esteem in settings of poetic charm or mythological memorability.

The quarry may elude us in the *Amores,* where the poetic situations were not set up to reveal esteem or any kind of reverence. The many trivial, annoying, painful, delightful, witty, and wistful encounters reverse normal morality and attack marriage, and widely acclaimed though they were a generation or so before the birth of Christ, they would have been totally incomprehensible or reprehensible to Christians, for though the historical Jesus may indeed have been far different, the established Christ of tradition was made morally severe and physically ascetic.

The irony that the poet of love seems on another planet from his near contemporary in Palestine who was the founder of a religion of love can scarcely be lost on anyone. And that irony is compounded if we try to follow the theology of the *Amores.* The poem begins by presenting a laughing, snickering Cupid, but he is soon directly addressed as a "nasty brat" ("saeve puer," 1.1.5) and the inducer of "savage passion" ("ferus . . . Amor," 1.2.8); and before we have finished the love god's attributes have all been interpreted, usually with lightly revisionary ratios. He is adorned with wings—this attribute goes back at least to Euripides—that must show his volatility; but these wings are also downcast, drooping (demissis). Cupid himself is *miserabilis* (pitiable, 3.9.9), and we remember that *miser* was a code word for lover. The torch is present too, but there is little revision of love as fire, though the flames, elsewhere so searing, are somewhat banked by Ovid's wit. The bow and arrow take on more literal meaning, for Ovid, though not original here, is more intent than most eroticists on military metaphors (love requires gusto and initiative). And although one is not aware of the old Hesiodic primal Erōs (Ovid is too skeptical for that), his triumphs (blown up into Triumphs) show the boy-god surrounded with pomp and magnificence but leading such whipped and bound captives as these (1.2.31–35): Conscience (mens bona), Modesty (pudor), Illusion (error), Passion (furor), and Flattery (blanditia). Ovid is a master ironist, but he does, in his own way, take his love god seriously, though not so seriously as does Propertius.

Modern liberal theologians, discovering that God is dead and his miracles unbelievable, turn to a gospel of good works. Ovid, also an unbeliever, finds the gods expedient, but his culture permitted no such recourse as the social tear. He does, however, reduce the vindictive fierceness of the older Venus (though she remains somewhat proud) and makes her tender, *tenera* doubtless referring to yielding voluptuousness, which some erotic philosophers were capable of claiming as a civilizing tendency, though no one ever accused it of being able to produce an ancient Man of Feeling. Ovid's Venus was the "tenerorum mater Amorum" (the mother of tender Loves, 3.15.1), surely one reason his amorous delights ("deliciae," 3.15.4) never let him down or seemed to him unbecoming. And a quality closely related to Venereal tenderness is the poet's desire to have cheerful women as company, not tearful lamenting ones like those of his own *Heroides:* let Ajax have his Tecmessa and Hector his Andromache, but for me—!

Anyone in search of the marital will have to say something about Juno, the brilliantly conceived divine villainness ("saeva Iuno" 1.114) of the *Aeneid.* In the *Metamorphoses* she seems mostly a nagging, jealous, vengeful being, in no way humorous or human and frequently unremittingly cruel and persecutory, while in the *Fasti* (6.27–28) she can be slightly ridiculous. Virgil's "Iovis et soror et coniunx" (both the sister and spouse of Jove, *Aeneid* 1.46–47) has been softened into a being with whom one can reason and even joke. In the earlier poems, in which the marital is sneered at or ignored, she might well have been presented as taking offense and demanding requital, but she is, instead, chastely sacred, her worshippers approaching her in hushed reverence, and perhaps we feel some sympathy for one whose husband swears falsely to her even by the river Styx.[2]

In the *Ars amatoria,* theory is much less relevant: Cupid is still present, but when "arte regendus amor" (love must be controlled by art, 1.4), the poet, not the god, is in charge, and the poetic speaker proclaims himself the teacher of love (ego sum praeceptor Amoris, 1.17). Is there here a distant echo of Socrates's boast in the *Symposium* or even of his female teacher Diotima's? The poet wants safe love (leave matrons untouched) but not moral love, though incest is a strong taboo, or marital commitment or a cessation of seduction and sexual victory (in other words, continue as before, but "gull only girls"). In the *Remedia* he ploughs up the very seedbed of elegy love, *otium*—leisure, laxity, the attractive drop-out alternative to aristocratic responsibility. Some conventional Roman values, close to those of matrimony, do seem to peep up from the erotic soil: the poet now recognizes a need for both energy and reason, *impetus* and *ratio,* in keeping intact the autarchic personality. And one can say that there is a delicate though insistent implication that permanence and commitment might be an attractive alternative to the alternative. It is such new glosses as these that the young Ovid made on the noun *Amor.*[3]

Ovid's exile for some seven years after the *Remedia* in a desolate place on the Black Sea (for having written an immoral poem, the *Ars,* and

committed a grievous error, never explained but evidently some kind of
lèse majesté) entailed separation from his third wife, whom he loved and
revered; a burning desire to have his relegation to loneliness and crush-
ing boredom revoked; and the necessity of keeping his wife active in the
cause of an imperial pardon. All these explain the intense seriousness
and the commitment to marital fidelity that characterize much of the
latest poetry. It would be naive to consider the poetry unworthy for being
generated out of self-interest and suffering, especially since the Roman
ideal of marriage was itself so hedged in with pragmatic considerations.
Of course the pursuit of pleasure also accommodates the ego, a fact that
has never yet thwarted its claims to be heard. In any case, the pleas to his
wife for *fides,* loyalty, dedication to his cause, cast in simpler but no less
artful language than the earlier erotic poetry and filled with mythology,
have much of the intensity, if not the charm and delicacy, of earlier erotic
persuasion. Again and again Ovid's unchallengeable sense of his own
worth and of the fame that even now as he writes he is bestowing upon a
faithful spouse anticipates the highly Roman stereotypes characteristic of
the younger Pliny in loving his wife.

Two qualities in particular need to be noted about the *Tristia (Matters for Grief)* and the letters *Ex Ponto (From Pontus,* where Ovid was
exiled). The vocabulary is mild, tender, amorous, recalling again and
again the addresses of the elegist to his beloved: the lady (domina) is
carissima, mea lux, maxima cura; and the *tenera* Venus (he seems to recall
and does not apologize for this adjective) has become the *mitissima coniunx* (the gentlest wife). But the mythological pantheon has changed. It is
now fixed, canonical, marital, and quite without flexibility, wit, or irrev-
erence. It includes many, perhaps most, of the marital heroines so far
treated in this book, and they are appealed to more than once as exemplary and as awaiting another poetized wife to join them. Penelope,
Laodamia, Evadne, Alcestis, and even Andromache, whose laments the
Ovidian poetic persona had earlier found distasteful, now seem to recall
the faithful, grieving spouses of the *Heroides,* deeply internalized.[4]

Such is Ovid's poetry in extremis, and it has its own kind of severe
and haunting *gravitas.*

But it lacks the range and brilliance of the *Metamorphoses,* part of
which was written in exile and which yields its marital meanings much
more indirectly and subtly. It is important to see exactly what the setting
for love is in this masterpiece. It is not the Age of Gold, which seems to
have had no sexuality in it but only eternal spring; it is, rather, the Age of
Jovian Iron, when every sin abounds, including familial ones, since loy-
alties expire, son-in-law plots against father-in-law, and wedded love

turns to murderous spite. Ovid's tale of origins provides no Eden, and there is no marital bower like that of either Genesis or *Paradise Lost*—no lovely erotic coupling exists, Cupid does not wave his purple wings, and there are no rites mysterious of connubial love.[5]

No more grimly realistic portrayal of what can happen to a family in this our life can be imagined than what overtook the mother, Niobe, all too boastful of herself and her *ornamenta* (her children, 6.146–312). Son after son is named and then with cruel suddenness dispatched by the unerring shafts of Apollo, and the once delighted mother kisses each of the seven icy faces and then turns to stone herself. In frighteningly effective verse Ovid cuts family beauty, pride, wealth down to much, much less than size. Niobe (6.193–94) and also others even less guilty of *hybris* violate Ovid's basic premises expressed in maxim after maxim: call no man happy until the end of his life; it is ill when majesty and love ("maiestas et amor," 2.846–47) coexist in one dwelling (in una sede); respect limits and boundaries (beware of Bacchic religion, it tends not to); and never forget that all life springs from *discors concordia* (1.433). The last is Ovid's somewhat wry contribution to the long history of this pre-Socratic oxymoron.

It is such Iron Age realism and disillusion that makes Ovid reduce to something less than heroic or mythic dignity the great Euripidean character of Herakles's wife, Deianira (9.134–58), and turn the majestic Trojan queen and mother Hecuba into a barking dog, filled with subhuman, even subcanine, hatred and anger (13.404–7, 567–69). The tone of the romantic story of Pyramus and Thisbe (4.55–166) may be hard to detect and define, but it strikes one as childish and sentimental, its violence overdone and kitschy. These qualities are dramatically motivated by having the tale told by the impious, voyeuristic, and somewhat pornographically inclined daughters of Minyas, who in their small, isolated, and sensually deprived society like to tell tales that embarrass procreative sexuality—tales of initial romance ending in suicide, adultery, or hermaphroditism. Ovid may not be speaking directly, but he clearly allows human potentiality to be dramatically undercut.

The voyeuristic and sex-starved offspring of Minyas (devotees of Minerva who are ultimately turned into bats for neglecting to worship Bacchus) do seem to be enemies of exogamy, and Ovid uses his very great skill to make extremely vivid and unpalatable deviations from normality in the brother-sister incest attempted by Byblis (9.454–665), in the father-daughter incest successfully prosecuted by Myrrha (10.298–502), and in the murderous magic of Medea (7.1–424), overwhelming her family piety and her deeply felt *erōs,* which may in part cause her crimes.

The clearest and most contrastive negatives produce the best positives, but this is not quite true in the complex art of the *Metamorphoses*. For over his direct portrayals of married couples of whose lives and loves he seems to approve he drapes the shadow of negation. The good Cadmus, still haunted by the fear that the snake he slew long ago may have been a sacred being, finds his doubts resolved as he himself turns into one, along with his wife, at her own request when she sees his fate (4.563–606). Their reward is to live on, their slippery bodies entwining, and to retain their gentle natures and soft spirits in snaky bodies. Not precisely a dignified immortality, and the serpentine embracings are repulsive to the comrades who witness the metamorphosis. But, again, this is the Age of Iron, and their fate is at least not torture or everlasting damnation.

The good Baucis and Philemon live in the country (not in a pastoral Eden) and in their humble but hospitable way entertain deities unaware (8.618–724). They are rewarded by becoming priests in Jove's shrine, which replaces their thatched hut, destroyed with their inhospitable neighbors. After that, but not before they have said farewell to one another, they become intertwining trees—perhaps a better fate than to become embracing snakes. Hospitality, so touchingly displayed by this couple, was of course one of the greatest virtues in the ancient world, where the survival of a traveler could depend upon it, as the story of Lot's doomed city in Genesis shows. But the piety here is accompanied by a kind of dignified marital devotion, which is rewarded with a decent natural life that may well outlast the human threescore and ten.

The story of the Locrian Noah, Deucalion, and his wife, Pyrrha, is stark (1.313–415). She moves from being wife to cousin to comrade, and like a Xenophontic couple they work together, though in a grim and destroyed land. No rewarding sexual union here, no command to be fruitful and multiply and replenish the earth. Only the command to throw stones, the bones of the Mighty Mother, over their shoulders, hers to produce women, his men. The other creatures spring up by an unaided act of the Earth itself.

So there are no romantic beginnings in Ovid, and against this creation story the fate of other loving couples in the *Metamorphoses* looks truly benign. In the narrative of Alcyone and Ceÿx (11.415–748), that favorite story of Sensibility and Romanticism, the ocean washes the husband's corpse back to the loving and distraught wife, who is ready to join him in a watery grave. But both are transformed into birds. Their loves last, and their marriage bonds hold. And when in winter they mate and breed, halcyon days of perfect calm succeed, and mortal men and women extol their love.

Into a section of the *Metamorphoses* (12.169–535, the battle of the Lapiths and Centaurs) that rivals the telling as it recalls the bitter cruelty of some of Homer's epic battles, Ovid inserts the story of the death of the centaur Cyllarus. This handsome creature, his human part covered with golden hair, his equine body silky black, his tail and legs white, is joined in battle and then in death by his beautiful female companion—his equal in beauty, battle, and death. This brief vignette of mutual love (12.407–416) that hushes momentarily the din of hideous battle is movingly human. It recalls a scene from the Elgin marbles that portrays sensitively a dying Centaur and also the ancient story of the lovely Amazon Achilles kills and in killing loves. Ovid joins those who pay tribute by high art to what society chooses to regard as the inimical Other.

Men and women producing life by throwing stones, loving couples becoming serpents, trees, or birds—this is not the stuff out of which romance is made. But such is in fact the mordant but haunting realism of Ovid about marital prospects in the Age of Iron, and the portrayal is not without modest hope and an austere and chastened dignity. One final example, the story of Cephalus and Procris, will show how the middle or late Ovid revised a marital story that the younger Ovid had first told in the *Amores*. Both the earlier and later renditions reveal the essential lineaments of his uxorial legacy.

What were the données of this myth? Procris was the daughter of the king of Athens. Her sister had been raped by Boreas, and Peter Green has observed that "winds with sexual characteristics seem endemic to this story." About a month after his marriage to Procris, Cephalus was seduced by Aurora, who then bore him a son and whose reputation among early-rising working people and lovers just leaving their illicit beds was not much higher than that of Donne's "busy old fool, unruly sun." Aurora gave him a swift hound and a target-seeking spear. But he had to leave his new wife, and he was gone for some eight years, hardly an auspicious beginning for a model marriage. On his return, deeply suspicious of his wife, he disguised himself and then seduced her, and after that they went their separate ways toward mutual adulteries. On one occasion they did hunt together, and the spear given Cephalus by Aurora found its mark in his wife's breast. The Areopagus refused to believe that it was an accident and in a fit of anger condemned Cephalus to exile for murder. What Ovid inherited was the squalid narrative of a stained marriage.[6]

What does he make of it, first in the *Ars amatoria* (3.686–746), then in the *Metamorphoses* (7.661–865)? In the earlier of these two versions he omits the rape by Aurora and presents Cephalus as relaxing in a siesta and calling upon the personified breeze Aura (whose name does indeed recall that of the dawn goddess) to relieve his sultry heat. The poet allows the sexual nuance to remain without leveling a charge and seems also to keep a trace of the old story that makes Procris suspicious of anyone named Aura and hence susceptible to the slander of a busybody who reports the language of Cephalus's solicitation to the wife. Procris searches out the compromising site and begins behaving like a crazed maenad. She finds it, lies down, and then hears her husband's voice calling once more on Aura, but this time as to a zephyr, without sexual overtones. The wife realizes her misunderstanding, recovers, speeds to her husband's arms, whereupon he, thinking this the rustling of a dangerous beast, hurls the infallible spear and dispatches her. But not before she can with her last breath declare her love and proclaim herself free of the misunderstanding, though she says that this mortal piercing is the last of many her loving heart has received—leaving us to wonder whether these were less often piercings of love's than of jealousy's arrow. The husband weeps copiously as he breathes in her last breath.

What is Ovid's lesson, for this is told in a book on the *technē* of love? Apparently it is directed to girls and bears the burden that the lady had been rash and thoughtless and had overreacted to gossip. He suppresses most of the inherited squalid details and leaves us with a devoted wife and an essentially loving husband, who did not compromise himself even if now and then he did lightly rattle his wedding chains. In other words, this is a not untypical Roman marital union that might be said to need a bit more tolerant and relaxed sanity in the wife, leaving the male the somewhat wider berth that he usually claimed as his right.

In the *Metamorphoses* Ovid moves even more decisively away from the squalor of the original Greek story. Cephalus is introduced as a handsome and impressive Athenian prince, fondling his great spear, here a weapon of Diana given to him by his wife. He himself with tears in his eyes tells the story of his great loss and of the marriage that had preceded it, a marriage mediated to him in the ideal Roman way, both by his father and by Amor himself. Two months into his marriage he is violated by Aurora, but she, a notorious androphage, uses force and is enraged that he should want to remain faithful to his wife. His mind twisted by the goddess, he wonders if Procris has been faithful and decides to test her by disguising himself, and after he tries many wiles this hitherto blameless woman yields to the proffer of a fortune and thus shows herself not a

Lucretia but a realistic Roman lady. She does no violence to herself but flees the house and becomes a devotee of Diana—a decent enough resolution for a while. When she returns home, it is she who brings him the spear and the hound, not here the gifts of that violator of his marital vows, Aurora, as in the original story. There follows a lifetime of mutual and glad affection (see 7.697–98, 707–10). Then comes the denouement, repeated with a few important changes. The address to Aura is now truly innocent, the slander is totally empty, and all is done as told before, except that it is Cephalus at the end who is frenzied when he sees what he has done. He rushes to pick up her bleeding form, pleads with her not to leave him guilty, disabuses her mind about Aura as a rival, allowing her to die smiling. In short, Ovid has given us a deeply pathetic tale about a married love that began precariously but finally attained stability, and was then tragically aborted by a cruel accident.

Or has he? Could he be ironic? This is the husband's tale, and is he to be believed? Would the sophisticated reader, recalling the original, wink, smile, or nod his head knowingly: I remember more than Ovid tells, the couple were both rogues all along? Such cynicism seems unwarranted. The best view is surely that Ovid is here very much the marital Ovid of the masterpiece in which the story is told: he has allowed life to provide a solace, which it poisons through illusion and suspicion. This is the Age of Iron. The story does not even provide the blessing of becoming loving and gentle serpents, trees, or birds. But a tender and austere, if somewhat qualified, beauty does nonetheless attend this, the latest version of Cephalus's and Procris's story, as it does almost all the marital tales of the *Metamorphoses*. Our next section, on the Greek romances, will radically change the severe Ovidian tone and so provide still another of those paradoxical contrasts that seem to inhere in Hellenistic-Roman culture.

The Greek Romances

The chiastic arrangement of this and the previous chapter taken together— Hellenism/Rome/Hellenism—brings us back, not always or often to Greece but always to Greek, the language of the broadly expanded, orientally influenced, mystery-inspired, Romanized, but still Hellenized world of the Mediterranean basin. Ever since it dawned on us disillusioned moderns that love and marriage do not always go together like a horse and carriage, it has been a continuing scholarly preoccupation to discover just when romantic love came into Western culture. The Victorian nineteenth century, Romanticism, eighteenth-century sensibility, the English Renaissance are all much too late, and so is that candidate of many nineteenth-century and contemporary thinkers and writers, courtly love. Nor will Christianity do, though it is a religion of love—at least in its earlier centuries. Late Hellenistic antiquity and specifically the Greek romances are now often favored as the chief begetters of romantic love sensibility. But there is New Comedy, to say nothing of the Sumerians and the semitic Song of Songs, whose marital eroticism modern scholarship will no longer allow us to allegorize out of existence. This tour d'horizon in search of etiology ought at the very least to dispose once for all of the notion that romantic love was necessarily bourgeois and middle class, since most of the periods and forms just alluded to were aristocratic and sometimes royal.

Since the surviving romances (only a fraction of the total written) number no more than seven and since some bear striking resemblances to one other, it may be instructive to set the type negatively by contrasting them with earlier works that can serve as a bridge back to Attic and Roman antiquity. Xenophon gave his name to several late romancers, and his *Cyropaedia* (after 362/61 B.C.) has been considered an influence.[7] But is it, in any illuminating, positive way? Pantheia, the most beautiful woman of Asia, proclaims her more-than-life love for her husband Cyrus (it is the word *timaō* she uses, meaning "I honor or prize"), and she hails their mutual *philia,* using that great Attic word we have seen significantly present in classical marriage. But more than anything, she wishes him to fight and, if necessary, to die gloriously; and he, as he leaves, though doubtless feeling deep emotion, only puts his hand on her head and prays, while the single action the author makes available for her is to lay her hand on the armored box of his chariot. When at the end his corpse is returned, the wife takes the severed hand of her husband in her own, kisses it, and then tries to fit it back on before she plunges the dagger into her heart. These are not the ganglia of farewells or reunions in the Greek romances.

Petronius's *Satyricon* from the first century of our era, a work that once may have approached the length of *War and Peace* but now exists only in fragments, possesses perennial appeal although it is highly individualistic and even eccentric and specifically tied to many local times and places. Some of its unforgettable scenes and themes show us precisely what the Greek romances are not, with its orgies homosexual and heterosexual, its Gargantuan gourmandism, its preoccupation both with impotence and Priapus, its deflorations of children after mock weddings, its thrusts at the Platonic: a "he" (denied the status of being a *totus vir,* or fully endowed male) says that "he" and "she" can become one soul in their embrace while the "she" will cruelly address him as "paralytice" (you impotent one) and vainly call for "voluptatem robustam" (a healthy voluptuousness). On the other hand, the Roman novel does resemble the Greek in its hair-breadth escapes, its encounters with pirates and rogues, its juxtaposing of the hetero- and the homosexual, and its use of tombs for more and other than death and burial.[8]

If we look closely at the most famous of the romantic tomb scenes, we see that it differs greatly from Petronius's. Chariton's supposedly dead heroine (we shall discuss his work presently) looks ahead to Juliet or, better, to Hero in *Much Ado about Nothing,* for she is "resurrected" and goes on to become an ideal wife. But Petronius (pp. 229–35), once he has placed a wonderfully virtuous, now grieving wife from Ephesus in her dead husband's burial vault, then proceeds in short course to have her accept the physical attentions of the tomb guard. These pleasures might be compromised if the amorous soldier should be blamed for criminal neglect on her watch: a body had been stolen from a nearby cross. The blame is deflected when the widow allows her beloved husband's corpse to replace the stolen body. Presumably the lovemaking can now be safely resumed.

It is the differences between the naughty Roman novel and the sentimental Greek romances that establish the taxonomy and tone of the latter. Their movements and adventures by land and sea all through the Mediterranean and Persian worlds are impelled by the sudden, overwhelming *erōs* that springs up early in the action between an aristocratic boy and girl. Her virginity or chastity—some are married near the beginning, others at the end—survives the hottest fires of trial and adversity, often close to those that tested Psyche. His may or may not be compromised, and we are frequently made aware that the venerable double standard is still in place. But we are also made to understand that the passion aroused early and mysteriously carries over into a calm and fruitful married life, which, however, is not depicted, only promised. And the adventures and trials are often interrupted by rhetorical or mythological learning, recollections or anticipations of Plutarch, and expressions of one or another kind of religion and sometimes of the spirit of philanthropy and forgiveness. As so often in this period, one feels at times strangely close to Christianity—at least to some aspects of that complex and varied aggregation of ideals and practices.

Chariton's *Romance of Chaireas and Callirhoe,*[9] formerly thought the latest but now regarded as the earliest of the extant narratives, is denominated by its author as a "pathos erōticon" ("an erotic incident" or simply "suffering" [1.1], the word *pathos* invoking both). Erōs is introduced as a god at once, and his aim is clear—to create an unrivaled couple, which in fact he does at the very beginning. But since he does not have the power to obviate *tuchē* ("fate" or "fortune," a most important Hellenistic word, as we have seen), love is given as chancily realistic a setting as in Ovid's *Metamorphoses*. And desire is a powerful presence in human life at all levels, a fiery power aroused at fleshly contact, as even the good and stately governor Dionysius learns as he brushes Callirhoe with a kiss. Erōs is given the usual tyrant role as he spreads unquenchable desire for the heroine everywhere, from the thrones of three states and of the great Persian empire itself on down to the masses. He seems to be effectually separated from *philia,* also a virtue in Chariton but not much stressed, at least within the marriage, although it is certainly present (the heroine bursting with love for her husband is described as *philousa*). Aphrodite is a continuing presence (the author, incidentally, comes from a town named after her), and all the good Greek characters are her devotees. She too is a uniter, the agency behind the marriage of hero and heroine, as well as a sanctioner of trials and testings; it is her special task to provide the resolution at the end, which, as the author says, is more pleasing than the brigandage, war, and capture that have preceded it.

To summarize the theology briefly: Both Erōs and Aphrodite create and sanction beauty and physical desire, both can conflict with reason, both support marriage and long-term union. But neither provides sentimental happiness or easy resolutions, and the underlying and motivating mythology thus provides little philosophical originality or unifying form but considerable beauty and much realistic force.

The leading characters are more than stereotypes. Callirhoe is ravishingly beautiful, though never proud or self-conscious about her attractiveness except to wish it away when it becomes a burden. She is certainly courageous, though she has moments of suicidal depression, and she is unswervingly loyal but also resourceful, calculating, and not above using guile to achieve immediately romantic and selfish but ultimately good ends. Thus in order to spare her and Chaireas's son for future glory in her home country, she will enter for a while into a state of bigamy (when she marries again, she herself is not at all sure her husband is dead). And she will allow her child to be raised by her second "husband," who is under the illusion the child is his. The ruse is bold and unconventional, but not spiritually wicked; it is not surprising that so versatile a heroine should acquire new virtues with each of her trials and finally fully merit the stable happiness that is vouchsafed her at the end. It is she who writes the masterful letter not unmixed with guileful diplomacy that reconciles the putative father to the final arrangement.

Chaireas, the lover and only true husband, entered at marriage with Callirhoe into fully reciprocal physical joy, and their brief time together before the adventures begin united *isorropia* (compatibility), *epithumia* (desire), and *sunousia* (sexual intercourse), on one level at least a kind of ideal partnership (B.8.4). Nevertheless, Chaireas has to be regarded as something of a cad at the outset, and he achieves a deep and abiding love for his wife only after unbelievable suffering. His suffering often takes place in a solitude that is partially mitigated by a firm but completely un-erotic friendship with a male colleague. Ultimately, distinguished military and other service fits him for leadership and also for the kind of forgiveness he metes out at the end to quondam enemies and rivals. Even before his feats as a commander, he shows himself erotically and morally (often the categories come close to merging in these fictions) superior to his royal rivals, including the great king of Persia himself—except, that is, for one.

That one is Dionysius, the governor, who buys the heroine from the pirates, falls desperately in love with her, and makes her the successor to his deceased first wife. His considerable piety is, like that of the heroine, directed toward Aphrodite, meaning that when he loves he loves passionately. But his emotional life is not entirely concentrated on the passionate and sexual: toward Callirhoe he is *philogunes* (a respectful word showing that his love includes enough respect to make her his wife, B.2.1), and toward his female subordinates in the house he is *chrestos* (kind) and *philanthropos* (B.2.1). He proves to be a formidable rhetorician in an exciting court trial before the great king, which presents a conventional but noble view of marriage. Of the boy he presumes to be his son he becomes a good father, and he is capable of treating the child with heartfelt sentiment.

In short, he is a highly civilized man, despite some pomposity, and we should not be surprised that he knows inner conflicts between passion and reason. But this psychomachia is not so conventional as it might at first seem: somewhat like Ovid, he wants his thinking being, or rational center, to be fully engaged by *erōs* ("sphodroteron psychēn en erōti philosophousan," B.4.5). In other words, his ideal is esteem enlivened by desire. In action this ruler is not a plaster saint, and he is not afraid to imagine his enemies and rivals dead, including the true husband of his new wife. But he is fully reconciled at the end, though not without an emotional struggle in which the boy finally assumes the affectionate place formerly held by the now unavailable heroine. Dionysius is a good, kindly, sophisticated, artistically sensitive man and fictionally an exciting one, providing drama, conflict, and a stable focus for much of the action that beats around him—worthy, in brief, of a place in the erotic pantheon.

The romance of Chaireas and Callirhoe begins in marriage and ends after searing trials in a reunion of the uxorial lovers. Longus's more famous and long loved and imitated *Daphnis and Chloe* (written perhaps after the middle of the first century A.D.) begins in innocence and ends in experience.[10] The action commences at the discovery in the country of both the boy and girl foundlings and ends with their urban marriage and return to the pastoral setting of their rearing and of their coming to sexual awareness. Chariton's novel, moving through much of the Middle Eastern world, subordinates time to place and is a novel of great international movement and moment. The motion of *Daphnis and Chloe* is temporal rather than spatial, set mostly in one rural place, and its gentle rhythms are those of the seasons as they change, each giving its own coloration to corresponding events and emotions. The characterization is more naive than that of Chariton's novel, and no one in it compares in depth or sophistication to the governor, Dionysius.

The children's earliest nurture is not administered by either the natural mothers or the wives of the shepherds who discover the foundlings with their birth tokens but by the animals who suckle them, a function they continue even after their adoption into respective pastoral homes. That most primitive nurture is loving, for the goat who suckles Daphnis is characterized by *philanthropia* (1.3) and the ewe who nurses Chloe is a mother whose gentle disposition it is to love the young child ("paidion philein," 1.6). No modern child psychologist could ask for more—the tender babes are loved, and the great Greek root, *phil-*, has been planted even in the animal world. Grace and the Graces also enter the pastoral world, for near the places of discovery is a lovely religious shrine presided over by delicate female deities, and toward it the pastoral "parents" who rear the children are worshipful.

Because of what happens at the conclusion, it is important to note that the setting, though decisively rural and pastoral, is not a rough or remote country but a beautiful and well-tended urban-dependent estate, an *agros* (field) that is *eudaimon* (prosperous, 1.1) partly because it is not far away from the great Lesbian city of Mytilene.

Erōs was introduced in the opening *ekphrasis,* and it is to him, the Nymphs, and Pan that the story is dedicated. Erōs begins assuming an active role when the boy is fifteen and the girl thirteen, in the long and erotically revelatory middle section of the tale. It is clear that the pert, pretty, and winged boy is about his usual romantic business of adolescent pair bonding, but here, it is also clear, he is intent upon creating an ideal pastoral couple. The rural "parents," who have shown and will later reveal status ambition for the children because of the birth tokens, also offer sacrifices to the rural Cupid, companion of the Nymphs, showing their at least unconscious wish for the union of their wards.

Much of the charm of the novel lies in the delicate but countrified way the frisky, childlike Erōs removes the veils of innocence from both girl and boy. In bathing Daphnis after he has fallen into a pit—there is plenty of dirt but no blood—the girl is the first to be erotically aroused. It is now Daphnis's turn to be aroused, and his awakening (after some slight quickenings at the kisses of Chloe) comes through a challenge from a crude, redheaded cowherd who attempts violence, which is quickly punished when he is attacked by dogs and as quickly forgiven when both Daphnis and Chloe treat his wounds. With the coming of summer heat, passions rise, and autumn brings the wisdom, mediated by an older musician-shepherd, that erotic pain can be remedied by kissing, embracing, and lying down together naked. The young people are still too shy to indulge in the climactic "cure," and successive seasons lead them both to swear eternal mutual love, Daphnis to offer to the country "father" a dowry of no less than 3,000 drachmas to which a dream has miraculously led him, and Chloe to learn domestic arts from her country "mother."

The most dramatic event in the sexual awakenings comes when a pretty, city-bred wife conceives a desire for Daphnis, divines that he is in love with Chloe and that both are still innocent, and contrives a ruse to permit her to instruct the youth in the ways of love, ministering to her own pleasure the while. Aided by nature, she succeeds in bringing about a consummation. But this initiation of the male is not followed by the third step prescribed by the shepherd-poet, that the adolescent lovers should lie down together. Why not? Partly because it is not yet time to end the novel, which by the already established generic rules must conclude with marital consummation. Partly because Daphnis, though he has enjoyed the encounter with the older woman, is almost as innocent as before. But mostly because his instructress had warned him of hymeneal blood, the thought of which now haunts him and makes him fear seeing his beloved in summer undress lest passion prove to be irresistible. There are, of course, precoital rewards, some of them presaging consummation, and Longus echoes Sappho in writing of the single apple left unplucked by the pickers high on the tree, which Daphnis now scales and brings the apple to Chloe as a gift. But it is not yet time for the full resolution, and Longus has given us so far only the preliminaries, which, however, constitute one of the subtlest explorations of dawning love in literature.[11]

It is important to see what the ending is not. Though a city is nearby, the resolution is not urban, neither of the realistic nor of the apocalyptic variety, for there is no hint of the New Jerusalem with the splendid geometry and sapphire-studded glory that the Book of Revelation brings to religious consummation. Nor is there a full country resolution either, like one Theocritus, Virgil, Horace, or even Tibullus might have imagined, to say nothing of a fully achieved Rousseauist nest. No, this novel ends in the pastoral garden described at the outset, whose absentee ownership and economic support lie in the great Hellenistic city nearby. Not all cities have been presented as worthy in this novel. Incursions into the country by the urban young have been criminal and impious: Daphnis was beaten and stripped, Chloe struck with vines and then driven off along with her goats, the Nymphs insulted, the ministrations of the great rural god Pan required to restore order and incidentally to deepen Daphnis's religious devotion. And now at the climax the great city sends to the country the drunken pederast, Gnathon, the most serious threat to the union of the couple yet, for he has conceived a desire for Daphnis and is himself politically connected by friendship to the absentee owner. This invasion by the city is the worst conceivable, since it directly threatens to undo the work of the country Erōs in making a beautiful and productive couple. Longus is not above making the corrupt urban invert disgusting and crass, though in the end the universal rejoicing is so infectious that even he is forgiven.

All this is brought about by almost apotheosizing the good father of the New Comedy into the tall, handsome, middle-aged, religiously named, and enormously rich but impeccably virtuous Dionysophantes, truly a Mr. Allworthy, the absentee owner of the great estate on which the babes were found, now revealed as the father of Daphnis, who is forthwith made as rich as the other children of the family.[12] But the couple, who had been nurtured by the animals and raised by the shepherds, do not want urban life; they wish to return to the place of their discovery, their rearing, and their erotic tutelage. And so back they go, after a sumptuous dinner and after Chloe's urban birth has also been established, to a wedding in the country, to the kind of ritualized naturalism that had fostered them, and to happy fruitfulness. They now come into the full joys of Philetas's third step, lying together in the nude, as Daphnis puts into play the skills into which Lycainion, the older married woman, had initiated him and as Chloe comes to realize how preliminary their country dalliance had actually been. But is desire enriched by esteem, by friendship? We do not know, but it is unlikely. Such is not the concern of this novel, which remains a suggestive and sophisticated idyl though always and insistently, in its central achievement of enduring rural union, a Song of Innocence.

The two great garden scenes are instructive. In the first, the garden of Philetas, a name known to pastoral poetry, the owner is vouchsafed a unique epiphany one noontide. He sees a naked little boy with a complexion like fire and skin like milk, a skin that shone as if it had just been bathed and oiled. Frisking a winning smile, he teases the old shepherd into desiring a kiss, but the boy is elusive. He finally reveals that though he looks young, he is older than Kronos and Time itself. What is the meaning? On one level that Erōs does foster a kind of childish homoeroticism that accompanied all growing up, an insight not unlike Freud's. But more pertinently here, he is also a great god, and creating a pastoral couple forever united is a task worthy of the Hesiodic view of him that we have already analyzed in an earlier chapter.

The other garden, the one owned by Daphnis's father, is disfigured, but not permanently, when its flowers are destroyed by a jealous suitor of Chloe shortly before the final revelations and reunions. This garden is a *paradeisos,* its plantations precisely arranged, the trees regularly spaced, the overhead foliage joined; it possesses a view of the city and seems to unite both venues. A temple to Dionysos, who apparently gave his name to the owner, stands exactly at the center, its interior full of pictures portraying Semele giving birth to the divine son honored in the temple, Ariadne sleeping, and Pan piping. Is this vision of structured nature central, and does it have the force of example? Only to the extent that it enforces what was already obvious and what we have already emphasized, that an urban economy supports the rural marital bliss.

The true dynamics lie elsewhere: it is not Dionysos but the divine *pais* (child) of the earlier garden who is now honored as the happy couple build an altar to Erōs the Shepherd and a temple to Pan the Warrior, the god who had, even though neglected by Daphnis, rescued Chloe and her goats and driven off the urban invaders. It is hard to regard this climax as progress into a more abundant life; the couple try to have their own experiences repeated and put out their male child to be suckled by a goat, their female by a ewe. This looks, rather, like a prototypical Romantic regression. Which is perhaps why it has been popular, for, as we saw in our introduction, psychological research shows that the modern dream of permanent romantic happiness may spring from a desire to find in marriage the lost paradise of childhood.

The remaining Greek romances can be dealt with summarily. Xenophon's *Ephesian Tale,* episodic, unnuanced, but historically important, tells forcefully the restoration in the end of the hero's homosexual rival to an ultimately gracious *philanthropia* after a manly but militarily cruel and criminal career—a story vastly different from Longus's account of the repulsive Gnathon.[13] (The theme needs to be noted as part of the marital vs. homosexual rivalry we shall continue to trace.) But the chief emphasis of the story falls on what can only be called a fanatical devotion to marital *fides,* to a *sōphrosunē* (a word regularly used for marital faithfulness, 2.1.4) that has become a fetish not very far from what early Christianity made of virginity. The hero makes it clear on his first night with his bride that he desperately longed for a *gunē sōphrōn* (a wise and faithful woman, 1.9.3), and that is exactly what he gets. The girl who revealed erotic aggressiveness on her initiatory night channels it with fearful concentration into unassailable monogamous loyalty.

Achilles Tatius, in a long, self-conscious, and sophisticated first-person narration, *Leucippe and Clitophon,* indulges in black humor, subtle satire, voyeuristic ironies, and both riotously gross and delicate parody, embodying a peculiarly masculine kind of sensibility surprising in this genre. It provides even bolder illustrations of what we have just noted in Xenophon and what in discussing Shakespeare I shall call the *paragone,* or contest, between the rival claims of love for boys and love for girls. And yet the power of Erōs stands unchallenged, the test of virginity and faithfulness can still be passed, and the marital and romantic themes we have come to expect stand intact even though they look a bit battered and tarnished.[14]

One work carries peculiarly religious meanings that stir resonances echoing backward and forward in time. In the *Ethiopica* of Heliodorus, the falling in love of the couple, done in slow motion, enforces the Platonic idea of the divinity of souls and the divine ecstasy of the *Phaedrus,* even anticipating Wordsworth's *Ode on the Intimations of Immortality in Youth,* and the initial attraction and absolutely indissoluble union of different races may not be far from the fusion of opposites Paul found in the gospel of Christ (Galatians 3:28), although the class involved is exclusively aristocratic, even royal.

If they have done nothing else, this and the previous chapter have at least challenged two eminent French writers on love and friendship: Montaigne, who sharply distinguished between the two and separated both from marriage, and De Senancour, who believed that "the principle of the institution of marriage has never been love, for which marriage is in no way necessary."[15] It may be too much to claim that any work of Hellenistic-Roman art or thought permanently enshrines friendship in matrimony, as, say, Tolstoy did, though many fictions and poems imply it. But marriage without erotic love, devotion, faith was certainly becoming unthinkable. Few husbands and wives in real life resemble the heroes and heroines of Greek romance. But however exalted and exaggerated, these fables redesign and reanimate old marital structures and establish new ones fully recognizable in the long-term unions of the historical reality that followed them.

We do not often enough know or remember the many and bewildering forms of erotic expression that in late antiquity, with its large cities and mobile populations, competed with marriage and long-term commitment. That highly successful student of ancient dreams, Artemidorus (second century A.D.), faced a vast array of erotic experience to interpret and base his predictions on: with wife, concubine, mistress; with the woman encountered casually; and with the servant or slave in the house, to mention only the basic types and classes of women.[16] And the following forms of liaison appear frequently enough to enter Artemidorus's manual of advice: with rich, beautiful, gracious, and well-dressed women but also with ugly, sloppy women; with male or female slaves; with well-known and familiar women; with married women; and endogamously with a grown son, a grown daughter, a married daughter, brothers and sisters, one's mother, and of course oneself. All these Artemidorus could conceive of as producing some good, though certainly not always, since much depended on circumstance, place, or even one's physical position in the act. Not only is the range wide, but no prohibitions seem to arise in the mind of the analyst. Nor does shock, or censorship, though of course some dreaming experiences augur ill luck. In all of this, marriage is given no place of privilege, except that it and death could signify each other reciprocally, both being a *telos* or end toward which life moves. So much we have certainly learned, not only from Sophocles's Antigone earlier, but also in this chapter from the penchant for the living heroes of romance to enter tombs and for the dynamics of romance to move toward marriage as tragedy does toward death. But marriage is never presented in thought or art as happily consorting with most of Artemidorus's rival forms, particularly the endogamous, though concubinage was often accepted in the home and of course prostitution outside it had coexisted with it in Mediterranean culture—and of course elsewhere too—from the earliest times to the present.[17]

Finally we must ask whether as the centuries move on into our era one has a sense that life is being softened or feminized, a sense that certainly arises in studying the course of culture from the English Restoration through the Victorian settlement. The course of art would seem to demonstrate such increasing tenderness, with the growing love of not only lifelike but softly sexual, alluring, sinuous, and delicate forms that seem to separate love from aggression. Cupid moves from being a fierce bearded man to a winged boy, often still hailed as a tyrant and capable of inflicting grave pain and suffering, but more delicately human, changeable, and forgiving than ever before. Venus moves from the house of ill fame to the marital chamber, though her demesne continues broad and varied. Michel Foucault has argued that that wonderful and civilizing Greek word *charis* now finds its full meaning and fullest expression in conjugal love and friendship, that *erōs* and *gamos* have come together, making it necessary to create a new erotic, and that there has been a philosophical disinvestment of boy love and a corresponding reinvestment of mental energy in conjugal love.[18]

As I have said before, Foucault is persuasive, but perhaps insufficiently precise. The strictly and purely religious aspects of Platonism enter Christianity, but that which in Plato is closest to life—boy love without consummation leading to a perception of the ultimate Forms—dies in the laughter of the New Sophistic or in many passages of roistering comedy in Petronius Arbiter or Achilles Tatius, for example. But the Aristotelian grounding of the *oikeios* (the homey, the familial) in nature and nature's sexuality (the universal friendliness of animal species and of human beings in ethnic and racial groups ultimately based on physical attraction)—this idea seems to have taken hold, and much of the literature of my Hellenistic-Roman chapters can be seen as a gloss on it. For both Cupid and Venus are in a sense surrogates for Aristotelian nature.

The idea persisted long past antiquity. Samuel Johnson, the greatest Christian of the eighteenth century, found that it was our duty to love all men but that "to love all equally is impossible." Selective love, however, both in friendship and marriage, he based fundamentally on nature:

> It has been ordained by providence, for the conservation of order in the immense variety of nature, and for the regular propagation of the several classes of life with which the elements are peopled, that every creature should be drawn by some secret attraction to those of his own kind; and that not only the gentle and domestick animals which naturally unite into companies, or cohabit by pairs, should continue faithful to their species; but even those ravenous and ferocious savages which Aristotle observes never to be gregarious, should range mountains and desarts in search of one another, rather than pollute the world with a monstrous birth.[19]

Such sexual force and ordering Johnson invokes as a "cogent principle"; it is that of the ancients we have studied in the last two chapters. Virtually all the thinkers of this period would have understood and approved his statement, for this reason, if no other: he had largely derived it from them.

Man lernt nichts kennen, als was man liebt, und je tiefer und vollständiger die Kenntnis werden soll, desto stärker, kräftiger und lebendiger muss die Liebe, ja Leidenschaft sein.

Goethe, Letter to F. H. Jacobi (1812)

The Jewish and Christian Testaments: Adam to Paul

*I*t may surprise some that those texts that have exercised the most powerful influence upon the sexual and marital mentality of the Western world are not numerous or indeed formidably difficult to understand. Their relative plainness of utterance has made the Bible easy to appropriate and therefore, despite their often formidable difficulty in application, the unavoidable source of most of our Western governing norms. The Bible constitutes a controlling structure without which revolution and deviation become little else than miscellaneous expressions of rootless neurotic force. Since the founding documents themselves include poems and fictions that contain restless energy and provide imaginative alternatives to all regulative standards including their own, revolutionary change has sometimes sprung directly from sacred scripture itself. I have referred to the clarity of the central texts, but this also needs to be said: even the legislative sections, though clear, are sometimes contradictory and always broadly applicable. Virtually every established position has been fought over, sometimes verbally, sometimes with coercive force—and even the covenantal inscriptions themselves bear the marks of struggles that preceded them.

Still, there is a core of meaning—or, more precisely, several related cores—that has created out of Judeo-Christian traditions from roughly 1200 B.C. to A.D. 430 (the year Augustine died) something of an organic body. The reader will notice that virtually every writer within these traditions whom I comment on directly appeals to or artistically reflects Genesis 1–2. Adam and Eve, both before and after the Fall, are living presences from the first book of "Moses" to the last book of Augustine. The burden of this and the next chapter is to bring forward the relevant doctrines and rules of the Hebrew Bible and reveal the continuing energies of some of its most memorable stories. The Christian Bible gives abundant opportunity for expository exegesis, less for literary analysis. But the period of transition from late Roman antiquity to established Christianity East and West, which will be the subject of chapter 7, does provide imaginative strivings as well as theological formulations and moral codes. Clement of Alexandria and John Chrysostom were didacts if not full-blown dialecticians, Hermas a preacher as well as an allegorist, and Augustine, one the greatest geniuses of any period to enter our story, a master of both discursive and poetic language and form.

The Hebrew Bible

In earlier chapters I have defined important erotic and marital words, trying to relate them both to regnant theology and their immediate artistic contexts. In the Bible, the rabbis, and the fathers, *erōs* and *amor* enter an austerer context than they have hitherto been accustomed to. The Greek word does not appear once in the New Testament; in the Old Testament its equivalents are never honored by being personified or deified and are often hedged in with legalities and prudential warnings. The equivalent of *erōs,* however, is very much present in Hebrew scripture, as we shall see—a fact that at once sets up a basic contrast between Judaism and Christianity. Other terms we have focused on (*oikos* for "house" or "household," *philos* for "friend" or "lover," *charis* for "grace" or "favor" or "bestowing and yielding love") are at once enlarged and concentrated. The God of Israel who filled the earth and the firmament as well as the human heart could be expected to enlarge the Xenophontic household (with its wife, ox, and plough) into the House of Israel, and the God of the New Covenant was almost at once impelled to nurture out of the *oikos* an *ecu*menical plant that would cover the earth. The *philia* that Aristotle denied was possible between a man and a god, Yahweh made not only possible but requisite for individual and corporate holiness: the patriarchs talked with God; Enoch, a friend of God, walked with God and was not for God took him; and the elders of Israel "beheld" the everlasting "I Am" on Sinai. Yahweh not only entered the house and the heart, he invaded the womb as well, to open or close it, to mould within it the human form, or even sometimes to impregnate it.[1]

Charis, so important to Greek marriage from Homer on, requires a special notation. Becoming the central Christian concept, grace almost lost the secular, domestic, amorous radiance that Homer, Pindar, and Plutarch gave it. In Hebrew its equivalents *ḥen* and *ḥesed* (sometimes translated *charis* in the Septuagint) are words of the deepest religious and political meaning, especially *ḥesed,* which has been luminously translated in the King James version by the English *lovingkindness* and which invokes the Covenant between God and Israel and other ties that bring out the noblest in mankind and lead to communal and individual salvation.[2] Did such ties of "leal love" (to use an early English equivalent of *ḥesed*) include for the Hebrews earthly love, betrothal, and marriage? Indubitably, as the Book of Ruth and the prophecy of Hosea both reveal. Hosea regularly uses the marital to exemplify the relationship of God and Israel: "I will betroth thee unto me in righteousness and justice, and in *ḥesed* and in compassion . . . and in faithfulness" (2:19–20).

Ḥesed, which I now narrow to refer to marital grace, was established amid the challenges of debilitating neighboring paganisms and amid temptations to sins among which are those that wound religious and civilized sensibility. Thus Levitical precept was forced to thunder against child sacrifice, temple prostitution, sexual profanations, homosexuality ("it is an abomination"), bestiality ("it is confusion"), incest ("theirs is thine own nakedness," with Lot and even Noah providing repulsive examples of sexual blood closeness).[3] One reason for the tempting nearness of such sins to the chosen people was that officially legalistic texts always kept warm the heterosexual allure despite their warnings, and could it have been otherwise in a people wishing to grow and thrive? The narratives we shall presently confront reveal that God was anything but a precisian when his heroes or heroines overstepped the strictest limits of regularity in pursuit of good ends.

Hebrew narrative makes us confront the romantic appeal of the maidenly Rebecca or of Dinah, the daughter of Leah, or of the favored wife, like Rachel or Hannah; Hebrew law includes that strangely nuanced prescription about how to make an attractive captive, necessarily an outsider, a bride. The regulations provided a liberal but cautiously guarded opportunity to the Hebrew warrior who sees "a beautiful woman" and conceives "a desire unto her" wishing to "have her to . . . wife" (Deuteronomy 21:10–14). First, she must shave her head, pare her nails, put off the raiment of her captivity, and be given time to bewail her mother and father. But then, if desire remains, she may become a bride. The regulation is male-oriented, to be sure, for if the warrior ceases to be pleased he can exercise the right of dismissing the woman in divorce (though without ever being allowed to sell her). It privileges desire aroused by beauty that such desire could thus easily and humanely be directed into legitimate channels and overcome the disadvantage of being induced by an enemy outsider.[4]

Hebrew wisdom literature combines as traits of the ideal wife that which much Western precept tended to keep widely apart, sexual allure and prudence. (Nor should we forget Sophia herself as bride [Proverbs 8:22, The Wisdom of Solomon 8–9, Ecclesiasticus 24].) Both wisdom and understanding are personified as female (Proverbs 7:4)—qualities that are in fact rather prudential than philosophical. The good wife is totally trustworthy and is given responsibility even in business and agricultural affairs: she appraises and buys fields and plants vineyards. Domestically, she is able and willing to work wool and flax with her hands, burning the midnight candle the while; some of the goods produced, like linen and girdles, she sells for profit. Not neglecting herself, she is clothed warmly and richly, in silk and purple. She rises while it is still dark to seek and prepare food for her family, nor does she forget the poor and needy.

Strong and honorable and far from silent, "she openeth her mouth with wisdom; and in her tongue is the law of kindness" (Proverbs 31:26). Such is the dignified and practical event, which begins in eros and continues in imaginative and perhaps even fetishistic renewal: "rejoice with the wife of thy youth. / Let her be as the loving hind and pleasant roe; let her breasts satisfy thee at all times; and be thou ravished always with her love" (Proverbs 5:18–19). Possessing such a collocation of solid and sexual virtues that might easily fly apart, the good wife assumes a high position indeed. She stands above lineage, the state, and friendship. "Children and the building of a city continue a man's name: but a blameless wife is counted above them both. . . . A friend and companion never meet amiss: but above both is a wife with her husband" (Ecclesiasticus 40:19, 23).

Too prudential ever to have a place on the Platonic ladder of philosophical eros, and lacking enough of the egalitarian to make it fully appealing to modern sensibility, the ideal still possesses a range and a complexity that have kept it alive for millennia. It must surely be seen as a considerable enrichment of the Xenophontic ideal of shared and divided labor, which it does, however, recall. Its power of emotional appeal will be demonstrated in some of the fictions and poems that follow.

The Age of the Judges: Samson and Ruth

The portrait of the Hebrew wife we have just contemplated contains surprising subtleties that a simple or extreme view of the Hebrew patriarchy might overlook. She is not a domestic slave, confined to the interior of the house. She has powers over real estate and agriculture as well as merchant control over the products of a goods-producing house. She is herself richly, attractively clad and possesses and retains sexual allure. Besides, the human covenant she has entered into is suffused with lovingkindness or grace, the great Hebrew quality of *ḥesed* that unites man and God and sanctifies good human relationships.

But a question arises at once, particularly in considering a sacred literature that has traces in it of matrilocality and even matriarchy and that recounts the story of a people tempted by the neighboring female defilements of mother goddesses, holy prostitutes, and luxurious queens: does the combination of prudential wisdom and sexual beauty endow the woman with dangerous power? Jeremiah inscribes a mysterious and haunting sentence in the midst of a stern prophetic warning against the backslidings and waywardnesses of Daughter Israel: "for the Lord hath created a new thing in the earth, A woman shall compass a man" (31:22). If we wend our way through the parallels to this verse and the interpretive bafflements that have attended it, we learn that the fear of woman's encompassing power and potential wickedness has long been allowed to sound a doleful and debilitating warning.[5]

This has never been more paradigmatically so than in the story of Samson, which seems to say that however physically strong or God-inspired the man is, he can meet his match in a designing woman. She need not always be as glamorous as a Mata Hari, but, as in children's Bibles and popular versions of this story, Delilah can provide a variety of temptations as cheat, hypocrite, prostitute, coquette, lustful herself and a cause of lust in others. To make things lethally dangerous, she is often socially successful and independent, bearing a name (unlike the nameless prostitute Samson visits) and owning a house of her own.[6] Such a woman is not entirely unrelated to the proud, partially independent, resourceful, and domestically tempting wife of wisdom literature, which also contains many warnings against the femme fatale.

But such is not my concern in analyzing Samson, whom I shall treat not as a prophet of God temporarily victimized but as an early portrait of a married man. Those who wish to enjoy variations on the more traditional appeal of this story can be referred to Milton, Saint-Saens, or Wolf Mankowitz. My aim is rather to lay stress upon Samson as a husband and to suggest that the ideal of Proverbs may also imply that the man needs to be made worthy of the woman presented in Solomonic wisdom. Samson, the Hebrew Hercules, whose very name embodies the word *sun,* which can destroy crops and ends in a dark dungeon every night, is an ascetic of the Nazirite variety dedicated from his mother's womb.[7] When the divine strength is in him, he can destroy the Philistine enemy threatening the borders of Judah and Dan, and he judges Israel for some twenty years. Nevertheless, he is very much in need of growing up. We should not always concentrate on the bald Samson, innocent, weak, speechless, resting on the knees of Delilah or on the hero-martyr meeting death, conferring it on his enemies, and freeing his own people. Let us instead shift the focus to Samson in his relations to parents, to women, and to lifelong marital commitment. Then we see that he is indeed something of a spoiled and despoiling child, as early Israel itself may well have been regarded during the time of the *beena* marriage by a later culture that had fully accepted the patriarchal *ba'al* arrangement.

Under *beena* the man leaves his own home, goes to the wife's country, allows her family to dictate terms, and follows the customs of the house and country new to him.[8] What does Samson leave? A pious father, to whose gravesite he is returned for his own burial, signifying that patriarchy has won and that the *ba'al* arrangement has now prevailed. He also leaves an equally pious mother, superior to the father in closeness to divine grace (she may have been impregnated by an angel of the Lord) and likewise in practical reasoning about the meaning of Samson's birth, of which she of course has direct practical experience and of whose sexual causes she seems to have intimate knowledge denied the husband. These fine parents Samson challenges by falling in love with an enemy girl, a Philistine, whom he petulantly demands as wife despite parental protests, "for she pleaseth me well." Perhaps it was a Deuteronomic scribe who added the explanation that God permits this wilfulness in order to provide an occasion of moving violently against the Philistines, but Samson is certainly presented in what must be the *ur*-text as spoiled, disobedient, and stubborn.

The folk hero has already acquired the superhuman strength of the tall tale, and he rends a lion as he would a kid—even the latter feat being itself difficult enough to conceive of. Returning to the Philistine city to claim his bride, Samson sees the lion's carcass now swarming with bees and filled with honey, which he brings to his parents to eat, keeping secret the place of its origins. The coyness towards the parents seems to fit in with the development of the lion-honey story into a sexual riddle concealing the paradox that rending can produce sweetness, that violation can be procreative: "Out of the eater came forth meat, and out of the strong came forth sweetness" (Judges 14:14).

Who are able to guess it? The groomsmen, the thirty Philistines provided by the bride's people in the foreign marital setting, and here again the older *beena* arrangements may provide the historical clue. In that more primitive tradition, which could of course be monogamous in the event, the wedding rites usually lasted seven days (as indeed they do here in Judges), and the bride was regarded as dangerous and her defloration as risky. Consummation took place away from parents and relatives, and indeed the bridegroom's task was sometimes turned over to others when it was not done artificially. Something like that seems to take place in the Samson story. The danger is now less magical than in very remote times. The wife, who wept and "lay sore upon Samson," teased the secret of the riddle out of him, a veritable proto-Delilah, and then she revealed it to her countrymen, who at the end of the seven days now know what is sweeter than honey and stronger than a lion. They know this because, in the full Hebrew sense, they have *known* the bride, as Samson's enigmatic answer seems strongly to suggest: "If ye had not plowed with my heifer, ye had not found out my riddle" (Judges 14:18).[9]

Samson becomes truly heroic only in death. But his marital adventures show him to be sometimes wilfully petulant, sometimes puerilely and even amusingly effectual (as in his scorched-earth policy with the foxes, his depredations with primitive armaments like the jawbone of an ass, or his folkloristic military strategies like embracing supporting pillars). But in his marital adventures he is always inferior to his noble mother, and even to his Philistine seductresses—such inferiority suggesting that both individual man and the Hebrew nation as a whole had yet to grow into a patriarchy which, though admittedly restrictive even at its apogee, could sometimes be wise and flexible enough to accommodate an equality of the sexes in shared maturity. Thus by negative implication the hero of Judges points to a different and sometimes better future, as a deficient *ur*-state can anticipate a more fully achieved condition. So there remains much in the story of Samson that invites the Psalmist's wry observation: "he that sitteth in the heavens shall laugh" at the human condition (2:4).[10]

God surely did not laugh at Ruth, who was as maritally successful as the blundering Samson was gauche and frustrated. For the Book of Ruth is a serious and lovely idyl also from the age of pre-Davidic judges, without the roistering panache of the Samson tales but still a story told with the highest narrative skills and the most attractive dynamics.[11] Though not set in the Wild East of the Samson story, it too has a frontier—that between Moab and Israel—but with this difference: the foreigner comes *to*

Israel for marriage and does not depart *from* it, as Samson did in seeking a mate. In an act of faith that is suffused with the practical wisdom of Proverbs, Ruth, guided by another woman to whom she has pledged Covenant faith, finds a fully mature man, who is also committed to divine initiative in family matters (to the noble ideal of *ḥesed,* that is), which he recognizes at once in the woman who seeks him (see 1:8–9; 2:20; 3:4, 9–10). He is spiritually mature enough to be led by the even more mature women who have sought him out. The older *beena* marital arrangements have been fully replaced by the levirate marriage, in which a relative of the deceased husband, usually a brother-in-law, marries the surviving widow and so ensures perpetuation of the line.[12] Here the canonical genealogist makes it clear that the second marriage Ruth entered into was handsomely rewarded by a line that produced Jesse and David—and in Christian revisionism, Jesus Christ as well. (One notes in passing how different the Hebrew emphasis is from that of many of the church fathers, who frowned upon second marriages as undesirable or even impious.)

In short, Ruth is likely to achieve the status of the ideal wife of Proverbs. What makes the story exciting? The grace under pressure displayed by this Other amid the alien corn and the sexual risks she courageously and unconventionally undertakes in order to execute the plans of her wise mother-in-law. The two women, as we have seen, dominate the story in character, will power, and imagination, proving superior in the end even to the good Boaz, whose great virtue is recognition of their worth, an insight mediated to him by the patriarchal God who is never just the helper of the poor, of widows, and of orphans, though he is that too, but a rewarder of courage, practicality, and even sexual attractiveness properly contextualized.

In fact, this story, its precursor text about Judah and Tamar in Genesis 38, and negatively the marital adventures of Samson are far from orthodox in their traditional meanings, privileging not the legalistic and the established but the irregular and the illicit.

All this makes the story of Ruth a fitting expression of the imagination that loves to adduce alternative ways, a story that reaches a climax of narrative art and enforces this kind of meaning in the marvelous night scene on the threshing floor. It is here that Ruth, after gleaning in Boaz's fields and after having won favor as Naomi's kinswoman, seeks him out alone and skirts the forbidden and the sexually dangerous in order to encompass her and Naomi's ends. The older woman, acting as mothers traditionally did in pre-Victorian societies, urges the younger to wash, anoint herself, put on raiment—in other words, to make herself enticing—and reveal herself to her benefactor only after he has eaten and drunk. All this goes beyond prudent planning, though it involves that too; it is rather more like maternal sexual advice before the wedding night, since both the instructions and the event itself are full of sexual double-entendres and ambiguities. Naomi instructs Ruth to uncover Boaz's legs—an act teasingly close to uncovering all the lower part of his body—and then to lie down with him. Scholars tell us that feet are a euphemism for the penis or the vulva, and narratively it is important that the Hebrew verbal structures, calling for repetition, here give to the older woman's proleptic speech the same kind of boldness the younger one enacts.

In the darkness, at midnight, as Boaz awakens to the carefully and boldly arranged situation, he finds the woman at his feet. She, who has uncovered his legs, now asks him to spread his garment over her, "for thou art a near kinsman" (3:9). The situation skirts transgression of the Levitical proscriptions: "thou shalt not uncover the nakedness" of "near of kin" (father, mother, father's wife, sister, half-sister, grandchild, daughter, or daughter-in-law: Leviticus 18:6–18). No forbidden frontier is actually crossed, and Boaz blesses Ruth and promises legal and official succor the next day. She rises "before one could know another" (3:14), and he warns her to keep their encounter secret. The terms *lie down* (used eight times), *uncover, know* all have unmistakable sexual meanings, enough to permit us to ask if the two did in fact enter into sexual relations, as Judah had done with Tamar in the precursor text. Rich ambivalence lurks in the delicate tissues of chapter 3, and the suggestion of deepest intimacy is strong indeed.

Such suggestions may *foreshadow* the ultimate marriage, but surely no overt act took place. If it had, could Boaz in good conscience have mentioned the other closer kinsman, whom the next day he asked to undertake the levirate task of marrying Ruth and raising offspring? He did not know until then that the alternative "redeemer" of the family was otherwise occupied or unwilling, and he could scarcely have been sexually hungry enough to have preempted the "redeemer's" role, which he promised to arrange for the next day. But even without literal fulfillment on the dark threshing floor, all the dynamics are in place—and the deeply intimate resonances of the scene reveal that both Boaz and Ruth instantiate the virtues of Proverbial sexuality.

This, then, is an exciting sexual story, the sexuality not less exciting for being implicit. Is it also a love-friendship story? Only in the sense of the mediated lovingkindness of *ḥesed,* which endows the adventure with religious sanction. That sanction, however lofty from some points of view, is at the same time part of what I have earlier referred to as the ego context that seems to be absolutely necessary for successful love in long-term commitment. Thus this lovely story is far from sentimental, though I think the word *idyl* is not inappropriately used of it. Love does not arise at first sight, nor do we see it developing into maturity of friendship and service. The context is too dramatically dangerous and temporally clamant for that; the narrator must concentrate on the more immediate persuasives of desire gratified and a dynastic family.

This is a woman's story, not a story of childishly sentimental or inexperienced girls seeking titillation. In fact during the night encounter Boaz, old enough to call Ruth "daughter," praises her for not having followed young men, "whether poor or rich" (3:10). The heroines of this story are mature women, fully seasoned, earlier grievously bereaved, and now seeking under divine government the larger satisfactions of stability, progeny, and place in a human society which one of them has had to enter as an outsider. And the wealthy and powerful Boaz is capable of providing just such a reassuring and satisfying context. Dare anyone say that Ruth, like an equally spirited but more romantically inclined heroine of Jane Austen, Marianne Dashwood, has merely settled for the sobriety of one who may soon need the constitutional safeguards of a flannel waistcoat? One trusts that only the very young and immature will laugh— Yahweh certainly did not.

The Love Gardens of Eden and of "Solomon's" Song

We have now noted the joyous though often mysterious and even perverse presence of sexuality in the Old Testament version of love and marriage. The great gardens of this mighty anthology, in Genesis and the Song of Songs, vividly illustrate this presence and explain its origin and meaning. The first three chapters of Genesis have of course received monumental commentary, which always reveals the mentality of the culture that produced it. Kant found in them the story of man's movement from sense and instinct to reason, which laid the groundwork for the greatest transcendence possible, that of nature by ethics and art.[13] In our own day these stories of origin are constantly being coopted to give sanction to vigorous contemporary religio-political programs, sometimes to condemn the patriarchy and its lack of sexual egalitarianism, sometimes to suggest a continuing counterculture within the dominant Hebrew ethos, and most memorably, by Harold Bloom, to reveal the universal genius of an ancient Hebrew author. In this and the next chapter we shall see how centrally Adam and Eve within and outside Eden figure in the New Testament and early Christian thought and propaganda.

My present purpose is to show how the later P version, the priestly redaction of the Elohistic version (Genesis 1:1–2:3), and the J (or Yahwistic) version (Genesis 2:4–3:24), both great works of differing kinds of art, establish for culture and therefore ultimately for erotic literary renditions the dynamics of long-term coupling.[14]

The brief, solemn, general, liturgical account of creation with which the Bible opens enforces the centrality and universal power of the Creator-Commander, revealed climactically in the creation of male and female in his image; but it does so without institutionalizing marriage, preaching monogamy, or envisaging friendship between the sexes. Having separated life from matter, divided vegetable and animal life into kinds, and given humankind a divinely replicative dignity not possessed by other creatures or forms, this account clearly establishes both differentiation and equality between the sexes.[15] Male and female are planned at once, the two great sexes that will animate the world are both created in the image of God, and both together are given dominion over all other living beings. These are highly important données, but the central and climactic emphasis falls on the divine command that accompanies each blessing (of sky life, water life, earth life, and finally human life), "Be fruitful and multiply." The P version is vitalistic, seed-oriented, sex-oriented, and the sexuality does not imply pleasure but generation. Here at the very beginning lies the great justification for intercourse, the act itself and the pleasure that leads to it—a meaning that is soon enforced when Genesis proceeds genealogically to itemize the descendants of Adam. The chronology is preceded by a repetition of the creation command to generate: "In the day that God created man, in the likeness of God made he him; Male and female created he them; and blessed them and called *their* [my emphasis here stresses the inclusion of both sexes in the generic noun] name Adam, in the day when they were created" (Genesis 5:1–2, a P text).

The J (or Yahwistic) version in Genesis 2:4–3:24 lacks the decisive compression of the first chapter and is more nuanced, more endearing, more social—a work of high narrative art in miniature. Here God is a potter, a sculptor, an artist, who creates by hand rather than fiat, by inspiring breath rather than signifying and organized words. He is given to first or primitive drafts or sketches, imbuing them with breathlike impulses that will drive them to fruition. Thus he creates *ur*-seeds before they are put into the earth and then an *ur*-being, an unsexualized earthling, before he separates "it" into the different sexes. As soon as this work is done, the sexually undifferentiated Adam is given "its" venue in Eden, and then "it" names the beasts, among whom no fit partner can be found. The implications of the naming, the deep sleep, the rib, "helpmeet," and the undifferentiated or androgynous physical oneness within the original earthling are still the subject of lively debate that does not seem quickly resolvable. But identity, love, the reuniting of the two human beings, and the institution of a nuclear couple living apart are at once decisively achieved. The Judeo-Christian "history" of our topic, the couple in early Western culture, has commenced.

We must not fail to notice the highly important differences that emerge between this earlier (more imaginatively artistic) account and the later priestly one with which Genesis begins. The great author "J" writes an erotic poem sung by the man to the woman, whose creation takes longer and can be regarded as more dignified than his: "This is now bone of my bones, and flesh of my flesh," a lyrical prelude to the naked man and the naked woman becoming "one flesh" in their own shared and private space (Genesis 2:23, 24). The hymeneal hymn and the nude cohabitation in isolated apartness, with no mention of a command to be fruitful and multiply, *do* seem to authorize something other than the exclusively procreative sexuality so strongly enforced in Genesis 1, and to sanction that embellishment of basic libido into an autonomous, attractive eros that the West has so abundantly celebrated and even, as in Milton, accorded the J story. Mutual help in the close vocational association of tending the garden may also suggest the possibilities of friendship, but just barely. The notion of a field of force that unites esteem, intimate association, and pleasurable physical contact must await later time and another place for its unfolding. But the seed may have been planted here in Eden.

The Fall has teased men out of thought as doth the eternity it did not abolish. We have already noticed that according to Kant it symbolized man's slow, somewhat tortuous journey from sensation to reason, ultimately leading to the civilized transcendence of nature through ethics and art. More popular homiletical-theological readings have alternated between, or at times blended, the belief that the disaster was caused by disobedient pride and the belief that it began in a stirring of libidinous sense and ended in full-blown lust and shame. My own interpretation tries to bring out the presence of aroused sexual desire: it makes the tree symbolize the awakening of sexual knowledge and power, a synthesis that thus blends both the erotic and the prideful.[16]

That blending appears if we contemplate one of the penalties imposed on Eve: "thy desire shall be to thy husband, and he shall rule over thee" (Genesis 3:16), J's Hebrew original being more specifically physical and less obviously hierarchical. Equal before the disobedience, unequal now, man and woman are saddled with a hierarchy, the rulership of man being compendiously ratified in both the Jewish and Christian covenants. But the verse goes beyond *locating* authority, in some interpretations it *relates* sexual desire and power: woman desires man, man therefore has power over woman. There is that in Proverbial wisdom which reverses the sex roles in the exercise of erotic influence and gives power to the woman in two ways: "Solomon" warns of the desirable woman's fatally mischievous power over man, as the earlier Samson story also shows, and "Solomon" envisages the woman as demanding and inducing desirable amorous pleasure for its own sake. Such powers have thrived outside marriage and are not unknown in it. The verse in Genesis that entails sexual desire on Eve as wife in the postlapsarian world has of course been used to enforce monogamous marriage. And, in a soberly realistic view, it would have to be said that the submissive wife does in fact obey and tolerate much even in the way of male infidelity because her yearning has indeed been "programmed" toward her husband. Eros, it will not be surprising to know, especially marital eros, can be an instrument of submission. It is not too broad a jump to the belief that the instilling of longing for God ("as the hart panteth after the water brooks" [Psalms 42:1]) can enforce divine authority and human obedience. The brilliant J author's Yahweh speaks at once simply and cryptically in laying the curse on woman: in David Rosenberg's translation in *The Book of J,* she is told, you will suffer labor pains and "to your man's body your belly will rise, for he will be eager above you." Being "eager above" a female would seem to invite multiple glosses, but later interpretation, like that of the King James Version, has sanctioned a union of sexual desire and power as a feature of the postlapsarian government, domestic and cosmic.

J has penetrated more deeply than is often realized into the nature of primitive sexuality by making the forbidden tree a tree of knowledge. (Perhaps originally there had been only one inaccessible tree, not two, the tree of life being added later.) The association of the tree with knowledge must surely bring in the sexual implications that the Hebrew word for *know* almost always bears: to know is to have sexual intercourse. This meaning appears so often in Genesis and elsewhere that the tree of knowledge must surely be consciously and sexually alive. But if, as Augustine and others believed, Adam and Eve before the Fall "knew" each other well enough to produce the offspring that would have filled the earth but for the mischievous aborting of God's plan, what needed to be punished? What does disobedient sexual knowledge add to the mere performance of the act itself? Some have said the forbidden fruit constituted a specific prohibition against eating one's own offspring, love of kind having become a form of irresistible cannibalism.

I am not in a position to deny or affirm such primitive traces in the Eden story, but I wish to suggest what I think is more plausible—an idea that is forcefully brought out in Umberto Cassuto's interpretive translation of the passage about the birth of Cain, particularly his expansion of the assertion, in the King James Version, that Eve has "gotten a man from the Lord" (Genesis 4:1): "Now Adam knew Eve his wife, and she conceived and bore Cain, saying, 'I have created a man equally with the Lord.'" David Rosenberg translates Eve's remark: "I have created a man as Yahweh has." The famous medieval Jewish exegete, Rashi, paraphrases Eve as follows: "When He created me and my husband He created us by Himself, but in the case of this one, we are co-partners with him." Teasing obscurity lingers in these and other versions, and it is present in the highly condensed, colloquial Hebrew. Did Eve become a mother after being impregnated by the Lord or one of his angels, as Sarai and as Manoah's wife and Samson's mother may have? Or did she understand merely that God opened her womb and that she is now grateful? Or does the passage also imply that she and Adam together have a sense of being able to do what hitherto only God has done, create a life? Is it possible that we have here a primitive trace that glances at dawning human consciousness—that Eve, and by implication the human race, has come to know the male role in procreation? The Trobrianders of today, who allegedly do not have such knowledge, believe in divine impregnation or some kind of superhuman miracle as the cause. And surely, though the woman's role cannot have escaped the very earliest observing consciousness, knowledge of the male role, some nine months earlier and easily concealed, may, without precise physiological learning, have been a long time in coming. And when it came, it may well have been regarded as an impious challenge to divine authority.[17]

Did the fruit of that forbidden tree contain such knowledge? If so, God, the maker of man and woman, would, quite consistently with the character the Old Testament everywhere gives him, want it kept to himself. The eating of such eye-opening sexual fruit would indeed be a sinfully proud affront—an act that required both expulsion from the Garden and a universal and inevitable mortality in order to prevent an overweening and untameable insolence by creative man, newly conscious of his powers.

Such an interpretation of the Fall would give it enormous consequences, not less epoch-making for being largely unconscious, and would make it perhaps a fall into patriarchy. Now that the deed had been done, God would have to adjust to it, and one way was to decree that the recently discovered male sexual power be surrounded by safeguards and sanctions. The consumed fruit would thus threaten lingering matriarchies, where the woman's role, so obvious and so visibly important, might enforce female authority. It would weaken the Magna Mater as the fundamental creating force. It would entrench the husband as a *causa causans,* as the primary and aggressive actor in the sexual drama. It would endow him with Godlike powers that he had not known before and suggest that he might be a governor or king in society as well as in the family, thus imposing familial order on ever-widening circles.

But might it also have the salutary effect of making the domestic man, now aware that he shares creative power with his Maker, want to exercise the divine *ḥesed,* or lovingkindness, that motivated Boaz when he discovered corresponding traits in Ruth the Moabitess gleaning in his fields? In fact, however much we may today dislike and wish to attenuate the mischiefs of patriarchy, we may have to give it this much credit—that in its day it could lead to a softening and feminizing of the man into a loving father, who might now regard the fruit of his loins as he had regarded Eve in innocence, bone of my bone and flesh of my flesh. Since postlapsarian marriage in Genesis is envisaged grimly enough, both in the prophetic curse and in the immediately subsequent stories of ancient Israel, like that of Cain and Abel, it may provide some mitigation to know that eating of the fruit of the tree of knowledge had beneficial results apart from the promised future redemption. And indeed it may have obviated and made obscene the older view (made prominent, however, in the intertestamental period of Jewish thought), whose mysterious trace Genesis 6:1–4 freezes in a moment of primitive time—that it was sons of God who mated with the daughters of men to create new offspring. Such unions seem now to be regarded by the Genesis author as much worse than the unequal marriages of ordinary life, which inflicted suffering upon the mother; these last led to the human generations that socialized humanity and promised a Messiah, while those produced giants, mighty men of old, men of renown, perhaps not unlike the immature Samson we have encountered earlier in this chapter, but demons for all that. The Yahwistic scribe makes this irregularly conceived race a prologue to the Flood, the creators of a blasphemously wicked age, and he damns them and their superhuman origins. As Blake was to see much later, experience, bitter though it is, has its advantages over innocence; one need not believe in a fortunate Fall to feel that Odysseus's choice was the right one, to leave the blandishments of the superhuman and celestial and as a mortal himself return to a faithful but inevitably transient wife. Eating the fruit brought its penalties, but in the long run it is better to "know" and to know together than to revolve forever in the rounds of an innocent idyl. In any case, we now have no choice. We know when we "know," and out of that knowledge we can create families and nations—even indeed a chosen and redeemed people.

It would for my purposes be irrelevant, even with the requisite learning, to try to probe into the origins of the Song of Songs. Did it once accompany fertility rituals? Was it a collection of marriage songs, perhaps for the *hieros gamos* (divine marriage)? From what Asian or Middle Eastern culture did it enter the Hebrew world? It has come down to us as aesthetically the most enticing part of wisdom literature, and if not written, as was formerly thought, by Solomon himself, it may have sprung from the wealth, luxury, and personal freedoms of his court. It is more germane to ask whether we should regard the garden of love in the Canticles as the prelapsarian Eden contained in the folds of our individual and racial memory and often divorced from the reality we know. In more official words, could it be, as has been suggested, a midrash (ancient Jewish exposition of a scriptural passage) on Genesis 1–2?[18]

Such dignity may not explain its origins, and may indeed have very little to do with them, but surely it has much to do with the insistent allegorization that has attended this quintessentially erotic work in both the Jewish and Christian worlds. My purpose, however, is not to view the Song as primarily an allegory of the love between God and Israel or between Christ and his church (views that of course account for its presence in both the Hebrew and Christian canons) but as genuine love poetry, however idealized—lyrical language uttered between fully human lovers in the situations of real though obviously exalted life. To this view even the orthodox of our day seem to be committed. The New Jerusalem Bible, for example, in its latest revision, has lent its enormous learning and Roman Catholic prestige to the view that the eroticism of the Song of Solomon refers primarily to married love, where it is not justified by procreation alone but ministers to affectionate and stable associations. Some contemporary Protestant commentators suggest that the eroticism of this text may indeed be precisely what modern marriages need most of all, and that to allegorize it is to evade what is pertinent and potentially useful. Traditional Protestant exegesis has urged that the pure and exquisite delight of this work opposes both asceticism and lust, two of the most prominent profanations of marriage. The enormously learned commentary in the Anchor Bible shows what abundant attention has been lavished on this work from antiquity even up to our own time, when it once more seems to be alive in Western, perhaps particularly American, consciousness.[19]

But to stress the literal over the allegorical is by no means to undervalue the venerable interpretations that have been enormously influential for centuries. These, encountering both clamant human physical desire and the need to transcend it, have led to those powerful and unforgettable examples of sublimation and projection that we find in the verbal sensualism of Bishop Ambrose of Milan, in the Canticle sermons of Saint Bernard of Clairvaux, and in Bernini's eroticizing of Saint Teresa's visions; indeed they may have lain behind Freud's brilliant and mind-opening discovery of love with an inhibited aim. Few cultures outside the West seem to have provided such stunning examples of the displacement of the erotic upon the divine as our own, and in the development of this phenomenon the Song of Songs has surely played a central role.

We can see the reason for this when we examine the text itself and allow its unconventionality and boldness to engage our spirits—qualities that in other modifications we have seen in both Samson and Ruth. But first, since we are stressing reality itself rather than its displacements, let us notice the presence of everyday concerns. A family seems to be present, for a mother provides a haven for the loving pair, daughters help the beloved search for her lover, and the beloved's brothers seem to be antagonists to the sexual couple. In the city streets which the beloved roams in her search, the patrolling guards strike her, wound her, and rob her of her veil. In these lyrics both enemies and friends pass across the stage. Consonant with the occasional realism of scene and setting is the frankness of the language. One modern translator renders as follows highly intimate allusions that are usually cloaked either in inoffensive translated euphemisms or sometimes in verbal displacements in the original itself: "the scent of your vulva [is] like apples"; "Your vulva [is] a rounded crater; / May it never lack punch."[20] The nut is another symbol of female genitalia, the bowels can refer both to sensibilities of pity and distress and to erotic emotion, and a keyhole can signify private female space, the zone of coital intromission.

Much has grown out of the apostrophe, "My sister, my spouse" (the phrase first appears in 4:9), not least during the eighteenth century and the Romantic period when the odor of incest hung over much erotic expression. But both Julia Kristeva and Billy Graham have denied the need for such implications in the repeated erotic addresses to a sister. Kristeva cites authorities for believing that "My sister, my promised bride," points to the virginity of the bride and that the carnal love here exalted is "conjugal, exclusive, sensuous, jealous." Graham, in the manual of his evangelistic crusade, paraphrases "sister" as "my lovely one" or "my darling bride."[21]

All these glosses seem just, and indeed one of the notable characteristics of the love relationship celebrated in this poem is not bloodcloseness but distance. We need not try to straighten out in detail the dramatic complications, but one certainly seems to be that a royal lover is successfully challenged by a shepherd boy. Not only social but racial difference is also implied: "I am black, but comely," "I am black, because the sun hath looked upon me" (1:5–6), where the last phrase need not mean that the girl is sunburned but may reflect the ancient explanation for African skin color. Indeed there is a long tradition, not growing out of the Song but surely related to it, that blackness possesses its own beauty, as witnessed by the many black goddesses, including black Madonnas, produced by white cultures. There is enough about love's conquest of otherness in this poem to make it congenial to modern ideals, a fact that in part may explain its nineteenth-century use in the early feminist movement and its popularity in our own day.

Closely related to the power of erotic love to challenge conventional boundaries and unify the culturally, economically, and physically disparate is the proud and persistent way in which the Song reveals female initiatives in love. The speaking lover is often a woman, using some of the frank language that we have noticed and appropriating to herself the full range of erotic experience. These male parts, for example, are celebrated: skin, head, hair (black), eyes, cheeks, lips, hands, belly, legs, countenance, mouth. Such range and frankness of physical reference are noteworthy features of the work that calls itself "The Song of Songs," that is, the greatest, the loveliest of all songs, a song worthy of the noblest of monarchs, Solomon himself. The girl is capable of saying: "My love thrust his hand into the hole, / And my inwards seethed for him" (Anchor Bible, 5:4). All this is not to say that there is no sexual differentiation within the sexuality itself; the man may be the somewhat more aggressive and his range of reference wider and bolder: he celebrates eyes, teeth, feet, thighs, navel, belly, breasts, neck, nose, head, hair, lips, and roof of the mouth. Though she does search in the night, the woman tends to long, the man to take action. Still, the role of the woman, given the context of sexual repression and puritanical evasiveness present in the cultures that have produced or embraced this amazing work of verbal art, is stunningly bold and revisionary. Some may be tempted to evade the force of the Song by saying that its seeming revolutionary energy merely reflects the mores of aristocratic or even royal society, not available to the masses. But such origins would in no way lessen the potential impact upon the wide and undifferentiated readership the work has enjoyed from its own day to ours.

Still, one cannot claim that we have here the full realization of heterosexual friendship or even the promise of intellectual growth through eros. But this much can surely be said: if the Song of Solomon recalls Eden, it does so not to invoke a lost dream or to hint at regression to childhood but to open adult eyes to infrequently envisioned imaginative possibilities in the realm of human sexual contact.

The Christian Bible

Coming to the New Testament from the Old, particularly from immediate contact with the Song of Solomon, and also more generally from the traditions of transmogrified and projected eros we have encountered historically in this study, is to experience a good bit of culture shock. What does the New Covenant say legislatively and didactically about love and marriage? Let us return to the important terms we have analyzed before in connection with the Old Testament and classical literature. The widely used and complexly exploited *erōs* of Greek antiquity (personified and unpersonified) and its derivatives make not a single appearance in the Christian Bible.[22] The nuclear and modular *oikos* (house, household) is broadened to mean the "household of faith" and beyond that becomes *oikonomia,* referring to God's plan of salvation for the whole world and creation. The great Greek word for friendship, *philia,* appears but once, and then it is used pejoratively in a denunciation of adulterers and adulteresses (James 4:4): "*philia* with the world is enmity with God, whosoever therefore will be a *philos* of the world is the enemy of God." *Philos* and other derivatives do appear, though the ratio of *agapein* to *philein* is about twelve to one. Jesus's redefinition of friendship in John 15:12–15 associates that most typical and almost unique New Testament word, *agapē,* with friendship. But it is friendship of a special kind, for love (agapē) is *commanded:* "This is my commandment, That ye love (agapate) one another, as I have loved you. . . . Ye are my friends, if ye do whatsoever I command you." And sacrificial martyrdom is the greatest love one can have for another: "Greater love hath no man than this, that a man lay down his life for his friends (philōn)." In commanding love, Jesus respects the Old Testament "Thou *shalt* love . . . ," but both the severe and single-minded commandment and the apocalyptic association with death and martyrdom tend to separate the concept from the lofty as well as the lowly—from the highest Aristotelian type of friendship and also from the grind of daily marital association however loving.

Charis (grace) demands special attention since it is perhaps the single most important Christian word, so important that its meaning of divine, redemptive, unmerited favor extending to all alike and mediated by faith and obedience tends to make it a one-way road descending from heaven to earth.[23] In its less Pauline and less theological meanings, it simply means a favor that requires reciprocation, but possible marital associations are not made. Jesus, theologically full of *charis* and *alētheia* (truth, John 1:14, 16), is as a man one on whom God sheds grace, as Athene did upon the head of Odysseus, who then became beautiful in form and persuasive of speech. Luke 2:40, 52 and 4:22 must have awakened some echoes in the minds of Greek speakers, for there we are told that Jesus is gracious in both mind and utterance, though beauty of body apart from stature does not enter. Can we make any connection between such grace and marital love? "Paul" (as distinct from Paul, the now acknowledged author of certain epistles) calls the husband the head of the wife as Christ is the head of the church, but the *charis* that Jesus the man possessed does not seem to have rubbed off on the "Pauline" husband, for the Greek word in Ephesians 5:23, *kephalē,* though it can mean the noblest part of the whole person (a notion that John Chrysostom was to make much of in enforcing love upon the husband) also means simply *caput* or "chief." Again, as in Jesus's love words to his disciples, the author of Ephesians introduces sacrificial martyrdom as being operative in husbandly love though, to be fair, we must note the basic roots in love of self and one's own body: for if the twain are now one flesh, love of the wife is like a love of one's own body. A considerable degree of Plutarchan shine has disappeared from *charis* in a marital context, if that context for the word can be said to exist at all.[24]

Jesus's teachings break completely with the Hebrew husband's right to divorce a wife on his own initiative, sending her out of his house with only a bill of separation. If Jesus perceived in this abrupt and brutal arrangement a censurable male desire to discipline a wife and keep her in line by exercising such immitigable authority over her future, he does not say so. But he does declare unmistakably, in a way that confounds modern interpreters who would flee this harsh text, that the married pair are indissolubly bound till death do them part save for adultery alone. There seems to be no taking into account whatever of a possible diminution of love and friendship, to say nothing of the intrusion of aggressive and cruel behavior. Moreover, commitment to Jesus as master could require harsh ruptures—with "house, or parents, or brethren, or wife, or children, for the kingdom of God's sake" (Luke 18:29).

Much of what Jesus taught on these matters must be seen in the context of belief in the apocalyptic end of the present world, ushered in by the Second Coming, which was thought to be imminent. And that apocalyptic tension continues to disturb the teaching about women in both Paul and "Paul" and in "John" as well as John, since end-of-the-age militancy would seem to obviate the feminine and the familial. In any event, woman was enjoined to be silent and not usurp man's prerogative in the churches, and the story of the Fall is read to mean that the deceiving woman was the first transgressor and can in a postlapsarian world be saved only in childbearing, if she remains believing, charitable, holy, and sober (1 Timothy 2:11–14)—words that entailed a frustrating and even enslaving legacy on woman in Western culture.

Such is a first view of New Testament teaching, and it is the first view that usually prevails. It cannot and should not be totally mitigated, for there is no escaping both a positive and negative attitude toward love in the founding texts. And if virtually all the love we have encountered in the cultures hitherto studied has proved to be ambiguous, Christianity can perhaps be said to add to the pressure of undecidability, making almost every commentator on Christian love and sexuality a sometime victim of ambivalent emphasis. The present commentator will be no exception, but a second look *is* requisite to see the total picture. Jesus's fullest though still very brief teaching in Matthew 19 may abrogate the Deuteronomic rule of divorce and set up another of granitic hardness, but it does accept the Book of Genesis and establishes what is known today as Creation theology, which among other things privileges the body, the material and the organic. Jesus invokes the creation of both sexes, fully differentiated and still fully capable of becoming one flesh in marital intercourse, without, note well, saying a word about procreation and offspring. He thus leaves the door wide open for regarding intimacy as a value that need not have reproductive results.

Paul (I now discuss what are today accepted as authentically Pauline statements), writing under the tense conviction of crisis shared by the first disciples that his Lord's return and the ensuing judgment were imminent, gives spiritual priority to virginity and celibacy: "it is good for a man not to touch a woman." But he concedes that "to avoid fornication" it is acceptable to marry monogamously and be governed by unshakable *fides,* though he would prefer "that all men were even as I myself." Let unmarried folk and widows remain as he is, "but if they cannot contain, let them marry: for it is better to marry than to burn." These famous verses from 1 Corinthians 7:1–9 have been much discussed, not least in our day, but they seem clear enough. Marriage is a good, continence after widowhood a higher good—and later in Christian history virginity also.

Two verses (1 Corinthians 7:3, 4), also much discussed, have, thanks to the King James Version, suffered the suppression or euphemizing of their central meaning. The Greek *opheilē* (Lat. *debitum*) was translated "due benevolence," and it has not always been realized that what Paul is discussing is a reciprocal obligation to satisfy the partner's sexual needs and demands. But the fathers understood this, the Wife of Bath gloried in it, and Montaigne chafed under it but fully comprehended it. It is indubitably related to that important purpose of marriage, just enunciated, to prevent fornication—for a sexually hungry husband, say, would have an excuse to sin if his wife withheld her favors. And vice versa, a subject often discussed in the Middle Ages and in the rabbinic tradition, which specified how often husbands in different professions were obliged to have sex. What has not been emphasized is that at the bedside man and wife were regarded as achieving an equality not otherwise vouchsafed them, and some may regard it as ironical that the gender aspects of the great Christian ideal of equality in Christ between Jew and Gentile, slave and free, man and woman (Galatians 3:28) found an easily available and fully sanctioned opportunity in the legalized carnality of married life. Of the realities of Christian copulation, Peter Brown has said, very wisely, "We simply do not know with what rituals . . . the Christian couple of the second century settled down to collaborate with their Creator."[25] We shall return to this notion of the marital debt in a far different context when we discuss the high Middle Ages and the Wife of Bath.

The reason for the relevance and importance of this Pauline injunction is that he also preached the resurrection of the body—not just the immortality of the soul or an airy blending of spirits in the afterlife or a vague opening up of future spiritual development, but a reassembly of the flesh atom by atom that establishes a continuity of present with future body and so a continuance of consciousness and the personality. The Pauline ideal of resurrected flesh is perhaps impossible for modern man to conceive. But the idea lives on in orthodox and fundamentalist circles, and in earlier centuries possessed widespread vitality and meaning. When in 305, for example, Saint Anthony, emerging from his cell at the bottom of a ruined fort, which he had occupied since 285, was met by the curious faithful, they were amazed that his body was neither thin and emaciated nor fat and overblown, but rather just as it had always been. What they assumed reveals strikingly the continuing power of Paul's resurrection doctrine after over two centuries.[26] Anthony's personal and open charm along with the purity of his flesh made them sure that he had either (1) begun to achieve the first state of Adam or (2) already received a portion of the spiritual body vouchsafed to the faithful in the resurrection.

There is no evidence that Paul revised his master by claiming that there was marriage and giving in marriage in the eternal life of the blessed, though there would be nothing in the amazing notion of a resurrected body to obviate a continuation of friendship and love. If it has been difficult to realize the biblical ideal of "one flesh" in sexual intercourse, which apparently often leaves a residue of unsatisfaction, tension, and unabsorbed aggressivity, it may be more difficult to avoid dismay at the Pauline idea of sowing dead, rotting flesh and reaping living, incorruptible flesh. But the idea certainly gave privilege to the body and provided the tools later orthodox thinkers needed to defeat the many articulate sects that denied this doctrine and related ones: the incarnation of Christ; the need for reproduction; and the goodness that can inhere in *sōma,* which in Paul never means just the whole man or his mind and spirit alone but specifically that part of him known as the body, though Paul uses the word *sarx* to refer to the sinful and unregenerate aspects alone of the flesh.

The Book of Revelation continues the paradoxes and oxymorons of Christian belief. Leaving aside the immediately and locally apocalyptic details of this strange and sometimes repellent work, we confront two symbolizations, each of which represents one side of the Christian love paradox. There is, first, the corps of 144,000 redeemed, who bear God's name written on their foreheads. They sing a new song before the throne, but who are they? "They are the men who have not been defiled by relations with women: they are celibates. It is they who follow the Lamb wherever he goes" (Revelation 14:4).[27] In other words, these are the ones who have literally followed Christ's command to leave and sacrifice all—including wife, family, and future generation—in order to become his disciples.

In the same book the redeemed church as a whole, now personified as a city, the New Jerusalem, is adorned as a bride to meet her bridegroom and has come to the marriage supper of the Lamb, which in the grotesquerie characteristic of this vision involves the cannibalism of consuming the bodies of kings, commanders, horses, and their riders—indeed the whole panoply of Roman paganism, but also all sorts and conditions of unredeemed men, slaves and freedmen, high and low alike. But in the final vision such obscenity is left behind, and the bride of the Lamb descends to dwell among men as a city, radiant, walled, highly geometrical, and thoroughly inhuman, quite unlike Eden or the garden of love in the Song of Songs. Gold is as transparent as glass, water clear as crystal, and there are no abominations or falsehoods. The tree of life flourishes on both sides of the river, but the life portrayed is rather more metallic and crystalline than organic or human, luminescent rather than vital—a vision luminously evoked in the medieval *Pearl*. Darkness and evil are banished, but they continue to exist, in the permanent division of cosmic space that ends the Bible.

In the Holy City a female principle is present, surely the seed of much future sentimentality. Every tear is wiped from every eye, and the gentle and tender ministrations of the Lamb go on forever. The marriage imagery has been inscribed as a permanent legacy. But in this female city all is, paradoxically, squared and measured, all is undifferentiated light and radiance. There is little that is rounded or voluptuous in this structured hierarchy, where some are rewarded more than others, though no grief or evil is known. The praised and the praisers mutually interact, and doubtless great music sounds through the colonnades and columns and the measured structures of the glittering city. But is the marriage of the Lamb and his bride, the redeemed, truly a marriage? Is there any creative tension, any fusion of opposites, any productive interpenetration of mind, body, or spirit? Would Augustine, Samuel Johnson, or William Blake, all passionate Christians, have thrived there?

Our biblical analysis would not be complete without pointing out forcefully that the marital legacy of the Hebrews also became the testament of the New Israel, equal in divine inspiration to the exclusively Christian. And so Eden lived on, the Proverbial wisdom and its sensuality, the Song of Songs, retaining considerable energy however much troped, redirected, and euphemistically reinscribed. The next chapter will display in patristic writings the dramatic and vivid contrasts we have already seen as inherent in Scripture, whose erotic force was translated into great art and enormously influential thought by the literary genius that Augustine applied to his religious heritage.

*When I love thee, what kind of thing is it that I love?
Not the beauty of bodyes, not the order of time; not
the cleerness of this light which our eyes are so glad
to see; not the harmony of sweet tongues in
Musique; not the fragrancy of flowres, and other
unctuous and aromatical odours; not Manna, nor any
thing of sweet and curious tast; not carnall creatures
which may be delightfully imbraced by flesh and
blood: They are not these thinges which I love in
loving God. And yet I love a kind of* Light, *a kind
of* voyce, *a kind of* odour, *a kind of* food, *and a
kind of* imbracing, *when I love my God: the* light, *the*
voyce, *the* odour, *the* food, *and the* imbracing *of my
inward man, where that shines to my soule which
is not circumscribed by any place; that sounds to myne
eare which is not stolne and snatched away by time;
that yieldeth smell which is not scattered by ayre; that
savours in tast which is not consumed by eating; that
remayns enjoyed which is not devoured by satiety;
This is that which I love when I love my God.*

Augustine, *Confessions* 10.6 (anonymous
translation of 1620)

*Why was it, Philoxenos of Mabbug would ask, that
night emissions seem to increase when the novices
grow in the love of God, so that their love appears to
take forms "akin to the passion of fornication?"
"Oh how difficult this is to understand! How the
knowledge of the scholar is tried!" For it was
precisely the intimacy of sexuality, and its apparent
position on the shadowy borderline of body and
mind, that enabled men such as John Cassian to
look to it for the first unmistakable signs of the
mighty works of deliverance wrought by God in the
recesses of the soul.*

Peter Brown, "Bodies and Minds" (1990)

SEVEN

The Earliest Christian Centuries: Augustine

 $\mathcal{T}$ he entry of Christianity into the powerful Roman world, especially its great cities, and the achievement by a relatively small minority of official toleration (A.D. 313), state power (c. 380), and transforming radiance during the course of a few short centuries of both persecution and indifference—these surely constitute one of the most amazing stories in Western history. No less amazing is the dramatic conversion of most of the barbarian invaders as they crossed the "civilized" frontiers, soon followed by the creation by the barbarian scholar Ulfilas of a written Gothic language to accommodate a translation of the Bible. It has not been difficult even for some who stand outside the Christian tradition to see the hand of providence in so unlikely an achievement, and it will certainly dissatisfy many that the best secular view, after many distinguished etiological attempts, remains modest and irresolute: the story continues to be both impressive and unexplainable. We have earlier noted striking consonances between classical and Christian artistic expression, but it is as an internal and external drama of extremes in tension that the growth of Christianity fascinates. And its complexities often pivot on matters of love and sexuality.[1]

Paul had encountered problems arising from licentious practices in the church at Corinth, leading him to excoriate the vices and abominations, often sexual, which he so passionately believed Christ had come to eradicate (1 Corinthians 5, 6). If this be done in the green tree, what will be done in the dry? Serious moral charges were leveled against the Christians, not surprising when we realize how much was at stake when the evangelical axe was laid at the root of the pagan tree. Tertullian, writing in 197, refers to the belief that Christians practiced group sex and even child sacrifice at their initiation rites. These extreme views may shock us, but it is perhaps small wonder that they should be held by pagans since the redeemed were themselves so adept at embarrassing one another with moral incrimination. In any event, it measures the polarizing paradoxes of this unbelievably riven period that the impression Christians made upon their pagan compatriots was that they were (1) impossibly puritanical and (2) individually and communally obscene.

The second set of charges need not detain us, since they faded away and now have mostly dated importance. But Christian asceticism challenged the marital ideals of Greek, Roman, and Jew; might well have swallowed them up, and so might have altered the practice of Western sexuality even more radically than it in fact did. The several forms of asceticism have been variously assessed and too often easily dismissed, and in some elementary ways we must get our modern perspectives adjusted in approaching this subject. Phyllis McGinley has found one extreme totally puzzling, and many of us today shake a finger at the fathers when we should be outraged by the Victorians, who formed our tastes and so our view of our religious origins.[2] An aristocratic, Roman Catholic Frenchman has said that if in his household a sexual word or phrase, however euphemistically softened, was uttered, it burned the tongue and seared the lips. Ascetic Christianity doubtless deserves some of the blame, if indeed any is thought to be attaching. But austere though the fathers were, delicacy of speech and sexual reticence were not usually their colloquial mode. Quite the contrary: they were as preoccupied with sexual dreams and images as Martin Luther, Samuel Johnson, and Sigmund Freud, and they openly discussed their own nocturnal emissions as signifying the state of their souls.

Many early Christians loved the physical presence of the anchorites and wanted to be impregnated with the "sweet smell of the desert," but modern commentators sense other odors emanating from the desert fathers, some of whom did not wash, prized their encrusted state, and even ate the worms and maggots that gathered in their clotted and ulcerated bodily filth. One of the quarrels with Judaism turned on sexual practices, even though the Hebrew tradition itself had developed houses of discipline and retirement, as is well known in our day of archeological discovery. Gibbon thought that with the coming of Christianity Jewish law became dominant, as in some ways it did, since Christians often practiced what Jewish moralists had preached; he seems to have blamed Judaism for pushing Christianity into making sexual frailty as disgraceful as poison, assassination, sorcery, or parricide. Gibbon's view will surely seem incomplete and skewed to readers of this book, which has pointed to many Hebrew poems and tales swelling with erotic juices, and he may have been surprised to know what early fourth-century Jews said to a

Christian bishop: "*You* have received a curse and have multiplied barrenness" (emphasis added). But if Gibbon is at one extreme, some twentieth-century scholars stand at another. One reforming modern commentator has found that the female virginal life arose as women themselves made it a practical reality in protest against the repressive social order, which legislated for them only procreative and domestic functions. Thus Christian orthodoxy allegedly accepted established female continence only after the subversive fact of serious female protest.[3]

These miscellaneous examples give some idea of older and newer scholarship responding to a complex and fascinating challenge. Fortunately, against this fermenting and often creative welter we are now able to set the authoritative and readable scholarship of Peter Brown, who, though he is by no means blind to the evils of "ferocious asceticism," has found appealing qualities in Christian virginity that make it early vogue less anomalous.[4] It valorized that original state in which every soul and every body were once joined, it encouraged an intense individual and corporate concentration upon the magnificent sociability of the invisible world, it revealed the mutual dependence of body and soul in a very important border area of the psyche even as natural flesh warred with Christian spirit. One cannot help remembering that William Blake, primitively Christian in many ways though very far from being ascetic, was himself intensely preoccupied with this very frontier between innocence and experience.

But whatever the life condition of the believer—layman, widow or virgin, priest or bishop (and clerical celibacy came late and, as Paul makes clear, was not characteristic of the primitive church)—the often passionate metaphors of marriage applied to the relations of God, Christ, and the faithful in the Bible continued sweet and strong in the believer's psyche. It mediated erotic imagery to whole congregations and communities, enlivened prayer, praise, song, sermon, and meditation, and encouraged the transference of active sexual desire and its projection upon the empyrean, something that was not necessary when Zeus and other Olympians openly descended to humanity for sexual adventures.

The traditional view of Christian marriage was that it followed Jewish example in a monogamy it made more intense by stringent prohibitions of divorce and remarriage, thus confronting a brutal, faithless, and permissive pagan society with a totally new and arrestingly austere ethic. In chapters 4 and 5 of this book we have confronted pagan *fides* in marriage, severe laws enforcing it, and literary art ennobling it. But the old view of confrontation and a radical break with the past should not be thrown out; Christian polemical tracts were not creating a quarrel where none existed, and marital probity, like virginity, was one of the most impressive refrains in the "new song." Galen (130–200?) was one of those greatly impressed with the structure and discipline of the Christian household—a discipline that might sometimes dictate complete abstinence from coition, that rejected divorce, and that viewed the remarriage of widows disapprovingly. The faith of the Annales school and Michel Foucault in the imperiously compelling change of episteme that took place outside Christianity in pagan Roman culture itself, creating ideals of unbreakable monogamous loyalty, personal love, and private intimacy *avant la lettre chrétienne,* may have to be reexamined and refined (see chapters 4 and 5). But the newer history is surely right in showing us that married Christians for centuries constituted an important city elite. That elite, which gives the impression of being guided by an already established marital tradition, certainly differed sharply from the desert fathers; from the roaming, fanatical ascetics who occupied dens, caves, crags, pillars; from separated organized communities of saints or "brides" of Christ; and finally from couples still in society and occupying a house together in an unmarried but continent state. These married Christians were the spiritual descendants of the Gentiles it was Paul's mission to bring into the new house of Israel. The wonder with which this chapter opened at the fact that in the course of only a few centuries emperor and court became Christian may well persist in the face of new scholarship, but that wonder must now be tempered by the knowledge that successful, often wealthy, married couples—the wives especially being dedicated to churchly support, financial and spiritual—lay solidly behind the establishment of Christianity. For it was not the rural poor or the laboring classes of the Christian villages of Palestine that accomplished this conquest, and the view that early Christians were usually simple, humble, and oppressed is, as Peter Brown has seen, a figment of modern romantic imagination.[5]

Much of the literature concerned with love and marriage that will presently be discussed addresses itself to or grows out of audiences of relatively sophisticated urban married couples, who would be fully capable of applying its instructions and appreciating its imaginative suggestiveness. Frequently the leaders and often the members of the Christian urban community had been exposed to an educational system not much changed since the Athens of the fourth century B.C. and so were trained in reading Roman and/or Greek didactic, rhetorical, and poetic texts, some of which must have been works already treated in the present study. At least among an influential minority there seems to have been a kind of cultural continuity, which made the specifically Christian challenge amenable to acculturation and liberal contextualizing.

Clement of Alexandria

Precisely such humanistic, Stoic, and Hellenistic contextualizing characterized the catechetical school of Clement of Alexandria, born in 150, who was about as close in time to Jesus as we are to Wordsworth or the French Revolution.[6] He read Philo; taught that gnosis could lead to a higher Christian perfection; accepted the Stoic ideas of self-sufficiency, frugality, and even *apatheia,* meaning "passionlessness" (an ideal of the desert) but not "insensibility to suffering" (specifically rejected by Christian teachers). In addressing his *Paidagogus* to the "little ones," he is not speaking to children alone but to all those in need of beginning instruction in the faith. The individual human body is fully accepted and is made a central preoccupation. In part the strategy of this emphasis is to permit warnings against lust and the sins of the flesh, as Clement excoriates adultery, effeminacy, sodomy, pederasty, all fruitless sowing of the seed, all unnatural methods of conducting intercourse or reversing sex roles, and even excessive copulation of the normal kind. But the centrality of the flesh also positively enforces the divine injunction to "be fruitful and multiply" and permits Clement to justify the sexual frankness of his catechetical language: it is not wrong, he argues, for us to name the organs of generation when God is not ashamed of their function. In brief, Clement gives the marriage bed due esteem, defends marriage for Christian leaders, and does not deny the attainment of Christian perfection to the marital state; but it is true that he considers marital sexuality the means for procreation and for little else. The husband is a "farmer" (a traditional Greek metaphor for procreative sex), but he must sow his seed only when the season is favorable and the land his own.

Clement, though sexually frank in speech, is also a "Scholemaster" in politeness and social delicacy: like Lord Chesterfield he does not approve of the loud laugh, and he derides ear scratching and loud burping. But though he writes in Greek we cannot apply to his vision of human love the great words we have analyzed earlier, *erōs, philia,* or *charis.* There is little room even for lofty Aristotelian friendship, to say nothing of intellectual or spiritual growth through shared sexual intimacy.

The Shepherd of Hermas

But the ideal of esteem enlivened by desire almost seems to touch Hermas, who is not a priest or a bishop or even a prominent layman, but perhaps a "prophet" active in the church a generation or two before Clement. Surviving papyri and John Cassian's writings show that his allegory had won a wide Christian readership, and Clement of Alexandria and Origen regarded it as inspired, though Tertullian condemned it and its author ("that apocryphal Shepherd of adulterers"). The identification of the author with the Roman Christian mentioned by Paul in Romans 16:14 was accepted by Origen and Eusebius; had it truly been a firm and persuasive one, the *Shepherd of Hermas* may well have been canonized. A partial copy of the work appears in that prestigious source of holy text, the Codex Sinaiticus.[7]

What does this combination of narrative, allegorical vision, and didactic sentence say about its author, his church, and his views of love and marriage? Hermas may have been a slave or a foundling, sold to one Rhode in Rome, a woman who had become a Christian. One day he meets her again after many years; he is now apparently married and has children. He begins to love (agapan) her as a sister (1.1.2), and since she is bathing in the Tiber he offers his hand to her to help her out of the river, wishing to himself that he had a woman of such beauty (to kallos) as his wife. His visions now follow, and from them we learn that Hermas's wife is something of a shrew or scold and that his indulgence of his children has made them corrupt, rebellious, blasphemous, and materialistic. To us Hermas appears to be curious (he is sometimes chided for wanting to know too much), simple (he seems not to absorb quickly the lessons of his experiences), and not terribly intelligent or logical (his lists of virtues and vices are dialectically unworked and miscellaneous, lacking internal coherence or priorities of value or meaning).

The church whose communicant he is is not a Montanist one, consisting of "separated" people, *les purs,* as it were, but a Catholic parish; indeed it contains all sorts and conditions of people, hierarchically valued, ranging from those who have to be expelled (lewd, partly exposed women, with loose flowing hair) to pure virgins. The church itself is personified as a virgin, whom Hermas the Roman confuses with a Sibyl since the visions take place near Cumae. She grows younger and younger in successive visions as Hermas's comprehension deepens. He ends (3.8.3–7) with greater singleness of mind and heart than he had possessed at first, with greater dedication to the poor and needy, and with a sense of spiritual enablement that can come by fasting, prayer, confession, and rededication to the Christian virtues (also personified as virgins) of faith, continence (akakia), fortitude (dunamis), longsuffering, simplicity, innocence, purity, cheerfulness, truth, understanding, concord, and love (agapē).

The lessons about love and marriage come from the narrative, the visions, and the "mandates." Hermas is severely rebuked for lustful thoughts when he helped his female owner from the river, though he was fully unconscious of them and thought he was loving her only as a sister, perhaps indeed as a "sister" in Christ. He is stunned at the accusation, since he had never made a coarse remark and thought of her as a goddess (there may of course be some hidden idolatry here). His sin can be atoned for by prayer, fasting, and confession, which in the end save not only the self but the whole household. Later it is clear that God was angered more by the shortcomings of Hermas's family than by the sin of unconscious lust in his heart, and one must draw the historical conclusion that this household must have been like many another, fatally divided between the pagan and the Christian world. Hermas takes the opportunity of didactically Christianizing his home; the head of the house must also be a proselytizer and a kind of internal domestic pastor, a role not unlike that of the angel of repentance who comes to dwell with him and gives him commands and parables, which he writes down for himself but also perhaps for his domestic charges.

Included in such instruction are mandates about marriage that revise Roman, specifically Augustan, practice. As under Roman law, a man must still repudiate an adulterous wife. But now, under Christian law, he may come to realize she has repented, and then he is obliged to forgive her and take her back. It follows that he must remain chaste and not remarry while he is waiting for her. After her death he is permitted to remarry, but it is better to remain single. Moreover, under the new law the wife—for so the mutual marriage bond is reinterpreted—must likewise forgive and chastely await the return of an adulterous husband, who is fully as culpable as an adulterous wife. Rome, we remember, condemned and severely punished female adultery—but stopped there, with hers alone. Now both were culpable though forgivable under charity. It is everywhere implied that man and woman alike must preserve chastity before marriage. All this is clear evidence that it was the necessities of Christian forgiveness that dictated a cleaner break with Roman mores and legalities than mere continuation of Roman monogamy and ideals of harmony would have required.

Hermas's confusion in thinking the allegorical woman a Sibyl is soon cleared up, and he now "matures" into a fuller loving relationship with the community that has mediated salvation to him and is now sanctifying his soul. The church is increasingly revealed as a virgin, and the ministrants are also virgins, who give commands to tall, noble, handsome, and strong young men about the building of the sacred tower (the church is now a structure as well as a person). These white-clad maidens are close to their Lord, who kisses them as he inspects the stones they are erecting, rejecting some, ordering others to be trimmed and fitted.

Hermas's relations to the virgins become more interesting and revealing after the inner angel-shepherd of instruction turns him over to them. He apparently continues to live with his wife, but in total continence now. Hermas fusses and worries at spending the night with the virgins, but they assure him they will be as brother and sister, not as husband and wife. The leader and the others embrace and kiss him, pursuing him around the tower, as he becomes younger and younger, dancing and thrilling childishly at the association. Their vigilance during the night consists only of prayer, their sole food the words of the Lord. The scene has charm, like a Blakean Song of Innocence, even though in Hermas the latent sexuality is more hidden and repressed than in the Romantic poet.

What strikes one about this fascinating glimpse into the mentality of a Christian of the second century? Jesus's words about the dangerous sin of subjective lust even without action ("But I say unto you, That whosoever looketh on a woman to lust after her hath committed adultery with her already in his heart," Matthew 5:28) have been fully internalized, and the tempted heart is as much a breach of the divine law as a rape. Paul's priorities have been institutionalized: marriage can be a good, but virginity is better. Christ forgivingly accepts sinners of all kinds, but especially rewards the pure in body and heart. "Verily I say unto you, Whosoever shall not receive the kingdom of God as a little child, he shall not enter therein" (Mark 10:15): this too has been fully internalized, and singleness of mind, innocence of heart, and childlikeness of disposition grow as the visions progress.

If regression to some version of childhood attended the early Christian experience of love, it would not be surprising: consider the many Gospel injunctions that we become as little children. Or does *The Shepherd of Hermas* in fact valorize a state of physically unconsummated affection, a kind of foreplay of the heart? Is this what Hermas's dance with the virgins suggests to us? The Clementine view of marriage—Hebraic as well as Christian in form and spirit, enunciated in the Eastern church a generation or two after Hermas had written in the West—has a robustness, a linguistic honesty, a mature concentration on the generative unknown to the earlier writer's allegorical fiction. (Recall that Hermas's work was in fact known to Clement.) Hermas impels one to conclude that a kind of unfulfilled and perhaps unfulfilling delicacy that delights in titillation without fruit is endemic in some aspects of Western eros, a theme to which we shall return. Delicacy is present in Clement, to be sure, but he has confined it to manners at table and less intimate features of social life. The verbal and physical dancings of Hermas and his progress from an unconsciously lewd thought to a fully continent marriage and to the childlike virginal dance we have noted are a legacy of—what? Could what we have found so prominent in New Testament appropriations and allegorizations of the Song of Songs be a source? Are the joys of Hermas the effect of combining strong erotic imagery with perscriptive denials of sexual fulfillment? We have not as yet seen the last of this kind of unconsummated religious sensualism. We dare not call it Platonic, for on this level it is without intellectual structure or resonance.

John Chrysostom

Hermas belonged to the Roman church, perhaps around the year 150; John Chrysostom began his lifetime career of service to the Eastern church in 381.[8] Both the similarities (priority given to virginity, requirement of chastity until marriage for both sexes, equal punishment for male and female adultery) and the differences of viewpoint (to be noted in detail below) are striking. The magnetic preacher of Antioch and patriarch of Constantinople was of course a devout, Bible-believing Christian, but like Clement before him he had studied classical culture and had also known some six years of monastic life in the hills before he was forced by ill health to return to Antioch, where he served as reader, deacon, and priest for some two decades. A skillful rhetorician close to his audiences, he must have soon come to realize how incongruous love was with the prudentially calculated marriages of the money-loving society that surrounded him and his church. He bent his rhetorical genius to define clearly what Christian marriage means. But clarity of definition in such matters has always proved elusive, and John did not achieve the codified and centuries-long definitiveness of, say, the older Anglican Prayer Book, with the threefold purpose of procreation, protection from sin, and mutual help or cooperation. He accepted the first two, but his emphasis even here wavered. The procreative aim had of course been present since Genesis 1–2. But now that the resurrection seems to be at hand and the world is already full, Chrysostom finds it necessary to break somewhat with this venerable purpose and say that there at present remains only one reason for marriage, to avoid fornication. This is to out-orthodox the orthodox, but in the event other traditional and more relaxed components remain fully in place. John sees clearly that the Pauline marital debt made husband and wife equally responsible for honoring the partner's need of sexual satisfaction. But John is blind to possible rewards for deepening mutuality through shared pleasure (the modern view in more than one confession), and the moralist takes over: denial of the marriage debt can lead to adulteries, fornications, and broken homes. The hierarchy established in the Epistle to the Ephesians receives strong endorsement: a household cannot possibly be a democracy, the husband rules, the wife respects and obeys. In other ways, John recalls Clement of Alexandria and the central orthodox tradition stemming from the New Testament: he loathes homosexuality, he hates harlots (harlotry was created by demons), and he fears rich wives (a threat to male headship of the household and an unwanted concentration of female power, since money could abet sexual attractiveness).

If that were all there is to John Chrysostom's analyses of marriage, there would scarcely be enough to sustain the claim made by modern Greek Orthodox writers that his teaching represents the best between Saint Paul and the twentieth-century church. There does in fact breathe through John's discourses a spirit of tolerance for the beauty of intersexual relationship and fellowship, which tends to mitigate without eliminating what a modern would regard as harshness. (Whether this gentler spirit owes anything to his long friendship with the widow and deaconess Olympias, others will have to determine.) He stresses mutuality in *fides*—that is, each partner must honor the other not only by permitting carnal indulgence but also by confining it, the husband-adulterer, as in Hermas, being fully as guilty as the wife-adulteress. Coition is a powerful binder of souls as well as bodies, and the "one flesh" retains its unity even if one partner remains an unbeliever. In other ways, John respects the attractive heterosexual bond, which is deeply planted in us, the one appetite that does not fade. This passion John calls *erōs*, and in quasi-Platonic fashion, this Greek writer suggests that such passion arose because Eve was even closer than a sister—she was Adam's own flesh. There is a respect here for androgyny not very frequent in the West until later times. The woman, who as we have seen must by both necessity and law remain inferior, nevertheless is regarded as embodying sexual allure. As a close student of the Old Testament and one who made frequent homiletical use of its powerfully human stories, John Chrysostom was attracted to Rebecca, whom he makes exemplary. She was a virgin of course and a beautiful one, her body reflecting her soul as in a quite different context Joseph's (another Old Testament favorite of the preacher) reflected his. She went out to work and serve and mingle in society, unlike many girls contemporary with the author. She was generous, modest, attentive to her duties, unabashedly hospitable, and kind. For the preacher she is the exemplary nubile girl—and it is thus that a touch of Hebrew sexual allure does in fact enter the Christian pulpit in Antioch.

Still, as I have hinted, John falls short of developing such qualities into the possibility for a ripening friendship, although he comes close.

Were a modern to put it to him straightly and boldly, he would perhaps acknowledge the desirability of such a vision of eros and love united. He gladly conceded that in the future life, when we possess resurrected bodies, men and women can enjoy mutual friendship.

But doctrine and Christian idealism hedge him in, and his homilies do have the considerable historical merit of revealing more clearly than anyone else's how an influential, highly placed, and popularly successful early Christian viewed marital love. We notice first that it is not a spontaneous or natural emotion but a commanded quality, a legalistic obligation, a compelling duty: "thou *shalt* love," as in John's Gospel quoted earlier (see chapter 6). The prerogative of love belongs peculiarly, it would seem exclusively, to the husband. It entails providential care, long-suffering patience, suffering on the wife's behalf, and even the giving of his life for her. In other words, the Christian husband is a surrogate Christ. To that level of love the wife (by the logic of the metaphor now a surrogate church) cannot attain, and John, echoing the Bible on Israel and on the frequently faithless and spotted bride of the Lamb, can become insultingly vigorous on what woman can descend to: she can be polluted, ugly, cheap, foolish, and blacker than darkness in her disobedience. Yet the Christlike husband must love her and even die for her, as his Master did for a sinful and unworthy humanity. It was a high but seriously fractured and certainly skewed ideal that the congregations in Antioch and perhaps also Constantinople heard from their priest and metropolitan. Some indeed have thought that his homiletical attacks on women may have antagonized Byzantine court ladies and contributed to the decision to exile him.

Is there anything in John of the regressive innocence that we found in Hermas? Perhaps when he addressed himself to the Subintroductae, those male and female Christian virgins who shared quarters in that abstinent intimacy that has been called *suneisaktism,* or "spiritual marriage."[9] That form of housekeeping may have derived from 1 Corinthians 7:36–38: let the man and his virgin marry if he has behaved himself "uncomely" toward her, but if he "hath power over his own will," he "doeth" even "better" not to marry. Moderns are capable of regarding these ascetic partners as "overachievers" and their unions as a kind of "refined torture," but many early faithful (how many? we have no way of knowing) must have considered them farther on the road to perfection than fully and formally married Christians. Some leaders of thought regarded the spiritually married with hostility or dismay. Jerome took a dim view of this institution (not attested in the first century but well known from the second on), accusing the couples of sexual relations. John did not go so far as to charge overt carnality; but this "new and incredible" form of heterosexual liaison he regarded as constituting a third and separate kind. The others were marriage ("ancient, licit, and sensible") and prostitution (demonically evil). The third kind he regarded as dangerous, if not demonic, as an insult to virginity, and as psychologically compromising. He thought virgins retained their beauty longer than wives, who tended to become increasingly less attractive through satiation and childbearing; virgins therefore imposed on their avowedly continent partners an incredible strain. John asks embarrassing questions: How is bathing handled? What about clothes? Why do midwives rush about visiting the virgins' houses if not to see who is violated, who untouched? Even if the midwife certifies the body, does one think that the rude touch or the sensual kiss can evade the scrutiny of our Judge? Is it true, as he has heard but does not charge, that these chaste couples lie down together at night and converse? John obviously does not know the facts, but as an imaginative writer of considerable skill he has managed a refreshingly vital rhetoric, which I have summarized by using the interrogative form—a rhetoric that effectually embarrasses the prolonged kind of foreplay portrayed in the maritally continent Hermas and present in many subsequent Christian epochs. I have earlier suggested that the tendency to associate intimately but not consummate may arise from imposing, upon the daily realities of denial and suppression, biblical metaphors of considerable erotic force and suggestiveness (the virgin bride of Christ; "thou art lovely, my Sister, my Spouse"). The situation envisaged in Chrysostom's rhetoric against the Subintroductae could of course also apply to the unconsummated eros of the Platonic circle, and it is not impossible that the sublimations present in Neoplatonism appealed to many Christian apologists precisely because they resembled psychologically the dynamics of postponing or elevating the satisfactions of those physical desires that the religious closeness of community life must surely have aroused.

Augustine

The greatest Christian thinker and perhaps the most influential writer that Western culture has ever produced, Augustine of Hippo (354–430), was subtly philosophical but at the same time popularly didactic and imaginatively creative.[10] He came to maturity during the flourishing of the ascetic movement, in an age when the climax of Jesus's parable of the sower ("But he that received seed into the good ground is he that heareth the word and understandeth it; which also beareth fruit, and bringeth forth, some an hundredfold, some sixty, some thirty," Matthew 13:23) received a special interpretation: in the exponentially larger harvests that the seed planted in the good ground of the Gospel produces, virgins reap a hundredfold, widows who do not remarry sixtyfold, and married women only thirtyfold.[11]

The mind-set revealed by this interpretation of the parable of the sower immediately suggests a potential tension between the man Augustine and the ambience of the church that surrounded him from his mother's womb. His powerful and highly trained mind and a turbulent personality rooted in carnal experience must have produced the vibrating clashes of struck cymbals. Though never a husband, he became the father of one son by his nameless mistress of many years, a woman shadowy to us but apparently loved. Augustine was obviously touched to the core of his being by his mother; she may have been more Christian muse and exemplar than beloved friend, a term he in all likelihood bestowed on no woman but reserved for his few abiding male relationships and the one passionate one that cost him his stability for a while. He was, finally, a man whose intellectual and artistic experiences embraced the classics of literature, the stage, and rhetoric and who began Manichaean and ended orthodox Catholic.

Such was the man who made love, marriage, and sexuality one of his most important intellectual subjects and personal preoccupations. The discussion that follows and that closes our sections on early Christian love will briefly provide an intellectual context, contrasting Augustine with Origen to bring out his ultimately wholehearted commitment to creation and the body, with John Cassian to bring out his conception of corporate friendship and brotherhood, and with Jerome to bring out the less austere elements of his views on marriage. These themes will be refined in the discussion of Augustine on marriage, both in his theological and practical discourses and also in what I can only call his strenuous idyl of Adam and Eve, in which he stretches his imagination to dramatize, sometimes grotesquely, his erotic message. Finally, Augustine Agonistes will fully appear in an analysis of the *Confessions,* which, even though written in prose, is one of the great love poems of our heritage, marital only by metaphor but as much deserving of the literary critic's intensest concentration as the masterpieces of Homer, "Solomon," Aeschylus, Plato, Euripides, Catullus, or Ovid.

The Context

We go back in time to Origen (185?–253) because his influence remained great and because Augustine's thought should be viewed against this predecessor's peculiar orientations. Origen tried to synthesize Neoplatonism, Stoicism, and Christianity and ended up uniting Logos with *apatheia* and separating matter and body from illumined and educated gnōsis. His learned synthesis is thus related to more popular and extreme ones: to the vivid dualisms preached by Valentinus, Basilides, Marcion, and Mani. With the followers of Mani Augustine had very close contact during some eleven years of his young manhood.[12]

We have repeatedly called attention to the paradoxes that reside in virtually all concepts of love, particularly in the Christian; none are more vivid than in the sects founded by the aforementioned leaders and by others, which spread through the Christian world, some advocating the austerest abstinence, others the most permissive indulgence. It does not need to be argued that the Christian Augustine resisted licentiousness of all kinds; he even thought for a while of having himself castrated, as Origen had done. But in the considered position of *De Virginitate* (401), he reveals that he had no intention on doctrinal grounds of following Origen's example and becoming a eunuch for the Kingdom of Heaven's sake: Matthew 19:10–12, he believed, must be interpreted as purely allegorical advice to renounce marriage for a pious purpose.[13]

Augustine found the Manichaeans disastrously wrong in believing that our flesh arose from some fabled race of darkness without beginning: how could we be exhorted under such madness to love our wives as if they were our own flesh (see Ephesians 5 and *De Continentia*)? But we can find more subtlety than this in Augustine's philosophical rejection of extreme asceticism, for he became in his maturity a reviser of that Origenic Platonism which regarded sexuality as a passing phase, in which social roles based on marriage and childbirth were, in Peter Brown's phrase, "as fragile as dust dancing in a sunbeam."[14] Origen was surely much too ambivalent regarding the body for the mature Augustine, who poetically celebrated the sexual relations of Eden and who couched the excitations of deity in the soul in proto-voluptuous terms: "you arouse" (tu excitas), he says to his God (*Confessions* 1.1; in Cicero the verb could mean "to arouse or provoke *amores*").[15] His subsequent paeans of praise in this great work and also in that amazing exposition of divine purpose, *The City of God,* make it clear that the divine muse stimulates, arouses, moves in the nerves, and stirs in the flesh. Augustine is thus capable of a kind of lyrical naturalism. It is not always easy to tell whether the Creator of the body had practical use or beauty uppermost in mind. But the body, which Augustine, like the Psalmist, found to be fearfully and wonderfully made, as a whole possesses a symmetry and musical harmony not yet discovered. If it is beautiful and useful in every organ we know, surely the hidden vital parts are equally beautiful and proportional to their function. What Augustine says here about the body, whole and part, he had earlier said in one of his most haunting passages about the totality of God's great creative fiats: "I no longer desired a better world, because I was thinking of creation as a whole: and in light of this more balanced discernment, I had come to see that higher things are better than the lower, but that the sum of all creation is better than the higher things alone" (*Confessions* 7:13).

Origen and other dualists Augustine came ultimately to perceive as crude and unrefined, even in their spiritual transcendences. His was a Trinitarian approach to the individual human being, who was made up of flesh, psyche, and pneuma, as in Paul. But these three spheres, though in constant conflict, were not separate or separable: "For the flesh lusts after nothing save through the soul, but the flesh is said to lust against the spirit, when the soul with fleshly lust wrestles against the spirit."[16] This is important psychology, for it does not simplistically endow the flesh with evil desires that can be cut off and so eliminated in some traumatic physical and spiritual elision. The real mischief of man's condition is that not flesh alone but flesh plus soul (that is, art, imagination, learning, what I have earlier called eros, the decorated libido) can destroy spirit and separate us from ultimate purpose. Flesh can insinuate itself everywhere, partly because flesh is potentially good; the same can be said of the psyche and the spirit.

Lest we have been too complex about the body, let us get back to the simple fact that the faith of the Christian Augustine came by means of the Incarnation, as the *Confessions* makes clear at its very beginning: "through the humanity of thy Son" ("per humanitatem filii tui," 1.1). And to the even simpler fact that in the sublimely romantic egotism of this, his greatest work, Augustine accepts the Old Testament belief that God operated creatively within the female womb and opened and closed it as he willed. But Augustine involved God in his father's sex act as well, when he refers—in a marvelously condensed Latin that echoes but makes more sexually precise Psalm 139:13–15—to "the progenitors of my flesh, out of whom [male] and in whom [female] thou createdst me [in the realm of] time" ("parentibus carnis meae, ex quo et in qua me formasti in tempore," 1.6). In those masculine and feminine relative pronouns (*quo* and *qua*) and in the prepositions (*ex,* which suggests the ejaculating male, and *in,* which suggests the receiving female) there lurks the whole act of copulation that produced him. Is it excessive to say that Augustine's very grammar has created a kind of primal scene? Let us recall the triangulations of Sappho and the *Phaedrus,* where we have found that to the loving couple is added a divine third party, and of course the Hebrew stories that hint at divine intervention (see chapters 2 and 6).

John Cassian, born in 360, was capable of being directly in touch with Hellenic thought, like Origen before him, whose follower he was.[17] It was perhaps inevitable, therefore, that out of a knowledge of different forms of traditional love (good and bad, family and tribal, instinctual and cultural) he should develop a refined and yet realistically compelling view of Christian fellowship. The *agapē* that united the fellowship to Christ was of burning intensity, and it extended "unto all men, especially unto them who are of the household of faith" (Galatians 6:10). But breadth of affection was not enough either, for not only was virtue required in authentic relationships but virtue of the same kind (a point that Samuel Johnson was to make in the eighteenth century). And then too there were the more specialized affections ordered and ordained by custom ("diathesis," more literally, "orderly arrangement"), parental, uxorial, filial; these could properly be unequal in strength, for did not Jacob love Joseph more than his other sons? Jesus, John more than the other disciples? John received greater love because of the virginity and purity of his flesh. And this last suggests there is a love that is "set in order" even above the human hierarchies, a privileged love, special because virginal and pure, based on singlemindedness and sacrifice. Above marriage, but not intellectual or Aristotelian or purely virtuous either, this is something new in the world and is only distantly related to the friendships of Aristotle and Plato, Cicero and Seneca. Augustine both before and after his conversion formed abiding friendships, which were always tied to his innermost being and sometimes tied to each other in religious or philosophical fellowship.

But Cassian's lovely, graduated, nuanced, and comprehensive vision does not seem consistently to animate Augustine, at least in his greatest or latest works, where the love is more intensely God-directed—a love that challenges the human even when the human is humane, virtuous, and noble, perhaps especially then, since it is devastatingly prone to becoming an idolatrous substitute for true *caritas*. Augustine, like Hermas, saw that the church was built of all sorts and conditions of stones, and he also saw that it was always threatened even from within by original sin and that its purity of doctrine and practice sometimes had to be maintained by state force. He had come not to trust even divine love always to work charismatically in a human situation to achieve the gracious ordering Cassian envisioned.

Jerome, born in 347, was in some ways closer in spirit to Augustine, and his priorities were often those of his younger contemporary. And yet he seems to have gone too far in a direction opposite to Cassian's.[18] He denied disparaging marriage, but he saw little chance of achieving holiness in a bustling household, loud, sensual, wrangling, discordant, with screaming, drooling children, disobedient slaves, and adulterous wives. Marriage is "vomit," to which no self-respecting Christian widow would want to return. The sole good of marriage was that it seemed to be the only way of producing the virgins the church now desired to accept ritually early in their lives, segregate, and form into communities for service and prayer. Jerome's angry attack on Jovinian for having placed married couples on the same level as consecrated virgins doubtless inspired many, but it also outraged Christians as late as the Wife of Bath. His view of Mary as pure *ante partum* and *in partu* separated her from normal sexual humanity and ensured the divine purity of Christ's flesh. But his insistence that she was a virgin also *post partum* effectually denied her a normal marriage to Joseph, forcing Jerome to believe that the Gospels' reference to Jesus's brothers and sisters had to be completely spiritualized and allegorized.

Augustine's position differs from Jerome's. Virginity is better than marriage, to be sure, but marriage is also a good, if a lesser one. Besides, virginity should not be too literally defined, for a rape does not deprive the soul of purity or even the body of its sanctity, and if the probing hand of a midwife should accidentally rupture the hymen, a girl would not have lost her virginity.[19] But literal loss of virginity does not figure in his view of the parents of Jesus, since he believed they lived together without physical contact. Values other than procreation apparently inhered in the married state, and it is significant, as Elizabeth Clark has said, that Augustine stands as "the first major Western theologian to argue that although Joseph and Mary remained celibate, they had a true marriage."[20] We now turn to a more detailed analysis of Augustine on marital love.

On Marriage: The Doctrine and an Idyl

Representations of Roman couples shaking hands on sarcophagi and of Marcus Aurelius and his wife Faustina the Younger on coins were not only marital symbols but symbols of concord that also figured forth all political and social harmony. Augustine's vision was not nearly so bland or stonily ideal. As a theologian and preacher he was capable of the didactic, simple, and direct; but his position was more often touched with fire produced by the extreme emotional and intellectual temperatures of both his psyche and his theological debates. His discussions of marriage are no exception, nor was he on this subject fully at ease in Zion.[21]

We have seen how intimately and complexly interactive was his psychology of *sarx, psyche,* and *pneuma;* his psychology of marriage was equally complex and dynamic, and to work it out he had to resort to a flexible, even sliding, scale of dialectics related to order and purpose. A simple antinomy of flesh vs. spirit will not suffice in applying Paul to the realities of life. All existence presents to consciousness not only the good vs. the bad, but the good, the better, and the best. Thus though health and immortality are both goods, immortality is a greater, and Mary is better than the good Martha. Marriage, too, is a good but chaste widowhood is better and virginity better still. These three together and in separate ways are related to three existentially inescapable, metaphorical, or sanctioned unions: Christ and his church, the husband and the wife, the spirit and the flesh, the first of course being determinative and preeminent. The marital, which by an inevitable natural juxtaposition participates in flesh vs. spirit, also bears an analogy with the central relationship of established religion and so entails the sacramental. This last is especially necessary for one so realistic about human sin and rebellion and divisiveness as Augustine; but its effect was that such a bond continued to be regarded as virtually indissoluble. And such has remained the prevailing view long past the challenges given it by the reformer Bucer and the poet Milton.

Even so, Augustine's logic led him to say that marriage and its attendant sexuality were not, like wisdom, health, or friendship, goods in and of themselves. It was necessary to impose upon the institution good and necessary ends, and Augustine gave it a threefold purpose that he codified out of Scripture and that has been enormously influential in the West. The first is to beget children, an aim not necessarily given priority, for circumstances could vary, but which remained the only justification for sexual intercourse. Without the generative aim, intercourse was venial sin, milder than mortal because of the good of offspring but nonetheless a sin, a poison injected into our semen and passed on by generation to the infant by the disobedience of the first couple. Because the natural instinct for physical relationship was powerfully attractive and placed in man to enable him to wax and multiply, the perversions of this God-implanted appetite were abominations, mortal sins, frustrators of the Creator's plan. To keep humanity from lust and to tie concupiscence to its original purpose, a second end of marriage became inescapable: to tame the libido and keep the couple unspotted from the world. This aim was realized in the mutual pledge and observance of *fides*.

The foregoing aims are conventional enough. Did Augustine leave any room for friendship, an aim implicit in and sometimes concealed by the often stated purpose of mutual solace (humanitatis solatium), of help or cooperation, of companionship, deriving from God's creation of a helpmeet for Adam? In the event, this purpose came to be related to the shared and divided labors of the Xenophontic household, but Augustine takes it much further, though not perhaps so far as Aristotle, who envisaged virtue friendship of the highest kind between husband and wife, whom he otherwise did not regard as equals. More nature-oriented in some contexts than is sometimes realized, Augustine regards not only the gift of sexuality itself as a great and natural good but also its derivative, the human social spirit, the desire to form friendships. This natural bond also goes back to Eden, for God created mankind out of one man to tie us together by the cord of kindred, making of humanity a single family. The great exemplar and prototype of this is the couple, man and wife, the power of whose union is signed in the flesh that binds them, since woman was created out of man. This of course had to be hierarchical; Augustine could scarcely escape Ephesians, which commanded the headship of the male and mandated that he love his wife following the example of Christ, who was at once the head and lover of the Church.

Even though he thus roots the bonds of "one flesh" in nature and God's creative act, Augustine remains blind to any possibility that sexual intimacy could minister to the deepening of marital friendship. That relationship is one totally of *caritas,* the central Christian virtue, and it is of course in no way related to *cupiditas.* Indeed, it is set off *against* the sexual desire, even that which is legitimated in offspring. Thus the marital friendship in Christian charity may be regarded as stronger and more lasting than the carnal bond, for grace is higher than nature. It persists, as marriage itself persists, beyond the childbearing years. And so the by now venerable tradition of marital continence receives Augustine's blessing. The glow of full physical maturity may depart, but there lives on in full vigor the order of charity between husband and wife. Indeed, so great a good is marital chastity that it should begin early, the earlier the better, since it is greatly praiseworthy not to do what one still has the power to do.

Doctrinally and didactically, then, Augustine respects esteem between couples, and he also accepts the coitus, though separately and somewhat grudgingly, like Paul. The union of libido and friendship comes, poetically and imaginatively and sometimes a bit grotesquely, in his conception of the human future and the human past, of Eden and the New Jerusalem.[22] For Augustine as well as other Christian thinkers, the human condition is a palimpsest as well as a prophecy, meaning that there is within us not only a legacy of evil but a remembrance of good things past and also the earnest of a glorious inheritance. Such recollections and premonitions accomplish emotionally for man what Freud's soberer superego was supposed to achieve somewhat more prudentially.

Augustinian postponements to the eternity of redeemed and resurrected flesh have received in the course of our more recent history tellingly fierce opposition: they divert our vision from present needs, pleasures, and fulfillments by the promise of celestial rewards in an unseen and remote world. But though Augustine was far from possessing a modern social conscience, he was as unsentimentally realistic about individual and corporate mischief as the most disillusioned philosopher or root-and-branch reformer. He did of course preach of future destiny—punishment as well as reward—but he never promised the pie in the sky of Marxism's crude parody of religion.

What purpose, then, did his idyl of Eden and heaven serve? Partly an artistic one, since as a verbal and rhetorical genius he must have loved to attempt the traditional *difficulté vaincue* of aesthetic creation. Partly, to mitigate through the polity of Christian love and mercy the harshness of his realism, of his portrayal of a God who proclaimed and enforced sexual prohibition. But also, I believe, to suggest that past and future could sweeten and beautify life, at least the mental life where metaphor and vision live, where possibilities exist that allow recollected and promissory fragrances to escape into and so embellish our present state.

Such a muse the primitive and pagan worlds did not, from a Christian perspective, possess, and Augustine becomes Swiftian in attacking their love fables and practices. The Great Mother stained the earth and slandered the heavens, effeminating life by her foppish eunuchs with their oily hair and powdered faces (*City* 2.4, 7.26). Her only peer was Saturn, who mutilated his own father; even the despicably immoral Jupiter was guilty of only one unnatural sin, in appropriating Ganymede to his service (7.26).[23] Augustine's portrayal of the deities required at a pagan wedding rollicks with almost Rabelaisian laughter. Jugatinus, God save us, is at hand when a boy and girl marry. But isn't Domiducus needed also to lead the lady to her new home, with Manturna thrown in to keep her at home with her husband? Friends decently go home, but the gods do not. They swarm in to help the groom and puzzle the girl. Virginiensis takes off her girdle, Subigus puts her in the right position, Prema keeps her from moving, and Pertunda (from *pertundere,* "to perforate")—but let this creature blush and go and leave the husband with something to do! And incidentally wouldn't one deity have been enough, Venus, say? But of course Priapus had to be there, for on his monstrous member a pious tradition required the bride to sit (6.9).

Augustine was not only aware of the contrasts and paradoxes of amorous love, but as a master of rhetoric himself he praised *antitheta, opposita,* or *contraposita* (*City* 11.18). And nowhere does he use them more effectively than when in *The City of God* he turns from the satire on pagan practice to Christian recollection and anticipation. Augustine is typically modest about heaven, which will be filled with resurrected bodies. The present reader is invited to consider after our discussion of *The Confessions* whether there is not the strong implication here that the ringing celebration Augustine derives from the love verbs *amare* and *diligere* will indeed join with *caritas* to hymn the everlasting wedding feast of the Lamb, though no human language can express it now. Our future spiritual bodies will surpass those of Adam and Eve before they sinned, but we cannot be sure that what Augustine imagines in *The City of God* about love in Eden will be replicated in the Golden City. Sexual differentiation will remain, for women will arise as women, their natural state remaining. No lust or deformity will exist, no one will be too fat or too lean, and the female parts will radiate a new kind of beauty. Obviously there is continuity between present and future, no traumatic annihilating of the body, no evaporation into pure spirit (*City* 22.17, 19).

Adam and Eve are of course treated differently, since the past may be imaginable where the future is not (*City* 13.19–21). They were married before the Fall, occupying real, not allegorical, space; their intended destiny was to produce children and fill the earth, and when that was done to enter an even more blissful state perhaps not unlike that of the redeemed future. The means of fulfilling the command to be fruitful and multiply was uncankered, lust-free copulation, something that it may strain our imaginations to conceive of, as it did Augustine's. Sex differences were exactly as we know them now. Passions existed but were never aroused contrary to reason, the sex organs moving at the command of the intelligent will, as we today move our hands. When need required, the seed was sown—a trope for human intercourse hoary with age. If it is difficult for us to conceive of such rational, purposive dignity solemnly attending the rites of unfallen human fruitfulness, Augustine may not help by invoking his homely illustrations (14.24). I now paraphrase what is a fully human and awkward vision, but one doubtless intended to give sanction to Christian couples even though they must now procreate in an ecstasy that is venial and a parturition that is painful. I have known, says Augustine, those who can move their ears or their scalps, swallow and regurgitate innumerable objects, mimic the voices of birds and beasts, shed copious tears, raise beads of perspiration, or fart songlike musical sounds. Such an idyl of innocence, his Edenic epithalamium, may not win us over artistically, and indeed his suspicion of the sex act in postlapsarian form may have unconsciously dictated his imagery from show, circus, and gymnastics to illustrate willed bodily movements. But we for-

FIGURE 9 Jacob Jordaens, *The Fall of Adam and Eve.* (Courtesy of the
Budapest Museum of Fine Arts.)

get sometimes that Luther and Augustine (and other deeply religious
teachers too) could be fully sincere and effectually poetic while offending
our lingering Enlightenment elegances and Victorian pruderies. And
one must take seriously Augustine's belief that Edenic sexuality was,
though grave, pleasurable, and though pleasurable, a great good—and
that it could filter down into a ruined world to inspire marital duty.

What about the Fall that followed? The first disobedience entailed
upon marriage sadness (post coitum triste), lust, pain, shame—we rightly
call our private parts *pudenda.* But of what are men now ashamed? Of the
exquisite, even cruel appositeness of the punishment (poena reciproca).
The first parents were disobedient and rebellious toward God, now their
own flesh rebels against itself and disobeys its quondam master. From the
beginning there has been disagreement about whether lust or disobedience precipitated the Fall, but virtual unanimity that its effect was the
creation of lust. Dawning libido was later a favorite painterly subject,
never more energetically portrayed than by Jacob Jordaens (fig. 9) and

William Blake. Augustine's verbal brilliance surely lay behind the vivid response to the calamity by painters of the Western tradition. He argued that the penile erection (that epileptic spasm), the orgasm, forepleasure, lingering afterpleasure, and sexual imaginings and fetishes defy the will and make the sexual emotions uncontrollable and involuntary. Man and woman cover themselves, and no other human being is now permitted to witness even the marital act, usually undertaken in darkness—though Blake wished, and many today act, otherwise. All copulation entails lust, and lust poisons the semen and produces infants tainted with a bias toward evil and excess (*City* 14.17–21), as a cocaine-using mother bequeaths her habit to her infant.

Augustine's mythologizing of original sin arose after and amid alternative Christian visions by others of greater humanity and permissiveness, especially in Eastern Christianity, and his vision was harshly judged as soon as it was known. And there is nothing new that can be charged against it now. It presented an unrelentingly cruel Deity; its fatality created sexual self-consciousness, inhibition, and guilt; its seeding of wilfulness deeply and inescapably within us has led to religious repression and even the use of holy force; it has laid a heavy, repressing hand on almost two millennia of Christian thought and practice, Catholic and Protestant, established and dissident. God the Holy Spirit has entered the bedroom and whispered in the innermost ear, "In Adam's Fall / We sinnéd all." If it is only fractionally right in its realism about the married state, original sin in its modern equivalences—now that both the religious sanctions and the redemptive graces and hopes that accompanied it have faded—may produce chaos instead of frustration and repression. But there is still a harsh and sobering realism in it which must be faced up to; and at the very least, in the long view of Western history, it establishes a polar contrary to vulgar sentimentality, to the simplistic and immediately gratifying sensibilities, to fairytales of flattering idealisms, to what Dr. Johnson called "commodious" self-deceptions. And it need not silence for us Augustine's own Song of Songs, *The Confessions,* written before he had developed the searing vision contained in his great *City of God* and yet possessing enough realism about human nature and our present state to keep anyone from complacency and lassitude.

Augustine Agonistes: *The Confessions*

Augustine names his own work, and that generic label accounts for much in it, where he praises God for delivering him from himself and his idolatrous involvement with the world, the flesh, and the devil: with fable, myth, grammar, rhetoric, the theater; with barbaric speech, honors, ambitions, the vanity of human wishes; with gluttony, brutal sports, astrology, magic. The confessor voluminously details his rescue from the whirlpool of assorted filthinesses in which he almost drowned. Long though our list is, it could have been much longer, and the word *confessio* does not come close to comprehending the full content and form. This masterpiece is also, in varying degrees, a narrative; a divine comedy; an autobiography of considerable intimacy; an apologetics against pagan, heretics, and conventional Christians; a theological, philosophical argument that analyzes time, space, substance; an exegesis of the creation chapters of Genesis; a veritable anthology of biblical quotations like much Christian utterance; and what, much later, dissenting sects, doubtless influenced however indirectly by the Bishop of Hippo himself, called "testimonies" to God's grace working in their lives. More centrally, it is a psalm of praise, though sometimes an imprecatory psalm addressed to the enemy, a hymn everywhere influenced directly by the Psalms, which are widely quoted or reflected as influential models and inspirers. (In view of my concluding and climactic stress upon spiritual sensualism, it is worth noting that these Hebrew poems can sometimes bring the Song of Songs to mind in their assimilations of erotic-naturalistic and religio-political desire [Psalms 42, 45].) This work is also a prayer, perhaps the longest stretch of submissive intensity in recorded history. One would have to say that it enlarges and vivifies virtually all the literary genres it recalls.

Above all it is a poem, even though only once (11.27) is Augustine overtly concerned with metrics, and then not with his own wonderfully rhythmic prose. Who is its muse? God the Father Almighty (the "Dominus," who is "magnus et laudabilis," 1.1), not primarily Jesus Christ, his only Son (though he often serves as mediator), or the Holy Spirit, the third person (who is doubtless the manifestation behind much of the spiritual ardor). Nor is the chief inspirer the Trinity itself, considered as a totality; though the Three-in-One moved Augustine's faith, he seemed to need a more individual and personal hypostatization for his erotic outpouring. His addresses to this mightiest of muses are a marvel of poetical apostrophe, ranging from the most majestic and awe-inspiring to the homey and even intimate, employing contrasting juxtapositions that melt into oxymorons. God is addressed as "most beautiful and strongest" ("pulcherrime et fortissime," 1.4), called "all-powerful and good" ("omnipotens et bonus," 1.7), while at the same time he is addressed as "thou most beautiful one" ("formosissime," 1.7). Like the "referential" swearing that delights us in Richard Brinsley Sheridan's great comedy—to compare the merely amusing with the sublime—the saint's epithets are adjusted with subtle appropriateness to the divine quality he is invoking, which is itself related contextually to the subject under discussion or the event or emotion being portrayed. It seems appropriate, when he recounts his joining the circle of Manichaean believers and friends, that he should suggest the strangely alluring ways in which that heresy seemed to seduce him through false beauty and truth, by apostrophizing the God who has saved him as "thou for me, father, the highest good, beauty of all beauties, O truth, truth" ("mi pater summe bone, pulchritudo pulchrorum omnium. o veritas, veritas," 3.6).

From his rich hoard of supple vocatives, I emphasize those that are the most erotically evocative, because I see this "poem" as being supremely a love poem. Augustine often and relevantly addresses God as "dulcedo mea" (1.6), and the feminine noun means "pleasure and sweetness." All this suggests that Augustine has indeed appropriated the rich traditions of *charis* and *erōs* in their highest sense and that his *amare* (perhaps, along with *cor,* the key word in this work) and *diligere* do in fact represent not so much sublimation (for their original force and meaning remain strong) as projection or transference or overwhelming concentration of original impulse, but without the kind of transcendental spiritualizing that evaporates the basic emotion.

I have already quoted Augustine as saying to God, "tu excitas" (1.1), and it is time now to ask what kind of temperament was prepared to receive such arousal. The "I" of this great work has a body, like Adam, and will always have one, which, though ultimately resurrected and spiritual, will remain a body still. That body has known lust, sin, searing loss of friendship, procreation (though not in marriage), an eleven-year concubinage, an intensely devoted mother-love. Clearly Augustine's body was a decisively sexual one, and there is every evidence from the *Confessions* that it was therefore (or also) a body capable of powerfully antithetical and conflicting emotions. To God, the confessor could say, "thou lovest and art not transported; thou art jealous but secure, or fearless" ("amas nec aestuas, zelas et securus es," 1.4); to himself he would have had to say, more often than not, simply *amas* and *zelas.* For many years he was "in misty affection" ("in affectu tenebroso," 1.18), but affection still, for love of one kind or another was at the core of his being. How torrential had been his lusts—mists, bubblings, fumings up, boilings over ("iactabar et effundebar et diffluebam et ebulliebam," 2.2)! He could refer to the powerful river ("flumen", 1.16) of custom; he could describe himself as following the force of his own stream ("sequens impetum fluxus mei," 2.2).

He loved much and many, he loved hard—and, most famously, he loved to love ("amare amabam," 3.1). Of the friend of his childhood and youth whom he lost, he describes the seething caldron of his emotions, from which it was still possible to create unity ("ex pluribus unum facere," 4.8). He details the thousand gracious movements that can come from lovers making and renewing their pledges in the joy (*laetitia*) of fellowship, souls blazing, affections rising in bone, tongue, eyes ("a corde amantium et redamantium procedentibus, per os, per linguam, per oculos, et mille motus gratissimos, quasi fomitibus [a strong Virgilian word meaning "tinderbox"] flagrare [the most powerful Latin word for "burn" or "blaze," often used of sexual delight] animos et ex pluribus unum facere," 4.8). Small wonder that he did not dare let Ambrose, his teacher and guide, know of "my private heats, nor of the pit of my danger" ("nec ille sciebat aestus meos, nec foveam periculi mei," 6.3). Small wonder that he feared to entrust himself to marital chastity! Small wonder that he had difficulty displacing his *amor* onto God! And small wonder that when the three-personed God finally battered his heart, it was with the arrows of Erōs, for he was also a lover of classical bent, having wept over Dido dead in his youth: "Thou hadst shot through our hearts with thy charity, and we carried thy words as it were sticking in our bowels" ("Sagittaveras tu cor nostrum caritate tua, et gestabamus verba tua transfixa visceribus," 9.2). And as God came closer and closer, Augustine remained his old tossed and tormented self, "I quaked with fear and boiled again with hope and with rejoicing in thy mercy, O Father" ("Inhorrui timendo, ibidemque inferbui sperando et exultando in tua misericordia, pater," 9.4).

The mysteries of eros in Augustine are great, and he has addressed some of them in the hymn to love of the tenth book of the *Confessions* (10.6, see the epigraph of this chapter), a poem much more richly profound than Paul's hymn to love in 1 Corinthians 13. The confessor's great hymn, structured chiastically like a psalm, is a wonderfully erotic poem of panting, tasting, hungering, thirsting, and final fulfillment. Is it too much to say that the soul which received such inspiration was itself by nature dionysiac, bacchic, for it surged, leaped, danced, rent flesh, spurted psychic blood, and frothed sentimental wine?[24] Can we say that it was truly calm even after it found repose in the great Sabbath rest of the Most High? Augustine asks of his God, "When I love thee, what kind of thing is it that I love?" And he then points to the order of time and the body and, having asked, How do I love thee? he counts the ways, invoking all the senses in order to transcend without dissolving them. I love "not carnall creatures which may be delightfully imbraced by flesh and blood [non membra acceptabilia carnis amplexibus]. . . . And yet I love . . . a kind of *imbracing* [amplexum], when I love my God: . . . the *imbracing* of my inward man, . . . that remayns enjoyed which is not devoured by satiety" (10.6). I have selected sexual enjoyment out of this resonant but tightly integrated poetic list in order to demonstrate that substantive qualities remain, only their direction changing as their adjectival qualities take on eternality. The generic essence (*quendam, quandam,* "a kind of") remains to be loved and enjoyed. The erotic, like everything else, is on a continuum—an essential Augustinian position that is obscured if we make of him a "thou shalt not" precisian or a vengeful Puritan. He has entered deeply into the sacramental meaning of creation, and indeed one of the last greatly energetic movements of his confessional symphony is a recapitulation of Genesis, which holds inescapable physical reality assertively before us, though it may be seen as complex and, without grace, destructive.

The key to this equilibrium in thought and sensibility is that the word *amare* widely but coherently ranges from earthly lust to love of friends to love of teacher (Ambrose), all the way to love of the heavenly bride and bridegroom. That ascent was not an easy one, and one purpose of the *Confessions* is to show how hard it was. The author's philosophical view that iniquity comes from a crooked will swerving away *from* God but that at the same time supreme substance resides *in* God and that God not only loves but *is* love helped him greatly as he climbed dialectically. Emotionally he is also helped by the sweet organicism of his faith (he not only addresses God as "my sweetness" ["dulcedo mea," 1.6 and elsewhere] but also, almost coyly, as "my delayed pleasure" ["tardum gaudium meum," 2.2]). This fiery man does not allow even his priestly and episcopal duties to cool him: he senses that he lives on burning with the fire of charity lighted by God's gift ("dono tuo accendimus," 13.19).

Augustinian love is also revolutionary, subverts individual and corporate systems, damming or diverting the great rivers of custom. Thus Augustine hurls the greatest of the commandments, to love God with all one's heart ("diligere deum ex toto corde") against what was to him and most early Christians the great sin of Sodom, and he regards the love that now animates him as both displacing and replacing the *morem* (*mos* or "custom") and *pactum* (the formal covenant) of great peoples and established traditions (3.8). But whether public or intensely private, Augustinian love was always seamless, never superficially divided into the earthly and the heavenly Venus, despite its inner tensions and despite dangerous temptations to idolatry of the lower. It is thus that deep within even the crassest corruptions and impurities that he knew as a youth, he senses the divine spirit wooing and beckoning. He now confesses his sins of long ago, not that he should in any way love them again, but that having known them he should love his divine muse more, his unfailing sweetness, his blessed and secure delight ("non quod eas amem, sed ut amem te [observe precisely the same verb], deus meus. amore amoris tui facio istuc, . . . ut tu dulcescas mihi," 2.1).

The *Confessions* is, then, a love poem with its erotic energies philosophically ordered but still metaphorically dynamic. It is an individual love poem, though of course the corporate body of the faithful is not forgotten and God is made to transcend literally conceived bodily form. It is a love poem at whose core are lover and beloved in nuclearly separated space but without intrusive institutional ordering. Thus it is not primarily an epithalamium, the church as bride and the Lord as husband (the spousal imagery of the Book of Revelation) being subordinated but not forgotten.

It may be hard to say why the marital is not a powerful or dominant strain. The centuries-long Christian drive toward virginity was doubtless having its effect, and in his own private life mother, mistress, "illegitimate" son may, for reasons now hidden from us, have hushed the creating muse on uxorial and familial matters. Sex and sensibility elevated intact to the seventh sphere, not erotic esteem developed in human marriage, is the gravamen of Augustine the confessor. Other sides have been more often displayed, and we have seen the great pessimist, the dark realist, the stringent legislator, the hunter of heresy. I have considered the time now ripe to elaborate another filiation earlier introduced: with the singer of the Psalms and the author of the Song of Songs, for Augustine has by his *Confessions* helped perpetuate the tradition of spiritual sensualism. We shall pick up the scent again and again of the greatest lover in the Christian tradition. Despite intellectual, moral, and emotional distances, he can still appeal because he ran the gamut of *amor* and never lost his dionysiac frenzy even in his highest ascents and most rarefied imaginings. His love affair with God eventuates in the longest of long-term couplings. It can inspire the marital even though it does not itself arise out of or reflect the marital. The application of his devoted love to so precarious a condition as even sacramental marriage may have given Augustine the theologian pause. But his art, if not his theology, reveals a kind of trembling joy that cannot be denied a place in our legacy of love from the past. His magnificent displacement of sexual desire and erotic longing upon his unseen Creator is perhaps the greatest verbal achievement in the extensive Western pantheon of physico-spiritual, religio-artistic monuments.[25]

They mistake the matter much, that think all adultery is below the girdle: A man darts out in an adultery with his eye, in a wanton look; and he wraps up adultery with his fingers, in a wanton letter; and he breaths in an adultery with his lips, in a wanton kisse. But though this act of love, be so defamed . . . , yet God chooses this Metaphore, he bids us kisse the Sonne. . . . *In this kisse, where* Righteousness and peace have kissd each other, *In this person, where the Divine and humane nature have kissed each other,* Love is as strong as Death; . . .

    John Donne, *Sermons*

EIGHT

The High Middle Ages (I): Intellectual Paradigms and Social Backgrounds

To the Romantics and the nineteenth century the medieval period constituted an attractive cultural watershed because of its discovery of intersexual courtesy and romantic and sentimental affection. To many in our own century the high Middle Ages have remained attractive for other, more complex and darker reasons: they were thought to have given paradigmatic expression to illicit passion, unappeasable but indissoluble, a passion that was inextricably and fatefully linked with suffering and death but nevertheless gave to life all it could know of devotion and delight. Readers of the present study, remembering Euripidean tragedy, the New Comedy, and the Greek romance, will know how wide of the proper chronological mark these judgments are. But our zeal for a more just and equitable distribution of credit—or blame—for erotic insights should not obscure the fact that the twelfth, thirteenth, and fourteenth centuries in Europe did indeed unite heterosexual esteem and desire as never before, discover intellectual bases for the long-term union of such qualities, and establish social, religious, and political sanctions for its realization. Such historical, intellectual, and quasi-mythological prototypes will be the subject of this chapter, while the next will be concerned with the "problematizing" of loving, long-term relationships in such a way as to make possible erotic fiction and art, notably that of France and England.

My epigraph from Donne reflects the paradoxical synthesis of Augustine, who hated sensual sin but kissed his Maker with an intensely sensual verbal kiss. The period we now consider was both rigoristic and naturalistic. Marital law derived from the Christian Bible remained governant, and the considerable interpretive energy of canon law was applied to it with casuistical amplifications and revisions. Augustinian rigorism was of course present, but Christian naturalism became a liberating force, abetted by the Hebrew Bible. Consider the upsurge of interest in the Canticles, as exemplified by Bernard of Clairvaux, who takes the prize for devout and brilliant prolixity in expounding the Song of Songs: in some eighty-six eloquent sermons he managed to get through all of two chapters.[1] Ovid, whose widely popular *Heroides* added secular married couples to the pantheon of lovers, kept classical and mythic story alive and available as influences poured in from the pagan North and the Moslem South.

The achievements of medieval culture in England and on the Continent in religion, architecture, law, painting, poetry, mathematics, philosophy, and astronomy have long been celebrated. But the dynamics that wrought changes in marital and long-term heterosexual love, as distinct from the subjective and lyrical intensities of *fin'amors* (courtly love), has not been sufficiently analyzed or appreciated by the general student. Yet such dynamism is everywhere apparent. In Arthurian romance erotic force and unshakable *fides* united to energize chivalric adventure, making knight errantry and honor sometimes incorporate marital love stories. Bernard of Clairvaux, who celebrated male friendship with fine, even erotic, fervor, also hailed married love and celebrated "one home, one table, one bed, and even one flesh."[2] Among female mystics, an increasing number of whom had been married, erotic, marital, and maternal metaphors became vivid and frequent, not without strange and surprising inversions that made of Jesus a nurturing mother. The homosexual vs. heterosexual debate, which we have noted as developing from Plutarch through the Greek romances, reappears in the Middle Ages, and in one influential poem Helen is allowed a decisive victory over Ganymede, whom she insults vigorously as even the pagan gods banish what is now regarded as an ancient heresy and a pagan perversion.[3]

Christine de Pizan (1364–c. 1430), the only independently professional, full-time female writer of the period, who made her living by the manuscript and book trade, holds that the Sibyls were greater than Old Testament prophets and proudly establishes female rights within *her* New Jerusalem (a "cité des dames," a feminine utopia) as she has her Lady Rectitude denounce male injustice toward women and indulge in a rhetorically powerful form of affirmative action. But at the same time, while she totally rejects *amour fou,* she opts for romantic marriage, with, however, many surprisingly conventional elements. Perhaps not so incidentally, Christine had herself been happily married, was widowed at an early age, and did not remarry. She wants women to be fertile and reproductive, but always subject to their husbands, rejoicing over the good

FIGURE 10 Renaud de Montaubon, *Wedding Scene,* MS 8073 fol. 117v. (Bibliothèque Nationale/Bibliothèque de l'Arsenal, Paris.)

ones, dedicated to reclaiming the wicked. Girls should remain virginal until marriage, widows pious and patient, and women of all classes virtuous in lives that would refute the slanders of men against their sex. I deliberately choose Christine, writing after high medievalism, thinking humanistically, and openly repudiating much that is medieval, to show that great respect for wedded life with continuing conventions from the past remained strong amid striking change and could easily be accommodated to an avant-garde sensibility.[4]

Perhaps this was true partly because art had sometimes succeeded in imbuing romantic marriage and coupling not with simple sentimental illusion but with the attractive worldly qualities that appear in the great fifteenth-century painting by Renaud de Montaubon (fig. 10). Here we see personal sophistication, intelligence, and wealth, as several carefully differentiated but generally comely individuals and couples process with the bridal pair, a kind of knowing modesty evident between lovers (the men wittily attentive and the women ironically reserved) as they move in flexible formality toward the promise of sexual initiation and fulfillment on the prominently placed wedding bed. The date of the painting is late, but its urbanity and panache were the gradual achievements of the immediately preceding centuries.[5]

Courtly Love

For many in our day the essence of medieval love is illicit and is revealed in courtly love and in the stories of Heloise and Abelard and of Tristan and Isolde. But the love affairs portrayed or implied in each of these clusters bear important, though sometimes teasing, implications for our story of marital affection, even as they present alternatives to it. The historical reality that lay behind *fin'amors* may forever elude us, and the artistic reality of the lyrics that constitute the corpus (minuscule in comparison to the criticism and scholarship lavished upon it, from the sixteenth century to the present) is itself varied, ranging from the ideal to the real, with many gradations between and with considerable variety in the individual poetical styles.[6]

That variety gives some plausibility to each of the three main strains in present-day criticism of courtly love. To one group, the poetic "I" is central but exists only grammatically, the dynamics residing discursively in what Paul Zumthor has called the verbally structured and synchronic "ego-nunc-hic," though he admits that in some troubadours temporal linearity is present in the following chain: encounter-desire-quest-sadness-favor-joy.[7] No firm conclusions about poet, lady, love, sexuality, or indeed any topos (except to say that content and form tended to be literarily conservative) can be drawn, the poetic energy being circular and self-contained, the aim being to produce beautiful and memorable song. The manifest social and moral limitation that resides in poetry so viewed is that of narcissistic isolation, this being a mirror world where similarity is subjectively and reciprocally reflected and where tragedy arises, if at all, from not being able to get out of the circle of unfulfilled desire that never reaches its distant object.

Such an approach may be called the "aesthetic." It differs from the "religious," propounded by Peter Dronke, who finds that lyrical "gentilezza" springs from "inherent *virtù*" and that the cult of the excellent object, far from being immoral and heretical, places God continuously on the side of such love. It is by no means unique to *amour courtois:* idealizing responses to the radiantly noble beauty embodied in the lady are found in ancient Egypt, Islam, Mozarabic Spain, and Greek Italy. Mutual love exists in real life and does not die with the coming of old age. In courtly love so conceived it would be impossible if not profane to separate the physical from the spiritual, for they are united as firmly as in the idea of the Incarnation. Such a critical vision is congenial to much in the present study, with its emphasis upon spiritual sensualism, ranging from the Song of Songs through Augustine's *Confessions* to Bernard's sermons. But the tendency of this religio-critical orientation not to emphasize sexuality while acknowledging its presence mostly through metaphor does tend to make courtly love less than fully relevant to marriage.[8]

That deficiency is decisively avoided in the criticism and scholarship of Maurice Valency and Moshé Lazar, where the troubadours are conceived of as secularly and even antireligiously celebrating an extremely sensual love. Every poetic detail comes charged with erotic electricity, and the poetic ego longs to see the naked body of the beloved as she undresses, to contemplate it, and to be couched with it (the husband, the while, being *vilain, jaloux,* or *ennuyeux*). It is thus, according to this line of interpretation, that the poet achieves *cortesia*—through exploiting the defining and central aim of *jovens* (while of course observing due *mezura*).[9]

One of the troubadours (Jaufre Rudel) was particularly noted for celebrating *amor de lonh,* but there lurks in all of this lovely and intense poetry, even at its most sexually suggestive, something of the far-off, the unattainable, the celestial that does not make it congenial to the renewed contacts of intimacy. Its sense of distance carries with it a strong sense of the Other, but not of the near and reachable Otherness of domestic intimacy that we have found and will continue to find in some literature. Chaucer's turtledove, in the *Parliament of Fowls,* caught the essence of courtly striving: "Though that his lady everemore be straunge, / Yit lat hym serve hire ever, til he be ded" (584–85). This is not the kind of mutual love the medieval French called *amistie,* and one would have to say that the erotic ideal of the troubadours is closer to the unfulfilled longings and unconsummated desires of the Platonic Erōs than to anything the Middle Ages developed for marriage.

Does this bring us back to Andreas Capellanus and the countess of Champagne? Husbands and kinfolk, as E. William Monter has seen, could scarcely have been reassured by Andreas's permitting the kiss, the embrace, and modest contact with the naked body in extramarital love.[10] The church would certainly have agreed with the King of Love's principle 29, "Non solet amare quem nimia voluptatis abunduntia vexat" (a man who is vexed by too much passion usually does not love). But it must have resented what lies at the heart of the countess's strongly negative response to the question of whether true love can exist between married persons. She wanted free and mutual granting of desires, without constraint, without the motives of necessity, whereas "married people are in their duty bound to give in to each other's desires and deny themselves to each other in nothing." She is of course referring to the marital *debitum*, which the church following Paul had made the cornerstone of marital sexuality.[11]

These several reservations about the possibility of extending courtly love to long-term, committed intimacy tend not to make it paradigmatic for this study. But, typically, works of the imagination have a way of subverting critical categories, and we shall find considerable *cortesia* of one variety or another in marital romance. Marie de France, like Chrétien de Troyes, both criticizes and absorbs courtly love. In *Chevrefoil* she reverses the usual image of clinging female vine and sturdy, supporting male elm: recalling courtly female dominance, she makes the male honeysuckle entwine the female hazel. In *Laüstic* Marie imbues an illicit affair with the religiously suggestive imagery of a bird's body broken by a crude and jealous husband, now wrapped in cloth by the lady, and then carried by the lover in a reliquary (could this be intended to suggest a saint's relic?). These two images (from nature and religion) recall the courtly. But in *Guigemar* Marie shows that amorous passion, which is presented as neither cupidity nor charity, can achieve the enjoyable erotic *surplus* and also be elevated by mutual loyalty: far from producing death, it leads to a solid and unshakable union. It is as though Marie could go to the heart of erotic love and make it richly mutual; in her approved relationships, no one is clearly dominant, no one *dangereuse,* and she does not pussyfoot about consummation. She seemed to be able to take from courtly versions what could become ennobling, give it both religious and natural sanction, imbue it with solemn symbolic and imagistic power— and thus make it sacramental and indissoluble. In other words, she rescued *fin'amors* for marriage by radically revising it and transposing its elements. That very process may prove to be exemplary as we come in the next chapter to consider the longer fictions of marital romance.[12]

Heloise and Abelard

These famous lovers, unlike the poet and the lady of the Provençal lyrics, have left us a perhaps authentic body of letters that tell a real story and were written by two gifted but highly different people. The letters record a period of intense and varied sexual encounters, a marriage, a brutal castration, a continuing love, and sophisticated reflections about the affair at all its stages. The story, by virtue of its power of persisting through centuries from its period of origin so distant in time and cultural geography, has assumed the quality of myth. But we must remember that it is rooted in history and that its flowerings were nourished by the sap of contemporary thought and sensibility. Besides being a dramatic story in and of itself, its historicity makes it an invaluable guide to what lies behind the imaginative literatures of love.[13]

The sexual relations, besides being initiatory for both the older man and the young girl, may have run the gamut of broad erotic experimentation and by the admission of Abelard included the imposition of raw physical power. For the lover was not above administering blows to work his will on the beloved, and she was submissive even to the point of "wanton impurities," such as copulation in a hallowed place sacred to the Virgin and the concealing of her pregnancy in the habit of a nun. Over most of the actual lovemaking a veil has been drawn, but we do know that Abelard in orthodox fashion regarded his sexual fall as resulting from a pride and vanity bred by his success as scholar, teacher, and preacher. *He* refers to "persuasion," which he apparently used before he resorted to blows, but we do not know of what it consisted. *She* says he wrote her many letters (not extant, alas) during their "courtship." Did their copulations include wooing, the amorous *peithō* of classical tradition, the language of "Solomon's" song? The blows he delivered, he said, were intended to avert suspicion and were prompted by tender love and feeling. Was the teacher acting the role of a loving and punishing God even in his seductions? We can only speculate. But we do know that what began as instruction soon yielded to loving and kissing and that years after the event Heloise regarded his emotions as lustful not loving, as desire not affection—a view she says she shared with everyone else.

The marriage that followed was compounded mostly of inherited compulsions. She opposed it for conventional reasons: though permitted for a cleric of Abelard's rank, it would have betrayed the ideal she had of him, that of a philosopher or teacher set above ordinary human ties. She marshals classical and Christian objections to marriage for the especially elect, arising from its grinding domesticity, lack of privacy, multitudinous interferences with intellectual and spiritual work. In this respect, and also in her traditional misogyny, she is religiously conventional. But she can also boldly invoke the illicit: she would rather be mistress than wife, and in drawing a surprisingly frank classical parallel she says she would prefer being Abelard's whore to being Augustus's empress. She wants freedom from compulsion in loving her paragon, who had every grace of mind and body, making her the envy of queens and great ladies. She wants him for herself alone, without the restraints or sanctions of marriage—her love is single, obsessive, possessive, eternal, extramarital. And nothing can overcome her passion, not his castration, not his unavailability, not his theological arguments, not her administrative duties in a convent, and certainly not her vows, which were far from freely or religiously taken.

Heloise turns to ecclesiastical business, and Abelard becomes increasingly theological. His castration, although a monstrous crime, was sent by God to punish him in the very place in which he sinned, the seat of his lust—like Augustine's God punishing disobedience in Adam and Eve with irresistible spasms of sexual arousal. Abelard seems to agree with Heloise that what he felt for her was quite simply lust, never love. For her continuing passion he recommends the homeopathy of more passion, of passion displaced or sublimated—passion for her Lord and Savior. As overtly and unabashedly as his archenemy Bernard of Clairvaux or the unlettered mystic Margery Kempe, he invokes the imagery of Christian sensualism and applies it to her emotional condition: "you who have been led by the king of heaven himself into his chamber [must] rest in his embrace, and with the door always shut [be] wholly given up to him, . . . and more intimately joined to him." Abelard could be suggesting a literal marital tryst.

The real tragedy of this story may arise, as Paul Zumthor suggests, because the "passions of love remained at the margin of the conceptual universe, and therefore all the more tenacious—unconquered, deprived of both language [but Heloise gives love passion uncommonly eloquent language] and of that relative security which results from insertion in an order." But not all amorous doors were tightly shut in medieval culture, and it is therefore possible to feel that the pity of this story may lie in the fact that the lovers were not in touch with—or perhaps were born just a little too soon to be able to sense fully—the forces that were transforming thought and the church, forces that *were* in fact finding a place in both the divine and human order for disciplined sexual love. Heloise and Abelard admittedly may have loved a little too soon to have felt the full impact of literary and artistic love.

Cicero on friendship, to which Heloise appealed as a model to replace marriage, was of course well known. The Ovid of amorous rebelliousness, whom she seems to echo in her preferring the illicit to the licit in love, may not yet have been fully revised and applied in her culture, but Virgilian love was very soon to be. Barely forty years after the lovemaking of Heloise and Abelard, the romance *Eneas* appeared, in which a pagan, fruitless, and exclusively male *amicitia* is cruelly parodied and then absorbed and replaced by *amor;* in which the desertion of Dido is regarded as a tragedy not of sin but of deprivation leading to suicide; in which the founding of Rome is accomplished by a political union that is also a union of lovers mutually devoted. With such models before them, Heloise and Abelard might conceivably have been less bound to traditional forms. In any case, the heroine Lavine possesses a composure, a self-knowledge, and a reward in real life that many earlier heroines lacked—and that Heloise may well have appreciated but was herself not fated to attain.[14]

Tristan and Isolde

In this legend the fires of passion that flame intensely in the heart of the troubadour and that flared up for two years in the lives of Heloise and Abelard burn eternally, mutually, illicitly. How is its popularity to be explained in a Christian society aggressively opposed to adultery and still fearful of passionate excess in marriage itself? The paradox deepens if we remember that the lovers' bonding in many ways parallels and even parodies the sacramental union: it is sealed by a lifelong *fides* that adversity and suffering cannot break and that seems to survive even death itself. And thus it seems that the taint of blasphemy and idolatry can be added to illegality, for the beloved rivals Christ and the lover's devotion challenges the saint's. Research and speculation about origins in Arab Spain, in Celtic-Pictish cultures, in classical Ovidianism or other pagan persistences, or in Christian heresy in Asia Minor and Provence are not decisive historically and certainly bring no agreement about either etiology or meaning.[15]

The fact that a love like Tristan and Isolde's has held the cultural stage from at least the twelfth century through Wagner's romantic opera and up to present-day Hollywood, giving to the most popular literary genre of modern times, the novel, its transgressive cast and force, led Denis de Rougemont to a stunning interpretation that has dominated or challenged twentieth-century criticism of the story.[16] This Christian interpreter is a believer in fruitful, productive marriage; the centrality of the body; and the need for repeated and renewed consummations, all under the disciplines of public and religious controls and all propelled by the natural forces of life. But the story of Tristan and Isolde, de Rougemont continues, is heretical and mortally fateful, sounding the united chords of love and death, bearing the terrible and unmentionable secret we all need to know, that passionate *amour* brings inevitable suffering and is lethal. A love of love itself ("amare amabam," as Augustine said of his idolatrous pre-Christian days) is circular and unproductive, not given to full sexual enjoyment and ultimately destructive not only of self but of family and society. This secret knowledge does reside in our unconscious, but the myth brings it out, thus serving the useful function of telling us that marriage, which cannot be built on ardor however fine, is more serious than love. Unfortunately, "happy love has no history," de Rougemont concludes, and the great lesson must therefore come negatively, from our hidden enemy, passionate love, which has compulsively dominated the art and belles lettres of Europe and America for centuries. Where would modern Western literature be without adultery, and where would we be if we allowed it to establish our sexual norms?

There is much to be said for this arresting thesis, if only to remind us that interesting art requires obstacles to felicity and the conflict of opposing social and personal forces. De Rougemont may have been correct about adulterous art, but he is too dismissive about good love in art. Our survey of subsequent literature will show what is all too obvious to the layman, that the hindrances beloved of the literary creator inhere in the married as well as in any other human state and have been fully confronted by artists sympathetic to marriage.

De Rougemont is historically unsound in ignoring the social, religious, and political forces I have already alluded to and will display in greater detail presently. Nor does he disclose accurately the dynamics of the Tristan story itself, which is much closer than he suspects to the medieval Christian ethos. We may lay aside for our purposes those versions that regard the love as only magically induced, so reducing both moral responsibility and personal enhancement, or that portray the love unsympathetically, enforcing one obvious and frequently drawn moral, that faithlessness to lord and overseer and an impious challenge to marriage bonds will inevitably be punished by exile, wandering, and death. Let us instead consider decisive moments in those versions that are sympathetically told (artistically the richest and best, as it turns out), in order to determine what the story says about love and implies about marriage.

In versions sympathetic to romantic love, like those of the Anglo-Norman Thomas d'Angleterre and Gottfried von Strassburg, the drinking of the love potion by Tristan and Isolde on shipboard en route to the wedding, instead of by the bridal pair as intended, is preceded by sexual attraction and by an ever-growing sense of love and is immediately followed by the deepest sexual enjoyment and a sense of total union, come life or death, come joy or sorrow. In hearing the story of the unbreakable love that follows, we must not fail to note that Isolde and her mother (who prepared the drink) are healers, in touch with deep and salvific natural forces; that Ogrin the hermit is on the side of the lovers and opposes the anti-Tristan animus of courtly society; that Tristan's baronial enemies are unpleasant creatures; that in some versions Mark is a cad or villain; that when Isolde is put to the trial of applying hot iron to her proud flesh, she wins triumphantly and saintlike she gives her jewels and clothes to beggars; and that the common people, cherished by God, are on the side of the lovers. Malory, drily but fully recounting most of the details of the consuming passion, exalts it by making these lovers virtually the equals of Launcelot of the Lake and Queen Guinevere, viewing Tristan as one of the two greatest of the secular knights of the Round Table, second only to Launcelot himself, his chivalric exploits seemingly fueled by his love. And in artistically the greatest of the versions Gottfried stresses the musicianship of Tristan the harpist without reducing his heroism and seems to find society too gross to be worthy of the fully physical but refined, sophisticated, and complex love that his hero and heroine share, most intensely on shipboard and in the isolation of the *Minnegrotte*. In the love grotto the two experience soaring joy, unfettered by convention and deepened by art, a true anticipation of Wagner's piercing music. And that love in Gottfried is endowed with *Moraliteit* (resonating spirituality), which the sadly shallow and joyless marriage of Mark in no way possesses. Such are some of the exaltations that accompany the illicit passion.

But what in fact does the story say about marriage? Gottfried does portray a loyal, happy, and long-lasting marriage in the characters of Tristan's foster-father and his wife as an important foil to the leading characters' passion. But Mark and Isolde's, so badly riven by accident and faithlessness, can hardly be considered normative. Nor can Tristan's desperate recourse to the arms of Isolde of the White Hands, whom he has made his wife. In Thomas she alternates between unbelievable innocence and jealous mischief, but it is Malory who gives that strange, late, and brief union its most memorable, if naive, definition by saying that when Tristan goes to bed with Isode le Blaunche Maynes, he suddenly remembers Le Beale Isode: "he was all dismayed, and other chere made he none [but] with clyppinge [embracing] and kyssinge. As for [other] fleyshely lustys, sir Trystrames had never ado with hir." Malory then goes on to make it clear that the lady too had "no plesure but kyssinge and clipyyinge."[17] Only osculation and embracing, only foreplay and no consummation—it looks suspiciously like courtly, *stilnuovo,* or Petrarchan relationships with their incomplete, frustrated, or delayed affections.

But it is not so with Tristan and the first Isolde in the best versions, though one must concede that some modern students remain deeply unsympathetic to the lovers and wish to believe that Gottfried is ironic. The lovers' is the mixed and common lot of humanity—joy, sorrow, treachery, manipulation, and of course death—and that human condition is poignantly portrayed. One is almost tempted to say that in their devotion the marital ideal of faith, trust, and loyalty is as exalted and undying as in sacrament. Their love is not shadowed by guilt, only by adversity, and though the venue is not right, the mutuality is nevertheless full and deep, evocative of great art. So far from being transgressive in its richest retellings, the love of Tristan and Isolde is celebratory however difficult, and it moves not toward extinction by death but toward exaltation and transcendence. Amazingly, Wagner's masterpiece comes close to portraying its essence.

Let me propose the following as a possible historical explanation of this staggering paradox: so profoundly and potentially antinomian is the central Christian conception that God *is* love that when a society is committed to it and exalts it, the boundary between the licit and the illicit cannot be firmly drawn. Even the adultery of this famous pair, like the homoeroticism of many Christian brotherhoods, does not always stand outside the divine radiance, at least in high art and thought. We now turn to intellectual and social history to see if there is justification for this perspective on medieval culture, subversively romantic though it may at first seem (we shall return to it at the end of chapter 9).

The Lessons of Intellectual History

To get a proper conservative context for the changes in mentality that were arising and that we shall presently consider, let us try to imagine what the results might have been had King Mark and Queen Isolde on their wedding night partaken together, as intended, of the potion Tristan and the future bride had accidentally drunk on shipboard, ostensibly to assuage an ordinary physical thirst. The supposition is not entirely whimsical. It was surely to bind the bridal pair together that Isolde's queenly mother, skilled in herbs and healing, had brewed the mixture in the first place. And the orthodox can always argue that the painful passions, the endless anguish, and ultimately death itself, which after the actual drinking fatefully attended the love and the joy, came from locating the love outside marriage and not from the chemically induced love itself.

But what if the location had been the correct one? What if the wine had awakened eternal romantic love in the legally espoused royal pair? Would sex and sensibility then have supported the marriage vows in a pleasing and passionate union of *erōs* and *gamos*? Would the skepticism about marital love expressed by Andreas Capellanus and by Countess Marie de Champagne have been decisively answered? Certainly, the scholarly scales would be tipped against those who have argued or implied that love was not a legitimate aim in marriage during the Middle Ages, that marriage was judicial and political, and that the intellectual conjunction of Amor and Hymen did not come until the bourgeois mentality of the late seventeenth and eighteenth centuries provided a congenial climate or even until the humane goodwill or the sentimentality of twentieth-century religious reform penetrated ecclesiastical authority in Canterbury and Rome.

Had Mark and Isolde been united not only by marriage vows but by bodily, mental, and spiritual love eternally flaming, they would, despite their royal and fully sanctioned marital status, have run extremely grave risks, the risks of what Daniel Defoe many centuries later was to call "conjugal lewdness." For the sin of adultery did not lurk only in the neighbor's house or in a secluded orchard tryst but on the marital couch itself when, as Chaucer's Parson said quoting Jerome, the couple "take no reward in hire assemblynge but oonly to hire flesshly delit" ("Parson's Tale," 904). In high chivalry the results could be disastrous, as they were, temporarily at least, for Chrétien's Erec when Cupid exerted his full powers on the hero's nuptial life, causing him for a while to love his bride overmuch, making his wife Enide his paramour, and so losing interest in his chivalric exploits. *Mezura* required a fine balance between the marital and the martial, and conjugal love became mischievous or tragic—and so of course aroused the keen interest of the dramatic poet—when the balance was upset. Persisting Augustinianism (of the variety so vividly embodied in *De Nuptiis et concupiscentia*) could easily compromise marital privacy and freedom, and the voice of ecclesiastical authority must surely have echoed in the bedroom: Are the positions assumed in coition proper since *mulier super virum* degrades the active nature of man? Is the wife's a forbidden condition? Is this a forbidden day, time of the month, or place? For amusing and instructive collocations of coition and the calendar, see Boccaccio's racy story about the judge in Pisa (*Decameron,* tenth story of Second Day), James Brundage's amazing chart of proper and improper marital dates, and Jean-Louis Flandrin's calculations that marital coition could properly take place about forty-four times a year, or fewer than four times a month. Jacques Le Goff has said that medieval man was watched at all times and placed under a "double spy system" by angels and demons. We might add that the eye of him who neither slumbers nor sleeps remained wide open also in the Christian bedroom.[18]

I have mentioned degrading retrograde coital positions that could weaken the activity of the male. These could induce feared and detested passivity, a fear in part inherited from classical antiquity. Saint Methodius of Olympus, who died around 311, writing on Genesis 6:1–7, thought the Flood was caused when men and women exchanged their usual coital positions. Pope Gregory the Great in the late sixth century believed it was virtually impossible to escape pure from the conjugal embrace. Historians disagree about the etiology of this fear of marital carnal risk and about the reasons for its persistence, but there seems considerable unanimity in the opinion that marital love might well lead on to what Flandrin has called *paillardise,* a lustful idling away of time and of healthy energy. So if the potion had been drunk in the marital chamber by Mark and Isolde, at least one tradition still strong in the high Middle Ages might well have challenged and dissipated the bliss that would surely have ensued. Quite apart from historical reasons, this tradition has continued to have vitality for the very cogent reason that lust anywhere can reduce a desired human being to a mere object, as both Coleridge and the present pope have said, and can lead to an obsessive idolatry that compromises the soberer ends of being.

I have called the tradition I have just been discussing Augustinian, with a considerable simplification that will not remain unnoticed by anyone who remembers what that great thinker said about lovemaking in Eden or who has been exposed to the sensuality of his vocabulary in the *Confessions.* In any event the austerities just outlined were by no means the only formulations available to medieval culture, and the legalistic prohibitions were, expectedly, the least fructifying for writers and artists.

It is a commonplace of philosophical history that Aquinas revised the central orthodoxy of Augustine by adding a rich substratum of Aristotelian naturalism to his unwavering commitment to divine *nomos* and so considerably softened the harsh doctrine of pervasive original sin. But it has not been often enough appreciated that this naturalism affects his view of the marital state. An ascetic strain remains, to be sure. He makes procreation a primary aim of marital contact and sees too intense a love of the wife as "in a sense" adulterous, while the *mulier supra virum* position is said to be a sin worse than rape. Nothing effeminates a man more than the touchings and fondlings a wife seems to require, and remaining a virgin is better than being a chaste wife or widow.

But Aquinas assures us that sexual dangers in marriage need not in any way jeopardize the overarching requirements of *fides*. And invoking animal sexuality, he closely relates marital sexuality and marital friendship ("an inseparable union of minds"), much as Samuel Johnson did centuries later: the greatest friendship (maxima amicitia), says the scholastic, is that between man and wife; they are coupled not only by physical intercourse, "which even among animals conduces to a certain sweet friendship, but also for the sharing of domestic life." Saint Thomas's dialectic—arising from his 3,000 uses of *amor,* of which *amicitia* is always an ingredient at all levels—is at once coherent and comprehensive.[19] The unbroken and graduated scholastic chain of love (which is "absolutely stronger than hate") consists of: sexual impulse, lineage, community, mystery (sacrament). This chain is also a veritable chain of being, for love penetrates all sorts and conditions in humanity and nature.

Aquinas's respect for nature and his use of the animal analogy leads us to consider the power and pervasiveness of medieval Natura, both secular and religious, and of the "law of kynde" so greatly admired by Chaucer. Aldo Scaglione, in a comprehensive and illuminating survey, traces the frank sensualism of medieval thought and art to one of its climaxes in the *Decameron,* a work we shall discuss in the next chapter. And he makes an important qualification that is especially relevant to a culture so religiously based as the medieval: "In no civilization can a naturalistic view of life be thoroughly and fully consistent."[20] Even more specifically pertinent at this point is George Economou's disclosure of the two *earthly* Venuses in medieval thought, a terrestrialization of the Platonic tradition that opposed the heavenly to the natural Aphrodite. Now a good earthly Venus contrasts with the lascivious and lustful Venus ("of the earth earthy," to apply a phrase from the King James Version); the admirable though physically oriented goddess supports a human love whose credentials ultimately come from Eden and which manifests itself in relationships in harmony with nature and the divinely established laws of the universe. This Venus serves Natura, God's great viceregent, as indeed does John Gower's and Jean de Meung's Genius, that combination of natural reason, ingenuity, creativity, and procreativity—truly Natura's priest and minister.[21]

It is here that the naturalistic philosophers and poets belong. Bernard Silvestris celebrates a female spirit in nature, which produces *bios* (life) and *erōs* (sexual love), and consecrates physical union because it propagates a sacred mystery. Alan of Lille also exalts an earthly Cupid, carefully distinguished from the infernal one. For him too Natura is the *vicaria Dei,* who has as subvicar Venus, who in turn works with Hymen, her husband, and Cupid, her son, to renew the human species. In creating unity out of sexual difference, Hymen could be said to recall Boethius on *concordia discors* and to embody the Coleridgean critical and marital principle of reconciling opposites. To the traditional marital virtues of chastity, temperance, and humility, Alan adds one not often discussed, *largitas* (general radiance), a quality not unlike the Greek marital *charis*, which we have described earlier and whose gleam we have accused earlier Christian writers of dimming. And across the channel from the School of Chartres there towers the Chaucer of the *Parliament of Fowls,* for whom Natura is the *mater generationis,* closely related to the Chaucer of other wonderful springtimes with their birds, of Troilus and Criseyde making love, and even of that Idea, now usually regarded as pallid, called Emily in the "Knight's Tale."[22]

It is something of a social leap to move from so aristocratic a story as the "Knight's Tale" to the ambience of an unlettered, illegitimately born girl in the French village of Montaillou, lying in remote isolation in the foothills of the Pyrenees, where most of the households were conjugal. But the strain of naturalism that I am tracing deserves both aristocratic and humble exemplification. Grazide Lizier was called before the inquisitor at twenty-one years of age as a Catharist suspect and as former mistress (from the age of fourteen or fifteen) of a libertine and heterodox rector, an affair broken off before 1320. The powerful current I have been describing reached this village in the Midi and, despite the violent antinaturalism of the Catharist belief strong in the region, may have predisposed the girl's mother to permit the priest to lie with her daughter in the earlier years, mostly in the daytime. It may also have endowed the girl's husband with the same tolerance in the later years. What views about this relationship and about similar matters did Grazide herself have? She believed in paradise but not in hell, though she did not wish to argue the point, any more than she wished to defend her inability to believe in the Resurrection. God created good and useful things for men but did not create wolves, flies, mosquitoes, the devil, or indeed anything evil. It is more proper to lie with a husband than with a priestly lover, but nothing that gives joy is truly sinful if the joy is mutual. No one would claim close relevance or typicality for this humble, unlettered, and untormented Provençal Isolde, for who now could possibly disentangle the echoes of Catharist dualism from occasional hints of internalized orthodoxy (the orthodoxy that had come to frown upon the marriage of even fairly remote relations), as when the girl says she would never have encouraged the cleric had she known he was a cousin of her mother? Still, the unsophisticated trust in natural and shared pleasure that gives the girl a kind of guiding philosophy strikes me as being related to the very naturalism we have been confronting, though here in simplified and un-tutored form.[23]

Other miscellaneously chosen examples of how in the Middle Ages a powerful Natura extended love into venues usually considered illicit may further support the perspective on Tristan and Isolde presented earlier. In *Fulgentius metaforalis* John Ridewall sees Jupiter as the Greek Zeus (or life), who is also fire and love (what a contrast to Augustine's fulmina-tions against the licentious king of the gods!), and on this mythological refocusing he builds a cosmogony of love, which he moralizes into *caritas*. Similarly, in *Ovide moralisé* the poet assimilates Jupiter's amorous transformations into the likeness of human flesh to the Incarnation, and Semele's death is seen as a kind of spiritual intoxication impregnated with truly divine love. Modern scholarship has perceived that the univer-sal exaltation of love was congenial to making passionate friendship the subject of much clerical poetry, persuading Saint Bernard of Clairvaux and others like him of the erotic element in their feelings, and disposing Saint Aelred of Rievaulx to give to love between those of the same sex a sensitive and profound Christian expression.[24]

And Marie de France was able to imagine in *Eliduc* that a happily married wife should be able to yield a loving husband to her rival and successor, while continuing to love and respect him, knowing the plea-sures in store for the girl, and realizing fully the high cost of their depriva-tion. So the wife enters a religious house, where she is followed by the new couple after they have enjoyed many years of perfect marital love, which also expresses itself in charitable deeds. Thus love stretches in a continuous line from the couch of holy matrimony to the altar of God, and even carnal desires and acts do not obviate but instead help to en-courage what William Blake called the sublimest human act—setting another before you.

In a Christian age such dynamic crossing of boundaries will re-quire high theological sanction, which I shall try to evoke after con-sidering medical opinion, which is surely relevant to Natura. We have discussed the love philter that united Tristan and Isolde, and surely all medieval concoctions of fact and fiction have some connection with natural soil:

> O mickle is the powerful grace that lies
> In plants, herbs, stones, and their true qualities;
> For naught so vile that on the earth doth live
> But to the earth some special good doth give.

> (*Romeo and Juliet* 2.2)

Friar Lawrence's naturalism is essentially that of the high Middle Ages, somewhat intensified.

Medieval medical opinion, like so much else in these centuries, tends to look two ways. Like Galen and other ancient healers, the doctors and dietitians of the later period preached moderation in coition, since excess can enervate and so shorten life. At the same time, with respect to the female sex (thought to be erotically the more energetic, enjoying twice the pleasure the male is capable of), the medical writers try to understand and foster the woman's pleasure. For good reason, of course: in medieval medical opinion engendering could not take place without her climax, and a frustrated woman, seeking her pleasure elsewhere, might easily become a social threat. But for whatever reasons, contemporary physiology, as John F. Benton has seen, regarded the erotic appetites of both men and women as driving toward intercourse and fulfillment; it saw sexuality as a compelling natural force that made necessary contraceptive devices and antaphrodisiac concoctions. Benton may well be right in suggesting that under then existing regimens and prevailing thought it is difficult to think of medieval men and women as being just a little bit carnal—as tepidly libidinous, as living lives of diminished energy.[25] Prohibitive sanctions were doubtless strong, they had to be. There was much that needed to be controlled before *mesure et goût* could be attained. Many, including the present writer, have accused Denis de Rougemont, with his frequent invocations of Wagner, Freud, and contemporary film, of being hopelessly unhistorical and anachronistic; but when outside the covers of *Love in the Western World* he confesses his own faith, he reveals a basic assumption, which I believe must have lain behind virtually every serious manifestation of medieval love: "the only monism that does not contradict the reality of the person is precisely that of Love, for the very being of Love—its existence, its power, and its essence—ceaselessly recreates the nonillusory multiplicity of persons, and preserves it at the heart of Unity, in order to love it and be loved by it."[26] The statement stresses the persistence of individuality within an energy of pervasive and compelling unity—essentially the paradox of the human family (and the Trinity).

We shall return to individuality in discussing social and legal history and in considering literary masterpieces. Now I wish to emphasize the unifying energy and its omnipresence. There was not, I believe, any serious orthodox dissent from the view of Boethius that the love that binds the universe also binds married lovers in chaste love. Hugh of St. Victor in the twelfth century stresses the absolute centrality—and the exuberance—of love: ". . . love is everything to you; . . . love is your dwelling and your blessedness. Love God, therefore, choose God; run, seize, possess, enjoy." No one can deny the powerful Augustinian separation of *caritas* from *cupiditas,* nor do I now forget what I said earlier concerning the scruples that were enforced upon marital sexuality. But so pervasive and unifying an epicenter as the creative, energizing divine love does not always permit drawing fine casuistical distinctions between body and spirit, as the examples already given in this chapter have shown. And Hugh himself, though fully acknowledging the two antithetical strains of worldly and God-directed love, regards the originating spring as one only, believing love to be "a single movement of the heart," "of its nature one and single, yet . . . divided in its act."[27]

In addition to the energetic stream emanating from the Godhead, two conceptions from Christian thought tend, when freshly and broadly interpreted, to drive sexual love within marriage beyond its primary and obvious procreative purpose: (1) theology insists on the primacy and persistence of the body even through the changes wrought by death; (2) practical Christian theology demands reciprocal sexuality in marriage. Both concepts I have discussed earlier in connection with Paul; they now need to be refined and amplified only slightly to fit the high medieval context.

The tympanum of the west facade of Bourges Cathedral (thirteenth century) is often said to portray resurrected souls (figs. 11, 12). It would be more authentically Christian and medieval to refer to its subject as resurrected bodies, since bodies, with some marks of decay still on them, are presented as rising from the graves, clearly on their way not to undifferentiated, spiritual essence but to individualized, resurrected flesh. The artist is in full accord with Augustine, who said of spiritual bodies that "they will . . . be spiritual, not because they will cease to be bodies, but because they will have a life-giving spirit to sustain them" (*City of God* 13.22). And Bernard of Clairvaux is clearly following the Paul of 1 Corinthians 15 when he says, "it is necessary that our longing and our love begin in the flesh: . . . And it is necessary that we bear the image of the earthly self first, then of the heavenly" (necesse est vt cupiditas à carne incipiat: . . . Et prius necesse est portemus imaginem terrestris, deinde coelestis).[28]

We have already confessed ignorance about what specifically the payment of the marital debt might mean in the earliest Christian centuries, and we have seen that the countess of Champagne made marriage ineligible for true love because its sexual favors could be traded in a kind of bedside marketplace. The Wife of Bath, whom we shall later interrogate, will throw some light on the matter, but much still remains dark.

FIGURE 11 Bourges Cathedral, west façade, central portal, thirteenth century.
(Giraudon/Art Resource, NY.)

FIGURE 12   Detail of figure 11: Resurrected Bodies. (Musée des Monuments Français, Paris, from plaster copy/Art Resource, NY.)

Did it, for example, permit only this kind of demand: I want a child, let's go to it? Could a partner sensing he or she was about to be aggrieved demand that relief be afforded at home to prevent sin abroad? Might the potential aggriever wish to obviate an oncoming sin and so make a demand for sexual payment? To the last question Albertus Magnus may have given a theoretical answer, when he says that if one partner discovers the lust to sin in the other even if not expressed or revealed explicitly, it would be wise to assume that he or she was being asked to pay the marital debt.[29]

It was not only medicine, biblical theology, and practical ethics that witnessed to the preoccupation with sex in marriage; religious mystics, especially women, internalized, subtilized, applied to their own lives, and brought to sharp and vivid focus the sexually tinged marital imagery of Holy Scripture. In defining the Christian virgin as a bride destined for a higher consummation, Caroline Bynum says, "she scintillated with fertility and power." And Bynum's many examples enforce the justness of her metaphor. Even on the paten and in the chalice Jesus might appear as a baby, as a bleeding and dying man, or, more pertinently to us here, as a glorious youth. To Mary of Oignies her beloved Lord revealed himself sometimes as a child, sometimes as a taste of honey, sometimes as a sweet smell, and "sometimes in the pure and gorgeously embellished marriage bed of the heart." Hadewijch, the Flemish mystic and poet, records her encounters with Christ as being mouth on mouth, body on body, "in language that seems to report the experience of orgasm." We shall return to such imagery in analyzing Margery Kempe in the next chapter.[30]

The mystics often suffered in their ecstasies, such sufferings effectually removing them from purely sentimental excess. Even as they honor the marriage bond, the metaphors of some of them reveal either that they are experienced and realistic about the vicissitudes and tortures of prolonged love (as was Margery Kempe) or that religious confinement at an early age could breed a festering eros. Thus marriage, when metaphorical, apparently does not obviate but rather intensifies and, realistically viewed, deepens erotic mysticism. All this is possible because Christians have not exclusively or always followed the Pauline injunction, "Walk not after the flesh but after the spirit": they do not always or indeed frequently make a dualistic separation of body from contemplative mind. Flesh and spirit stand on a continuum of interacting and related forces. Thus even fasting is not an escape from but a flight into the body. To return to the love of Heloise and Abelard, we now know that the tomb that housed both their remains was reverenced by their contemporaries as witnessing to their loving union on earth; it was also regarded as a seedbed for heavenly fulfillment. In a wonderfully revealing letter to Heloise after Abelard's death, Peter the Venerable consoles her with these words: "God fosters him, my venerable dear sister in the Lord— him to whom you have been attached, first in carnal union, then in the stronger, higher bond of divine love [Peter apparently does not know or chooses to ignore how weak Heloise regarded that bond to be]; under whom you have long served the Lord—God fosters him, I say, in your place, as your other self, in his bosom; and keeps him to be restored to you, by his grace, at God's trumpet call."[31]

The Lessons of Social History

Historians tell us what it is very important for literary critics of medieval culture to know—that in contrast to the domestic situation prevailing in the ancient world the medieval family was commensurable and comparable all across society. The ancients lacked a concept of the family as a moral unity common to all social levels, but from the seventh and eighth centuries A.D. the family could serve as the standard unit of the census. For tax purposes censuses counted hearths, not heads or houses or even heads of households. And the extraordinary Florentine *catasto* of 1428 reveals a family size fairly typical of Western Europe, an average of 4.42 persons per hearth; small to moderate-sized households seem to have been the medieval norm. The nuclear family was clearly in place, with the couple at its center and the marital bed symbolically honored as one of the most cherished of possessions in an age that dearly loved domestic goods and objects.[32]

The creative legalistic outburst within canon law of doctrinal definitions and speculations, a development that took place during the twelfth and thirteenth centuries and has been intensively studied in our day, is rich in marital-sexual details, but it does not come close to exhausting a reality that is an intricate and bewildering maze.[33] Fortunately, two basic models for the medieval family, one lay and the other clerical, help clarify the situation, though there is considerable overlap between the two. Perhaps a profile of each may be helpful, though inevitable simplification must be acknowledged. The lay configuration is the earlier, predominating from the collapse of Roman power well into the period of Charlemagne. The later clerical ideal was born in Carolingian times and ultimately became powerful and regulative, with enormous consequences for high medieval and later societies, reaching its apogee in the papacy of Alexander III (1159–81).

In the time of lay dominance, a time of considerable brutalization when church and state alike were weak, a decisively empowered male was in full charge, and feudal marriage was in some respects highly private and autonomous. It served the ambitions of the wealthy family through dowry or bride-gift, inheritance, the extension of property, and systems of interfamily alliance. The Roman city having been eclipsed by the countryside, urbanity in some places collapsed almost completely. Rural indulgence in food, unregulated by genteel custom or sophisticated hygienics, may have been related to abundant attempts at procreations in order to overcome high mortality rates, to frequent adulterous sexual relations (a Burgundian law referred to the "stench of adultery"), to little positive use of the word *amor,* and to a pervasive ravaging by physical passion, which could therefore be officially regarded as unreasonable and consumingly destructive.[34] Contemporary penitentials put three sins at the top, fornication, acts of violence, and perjury; and fornication, which headed the list, referred to sexual sins of all manner and degree. When sexual impulses were regulated, it was usually in the exclusive interest of patrimony; and since monogamy was not universally required, one could encounter segments of rich and privileged society where no blame attached to polygamy. Since great powers were accorded the autonomous family itself, it is not surprising that there was a strong tendency toward endogamy.

In another sense the earlier feudal family was anything but private. Marriage was not supposed to be clandestine, and its celebration was notably public. The marital *pactum* was too important to be created by the individuals concerned; instead, it was forged by the two men who headed the two families involved. Negotiations resembled statecraft on a smaller scale, but it would be a mistake to think that all was coldly ambitious or male-serving in the largely secular if not outright pagan family. Germany continued to enjoy the reputation Tacitus had given it in antiquity of treating its women rather better than its neighbors did; in old Irish society descent through the woman was very important; Wales, if we can judge by the saints' lives, gave unaccustomed honor to women and to marital and familial affection.

The clerical model, though it moved in different directions from the lay and ultimately triumphed after years of fierce confrontation, was itself divided and confusing. This arose in part no doubt because it inherited the austere prohibitions from the Gospels and the epistles of Paul, rigid flesh-spirit dualism from Augustine, and fear of sex even within marriage from countless patristic sources. The requirement of the marital *debitum* and the conception of marriage as a bulwark against fleshly sin remained central. Procreation lost something of its primacy and prestige as a reason for marriage and became more nuanced and adaptive; but it was still in force, for God continued to need denizens of heaven to replace the fallen angels. Marital *fides* was deeply honored, and adultery was regarded with fear and contempt and sometimes strictly punished by church and community.

But strikingly new, even revolutionary, ideas were being introduced by the medieval church as it moved into the twelfth century and beyond. Exogamy, supported by an almost neurotic clerical fear of excessive closeness of degree in marriage, tended to push young founders of families outside their wonted bounds of neighborhood and sometimes even class. It is not often enough realized what a profound opportunity for adventure, travel, conflict, and the fermentation of unwonted ideas and habits this new emphasis provided, with incalculably enriching results for the imaginative arts. But it was the new sanctioning of free, secret, and sexually fueled choice and the privileging of love and therefore personal beauty that constituted the most significant steps toward freedom of choice and enhancement of individual taste and desire.

Consensus facit nuptias had been a principle of Roman and early canonical law, and the church was therefore not fully innovative in resurrecting it in its struggle against secular feudal familial authority. Still, the results are astonishing, and they may have been unexpected even by the ecclesiastical hierarchy. The church wanted a union of hearts as well as hearths, and so private mutual vows and promises with or without consummation were understood to constitute a valid marriage, and the *desponsatio* (betrothal) became more important than the final ceremony. (The church of course preferred the fully licit to the merely valid marriage, the licit being attested by financial arrangements, betrothals, public banns, exchange of consent at the church door, delivery of the bride to the husband by the father, the exchange of rings, and the bridal mass in the church edifice.) Not only was the consent of both spouses absolutely necessary but in time, as Michael Sheehan has said, "the consent of no other person was required," with the result that "medieval society had developed a theory of matrimony that enabled the individual to escape the control of the family, the feudal lord, and even the king in the choice of a marriage partner."[35] Consent was regarded as so binding that it was given first priority: if necessary it could require a divorce between a man and a woman solemnly married in church if one of them had earlier joined in a bona fide mutual marital promise with another. The new legalities not only confirmed the old tradition of male-female equality at the nuptial bed when exercising the marital debt; they now established equality in the very promissory stages of union (clerics considered the woman as a "*consors* de plein droit" [a consort with full rights]), and these included the right of refusal, as much art and literature demonstrates.[36] There was a recognized place, a real category of life if not of canonical beatitude, for the loving and beloved married woman, though it may have been a median one—between the prostitute or adulteress (the despised woman) and the nun or the Virgin (the idealized love object).

Clandestine marriages figure centrally in Gottfried's *Tristan,* in

Aucassin et Nicolette, and perhaps also in Chaucer's *Troilus.* Since some canonical schools required consummation to bind the couple into indissoluble legality, though some did not, it is clear that sexual attraction was honored, which in effect means that beauty of body was privileged, another revision of primitive Christian rhetoric, perhaps providing an additional reason why artistic efflorescence accompanied churchly liberalization. In fact, Peter Lombard is quite explicit in interpreting common consent as being closely related to the beauty of man and woman alike, which enflames the heart and moves the desire toward consummation. It is not by chance that love at first sight becomes for centuries a sanctioned norm in much romantic Christian literature. It may even be possible to regard the church in its reformatory moves as in effect opting for something like the passion of Tristan and the first Isolde and decrying the unconsummated fondlings of Tristan's marriage to Isolde of the White Hands and the historical *mariage blanc* of Henry II and Cunégonde in the eleventh century, in which she retained her virginity all through marriage and was popularly revered for it.

Augustine had recognized the importance of friendship in marriage, particularly to couples who had piously renounced *cupiditas* for *caritas.* Maternity was of course regarded as a high expression of Christian charity, and the Virgin herself was the exemplar. But the new religious ethos that stressed *maritalis affectio* seems to have gone beyond both maternal love and Augustinian *amicitia.*[37] Innumerable treatises emanated from religious houses showing that marital affection was considered an essential component of marriage, particularly when marriage is being used as an analogy for divine or mystical love: commentaries on God's love, on energetic love within the Trinity itself, on the Song of Songs; poems, letters, *miracula, exempla,* hagiographies; as well as disputes on canon law and records of actual marriage cases. We should note that the very rhetoric used in proclaiming marital love was strong. Deny le Chartreux said that man and wife should love each other with a love "multiple, special, cordial." Ecclesiastical authority "quizzed the family strenuously on whether love existed between the couple" (inquirit de parentela fortiter, si est amor inter illos).[38]

Ekbert de Schönau (d. 1184) stressed *unitas mentium* (unity of minds) between spouses, and this phrase, recalling Aristotle's highest ideal of friendship, leads us to ask whether the marital love envisaged rose to such heights, or whether it meant humble service and obedience only, of the kind that bade a spouse follow an afflicted partner to a leper colony. The powerful marital imagery of the mystics does not answer our question, for it too could imply submission and not mental sharing, and the forms of domestic address, *mon seigneur* (my lord) and *ma par* (my equal), seem to point to both hierarchy and equality.[39] Still, some of the canonical decretists, following Gratian's *Decretum* (completed in 1140), did argue that the joining of bodies be accompanied by a joining of souls in solid friendship (firma amicitia), and Huguccio, though he attacked Gratian on other points, said that matrimony did not exist unless there was a union of souls (matrimonium non est nisi coniunctio animorum).[40]

Such at least was the ideal, embodied in the powerfully realistic and startlingly animated row of dignified married couples (Hermann and Regelindis, Ekkehard and Uta, among others) portrayed in the west choir of Naumburg Cathedral around 1240 (figs. 13–15). Each person is individualized in face and form, and the dynamics of the art suggests the equality of the sexes in stature, attractive physical endowment, moral worth. It also suggests that each couple is tied together in bonds of truly endearing unity. That ideal finds expression in the writings of two articulate popes, a lofty norm toward which an institution that possessed powerful sanctions was trying to push the society it led spiritually. Both art and life reveal that the vision was not fully realized. Only a totally unreconstructed sentimentalist could believe otherwise. But the ideal pattern had its effects, and these appear with revelatory power in images that adorn all aspects of medieval life and art. Let us cast our minds back to the somewhat cold and remote urban architecture and ambience of "John's" New Jerusalem in the Book of Revelation, with its squared geometrical space, its dazzling white light, and its hierarchical arrangements. The medieval mystics conceived of heaven as a great white house, often an eroticized house, which they superimposed on the *urbs* of the Apocalypse. It may not be easy for us to know what the white house of the mystics really looked like, but historians of private space tell us that we must abandon our image of the medieval castle as a place of sadness and terror, and think instead of richly dressed people in gleaming roseate candlelight filtered through silk hangings as they proceed to a sumptuous repast. Gold, silver, music suggest dreamlike images, to be sure, but we are assured that these do not in fact constitute a dream; they are "an amplification of what we can detect on the fragments of 'positive' evidence, which permits us to conjure up images of a strange yet familiar feast."[41]

Georges Duby, in surveying the Christianization of marriage that began in the Frankish church under Louis the Pious and culminated in the

FIGURE 13 Naumburg Cathedral, west choir, south wall, Married Couples, c. 1240. (Foto Marburg/Art Resource, NY.)

FIGURE 14 Naumburg Cathedral, detail of west choir: Hermann and
Regelindis. (Foto Marburg/Art Resource, NY.)

FIGURE 15 Naumburg Cathedral, west choir, north wall, Ekkehard and Uta.
(Foto Marburg/Art Resource, NY.)

twelfth and thirteenth centuries, sighs at one point and says: we do not know if love had anything to do with this development and no one ever will. "About the passions that moved body or spirit I can say nothing."[42] But Chrétien de Troyes, Boccaccio, Chaucer, Malory, and many others can and do, and it is to them that we turn in the next chapter.

The only metaphor for agapē *is* amor.
  J. B. Broadbent (1964)

French poets, in the eleventh century, discovered or invented, or were the first to express, that romantic species of passion which the English poets were still writing about in the nineteenth. They effected a change which has left no corner of our ethics, our imagination, or our daily life untouched, and they erected impassable barriers between us and the classical past or the Oriental present. Compared with this revolution, the Renaissance is a mere ripple on the surface of literature.
  C. S. Lewis, *The Allegory of Love* (1936)

The High Middle Ages (II):
Imagining Long-Term Love

*f Johan Huizinga is right that in no other period did the ideal of civilization so closely amalgamate with the ideal of love as in the high Middle Ages,[1] then it should be no abrupt transition from the social and intellectual history summarized in the last chapter to the literature to be analyzed in this. The close relationship that unites the history of love and of the art that celebrates it is reflected in the coincidence of views between the historian and the literary critic I shall now cite. Michael Sheehan regards the consequences of the new theory of matrimony that permitted escape from the control of family, feudal lord, and even king in the choice of a married partner as "immense"; after much ebb and flow the tendency was toward "the individual's freedom" and "an astonishingly individualistic attitude to marriage and its problems."[2] And Robert Hanning sees individualism as strikingly present also in literary love, notably in chivalric romances, where affection tends to concentrate on one person who is singled out from all others—a literary situation that "emblazons the fact of radical individuality in acknowledging love's dominance." But the "exploration of individuality that animates the romances" comes not from fulfillment in passionate love alone but from its association with the public pursuit of honor through prowess.[3]

As it has done immemorially out if its own nature, the artistic imagination thus carries over into its own creations the stimuli it has received from life and thought. Perhaps more intimate, however, than the relationship between history and belles lettres is the closeness of metaphor between the religious mysticism we have already confronted, particularly that of women, and the imaginative works we shall now consider. Both the religious and the literary drew on the long tradition of biblical eroticism we have earlier displayed, but this difference appears between the two: In the religious the imagination tends ultimately to resolve everything in the putative satisfactions of a heaven in which a kindly God will wipe away every tear from every eye; the literary, usually earth-bound, comes to more precarious resolutions achieved only after many vicissitudes. But still, even in the chancier world of letters, final resolutions suggest some kind of fulfillment of early attraction in an improved and enriched relationship (usually the matrimonial), even when the event is tragic. In literature such enhancement of love is bestowed persuasively only after obstacles have been overcome and hindrances transcended or removed. Love from afar (the famous courtly *amor de lonh* we have commented on) provides rich opportunities for romantic complication, and the best romantic art is never cheaply sentimental.

It follows that imaginative works were often paradoxical combinations of the ideal and the grimly realistic. In a preliminary way the visual arts can provide us with an introduction to the coexistence of the lofty and the lowly in various combinations. Religious art sometimes further heightened the already exalted by bringing together figures who were usually treated separately: thus familial values were enhanced when the Virgin and St. John were brought together as mother and son. Feelings of intimate love could be intensified and elevated when a married couple commissioned paintings of themselves and their offspring for their own private devotions, paintings that might retain the homely details of bourgeois life. The same visual image could be at once moralistic and sexually frank. Thus a dog represented either fidelity or sensuality; red was the color of sexual love and of the Crucifixion; long hair could symbolize virginity or prostitution; a unicorn emblematized chastity but its horn was phallic, as when a woman cradled it on her lap. Rabbits and mandrakes symbolized fertility but so did the act of urination.[4]

In the literature I shall now consider (first of the Continent, especially France and Italy, and then of England) such ideal-real juxtapositions will appear frequently, along with the time-honored oxymorons love seems always to produce. That literature will also serve a much more important and pertinent aim: it will bring into new perspective the epoch-making developments recorded by the social and intellectual history we surveyed in chapter 8, and at its best it will also do what the imagination has always claimed the license to try to do, bring new worlds into being.

Chrétien de Troyes

As the greatest romancer of medieval marital love, Chrétien had imaginatively absorbed the Christianization of marriage, and his fictions gladly and naturally embody the mutually romantic marriage of consent and choice, while remaining realistic about the dangers inherent in any human condition and fully aware of the importance of political, social, and religious contexts for domestic affection. Of the three paradigmatic loves earlier discussed (the courtly, that of Tristan and Isolde, and that of Heloise and Abelard), he with a full consciousness adapted the first two to his artistic purposes. He applied to matrimony his own carefully thought-out version of the courtly ideal, and he was a cogent critic and reviser of the Tristan legend. None of his romances more fully establishes his credentials than his first full-length extant work, *Erec et Enide.*[5]

Before meeting Enide, Erec was already a respected and beloved knight of the Arthurian circle, courteous to ladies and mighty in chivalric prowess. Soon after the romance opens he meets Enide, who surpasses him in dramatic interest, though he too remains at the center of our fascinated attention. In their initial meeting we see Natura at work and are reminded that Alan of Lille and the School of Chartres are exerting their romantic, sensual influence. The girl is plainly clothed, for she is the daughter of a *vavasseur* (the vassal of a noble but not of a king) and so in no way the social equal of the future king she loves at first sight. But her beauty and courtesy shine through the simple dress, and at once a magnetic mutuality that must be called both bodily and acculturated seizes them. In very short course a splendid wedding takes place, bride and groom having won the accolades of noble and commoner alike and received the full support of the loving family from which she springs, which, as it turns out, is of high lineage on the mother's side. Chrétien goes out of his way to praise the family love, which explains the tenderness of the girl's farewell to her parents: "Such is love [*amors;* notice that this love word is not confined to the couple], such is nature [Natura sanctions family as well as sexual love], such is the pity [an obsessive word in courtly love here transferred to upbringing] of her upbringing" (lines 1451–52). The romantic beginnings display unalloyed attraction and radiance, but not without a touch of the selfishly ambitious in Enide: when she first laid eyes on Erec, she knew that he would be a king and she a queen.

The first real crisis of the romance arises in the marriage itself. These evenly matched and extraordinarily beautiful bodies—it is impossible to say which is superior—are also one in spirit, wisdom, courtliness, nobility ("d'une meniere, / d'unes mors et d'une matiere," lines 1495–96). But now the sexuality, for which the beauty is here as elsewhere a euphemism, takes over; after a most delicate rendition of the bridal-night deflowering when she became a new woman ("ot perdu le non de pucele; / au matin fu dame novele," lines 2069–70), Chrétien makes clear how in the first phase of marriage his hero committed the sin of loving his paragon overmuch, having no delight other than her body, arising long past noon, neglecting his chivalric occupation, and thus arousing scorn and contempt. It is given to Enide to reveal to him his own true state and his diminished reputation, producing in him simultaneous dismay and gratitude and in her what is, for a modern at least, her first clear fault, excessive abjectness and self-censure.

Erec is now aroused to crisp decisiveness: off they must go together for adventure, but under the strictest discipline, for she must remain silent even when mortal danger threatens. No Griselda, she of course does not obey when his life is at stake. Though troubled by having to disobey, she alerts him, arouses his anger, each time promises future silence—but continues to take the humane and sensible course.

At one point he approaches death so closely that Enide believes he has in fact succumbed. In this supreme trial, in addition to continuing her defiance of her husband's command, she shows the ability to manage a ruse: encountering a passionate male, she is willing to make use of her sex appeal, which we know to be considerable: "She well knew how by words to arouse a scoundrel when she gave the matter her attention" ("Bien sot par parole enivrer / bricon, des qu'ele i met s'antante," lines 3380–81). At the nadir of her trials, when she thinks her husband dead[6] and when she is forced into marriage with a villainous count, who strikes her, Chrétien portrays a hideous parody of the true marriage of Erec and Enide that is now being so sorely tried: the count treats Enide like a chattel and proclaims loudly that she is his and that he will do with her what he will, striking her again when she says she can never be his. Erec of course comes to life again and dispatches the villain; invoking the Song of Songs, he calls Enide his sweet sister ("ma dolce suer," line 4872), and announces the end of the test. Reversing their roles completely, he now wants to be entirely at her command, thus striving to domesticate and so prolong premarital courtesy. During Erec's years at Arthur's court and after his assumption of the throne of his father, Chrétien demonstrates that marital *fin'amors* could coexist with chivalry and governance.

Wherein lies the cultural force of this marriage? Certainly in Chrétien's direct refutation of Andreas Capellanus's contention that romantic love could not exist in marriage. But some traditional *données* remain and are enforced strongly, husbandly dominance being the most prominent. The new consensual marriage, conceived of as virtually a *pactum inter aequales,* could of course not ignore the clear Pauline command that the husband must be the head of the wife as Christ was the head of the church. The inherent contradiction was stubborn and problematical: it agitated Chaucer in his marriage group within the *Canterbury Tales*. Clearly a working dialectic had to be formed. One solution goes back to Xenophon, that the man rules outside the home, the woman in it; but this is much too simple—and of course déclassé—for Chrétien. Sexual attraction, absolutely necessary in beginning and grounding a relationship, must never at any stage be allowed to weaken the man's political, military, and social duties and skills. But in these the wife also can and must take a part, for Chrétien gives to Enide a real presence on the field of adventure, where she is often more strategically perceptive if not more courageous than Erec. Moreover, he gives her a will independent of her husband's, for she often disobeys him and employs her own wits to win the greater good of his life and their common safety. Romance does not obviate calculation, what I have earlier called the ego context of love, and ecstasy joins with the new sanctions of church and society to support the coming together of heterosexual equals.

In *Cligès* Chrétien gives us one of the most arresting of the many medieval unions of the ideal and the real. The real he extends daringly through long stretches of narrative time and makes it challenge the courtly elements he weaves poetically into the domestic bliss. The story is presented in two parts, in which the loves of two generations of spouses are played out against combats of a fierce and cruel kind. Moshé Lazar says of these two narrative parts, "One describes, the other polemizes."[7] The differences between the parts should perhaps be described somewhat less literarily and rhetorically and should be seen more deeply and subtly as the social and personal revelations of the characters themselves. The story of the first generation is relatively simple, the *fin'amors* fully obvious though it is cautiously and indirectly elaborated. In this first part a love potion (though none exists literally) must surely have been symbolically drunk by the marital pair, for the romantic affection that is maritally sustained after the initiating eye contact is deep, binding, physically satisfying—and in its verbal expression a bit tiresome. Has Chrétien added a dash of satiric salt that shows him somewhat more revisionary of courtly love here than he had been in *Erec et Enide?* Arthur's queen may be his raisonneuse when she urges the lovers to cease killing themselves by secrecy and to get honorably married so that a social framework might stabilize what could otherwise be volatile and evaporative.

The second-generation passion, in which the son of the first married lovers is the title character, flames in equal intensity, but the love is streaked with irony and qualification, showing, if nothing else, that the author has "problematized" the affair—that is, wrestled with it, ethicized it, and perhaps himself been a bit dismayed by the intensity of the intimacy.

It is not necessary to consider all of the fifteen or so recollections of the Tristan legend that are present in *Cligès*. In the first-generation affair the illicit love of the precursor work was transformed by changing its venue to marriage, where it burns on with undiminished heat. But in part 2 the love is presented as a complex and radical revision of the Tristan text. That revision appears starkly because the amorous situation is in structure precisely that of the famous trio in Cornwall: the hero Cligès passionately loves and is passionately loved by Fénice, the heroine, who through much of the story is married to her lover's uncle. And love philters play a role to solve crucial problems in the plot. Though the lovers come to feel that somehow Fénice must escape her unhappy marriage, she rejects Cligès's proposal of elopement as vigorously as Jane Eyre disdains Rochester's, turning instead for a solution to the herbal juices her skillful attendant can prepare. And so she "dies," is buried, is resurrected, and ends up in what one can only in honesty call a passion pit. The joys of that kind of secret place will of course exact a dear price, and Chrétien subjects the beloved to torture before the ruse of her "death" and subjects both of them to harrowing discovery afterwards, perhaps in flagrante delicto. Now the old husband conveniently dies of rage and madness, the lovers marry, and putatively the story ends happily.

But before the happy denouement, the love in its time of secrecy comes close to idolatry, and its furtive obsessiveness keeps the lovers from human society. It may be significant that the romantic marriage that follows the long romantic liaison, unlike the earlier marriage of part 1, produces no children. Romantic love is left without heir or successor. And yet it is honored, as the church honored clandestine commitments honestly made. Compared to the warm and lifelong *fides* of the romantic passion, the "official" royal marriage that binds a burning girl to a foolish ruler is a sham of cold arrangement and vividly illustrates the incompatibility of young and old, later to become the topos of the *couple mal assorti*. And thus there are after all some positive parallels between Cligès-Fénice and Tristan-Isolde. If, as I argued in the previous chapter, even the faithful though adulterous pair could be thought of as standing within the divine radiance, the lovers of this story must be seen as kindled by it. We should not be surprised that they are rewarded with holy matrimony after merited sufferings. Under the newer ethos they had been spiritually, though not literally, married all along.

The potion used to produce Fénice's death-in-life does not so much recall Tristan and Isolde—to say nothing of burials and resurrections in Greek romance—as it anticipates *Romeo and Juliet*. But another potion in *Cligès,* more important and problematical, not only recalls the Cornwall story but in its tortuously suggestive way actualizes the supposition I proposed in discussing the Tristan legend earlier—what if King Mark had drunk the potion as intended? Here the royal husband, Alis the emperor, does imbibe his draught nightly, but what a difference there is between his drink and Isolde's mother's Irish concoction! This one is an illusion-creating potion (could Chrétien be suggesting that Isolde's was also, though in a vastly different way?), prepared by the wife's maid, who is described as mistress of the black art of necromancy. The husband relishes it, since it makes him dream that he achieves, nightly, full and uninhibited delight in his wife's arms. All the while she remains a *virgo intacta* against the day when her true lover can perform the rites of defloration in holy matrimony. No need here for a Brangain or a bed trick. The wife rejects by name the illicit ways of Tristan and Isolde and by magic can keep her coeur and her corps unitedly intact for the lover, to whom the plot in its own good time will deliver her. We are surely intended to admire the fortitude, the persistence, the unwavering demand for free choice, and the religious idealism of the beloved—all highly consonant with the churchly model of wedlock discussed in chapter 8.

But poor old Alis does not easily slide out of mind. This uncle-husband-emperor did, to be sure, violate a promise never to marry in order to keep the throne open for his nephew, and so caused the sufferings of the true but frustrated lovers. It may measure the author's commitment to romantic marital affection that the human obstacle to it is so unrelentingly and ironically reduced to ridicule. *This* January suffers the indignity of being "deceived" by a pure and virginal wife, while he nightly dreams his blissful dreams. Illusion was not taken lightly in the Christian centuries; Bede reports that Pope Gregory forbade the first archbishop of Canterbury to allow the administration of the sacrament after sexual illusion in a dream. So the husband here was not only deceived in life but may have been damned to boot.

What, then, do we have in *Cligès?* Perhaps a finally unsuccessful poem with too many literary and intellectual loose ends. Certainly a picture in its first part of an ideal marriage in which *fin'amors* is fully reconciled with marriage. But what compels attention today, and what greatly interests a student of marital affection in its Western continuities, is that the author, after allowing only one generation to pass, shows how reality tortures the original, uncluttered ideal into daily complexity and evasiveness. The paradoxical and deconstructing duality of this diptych, in which an early ideality becomes ambivalent and even grotesque while remaining devoted love, is highly typical of love in the Western world. Still, though Chrétien may buffet the ideal and wrench it out of shape, he does not abandon it. If we use the flexible canons of Romantic or even modern criticism, the romance seems to rise to the status of a multilayered symbol of extensive suggestibility whose force can be appreciated in radically differing cultures.

We shall return to Chrétien's *Lancelot* when we come to Malory, and it would be pleasant also to analyze the rich mysteries of this author's masterpiece *Yvain.* In the latter's Laudine Chrétien has created a dignified but authoritarian woman and in Lunete a combination of comeliness, courtesy, and intelligence, through whose arguments with her mistress about early remarriage the author is clearly revising the codes of courtly love and the long tradition of honoring Christian widowhood.[8] All in all, Chrétien de Troyes proves himself a grim realist and an ironical commentator on emotional sham but also a warm-hearted, subtle, fairminded, and highly skillful celebrant of that signal achievement and troubled legacy of the high Middle Ages, romantic marital love.

The Italian Idealistic Tradition: Dante and Petrarch

The Italian poetry of love tends toward a greater bifurcation of the ideal and the real than is present in French romance, setting up Dante at one extreme and Boccaccio at the other. I shall conclude the treatment of Italy with the *Decameron,* but I must first consider the idealizing poetry of Dante and Petrarch, apologizing for the brevity of my analyses and recognizing that Florentine Neoplatonism is of remote relevance, as are many lyrical poems of great intellectual subtlety, notably those of the more earth-oriented Guido Cavalcanti.

Dante in *La Vita nuova* (written 1292–94), like many *stilnovisti,* makes woman an angel through whom man reaches God. She forms part of the love triangle, along with man and Amor—a triangle of ancient origins and subtle Ovidian elaborations, but which usually remains an intellectual and spiritual configuration along which energetic meaning can flow without breaking the hierarchical shape. But, as Joan Ferrante notes, "the *union* of man and woman, whether literal or figurative, has little importance in this literature" (my emphasis).[9]

In Dante's spiritual autobiography the earlier years are not devoid of physical reality: women meet and talk, they sneer at his passion, and a simple greeting from Beatrice makes him swoon. The imagery is sometimes grotesquely unnatural, as when Love makes Beatrice eat that fiery object, the poet's flaming heart, an anticipation of the sacred-heart extravagances of baroque and mannerist Catholicism. Love in Dante's increasingly spiritual account is a key—to what? It is "la chiave d'ogni pietà," where *pietà* can refer to the courtly and sentimentally amorous and also to the theologically religious. The famous sonnet that unites love and the gentle (or noble) heart anticipates centuries of sex and sensibility, the central equation of the whole work being the fusion of love and courtesy ("Amore e'l cor gentil sono una cosa," p. 37), as close in fact as the rational soul (alma razional) and reason (ragione) itself. But the drive is toward eternity, and toward Beatrice, who has been and will always remain a "bella persona," with an "anima gentile," her whole being a "sì gentile cosa." And in the end she takes her place with the Virgin, "piena di grazia." We should of course remember that both Dante and Beatrice in real life were married, but not to each other. This love does not therefore ever have even a remote possibility of marital fulfillment.

The idealizing movement is resumed and reaches its climax in the *Paradiso,* with its apocalyptic poetry of light, sound, fire, and geometrical form, in which, however, resurrected flesh is not lost sight of, since Beatrice retains her full identity. For this is a Christian, not a gnostic or Hindu climax. Dante's journey may be described in another way more relevant to our previous chapter: he moves from the secular Arthurian *cortesia* of French romances in prose to the God of the *Divine Comedy,* who is the "sire de la cortesia." But Dante can still weep and even swoon over the lovers, as he does when in the *Inferno* he encounters the adulterous Francesca and Paolo (*she* deserves to be mentioned first as being the more dominant, a true *domna* herself). As everyone knows, they had fallen into the trembling sensual kiss (surely a euphemism for ensuing full climaxes) on reading the story of Lancelot and Guinevere. The story is as flutteringly delicate as the lovers' literary kiss, and there is something congenial in Blake's view that Dante swooned in pity for a humanity caught in the wrath of an avenging deity. Francesco de Sanctis's idea is also appealing, that Dante has made Francesca his first-born daughter, "the first truly living woman to appear on the poetic horizon of the modern age." [10] But the soundest view remains the one that sees Dante as enforcing, though with deep feeling for the lost, the divine laws against fleshly sin and the seductive titillations that romantic literature can arouse. One cannot in good conscience argue that Dante belonged to the tradition of Christian sensualism I have been at pains to disclose. Indeed, if he was ever attracted by it, he seems to have ended in a more centrally orthodox ambience that rejected it while sensing its allure.

Must we say the same of Laura and Petrarch, obviously cultural successors of Beatrice and Dante in the spiritualization of love? The differences are great, apart from Petrarch's obviously being the lesser genius: in his amorous verse he is more insistently subjective and secular; his emotions, less structured by institutional religious formulations, are more tightly reined in by poetic conventions and grammatical constraints; and his sense of daily, natural, and cultural reality is less potent and particular. Yet the achievements of this inward-looking egotist relevant to my topic, notably in the *Rime sparse* and related lyrics, are psychologically as well as artistically noteworthy and have exercised a stunningly broad and long-lasting influence. They have been likened to a wildfire spreading literary mania and have been described as "one of the widest, subtlest, most enduring cases of personal influence in the history of literature," opening the way to Cellini, Montaigne, Alfieri, Rousseau, and Proust—and even anticipating Freud by disclosing the unstable, complex, and contradictory human ego.[11]

In one late poem (no. 323) Petrarch gives us a highly suggestive and useful recapitulation of the obsession with Laura that held the poet captive for some twenty-one years of what he called "love and error" (compare no. 364), both the nouns being equally important. Standing at his window (no. 323), the poet is visited with a series of brief visions, each image representing Laura and recalling language and events peculiarly hers. First a wild creature appears, and we remember that *wild* and its synonyms appear frequently in the oxymorons the poet applies to the lady's psychological effects upon him. The landscape sites that conceal her are mountainous and wild ("alpestri" and "feri," 37.104). She herself is disdainful and fierce ("disdegnosa et fera," 112), composed of disdain and anger ("disdegno et ira," 44). She is a wild beast that is lovely and tame ("bella et mansueta," 126.29). Her fierceness persists through the years: "she, humble beast, with heart of tiger or bear" ("questa, umil fera, un cor di tigre o d'orsa," 152). The two black and white hounds that destroy her and cause this quondam beauty to be encased in stone (this last is ironical since she herself had had a Medusa effect on her patient lover) recall Laura's dark eyes, black and white becoming a synecdoche for the lady herself, but are obsessively destructive images for the poet, who is captivated by their dark and dangerous beauty. Now the lovely-perilous eyes, transformed into a beast, destroy their possessor.

The next vision, that of a ship with ropes of silk, sails of gold, adorned with ivory and ebony (another black-white image recalling Laura's eyes), must also recall the handsome dress of the beloved, just as the succeeding vision of the laurel tree recalls her slender hands, noble arms, and sweetly haughty gestures as the place itself, a locus amoenus, recalls Eden. Both these images are destroyed: the ship is wrecked in a tempest, the tree is destroyed by lightning, just as a chasm swallows up the next image, a lovely fountain, recalling the area where both Laura and Petrarch lived. Seeing the uprooted laurel and the dry fountain, the phoenix (compare no. 280), which arrives next, disappears at once—as a symbol of resurrection it cannot very well die. Its splendid purple and gold coloring, like the ship's, must recall the stuffs and silks, the veils and garments with which Laura was wont to hide her face, showing only her shadow, a movement recalled when the phoenix turns its beak before departing haughtily.

In the final image of the poem Laura returns to grass and flowers, often her locus in real life—in one important series, nos. 191–201, Petrarch intensifies the beauty of the lady by associating her with rain, pearls, green grass, flowers—with all that art, genius, nature, and heaven ("Arte, Ingegno, et Natura e'l Ciel," 193) can provide. As a kind of climax to the many paradoxes of her very being as a beloved, she unites humility in herself and pride against love ("umile in sé, ma 'n contra Amor superba," 323.64). Bitten in the heel, presumably by a serpent, the lady dies, and we recall that the curse Yahweh has mounted against fallen humanity in Genesis 3:15 establishes enmity between woman and the serpent, not inappositely if we make the almost inevitable interpretation that the serpent stands for sexual, specifically phallic, love, an enmity inscribed in the lifetime of denials love imposes on the suffering poet. In no. 188, lines 3–4, Petrarch compares Laura to the unfallen Eve, with the traditional misogynist interpretation of her as the first female temptress: "she flourishes without equal since Adam first saw his and our lovely bane" (". . . senza par poi che l'addorno / suo male et nostro vide in prima Adamo"). (Very subtly Petrarch rhymes the *Adamo* of line 4 with the *amo* of line 1, making the name of the First Man in Italian mean "I love toward.")

If there is any hope at all, it can come only from the Christian allegorization of the Genesis verse, where the threat is followed by a promise. Though the serpent may bruise the woman's heel (as Satan already has by tempting her with immortal ambitions), she will (through Mary and her Son) bruise his head on the cross. (We remember that the first meeting of Laura and Petrarch took place on the anniversary of the Crucifixion.) Each of the imagistic vignettes of this splendidly subtle recapitulation of the series ends in the death or destruction of the beloved object, except for one that ends in departure and another that inflicts a snake-wound.

Ultimately, Laura is replaced by the Virgin at the climax of the sequence; and it is to her that the love sufferer, who in religion finds equivalences for what Laura had never given him on earth, accords his final accolades. We know the consolations that religion through Mary and Laura now in heaven can provide only through the imagery, brief but clear, of nos. 284, 285: in place of the burning chastity of her earthly life ("onesto foco," 285) we now perceive the gentle lady set in an ambience of home and family. Mary was often regarded as the fruitful mother, the sponsor of procreation, and Petrarch's Virgin stands in that tradition. Thus the fruitlessness of earthly denials and endless tears has been supplanted, albeit only metaphorically. Some of the married mystics may, as we saw in the last chapter, have transferred to Christ and heaven the erotic joys they knew in life, pretty much intact, but Petrarch provides fulfillment by way of contrast to the feelings of doubt and insecurity he had known during his twenty-one years of love agony. And these redeemed values turn out to be very close to the values of the traditional church—motherhood, progeny, and home.

We may, with some adaptation, apply to Petrarch's more than two decades of amorous suffering the famous troubadour phrase, *amor de lonh*. However we judge the religious recantation at the end, the life that preceded the turning to the Virgin looks suspiciously like a major version of the *via negativa*. Though a secular one, it is even more life-denying than Christianity at its most ascetic: until the very final recantation it may possess love, but it stands without hope or faith. About the best that Petrarch can claim for his long purgatory is that it gave him a glimpse of maturity ("la età matura onesta," 317), not a strikingly original thought if we recall patristic privileging of lifelong chastity and denial. Almost totally lacking in mutuality, Petrarchan devotion produces disdain and anger ("disdegno et ira," 44) and the greater mischief of praising (and so abjectly accepting and sanctioning) the lady's great refusal ("ringrazio et lodo il gran disdetto," 105). After fifteen years he professes being more dazzled by her rays (107) than on the first day of their encounter, but these rays are rays only, obviously coming from afar. As he returns to his pain, they only make his unrequited fires immortal. He does get some relief by brushing past Laura now and then on his walks (recalling the fleeting encounters of Dante and Beatrice in *La Vita nuova*), but it is only temporary, the faint mutuality consisting of only a returning nod or bare acknowledgment of presence.

The death of Laura is said, somewhat blandly and unconvincingly, to mediate great spiritual benefits hitherto unknown, but its more realistic description in anticipation of the event (297) really bites. Death has separated those two great enemies, beauty and chastity. Beauty remains on earth—the girl is in her grave—dust now mantles the eyes from which amorous darts once glinted forth. Pen-weary (297), the poet is now bitter, and he decarnalizes himself ("or me ne struggo et scarno," 308). He had done so many times before, but now he turns to a holy and chaste art in a poem in which her sigh becomes a holy word but in which there is neither fulfillment nor growth. For this kind of aged meagerness we have been fully prepared by the decades of deprivation. Provided with such hunger-sharpened weapons, the poem cuts with a bitter edge that has more efficacy in its bareness than the religious envoy in its fullness.

He repents, and he has much to repent of. But has he understood his offense? Perhaps the positive names of mother, daughter, bride he finally discovers in the Virgin (366) imply lost values more powerfully than a recapitulative confession possibly could have. For in a sense the whole love sequence of the *Rime sparse* is the sin, though it is deprivation not transgression, omission not commission. Youth had been wasted, tears fruitlessly shed, unions and consummations proudly denied or scrupulously avoided. Endless verbal foreplay without benefit to man or woman, no touching except furtive brushes, or highly chaste and euphemistic displacements mediated timidly by natural images like leaves, grass, and water—these have replaced the full-bodied joys and sorrows of French romance. They recapitulate the delays and deferrals of Plato's erotic legacy, though without philosophical rewards. Artistically they fill the echoing distances of courtly *amor de lonh* with exquisitely breathed sighs and daintily shed tears. They of course lack the narrative fulfillments in long-term intimacies provided by courtly romance. But the centuries-long Petrarchan vogue indicates that the poet had struck a sympathetic chord in later cultures that has vibrated in response to his subtly expressed and amply displayed denial.

My treatment of Plato, Hermas, Petrarch, and related love syntheses that defer or evade consummations (a linked theme announced in my preface) has not always been without censoriousness. But I must make clear that I cannot regard these powerful philosophies and emotional expressions as mere interruptions of the main current of this study. They have often constituted serious intellectual challenges to my theme, and they have received artistic embodiments that rival the best in the tradition that united eros and esteem. Hence no student of Western erotic culture can afford to ignore or underrate them.

Transitions to Boccaccio

To plunge into the harsh and wry realism of the *Decameron* after the pure or qualified idealizations of love we have been considering could induce something like culture shock. We need to establish more delicate transitions, and they are provided by comic or ironic elements within the French romantic tradition itself. One such transition—others might be provided by *Les Quinze joies du mariage* or by Eustache Deschamps's *Le Miroir de mariage*—is provided by a fairly late work, dated variously in the thirteenth or fourteenth centuries, *The Pilgrimage of Charlemagne*.[12] There the old French word *gaber* (from the Occitan *gabar,* related to that part of comedy known as the *gabs* or "jests," meaning "to boast, to praise, to ridicule, to praise excessively or falsely") is used, with cognates, some thirty-seven times, prominently, even structurally.[13] And appropriately, for the royal eponymous hero is, for all his fame, a blusterer and a braggart. This quality appears at once, when Charlemagne's wife insults him by saying she knows a king in Constantinople, superior in splendor and power to her husband. He threatens several times to behead her for her impudence but decides, rather more sensibly, that on his pilgrimage to the Holy Land he will stop to visit this king Hugo to test his queen's evaluation, which if inaccurate will then lead to her death. The court proves to be splendid indeed, and, as is the human wont when overly impressed, the king and his men, occupying a sumptuous nocturnal chamber, decide to jest, *gaber*. In fact they are ordered by their emperor so to perform some twelve separate times. We need pause on only one of these boasts, the one that involves sexual comedy (28–44). Count Oliver's bravado is that if the royal host will entrust his daughter to him, he will forfeit his head if he does not, on her testimony, enjoy her (the verb is *aveir,* not much different in meaning from modern French or English equivalents). The spy who hears this boast (the king of Constantinople had placed such informers in the chamber to detect mischief) breathlessly reports it to his master, who is shocked but complies. The next night Oliver succeeds and, to the accompaniment of his and her courtly addresses, "has her" (or "does it," "li fist") some thirty times. But when the next day her royal father asks her if he had "done it" one hundred times, the girl replies, "Yes, my lord the king." The king spares Oliver on the grounds that he must have been a magician.

The jesting here does not embarrass and drive off the stage, once and for all, the sexual-romantic love that has undergone such intense *gabbement* (the substantive is used three times in the romance). Nor does it provide an alternative, for the medieval theory of irony does not envisage replacing a marred or destroyed semantic surface, it merely sets up aesthetic distance. Something not unlike such humorous detachment appears in the charming chantefable, *Aucassin et Nicolette,* the scholarly consensus now assigning it the date 1270.[14] This is late enough to justify the ironic contemplation of romantic love by its highly sophisticated northeastern French author. The essential values of marital romance remain intact, however, in the surrounding lightness and airiness, and the action is appropriately commenced and ended in a courtly Provençal setting on the Rhone River. There the final felicity is won in irregular but appealingly human ways, since the work removes some of the reservations modern sensibility feels in reading more normative chivalric literature. These new elements, which are embedded in a prose-verse form traditionally congenial to satire and humor, need to be noted carefully.

The coming together of the princely hero (son of an old-fashioned feudalistic tyrant who desires war with his neighbors and a profitable alliance in his son's marriage) and the girl (the father, and apparently Aucassin too, thinks that she comes from afar and is a slave) provides the serious complication that sets the plot in motion. The boy regards his sweet friend, whom he so much loves ("douce amie que je tant aim," 2.21) as worthy of any throne in the world, France's, England's, Germany's, or Constantinople's, although all he has to offer is the stronghold of Beaucaire on the Rhone. With an appealingly Shavian kind of contempt, Aucassin scorns the promise of paradise (where old priests, old cripples, threadbare beggars, and the groveling maimed and dying go), preferring the hell his father warns will be his destiny if he beds Nicolette—an inferno which the son rehabilitates by imagining its denizens to be gallant knights, handsome clerics, and beautiful courtly ladies and their lovers.

The same tone of civilized mockery attends Aucassin's escape from his father's prison (into which he was thrown for his military recreancy), his travels at sea with Nicolette (recalling, at least to us, many Greek romances), and their three years of adventure in the somewhat abnormal Utopia of Torelore. This is a place where the queen leads an army (the weapons of war are rotten crab apples, eggs, and fresh cheeses), where the king prohibits lethal warfare and so discourages the participation of the young French prince, where Aucassin rebukes the king for pretending he is with child, and where Nicolette lyrically censures "unnatural" love practices that must be homosexual (her song stands in the tradition of the Latin dialogue between Helen and Ganymede and the many confrontations of homo- and heterosexual love in Greek romances and Plutarch). She knows she will be thought a fool in this culture, but she must insist on her—and her lover's—erotic rights. Her plaint is naive and straightforward but comes from a *coeur sensible:* my sweet friend embraces me for he feels me plump and soft; this gives me great pleasure; no dance, no music, no game can match what I then feel. Period.[15]

In vindicating the pleasures of heterosexual love against forms of effeminacy; in revealing Nicolette's very high position as a princess though of Saracen blood; in ultimately establishing Aucassin's courage in confronting supernatural danger and his prowess with conventional arms, though he still gives the safety of his beloved priority over anything else; and finally in giving his characters, both virginal during their trials, a long life of pleasure and true joy as lord and lady of Beaucaire, the learned and civilized author shows us that he has not abandoned the chivalric formula. But in realizing it he has provided his reader with an uncommon amount of spirited, unconventional, and truly humane joy. He celebrates the newer ethos of *amor* and of the marital *ami-amie* while satirizing romantic *gabbement,* feudal and patriarchal callousness toward individual values, and the all-too-easy way in which traditional chivalry places sword and spear in the hands of its heroes.

To smooth further the rough transition from romance to the *Decameron,* we may need to taste even stronger meat, and that is provided by France as well as Italy in the fabliaux. It has been calculated that about 160 surviving texts treat erotic subjects, among which the following are marital: some 40 *contes à triangle* where wife and lover oppose the husband, about 20 in which two married protagonists encounter difficulties, and 20 or so others which are tales of seduction.[16] The satiric vulgarity or grotesquerie of these tales, which may distort downward as much as romance upward, appears in much visual art. Manuscript illuminations, some with savage relentlessness, portray battered wives, husbands, and lovers.[17] Even medieval churches, in odd places, mostly on the underside of choir seats, sometimes provided shocking visual examples of forbidden practice—oral sex, for example. (These underseat sculptures were called "misericords." Since sitting during the holy offices was forbidden, the seats were often in an upright position; the misericords gave the aged or infirm something to lean against, and the portion of the anatomy resting on them no doubt helped determine the subject matter of the sculptures.) Thousands of such medieval carvings also portrayed mermaids; ancient fables; early liturgy; popular romances; Adam, Eve, and the serpent in the garden; venues of prostitution or of sexually charged domestic intimacy; scenes of domestic vanity with comb and mirror; domestic couples totally in the nude (in one case the husband playing a fiddle, the wife a flute); and, in Holy Trinity church in Stratford-upon-Avon, a sexually aroused woman wearing an enticing smile.[18]

Before analyzing Boccaccio himself, we should return to Italy for a late medieval or immediately pre-Renaissance historical context. It will provide, in degrees impossible to determine and relationships difficult to disentangle, the by now familiar combination of realistic and idealistic data. It was a society in which wives were subjugated, even beaten. San Bernardino of Siena addressed the men in his congregation: "And you, husband—do not beat your wife when she is pregnant; that is a great peril, I insist. I don't say—never beat her; but choose your time." Intimacy was regulated by the church; conjugal sodomy was common in Tuscan cities; priests and monks were so active sexually that the sex act was sometimes referred to as a "psalm" or a "Pater." And yet friendship, exalted by both classicizing and Christian influences, was a paramount virtue, surpassed only by conjugal love. Love in the home was regarded as warmer than anywhere else, and the conjugal bed was a prestige item of purchase, given symbolic priority in the home. Woman was trusted to produce marital and familial concord; usually younger than her mate by seven to ten years, she was nevertheless the chief educator of the children. Memoir writers testify to but also try to foster respect for the mystique and dynamics of family life.

An early sociologist, Fra Paolino in 1314, delineated three progressively more exclusive and intimate communities: (1) the overarching political group (city, kingdom, or other entity); (2) the neighborhood (the *vicinato*); and (3) the household.[19] Anyone who knows Italy today can testify to the important overlap between the last two categories. And late medieval Italy undoubtedly put the essentially nuclear family of husband, wife, children, and domestics (with an average total size of only 4.42 people in 1447) in energetic contact with neighbors and friends. This virtual synonymy of neighbor or friend and family member is a feature not notably present in the French literature we have studied, but it does creep into episodes of Dante's *Vita nuova* and Petrarch's *Rime,* where neighborliness can be more intimate than love. Such was not the priority of the real Italian setting, but it is important to realize that *vicinanza* pressed upon the sorrows and joys, even the ecstasies and infidelities, of family life. We are now ready to consider Boccaccio's masterpiece and its erotic ambience.

The Decameron

It will introduce us to a central aspect of Boccaccio's literary personality if, remembering the delicate pathos but inexorable fate of Dante's Paolo and Francesca, we consider the later writer's retelling of the story. He aims to get at the truth, and it is grim and sordid. The domestic tangle arises from a not unusual situation in which Francesca da Polenta, who loves the handsome Paolo Malatesta, is for reasons of prudential family alliance given to his elder brother, the deformed Gianciotto. When the unloved, unattractive husband goes off on business, a sensual opportunity arises for the lover, now a middle-aged family man, and his beloved, now the mother of an adolescent daughter. They are surprised by the deformed husband. Paolo jumps into a sluice that opens upon a sewer, but his shirt is caught on an iron hook. Gianciotto thrusts at him; Francesca, interposing her body, is run through, and the husband, berserk with passion, kills Paolo too. Here there is no pandering work of art, like the Lancelot-Guinevere love in Dante, to relieve the circumambient stench—no sweetness, no freshness, no melting tenderness. But the two lovers *are* buried in the same tomb.[20]

This sordid story is far from doing justice to Boccaccio's wide-ranging imagination, nourished by his high Sidneyan view that poetry is a kind of fervid and exquisite invention.[21] It does not prepare us for the *opere minori,* Boccaccio's interesting canon of early works, all devoted to love except for his first substantial work, the *Caccia di Diana* of c.1334. These works, both in poetry and prose, enforce the classical view that passionate love is a dreadful fatality, a warped destiny, illustrated by the story of Madonna Fiammetta of the *Elegia,* whose commitment to libido is an incurable psychic sickness. But eros (decorated love) can also rise to the sensory beauty of the *Ninfale fiesolano,* and this early work passes in review Arthurian heroes, Tristan and Isolde, medieval romance—and the locus amoenus of Venus and Diana. Still, the eros of art and legend can also be dauntingly ambiguous. In the *Teseide* Venus's temple stands in a delightful garden that is perfumed with the flowers of courtesy, kindness, and beauty, but flattery, pandering, idleness are also present.

Boccaccio frequently rises high enough to suggest the beauty of exalted Christian love. The Fiammetta of the *Amorosa visione* (1342–43) is a *donna angelicata* and symbolizes *caritas*—and the narrator kisses her in devotion. But in the largest and most ambitious panel in this allegorical house of iconic vision, that devoted to love, where the author finds it valuable to see how beautiful what has often been presented as evil could be, it is noteworthy that profane love never seems to rise to the divine, as in Plato, Dante, or even Petrarch. The kissing of *caritas* comes only on the panel devoted to Fortune, where apparently stark necessity calls for an austerely moral guide. Is there, then, no norm at all involving the natural, the sexual, the erotic? Has one of the greatest naturalists of medieval culture failed to honor Natura and her procreative Venus? Did the School of Chartres never enroll Boccaccio as even a part-time visiting scholar? A final answer must await our imminent analysis of the *Decameron.* Here we can only say that the author of the varied and attractive early minor works has relentlessly exposed the illusions of love religion in his parody of courtly amorousness but has now and then suggested or implied as an alternative, not the renunciations of Christian love, but a marital love embodying choice of partner, sexuality, and procreation. In other words, the churchly settlement that defeated feudalistic arrangement and substituted consensual marriage based on sexual attraction and free choice had entered Boccaccio's soul as a sane hope if not a fully realistic norm. As we saw, even the grim retelling of the story of Paolo and Francesca implies as much in the common burial of the lovers.

If this understated view is valid, then the *Decameron* does not constitute a plunge from idealism to realism but is a more subtle movement on an artistic continuum. We note first of all that its final and climactic story is that of the patient Griselda. De Sanctis sees her as the successor of Beatrice and Laura, and the continuing appeal of her patience and self-sacrifice must have served a deep cultural need, as is attested by the importance Chaucer accorded her in the marriage group of the *Canterbury Tales*. At the same time, de Sanctis has said of Griselda that she has suffocated everything of value in her humanity, including her own free will, and Thomas Bergin calls her "a pathological case verging on the monstrous."[22] It is hard for a modern to escape these judgments, and attempts to rehabilitate her in our own day as an example of love on the sacrificial level, making of Gualtieri, her noble husband, the testing, judging "Divine Father," seem considerably less than compelling. But if we deny that the story of the patient, lowly born, and beautiful Griselda can represent the disillusioned, hard-headed author's own ideal—and we note that its telling produced disagreement in his own day—what can we say of it? Only that the discovery of worth in the kind of humble cottage where the aristocratic suitor found her has the ring of humanity about it and that the story ends with Gualtieri's loving her "over all else." His discovery of a beautiful body in humble dress and his determination to love and reward it has had high sanction (we saw this most recently in Chrétien's *Erec et Enide*), and here it constitutes one of Boccaccio's many tributes to the power of nature over all else. But the husband's kindness is compounded of a repellent condescension and morbid insecurities, and may of course have been solicited by *her* abjectness and devotion to him. And so we have a right to doubt the purity or strength of the affection at the end, and we suspect that Boccaccio shared those doubts. We must remember, however, that determining the author's stance is always difficult in Boccaccio, as it is in Chaucer. Interpretations here must be affected by the character of the speaker; by the nature of the response by the aristocratic young people, who have left Florence to escape the plague; by the positioning of the stories within a thematic series established by designated leaders; as well as by the imaginative dynamics of each tale.

Though this final example of love falls far short of being a satisfying norm, there is no doubt that the *Decameron* is love-obsessed and that it gives enormous prominence, hitherto unexampled in fictional art, to women. Thomas Bergin's census shows that of the 338 characters in this collection, 83 are women, a great increase over Dante's 20 or so women in a total fictional population much greater than Boccaccio's. Of his 100 stories, 32 place women in central roles, and the stories and their resolutions, quite apart from statistics, reveal a woman-oriented world.[23] The seven women who help constitute the company of ten are fair, well mannered, sprightly, of noble blood, none over twenty-seven and none under eighteen, three of them mistresses of the men present, all united in the bonds of friendship and neighborliness we saw as being characteristic of contemporary Florence. Nevertheless, the minority of men (only three of the ten in the company) are assertive and express insistently masculine points of view, which they regard as desirably didactic and reformatory.

For though the *Decameron* is a book of laughter, its circle of interacting narrators constitutes a kind of amorous professoriate, complexly related to the famous work of Andreas Capellanus; two-thirds of the tales are concerned centrally with a sexual relationship. What lessons are taught in this school of love? Two stories, though subtle, are of prerequisite importance to the later courses for credit. The first comes in the introduction to the Fourth Day, addressed to the ladies by the "king" for that day and containing the following story, *hors du jeu,* as it were. It concerns the son of a rich man of Florence, Filippo Balducci, of mean extraction. He loved his wife "with an exceeding love," as she did him. Their peaceful life was devoted to the one pleasing the other, and when she died he felt so great a loss that he renounced the world and raised his two-year-old son in the mountains away from society. When the boy is eighteen, he desires company, but of course he conceives of the human community as consisting only of others like himself and his father. The boy marvels at the city, and when he sees a group of women coming from a wedding, he asks his father, who are these? what are they called? The father, now an old and devout man, says, "green geese," and the son says he wants one, to bring back to the mountains and to feed and care for. The father refuses, and, seeing that nature in the boy is stronger than the wit of his metaphoric appelation, says, "You know not whereat they are fed."[24]

The implications being potentially offensive, the king for the day must reassure the ladies, and he tries to do so by confessing that he is himself overmuch pleased by ladies, attracted by their dainty manners, beauty, grace, and courtesy, to say nothing of kisses and embraces. And he asserts that the boy's attraction at first sight is natural, and he gives to his naturalism the religious twist of the School of Chartres, asking if heaven itself had not created such appropriate love of the female body. He then uses a mysterious metaphor, "a leek has a white head, the tail thereof is green." For an explanation we must turn to another tale (the tenth story of the First Day), told by the queen for that day, who gently censures her own sex for adorning the body, rather than the mind through wit, even justifying lack of conversational skill as a modesty proceeding from purity of mind, when it is really a lack of what we shall come to know Boccaccio greatly prizes, mental astuteness (*ingegno*).

The story concerns a famous Bologna physician, now seventy years of age, who no longer feels natural erotic heat but nevertheless courts a beautiful and sought-after woman of forty-nine. He replies to the taunts of her friends by saying that though old men may be bereft of vigor, they are not thereby bereft of wit and the will to be loved worthily. He then introduces the metaphor of that humble vegetable, the leek, and chides the ladies for munching the leaves (which are not good for much and are smelly besides) and merely holding the head (the bulbous and only really edible part) in their hands, a perversion of the normal process. The implications are naughty but complex, and the women do not understand them, the lady being courted saying: you may command me but be sure to save my honor. In making this large essential exception, she had obviously misunderstood the leek metaphor, and deserves the laughter of the older suitor and his companions as they abruptly walk out. So she who thought she had discomfited another was herself discomfited. But how? The man had quite modestly meant that women are known to choose the sexual safety of liaison with an aged man and so munch only the leaves of the leek while they forego the vigor of a younger man (the best part, the head, the bulb, the meat). The old physician, though he may be past his prime, knows that the lady who accepts his suit but guards her honor has thus unwittingly missed the point, although he may not himself be able to deliver it. So once more Boccaccio stresses the essential naturalism of his vision and strives to bring women to modify their inherited and socially imposed modesty, acknowledge their natural endowments, cease acquiescing in arranged marriages that tie them to older and unattractive men, and by doing all this increase both their honesty and their pleasure.

It is an argument for the mutuality and equality that come of recognizing that nature has not exempted women from its universal, life-enhancing endowments. The female need for such instruction is revealed at the end of the story, when to accompany Lauretta's dance Emilia warbles out a confession that, "I burn for mine own charms with such a fire, / Methinketh that I ne'er / Of other love shall reck or have desire." That kind of narcissism is at a pole opposite to the honest naturalism Boccaccio is teaching in the revisionary curriculum of this school of love.

Fortunately, the tales we shall now consider are not so archly witty and metaphorically indirect, although the Boccaccio of the *Decameron* more often than not remains sly and elusive—and determined to amuse at all costs. To reveal the essential shape and force of his erotic ethos, I shall have to establish a set of categories of my own that adjusts for expository purposes the author's own taxonomy, suggested by the topics of each day and by the order in which the tales are told. As seen from the perspective of my entire book, the *Decameron* (1) attacks arranged marriages and other examples of incompatibility, the bloodless couplings of the "mal assorties"; (2) recommends a self-serving cleverness, or *ingegno,* that impels people to demand that all their human needs be met, in this case the need for sexuality; and (3) creates situations that impel attractive and attracted women and men toward equality by heightening the position of woman in recognizing her humanity, lowering the artificial and often ridiculous superiority of the male, and therefore leading to a severely moderated ideal of consensual union that can be, whether licit or illicit, both long-lasting and basically satisfying.

Several categories, but especially my first one in which the stories attack the merely prudential and calculating in establishing heterosexual relationships, support, even when aristocrats are involved, the truth of Vittore Branca's description of the *Decameron* as a "mercantile epic," an epic of the autumnal waning of the Middle Ages in Italy.[25] From this perspective we see why life is competitive and often cruel, why such qualities as *ingegno* are necessary, why excess of sentiment is usually undesirable, and when it comes why it is escapist. But this ambience also explains why, if the realities of human nature are not lost sight of, some modestly conceived long-term couplings have a chance of success and of life enhancement, for commercial relationships require a degree of stability and trust if there is to be any kind of society at all. Erich Auerbach is surely right in believing that the *Decameron* develops "a distinct, thoroughly practical and secular ethical code rooted in the right to love," but he is excessively simple when he accepts at face value its anti-Christianity.[26] As we shall see, if we melt the hard icy surface tiny sprouts of truly Christian marital value do appear in time, and we err if we think these actually to be what they merely seem to be, blasphemous bravado, though the cynical tone is valuable in removing the stifling encrustations of ages past.

The sixth story of the Third Day (a story told by a woman) requires five characters, a curious and noisily aggressive Neapolitan neighborhood, and a considerable amount of Restoration-like deceit and manipulation to expose the hollowness of the marriage between the wealthy, noble Ricciardo and his fair and lovesome wife. He falls in love with a virtuous beauty, the wife of a young gentleman she loved and cherished. But he cannot accomplish his designs upon this Catella without spreading word that the husband she allegedly loves is also casting *his* eyes elsewhere and without Ricciardi's own feigning of love for another, a shadowy fifth actor in this complicated chain of affairs. A Machiavellian ruse brings Catella and Ricciardi together in the dark chamber of a bagnio, she thinking she has encountered her "beloved" husband out for an adventure. Their encounter is not without its risks, and at times she becomes almost uncontrollably angry; but before she knows she has been in the arms of Ricciardi, her lover, she denounces her putative husband for his briskness with someone he supposes to be another when he is so impotent and forespent at home with her. Ricciardi then reveals himself and says (for once Boccaccio allows a traditional erotic personification) that Love has taught him what he knows. The story is hard-bitten, and Catella has to be threatened with exposure and a potential blood-feud between her men. She becomes reasonable, now knowing that the kisses of love are better than those of an indifferent husband, and knowing too that an adulterous relationship will have to do if the licit one is life denying and deprived. Moreover, the illicit turns out—under proper safeguards, of course—to achieve tender mutuality and much joy, ending with the female narrator's prayer that God may grant all of us joyance in our lives. It is only a little too abrupt to say that Boccaccio much prefers a mutually rewarding adultery to a life-denying marriage, the kind of lifetime liaison characteristic of so much aristocratic life and featuring what Samuel Richardson's Mr. B in *Pamela* once called a "a yawning husband and a vaporish wife."

Other stories in different ways show what nature makes inevitably happen when the couple is ill matched for whatever reason—bourgeois man with aristocratic wife; a clod-pated dullard with a clever woman fair and plump as an apple; an old, avaricious, jealous, precisianist, loutish, or drunken male with a young, spirited, sexually hungry, frustrated, educated, courteous, or intelligent female.[27] Illustrating the exaggerated rhetoric of shock and surprise, Boccaccio's illicit alternative, when it is not allowed to become so passionate and romantic as to be foolish and imprudent, often brings much more joy than had been known under the stifling *nomos* of law and respectability.

As for my second category, many of Boccaccio's cleverest and most realistic narratives seem cynical. We must keep reminding ourselves that they intend no more than to enforce the importance of what in my introduction I made basic to all long-term love and called its ego context. If that remains unserved, all is lost. Every person, female or male, is entitled in love to a decent degree of life (exuberance), liberty (along with the wit to escape desire-thwarting restrictions), and the pursuit of a happiness that serves the whole person (female or male body as well as spirit). The male teller of the second story of the Seventh Day brings out the female *ingegno* of the lower-class Neapolitan wife in a crude and uproariously funny *fabliau,* but the story honors Peronella's quick wit, flexibility, and natural acting ability in seeming to be aggrieved when she herself is the "sinner." With such histrionic ability she imitates her "betters" in higher society and shows that a girl of mean condition need not remain joyless. The fourth story of the Seventh Day, told by a woman, is more delicate as it shows a stupid jealous man outwitted, sometimes cruelly, by a clever and mischievous woman, using his weakness for wine to get him to a domestic arrangement in which some discreet and carefully regulated libertinism does not destroy a marriage but does allow female fulfillment within it. The immediately following fifth story, also told by a woman, deceitfully cures a cruelly jealous husband who has virtually imprisoned his handsome and agreeable wife by having him cuckolded in a witty plot by a learned priest, who provides the starved wife with merriment for a long time—much to the approval of the women in the audience. Other stories that endow the wife with the kind of conquering and aggressive cleverness that sees to it that her wants are respected and satisfied include the sixth of Day Seven (a woman's tale), the seventh of Day Seven (also a woman's), and the eighth of Day Seven (a woman's). Admittedly the means used to achieve these ends will offend the pious and the legalistic, and also many decent people who rightly believe in the need for order. But the bold Boccaccio is engaged in a kind of affirmative moral action, however shocking, which Chaucer later was also to use with unforgettable effect.

It should now be clear that I think it possible to regard many of Boccaccio's racy marital stories as embodying a drift toward equality (my third category), a drive that might even serve the purposes of greater compatibility and hence greater friendship in marriage.

We have seen him try to achieve this condition by "reducing" woman to the level of only appetite, the condition of many men. But such equality would be sure to do no more than trigger the older rigoristic ethic. Still, unless we (minimally) believe of women that if we prick them they will bleed and that if we oppress them they will seek revenge, any thought of friendship or reciprocality between the sexes is totally beside the point. My ventriloquizing of Boccaccio in these matters may not seem completely beside the point if we consider the bold attack in the seventh story of Day Six (told by a man) on the statute that an unfaithful wife caught in flagrante delicto should be burned at the stake. The amorous wife Filippa was so discovered by her husband Rinaldo, who seeks the vengeance of the law. Against the advice of a friend and even of the judge, she boldly confesses all, which is that she had enjoyed Lazzarino not only on the night of the discovery but for many nights of "great and perfect love." Portia-like, Filippa accepts her punishment but argues that the statute should apply to all, men as well as women. Then without waiting for the provost to decide, Rinaldo the husband jumps into the argument, admitting that as a wife Filippa had fully respected the marital *debitum,* acceding to his every request and fully satisfying him. Bolder than ever, the wife says: "If he has always taken of me that which was needful and pleasing to him, what, I ask you, was or am I to do with that which remains over and above his requirements? [Recall the sexual "surplus" in Marie de France, in chapter 8.] Should I cast it to the dogs? Was it not far better to gratify withal a gentleman who loves me more than himself, than to leave it waste or spoil?" The people cry out that she was right; the provost, with popular approval, modifies the cruel statute, making it apply only to those who are unfaithful for money; the husband leaves, embarrassed; and the wife returns to her house, joyful and free. The story is modern in feeling: a woman boldly asserts her right to be satisfied, she claims equal treatment before the law, she accomplishes a radical revision of the law, and she embarrasses a conventional and legalistic husband. Moreover, she seems to praise as well as illustrate an entirely secular and even irregular ideal, but still an ideal for all that (a "great and perfect love"), which is articulated and instantiated by an admittedly wealthy and privileged woman but which wins the plaudits of the people as well. All this is bolder than anything in Shakespeare. It inscribes over one domestic hearth Dante's three great themes in *De Vulgari eloquentia* of *salus, venus,* and *virtus,* now slyly rethought and suggestively (even

shockingly) reapplied. For this is not just another case of the all too familiar furtive libido sneakingly finding its appropriate satisfactions. Here an
adultery is given considerable dignity and force.

But Boccaccio is not content merely to energize and so exalt the
woman; contemporary conditions and a long tradition made it necessary
also to demote the husband, and he does so with a gusto provided by
both male and female narrators. Many of the stories already summarized
or alluded to show how frequently the conventional male is deflated as
his cruelty, stupidity, avarice, jealousy, or domination are cleverly outwitted. Since Boccaccio's aim could not possibly have been to remove man
from the romantic scene altogether or to reduce everything to an equality
of impotence or mere propriety, he has been careful to create as well a
small but impressive pantheon of loving, spirited, intelligent, civilized
males. Some of these are clerics, to be sure, as if to show that the achievements of reading, writing, thinking, and courtesy, however inconve-
niently or irregularly located, are appreciated by the female sex. To be
sure, some laymen (even of poor family background) also have lovable
and attractive qualities, as does Zima in Elisa's spirited story (fifth story
of Day Three). He is as witty and ingenious as any female, he is fully articulate and capable of verbally parodying the conventions of courtly love,
and he is an actor of impressive versatility, able to ventriloquize even the
woman when necessary.

And of course the sexual endowments Boccaccio has so honored in
the woman cannot be lacking in the successful male, or the project of
erotic reform is doomed from the outset. Thus the account of Cimone,
the first in a series told in response to a request of the queen of the day for
"fair-fortuned" stories, is crucial (first story, Day Five). It is classically set
and features a decisively masculine Eros, albeit a well-educated one. It
concerns a handsome, well-born, but at the outset sluggish and witless
lout, who is civilized by nothing other than sexual desire aroused by the
beautiful sleeping Iphigenia. Inspired by that desire, he begins to climb
the ladder to civility, ultimately becoming a judge of beauty, a man of
fashion, a literatus, a courteous and seemly speaker, and a master of song.
Like a hero of Greek romance, Cimone must go through fiery trials after
his sexual arousal to attain such heights, but he succeeds. The progress is
not unlike the dialectical ladder Socrates raises in Plato's *Symposium,*
with this difference: Boccaccio's hero, though he climbs high enough to
become a philosopher, never deserts sexual passion, even though he is
perceptive enough to see that it can be associated with violence and rape.
And he is rewarded at the end with a long and happy marriage. Boccaccio

has thus revised a venerable tradition to make sex itself not only an ini-tiating force (that too is a feature of the Platonic *erōs*) but a force for civility that continues without suffering any diminution of energy. This is esteem enlivened by desire, properly founded and long in duration. It is also desire enlivened by esteem.

Before we consider a complex and beautiful story that shows how a long-term relationship that embodies both friendship and love can over-come what there is of a challenging Otherness in the narrative donnée, we must consider that the open-eyed Boccaccio would never present an unqualified or sentimentalized ideal. He of course does not suggest a guaranteed permanence in the relations he sets up, since he is not the writer of fairy tales, and all human contact requiring or producing pas-sion must be hedged in with common sense, good humor, social pru-dence, and moderation.

These qualities appear as implied or stated requirements in the sto-ries with romantic plots of Day Five, all told under the rubric of tales with happy endings. In one (the second, a woman's story) the long, peaceful repose of a couple in their wealthy home in the Italy of their origin arises not only from mutual love at the start but from the demonstrated courage and persistent practicality of the wife Costanza when alone at sea and the courage, cleverness, and diplomatic skills of the lover and husband who makes his way by good counsel and hard work to high favor with the king in Tunis. In another romantic story (the third, also told by a woman) the love of the eloping couple does not stand alone but receives the blessing of a great lady of the powerful Orsini family, who is strongly committed to the churchly view of consensual marriage and the validity of clan-destine unions, and therefore sponsors the nuptials of the already com-mitted pair, who live to a ripe old age in peace and pleasure. Even the unsentimental and slightly naughty story (fourth story, Day Five, with its hilarious nightingale euphemism), told by a male and featuring a tartly witty and disillusioned father, respects fully the canonical definition of marital validity—consent followed by consummation—an ecclesiastical minimum that is fully honored here. It is a romantic plot, no doubt of that, but it is supported, however crassly, by family and good financial prospects. And so it is everywhere—things amorous succeed when they combine what that other commercially oriented writer, Daniel Defoe, called "religion and the prudential."

Open-eyed moderation is the desideratum, and excess is silly even in friendship: Boccaccio, in the story (eighth of Day Ten) of the impossibly altruistic friendship of Gisippus and Titus in the time of Octavius Caesar, makes them as much monsters of goodness and sacrifice as Griselda ever was. The female narrator's concluding praise of friendship as being above family and household sounds somewhat fulsome and hollow. It is of course not impossible that Boccaccio, deciding to exalt classical, masculine virtue, is not at home doing so and treats the matter with clumsy exaggeration. In the eighth story of Day Eight (a woman's story) a ménage à quatre, where there is some infidelity, does seem to succeed tolerably well because expectations are lowered: if you are mildly aggrieved sexually, avenge yourself in a moderate and tolerant spirit. Boccaccio's version of *The Taming of the Shrew* (ninth of Day Nine told by a woman) outdoes in crude directness the more nuanced Shakespeare and so offends the ladies. But even here the cruelty of the husband who learns from a muleteer to beat his wife into submission is allowed to stand in flat contradiction to the Solomonic injunction with which the story opens: if you wish to be beloved, love. Surely this, not the crude cudgeling, must be Boccaccio's norm, which is in accord with the general moderation of his ethos. Its failure to be followed points up human weakness.

In a strangely rich and beautiful story (ninth of Day Ten, told by a man) Boccaccio confronts what we have noted, in our discussion of Plato's *Lysis* (chapter 3), as an important obstacle that love must and can overcome, the proximity of the Other. Otherness arises in this story from the presence in Italy of a disguised Saracen monarch and his attendants, who have come to spy out the Christian preparations for a crusade and whom Torello, quite unaware of the leader's royal status and and purpose, lavishly and quite disinterestedly entertains. As he leaves for his duties as a Christian soldier, Torello gives his loving and distraught wife a year and a day before she may marry again, and she weepingly says, as she gives him her ring, that she will always be his wife. As it turns out, the husband is captured and taken as a prisoner to Alexandria. There, like Joseph in Egypt, he rises to the top of the realm, obviously because the sultan remembers the Italian's kindnesses and also has found in him an extremely able man. Torello, having heard that his wife's remarriage is about to take place, falls into a deep depression: the sultan's consolation that her beauty will fade does not reconcile him to the loss of her other virtues of good manners, fine fashion, and pleasing demeanor. Though he is now about to become almost an equal in governing the realm, Torello is delighted when the benevolent sultan relinquishes him and arranges through necromancy to have him set down in his home. He arrives in time to come to the wedding, dressed in Saracen clothes and with a great beard. But the wife sees at once who he is and in the exuberance of her love kicks over the table and cries, as if mad, "It is my lord." Even more joyous nuptials, those of renewal, now replace the second wedding, and the first marriage is allowed to reach its true consummation in a lifetime of devotion.

It would be easy to see this as merely a restatement of the importance of consensual marriage, which Torello's certainly was, and respect for which Boccaccio, as we have seen, has elsewhere shown in subtle and indirect ways. But we need to consider what Otherness has wrought. The Italian husband's first kindness ignored the total strangeness of his Arab visitors, and he is allowed to ignore, albeit unconsciously, the mission of military threat, as though the dynamics of the story placed other matters in a vastly more important position. The sultan himself later ignores cultural difference in magnificently promoting a Christian stranger and enemy of war to virtually the highest position in his land. But the splendor of such success yields to the homecoming, where the wife at once sees below her husband's new and superficial otherness and in the exuberance of her continuing first love brushes away the new obstacles. We have a right to ask if there are deeper connections between the political Arabic elements and the domestic Christian. It is difficult to prove that Boccaccio in synthesizing these historically inimical and mutually threatening powers and in making one serve the other did anything other than act unconsciously as an artist.

But the questions persist: why does a powerful Arab otherness serve Christian domestic love and unity? why does state power yield to domestic happiness in so unsentimental a writer as Boccaccio? Could it be because this usually wry and disenchanted man perceived that the Italian couple had already overcome a more stubborn otherness than that which inheres in racial and cultural distance—inherited gender difference between the sexes and the Sartrean gulf that yawns between unyielding individualities? Boccaccio's plots often subject his characters to all the rigors of Greek romance before a final rewarding resolution is reached. This story with its distantly sounding trumpets of Christianity vs. Islam and its external obstacles of bitter conflict, of wind and weather, of suffering and separation shows that all these can be handsomely overcome. This story may therefore be regarded as exemplary in removing what Boccaccio has so frequently shown elsewhere as more familiar but more grievous obstacles—those of close-at-hand differences, of problematical domestic proximities. When these have indeed been overcome, as they had even before this heartwarming story began, Boccaccio can without qualms reward his actors with a deep and abiding joy that might seem sentimental in a lesser genius. But why, then, does he remove the obstacles by magical, not natural, means? As a realist Boccaccio may not have wished to risk being unpersuasive at this point by portraying an entirely naturalistic venue and so risk arousing disillusioned, cynical questions. And he may well have been willing to suggest that marriages succeed best when divine grace has been mediated, as it has been here, by the charity of both husband and wife. Boccaccio should be allowed to remind us, despite enormous cultural differences, of that other preceptor of love, Ovid. For out of much witty and seemingly frivolous indirection each is able to find his own version of the direction that guides this study.

An English Context for Chaucerian Love

Medieval Europe not being the patchwork of rival nationalisms it later became but an intellectual fraternity (however vigorously challenged) ruled by a Christian establishment, virtually all of what we presented as the medieval erotic and marital background in this and the previous chapter is relevant to the England of Chaucer. Still, a few adjustments and reminders are necessary to plant us firmly on English soil. It was his work on an Ely Register of fourteenth-century England that led Michael M. Sheehan to the important conclusions we quoted earlier; here we need only note that the records he studied, from Thomas Arundel's reign as bishop of Ely (1374–82), confirm the view that the Western church did indeed have a theory regarding the purposes and practices of marriage—that consent constituted the marital bond—and that that belief was becoming incorporated into local law among people of various traditions. The astonishing results were that parental consent came to be only occasionally and incidentally present and that there is no evidence of familial or seigneurial pressure on the choice of mate or the time of betrothal.[28]

It is always important, of course, to realize that canon law and clerical ideals are neither always nor usually regulative of life and certainly not of literature, though they do constitute an effectual presence that presses upon all relations, real or imagined. Wife beating and child abuse continued, and subordination and even ill-treatment of the female spouse were popularly sanctioned by continued insistence that woman was created from Adam's side: if God had wanted a higher status for her he would have taken her from the man's head. Even at the level of authority, the new privilege accorded consent was soon abused by being hardened into an almost legalistic-magical formula; the bishop of Salisbury in 1219 issued a rule forbidding a man "to encircle the hands of a young woman with a ring of rush or other material, . . . lest while he thinks he is joking he binds himself with the burdens of marriage."[29]

Familial breaches of regnant standards were not uncommon: in England and London especially, adultery seemed to be very common among married men, and unmarried girls were closely watched. Reaction to libertinism was both official and popular. Penalties for adultery were enforced, and among the lower middle class of artisan there appeared a streak of rigorism. Still, the new Lollardy, though it thought that celibacy was an impossibly high standard that encouraged unnatural vice, was nonetheless often puritanical in its influence. With respect to the position of the married woman, one scholar has concluded that she clearly had command of the household and that affection and tranquil love "came more often than not." Lord and Lady Lisle seem to have treated each other tenderly, using such terms of endearment as "mine own sweetheart" and "my very heart root and beloved bedfellow"; they had escaped outside pressure by marrying relatively late as widow and widower, and they took special care not to interfere excessively in their own children's marriages. On the other hand some families show lingering traits of familial feudal autarchy: The Pastons knew at first hand the power and determination of the church to recognize clandestine marriages as valid, but their experience did not prevent the family from ostracizing the seventeen-year-old Margery and permanently barring her from the home after she had clandestinely bound herself to the bailiff—and this was as late as 1455.[30]

Literature, tending as usual to be more innovative than social life at any level, embodied, in the new dialect of Old French that developed after the Conquest, new themes in old forms. In Anglo-Norman romances and the Middle English versions of them, courtly practices were revised, and a new insularity toward love and chivalry developed that tended to be skeptical of *fin'amors*. One result was that love was not usually allowed to help shape heroic identity, and the hero did not often suffer a serious conflict between society and his own desires. Still, the story of Tristan was retold in ways that emphasized an unending conflict between the social order and love—love being defined, however, not as unrealistically ideal but as potentially reconcilable with human frailty. In the 1180s Hue de Rotolande, the insular Anglo-Norman poet from Herefordshire, author of *Ipomedon,* uses parody, both witty and obscene, to challenge and enliven his eroticism, and he implies that courtly love and selfish desires are not by nature contradictory forces. One scholar has concluded about English romantic literature in general that heroic love was less often regarded as idolatrous than on the Continent, that marriage received greater emphasis, and that loyalty and modesty were of considerable importance.[31]

Confronting love in language, we need to remind ourselves that obliqueness and troping are common in authoritarian societies not only because of the nature of language itself but in order to veil subversion and protest, though despite official frowns medieval utterance can at times be raucously and brutally frank. English and Scottish popular ballads reveal a surprising amount of hidden meaning, euphemistic concealment of embarrassing sins and perversions, a richly suggestive collection of metaphors, and other linguistic indirections. Thus—and here I am highly selective—coarse woolen cloth can stand for the maidenhead, and *sew* and *sow* are frequent sexual puns; wind, blowing, and the horn have sexual connotations, as do the knife and the sheath, the sword and the scabbard, and the letting fly of an arrow. A desiring brother approaches his pious and newly married sister in a garden, and she is horrified at what he invites her to: "To such a Hellish crying Sin, / Which none but *Sodom* wallow'd in."[32]

The richly layered allusiveness of the short medieval lyric has been long appreciated, and we need invoke here only one familiar example. A lovely song, scored for two voices and written by an unknown author, is metaphorically and semiotically sophisticated:

> Foweles in the frith.
> The fisses in the flod,
> And I mon waxe wod.
> Sulch sorw I walke with
> For beste of bon and blood.[33]

At first this seems to be a human love song sung by a man to a woman in the spring, but the "beste" of the last line is an ambiguity (could it be *beast,* thus invoking the lustful, or is it *best,* thus invoking an ideal?). It is highly likely that "the best of bone and blood" is not only the beloved but also Christ, and, once more in the manner of responses to the Song of Solomon, the delicate lyric at once celebrates human eros and laments the crucified Savior. Such troping, which gives us a wide range of interpretation, from sexual to sacred, is surely cousin german to the medieval recantatory envoy present in more than one masterpiece of Chaucer.

The copresence of eros and religion reminds us of how close mystical and literary expression could be. We have already confronted frequent marital and overtly sexual metaphors being applied to Christ and even God in Continental female piety, but the greatest of the English mystics, the Anchoress Julian of Norwich (died between 1416 and 1419), seems, like the whole English mystical tradition, more reserved and modest in her *Book of Showings,* written in Middle English, where, however, she says that love is the central message of the revelations she personally has received and where, in the longer version of the work, she uses the words *loue, love,* or *luff* at least 542 times, while *charity* or *chartye* is used only 25 times. God is her "Maker, her Brother, and her Lover"—and also, very positively, her Mother. It is the familial, the "homely," which seems best to characterize her emotions. She stresses these effects of God's love: "marvelous homelyhed," "gentylee curtesse," and "endlesse kyndness" (this last not necessarily totally without sexual connotations because of the first syllable *kynd*). And God is said to enjoy cherishing a wife, but there is more emphasis on Trinitarian espousal than on Christ as lover or husband.[34]

The emphasis of Dame Julian moves dramatically to the physical in the visions of Margery Kempe, whose *Book,* lost for centuries until its discovery in 1934, the illiterate author dictated to a clerical scribe in her own colloquial English, which is only seldom interrupted by what looks like extraneous clerical learning.[35] There is room here only to note, first, some of the striking realities of her marriage and then the marital and erotic tropings present in her visions. Married at twenty to a worshipful burgess of Lynn (now King's Lynn in Norfolk, where she was born c. 1373), she ultimately became the mother of some fourteen children, who are scarcely ever mentioned in her narrative—a not inconsiderable achievement for one who went out of her mind for well over half a year after the first birth and who sometimes found uxorial intercourse irreligious, particularly after having heard such sweet and delectable music when in bed with her husband that she thought of paradise, not of her marital duties and pleasures. We must note well the lack of disjunction here: apparently what she heard in bed was heavenly sound beyond anything she had known of sensual joy but not totally unrelated to its sweetness. Her full-bodied sexuality appears when she is mightily tempted to adultery by a man who later told her he would rather be chopped up like meat for a pot than unite with her. Her passion for him became so strong that she could not think a good thought, attend evensong, or say her paternoster.

She and her husband dedicated themselves to chastity, but domestic life did not always continue on a smooth course after that. He forced her to confess that she would rather see him being killed than have them turn back to their former uncleanness, and she forced him to confess that he had been able to lie with her untouched only because of his great fear. They bargained—if she would give up fasting on Fridays, he would never make the marital sexual demand—and she used her real collateral, her father's legacy, to pay off her husband's debts in return for being left alone. After she received guidance from Christ (she thinks God loves virgins more, but he assures her, to her great surprise, that he is just as pleased with good wives), marital abstinence won out, and she agreed to eat and drink on Fridays at her husband's bidding. Apparently the couple's vows of abstinence were widely known in her circle and neighborhood but perhaps not widely approved. In any event, Margery scrupulously cared for her husband when he became old and childish, unable even to relieve himself. One of the recurring charms of her narrative lies in its persistent naivete and all too human inconsistencies. Thus she consoled herself in these unpleasant trials by recalling the many delectable thoughts this now repulsive body once provoked; she may in fact be reenjoying her youthful marital ecstasies. But since these were often inordinately physical and lustful, she now can rejoice that she is being "punished by means of the same body," a reminder of Augustine, who believed that God cursed the first man precisely in the place of his lustful sin by endowing him and his descendants with uncontrollable tumescence.

When we now turn from the autobiographical realities to the mystical metaphors, we have not left the world of Margery's flesh very far behind. For she forthrightly reveals how close her body was to her believing and praying soul. She says she often felt literal heat in her body when she thought of the love of Christ. Small wonder! The Christ she worshipped said to her, "I must be intimate with you, and lie in your bed with you . . . and you may boldly, when you are in bed, take me to you as your wedded husband, as your dear darling, and . . . I want you to love me . . . as a good wife ought to love her husband. Therefore you can boldly take me in the arms of your soul and kiss my mouth, my head, and my feet as sweetly as you want" (126–27). Facing such competition in the marital bed, the husband not surprisingly settled for good and hearty meals on Friday instead of sexual intercourse. But at least this much can be said for the good burgess of Lynn, that he contributed to the abundant and loving marital-sexual metaphors that lay at the center of his wife's religious life.

Margery's images must in part surely have been highly sensualized substitutions for a somewhat less than glamorous reality. And in this masterpiece of naive art we feel certain that the literary imagination has been fed not by courtly idealizations and heroic exploits but by the real experiences of life itself, doubtless sometimes fetishistically embroidered into a kind of humble eros. In any case, Christ came to her as a most seemly and amiable man, for so she imagistically appropriated what for her was the central doctrine of her faith, the humanity of the incarnated Jesus. Her Lord is also paternal, and his favorite epithet for her is "Daughter," which does not, however, expel the uxorial. Nor does it always imply that Jesus is a father: an anchorite and fellow mystic to whom she confided her revelations interprets them as follows: "Daughter, you are sucking even at Christ's breasts" (52). We have noted that the melodies she hears while in her bed make her certain that it is "full merry in heaven" (46), and we shall not be far wrong in thinking that her own experiences of dalliance contributed more than did the Book of Revelation to her vision of the future life. The centerpiece of her personal religious iconology, deriving from the doctrine of the Incarnation, is a male youth: "And if she saw a handsome man, she had great pain to look at him, lest she might see him who was both God and man. And therefore she cried many times and often when she met a handsome man, and wept and sobbed bitterly for the manhood of Christ" (123).[36]

Nothing more fully reveals the closeness of Margery's metaphors to the sensual realities mediated to her by her own body than the fact that in moments of what we today would recognize as depression and paranoiac fetishizing she indulges in foul thoughts and foul recollections of lechery and uncleanness, in which she sees exposed (sometimes indeed by priests Christian or pagan) men's genitals and other abominations. In her view these horrible inversions are sent to her by her chastising Lord, but her somewhat simplistic theology is not quite adequate to the subtle intermixture of sensual good and evil in her imaginings: the devil dallies with her as the Lord dallied with her. Her religious sensuality is deeply tied to the carnality of her earthly ways, licit and illicit.

The turning of the high medieval church to love marriages did not in itself induce such mysticism as this, which has older and deeper roots in the venerable tradition of Christian sensualism, one of the main themes of the present book. But Margery Kempe's is an honest example of its medieval version, revealed in straightforward, unpretentious narrative art, close to an intimate diary brimming with the juices of life, while at the same time it shows itself a carefully thought out transformation of spiritual exercises derived from meditations on the life of Christ. Her travels to the Holy Land and to Continental shrines and her confrontations with clerics, neighbors, and traveling companions also contribute greatly to its full charm. Church historians and students of religious culture in general and mysticism in particular will be attracted by Margery's many allusions to other mystics and her relations to ecclesiastical institutions and established forms of worship.

Chaucer

If Margery is susceptible of multiple approaches, consider the critical opportunities opened by the many-faceted Chaucer. I have chosen one that concentrates on the *Canterbury Tales,* a dramatically conceived masterpiece that conceals the author behind its characters and that buries the didactic in mimesis and irony. I have thus placed this witty and elusive portrayer of Eros in a category similar to that occupied by the Ovid of the *Metamorphoses* and the Boccaccio of the *Decameron.* We shall therefore have to dig for marital meanings and insights and take sightings and soundings based on an uneven and irregular terrain.

But we need not begin there, and it may tie Chaucer to several of the traditions we have already analyzed if we look (without being too categorical) at his own confrontations of pagan antiquity, Christian orthodoxy, courtly love, Chartrian naturalism, and the ecclesiastically sponsored marriage of individual choice. These confrontations take place everywhere, and I therefore use a topical rather than a chronological approach. But wherever authentic Chaucerian love appears at its witty and luminous best, one donnée is never far to seek. It is present in the racy "Miller's Tale," where Chaucer blesses sexual indulgence that is natural, free, simple, and universal, and where the longings of love that Absalon feels are, as has been well said, "positively epidemic in the Middle Ages."[37] One thinks of Boccaccio, but Chaucer's urbane and worldly detachments should not obscure the connection of his realistic art with the theology described in chapter 8—the theology that defined God as love and so electrified the whole of existence with amorous impulses that cannot easily be denied. I wish to assert, perhaps controversially, that if there is any one perspective that will give central unity to Chaucerian diversity, it is this, that a universal love radiance conceived of as divine cannot be confined legalistically to any institution of culture or religion, especially if the central tenet of that religion is that God not only commands but *is* love. If this perspective is right, it is wrong to apply narrow

Augustinian or orthodox standards to Chaucer's literary practice, even though he knows them well and at times nods in their direction. His intellectual milieu is newer, broader, more creative—and culturally more universal. How does Chaucer confront the erotic traditions of (1) the pagan, (2) the courtly, (3) the orthodox Christian, and (4) the naturalism of the School of Chartres?

The world of pagan antiquity is the setting of two of Chaucer's greatest works. The "Knight's Tale" ends coldly enough, with an aristocratic stress on prudence, biology, and established religion (Jupiter is put back in charge of cosmic affairs), and with little concession to individual joy or grief but great stress on the generative reduplication of both the dynasty and the human species. So when we are told that the decreed marriage, at the end, of Emily and Palamon will bring total happiness, without jealousy but with abundant female tenderness and full male fidelity, we are not moved: these medieval values are here inscribed glacially, monumentally. Still, I am convinced that some values emerge, however qualified, from Chaucer's contemplation in the "Knight's Tale" of what V. A. Kolve has called "the pagan moment in history." The range of interpretation, from idealization to disillusioned denigration of the best candidates for some kind of approval, Emily and Theseus, is distressingly wide, even for Chaucer. And yet pagan sensual values, even though standing alone they are dangerous, also seem capable of some kind of redemption. Which ones? Surely not the universally mischievous Mars or the ultimately life-denying Diana. Venus, who has, to be sure, her own peculiar mischiefs and even terrors, is supported by Saturn, who is older and cosmically more powerful than Jupiter; *her* man wins both life and love in marrying that attractive "idea," Emily, one of Chaucer's dearest concepts though far from being one of his most vivid creations. And Theseus, the Knight's—and surely in part Chaucer's—raisonneur, welcomes sexuality once it is stabilized in familial order.[38]

The Christian palinode of *Troilus and Criseyde,* another work set in pagan antiquity, has provoked much deep disagreement, but if we draw our lessons not from orthodox theology but from the energies of Chaucer's art, the meaning—though it remains only a part of the work's final effect—seems inescapable: that the author has once more credited pre-Christian culture with the discovery of sexual joy and romantic commitment.[39] But he here makes it evanescent, though lovely, and allies the motif with tragic fear and piteous poignancy (the poet weeps as he writes). From his perspective in the eighth sphere, Troilus may enforce on us the transience of the romantic rose he had plucked, but he cannot

erase the Chaucerian celebration of its fresh, young loveliness and fra-
grance on the "blisful nyght," when even then the "hevene blisse" is
posed "bitwixen drede and sikernesse" (3.1315, 1317, 1322). Nor can
the redeemed hero erase the association of his quondam consummated
joys with both "gentilesse" (3.202) and the increased heroic prowess that
follows them. And the concluding recantation, admittedly beautiful and
moving, cannot make us forget the highly sympathetic narrator's eleva-
tion of joyful ancient eros into the Boethian principle that love rules
earth, sky, and sea; creates amity between states and nations; establishes
laws of friendship; and joins couples in a holy tie.[40]

In the *Legend of Good Women* Chaucer adapts to his purposes another work from pagan antiquity, the popular *Heroides* of Ovid. His purpose is to create an additional palinode to the *Troilus*, this one asking
directly for forgiveness from the ladies for his portrayal of the faithless
Criseyde. With an unerring rhetorical eye he draws upon a very popular
work from pagan antiquity to portray the faithfulness of loyal long-term
lovers in myth and legend. In the prestigious pagan context of this envoy
(so unlike the Christian recantatory conclusions of the *Troilus*) he shows
more flexibility and grace than he does in exalting the courtly and chivalric wooing, waiting, and grief of John of Gaunt, who had shortly before
lost his first wife in death.

Chaucer confronts the courtly in *The Book of the Duchess,* where his
conventionality and stiffness of manner may show embarrassment at
writing in the called-for manner of aristocratic flattery[41]—but, as we
shall see in the *Parliament of Fowls,* when the literary occasion is royal
and structured by class, he is by no means put off provided the subject
matter is congenial. We may conclude, too summarily, that the heritage of
courtly love was not a permanently engaging or enduringly fruitful one
for Chaucer.

Chaucer's relations to the tradition of Pauline and Augustinian orthodoxy regarding marriage are more complex than to either the pagan
or the courtly moment. He allows his Parson to express that tradition in
the *Canterbury Tales:* in his tale marriage is "sacrement" whose "auc-
tour" is "Crist" (881) and whose aims are conventional (engendering
children for the service of God, payment of the marital debt, and avoid-
ance of sin, 880–85). It can be threatened by sexuality both before and
after nuptials. All sexual love is emblematized by the devil's five fingers:
looking, touching, foul words, kissing, and "the stynkynge dede of
Leccherie" (861). The Parson sweeps away with these five fingers not
only raw libido but cultivated eros as well. He expectedly regards vir-

ginity as the "hyeste degree that is in this present lif" (867) and the sin of defloration as heinous precisely because it keeps the girl from the highest holiness: she may repent but she is always "corrupt" (871). The most important conclusion to derive from such a forceful and direct statement of orthodoxy by a character Chaucer admires is the author's virtually complete artistic ignoring of its tenets when he is writing at his best about love and marriage.

What norm, then, does Chaucer seem to adhere to? We must turn to a difficult work, which is not, however, finally ambiguous in its views of love and commitment, *The Parliament of Fowls*. At first many of the speeches by birds on the highest social level seem to be a distillation of courtly amorous experience—Peace and Patience are friends, Delight accompanies Gentilesse. In his suit the royal tercel eagle promises to serve the formel eagle in obedience, truth, and faith and now seeks her mercy and grace—or death will follow. But for the most part his suit is moderate enough, a kind of modified, essentialist courtliness, and we may therefore be somewhat surprised that the cause of his pain and the object of his devotion blushes red in shame and modesty: "Ryght as the freshe, rede rose newe / Ayeyn the somer sonne coloured is" (442–43). Perhaps this sensible royal woman is put off by even hints of the courtly tradition.

In any case the *essential,* though certainly not the exclusive, force of this work comes from newer philosophies and theologies in which the accents of Alan of Lille are clear and strong. Nature is fundamental and all-determining, powerful as "the vicaire of the almyghty Lord" (379). And the clerical ideal of free and equal choice is fully in place: the formel eagle is given "my choys al fre" (649), which she will exercise according to her heart's desire. Inclination is thus respected and may explain (more seriously than in my light comment about the courtly a moment ago) that the lady's blush is a modest acknowledgment of the presence of sexuality in both the suit and her heart. The males are not abject, though they are polite and distantly courtly; each of the three contenders for the formel's hand has, until the decision is reached, equal rights though not all have the high rank of royalty. By Nature's decree her decision will not be made until a year has elapsed, allowing time for a mature and fully independent reflection. The separate elements and the total structure of Chaucer's own code of love stand in clearest light in *The Parliament of Fowls.*[42]

Chaucer's code of love has also been thought to appear in the *Canterbury Tales,* where love and marriage have been long known to be a major preoccupation. The fabliaux-like narratives have, of course, something to say on the subject, often in the wry, indirect way of Boccaccio, who is the source of some of them. Chaucer, a master ironist and imagist, often uses contrast to arouse attention and suggest alternatives to what he presents grimly and realistically. The "Merchant's Tale," a peculiarly grimy story that does not keep the young and lovely May unsullied for very long, presents a *couple mal assorti,* if there ever was one. And the sordid touch of January, perverting the ends of marriage to serve his cramped and commercial spirit and then applying the highest hopes to what he so calculatingly arranges, makes his comeuppance at the end seem both just and comic. We may indeed feel some compassion for May when she sees what she has been united to for life "sittynge in his sherte, / In his nyght-cappe, and with his nekke lene" (1852–53), but against the ideal of the *Parliament of Fowls* the marriage of January and May looks perverse and degenerate. January's literal blindness near the end is a narrative ratification of what he has been spiritually all along, while May's brief and joyless consummation in the branches of a tree is all that can be expected of a flirt full of what Talbot Donaldson calls "superficial honesty and subcutaneous deceit." She stands well below Boccaccio's assertive, witty, and ingenious wives.[43]

To get the full dialectical force of the marriage tales we must contemplate those narratives and autobiographical confessions that have often been thematically related and evaluatively compared. In the light of the categories of this study, the Franklin, the Clerk, and the Wife of Bath will be related somewhat differently than hitherto, and I shall attempt a radical shift of emphasis *from* what has usually and all too easily been taken to be the norm *to* what has much too frequently, though of course understandably, been regarded as heretical and reprehensible.

What is wrong with making the "Franklin's Tale" the synthesizing resolution of the stark alternatives of idea and practice that appear in what has been traditionally regarded as the marriage group? For one thing, the norm stands at the beginning of the story and not the end, and what comes after it seems to make us uneasy about it in profound and crippling ways. Like Chrétien in *Cligès,* the Franklin begins his story of marriage with an ideal, a very lofty one, which he then allows reality to modify and darken, if not eclipse entirely. Chaucer initially shows the "grete worthyness" that is in married love, which he heats up enough to melt away stubborn considerations of domestic governance and ultimate control so prominent in other tales. "When maistrie comth, the God of Love anon / Beteth his wynges, and farewel, he is gone!" (765–66). True enough! The point had been reiterated often since Andreas

Capellanus, who, however, had the countess of Champagne's circle vote that this very truth made love and Christian marriage totally incompatible, with the latter's desired stress on husbandly headship and the obligations of sex on demand enforced by the uxorial *debitum*. Over such difficulties as this Chaucer's unimpressive dialectician, the Franklin, skips much too lightly. Obviously mutuality and forbearance can be said to lie in shared humility. The man must remain in marriage the same servant of love that he was in courtship. The lady too must be committed to being a "humble trewe wyf" (758) and friend, knowing that "freendes everych oother moot obeye" (762). But it all seems too easy in the very formulation, which the subsequent tale, advertently or not, proves it to be. For real life imposes qualifications and evasions, and magic, remoteness (this is a Breton lay), and naivete of mind and character are with scant conviction summoned to untie knotty problems and explain difficult decisions. Finally, an ecclesiastical *nomos,* not fully consonant with the new churchly ideals of free choice, consent, and continuing love, returns to organize somewhat too rigidly or self-righteously the freer, more spiritual agape of the opening. This last point has been made by R. E. Kaske in the most satisfactory interpretation of the *Tale* that I know: "If man is indeed woman's intellectual superior—as holy Church tells us, and as I duly believe [Kaske is here ventriloquizing Chaucer]—he will of course be able to stay one jump ahead of his wife, and to rule her the way Arveragus ruled Dorigen. Won't he?"[44] "Chaucer"-Kaske's sly question at the end—"Won't he?" doubtless accompanied by a wink of the scholarly eye—throws the fragile equilibrium of this delicately posed tale out of balance. Doesn't it?

Instead of imitating the order of *Cligès,* as the Franklin's story did in moving from the ideal to a kind of ambiguous reality, the Wife of Bath inverts it, beginning with the assertively real and ending with the authoritatively ideal. Through her, Chaucer presents his meaning, not less subtly, not less indirectly, not more consistently, but more robustly, more imaginatively, and therefore with greater aesthetic compulsion. But before discussing the "Wife's Prologue and Tale," I must make another comparison. Griselda and Alisoun have often been regarded as the opposite extremes of abject humility and tyrannical pride that must be avoided if one is to strike the ideal matrimonial balance envisaged in the first, theoretical part of the "Franklin's Tale." I view things somewhat differently, regarding both women as powerful and attractive, each in her own way. Griselda is greatly superior to her testing husband in both narrative and moral worth, and an authentic heroine within the strict param-

eters set for her by the "Clerk's Tale."[45] But she paid too high a price for
her exaltation, as I think Chaucer himself saw (in his envoy to this tale
the narrator wants no husband to imitate Walter nor wife to follow
Griselda); she sinks the mother in the wife, and her wifeliness consists
much more of obedience than love, as her husband's "love" consists
much more of the bestowal of a haughty and established grace in return
for compliance than it does of attraction to her beautiful body and respect for her formidable will. And there can be little doubt that it is the
Wife of Bath who has laid a powerful hold upon the sensibilities of our
own day. Do we find intimations of nobility and norm in her "Prologue
and Tale"?

The autobiography and the story told by Alisoun are as "boold . . . ,
and fair, and reed of hewe" as was "hir face" ("General Prologue," 458),
imbuing the married state with more sordidness and pain but also with
more delight, insight, and immediate vibrancy than one usually encounters at any time or any place. As is true of all great imaginative creations,
the Wife's roots go deep into her culture's soil, and the effectiveness of
her challenge to its frustrations and oppressions is in direct proportion to
her knowledge and mastery of its ways. Had space permitted an analysis
of the *Roman de la rose,* we would have met one of her several ancestors in
Jean de Meung's learned and cynical old woman, La Vielle, once a beauty
but now wild and foolish, who, however, stands on a considerably lower
literary and human plane.[46] There is scarcely an idea that has been raised
in this and the previous chapter on the Middle Ages that does not appear
in some form or other in Alisoun's exposition and narrative. She belongs
with us on this subject, if anywhere, for she is very much a wife—
sometimes only fashionably and commercially so but at a deeper level
totally so in body, soul, spirit, in reality and dream. She is, you might say,
das ewig weibliche (in the sense of wifely, not generally feminine) in her
essentials; more narrowly and pertinently, she is present in a work where
characters are defined not only by social roles but also by the work they
actually do, the Wife possessing a position defined by the institution of
marriage. When she loves, it is mostly, if not quite exclusively, in marriage: "I wol bestowe the flour of al myn age / In the actes and in fruyt of
mariage" ("Wife's Prologue," 113–14). She understands—and makes
full use of—the essential drive to sexual equality that, as we have seen,
inheres from Christian antiquity through the Middle Ages in the marriage debt. She has chafed under the clerical tradition that found sin even
in marital acts, and she attacks it directly. Like a doughty chevalier in
Chrétien, she loves *and* fights, veritably a Venus and a Mars in one. She

strikes her husband and is struck by him, and her blow is also intended for the long literary and clerical tradition of antifeminism. That she loved and struck Jankyn and that he loved and struck her in return puts both of them in the company of Abelard, who, as we have seen, combined embraces and blows, punishment and instruction, "to bend [Heloise] to my will if persuasion failed." In her full-bodied physicality she surely belongs to some version of the naturalistic tradition. In the art of love she "koude . . . the olde daunce" ("General Prologue," 476), was never discreet, and forced her partners to do what some medical opinion demanded—to pay attention to the needs of women. She is mightily endowed with erotic desire, she scolds, she can be cruel, she demands mastery, and with at least her first three husbands she plays that commercial game which society has set for her, buying and selling property and marital flesh equally. In many ways she illustrates the belief of many in her time, but more especially a few centuries earlier, that marriage was nothing but *iurata fornicatio.*[47]

Thus with the Wife of Bath we begin realistically enough—gamily and even grimily, but with no lack of attractiveness and literary energy. Where do we end? With the tale. And I confess to being one of those who believe that an organic nerve ties it to the prologue. Through that nerve flow impulses in the form of witty recollections of the Wife in her autobiographical account. *She* wants mastery, and she believes *all* women want mastery over men. With an earthy reminder in her own autobiographical voice of her own attractively assertive personality, the work ends. These last lines remind us that Chaucer is an ironical realist and also wants to tie his parts together, finally establishing the wholeness of his unforgettable character and of the two parts devoted to her.

But surely in both aesthetic and human terms these impressions of an unreconstructed Wife continuing to dance the old dance, vigorously human though they are, must in our final judgment be subordinated to what is new, rich, strange, and even ideal in the tale—to human and humane qualities and to visions that Arveragus in the "Franklin's Tale" never achieved and that make *his* final mastery seem by comparison self-righteously egotistical in theory and thin and watery in practice.[48]

It is a central thesis of this work that aesthetic power is often generated through the creation of an imagined state that at once transcends and shames the circumambient reality. We must so interpret these less realistic and loftier elements of the Wife's final vision. The raped solitary country girl of the Arthurian landscape in the tale surely symbolizes what society had done to Alisoun in her loveless marriages. Running on a continuous line, the story transforms the wronged girl—and by implication Alisoun too—into a crone (any person's fancy since we are all fated to observe our own decline). But then the crone becomes a maiden again, as Britton Harwood has suggested, when her honor is perceived, respected, and so restored, and her judgment and goodwill trusted: *you* are good and wise, *you* decide, a confidence that is surely the greatest gift any knight can give to any lady.[49] The sermon on *gentilesse* preached by the Wife as crone may be conventional; it appears, as Lee Patterson has suggested, to derive from John of Wales's preaching handbook, the *Communiloquium*.[50] But though not original with Chaucer, his use and placement of this sermon, with its tender consideration for the lowly, the old, the poor, and the deprived, in the mouth of one whose own experience had included so much that was base and harsh, is surely intended to valorize her. And it also represents a powerful inversion by Chaucer of the medieval topos of the ugly old woman as the quintessential type of all that is undesirable. Chaucer has ratified the Wife's full humanity by letting her express the sublimest philosophy he or his culture knew.

In chapter 8, when discussing Tristan and Isolde, I asked what the results might have been had Mark and his wife together drunk the potion as intended. Dare we now ask if the Wife had drunk the cup of everlasting romantic love? She must have, for no one could have dreamed the dream of sexual fulfillment that closes the Tale, so often considered totally unrealistic and sentimental, without such a rich infusion. And she places the perfect romantic delight *in* a marriage upon which she bestows an intense mutuality. The Wife is not often regarded as a romantic, but Chaucer, perhaps unconsciously mindful of the tradition outlined in my study of the Middle Ages, endows her vision of romantic mutuality with the richness and mystery of Christian paradox, as indeed he did in introducing the "Franklin's Tale." The wife may preach sovereignty for herself and her sex, claiming rights as the head of the domestic state. But at the same time,

> . . . she obeyed hym [her husband] in every thyng
> That myghte doon hym plesance or lyking.
>   And thus they lyve unto hir lyves ende
> In parfit joye; . . . ("Wife's Tale," 1255–58)[51]

This joyful verbal and human exuberance is more compelling than the male domination, however genteel, that the husband of the "Franklin's Tale," Arveragus, gives us as legacy. In the Wife's concluding dream Chaucer may be redressing a balance or undertaking a bit of affirmative action in the only way open to him, the way of literary imagination. Does he present the demand for sovereignty (which he believes, on the domestic scene at least, to represent a universal feminine desire) as extreme or outlandish? On the contrary, it is precise and culturally induced: "Wommen desiren to have sovereynetee / As wel over hir housbond as hir love" ("Tale," 1038–39). Are not Chaucer's women demanding what sooner or later the courtly adulation of the lady would suggest as being inevitable—that the respect accorded in courtship be carried over into marriage, that the courtier and the husband should be integrated into one human being? Is such a demand totally unreasonable? That unity Chrétien had clearly envisioned, and it could not have been far from what the church wanted when it called for a freely achieved prenuptial consensus. The preliminary ideal of the "Franklin's Tale," whatever we think of its conclusion, establishes a "lawe of love," which requires that that traditional tyrant, the husband, abandon constraint and "maistrie" and put the will of his wife above his own, "As any lovere to his lady shal" (750).

There is of course the danger of substituting one tyranny for another or of ending in a stalemate. And there is in every great realist—and Chaucer is surely one—an awareness of the ever recurring presence of human mischief. After the crone's vision (also the Wife's, also Chaucer's, also ours?), Alisoun reminds us that she remains very much herself: even in her final prayer she asks for meek, young, fresh husbands, for the benefit of outliving them, for the right to rule them. And what about the sexually niggardly and the physically stingy she had known so well, brokers and buyers in the commercial marriage market, the "olde and angry nygardes of dispence"? Well, as for them, "God sende hem soone verray pestilence!" (1263–64). We are reassured, the Wife is still wrapped in her own individual and unforgettable humanity. For Chaucer to have ignored that would have been to lose artistic credibility and authority.

So we may allow the loving mutuality central to the crone's vision to stand uncompromised in its intensity and in the responsiveness of one partner to an other—refined, sensitive, and continuous. In this sly way Chaucer has signaled that that vision is not the product of a deranged mind prone to illusions. But why the submission to female sovereignty, which the crone requires of the knight? For one thing, it is in character, and Chaucer wants us to remember the real humanity of his creation. But it also seems more like an initiatory ritual gesture than the prolonged imposition of what Blake called "the Female Will." Would a tiresomely jokey recollection of a fabliaux stereotype consort well with what Chaucer's genius has created—a powerful woman who has known the bitterness of marital commercialization, who has attacked the misogynist stereoptypes of high religious culture, and who has been given a climactic moral vision that recalls Boethius? I suggest that we trust Chaucer's power as an artist and reverse one important scholarly and critical tradition by giving the palm for vivacious, complex, and central marital meanings to the Wife of Bath and not the Franklin.[52]

Malory

Malory, though he is not without complications, is a much more straightforward and direct writer than Chaucer, and in the matter of Britain, which he so influentially and unforgettably exploited, he brings us back to Continental romance and so provides a fitting climax to our consideration of long-term love in the Middle Ages. We have already shown how his treatment of Tristan and Isolde—and this is true of his source as well, the *Tristan en prose*—transformed Mark from sympathetic to villainous and Tristan himself, without sweeping his love under the rug, from a deceitful lover breaking alike the laws of marriage and knighthood to a heroic Arthurian champion. It now remains for us to consider his friendly rival, Sir Lancelot of the Lake, whose stories constitute the largest branch of the Vulgate Cycle and the most memorable sections of Malory's *Morte Darthur.* In these stories the author, though subordinating and subduing the adulterous passion for Queen Guinevere, allows it to stand paradoxically juxtaposed with the hero's deserved reputation as the greatest of Arthur's secular knights, kept from being the greatest even among the Grail heroes only by the earthiness and irregularity of his affectionate obsession, a paradox inherited from Chrétien de Troyes, who may well have invented the story of the love of Lancelot and Guinevere.[53]

Parallels to the present paradox we have encountered earlier, but they have seldom been so honorifically placed—close to the center of chivalric government and official piety. It would be wise to analyze central episodes in the Lancelot-Guinevere story as reinscribed by Malory to bring out their artistic appeal and their relevance to our story. After the Grail search, the queen and the knight love more hotly than before, and many speak of it. Its heat inevitably creates misunderstandings, particularly on the queen's part—misunderstandings that lead to a statement of Lancelot's philosophy of affection, when he is himself courted by a fair maiden, Elaine le Blanch, who dies of her unrequited affection. For Lancelot is so compounded of courtesy that he encourages closeness of contact, forgives passionate zeal, converses intimately with and kisses those who love him. With this particular Elaine, however (he had been loved by another of the same name earlier), he makes it clear that he will never marry ("truly I caste me never to be wedded man"), and he recoils at the thought of being her paramour (such a relationship is "full evyll," and he cries out "Jesu deffende me" [lines 17–23, 2:1089]).

It is not only Chaucer who has his lusty months of May (obviously created in honor of Natura and the good earthly Venus); there are at least two in Malory, and one of them, while praised for its renewing fecundities, leads to the authorial reflection that modern love, so unlike that of Arthur's time, lacks stability and wisdom. Then, in the kind of passage we so often long for in the midst of complex narrative art, Malory defines "vertuouse lofe" as loyalty first to God and then to the single person to whom one's faith has been pledged: "for there was never worshypfull man nor worshypfull woman but they loved one bettir than another" (lines 25–32, 3:1119). No direct mention of marriage here, only a long-lasting *fides* arising from solemn and joyful promises scrupulously kept.

We return to the lovers. Did extramarital long-term commitment resemble the marital in sanctioning sexuality? Or was it like the love of yore, when "men and women coude love togydirs seven yerys, and no lycoures lustis was betwyxte them, and than was love trouthe and faythefulnes" (lines 1–6, 3:1120)? On this crucial and much debated question, Malory seems to hedge, so revising Chrétien, who makes fleshly consummation unmistakable in this love. But there is no escaping the amorous heat between the lovers (that we have already noted) or the impossibility of regarding at least one dramatic episode as being other than sexual consummation. Coming to rescue the queen from her captor, Sir Meliagrance, who had loved her for years, Lancelot romantically sets up a ladder to her window and asks her if she wishes in her heart to be with him, evoking a "Ye, truly" (lines 12–20, 3:1131; observe the emphasis on accordant desire somewhat ceremonially stated, as though in a betrothal). Here, as elsewhere in chivalry, love leads to superhuman strength—and a wound, for Lancelot breaks out of its place an iron bar set in stone and cuts his hand to the bone. That night, he "wente to bedde with the quene and toke no force of hys hurte honde, but toke hys pleasaunce and his lyking untyll hit was the dawning of the day" (lines 28–31, 3:1131). Whatever hedging, lying, deceit, or hypocrisy this inevitably led to (all of course presented as serving a pious and political cause, like Luther's alleged injunction to tell a great lie for the sake of the Gospel), Malory and of course we too have to live with it. Lancelot and Guinevere indulged at least once in consummated carnality, though no one can say that the author has made them dissolute or promiscuous. They remain faithful to one another, and the *imitatio nuptiarum* can be said to be made complete by their physical union.

This amazing paradox causes many jarring notes to sound as Lancelot is forced in the climactic battles that lead to the dissolution of Christian knighthood to defend before Arthur his queen's honor and bend the truth to his lofty aim. But his honor seems somehow to remain unsullied in the mind of Malory, his last and climactic medieval redactor. And few even today can respond without emotion to Malory's soberly beautiful beatification of his hero after the confession of his sins, where he retains his full humanity. Guinevere does not, and she can be accused of becoming a precisian, refusing his kiss, dismissing him to an unbreakable earthly separation from her, and dying before he arrives for the last visit, which she did not desire. He does not rejoice in recollections of his sin, but he cannot forget her beauty and nobility; when he sees her and Arthur's bodies lying together in the tomb, his heart cannot sustain his body ("truly myn herte wold not serve to susteyne my careful body," lines 29–32, 3:1256), and his pride is laid low. He dies not long after. Even in such simple, understated prose the pathos rises higher than that evoked by Dante for Paolo and Francesca and approaches that of Chaucer uniting and then dividing Troilus and Criseyde.

This late medieval masterpiece is our last example of how the Christian literary and rhetorical spirit of the high Middle Ages privileged love and allowed it to transcend the legalistic and institutional. Chaucer, as in many late medieval sermons about Mary, does more than skirt the paradoxical when he has his Prioress pray to the Virgin and use the powerful word *ravish* (to allure, seduce) of her role in the Virgin birth:

> O bussh unbrent, brennynge in Moyses sighte,
> That ravyshedest doun fro the Deitee,
> Thurgh thyn humblesse, the Goost that in th'alighte.
>
> ("Prioress's Prologue," 468–70)

The paradox is so bold and contains such volatile elements that it was destined to fly apart. Lancelot and Guinevere provoked a moralistic rebuke from Roger Ascham in *The Scholemaster,* who found that "the whole pleasure of [Malory's] booke standeth in two speciall poyntes, in open mans slaughter and bold bawdrye: In which booke those be counted noblest Knightes, that do kill most men without any quarell, and commit foulest aduoulteries by subtlest shiftes: as Sir *Launcelote,* with the wife of king *Arthure* his master."[54] The Protestant and puritan responses to the medieval achievements in honoring eros in and out of marriage will concern us next, when we study the Renaissance. But one child of the new day, Lorenzo the Magnificent, though he is discussing neither Malory's work nor the Arthurian legend, seems to have some feeling for the fiery juxtapositions of medieval love and law. He proclaims that pure and chaste love may come to sexual fruition without diminishment or self-destruction, saying that "they are to be praised who pursuing this end, love one object only, day in and day out, with firm and constant faith."[55]

Amorous constancy may be peculiarly associated with holy matrimony by theologians, statesmen, philosophers. And by imaginative writers, artists, and mythmakers too—remember Chrétien, and consider the inner bond of marriage, without formal betrothal, exchange of oaths, priestly blessing, or nuptial mass that binds Parzival and the queen in Wolfram von Eschenbach.[56] But imaginative writers also find *fides* elsewhere (consider Isolde, Troilus, Lancelot, the troubadours) and are capable of honoring it imaginatively wherever it is located and however unconventionally and riskily the union is compounded (consult Boccaccio). It is not surprising that for centuries the Middle Ages has been considered the venue par excellence of romantic affection. This view needs chronological correction, as our discussion of antiquity (both pagan and Christian) has attempted to show; and C. S. Lewis, in the passage quoted in the epigraph of this chapter, claims too much for the medieval love synthesis. But still the Christian centuries reflecting their belief in a pervasive, divine, amorous radiance are intense, if not revolutionary, and they continue to surprise us with their artistic embodiments of long-lasting committed affection both inside and outside established marriage.

The divine radiance is somewhat different from ascetic prohibition; evasions, envoys, and apologetic deferences to orthodox authority show that we are left with a profound paradox that is perhaps unresolvable. Both the expansive and the restrictive must somehow be accommodated, and the amorously expansive is vastly more difficult to analyze precisely or appreciate fully. That bizarre masterpiece, Juan Ruiz's *Book of Good Love,* with its polarities of orthodox theology and ethics and of erotic mischief and even blasphemy, resists consistent interpretation. In a section in which Venus is invoked and then indeed undertakes to guide the Archpriest in his major seduction, the goddess is not only hailed as "holy" and "blessed," but as the bride of Love, "our Savior-lord divine." The best minds and the most sensitive spirits were aware of the ambiguity and the conflict, which they embody usually without discussion, as Chaucer did in the *Troilus* where he haunts us with consummated love but in the end just as beautifully recants.

In Gottfried von Strassburg the paradox rises to the surface but remains resistant to interpretation, at least to easy interpretation. King Mark orders an ordeal by hot iron to test Isolde's innocence, and it is staged with the full panoply of church and state. To prepare for it Isolde indulges in extravagant charities, giving away silver, gold, jewelry, all the horses and clothes she possessed. To keep herself technically free of lying, she arranges for Tristan to disguise himself as a pilgrim, to carry her from her ship to land, to stumble with her, and then to lie in her arms and lap, a position that all who saw thought was inevitable and totally innocent. The ruse permits her to take an oath that she has lain with no man except her husband and now, accidentally, with the pilgrim. Not only does the king approve the oath, but Christ does as well, and she seizes the glowing iron without injury. Of the Christ implicated in the ruse, Gottfried says:

> Thus it was made manifest and confirmed to all the world that Christ in His great virtue is pliant as a windblown sleeve. He falls into place and clings, whichever way you try Him, closely and smoothly as He is bound to do. He is at the beck of every heart for honest deeds or fraud. Be it deadly earnest or a game, He is just as you would have Him. This was amply revealed in the facile Queen. She was saved by her guile and by the doctored oath that went flying up to God, with the result that she redeemed her honour and was again much beloved of her lord Mark, and was praised, lauded, and esteemed before the people.

This amazing passage is surely not an attack on Christianity, since other passages attest the author's piety. It may be an attack on ordeals (outlawed by the church a few years later) or on established religion, the court, and the people, who bribe the Lord to favor illicit ways. If so, it is an astonishing anticipation of William Blake's Christ of the established churches and schools, the "Divinity of Yes & No too, The Yea Nay Creeping Jesus" who supposes "Up & Down to be the same Thing." Gottfried is sophisticated enough to create a telling satire. But he is also the artist of the erotic, the creator of a richly musical mutuality between Tristan and Isolde the Fair. And the difficulty of letting the satire on the corrupt church and aristocracy stand as final and definitive is that the oath *is* efficacious, the queen is spared, and in its most deeply artistic tellings the story privileges illicit love over arranged and officially sanctioned relationship. The best interpretation may be to let the paradox stand un-resolved. Law prohibits and is rule-bound, the Gospel is free and can be permissive. God's punishments of antinomian liberty can be terrible and eternal. But truly committed love can win divine approbation even when moral law is flouted. If we have emphasized the law of love over the letter that killeth, it is perhaps because this is primarily a study of art not phi-losophy, of products of the imagination and not reason.[57]

Thou tellst me, Mall, *and I beleeve thee must,*
That thou canst loue me much with little lust; . . .
Trust me, I find an aptness to mistrust;
I cannot loue thee long without my lust.

Sir John Harington, "To his Wife" (between
1585 and 1603)

TEN

The Renaissance (I): Struggles to Unite Eros and Marriage

*N*uptial love maketh mankind," wrote Bacon in "Of Love," "friendly love perfecteth it; but wanton love corrupteth and embaseth it." Although Bacon—and also Montaigne more vividly—separated these three loves, it does not today strike us as fanciful to think of them as united. The Renaissance itself and also more recent cultures, with perhaps greater delight, have habituated us to thinking of the nuptial, the friendly, and the wanton as constituting a consistent and satisfying pattern. Wordsworth hailed his wife as a "phantom of delight," who possessed "a reason firm" and "a temperate will" and who also bestowed "love, kisses, . . . and smiles," retaining, as she trod a household floor, the power "to haunt, to startle, and waylay," the last verb being particularly delicious in an uxorial context. I shall argue that in the Renaissance powerful forces were striving as never before to bring together into one relationship both the love that makes and the love that perfects. And even the more ambitious—and certainly risky—aim of redirecting "wanton" love in such a way that it was relieved of Bacon's traditional implication of corruption and baseness without losing its sensual charm was a major cultural undertaking. To mold a form of love that could contain volatile and conflicting forces challenged poet and artist; their achievements will be the subject of the two following chapters. But such complexly constituted love in artistic form did not arise in isolation, and it is the business of the present chapter to analyze intellectual formulations and also the religious, social, and political energies that stimulated the creating imagination. Of these energies the most transforming arose from the Reformation.

The Strengthening of Eros

Again and again in these pages, I have tried to show how problematical matters associated with human sexuality in its essence seem to be; they become more deeply so when new ground is taken, when new horizons open. And it should be no mystery as to why the struggle to unite eros and marriage becomes more difficult and intense if the libido is encouraged by greater tolerance and frankness than the preceding Christian centuries knew and if eros is allowed unabashedly to display and assert itself. It was precisely that which took place in the Renaissance, for it was not always a tamed or a childlike or a playful Cupid taking a cozy place in the domestic nest who was effectual and active but often a mature Eros of primitive strength and menace.

Nothing shows this more clearly than the visual arts. We can count on the honest and often disillusioned Caravaggio to bring out the seamy side. He did, to be sure, portray a sunny and radiant Cupid in *Amor Victorious,* now in the Kaiser Friedrich Museum in Berlin, but his view of Cupid is realistic and disturbing in *Sleeping Cupid* in the Pitti Palace (fig. 16). In this deeply shadowed painting, which almost conceals his wings, Amor is fat, even pot-bellied, though young; his navel is large, the features of his large face heavy and gross, his feet and toes gnarled, his eyebrows and locks black, with a suggestion of hair on his upper lip. He could be a teen-aged Bacchus or in our day a very juvenile member of a street gang. It is hard to view him and be comfortable about what he represents. In Bronzino's *Venus, Amor, and Jealousy* (fig. 17) Cupid is mature, almost as large as his mother Venus in size, with a penis matured though not in tumescence, but he is red-haired and fresh in appearance. Mother and son make a handsome aristocratic pair, as she looks at him proudly and longingly and as he confidently holds his bow and arrow. But in back of the son lurks a black-haired figure with a darkly brooding, hideous face whose mouth seems about to bite a snake. He represents jealousy and "balances" with ugly menace the smiling *amorini* to the right. Like its sister piece in the National Gallery, London (Bronzino's *Venus, Cupid, Folly, and Time*), this painting is at once artificially beautiful and deeply disturbing, with its hints of incest and excessive amorous similitude.

Venus herself is often as ambiguously poised and potentially contradictory as her son. Even that nobly unambiguous celebrant of uxorial love with a powerful sexual ingredient, Edmund Spenser, presents her as a lightly veiled beauty who is, however, both male and female: "She syre and mother is her selfe alone, / Begets and eke conceiues, ne needeth

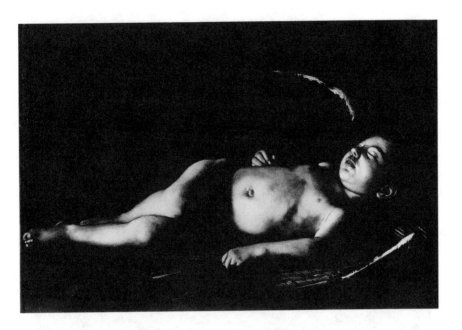

FIGURE 16 Caravaggio, *Sleeping Cupid*. (Pitti Palace, Florence; Alinari/Art
Resource, NY.)

other none" (*Faerie Queene,* 4.10.41). Venus is not frequently androgynous, certainly not Spenser's love goddess at her most typical. In
the visual arts she usually displays unmistakably positive sexual allure as
a nude lying on a couch, and she does not always beckon to illicit adventure. Modern scholarship has persuasively argued that Titian's famous
Venus of Urbino (fig. 18) in its direct appeal portrays a nude woman offering herself, but that many obvious hints make her primarily a bride awaiting her husband, accompanied as she is with epithalamic imagery and
traditional uxorial signs.[1] Indeed, some of the most memorable painterly
embodiments of the love goddess invoke, along with bodily allure, the
intellectual, the chaste, the delicate, the maternal (a Veronese Venus recalls the Madonna *lactante*), and several other manifestations of the domestic and the wifely.

Two charming painterly *poesie* are worthy of especial attention. The
first, by the Venetian artist Lorenzo Lotto (1480–1556), *Venus and Cupid*
(fig. 19), is unmistakably epithalamic. The ivy behind Venus and the
myrtle wreath, her headdress and earrings are insistently conjugal; and

FIGURE 17 Bronzino, *Venus, Amor, and Jealousy.* (Courtesy of the Budapest Museum of Fine Arts.)

FIGURE 18 Titian, *Venus of Urbino*. (Uffizi Gallery, Florence; Alinari/Art Resource, NY.)

the pleasant-faced love goddess may well be blessing a bride, who should be imagined as standing before the canvas. It is Cupid, however, who is unforgettable: he directs a stream of urine through the wreath in an arc onto the rose-covered pudenda of his mother, and the best interpretation says this augurs offspring and fertility. Have Venus and Cupid ever before or since been domesticated in so coyly original a way?

Somewhat earlier, in 1470, Francesco del Cossa, in a fesco of the Palazzo Schifanoia in Ferrara called *Venus and Her Children* (figs. 20, 21), introduces the social and the premarital on the border of innocence and experience, a psychological zone extremely important in Spenser, Shakespeare, and many lyrics of intimacy, the place where couples are formed and courtship takes place. Venus is crowned with flowers—the time is April—and the genre is a Triumph, Mars kneeling at her feet and bound in chains. Venus herself is imbued with a richly ambiguous pensiveness that extends to her children, male and female, all elegantly and modestly dressed. Some are disposed in couples and more in triples, either one man and two women or one woman and two men. Some kiss, some talk, some gaze, some touch—and there may be suggestions of jealousy be-

FIGURE 19 Lorenzo Lotto, *Venus and Cupid.* (Metropolitan Museum of Art, Purchase, Mr. and Mrs. Charles Wrightsman Gift, 1986.)

tween the girls in some of the triples and perhaps even of present and future mischief (one of the males extends his solicitations beyond the bounds of propriety for a group scene). Neither joy nor ecstasy is indubitably anticipated, as in Watteau. Still, despite the subtext that gives us weird rock formations and swans that look a bit like aggressive geese, the scene is mostly one of pleasure, heightened by modesty and a pervasive current of trembling delicacy. This splendid painting suggests that courtship is indeed what Shakespeare made of it in his romantic comedies, a not unprecarious time of muted joy being tested, pregnant with possibilities of either the abortion or fulfillment of desire.[2]

If we move from mythology to the realism of the domestic-bourgeois, we find the scene no less ambivalent. Frans Hals portrays in two companion paintings a married couple from the new merchant classes. She offers him a rose, he holds out a gloved hand to receive it.

FIGURE 20 Francesco del Cossa, *Venus and Her Children.* (Palazzo Schifanoia, Ferrara; Alinari/Art Resource, NY.)

"Their hands combine . . . to say 'dowry'." The wife is charming but calculating; she might tell the truth but only when giggling or drunk—and the truth would show that she knows her man's weaknesses. He is self-satisfied and lecherous. Will his ungloved hand undo her bow, which "whispers *undoing*," or will he leave without taking off his cape and visit his favorite prostitute?[3] Whatever he does, it is clear the husband knows he has made a good financial arrangement. Hals has represented both countenances without the slightest suggestion of love, and any age could provide abundant examples of this kind of marital unlove.

Other portraits of married couples coming from a northern ambience are less lightly cynical and reveal idealistic marital possibilities in real life. A Van Dyck painting in the Hermitage (fig. 22) portrays a chubby child fully dressed; a father on whose dignified, intense, deeply human countenance love is written but worry and responsibility also (the

FIGURE 21 Detail of figure 20: Group of Venus's Children. (Alinari/Art Resource, NY.)

one visible hand is tensed); and a wife, lovely in her lace collar, who catches our eye with her gaze, the play of a knowing near-smile on her face that seems to say, "I *do* know how babies are made. It was fun but don't ask me to express it." Rubens's portrait of his own family, *Rubens, His Wife Helena Fourment, and Their Son Peter Paul* (fig. 23), is a lovely

FIGURE 22 Van Dyck, *Husband, Wife, and Child.* (Courtesy, The Hermitage, St. Petersburg/Jean Hagstrum and Russell Maylone.)

FIGURE 23 Rubens, *Rubens, His Wife Helena Fourment, and Their Son Peter Paul.* (Metropolitan Museum of Art, Gift of Mr. and Mrs. Charles Wrightsman, 1981.)

FIGURE 24 Rembrandt, *The Jewish Bride*. (Rijksmuseum-Stichting, Amsterdam.)

expression of esteem enlivened by desire, the sexually alluring wife looking at the child, Rubens looking in mature and grateful amorousness at
the wife.[4] The painter has added erotic resonance by placing himself near
a statue betokening fecund art and by associating his wife with vividly
beautiful flowers and so presumably with nature and procreation. The
energy of circular linear motion ties the family and the icons together,
and the canvas can without exaggeration be called libidinal, though in a
subdued and thoroughly gracious way. Rembrandt's more serious *The
Jewish Bride* (fig. 24) presents subdued eros but undiminished love and
may well have been inspired by the story of Isaac and Rebecca in Genesis
26:8 and also by the passages in Proverbs we discussed in chapter 6—the
coincidence of Protestant and Jewish values being well known. The husband is older, the wife modest but richly garbed, and maturity and
seemliness do not seem to impede the sexual currents. For his right hand
touches her fully covered breast, her hand touches his hand that touches
her heart, while her other hand is placed on her pudenda, hinting per-

haps at the Venus Pudica, who may be sexually shy but is of course Venus still.

If this preliminary visual survey were more ambitious, it would have to include other bourgeois couples—stiff, separated, unattractive, and substantial in girth as in gain—and it could not possibly ignore the realistic satirical tradition of portraying the *couple mal assorti* (consider the elder Cranach's wonderful union of his version of "January" and "May" in *Das Ungleiche Paar* in the Kunstakademie of Vienna). And innumerable representations of Eden, the Fall, Judith, and Salome, and pictorial narratives of Cupid and Psyche, notably by Raphael and Giulio Romano, would enforce the view that the Renaissance, southern and northern, invigorated both Cupid and his mother even when it placed them in a marital context. So important though sometimes so complicating and controversial a matter is this erotic heightening that I wish to ally myself with the bold (some will think overbold) insights of two scholars from different fields. Adrian Stokes comments on the nature of the apotheosis achieved in the famous monument of Rimini to an affection that began as extramarital and then became marital. The critic finds that erotic energy comes from real life directly to the bas reliefs by Agostino di Duccio in this small and exquisite Taj Mahal of the West, the Tempio Malatestiano, an energy that affects our perceptions and sensations of the marble itself. We see the stone pristinely as primitive organic matter and water—and we are asked to believe that Isotta's "pervasive magic stimulated in the sculptor . . . fantasies . . . of fecund moisture in stone, of glimmering forms seen under water, of suctional forces congealed in shapes on the surface of the marble."[5] If indeed the stones at Rimini are so sexualized, we would have further evidence that art was bringing erotic energy, what Bacon chose to call "wanton" love, into the marital context at the very same time that that venerable estate was being elevated into something approaching Aristotelian friendship (esteem, in fact).

The erotic force Stephen Greenblatt finds in art is less concentrated and more diffused but no less powerful. He is right in believing that "great creating nature" is the inspiration of Shakespeare's comic magic—a conscious inspiration, I would add, since the playwright makes so many eulogistic invocations of it. Greenblatt is also right in noticing that though the comedies move toward the marriage bed, the sensual courting that precedes dramatic closure becomes the focus of dramatic attention. The "special pleasure of Shakespearean fiction" is "friction," a "generalizing of the libidinal" that is diffused through the comedies as foreplay. The theater is the venue in which sexual heat is generated, but I would urge that such literary libido is rather closer to eros as I have defined it earlier than to instinct and so is an achievement of the author's imagination.[6]

The Aims of Marriage and the Great Reformers

Erotic heat may not often be associated with theological or humanistic discourse, but in Renaissance thought, as in some medieval naturalism, it warms more than one category. Consider the aims of marriage as codified in theological treatise and canon law. The presence of libido is obvious in what was usually regarded as the first aim of marriage, procreation. It is also openly present in the marital debt, as we have seen, since there could be no insurance in marriage against sin (the second aim) unless the partners were sexually willing—and on request. Archbishop Cranmer in 1549 added a third reason for marriage to the Anglican Prayer Book, "mutual society," which was variously thought to mean help, comfort, cooperation, love, sometimes even friendship.[7] One of the questions that will detain us is whether this new motive envisaged a union of mutually interacting eros and esteem. In other words, did the strengthened eroticism of Renaissance art effectually enter the ideal of the marriage of true *minds?* If so, the sixteenth and seventeenth centuries in Europe would represent a true watershed.

Some students of culture have denied that there was much change in relations between women and men or in the status of women as the high Middle Ages waned, and some have even seen a deplorable regression. Evidence from history and culture gives considerable support to these views, particularly with respect to southern Europe. But to get a right perspective, we must concentrate on that profoundly culture-shaking event, the Protestant Reformation, notably its attack on clerical celibacy and its insistent and widespread propaganda for the dignity and attractiveness of marriage, not only for the clergy but equally for every Christian in the newly defined priesthood of all believers. Let us therefore try to put flesh on the bones of John Harington's epigram on the expanded rationale for marrying: " . . . late writers, men of passing piety / Have found a thyrd cause, mutual society."[8]

Paradoxes continue to abound. "Mutual society" would be expectedly more available but at the same time might be more difficult to achieve in an association more complexly constituted than Xenophon's famous separation of male labor outside the house from female labor inside. But whatever the opportunities or risks, the husband now regarded the marital enterprise as a kind of joint stock company, in which the wife was "a ioynt Gouvernour of the Family, with himselfe."[9] Such an arrangement can scarcely be said to be unproblematical and would have seemed to require the divine sanction of a marital-specific grace, but the reformers denied marriage the status of sacrament and made it a civil contract, though most of them and all of the societies they influenced refused to consider divorce when love and companionship failed. The church of the Middle Ages had given its blessing to consensus in marriage, to the free and untrammeled choice of mate, even in clandestine situations. The reformers, while calling for companionate marriage, strengthened fatherly rule, frowned on secret unions, and made parental consent as well as guidance de rigueur. We have in our pictorial analysis argued for the intensification of eros. Intensification can be seen everywhere, not only in the praise of marriage and the strengthening of its affective bonds, but also in the unrelenting Protestant-Puritan attack on licentiousness. It is not difficult to see that a fully sanctioned concentration of erotic energy in the home made less necessary its dissipation in illicit venues, which were now treated with unmitigated scorn and even horror. Post-Reformation mentality required the bride to be more than "bonere and buxom in bed and at the borde." (The phrase comes from the bride's vow in the Sarum Manual of 1542 and is used in the Oxford English Dictionary to illustrate *bonair,* meaning "well-bred, gentle, courteous, kind, complaisant.") She should also be "clubbable," in the important social sense associated with Dr. Johnson and his circle, but not punished corporally, though, amazingly, that savagery was sanctioned by some as a last resort. The woman was endowed with absolutely equal status before God, but in her relation with man the requirement that this lovable creature be also cooperative and obedient was enforced with the considerable strength that Protestant rhetoric seemed always to possess. That it was often amazingly effectual is attested by the fact that the reformed Christianity took strides in creating a new man that make communist attempts pale by comparison. For the "new creature in Christ Jesus" was often able to attain, in a psyche stirred by religion to its emotional depths, a steady and lasting control in directing and enjoying eros without the more relaxed and relaxing rhythms of sin-confession, confession-sin characteristic of other cultures.

Let us look at the writings, sometimes vivid, of the three greatest reformers, Luther, Calvin, and Erasmus, using mostly texts that have some claim to being more than discursive or homiletical. Luther's Paradise Lost appears in his lectures on the first five chapters of Genesis, which, without Milton's sophistication of language, are characterized by a vivid and self-revealing prose that sensitively reflects changes in mood and paradoxical ambiguities.[10] These last do not, however, abort the steady emergence of new and surprising insights. In Luther's Eden woman shares with unfallen man his mental gifts, including his full knowledge of astronomy. The commentator bridles at Aristotle's view of woman as a maimed man (she was not a whit inferior to Adam even in reason) and apparently at those commentators who find her monstrous for having introduced evil. Those who speak so are themselves "monsters and sons of monsters." He praises the beauty of naked flesh that characterized Adam and Eve; even though she was the moon to his sun, the pair were imbued with "the greatest dignity of the human body." But "this glory has perished," and it perished soon, for Innocence, which might have been fruitful, producing generations of families living in nuclear households under separate trees, lasted only a few hours of real, unallegorical time.[11] Thus Luther's vision of Eden is briefer than a day and lacks the detailed celebrations that Augustine provided with his sometimes grotesque elaborations of unfallen libido. The reformer's realistic imagination is forever pushing us ahead to our present condition of leprous lust and sexual shame, that is, to our world, the only place in which we can now achieve our destiny. In the experience of real life alone arise the possibilities that can transcend the taint which tainteth all, poisoning even the intimacies of postlapsarian marriages, which can be shaken by "epileptic and apoplectic lust" (the phraseology again recalls Augustine). It is appropriate to recall the Fall in Jordaens's vision, which is a powerful visual counterpart to the belief of Augustine, Luther, Calvin, and many others in the transformation of love to lust, which that catastrophe accomplished (fig. 9; see chapter 7).

Still, stubbornly lustful though postlapsarian life tends to be, Luther draws out the possibilities of transcendence, and these grow as the commentary proceeds. After the Fall, God does not repudiate Eve: she keeps her flesh, remains a woman, and is invited to achieve motherhood and create the lineage that will ultimately produce Jesus Christ. Theologically, Luther of course wishes radically to reduce the importance both of the Virgin Mary and virginity itself, but in the event his interpretation of the Hebrew word *know* envisions new and purely human horizons. *To know* is unabashedly to have sexual relations, but it also reaches out to broader meanings that include abstract knowledge. Luther goes beyond even that: Adam "knew" Eve not just "objectively or speculatively, but he actually experienced his Eve as a woman." I see the germ here, despite much traditional chaff in the presentation, of a new vision of esteem and intimacy combined and arising from the procreative sex act—a seed out of which might well grow, nourished of course by other forces economic and political, the homiletical and belletristic lyricism with which the Renaissance hailed wedded love.[12]

The sexual rigors of Calvinism are so well known and their blights have been so vividly expressed (as in *The Scarlet Letter*) that they need no elaboration here or even a tracing to their source in the learned reformer's thought. But if we are to disclose fully the emergent marital ideal, we need to extend to John Calvin himself that major rehabilitation of Puritanism which modern historians have undertaken so voluminously for England and America. The rigor of Calvin's thought is accompanied by greater respect for chastity and virginity than was shown by Luther, and the society of Geneva under his guidance constitutionally prescribed precise and graduated punishments for fornication and adultery. But equally with Luther and Erasmus, Calvin attacked universal clerical celibacy as a "dire murderer of the soul," whose effect was to shut priests up in "a furnace of lust, to burn with a perpetual flame," priests who taint the whole world with the hypocrisy of their teachings, the impurity and the grossness of their personal sins. On the positive side, Calvin interprets the faith much as some medieval Christian naturalists did in celebrating the intensity and boundlessness of cosmic love. When he says that "all the powers of our souls [are] under the influence of love," led by popular stereotypes we might have expected him to say "sin" instead of "love." But in fact he does say "love," which he conceives of as controlling all the energies of our psyche. Calvin interprets the heart-mind-soul love of God as being more than reverence, obedience, and trust: it also means "such vehemence of zeal, that there be no place in us at all for any thoughts, any desires, any intentions which conflict with this love for him." Such vehemence could of course be regarded as a source of the persecutory zeal that sometimes drove Calvin himself and that has bedeviled more than one Calvinistic society, but it can be shown equally to anticipate the eagerly sentimental praise of married love by Protestant, notably Puritan, homilists. For Calvin extends the scriptural love of neighbor to those "unknown to us, and even enemies," and such love, he holds, should so rule in us that it governs every part and becomes the principle of all our actions. If intense love can be commanded for so generally defined, remote, and even inimical a neighbor, it can surely, and with appropriate ease, be directed to that neighbor of neighbors, the lifetime wife. And so indeed it was, though one must add the caution that proximity of course does not ipso facto ensure the companionable.[13]

Erasmus brings us to the verge of literature in his *Colloquies,* tales and dialogues designed to improve the skill in Latin of upwardly mobile young men. The work became a bestseller and influenced generation after generation in western Europe and England as a standard textbook.[14] It is the maritally oriented portions of these popular but learned and socially wise *conversazioni* (said by Johan Huizinga to have placed their author in the constellation of sixteenth-century followers of Democritus: Rabelais, Ariosto, Montaigne, Cervantes, and Ben Jonson) that provide us the best possible context for the literary achievements to be analyzed in the next two chapters of this study. Though he himself never broke with the Catholic Church or abandoned his vows as a priest, Erasmus mounted a brilliantly effective attack on clerical celibacy and its attendant hypocrisies and delinquencies, but beneath the wit and urbanity of his reformatory zeal there remained a residual conservatism. For example, in his attractive portrait of More, he praises the subject of his epistolary sketch for his skill as a husband. When he married a second time within a few months after the death of his still youthful and productive first wife who had borne him several children, More chose a plain widow (observe how the age-old prejudice against second marriage has vanished!) on the edge of old age and greatly skilled in domestic management. He undertook to train her on the cithern, the lute, the monochord, and the recorder, and he managed to continue what he had known before, a quarrel-free household. Erasmus is all admiration for the way in which More achieved domestic concord—by cajolery, jests, high spirits, and merriment. Erasmus, however, also implies without saying so that his subject's merry way with women was in the end used to enforce submission. Thus the brief biographical sketch, while showing an ideal of a refined and gentle domestic love, manages to keep the ambience hierarchical, and there is no mention of passion and intimacy.

A similarly gentle and intellectually aristocratic spirit governs the complexly conceived rhetoric of the *Colloquies,* where Erasmus shows that he distrusts mixed marriages, that he prefers similitude between partners, that he respects class distinctions, that he loathes selfishly arranged commercial marriages, that he desires mutual physical attractiveness—all this being both expected and understandable in one who, like other reformers, is determined to discover an ethos that will make marriages work and who is only secondarily interested in improving the status of that sex which was universally called "the weaker vessel."

Passionate love appears in some of the *Colloquies,* showing that Erasmus, like the Protestants, understood its efficacy as a binding and civilizing power when properly contained within marriage. But wherever he finds sexuality, even in prostitution, which of course he roundly condemns, he usually reveals an ability to understand sympathetically the mentality of the girl, fallen or unfallen, prostitute or postulant, but especially a high-spirited virgin being courted. This last is the situation in one of the most attractive of his eight marriage conversations, the one entitled "Courtship" ("Proci et puella"), first printed in Basel in 1523. If at the end the girl seems excessively coy in refusing her lover's kiss, we must remember that even a kiss, accompanied by certain language and witnesses, could constitute a spousal *de praesenti.* And the girl's witty quibbles urging delay or disagreement are also uttered for prudential reasons. For this is a careful and calculating couple, not a romantic pair, sensible, northern, with deep respect for the family and desiring its approval. Still, one gets the impression of a full and spirited de facto equality. Both boy and girl are scholastically witty in the manner of Donne and reveal full intellectual compatibility, though there is acceptance by both of sexual differentiation in love (he active, she passive). Christianity is foundationally present though it is not obtrusive, and there is an easy familiarity in invoking pagan mythology. Compatibility in brains and beauty, social status, personal hygiene (the new ethos calls for cleanliness as a sine qua non), education, temperament, and age shows that excellence is not enough. It must be matchable excellence. The boy stresses sex, calling it a vice not to have intercourse, and of course he desires children, who will be well brought up. She disagrees with none of this, but she insists on a rational decision and parental approval. And when they shake hands at the end, it is, she says, a "symbol of our mutual love." No one-night stands here, no union for life with a half-stranger, no *falling* in or out of love, and not even the remotest sense that the two were approaching a heaven-made marriage. The most heaven could do, apparently, was to seal what had already been wrapped up on earth and then bless it. But an ideal is unmistakably being acted out, and under it the whole person is somehow subsumed.

When Erasmus was attired in the middle and late sixteenth-century English dress of Wilson's *Arte of Rhetorique,* the Dutch reformer is made to judge the single life as "barraine, and smally agreeing with the state of mans Nature," while he presents marriage as a state that matches hearts and minds, bodies and souls, in a union that is deeper than friendship, sealed sacramentally, and imbued with joys transcending those of friendship: "For what can be more pleasant than to liue with her, with whom not onely you shall be ioyned in fellowship of faithfulnesse, and most heartie good will, but also you shall be coupled together most assuredly, with the company of both your bodies."[15] The English soil was obviously being prepared for the comedies of Shakespeare—and also for the changes that he rang upon this ideal.

Italian Humanism

In 1549 John Morisotus wrote colloquies guided by the strictest Roman Catholic standards to replace those of the flexible, suggestive, and sometimes ambiguous Erasmus (was the Dutchman only superficially Christian but essentially pagan?).[16] But our purpose in now swinging south in our survey is not to study the Catholic response to the northern Reformation but to bring Italian humanists and the Neoplatonic tradition into our picture. There are no surprises in the Venetian humanist, Francesco Barbaro.[17] He himself had had no personal experience of marriage, and the deficiency is evident. He hoped to transfer to the domestic scene the tranquility and perfect harmony that were sentimentally alleged to be uniquely characteristic of Venetian society, but in his *On Marriage* he was able to define only in a mischievously skewed and unbalanced way the love that he required of both husband and wife and the internal leadership he was willing to grant the woman. Sex in marriage exists for procreation solely, and it is thus deprived of much of its potentially equalizing power. The woman exists to please her husband above everything else, and Barbaro has at least the merit of making clear what some of us have suspected all along—that the age-old Christian requirement that there be love in marriage was often interpreted as a one-sided obligation that meant serving and gratifying the male. It is assumed, to be sure, that the husband will be kindly and thoughtful, but here at least the odor of a patronizing air is unpleasant and inescapable. Thus the clearest admonition to love appears in this form: "I should like a wife to love her husband with such great delight, faithfulness, and affection that he can desire nothing more in diligence, love, and goodwill"—in the exercise of which qualities she must be subservient but at the same time be a good manager in her own domain. Admittedly such views find indirect sanction in St. Paul, and even so liberated a spirit as Erasmus was capable of making women themselves talk in the manner of Barbaro.

The circle of Castiglione's *Courtier,* with its commanding presence of assertive aristocratic women, promises greater equality—promises more than Boccaccio ever claimed for his spirited male-female company.[18] But unlike Boccaccio's *Decameron,* Castiglione's widely esteemed work proves disappointing to the modern reader. Every time the group comes into the presence of the duchess, each male mind conceives of "an high contestation" (Hoby 1577, C iii verso), and some agreement through discussion is achieved on important issues like male friendship, the status of women, love, grace, *sprezzatura,* and even sexual difference. But after a steady dialectical movement that respects man *and* woman, soul *and* body, the humanist and Neoplatonist Pietro Bembo's climactically placed hymn to love turns out to be another grand evasion of the human and an exaltation of angelic beauty and virtue in the tradition of Dante, Petrarch, Lorenzo de'Medici, Pico, Ficino, and Bruno. Bembo's effusion deserves Lady Emilia's rebuke: "Take heede (M. Peter) that these thoughtes make not your soule also to forsake the bodye" (Hoby 1561, p. 363).

But there are other constellations in the southern sky that give out more light. Leone Ebreo does not of course escape otherworldly sublimations; but, because of a strong infusion of Old Testament realism, favorably opposing the sexual differentiation of Genesis to the androgyny of Plato's Aristophanes in the *Symposium,* he gladly admits sexuality to pleasure and pleasure to marital friendship, and he frequently uses the term *copulation* to vivify his most exalted flights, as when the Active Intellect (God) unites with potential intellect (ours). Admittedly man could sink to the level of bestiality and viciousness, but above that unpleasant plane there stood the moderated corporeal, not so high, to be sure, as the intellectual (the realm of the absolutely virtuous) but containing realistic promise for at least some sublunar intersexual happiness.[19]

Among the many defenses of women produced in this period—some rhetorical exercises only, others passionate and eloquent pleas for the rectification of injustice and the long overdue recognition of worth—one work presents an inversion as striking in its way as Blake's *Marriage of Heaven and Hell.* It was Englished under the following title: *Female Pre-eminence: or the Dignity and Excellency of that Sex, above the Male. An Ingenious Discourse: Written originally in Latine, by Henry Cornelius Agrippa, Knight, Doctor of Physick, Doctor of both Laws, and Privy-Counsellor to the Emperour Charles the Fifth.*[20] Granting that before God both sexes are equal, possessing "the *same* innate worth and dignity," Agrippa asserts bluntly that "in all other respects the *noble* and *delicate* Feminine Race, doth almost to infinity excell that *rough-hewn boisterous* kind, the Male." He then goes on to prove his point in the usual humanistic way by citing literary, religious, mythological, and artistic examples. The female powers include a body that is "plump, juicy, and attractive," with all its "partes . . . well furnished with humour" (the translator had promised in his title that he would provide his "English, with Additional Advantages"). Agrippa defines marriage as a "Holy and honorable sacrament," "more excellente, then other mysteries and loves." He endows this state with one of the most progressive interpretations of the newly prominent aim of companionship that the Renaissance produced, rooting it in what he called a love "out of measure." The "one fleshe, one minde, one concorde" achievable in marriage approaches the very highest type of friendship conceived by an Aristotle or a Montaigne, "one agreable mynde in two bodyes, in two bodies one mynde and one consent."

One last defense needs to be examined, this one in the form of a dialogue (1595) between Hercole Tasso and his famous cousin, Torquato Tasso, a work still known and admired in the circle of Blake and other disciples of Milton in 1796. Hercole's attack on women is a tissue of mysogynistic commonplaces (though the allegation that the rib from which Eve was formed was a "Non Ens" is new to me and also unclear); the attack is later recanted. Torquato's defense is warmly and learnedly written. (One should not miss the irony that the defender of women and marriage is a bachelor and the attacker a married man, whom, however, Torquato praises as being wise in his life and witty only in his writing, which is "full of scandall and disgrace.") His defense contains a direct refutation of centuries of Christian ascetic moralizing and of Plato himself, who, as we saw, admits no cognitive value to the married state and denies the uxorial a place on his ladder of ascending values. But Tasso says that matrimony is a great help in the active life while it in no way impedes the contemplative, pointing to the examples of Pythagoras, Socrates, and Crates, married men who thought high thoughts and cultivated the virtues of the mind. Thus he has prepared the ground for what he himself finds desirable and possible, a lasting "amitie" that loves virtue, a union of respect and desire where "honour . . . [is] conioyned unto delight." He is able finally to call marriage a "patrimonie" which is preferred above love of parents and conceived of as "the flower of friendship."[21]

Protestant Propaganda

Agrippa and Tasso can be rhetorically daring and memorably eloquent, but they do not quite prepare us for two qualities in the Protestant, largely Puritan, homiletics that spread Reformation views of marriage to a wide audience in the British Isles: (1) the enthusiasm with which the pleasures of sexuality are linked with marriage (given the reticence that is usually and perhaps necessarily associated in homiletics with sensuality, such exuberance is noteworthy); and (2) the persisting determination with which equality between the sexes modified the still strong desire to put woman in her place. The preachers praised and elevated woman while at the same time reminding her that "*Mine husband is my superior, my better:* he hath authority and rule ouer mee."[22]

It is now widely recognized that the Puritans gave an honored place to the flesh and that in the "league of friendship" which marriage is surely intended to be, the appetite needs a "dayly whetting," as the Calvinist preacher Daniel Rogers (1573–1652) put it, since marriage is "a sweet compound of both . . . religion and nature." The words *delightful* and *pleasant* are almost compulsively used in connection with the woman and relations with her. It was natural to invoke Eden, "that most joyful garden of pleasure" where marriage was instituted—and that with more enthusiasm than Luther showed, for the very central and controlling heritage of marriage is that one man and one woman "are coupled together in one flesshe and body . . . by the free, lovinge, harty, and good consente of them both," in the words of Thomas Becon, a Protestant divine of Norfolk (1512–67). I solicit attention to these strong, cordial adjectives because they are not untypical; admittedly we can find stretches of sandy sameness and dullness in the pamphlets and sermons, but enthusiasm bubbles up everywhere to create a vision of a pleasurable earthly paradise. The Anglican Church has been rightly censured for being traditionally wary of the new spirit abroad in the land, but it did include in the Prayer Book the sentence, "With my body thee I worship," a liturgical phrase which Paul Elmen, who has traced its fortunes, calls on one level a "euphemism, a pious fig leaf, by which the church could accept the glad cry of a suitor in sight of his goal."[23] Nicolas Breton, a pastoral poet but also a religious writer, in 1616 gives us a just summary of the qualities cherished overall, which include the following sentimental, even passionate ones: "A good wife is a world of wealth, . . . the heart of love; a companion of kindness, a mistress of passion."[24]

The other saliency in the hortatory writings brings into view the idea of equality. The headship of the husband was almost universally enforced, as it had been all through Christian history. In the Book of Common Prayer the homily on marriage, read periodically in the churches from 1562 on, does put woman in her place, saying that "the woman is a weak creature not endued with like strength and constancy of mind." But the famous Puritan divine William Gouge (1578–1653) chooses to put matters otherwise, referring to that "small inequality which is betwixt the husband and wife: for all degrees wherein there is any difference betwixt person and person, there is the least disparity between man and wife." This and many other such passages led William and Malleville

FIGURE 25 Rembrandt, *Portrait of the Mennonite Pastor, Anslo, and His Wife.*
(Staatliche Museen Preussischer Kulturbesitz, Gemäldegalerie, Berlin.)

Haller to conclude in a classic article that "too great subordination" was
as undesirable as insubordination, and that in the "nice and subtle happiness these men conceived for themselves," "woman is less than man, but
so little less that it is easy to fall into the error of supposing she is not less
at all."[25] And, as we have seen, some controversialists like Cornelius
Agrippa argued that she was not only not less but was naturally, culturally, and obviously more.

One feature of the post-Reformation ethos that gives to the marital a
quality of adventure arises from the fact that the marriage of the clergy,
after more than a millennium of decreed Christian celibacy, teamed pastor husband and "clerical" wife into what must have been often regarded
as a new cooperative enterprise that gave deeper meaning and wider
scope than ever before to the marital aim of fellowship and cooperation
and that radically revised the Xenophontic model of man outside and

woman inside the house. It put onto the cultural landscape a new kind of man-woman coupling that has been a feature of Protestant life ever since. Rembrandt gave expression to it in his portrait of a Mennonite pastor and his wife (fig. 25). He is bearded, and wears a hat on his head and a starched collar around his neck; she is a distinct person in her own right, perhaps even lively—by no means a Griselda. The large open book before them must be the Bible, which he may be explicating for her understanding or for the strengthening of her faith or for her future participation in the evangelical task; in any case it certainly establishes a bond between them either at home or abroad. Because of the redefinition of the church that followed the Reformation (all believers are priests and pastors), this couple should not be regarded as set apart but as a kind of model for all men and women, lay and ordained, engaged in the creation of a domestic state that epitomized the larger communion of the saints on earth.

Relevant Social History

The exact coincidence between history (what really happened) and belles lettres (what may or may not but could or might have happened) will never be known, especially not in love. It is easier to see the radical disjunction between intellectual and actual history, between discursive precept or structured mental discourse and the buzzing confusions of daily life. But since the polarities just mentioned interact, we must at least ask ourselves what reality lies behind philosophical formulation and imaginative portrayal, and consult those who are trying to find out. The artist Lavinia Fontana, who was born in Bologna in 1552 and who died in Rome in 1614, was an almost exact contemporary of Shakespeare. She has left us the portrait of a family (fig. 26). At the left and right extremes are grandfather and grandmother, in the center a couple, to the left a brother and younger son, to the right a little girl with mother and grandmother. The old man points to a dog, the symbol of faithfulness. Dynastic values are enforced, the couples are not placed close to each other, females and males are decisively separated, and there is little sentiment. But the more one looks at the painting the more one senses respect for all. Animated, decisive gestures, not positioning, tie the family together; the women and the girl are somewhat more interesting than the men and are given fuller humanity and greater individuality. The whole expresses what has been called the "tonality of togetherness" (l'intonazione d'insieme).[26]

Does this extremely rare kind of art, a family portrait created by a

FIGURE 26 Lavinia Fontana, *Ritratto di Famiglia*. (Pinacoteca Nazionale di Brera, Milan/Jean Hagstrum.)

woman, express her own or her sex's personal view of actual matrimony? Who can say? But who would not wish to say? Contemporary Italian life opened only two viable options for the respectable woman, marry or enter a convent. And Fontana's portrayal makes the married alternative look stable, attractive, and life-enhancing. But for many who married, existence must have indeed been what one of our contemporary interpreters calls "savage"; some men were so jealous they might confine their wives to the home for an entire year. Many domestic prisoners may have longed for convent life, particularly since nuns were often not cloistered at all but could enjoy at least some of the pleasures of Venice—cosmetics, jewels, dancing, perfumes, gardens, gondolas, masks, liveries, comedies. Of these women one patriarch said in 1629: "If they had been of the other sex, they would have commanded and governed the world." Yet Archangela Tarabotti, a nun from the age of sixteen and a firm believer in female superiority (Eve came from Adam's rib, he from the mud), attacked the "monastic inferno" and unwittingly illustrated many of

Erasmus's grave charges against "celibacy." Were there many like this religious? Who really knows? Who would not wish to know?[27]

Still, we do know enough to qualify some of the purely intellectual formulations we have quoted in the chapters on medieval culture and earlier in this chapter. We have stressed the growing respect and unshakable legal status accorded the couple's consent in marriage, a religio-didactic achievement of unparalleled importance for literature. In the Anglican Church, the priest specifically tries to determine mutual consent, asking, "Wilt thou have this man [woman] for thy lawfully wedded husband [wife]?" But also important for the arts is the patent truth that reality does not permit us to make a strict dichotomy in large social units between arranged and personal marriages: The investigations of the present study bear out what the anthropologist, Robert Lowie, has affirmed, that in most societies practical points of view are foremost in inaugurating and maintaining conjugality of whatever kind.[28] The lingering old and the preempting new were closely juxtaposed, and the resulting conflict was a fruitful seedbed for drama; without the sparks from potential conflicts between radically opposed customs many a literary blaze would have remained unlit. Moreover, the very processes and the indispensable contracts of courtship and marriage, stressing *verba de praesenti* or *de futuro,* privileged words *and* witnesses, and contained in embryo the situations exploited on the stage of the Globe Theater. One story from 1549 involves a man of the establishment acting out a personal role quasi-publicly. On a midsummer evening as a group of young people out for a stroll passed an empty house, a man said to his female companion in the presence of the others, Let's make love. She insisted on a public pledge of marriage in front of their companions. This was sealed with a kiss. The man then asked the other walkers to go on ahead toward the village, saying that he and Alice "wold shortlie come after." The speaker was a man of the cloth.[29]

The socio-moral position of love at the very time of this incident from real life was especially problematical. It has been shown that after the Reformation, during the first half of the sixteenth century, there occurred a stern repatriarchalizing of the family, endowing the paterfamilias with renewed powers, unprecedented for centuries. Shakespeare was not out of touch with such paradoxical realities of familial love and of marriage, either when he portrayed his many conflicts between stern father and disobedient daughter or when he staged, with amazing consistency, the ultimate triumph of the latter. But quite apart from what happened either on the stage or in the minds of molders of ethical and religious opinion, it is well to remember that much of society, perhaps decisive majorities in it, continued to follow the old practical ways of prudential consideration (with plenty of time out for libidinal relaxation of many kinds). Conjugal love was rarely regarded as sufficient in and of itself, and only a few—and those among the highly privileged—trusted marriage based only on mutual affection. Romantic love perhaps appealed more often to men than to women, and betrothal and marriage were not often purely private affairs. Such cold-water douches as these, provided by the social historians, are wholesome in helping us adjust our perspectives and in showing that literature arose from a reality that was conspicuous for its inability to provide firm guidance or clear perceptions about the wave of the future or emergent forms of life enhancement.[30] Since no one today trusts simplistically in art as an imitation of reality, it should not be hard to believe that there was much work left for the imagination to perform. The wide gap between what happened in Denmark (to say nothing of what may have been happening in London) and what happens in *Hamlet* is a standing challenge to creator and critic alike in any epoch.

The Renaissance, like antiquity, made certain values and practices dominant and enforced them by regulations supported by a large or influential social consensus. Still, there were many competing forms of sexuality, widely practiced, widely discussed, and therefore plausibly and sometimes ambiguously presented in the arts. Homosexuality was widespread enough to occasion a renewal of the Plutarchan debate about its competition (*paragone*) with heterosexual love; and male friendship, erotic or not, entered the making of wills and testaments and sometimes received the accolades usually accorded to lifelong uxorial relations. Lesbianism was one of the major preoccupations of women at the court of Henri II in France, though lesbianism was often treated as no more than a preliminary to lovemaking of the dominant kind. The prostitute in Venice did not remain on the margins of society but as a courtesan helped create an authentic *civiltà puttanesca,* for with her bodily, magical, quasi-religious powers she helped shape the sexuality that Aretino portrayed so vividly. Although the emphasis varied from nation to nation and even decade to decade during the Renaissance, prostitution by no means threatened established marriage but could be thought, in ways unimaginable by reformers and Puritans, to strengthen it. Scholarship has shown that in Venice the fornications which throve in that enchanting city paradoxically created amorous situations that stimulated the affections and produced mutual attractions that were increasingly regarded as fuel for marriage. So far from threatening the hearth in certain parts of France, even its small towns, the *prostibula publica* belonged to the community, and the private brothel in normal circumstances seemed in no way illicit and was often presided over by a woman called the *abbesse.* And everywhere even the granting of personal choice to the young in love, which moralists had been enforcing upon the heads of families since the Middle Ages, was in part related to the greater freedom of sexual life before and even outside of marriage. It is for this reason among others that the Protestant-Puritan attack on clandestine marriages was so unrelenting.[31]

Daily life everywhere—exalted and low, south and north—provided stiff and varied competition to the concentrated romantic personalism of the newer marital ideal. We should not forget that in some ways this ideal was intended to take the high place that illicit romantic affection had sometimes held in the old dispensation of politically and economically arranged marriages. Lucrezia Borgia's first marriage, carefully arranged and later annulled after the spread of vicious rumors on the grounds of lack of consummation, took place when she was thirteen. Her second husband, married to her when they were both eighteen, was the bastard son of Aragonian royalty and was murdered at the age of twenty, for reasons now unknown. Finally she was married to the scion of the Este family of Ferrara, who drove a hard bargain and who as husband remained uncouth, loved whores and the machinery of war, and had a touch of the pox. It was against that background that Lucrezia exchanged "the prettiest love letters in the world" (the phrase is Lord Byron's) with Pietro Bembo and indulged in the erotic metaphors that on his part consisted of fiery bliss expressed in an exquisite language suffused with religious imagery and on her part of real images and objects upon which she could displace her ardors and desires.[32]

The revived Neoplatonism of the southern Renaissance must have sometimes opened an escape from marital routine or indignity that the Greek hetaira or the Roman *amicus* (or *amica*) provided the ancient husband. In the Protestant world such subtle or exalted or intellectually adventuresome love did not frequently compete with the new domesticity—but perhaps business did. We should not forget that the Puritans, who produced so much warm rhetoric about marital love, were themselves a fairly small but powerful elite, who, as Daniel Defoe put it much later, combined religion and the prudential. What, then, in the northern Reformed world competed with love marriage and strict fidelity? Perhaps more than anything else the lingering traditions of the older medieval world. Both new and old were Christian, and hence one does not always find disagreement in formulation of doctrine. But the congregation of the saved, the elect, the redeemed, or the pure was greatly different from the inclusive parish with its more flexible and varied standards.

Consider the situation in Somerset, England.[33] Its marital norm was one that had prevailed for centuries: intercourse between husband and wife for purposes of procreation was to take place in the missionary position (woman on her back, man lying on her and facing her) and not at prohibited times in the church calendar or in proscribed wifely conditions (pregnancy, menstruation, recent childbirth).[34] This is orthodox and remained unchallenged by law and decree. But the court and diocesan records reveal a quotidian life in which premarital and extramarital sex (the latter often a continuation of the former with the same partner) was frequent though risky; women were often sexually aggressive in soliciting the male member; mutual masturbation was known; women accepted a dual morality for men and women; women's rights were scantily regarded; and violence was a regular part of the sexual scene. Scholarship concludes that in Somerset chastity was not an economic asset for most of the destitute or poorly paid rural population.

Irregular conditions like these must have obtained on many social levels throughout much of England and the Continent both before and after the Reformation, resisting revolutionary change in mentality and custom. These conditions perhaps constituted the severest competition that the new marital romanticism faced; they have been called "patriarchal, parochial, public and precarious."[35] Each adjective alludes to a feature of life that might make the ambience competitive—both respectably and illicitly so—with the marriage of esteem and desire. But traditional, conventional life did not subvert the institution itself, though it may have made its reform slower and more difficult. It placed a dragging, traditional chain on a progress that required a fervently dedicated spirit, which was not always easily or willingly achieved.

Do demographic conditions bear any relationship to the literary and artistic scene we shall confront in detail in subsequent chapters? Certainly the great Florentine census of 1427 has some bearing on the entire Western situation. The *catasto,* which counted some 60,000 households and some 260,000 people, draws special attention to marriage as the most important vital event in a society which owed to that institution the creation and prosperity of its great dynastic and commercial families and the stability of its common people. The census shows us that the creative center of Renaissance culture was moving toward what J. Hajnal, the great English demographer, disclosed in 1965 as the west European pattern of first marriages, which occurred at twenty-six or twenty-seven years of age or older for men and twenty-three or twenty-four or older for women, with a high percentage of both men and women never marrying at all. I shall not pause to note the several variants from this model, variants that were generally lower in age even for Florence and that among the Irish nobility, for example, were considerably below.[36]

In England in the age of Shakespeare demographic conditions approximated the west European paradigm. The median age of marriage for all male children of people in the rank of squire or above was lower, but not much lower, than the norm: twenty-one before 1550, up to twenty-three in 1550, staying at that level until 1628 or 1630. For females of those ranks the age was twenty in 1550, down to eighteen in 1575–1600, when it began to rise. The children of peers who never married before fifty years of age or more was about 14 percent of the relevant population in 1575, rising sharply to 23 percent in 1600, sinking to 15 percent in 1625.[37] The important conclusion to be drawn from these statistics is that the newer Protestant opportunities in and standards for marriage were being contemplated by fully mature young people capable of enjoying and insisting on their individual rights of making a free choice or of delaying choice for several years. It is especially important that in Shakespeare's productive years almost one-fourth of the young people of rank chose not to marry at all and must have given serious thought to competing modes of sexual gratification, including friendship, which of course did not need to be erotic. The *res uxoria,* always a complicated matter, was now being contemplated by mature young people given the opportunity of making essentially their own decisions outside strict family control with their own tastes and interests largely determinative. Marriage was therefore worthy of careful thought and preparation, and it is not hard to believe that society was producing readers and spectators receptive to anything that might be said, realistically or imaginatively, about amorous choice and about how and when it should be made.

Other pivots in social history are also important. Many of us tend to forget that the sexual act does not require love, admiration, or even intimacy, but that usually—though not always—it prefers privacy. Such privacy the young people contemplating liaisons were increasingly able to arrange.[38] The revolution in housing between the accession of Elizabeth and the Civil War was creating more and larger rooms, disposed along the walls of a corridor to permit separate entrance. Gardens provided rooms for private functions and mounds for couples to sit on. Didactic literature, like Alberti's on the family, stress privacy, and many paintings show the bridegroom presenting a private room, sometimes sumptuously and traditionally appointed, to his bride. Van Eyck's famous Arnolfini picture of 1439 seems to portray a ceremonious celebration of intimacy taking place in a new chamber. Even within a chamber that could sometimes be entered by family or guests, some privacy for the exchange of love confidences (or of course for business and politics as well) was ensured by the *ruelle,* a newly popular space created between the wall and the bed when it was moved from the center of the room closer to the wall.

The widespread valorization of privacy became at once cause and effect, strengthening eros, both licit and illicit but mostly licit. Jacob Burckhardt's nineteenth-century insight about the Italian Renaissance is still sound: the profligacy that existed, and he thought it was rife, did not jeopardize or even disorganize marriage.[39] More positively, the new propaganda among reformers and humanists for companionate marriage in the long run actually strengthened the institution in both the Catholic and Protestant world. Challenges to the marital state from many quarters served only to inflame the zeal of its defenders, who were often skillful in the then intimately related arts of rhetoric and aesthetics.

Since this is a book that encompasses a long span of time, it is not inappropriate to note that there played upon Renaissance reality a thousand points of light, some of them flickering from the remote past. Newly discovered ancient texts opened hitherto restricted vistas—and that opening, as we shall see in chapter 11, gave a new perspective upon love. Here we take notice of a dark subterranean stream that seems to have flowed into Renaissance consciousness from mythical prehistory. Marco Antonio Altieri, an early social historian, who published his *Li Nuptiali* shortly after 1500, provides a highly suggestive hypothesis. After a lengthy description of Roman nuptials in which he pays tribute to the church and its influence, he takes a long and deep look at Renaissance practices in relation to some dark corners in antiquity. He remembers that Rome was built on murder and marriage by force, and he concludes that "every nuptial act recalls the rape of the Sabines." He commends Rome for having achieved pacification after such violent beginnings, and he credits the church and its ritual acts that celebrate divine mysteries for having maintained the anciently created social equilibrium. This amazingly modern ethnologist of marriage sees that marriage even when regarded as a sacrament is the product of a long social and dialectical fusion of violence and friendship.[40]

Shakespeare seems to have had more than a glimmering of the same insight. Notable instances occur in plays like *A Midsummer Night's Dream* and *The Two Noble Kinsmen,* in both of which Theseus appears, his nuptials being intimately related to the courtship and the ultimate union of the more centrally placed youthful lovers. This man of quondam violence and licentiousness has become a sponsor of marriage, even of the newer marriage of choice; and the reader gets a strong sense that a pacification of conflict between the sexes has taken place before the comic action begins. In *A Midsummer Night's Dream* Theseus says to his Amazonian queen, recalling the well-known and bloody conflict between warrior women and Greek heroes: "Hippolyta, I wooed thee with my sword, / And won thy love, doing thee injuries; / But I will wed thee in another key . . ." (1.1). And in *The Two Noble Kinsmen* Theseus's wedding is interrupted by the request of the three widowed queens of Thebes, who wish him to take military action to ensure burial of their dead spouses. He reluctantly agrees. Such juxtapositions of warfare and marriage may not recall the rape of the Sabine women, but they have deep, mythic, ancient resonances that are enforced by opening speeches. One of the grieving queens from Thebes in *The Two Noble Kinsmen* reminds Hippolyta of her past: "with thy arm, as strong / As it is white, [thou] wast near to make the male / To thy sex captive" (1.1). And Theseus himself regards marriage as being a challenging undertaking that rivals warfare itself: "This grand act of our life, this daring deed / Of fate in wedlock" (1.1).

Shakespeare is the subject of the last full chapter of this book; here we conclude by assessing the reformers' and the humanists' contribution to the marital ideal. It falls short of being a product of twentieth-century mentality (by which it should not of course be judged), when the scales have fallen from our eyes about the mischiefs of colonialism, including the exploitation of women. But judged in the long annals of written human history, the Renaissance achieved a more humane and human view of marriage than had characterized earlier periods, though they provided striking and influential adumbrations of it. If we look ahead to what historically followed the attempts of the Renaissance to unite desire and esteem to achieve stability, lineage, friendship, and mutual personal and psychological growth, it appears that the synthesis we are studying has had rather steadier success than most ideals that have been more or less adopted by a mass consensus. For until the twentieth century, when the powerful economic-social thought alluded to in chapter 1 mounted an attack upon marriage, and when women entered the work force in great numbers to compete with men, the fifteenth-century ideal has demonstrated remarkable staying power. For centuries it stabilized even as it concentrated sexuality for millions and provided many of them with the spiritual comforts of loving intimacy—or at least with the illusion thereof. If it did not weaken the patriarchal order sufficiently to give woman the freedom she needs and deserves, it often allowed her effectually to rule while the putative head of the household only reigned. That ideal apparently still retains the power to attract uncounted multitudes the world over, among whom are some of the most liberated. We may not have seen the end of it yet.

That which doth join our souls, so light
    And quick doth move,
That like the eagle in his flight
It doth transcend all human sight,
Lost in the element of love.

You poets reach not this, who sing
    The praise of dust
But kneaded, when by theft you bring
The rose and lily from the spring
T'adorn the wrinkled face of lust.

    William Habington, Castara *(1640)*

ELEVEN

The Renaissance (II): Literature and the Problematics of Marriage

rom the vast literature of purpose and its accompanying religious and social history treated in the last chapter, we may draw three conclusions highly relevant to the belles lettres we shall consider in this and the final chapter. First, marriage was vitally central to Protestant morality, which endowed it with the potentially aesthetic values of adventure and pleasure. Earlier ambiguities about the status of matrimony had been sufficiently resolved to make it a quickening and positive force in even religious life and thought; the married woman came to be regarded as chaste even when sexually active, fully as chaste as the religiously committed virgin. Indeed, she was elevated in spirituality above the celibate nun, as Eve was rehabilitated and Mary dethroned. Second, naturalism, decisively and creatively present in the high Middle Ages, was in the Renaissance deeper going and considerably more transformative. It joined scriptural hermeneutics in reinterpreting Genesis 2 and other Old Testament texts (the reformers were especially fond of considering the Old Covenant exemplary and instructive in these matters), helping to make marital sexuality an end in itself, an instrument of pleasure and a means of uniting minds and souls. This aim, however, was not often directly or openly discussed. Third, the purposes of marriage were expanded and restated in such a way as to give greater prominence to the aim of companionship, even friendship. Some indeed located the sacramental or religious essence of marriage in its friendly rapport, though few if any beside Martin Bucer (1491–1551) and Milton carried this idea to its logical conclusion and called for divorce when love and compatibility died.[1]

All these changes in mentality could be as congenial to aesthetic discourses as to homiletical persuasion, and they entered literature with much of the élan that accompanied their rhetorical and didactic presentations. Earlier intellectual historians believed that "the moralists preached the code [of love], and artists like Spenser, Shakespeare, and Milton fortified the preaching with the fruits of their imagination." To fortify preaching is scarcely to cultivate Mount Parnassus save perhaps on its lowest slopes, and recent historians and literary historicists are much subtler about art, even as they dig deeper into social realities. Stephen Greenblatt has said that Shakespeare and his theater "functioned neither as a simple extension of constituted religious or political authority nor as a counterchurch or subversive assault upon that authority. We have instead a far more complicated pattern, in which risks and advantages, pressure and protection are continually renegotiated." This fine insight can be applied to all belles lettres, and we must therefore examine our texts with a sensitivity appropriate to the complexity of their social and intellectual relationships. But unless I err greatly, long-term love bears the unmistakable marks of a major struggle between the emergent and the residual, in which it is clear, to this investigator at least, that the emergent was, in most essential respects and with many accompanying reversionary trends, winning the day.[2]

Ambiguous and Changing Legacies

The traditions we have earlier examined in detail stemming from the Hebrew and Christian Bible—sometimes called ascetic, sometimes dualistic, sometimes Augustinian—were traditions that feared and limited the sexual, and they were of course present in Renaissance literary and artistic expression, north and south. All Renaissance cultures were more than residually Christian, though there were many new and sometimes powerful challenges to religious establishments. The ascetic tradition lies behind Bacon's typical statement that "it is impossible to love and be wise," and Iago plays diabolically with that tradition in making Othello feel that marriage is sin-riddled and mischief-prone.[3] Similarly, Platonic and Neoplatonic and also Petrarchan evasions of the clamantly physical, leading as in earlier periods to etherealization, postponement, and escape, were both present and resisted—and often transcended. Romeo's language undergoes a subtle transformation from the stiffly artificial, conventional, and effectually unsuccessful to the flexibly lyrical and erotically consummatory as his love shifts from the fair Rosaline (a Petrarchan paragon) to Juliet (all flesh and blood).

The small poetic legacy of Pernette du Guillet (c. 1520–45), who supposedly died at twenty-five, is fascinating because of a similar transformation.[4] She learned a fashionably Renaissance and Neoplatonic doctrine of love at the feet of Maurice Scève, the famous humanist teacher of high love in *La Délie,* of which she allegedly was the inspiration. She loved her teacher for some nine years, and in her verse she transformed that emotion into a love whose principal ingredient was a sexuality that she believed ought continually to be nourished. Such love was also capable of rising to spiritual heights in a *contentement* that remained sexual enough to ravish even the highest self. The French girl in the space of very few years and lines of poetry achieved, in a tutorial situation outside marriage, a synthesis that had eluded Héloise but that has ever since lurked in the groves of academe.

At the opposite pole to any kind of idealizing, even the kind that refines but does not dissipate the libidinal, is the fabliaux tradition that remained strong in many lands. Shakespeare's bawdry is now well known and its vocabulary, direct and allusive, well understood; city comedy is filled with bawds, pimps, procurers, seducers, and love magicians, and adultery and seduction retain perennial fascination even in the higher genres.[5] The fabliaux tradition, or indeed any realistically erotic art, takes on peculiar richness and relevance for two reasons: (1) the marital ideal is not forgotten even when it is flouted in sexually explicit or suggestive art; and (2) the sexualized state of marriage becomes available as never before for verbal troping. Carew's wonderful and justly famous "Rapture" is sexually frank but not obscene: its images of travel and discovery, not unlike Donne's exploration of his Newfoundland, keep us intellectually and morally alert and so fully human as we soar above the Monster Honor to a totally sexual Elysium. But even here, where "wedlock bonds" are not broken but simply banished as irrelevant, the ideal does subtly intrude, from the wings as it were of this blissful bower. Venus presides, to be sure, but not alone; she shares her rule with "Innocence, / Beautie and Nature." In the prologue of *The Two Noble Kinsmen,* beginning with prostitution and then turning to the uxorial, Shakespeare and Fletcher boldly trope the experience of witnessing (also producing?) new plays:

> New plays and maidenheads are near akin:
> Much followed both, for both much money giv'n
> If they stand sound and well. And a good play,
> Whose modest scenes blush on his marriage day
> And shake to lose his honour, is like her
> That after holy tie and first night's stir
> Yet still is modesty, and still retains
> More of the maid to sight than husband's pains.
> We pray our play may be so.

One final aspect of the problematics the Renaissance insistently asso-ciated with marriage, even the newer marriage of consent and love, re-sists definition. The repatriarchalizing of the family and the reinvocation of Levitical standards, which followed the Protestant Reformation and which we have already noted, raised the stakes in marriage for both mis-chief and joy. If, as Hooker says, "obedience of creatures unto the law of nature [Puritans would have substituted the law of God] is the stay of the whole world," then disobedience becomes, as Jonathan Dollimore has said, literally world-shattering.[6] I would add that disobedience in that little proto-state, the family, was equally momentous. Furthermore, the confluence of scriptural and classical influences made definitions of mu-tuality and marital unity infinitely more complex than they had been. Even the uxorially oriented Edmund Spenser, who memorably associ-ates his Venus with Concord, Christ, and Womanhood, is also capable, as we have seen, of conceiving of her as a hermaphrodite (has he forgotten Genesis 5:2, "Male and female created he them"?): "she hath both kinds in one, / Both male and female, both vnder one name" (*Faerie Queene* 4.10.41). Tolerant of the androgynous, Spenser is not notably censorious of Ganymede; homosexual love is during the Renaissance, as in one ven-erable and important Western tradition, often competitively juxtaposed with intersexual love. Harry Levin has said of Christopher Marlowe's *Edward II:* "The most wholehearted treatment of love in any of Marlowe's plays involves the erotic attachment of man to man."[7] Indeed, the king is capable of singing a kind of *Liebestod* music when separated from his beloved friend: "my dearest Gaveston . . . / My lovely Pierce, my Gaveston, again" (scene 1, lines 1–9).

All the foregoing survivals and adjustments of tradition in the Re-naissance obviate simplistic approaches. The texts we shall confront and the many more we necessarily omit make it egregiously wrong to con-clude either that "it's a jungle out there" or that "love makes the world go round."[8] Both extremes are mischievous, the sentimental as well as the pessimistic (most of us incline to gloom and doom these days). Either one can simplify reality dangerously and also frustrate the imagination. That faculty has the power to transform external reality even as the artist ob-serves it and so change the very nature of the nature that art is imitating. Besides, the imagination is closely related to love and can deepen the creator-observer's sympathy, thus changing not only the "objective" out-side but also the subjective inside, the mind itself as it strives to render nature.[9] Our theme (love) and the faculty that artistically appropriates it and embodies it (imagination) are thus capable of a subtle "interinanimation." The resulting hermeneutical situation becomes subtle and evasive indeed but, one hopes, rewardingly rich.

Lyly and Spenser

The heritage of the past was tortuous and ambiguous not only because of what the Renaissance was doing to it but also because some of its greatest ancient masterpieces and most revered authors arrived with built-in paradoxes and oxymorons that rival those of the Shakespearean sonnets. Ovid, powerfully influential in the Renaissance, had seen that sexual life could be grotesque, awkward, savage, ludicrous while at the same time it was exciting, compelling, beautiful, revealing us to ourselves, displaying an essential part of what it means to be human. But to be alert to the ambivalences that reside in love or marriage does not require us to cast the suspicion of hypocrisy or selfish interest upon expressions of it. Yet that is precisely what some current thought has done, and we should face up at once to the implications for criticism of such deconstruction. What is fast becoming a new orthodoxy in Renaissance studies tends in effect to truncate Shakespeare's famous line to read simply "love is not love . . . ."[10] What is it then? Power or the flattery of power, rivalry for power, and envy produced by an insistent upward mobility—all these, translated into the idiom and imagery of love and sexual jousting.

Let us concede at once that this new perspective, though limiting, is at times extremely helpful and usefully deconstructive, for who can deny that Cynthia is not Cynthia in much of the mythologizing of the English Renaissance. Consider John Lyly's *Endimion, the Man in the Moon* (1588), an allegorical play in which the author surveys many kinds and ways of loving, from the ludicrous and grotesque to the sublime, and does not hesitate to point up the ambition and self-interest that bedevil love.[11] Tellus, the Earth, not a mother here but a virgin, is jealous of Endymion's love of Cynthia, suggesting that since he cannot love her (Tellus), his love of Cynthia is suspect. Tellus is proud of her potentially fertile beauty, and Lyly is capable of presenting her earthy growths with a wit that anticipates the paintings of Giuseppe Arcimboldo, who, we may remember, figures the body and its parts by means of flowers, fruits, grains, grass (of the last-mentioned, Lyly-like, the painter makes human hair). As the play proceeds Tellus reveals herself as changeable, vain, dissembling—in short conventionally feminine and romantic. In the end Cynthia forgives her all, except her use of a magician to bewitch Endymion into sleep.

Sir Thopas, a version of Mars, is rough, barbaric, bloody in thought: "That pelting [paltry] word 'love,' how waterish it is in my mouth! It carrieth no sound. Hate, horror, death are speeches that nourish my spirits" (2.2). How did he get that way? Perhaps because he once thought that all amorousness is sweet and was completely blind to its terror. If so, he was a fool; but like many sentimental fools, at the first touch of sobering reality he turns around and with his mouth full of Ovidian tags inverts sweet to sour, the beautiful to the ugly. Delusion turns to perversion. Eumenides, who appears late, comes in to introduce the theme of friendship, but since he is tormented by passionate love for Semele, such doting must be eliminated root and branch to preserve the nobler love—exactly what the play tries to do. The hapless Eumenides sometimes sounds like Shelley: "Ah. I faint, I die! Ah, sweet Semele, let me alone, and dissolve by weeping into water" (3.4). In strokes of dazzling virtuosity Lyly here embodies most of the clichés that have attended romantic love up through Keats at least. And in developing a contrast that will be closely relevant to our discussion of the love *paragone* in Shakespeare, he suggestively juxtaposes sentimental, romantic silliness and "the rare fidelity of a tried friend" (3.4): "the love of men to women is a thing common and of course; the friendship of man to man infinite and immortal" (3.4).

Endimion's love of Cynthia is expectedly the capstone of Lyly's elaborate arch. She is early revealed as a petulant arbiter elegantiarum and a thought-controlling tyrant, suggesting that Endymion's infatuation has something forced and unnatural about it. In the climax, which is achieved by easy, magical fiat, certain kinds of love remain intact, such as the friendship between Eumenides and Endymion. But Eumenides continues to love his mistress (now his wife), and though he experiences a sudden (and traditional) shudder of fear that his paradise may be lost through the excess of his joy, he resigns himself to rapture. Lyly apparently has absolutely no thought of uniting the values of romantic love and male friendship, and the two remain separated. Sir Thopas is forced to be content with loving someone his own age, thus obviating another *couple mal assorti,* a common enough worry. Kissing Endymion awake after all these years but unable to restore his youth, Cynthia does, however, restore him to her favor—and that, apparently, is intended to be the summum bonum. Seek ye first the kingdom of Elizabeth, and all these things (the conventional goods of life and love appearing on Lyly's ladder) shall be added unto you. *Endimion,* written some ten years before *The Faerie Queene,* is a fascinating document that begins promisingly and entertains us almost to the end. But then it sinks to political flattery and must finally be adjudged a flawed and failed vision.[12]

We have already confronted one of Spenser's mythological ambiguities and complications, but his lifelong attempt to harmonize body and spirit does culminate in the beautiful and untroubled serenity of marriage, a state he chooses not to explore in depth. (The ambience [liberalism] and the genre [the novel] congenial to the expanded revelations of a Richardson or a Fielding had not yet arrived on the cultural scene.) Spenser's bias is strong against arranged marriage and in favor of free choice (consider the love of Bellamour and Claribell in *Faerie Queene* 6.12.3–8), and his imagination is drawn to grace and civility with an evident but delicate sexual implication. His Graces are "daughters of delight": "And all, that *Venus* in her selfe doth vaunt / Is borrowed of them" (*FQ* 6.10.15).

His allegorical epic and other works do not entirely escape the charge that Spenserian amorousness is sometimes being displaced onto a royal personage, and so his purest and most untainted celebrations of the marital are those closely related to his own personal life, specifically to his second marriage. Are not the *Amoretti* and the *Epithalamion* the first love poems we know to have been written by a poet to his bride? Is not the fusion in the marriage song of bridegroom and poetic speaker entirely original? And—to consider the author as being what he perhaps in actuality was, a not untypical Elizabethan male—does not the consummation lead directly into the peace of a husband-regulated stability?

A perspective on the last question may be provided by the *Faerie Queene* (4.4–6). Artegall, Britomart's lover, is conquered by Radigund, the queen of the Amazons, for whom he must perform womanly tasks; but Radigund is in due course vanquished by Britomart, at once deeply in love and irresistibly heroic, who finally restores male rule and for the future forbids female government, freeing the male knights to govern and achieve true justice. Furthermore, Cupid appears to diminish in importance in the last books of Spenser's epic, but this diminution takes place after a long career of active intervention in the affairs of heroes good and bad and after his powers for weal and woe have been displayed with unprecedented lavishness.[13] Is it just to consider this Cupidinal decline as an approbatory allegory of what does and should take place in marriage, where other values compete with and dominate the erotic? Perhaps. But we must look at the love lyrics themselves.

The *Amoretti,* whose linkèd sweetness has been regarded by many as too long drawn out, end ethically and piously, like so many love sequences of the author's southern predecessors. Number 79 elevates love to the "trew fayre, that is the gentle wit, / And vertuous mind," and the very last sonnet (89) climaxes in a "pleasauns" that is "unspotted" and

moves both God and man. The *Epithalamion,* after one of the most delicately rendered erotic scenes in all literature (*amorini* flutter around the
bed, carelessly dallying in a paradise of joy), ends in morning light with
thoughts of procreation and family. Spenser keeps the traditional supporting structures of erotic love very much in place and chooses not to
invade them with the natural joys he has so exuberantly and memorably
painted. As do Boccaccio, Shakespeare, and even many ancient writers,
Spenser suggests (especially in number 67 of the *Amoretti*) that in the
bride a "wyld" deer has been tamed and that courtship and promised
sexuality have homeopathically created a welcome and enduring calm, a
kind of pacification (that is, the opportunity of extended licit passion has
calmed passion). But Spenser nowhere hints that in that erotically tinged
calm the mind and spirit will grow and friendship will flourish, transforming erōs into *philia.*

Still, the achievement in the sonnets of splendidly and opulently
using nature to decorate courtship and premarital love is a high point in
erotic literature. Early in the sequence Spenser transcends the Petrarchan
injustices and imbalances he finds in literary love, where the lover suffers
unrightly, and the beloved "lordeth in licentious blisse / Of her free-
will, scorning both thee [Cupid] and me [poet-lover]" (10). There are
also traces of Catholic devotion (in number 22): the lady is "my sweet
Saynte," a "glorious ymage" in his mind, his thoughts being priests tending the altar on which his chaste and pure desires burn. Like Petrarch,
Spenser conceives of the lady ferally—she is first panther, then tiger, but
finally to the weary hunter she is a "a gentle deare," whom, trembling, he
ties fast with "her owne goodwill": "Strange thing me seemd to see a
beast so wyld, / So goodly wonne with her owne will beguyld" (67). *Will*
may mean both her assent and the sensual desire which impels the acceptance—either alternative or both closely related to the Protestant marital
dynamic. And it is not inappropriate that after this central climax there
should be a ratifying Easter hymn ("Love is the lesson which the Lord us
taught"), where the "deare" is cleansed, along with her suitor, by the
"deare blood" of Christ (68).

In Spenser religion does not abolish the sensual. Sonnet 64 delightfully recalls the garden flowers of the Song of Songs, and 76 invokes
Eden, where the lover's thoughts are sensual indeed, nesting between
"her paps like early fruit in May," a fancy so bold that the poet momentarily wonders if he has been led rashly astray by his beloved's ravish-
ments. But no! these are not abolished as sinful or even subdued for very
long. They appear in Spenser's *Epithalamion* in full blaze, the most con-
summately satisying expression in English of marital desire on the verge

of fulfillment. Even inward beauty is garnished with the physical, and though some "affections" can be regarded as "base," these too "yeeld their services unto her will" (line 197, where *will* may combine the meanings of command and sensual desire). The libidinal excitement mounts— Graces dance, maidens carol, Jove and even his illicit loves are invoked, wine is poured out "not by cups, but by the belly full" (251), and the posts of the bed and walls of the chamber are sprinkled with Bacchus's potion until they sweat and are drunken. But the poet has reminded us that the bride is modest as well as beautiful, queenly as well as humble, sexually alluring as well as good, one whose mind is "honors seat and chastities sweet bowre" (line 180). Is she also intelligent? The poem does not say so, nor does it promise a marriage of true minds; the affection is likely to be an ever-fixèd mark, though of the tempests that may shake it nothing is said or implied.

We are justified in finding in Spenser's initiation of marriage all the verve of the Nature he hails in the "Two Cantos of *Mutabilitie,*" where "*Life* was like a faire young lusty boy, / Such as they fame *Dan Cupid* to have beene" (*FQ* 7.7.46). On the uxorial poet has fallen the mantle of Alan of Lille, the School of Chartres, and the Chaucer of the *Parliament of Fowls.* But he did not follow up the vigorous Protestant ethos he expresses in "*Mutabilitie,*" where human beings

> . . . are not changèd from their first estate,
> But by their change their being doe dilate:
> And turning to themselves at length againe,
> Do worke their owne perfection so by fate;
> Then over them Change doth not rule and raigne;
> But they raigne over change, and doe their states maintaine.
> (*FQ* 7.7.58)

Such an inward turning, such dilation of being, such a free working out of one's own salvation unenslaved by mutability Spenser may well have envisioned as possible in marriage and intersexual friendship. But he did not say so, nor did he attempt what was fully exploited only after the birth of the modern novel, a portrayal of the domestic scene. Still, he was more concerned with the personal than any of his predecessors in the venerable epithalamic form, who tended almost without exception to celebrate the institutional order attained by union. Spenser achieved an erotic music that can haunt the mind through a long lifetime. And his vision is vastly more compelling, as it is more deeply rooted in emergent cultural values, than that of the courtly and politically oriented Lyly. For though Spenser in the totality of his vision keeps an important place for

order and degree, his essentially individualistic (Protestant?) ethos preserves, to his great credit, the intense moment that fuses lyric and life.[14]

Miscellaneous Triumphs of the Shorter Lyric; Ben Jonson

Petrarchan love was bound, sooner or later, to weary the spirit—Marvell
said it was "begotten by Despair / Upon Impossibility"—and one approach to the lyrical Renaissance is to see it as an escape from such an
artificial and fated malaise. Old ascetic beliefs also enter the lyrist's consciousness, to say nothing of the pressures of both personal experience
and reformed society. We have seen Spenser, for all his putative Calvinism, using Catholic imagery; avowedly Catholic writers, making no
abject or long-winded apologies for the need to escape the sexual passions, must have found Petrarch's persisting passion, with its evasions
and interminable postponements, mischievously idolatrous (though, as
we have seen, its final lyrical ritualism is unmistakably Catholic). Here is
Crashaw's wish in "On Marriage": "I would be married, but I'd have no
wife, / I would be married to a single life." The Jesuit Southwell is
abruptly dismissive about "Love's Servile Lot": "She is delightful in the
rind, / Corrupted in the core."

Echoes of the medieval courtly tradition resound everywhere. Skelton
in mid-century stresses beauty *and* good breeding, praising "Mistress
Margaret Hussey" for being "So maidenly, / So womanly" in demeanor,
"Steadfast of thought, / Well made, well wrought," a midsummer
flower, "Gentil as falcon / Or hawk of the tower." John Heywood in
1557 harked back to the woman of yesteryear: "Truly, she doth as far ex-
ceed / Our women nowadays / As doth the gillyflower a weed, / And
more, a thousand ways." Sir John Davies in *Orchestra* goes much further
back, ultimately to the pre-Socratics, using the dance to symbolize the
discordia concors that brought the universe into being and order and that
is repeated in the nuptial dance and the consummation it prefigures.

Wyatt early breaks away from the classical-courtly tradition, and his
masculine ruggedness makes even hoary clichés (woman's fickleness, for
example) become starkly dramatic as former love turns to hate. He compares the erotic suppliants he has encountered to political suppliants and
place seekers, and in his quite wonderful "They flee from me," he reifies
the post-Reformation woman. She is no longer "gentle, tame, and meek,"
nor is she feral in the Petrarchan or even Spenserian way; she is by implication more aggressive, not wildly shy and furtive but ready consciously to "use newfangleness."

Sidney, for all his toying with the Neoplatonic ideal and his initial exaltation of the eye as formed to serve the "inward light," ultimately moves to individual passion ("the very face of woe / Painted in my be-clouded stormy face"), which of course still invokes art and artifice but at the same time achieves a poetic honesty that is rugged, direct, and personal:

> Then think, my dear, that you in me do read
> Of lovers' ruin some sad tragedy.
> I am but I, pity the tale of me.

Sidney's sonnet sequence satisfies on more than one level: there are moments of passionate love, but there is also, up to sonnet 32, an extended anatomy of love, which in the sestet of sonnet 14 includes the expression of an ideal:

> If that be sin which doth the manners frame,
> Well stayed with truth in word and faith of deed,
> Ready of wit and fearing nought but shame;
> If that be sin which in fixed hearts doth breed
> A loathing of all loose unchastity,
> Then love is sin, and let me sinful be.

This is a ringing defense of an eros that does not compromise chastity, of the civilizing power of love, of a stabilizing troth, and of intellectual liveliness ("wit") that could be the ingredients of long friendship. It embodies the conditions laid down in theological and ethical matrimonial defenses and represents the emergent ideal. But an irony is present because the underlying situation, either literary or real, is in fact extramarital. That irony may be signaled by the insistent revisionary curve indicated by the conditional grammar of the "if" clauses—a bold and paradoxical hint that the poet would, if necessary, inhabit a state of sin to achieve his ideal.[15] Renaissance secular liberty should not shock us when even in its idealized form it risks the state of sin. We have been taught by earlier ages to conceive of long-term erotic relationships, officially unblessed, that somehow partake of divine, if not sacramental, grace.[16]

Ben Jonson's exquisite erotic lyrics, particularly those addressed to Charis, occasionally recall but do not closely resemble any of the patterns so far adduced.[17] The very name of his mistress brings us back to Homeric and Attic Greece and should recall our discussion of *charis* and *gamos*. Jonson's definition of marriage, which he imbues with metaphysical dignity, goes even deeper into antiquity, to the pre-Socratics' *discordia concors* we have so often mentioned. Marriage is "That holy strife, / And the allowed war: / Through which not only we, but all our species are"

(p. 243); the "allowed war," of course, cannot possibly refer to marital quarrels but must reside in reproductive sexual union itself, which is of course invasive and can initially be traumatic. Marriage is cosmic, social, and individual, a union that binds "the fighting *seeds of things,* / Winnes *natures, sexes, minds,* / And eu'rie discord in true musique brings" (*Hymenaei,* lines 100–102). The allusion to creation is not always heavily philosophical or lexical; it sometimes darts out from facial grace, where "alone there triumphs to the life / All the gain, all the good of the elements' strife" (p. 132). Jonson is everywhere learned and allusive, though not always cosmically so. On one occasion he takes our breath away by seeming to anticipate the present-day critical scene with its intertextualities: a graceful girl and a noble man unite, "With light of love, this pair doth intertext" (p. 244). (Of course, the word here may not be bookish at all, *to intertext* meaning primarily "to weave together.")

By calling his beloved "Charis" in the charming lines devoted to her, Jonson suggests that he wishes his poetic speaker to invoke Charis's husband in Homer, Hephaistos, the skillful maker who was also lame and ugly. Jonson knew exactly where his own gifts lay, in his inventive mind but not in his person, for he creates an "I" here and elsewhere who is fat, middle-aged, bald, and unkempt. The addressee, perhaps a lady of the court of James I, is well named, for she is exquisitely dressed, beautiful, intelligent, and above all graceful and delicate. She is not so delicate, however, as to obviate sexual entendres. Cupid, who makes a nest in the valley between her breasts, confuses her with his mother, Venus. But the lady has more than Venereal allure and the outward grace of youth and beauty; she is also intelligent and dignified: ". . . she's Juno, when she walks / And Minerva when she talkes" (p. 135). Jonson, courtly, classical, Catholic, humanist, does not of course express the Protestant-Calvinist synthesis. But he does not embody the patristic or the high medieval either. A celebrant of marriage, he can like Spenser hail the beauties of a lady, but unlike Spenser's bride she may not necessarily be nubile or on her way to the nuptial chamber. His most alluring physical verses may indeed reflect the essential Platonic *erōs,* which always implies distance and separation in longing, and hence the lady becomes an object of contemplation amenable to troping rather than touching. (Has the poet, conscious of his mountain belly and rocky face and unwilling to risk real-life contact, displaced onto exquisite metaphor the desires of his abundant flesh?)

> Have you seen but a bright lily grow,
>   Before rude hands have touched it?

Have you marked but the fall o' the snow,
　　Before the soil hath smutched it?
Have you felt the wool o' the beaver,
　　Or swan's down ever?
Or have smelled o' the bud o' the briar?
　　Or the nard in the fire?
Or have tasted the bag of the bee?
O so white! O so soft! O so sweet is she!
　　(pp. 313–14)

All the senses are invoked here except those of the ear, which the verse itself delicately satisfies. Jonson achieves the exquisite and comprehensive sensuousness of Spenser's *Epithalamion,* without the organizing intensity and immediacy of the wedding plot. The breathless excitement of narrative movement has been here replaced by a static lyrical construction, a synchronic, atemporal enumeration of sensual allurements that fulfills another classical ideal, the stillness and silence of an icon like Keats's Grecian urn. Ut pictura poesis.

Two French Utopias

The juxtapositions of this section and others to follow are not intended to match excellence with excellence but to do quite the opposite: match works of differing worth and values in order to suggest aspects of our topic not apparent in separated analyses. Two sharply unlike utopias from Renaissance French literature bring together the Eden of the Huguenot Guillaume Dubartas (a middling author at best but one closely related to the Continental and English Protestant tradition) and the Abbey of Thélème in Rabelais (a witty, eccentric, and satiric genius, one of whose continuing preoccupations was the married state, on which he applies a perspective that arises from the filiation that has threaded its way through these pages). We begin with the lesser and later work.

Dubartas's fame attracted the young Dryden, who confesses he once was ecstatic about the French author's hexameral poem, *La Semaine* (1578), in its pungent English translation by Sylvester (completed 1605–6), which made Spenser seem mean by comparison; but in his full maturity, in 1681, Dryden was of a different opinion: "I am much deceived if this be not abominable fustian." Wordsworth in 1815 had much the same view: "Who is there that can now endure to read *The Creation* of Dubartas? Yet all of Europe once resounded with his praise."[18] The French Protestant's Eden is both reformist and humanist. The latter aspect seems to predominate at first, for Adam possesses the highest human power in its highest form, reason, and he is fully in command of all his potentially rebellious members that might fall into lust or sloth. His eyes, those organs so voluminously honored in the Platonic and Neoplatonic traditions, are not only rational guardians placed in the noblest part of the human "Cittadell," but are also sexualized into

> . . . lovely Lamps whose sweet sparks livelie turning,
> With sodaine glaunce set coldest hearts a-burning,
> These windowes of the Soule, these starrie Twinnes,
> These *Cupids* quivers, . . .
>   (1.6.539–42)

Eve is both sexual and civilizing, whose "rapting features" (1.6.1006) invite to delight and without whom Adam would be "but halfe a man, / But a wilde Woolfe, but a Barbarian, / Brute, ragefull, fierce, moodie, melancholike" (1.6.1007–9). Can this be Eden? we ask, when such alternatives are considered possible. But it soon becomes clear that Dubartas's paradise is nothing if not this-worldly, lacking the austerities of Augustine's and the total separation from postlapsarian sin that characterized Luther's. Here Adam is ravished at the sight of Eve: "in his hart he gan to leape and laugh" (1.6.1046) in all too human fashion, and the union with Eve constitutes a fully human marriage attainable in our present state.

> Source of all joyes! sweet *Hee-Shee*-Coupled One [amoureux
>   Androgyne]
> The sacred Birth I never thinke upon,
> But (ravisht) I admire how God did then
> Make Two of One, and One of Two againe.
>   (1.6.1051–54)

The final "One of Two againe" does more than envisage procreative copulation—it embraces the highest Aristotelian traditions of friendship as well, moral and intellectual companionship, two minds and souls in one body, for it is "chastest friendship whose pure flames impart / Two Souls in one, two Harts into one Hart!" (1.6.1057–58). The Book of Genesis—and here the author's point of view is highly Lutheran—does not give us an allegory, a fantastic, mystic, or feigned paradise, but a true garden, literally plenteous and fertile, the seat of the graces, where joy was as real as later pain. When the poet recovers his senses somewhat, he of course must make it clear that Edenic sexuality was without our "tickling flames" (2.1.1.653) ending in "Epilepsie" (2.1.1.654, recalling both

Augustine and Luther); but he makes it clear that if Eden had been asexual and without issue, the creation of the two sexes had been in vain. One comes away from this naive and sentimental imagining with the strong feeling that it is meant to be a model even though after the fall spirit and flesh are continually at war. One cannot be sure that Dubartas foresaw the unrelenting and surprisingly successful post-Calvinist determination to reinscribe Eden in the Christian home, but it is hard to believe that he would have stressed so many purely human features of prelapsarian bliss had he not felt that they could be somewhat approximated in the elect community.

Rabelais introduces us to a greatly, but not entirely, different world.[19] Modern scholarship has shown us that this witty, irreverent, realistic, and boisterously frank explorer of the nether realms of the body and of society had affinities with Renaissance evangelism. He created what can be called Christian comedy, he broke with the misogynist tradition of priests and monks, but in the end he regarded marriage as being, like celibacy, neither good nor bad. Both states were what Paul called indifferent things, depending on the use to which they might be put. Rabelais's characters, some grotesque, some merely eccentric, some humane and wise, some literally larger than life, explore all sides of the question at stake (notably marriage), using the full panoply of Western learning— often ambiguously and with irresistible undecidability, sometimes hilariously, and almost always with a verve that celebrates life in all its force and forms. But it is the utopia called the Abbey of Thélème that is most relevant to our considerations here.

It provides an illuminating contrast to Dubartas's Eden. Eden was intended to be historically real and, in part at least, reattainable, the abbey is imagined. Eden was marital, the abbey premarital. Eden was a primitive utopia created by a good God, and it constituted man's first historic home. Thélème is a satirical utopia intended, like Swift's land of the rational horses, to embarrass by contrast to the glaring deficiencies of circumambient reality. Eden was nude and essentialist, in some respects like Husserl's phenomenological Reduction, or Bracketing; the abbey is fully clothed with the trappings of aristocratic society, immediately attractive through its highly selective array of civilized delights. But both Eden and Thélème are places new and youthful, congenial to "yonge fresshe folk," and each has its own admixture of real or implied sexuality.

In Rabelais's story the time has come to reward a monk who had fought for Gargantua, but the cleric refuses to become an abbot in real-life Seville and turns down other such offers, desiring instead to found an abbey and structure it to his own desire. Gargantua is pleased at what he

hears of the plans and gives his protégé the country of Thélème along the
river Loire. The name comes from the Greek *thelēma* (will), not much
used in antiquity, meaning "spontaneous, instinctive desire" or "appetite" as opposed to reflective reason. In the Septuagint it translates the
will of God. The word could carry the large burden of mediating between Nature and Grace and of inspiring into harmonious activity both
desire and will. The new society is carefully created, like a work of art, by
selecting, excluding, arranging, and refining the materials of real life and
ordering them according to both desire and reason. No clocks or sun-
dials or tolling bells measure time, no wall is built to include or exclude.
Men and women are both admitted: among the women none are blind,
lame, crooked, ill-favored, misshapen, or foolish; the men, exactly equal
to the women in number, are also comely, personable, well educated,
brave, and witty. Both sexes are richly appareled. The architecture is
sumptuous—though, one might add, a bit too geometrical for some
tastes, not entirely unlike John's New Jerusalem in the Apocalypse. Art is
everywhere present: an alabaster fountain features the Three Graces,
and tapestries, hangings, and frescoes recount heroic story and provide
descriptions of the world. The library is generously supplied with books
written in many languages, the park is full of deer, and there is a pleasure
garden with labyrinth and orchard. In short this community is a direct
and total reversal of Christian asceticism, with its vows of chastity, poverty, and obedience. The rule is one not of law but of free will and pleasure, the motto being, "Do that which thou wilt" (Fay ce que vouldras).[20]

The rule of life may at first suggest that what the monk has created is
a place of licentious indulgence, an embodiment of the deadly sin of *lux-
uria*. But on further reflection it seems rather to be a community of people living in what Paul called—in words invoked by Milton in his divorce
tracts—"the liberty wherewith Christ hath made us free" (Galatians
5:1). Plain, honest expositors of Scripture are welcome, the Holy Word is
revered; and one remembers that the reformed religion was biblio-
centric. Marriage is honored, though in special ways. Needless to say, it is
not arranged authoritatively, from on high or from without; it arises from
amity and the shared good life of the abbey. But when a couple marry,
they leave the abbey, bringing to outside life the friendship and mutual
devotion they have known within—except that their love attains greater
fervency in the married than in the single state and prolongs the initial
ecstasies until death itself. Thus though there may not be marrying or
giving in marriage in Thélème—it is like heaven in this respect—there *is*
courtship, the creating of lasting bonds, certainly intellectual and emo-

tional ones, and by implication the physical too, in preconsummatory
ways mostly but perhaps not exclusively, for no vows of chastity are here
ever made.

To modern sensibility there is something cloying about the pleasant
aristocratic sameness of it all, and some regulations are positively off-
putting. The freedom of the abbey did not always tolerate variety. "Do
what *thou* wilt!" to be sure. But if *one* chose to do something, then *all*
followed suit, this not being seen as compulsion, yet surely such sheepish
subservience to a suggesting companion is one of the worst tyrannies
imaginable. (Who could possibly "just say no"?) And the hopes for marriage may be as sentimental as anything that has ever come out of Hollywood.

We should remember, however, that this is satire by inversion; it is
fierce and unrelenting, since it wins our assent before it is directed toward reality. Fewer more devastating attacks on monastic life, character,
and practice have ever been mounted. We should not ask, therefore,
whether we ought to go out and establish a real Thélème or even raise the
question of whether we could in fact tolerate living in such a utopia, any
more than we should ask whether we could inhabit a Shavian hell or
heaven, or Houyhnhnm-land, eating oats with the rational horses, or the
Blakean Hell with its consuming creative and revolutionary energies.
What we need to see is that this French document, produced as reforming forces were being unleashed, contains a vision we have encountered
before, albeit in bits and pieces. It is a tribute to great creating Nature
as a modifier of convention, it renews the energies of the School of
Chartres, it ratifies youthful choice in marriage, it stresses compatibility
and friendship, and it recognizes that human love does not thrive in deserts of poverty and denial but in places of creature comfort and the satisfaction of both the outer and inner person. It is not a realistic blueprint—
who could think so who knows Rabelais's portraits of reality?—but it is a
sharp challenge to discover how and where human possibilities can be
enlarged and what needs to be changed politically, socially, religiously,
psychologically in order to open them up.

Apparently the erotic commitment induced by the Renaissance and
Reformation was capable of firing the creative mind, and the delicious
foreplay of Rabelais's Thélème, only preliminarily related to marriage,
finds richly suggestive reinscription in some of Shakespeare's comedic
courtships or indeed wherever Western man imagines, from Hermas's
Shepherd to Keats, the prolongation of antipicated erotic-asethetic delights.[21]

Marlowe and Chapman

Because of the illuminating contrasts in its millennial retellings, the story of Hero and Leander may well serve us for the Renaissance, as the myth of Amor and Psyche did for late antiquity, as a paradigmatic myth of love and marriage. Beginning as a folk legend, made the theme of an *epyllion* (little epic) by an Alexandrian poet, famously memorialized in an exchange of letters by the lovers in Ovid's *Heroides* and so kept alive in the Middle Ages, the versions we will consider here are those of the *grammatikos* Musaeus (c. A.D. 465–528), Christopher Marlowe, and George Chapman. The three together form a kind of chiastic structure, the late ancient poet being uxorial (A), Marlowe celebrating passionate pleasure (B), and Chapman returning to the marital and richly amplifying it into a kind of proto-baroque (A'). The appropriateness of tying late antiquity to the Renaissance is clear from our discussion of the Greek novel. The present chronological filiation should enforce what I hope no one has missed, that my theme has not unfolded itself along simple developmental lines.

Many verbal and situational parallels connect the fiction of Musaeus to those of Chariton and Achilles Tatius.[22] Hero, a priestess of Aphrodite, lives alone with her parents by the sea, sheltered by them to protect her from human contact and leaving her abode only to serve at Venus's altar. So beautiful is the maiden (also innocent, despite the high eroticism of her vocation) that many a young man has burned to bed her, but it is not until Leander arrives from across the Hellespont that she, sensing his ardor, falls in love. Though she is modest and protests that it is illegal to touch a priestess of Venus, he rejoices in perceiving at once her reciprocating emotion. And so that evening under the shining Evening Star he presses her rosy fingers and kisses her perfumed neck. He asks her at once to celebrate the conjugal mysteries ("gamēlia," 42) with him, and having been warmed by the sweet flame of Erōs ("glukerō puri," 168, the adjective recalling Sappho's famous oxymoron, "bittersweet"), she gives silent consent—the suddenness and the romantic nature of the passion indicated by his being a total stranger who must give her his name and address. After they talk and make arrangements to meet, he becomes her *posis* ("spouse," 220). He departs and soon returns, but Erōs, as so often, has been cruel; after the waves have buffeted Leander in his natatory crossing, he arrives salty and smelling of fish. But Hero anoints and perfumes his body and calls him husband. They meet often, but then come winter and storm. On one fatal occasion the wind blows out the light in her tower that had formerly guided him, and he perishes in the waves, to be joined in death by Hero, who makes a suicidal plunge into the sea from her tower. Through divine intervention the lovers enjoy each other eternally.

We have already noticed two important marital words in this pagan story, *posis* (husband) for Leander and *gamēlia* for the spousal rites; and the Greek of Musaeus, though it rings changes on the word *erōs* and involves Erōs himself at every turn of the plot, stresses the marital and those love words that are most appropriately associated with it. Thus, besides *gamos,* the following words and their cognates are most prominent: *philos, agapē, lektron* (marriage bed). Such words give to this Wagnerian passion the respectability of medieval consensual marriage, but Musaeus may confer upon it something additionally dignified, even religious, for in asking for Hero's hand Leander invokes not only Cypris, the girl's divine patroness, but Athene as well. In using the term *makartatē* (apparently "being in the most blessed or blissful of states"), the author seems to add even a religious dimension, recalling the divine blessing of Israel in Deuteronomy 7:14 and the unknown woman who calls blessed (*makaria*) the womb and breasts of the woman who bore and nurtured Jesus. Jesus reciprocates by calling blessed (*makarioi*) those who hear and keep the word of God (Luke 11:27–28). I have no wish to suggest an influence from the Septuagint or the New Testament upon the *grammatikos* in retelling the ancient pagan legend, only to say that the context for the marital emphasis is made to resonate with meanings and words that suggest the Christian, as is true so often in late secular antiquity.

There is no such resonance in Marlowe's retelling.[23] It combines the following pairs of antithetical elements: pathos and comedy (he calls Hero a "holy Idiot" [1.303] for trying to serve Venus as a "nun" [1.45, 319]); the hetero- and the homosexual (Neptune wantons with the swimming Leander, trying to steal kisses and forcing the youth to say, "I am no woman I" [2.192]); gnomic sentence ("Who euer lou'd, that lou'd not at first sight" [1.176], and "It lies not in our power to loue or hate, / For will in us is ouer-rulde by fate" [1.167–68]) and passionate pleasure. It is the last which predominates, and we are inclined to ask how Marlowe would have treated the erotic if his plot had allowed it to move into marriage. As it stands, the tale celebrates, though with wry touches here and there, a heroine who is naturally alluring and who wears clothes almost comically stiff with mythological decoration, while Venus's temple, though it is beautiful, has a glass pavement on which we see gods and goddesses committing "headdie ryots, incest, rapes" (1.144–45). Marlowe (as we would expect from an author who might well have looked with Neptune's eyes upon his hero) makes Leander more plausibly human and attractive than Hero: he is articulate, athletic, but above all else "amorous, . . . beautifull and yoong" (1.51), with a dazzlingly white neck, a smooth breast, wonderful eyes, cheeks, lips. Small wonder that he is narcissistic and tries to kiss his own shadow—how easily Marlowe's poetic eloquence slides toward the illicit! The uxorial of Musaeus has not entirely vanished in Marlowe: Hero gives Leander all, "both to each other were *affied*" (2.26). But the *fides* does not last long, for soon thereafter she becomes passionately jealous and throws herself on her lover, in completely un-Spenserian and untraditional fashion, and we have perhaps a right to conclude that had the lovers survived into marriage, it would have been a stormy one. Marlowe's very brief skirmish with the *res uxoria* does not promise serene fulfillments.

Marlowe's unfinished poem left the lovers alive, their love fully consummated but by no means exhausted; in his continuation George Chapman completely changes tone and perspective—and he wants us to know it.[24] He refers to his "sterne Muse" and calls the subject "trifling" (here he may be deliberately coy, for he adds quickly, "he that shuns trifles shuns the world," noting that the story made Musaeus, its first author, "eternall"). Distancing himself from Marlovian passion, he refers wryly to Leander's "Hero-handled bodie," and he moves from young passion to the need for mature judgment: "Loues edge is taken off, and that light flame / . . . Must now grow staid, and censure the delights, / That being enjoyed aske iudgement." Such a shift to reason gives Chapman an opportunity to outdo his predecessor in aphorisms, some of which are wise and witty. He moves to allegory, and a splendidly panoplied figure descends: she first appeals to "Sence" in her radiant beauty but then to reason and faith, for she is attended by Religion, Devotion, Order, State. She is Ceremony, and rebuking Leander for "bluntness in his violent loue," she inspires him to go to his father and resolve on a celebration of the marriage vows already sealed. Masculine government is beginning to emerge, and the Elizabethan world order is being restored, not excitingly or originally perhaps but with dignity and skill.

Chapman pauses now to renew his inspiration, that "most strangely-intellectual fire," as he calls it, and he ventures to hope that it will guide Hero's "burning faculties." His artistic virtuosity does not desert him as he turns from public masque to individual character, whose emotional conflicts he explores plausibly and compellingly. Left alone, her maidenhead and Leander gone, her religious vows broken, her once peaceful abodes invaded and despoiled, and herself a prey to violent thoughts she never before knew, Hero discovers she is "euen to her selfe a stranger." Chapman has here opened a promising vein of rich Renaissance individuality, and we would like to follow this skillful and intelligent analyst into a fuller exploration of his conservative thought, now individually directed to his subject's psyche. But he disappoints us, for the public proto-baroque manner returns too soon, and he brings Hero to her temple, a sacred venue that once more invites elevated elaboration. He has his heroine wear her crown of icicles that nothing could melt and further stiffen her priestly robe with new embroideries that now incorporate her late experiences and also the mottoes and proverbs of the morally learned author. Writing iconically he tries to outdo the most stately of epic *ekphrases,* a mode that continues through the hymeneal feast and masque that accompany the wedding of a betrothed couple Hero sends for and unites ceremonially. Some dramatic interest attends her attempt to enjoy what she hoped might be a surrogate for her own union, and Chapman's epithalamic verses are not without grace and delicacy.

The deaths of the lovers, decreed by hoary tradition, Chapman recounts solemnly and at times realistically (Hero hugs Leander's torn and buffeted body and dies breathing his name), and Chapman has not failed to enforce his theme that "Joy grauen in sence, like snow in water, wasts." But artifice and conventionality return to crown a poem already overladen with them: Fate is somewhat evasively and conventionally blamed for the accident, and in the spirit of the Ovidian genre Neptune in pity (the homoerotic desire with which Marlowe imbued him having entirely disappeared) transforms the lovers into a pair of immortally sweet and loving birds, the Acanthides.[25]

Two Married Women Killed with—

It is difficult to know precisely how to relate the Jacobean court to the literature of love and marriage. If the king loved profoundly, he often did so in his own "twisted fashion." He was "shockingly inquisitive in matters of sex," and it has been suggested that lines in Webster's *The White Devil* epitomize the moral and educative effects of the court of James I: " 'I visited the court, whence I return'd / More courteous, more lecherous by far' " (1.2.315–16).[26] Of the many tragedies that seem in one way or another to be related to the spirit if not the letter of the highly emotional and tortuously ambiguous royal life, I have chosen two that unforgettably deal with the institution of marriage. One of them, the one that achieves truly tragic force, opens cesspools of monstrous iniquity and villainy in the highest places; the other introduces more easily recognizable evil among the rural rich. Both plots turn marital situations of love, devotion, and promise into venues of suffering and death. It will be our aim to determine whether Heywood's *A Woman Killed with Kindness*[27] (printed 1607) and Webster's *The Duchess of Malfi* (1613–14) affirm or annihilate, strengthen or weaken, or keep precariously ambiguous the ideal they place under such extreme stress.

Two plays could not bear more sharply contrasting features. The first is set in rural Protestant England among the gentry; the second in corrupt, courtly, ecclesiastical, aristocratic, backward-looking southern Italy. The first is domestic drama, what T. S. Eliot has called "a drama of common life."[28] It is simple and direct in expression (the dramatist self-consciously refers to "our poet's dull and earthy muse," Prologue, 11), sometimes effectively realistic in its portraiture and delicately tender in its sentiments. The second is tempestuous in mood, tenebrist in coloring, often metaphorically invoking an external nature that is feral and ruthless, and poetically, though not always structurally, sophisticated.

Heywood, a most productive and highly successful playwright, opens this, his best and most famous play, with marriage festivities that involve the whole community. Anne, the bride, is praised for ornaments of both mind and body, her birth is noble, and she has been educated in music and languages. Her brother, Sir Francis, ends his praise of her by stressing her meekness and patience and by quoting an old saying, "In a good time that man both wins and woos / That takes his wife down in her wedding shoes" (1.47–48). But the speaker has a reputation for "wild blood," and the dramatist surely intends to rule out such uxorial taming as inconsistent with the progressive ideal that another much more sympathetic character, Sir Charles, implies in describing the new union:

> There's equality
> In this fair combination; you are both scholars,
> Both young, both being descended nobly:
> There's music in this sympathy . . .
> (1.66–69)

It is such promise and high harmony as this (surely related to the great concord of Spenserian and other Renaissance thought) that the melancholy villain, Wendoll, a friend and currently a house-guest of the happy husband, Frankford, shatters when he rushes in upon the young bride with a sudden outburst, "I love you!" (6.106), stunning her with his abruptness but in the end winning her body. The time-honored emotion of pity for his Cupidinous plight softens her for her fall. Frankford, informed by servants, unlike Othello gets the full ocular evidence he seeks but, reminding us of Hamlet, he cannot dispatch the guilty pair "with all their scarlet sins upon their backs" (13.47). The aggrieved husband might have been sanctioned by an old convention had he resorted to blood revenge, but instead he chooses this solution: he will not martyr his wife or label her a strumpet "but with usage / Of more humility torment thy soul, / And kill thee even with kindness" (13.155–57). He sends all her possessions out of the house in order not to be reminded of her, and she is not to see the children. Frankford's verbs *torment* and *kill* should give us pause, for his kindness is indeed cruel and lethal and is intended to be. Ultimately he has this motto engraved in gold letters on her tomb, "Here lies she whom her husband's kindness killed" (17.140). No doubt such a solution is better than immediate bloody murder, but by how much? Killing as it does both spirit and body, it can scarcely be said to have the relish of Christian salvation in it even if the wife's soul is finally saved. To a modern, the husband is likely to seem a bone-chilling monster of self-regarding and cruel complacency.

Such feelings are not dissipated by the conclusion. Given one of his manors and all her material possessions but denied everything that might make life worth living, Anne starves herself to death. She regards herself as polluted, for though her soul can be saved, her earthly tabernacle has been desecrated beyond cleansing. It may be of no great moment that her theology is not wholly orthodox (she believes that her own salvation depends on her aggrieved mate's forgiveness of her), though it does show what God-like authority he seems to have exuded. That forgiveness, necessary for her salvation or not, she receives before she dies, in the arms of her husband and in the presence of her extended family. Her brother, Sir Francis, opines that threats and bad usage would not have led to such true sorrow and repentance as this, but here again we must ask if this somewhat compromised character can possibly be Heywood's raisonneur. Frankford's own grief may come closer to the playwright's perspective: their souls are now united but her rash acts have separated their bodies and thus aborted what had been so generously promised at the outset. Heywood would like us to feel tragic emotions over all that has been lost, including the union of bodies in holy wedlock.

Up to a point such an aim is realized. There are many scenes of genuine poignancy, expressed in simple beauty, more often by the suffering wife than by the suffering husband. When he discovers that Anne's lute has been left behind, he says:

> Her lute! O God, upon this instrument
> Her fingers have run quick division,

Sweeter than that which now divides our hearts.
These frets have made me pleasant, that have now
Frets of my heartstrings made.
    (15.13–17)

Anne, on the road from her home to exile, when a servant overtakes her
and gives her the instrument, speaks more simply, more pathetically, less
punningly (though not without some word play), revealing a deeper and
tenderer spirit than her husband's: "I know the lute. Oft have I sung to
thee; / We are both out of tune, both out of time" (16.18–19). The lute is
then by her order broken against the coach wheels, "As the last music
that I e'er shall make."

But if Heywood wished to achieve, in addition to the pathetic so
often associated with domestic tragedy, a deeply tragic emotion, his wish
remains unfulfilled. We must of course be realistic and historical, remembering that current mentalities cannot be escaped or ignored in art and
can be transcended only in the best. To the lovely marital ideal so compellingly presented at the outset and so typical of the dreams of the larger
society, no greater threat than adultery existed—a point made from the
earliest antiquity, pagan and religious, and after the Reformation enforced with stern and blazing language by religious publicists known for
their rhetorical power. When Frankford approaches his wife who, he
knows, is in the arms of his dear friend and guest Wendoll, his speech is
sincere and piercing:

    Astonishment,
Fear and amazement play against my heart,
Even as a madman beats upon a drum.
    (13.24–26)

Why then does *A Woman Killed with Kindness* fall short of tragic
sublimity? Because, I think, of a deficiency in moral vision and also in the
ability to portray multidimensional character. We are surely grateful that
Frankford did not take the often sanctioned route of murderous violence
upon the guilty pair, but can we escape feeling that a husband so mon-
strously kind would sooner or later have been insufferable in one way or
another and that so submissive a wife would only have flattered his power
and never resented or corrected his pious vanities? The alternatives to
overt violence complacently instituted by the husband remain themselves convention-ridden, without grandeur, small, petty, mean-spirited,
only verbally religious, if that. The Christian command to forgive has
been materialized and cheapened—it would have been better to senti-

mentalize it. The wife too is well below the heroic, and comes nowhere near the exemplary force of a Lucretia, the unquenchable determination of a Griselda, or the grandeur of the repentant Clarissa. We of course feel some sympathy, as we do for all suffering, but there is no *depth* of pity or fear or admiration, for there has been no depth of character. The lyrical and promissory opening vignette is only that, a little vine that does not bear fruit, an epigraph under which not much has been written out.[29] All this may be by way of preparing for Shakespeare, who has honored our theme by applying to it the full range of his genius and who, a century before Fielding, Richardson, and the bourgeois milieu of the eighteenth century, truly realized an aim of the later period, to actualize the truly heroic and tragic on the domestic scene. Heywood has not done so.

Webster has come close, though his chosen milieu is vastly different. His highly Italianate world is one of ruins.[30] He was in general "much possessed of death and saw the skull beneath the skin," in T. S. Eliot's famous language, and he so envisaged institutions and civilizations. "Churches and cities which have diseases like to men / Must have like death that we have" (5.3.20–21). In *The Duchess of Malfi* Bosola, a villainous spy for the Arragonian brothers, even deeper-dyed in villainy than they, says, "We are only like dead walls or vaulted graves, / That, ruined, yield no echo" (5.5.131–32). But the two friends, Delio and Antonio, good men in a mad and corrupt world, think otherwise: ruins can be loved since treading them we set our feet on history, and they *do* produce echoes, "hollow," "dismal," but "plain" (5.3.7–8)–that is, spiritually clear. The final speech of the play comes almost like an echo from the duchess's grave and from the great all-encompassing ruin wrought in the play itself, which includes centrally the destruction of a marriage. The message of that concluding speech may direct our vision toward the future, to life, lineage, and all-creating Nature. But its aphoristic climax turns us back to the play:

> I have ever thought
> Nature doth nothing so great for great men
> As when she's pleased to make them lords of truth:
> Integrity of life is fame's best friend,
> Which nobly, beyond death, shall crown the end.
> (5.5.153–57)

If we do not see the duchess as, despite some human failings, a "lord" of truth and a woman of integrity, we deprive the play of its tragic dignity and power.

That dignity has been traditionally thought to reside in the duchess's lofty fearlessness and nobility in facing persecution and death, and I have no wish to deny this insight. The Iago-like spy and informer Bosola seems to have come to a central truth about her before he dies: she is one who "gives a majesty to adversity" (4.1.7). She is, furthermore, a modern woman, modern in her and our day, one who faces death without penitence or submission, without rite or ritual, for which she sees no need. She is also modern in breaking with the hideous class distinctions and almost incestuous family pride of her totally villainous and backward-looking brothers, who represent both church and state. All this is true and contributes reasons why a modern may without qualms regard her as a heroine.

Still, I wish to shift the focus somewhat and place her clearly onto the landscape of this book. There she stands not so much *larger* than life as fully *capable* of life, an enemy of jejune custom and sensitively absorbent of Nature, its joy-producing energies as well as its truth-sanctioning standards. She opts for choice in marriage, and the steward she chooses as her mate joins her in clandestinely celebrating their rites, not unlike the lovers in Chapman's *The Gentleman Usher;* they are mindful in their home-made vows that what they are doing is fully valid, sanctioned now by religion, altered custom, and evangelical propaganda. Thus Antonio, the bridegroom, adverts in the manner of the homilists, to the union in Eden, "that first good deed began i' the world, / After man's creation, the sacrament of marriage" (1.1.475–76). And the eager bride, trying to arouse an understandably diffident bridegroom whose station in life is so far below hers, asserts that she is not an alabaster statue worshipping a dead husband: "This is flesh and blood, sir" (1.1.560).

Thus from her high social position she is imbuing the marital sexual act—and that of a second marriage, to boot—not only with the equality at the marital bed between the sexes that had been inherent in Christianity all along but with a social egalitarianism that could be truly subversive and destructive of old privilege. It is not by chance that Webster, in a stunningly dramatic scene, has his heroine confront one of the chief enemies to her private happiness immediately after, virtually *during,* a moment of intimate domesticity. She can be said to perish as a martyr to the reactionary forces which in her society, even within her own patrimony, were determined to destroy the emergent marital freedoms that were beginning to open vistas upon possibilities of human development within the freely established nuclear family.

It is therefore not irrelevant to celebrate the flesh-and-blood duchess, a fully human being embarked on a marital adventure riskier than most, one in fact mortally dangerous, who gives human poignancy and warmth to the majesty she surely possesses. I recognize her faults, but I do not wish to ally myself with those contemporary critics who reduce her stature, finding her to be foolish, imprudent, deceptive, sly, and criminally rash in risking so much. I do not choose to answer these charges point by point, except to say that guilt of some of them partly constitutes her greatness while others can be contextually excused. But I do insist upon her humanity, which of course by definition includes frailties. The striking scene I have just referred to shows that what is lost in the catastrophe of this searing tragedy is not just goodness, greatness, and individual initiative but those qualities placed, however precariously, in daily life—specifically in the family. The duchess now married to Antonio is combing her hair, preparing for bed. She has been fast wedded long since, though she is still fearful of discovery. *We* know, though she and Antonio do not, that her brother, the jealous and perhaps incestuously inclined Ferdinand, is present. This fact throws a dark and dramatic shadow over the domestic conversation that is witty, intimate, and perhaps a touch salacious. "My hair tangles," the duchess says and proceeds with her combing. "When were we so merry?" she asks (3.2.63). Antonio and the maid depart. Thinking they are still there she continues to talk and comb, the words accompanied by the motions of her arms in the shadowed, candle-lit boudoir, a scene any director would love to render. Trying to be lightly ironic, she becomes inadvertently grim when she says, "We shall one day have my brother take you napping" (3.2.75). And then suddenly she knows a brother is in fact there—and the world of gross sin and cruelty intrudes on a loving though perilous domesticity. Ferdinand hands his sister a poniard. With a sudden change from bedtime banter to authority she takes it and says, " 'Tis welcome, / For, know, whether I am doom'd to live, or die, / I can do both like a prince" (3.2.83–84).[31] Against the unmitigated horror that now ensues she rises to moral dignity, but we are not to forget the human warmth, even the rapture, of her second marriage and the boldness of its disobedience to church and state, to family and property, to class and tradition (for one, the venerable Christian tradition that second marriages were undesirable). Much of the force of the tragedy resides in the loss to corrupt and cruel political and ecclesiastical power of a domestic happiness well begun, greatly enjoyed, productive of three children, and big with the promise of long continuance.

Modern scholarship has documented historically the tribulations and occasional triumphs that attended romantic marriage in late medieval and Renaissance times.[32] Literature like that of Webster and others

FIGURE 27 Titian, *Flora*. (Uffizi Gallery, Florence; Alinari/Art Resource, NY.)

analyzed in this chapter demonstrates the truth of the observation that
"the movement of lovers toward each other may well be the most important single motive force in Elizabethan literature."[33] That movement animates the Shakespearean oeuvre, and so avant-garde a commentator as
Germaine Greer has said in *The Female Eunuch* that Shakespeare was

FIGURE 28 Rembrandt, *Saskia with a Red Flower*. (Gemäldegalerie Alte Meister, Staatliche Kunstsammiungen, Dresden.)

"one of the most significant apologists of marriage as a way of life and a road to salvation."[34] That statement will need to be qualified by the problematical ambiguities that attend Shakespearean love as it has attended all love everywhere; this will be the subject of the next and final full chapter of this study.

Our central focus on marriage and the erotic will be sharpened if we

FIGURE 29 Rembrandt, *Saskia as Flora*. (Courtesy, The Hermitage, St. Petersburg/Jean Hagstrum and Russell Maylone.)

return briefly to the visual arts in concluding our discussion of the extra-Shakespearean Renaissance. The blondish *Flora* painted by Titian (fig. 27) obviously possesses sexual attractiveness—her pensive eyes and facial expression reveal some longing. She *could* be uxorial, as she holds cut flowers in her right hand and with the other modestly covers her breasts. But Rembrandt has gone further in portraying his wife "Saskia with a Red Flower" (fig. 28), presenting a flower with her right hand and touching her covered breasts with her left. He is doing more than meets the eye. More obviously and more powerfully in the Hermitage painting (fig. 29) he recalls the Flora of a long and varying tradition: the same Saskia, now obviously pregnant, her hair wreathed in flowers, holding in her right hand a staff adorned with a bouquet, she touches her abdomen and looks coyly at the spectator. Rembrandt unmistakably gives his Flora the radically new and different environment anticipated by the high Middle Ages in consensual marriage and firmly established by post-Reformation culture. The *Flora Meretrix* of the church fathers has been revised and redeemed and, without loss of sexual allure, placed solidly in the home.[35] In portraying the founding marriage, Milton was to effect a comparable conversion of the Flora image. His Eve lies still unawakened, "with tresses discompos'd, and glowing Cheeks," as Adam "hung over her enamour'd." He beholds "Beautie, which whether waking or asleep, / Shot forth peculiar Graces; then with voice / Milde, as when *Zephyrus* on *Flora* breathes," he touches his wife's hand and awakens her (*Par. Lost* 5.10, 13–16).

*Unlesse there be a ioyning of harts, and knitting of
affections, it is not Marriage indeed, but a shew and
name.*

    Henrie Smith, *A Preparative to Marriage*
    (1591)

At length the candle's out, and now
All that they had not done they do;
    What that is, who can tell?
But I believe it was no more
Than thou and I have done before
    With Bridget and with Nell.

    Sir John Suckling, "A Ballad upon a
    Wedding" (1641)

TWELVE

The Renaissance (III): Shakespeare

*I*t is no longer necessary to say that though Shakespeare may be for all time, he is also supremely of his age. Others may abide our questions, but *he* is by no means free of ours. I hope to interrogate him about our theme as rigorously as I have the many authors in my millennial canon of amorous utterance. And he certainly ought to be considered in the context of the intellectual and social history we have sketched both for his own and antecedent ages. But whom are we to interrogate? Too little is known of Shakespeare the man to provide us with a mentality to explore, and the author within his works is as elusive as he is important. Nevertheless, on our topic, love and marriage, I believe we can locate an intellectual center and that norm I shall refer to, at least for the time being, as "Shakespeare." It should, however, be clear that, though I put aside the historical Shakespeare as unavailable for analysis, I do not ally myself with the current "bardicide" that celebrates "the death of the author" and brings the literary equivalent of the Death of God to Shakespearean criticism.[1]

Locating "Shakespeare"

"Shakespeare" identifies himself as supporting consensual marriage of, by, and for the young and therefore as an enemy of arranged unions, even those in the highest places. Judging from the dynamics of his fables, the energy of his language, and the omnipresence of the marital theme, we can see him as partaking in the post-Reformation celebration of marriage; he would have agreed with the famous sermon of 1591 which proclaimed that institution as possessing more honor than any other ordinance: "Before man had any other calling, he was called to be a husband." Margaret Ranald has said that "in Shakespeare marriage is the one human relationship portrayed in almost every play. It forms the denouement of every comedy, and it is usually described in affirmative images of harmony, order, and even transcendence." Shakespeare's bleakest play, *Timon of Athens,* "demonstrates the horror of a world completely devoid of marital love."[2]

He was also a full inheritor of the Judeo-Christian tradition of physical naturalism, which we have seen lying behind and sanctioning the institution and which animates classic utterances in the Bible, the fathers, and high medieval reformers. We have noted that on her wedding day the duchess of Malfi tries to arouse an understandably diffident bridegroom of much lower degree by asserting she is not alabaster: "Awake, awake, man! This is flesh and blood, sir." In one way or another all of "Shakespeare's" great women make the same assertion, sometimes with the help of disguise. Some have found it charming and appropriate that marriage plays should drive on, though at times somewhat prematurely, to pillow talk.[3] But I find "Shakespeare's" comic and tragicomic sexuality rather more related to the traditions I have disclosed earlier—the placing of desire in holy matrimony. And the healthy, unconcealed erotic hunger of his heroines often expresses itself in what we might call a kind of baptized bawdry, free, as low-life joking often is not, from dullness and exaggeration.

All this is far from saying that Shakespeare does not present a perverse side of the uxorial or that he does not allow it to be scorned, tested, threatened from outside and inside, challenged by other forms of greatly admired love. For Shakespeare often places the theme itself in extremis, along with his heroes, but it should be noted at once that that most potent of challengers to marital happiness, Iago, is well outside our tradition—a rationalist not a naturalist, a misogynist not a feminist, an exploiter not an enjoyer of erotic desire, an egoistic enemy of amorous integrity and familial stability not a supporter of wedded esteem and desire. But even he, though he can heartrendingly destroy the bliss, does not succeed in dispelling the ideal from the mind of anyone, least of all the grand sufferers. This "Shakespeare," whose character I have so briefly sketched, appears in play after play, in all genres of literature and forms of love, in merriment and in tears, in construction and destruction.

But "Shakespeare" is more dynamically bound to social reality than to philosophy, ethics, or theology, and it will throw light on his art if we compare the Shakespearean world to the contemporary life that emerges from the voluminous notes kept by Richard Napier, a seventeenth-century astrologer and physician, on his medical practice among middling and lower class people.[4] I concentrate on the relations of spouses. Passionate attachment was common among the doctor's clients, romantic love was extremely important in choosing marriage partners, many people (*pace* Rosalind in *As You Like It*) actually *did* die of love, new ideals were eroding arranged marriages, "first liking" came to be deemed as essential to a good union, and most wives desired and expected close affectionate ties with their husbands. The tragedies of humble or ordinary life arose from the frustration of such desires as these, and madness and misery attended—and were expected to attend—the breaking of close amorous bonds. *Othello* and *King Lear*, it appears, were not out of touch with real life when they presented the tragic consequences of cutting familial or uxorial ties; indeed, one can say that Othello's madness and Desdemona's numbing grief were ordinary life writ large. And one also has a right to assume, since the sense of loss is always proportionate in intensity to the perceived value of what is lost, that "Shakespeare's" many moments of exuberant and jubilant joy also evoked an echo in many breasts accustomed to the trials of love in real life. When the witty, verbally dexterous, high-spirited, and not easily duped Rosalind utters her piercing love cry to her dearest female friend, the playwright, we may feel sure, was electrifying his auditors of every social class and psychological condition: "O coz, coz, coz, my pretty little coz, that thou didst know how many fathoms deep I am in love. But it cannot be sounded. My affection [a strongly charged word that could mean passion] hath an unknown bottom, like the bay of Portugal" (*As You Like It* 4.1).

There is thus a paradigmatic "Shakespeare" compounded of life experiences close to those of his contemporaries and of inherited intellectual formulations—how he loved at times to expatiate on degree, power, sorrow, order, or indeed "the unity and married calm of states" (*Troilus and Cressida* 1.3). But to that must always be added the imaginative power of the genius Shakespeare, which is applied to our theme as much as to any other—the power to create worlds alternative both to established philosophical tradition and the circumambient status quo.

I now give four glimpses of "Shakespeare" on marital love, the first two (from *A Midsummer Night's Dream* and *Romeo and Juliet*) exemplifying intellectual formulations abundantly present in his age but anticipated for millennia in documents of high authority, and the second two (from *Julius Caesar* [surprisingly!] and *The Merry Wives of Windsor* [expectedly]) reflecting contemporary social reality.

We have assimilated the patients of a contemporary alienist to Shakespeare's characters in love, not inappropriately since Theseus in *A Midsummer Night's Dream* tells us that

> Lovers and madmen have such seething brains,
> Such shaping fantasies, that apprehend
> More than cool reason ever comprehends.

> The lunatic, the lover, and the poet
> Are of imagination all compact.
>   (5.1)

These oft-quoted lines, though they are pertinent to the confusions and mischiefs of the Midsummer Night—to love's madness and arbitrariness in the play—may reflect Bottom's observation that "reason and love keep little company together now-a-days" (3.1), but they do not epitomize "Shakespeare" on love. Hippolyta's immediately sequent lines do, making her the raisonneuse of the play:

> But all the story of the night told over,
> And all their minds transfigured so together,
> [the Elizabethan preoccupation with mutuality was obsessive]
> More witnesseth than fancy's images,
> [a direct hit at her husband's analysis]
> And grows to something of great constancy;
> [the Elizabethan marital ideal *in parvo*]
> But, howsoever, strange and admirable.
> [Illusory and even mad beginnings can and do lead to
> stability, although retaining some of their original wonder.]
>   (5.1)

Such wisdom—true both to what is mysterious and awesome in how love begins and grows, and also to healthy transformations by love and its stabilization in and by society—is truly paradigmatic and controlling. Musical responses, too delicate like Mendelssohn's or too passionately concentrated like Berlioz's, though they exquisitely or intensely express elements in the play, do not evoke its effectual form and integrating spirit. And Fuseli's portrayal of Puck, not pleasantly impish but sinister and diabolical, had better remain on the margins along with Jan Kott's animalism. To Kott, Bottom is a phallic quadruped; Helena's line, "I am your spaniel," is brutalized; the forest is inhabited by devils and lamias, by slimy, hairy, sticky creatures (without noting that these are neutralized or frustrated); and Titania's court is made up of toothless old men and hags, their mouths wet with saliva. To keep my point of view in focus, it will be helpful to invoke the categories of chapter 1 (libido, eros, tender affection, friendship, *agapē,* the ego context) and ask which predominates in this frequently eccentric play. Eros would seem to win the day in the body of the play, with friendship climactically envisaged in Hippolyta's stress on "something of great constancy."[5]

I have earlier referred to Rosaline, Juliet's predecessor, who is present to us only as an ensemble of Petrarchan conceits in the mouth of Romeo, otherwise being invisible to us. The passion of the flesh-and-blood Juliet is, to be sure, not without its own conventions and conceits, but it also possesses linguistic verve and resonance. One line (3.5.43) seems comprehensively paradigmatic, a philosophical epitome, worthier of "Shakespeare" himself than the young teen-ager who utters it. Juliet hails her departing lover as follows (I give the readings of the first two quartos and the first folio):

> JUL: Art thou gone so, my Lord, my Loue, my Friend? (Q1, 1597)

> IU.   Art thou gone so loue, Lord, ay husband, friend, (Q2, 1599)

> IUL.   Art thou gone so: Loue, Lord, ay Husband, Friend. (F1, 1623)

The original wording and the changes show that the speech was taken seriously and was meant to be emphasized by the actor. Each item is given metrical weight, and the interjectory *ay,* added in Q2, suggests a separation of the first two nouns (already established, as it were) from the last two, which yet await time and circumstance for their fullest realization. The second quarto and the first folio place *Loue* first in the series, a logical step since it is of course primary and causative. The addition of *husband,* in some ways a synonym of the hierarchical *Lord,* may point to a verbal betrothal (verba de futuro) which, when consummated, would constitute a binding marriage that family rivalry and parental opposition could not legally overturn.

The stable presence of *Friend* at the end of the series suggests a climax, which at once transcends and absorbs the other values. But are we certain what the word means? It could mean—especially when used in the plural—"ally," "relation," or "sponsor" (*Cymbeline* 1.5.59), and here it might suggest what was very important to the young girl, that Juliet Capulet was now a Montague, entitled to all the benefit and security thereto appertaining. The word could also mean "sweetheart" or "mistress" or "wife" or "sexual companion" (*Love's Labour's Lost* 5.2.404, *Winter's Tale* 1.2.109–11, *Measure for Measure* 1.4.29); if so, it is here redundant and merely reinforces *Loue*. The best interpretation, though the others are not necessarily obviated, is that *friend* means "friend," more or less in the highest Aristotelian sense of an esteemed and beloved long-term companion. If so, we have the full Reformation ideal here adumbrated, one that was to receive climactic expression in Milton's Adam and Eve.

Shakespeare's predecessor, Arthur Brooke, a Puritan who represented the backlash of extreme Protestant fear of breaking arrangement and encouraging independent consent, is far from such an ideal. In 1562 he moralized the story of Romeo and Juliet as follows: "To this end, good Reader, is this tragical matter written, to describe unto thee a couple of unfortunate lovers, thralling themselves to unhonest desire, neglecting the authority and advice of parents and friends; conferring their principal counsels with drunken gossips and superstitious friars, . . . abusing the honourable name of lawful marriage to cloak the shame of stolen contract; finally by all means of unhonest life hasting to most unhappy deaths."⁶ Shakespeare's version completely overturns such moralistic precisianism, and his lovers' love, though tragically aborted in death, does in the end heal the familial and communal breach. The underlying concept of the play stands in the main line of the high medieval and Renaissance Christian naturalism and of the reforming revisionism we have studied at length in earlier chapters. The epitomizing line I have just analyzed embodies, with amazing condensation and resonance, the cultural achievement of consensual and companionate marriage.⁷

Julius Caesar brings us inside the home and lets us glimpse the marriage of Brutus and Portia, where the scene, however, is not Roman but Christian in the sense just described. (For a stereotypically submissive and silent Roman wife, see the devoted Virgilia in *Coriolanus*.) Shakespeare has, as it were, rendered a real-life, contemporary scene of a loving couple in deep crisis and potential grief, trying to actualize the new status for woman in the home and the amorous mutuality enjoined by religious thought. Portia speaks:

> No, my Brutus,
> You have some sick offence within your mind,
> Which by right and virtue of my place
> I ought to know of. And upon my knees,
> I charm [implore] you, by my once-commended beauty,
> By all your vows of love, and that great vow
> Which did incorporate and make us one,
> That you unfold to me, your self, your half,
> Why you are heavy.
>   (2.1)

Brutus bids her rise, although she, and surely he too, must recognize his authority, but she persists in her demand and continues her definition of a Christian companionate marriage in which the twain are one flesh, one spirit:

> Am I your self
> But as it were in sort or limitation?
> To keep with you at meals, comfort your bed,
> And talk to you sometimes? Dwell I but in the suburbs
> Of your good pleasure? If it be no more,
> Portia is Brutus' harlot, not his wife.
>
> (2.1)

Conventional attitudes linger on here, but the spirit is new, fresh, emergent. And those critics who wish to remand the Shakespearean heroine after her marriage to the hierarchical stringency of a marital status quo should ask themselves if Beatrice, Portia of Belmont, Pauline, Imogen, or Rosalind could ever be content in an intellectual and emotional suburbia and if their creator intended them to. The social "Shakespeare" speaks with amazing directness in the words of the Roman Portia.

There is much room for disguise in the pranks and high jinks of *The Merry Wives of Windsor,* not least in the "ritual" embarrassment and ultimate rejection of Falstaff at the close. Can we believe that either Mistress Quickly or the song provides a normative perspective when *she* calls Falstaff "corrupt, and tainted in desire," or when *it* says, "Lust is but a bloody fire, / Kindled with unchaste desire" (5.5)? But in the wooing and winning of Anne, in a play closely leveled with the real life of country squires and full of references to contemporary society, our "Shakespeare" does appear with even greater clarity and finality than in the Roman tragedy. Consider the arranged marriage which the elder Pages, with divided counsels, wish to foist on their "pretty virginity" (1.1) of a daughter, nubile, seventeen, and the heiress of a decent competency. The otherwise astute father favors Abraham Slender as a suitor, rich enough in land but a bumbling innocent of a man who in hilarious malapropisms tries to articulate the widely held conservative position that love need not precede but can be counted on as developing within marriage: "I hope upon familiarity will grow more contempt. But if you say 'marry her,' I will marry her. That I am freely dissolved, and dissolutely" (1.1). One shudders at the verbally bright and sprightly Anne having to face a lifetime of cutting through such a linguistic wilderness as that! Her mother's choice for her is not much better, the "well-moneyed" (4.4) but irascible, foolish, and thick-accented French physician, Dr. Gaius.

Anne's own choice is not perfect, and "Shakespeare's" position gains credibility for not being guilty of sentimental idealization. Fenton has been dissolute and is of the upper classes—much too high in status for

Anne, thinks her father. And he himself confesses that he began his suit with her father's wealth as a first motive but that he grew into discovering her own personal riches, "the very riches of thyself / That now I aim at" (3.4). Some growth—the kind that the dim-witted, spiritless, and easily led Slender had hoped for only after marriage—has apparently taken place during courtship, perhaps providing a clue as to why such preliminaries to marriage occupy so decisive a position in the comedies. Fenton's protestations do not entirely reconcile us to his worthiness, for he seems glib at times, but it is understandable that a high-spirited and beautiful girl should trust herself enough to take her chances with a dashing ex-libertine.

Particularly since—after the final "ritual" disgraces the other suitors, who in disguise manage to choose boys instead of girls for partners —Fenton is given a speech in which "Shakespeare" seems to reveal himself. The handsome suitor says that had Anne's parents' wishes been followed, she would have been married "most shamefully, / Where there was no proportion held in love" (5.5). In exchanging vows with him, Anne "doth evitate and shun / A thousand irreligious cursèd hours, / Which forcèd marriage would have brought upon her" (5.5). These sentiments[8]—nowhere else in "Shakespeare" so clearly and eloquently stated—are ratified and made unmistakably "Shakespearean" by the parents' immediate acceptance of the young people's choice, which the father blesses as the wife acquiesces. Then all are invited to laughter and joy "by a country fire."

The Marital and the Political State: The Early Plays

By the time of his great second tetralogy of historical plays in the middle or late 1590s (*Richard II*, the two parts of *Henry IV*, and *Henry V*), the "Shakespeare" I have just adumbrated had achieved a recognizable identity. Of him we catch only glimpses, but he is obviously at ease with his marital ideal. In Richard II's queen—historically only nine years old at the time her royal husband went to Ireland—he creates a gracious, lyrically perfumed presence. As he is led to the tower of London, she says: "But soft, but see—or rather do not see— / My fair rose wither"; "thou most beauteous inn: / Why should hard-favoured grief be lodged in thee?" (5.1) Hotspur's Kate is of an altogether different kidney. Though deeply concerned, like Brutus's Portia, with her husband's worried state of mind and body, she is quite unlike the Roman wife when she calls him a "mad-headed ape," compares him to a "weasel," and threatens to break his little finger (2.4). I take this indignant playfulness to reveal as much love and devotion as Portia's serious protestations do—and perhaps a good bit more relaxation in her knowledge of the essential equality of their partnership (*1 Henry IV* 2.3). Henry V is cut from the same cloth as Hotspur, at least when the great victor of Agincourt speaks "plain soldier" in wooing his French Kate. And values appear more decisively: sexual attraction, love (though not of a sentimental or romantic variety), and a pledge of "plain and uncoined constancy" (*Henry V* 5.2).[9] To go back to the Kate-Hotspur dialogue, we derive the reason for the brevity and briskness of amorous encounter in this tetralogy: Hotspur calls his loving and beloved wife a "trifler" since her importunities interfere with the urgent military business at hand. There is simply no time now "to play with maumets and to tilt with lips" (*1 Henry IV* 2.4).

Nor was there time in the first tetralogy from the early 1590s, in the three parts of *Henry VI* and *Richard III*. But here Shakespeare *takes* the time to look closely at dynastic marriage. Why? I suggest that the author is himself wrestling with the meaning and value of political marriage, with the presence of larger-than-life women on the political scene, with what of intimate human value was lost in a time of foreign and civil strife—this last, we remember, being one of Homer's poignant concerns in the *Iliad*. It is certainly clear that in scenes of tyranny or terror, of weakness and indecisiveness, Shakespeare, almost obsessively, has his characters use the great words *love, friendship, loyalty, faith*—often with cynical and base political motivations and meanings.

It is worth considering the memorable women that cross this troubled and terrible stage. The first, Jeanne d'Arc, is chauvinistically knocked off the pedestal on which many of the French had placed her as "a holy maid," with the "spirit of deep prophecy" or a great warrior wielding the sword of Deborah or a "bright star of Venus, fall'n down on the earth" or a "Divinest creature, bright Astraea's daughter." To the English heroes she is a slut, a trull, a sorceress, even a "Devil or devil's dam"—and it seems clear that the author allies himself with the bluff and unpleasant prejudices of his own people (*1 Henry VI* 1.3, 1.8). She need not detain us, since she is not placed in any recognizable amorous-marital relationship.

But another Frenchwoman, Margaret of Anjou, *is* so placed, by the political diplomacy of the English side. She appears in all four plays of this tetralogy and is their most interesting dramatic presence. Shakespeare apparently caught fire at what one of his sources said of her, that she "excelled all other, aswell in beautie and fauor, as in wit and pollicie, and was of stomack and corage, more like to a man, then a woman."[10] He made her a "fairest beauty" (*1 Henry VI* 5.2) capable of bereaving men of their wits, a woman laced with fatality—fearfully ambitious, formidably articulate, monumentally hypocritical, and terrible in her pride and persistence. She is first placed in contrast with her weak, pious, and indecisive husband, to whom apparently she was unfaithful in an adultery with the man who officially wooed her and brought her to the English royal bed—an adultery that lacked erotic charm and allure, where illicit passion was consumed by political ambition and personal revenge. Later the queen's force is contrasted with the brutal decisiveness of Richard III, and her vocabulary of invective toward him rivals his toward her: Crookback is a "foul mis-shapen stigmatic" (*3 Henry VI* 2.2) who (if it is not inappropriate to invoke Dryden) now curses Nature though Nature first cursed him. She thus has the important dramatic role of bringing the spectator a considerable degree of emotional relief in her taunting of the "rudely stamp'd" royal monster, making us forget her own earlier cruelties and enormities.

Queen Margaret is called the "she-wolf of France" but I am given greater pause by another epithet, "an Amazonian trull" (*3 Henry VI* 1.4), not because it relates her to the Maid of Orleans but rather because it recalls what we have earlier said in invoking the Theseus of *A Midsummer's Night's Dream* and *The Two Noble Kinsmen* and in recounting the wars between the sexes of classical antiquity (see chapter 10). The Amazons were a considerable presence in Elizabethan plays, but not always, surely, because of their presence in ancient myth. The titanic struggles among female rivals for the British throne, the quarrel over the Salic law in France, the literary heritage of the great women of myth and classical drama, and the continuing force of the misogynist satirical and fabliaux tradition—with these contemporary Englishmen had to come to terms. Some kind of settlement was necessary before one could contemplate the recently and widely propagandized marital state of mutual love and fruitful peace. And before Shakespeare created the great women of the marital comedies, the terrible woman of political alliance had to be exorcised. And Shakespeare has done that in the first tetralogy.

It is fascinating to see him working his way through this particular kind of pacification. Hypocrisy, as we know on high authority, is the tribute that vice pays to virtue. When Suffolk, who will be Margaret's adulterous partner, describes her to his weak royal master, he utters home truths about marriage as he urges rejection of financially attractive alternative proposals to the one whose cause he pleads. What is wealth compared to "perfect love"? Dare we make a sheep-and-oxen affair out of wedlock, which, when forced, is hell while its contrary is "a pattern of celestial peace"? "Marriage is a matter of more worth, / Than to be dealt in by attorneyship" (*1 Henry VI* 5.7). Another revealing scene even more clearly, though not by so stark an inversion as that we have just seen and though with considerable ambiguity, brings out newer, more personal, less political values. King Edward IV (called by a youthful enemy "lascivious Edward" [*3 Henry VI* 5.5] and by Hall, Shakespeare's source, one "given to fleshly wantonness") courts an attractive young widow, whom Hall characterizes as "very wyse" and of whom Samuel Daniel writes, in an account that makes love win out over ambition in the breast of the English prince: "An English Beautie, with more worth indue'd / Than *France* could yeeld." The king rejects an arranged marriage with a French lady, and the scene (*3 Henry VI* 3.2) of wooing and winning Lady Gray and making her Queen Elizabeth describes the beginning of a marriage of choice that stands in pleasant contrast to the cynical calculus of political matrimony. Besides, the scene is one of considerable verbal nuance, wide-ranging allusiveness, and moral and intellectual depth and independence in the woman—along with being a brisk reciprocation in smart, economical language. Samuel Johnson said of this scene, "This is a very lively and spritely dialogue; the reciprocation is quicker than is common in Shakespeare."[11]

   I have emphasized here what the history plays emphasize, the confrontation of powerful political women and the implication or adumbration even among them of the norm that will both stimulate and regulate desire in the comedies. It may at first seem strange to postulate a connection between political marriage and the purely private, but not if we reflect that the Protestant ideal extended uxorial *philia* not only to the clergy and the church but to the state as well. The priesthood of *all* believers went up as well as down and laterally. The historical subject matter necessarily turned Shakespeare's gaze toward the Middle Ages for this form of precomic pacification. But even in his adaptation of a classical Roman play, approximately contemporaneous with *Henry VI*, we find Shakespeare revising Plautus in such a way as to modernize, civilize, and partially Christianize him. Adriana, the wife who thinks she is aggrieved, mostly because of mistaken identity between twin men in *The Comedy of Errors,* is even in this context given a cri de coeur not unlike Shylock's plea to be treated as an equal human being. She has no intention of breaking with the ancient topos that the husband is the elm and she the clinging vine, but she does cry out, as many church fathers and divines had, against the sexual double standard in marriage. To make her point she passionately explores the implications of marital union as incorporation, the "one flesh" of Genesis, the same ideal that another Shakespearean pagan, Portia, invoked in claiming a central place in her husband's political life. (It does not distract from the force or meaning of Adriana's speech that she is unwarrantedly jealous of her husband, who has been tardy for a meal, and is here addressing not her husband from Ephesus but his twin from Syracuse and is therefore under an illusion about the confusion, indifference, and ignorance that now confront her.)

> How comes it now, my husband, O, how comes it,
> That thou art then estrangèd from thyself?—
> Thy 'self' I call it, being strange to me
> That, undividable, incorporate,
> Am better than thy dear self's better part.
> Ah, do not tear away thyself from me;
> For know, my love, as easy mayst thou fall
> A drop of water in the breaking gulf
> And take unmingled thence that drop again,
> Without addition or diminishing,
> As take from me thyself, and not me too.
> How dearly would it touch thee to the quick
> Shouldst thou but hear I were licentious,
> And that this body, consecrate to thee,
> By ruffian lust should be contaminate?
> Wouldst thou not spit at me, and spurn at me,
> And hurl the name of husband in my face,
> And tear the stainèd skin off my harlot brow,
> And from my false hand cut the wedding ring
> And break it with a deep-divorcing vow?
> I know thou canst, and therefore see thou do it!
> I am possess'd with an adulterate blot;
> My blood is mingled with the crime of lust.
> For if we two be one, and thou play false,
> I do digest the poison of thy flesh,
> Being strumpeted by thy contagion.
>
>   (2.2)

One wonders what Plautus would have made of this Christian sermon, with its eloquent and subtle application of Christian doctrine. We should perhaps recall that a wife deeply united in equal bonds with the husband was known to antiquity, notably in Ovid's *Heroides,* a work that remained popular in Shakespeare's England. Still, the point remains: The young Shakespeare in his earliest comedy is wrestling with the problem of an assertive woman and her position in marriage, and the tirade of Adriana, though it would never be uttered in this form by one of his great comic heroines, does show that the apprentice playwright is consciously deriving sexual rights from learnedly uttered and popularly accepted doctrine. This, too, is part of the pacification-after-[intellectual] struggle that seems to be occurring before the attainment of the comedic vision, to which we now turn.

Comedies of Love and Marriage

The comedic vision is complicated by Shakespeare's addressing, complexly and ambiguously, what had earlier exercised Chaucer and many theologians and propagandists of Protestant marriage, the matter of domestic government. The Christian command was clear and uncompromising: the husband is the head of the wife as Christ is the head of the church. But the practical working out of governance in the home could make royal government seem simplicity itself, so constant and inescapably nagging are the domestic challenges to order and established practice. Shakespeare the marital poet could not and did not escape such concerns, and the baffling and paradoxical *Taming of the Shrew* is his contribution to the age-old preoccupation. Having referred, as we have seen, in widely varying contexts to the defeat of Amazonian women, he could not escape confronting the contest not in the remote past, not on the highest levels of society, but at the local hearth itself. Though George Meredith in the nineteenth century could say with confident assurance that no high comedy is possible without equal intellectual status for woman, Shakespeare, living when and where he did, must surely have recognized that the brawling, Amazonish, shrewish wife of popular art and humor was as much an enemy to domestic comity as the tyrannical male. And wisely he chose to tell his story partly in farce, with wild exaggeration and implausible overstatement, not in the sophisticated milieu of high or civilized comic art. And yet the male voice that points the moral and adorns the tale at the end is not an uncivilized one, at least as we and Shakespeare have known civilization.

The play must not be sentimentalized to flatter our own consciences, nor should its stark conclusion be weakened. Let me try to catch the drift of the play's ideology. It brings a loud-mouthed, aggrieved, and aggressive girl to a state of compliant modesty—a state in which she can at the very least realize the Prayer Book injunction to "love and obey." It establishes the authority of the husband and only up to a point (for we cringe at much that takes place) justifies his high-handed methods of achieving peace. The man who came to wive it wealthily in Padua has succeeded beyond his own wild expectation—his dowry being increased at the end by the relieved and happy father by some 20,000 crowns. And when asked what Kate's final obedience bodes, Petruccio replies calmly and with superb self-assurance, but with an uncanny sense of what the exigencies of life together might require:

> Marry, peace it bodes, and love, and quiet life;
> An aweful rule, and right supremacy,
> And, to be short, what not that's sweet and happy.
>
> (5.2)

"Sweet and happy" could come out of sentimental Hollywood, but "aweful rule" and "right supremacy" place any joy that may ensue in the firm context of a traditional order imposingly sanctioned by church, state, and popular opinion. Love exists, one is ready to grant that, and the effectual operation of the play suggests that friendship is not inconceivable; but there is no escaping the fact that wifely submission lies at the base of whatever comely order may be achieved in this little state.

And what finally has our Amazon learned? First, the importance of amenities: you do not strike or brawl or bellow; you do not hate men and cuff with them; you do not conceal, mask, subvert, or otherwise mar your own beauty; you keep all the procreative and recreative sexual doors wide open. Second, the importance of the friendship ideal (as stated, for example, by Vives, "matrimonie is the supreme and most excellent part of all amitie"): you do not validate male misogyny by being shrill, shrewish, stubborn, or dogmatic; you temper life with good humor, play, and high spirits. Many religious tractarians and what female writing there was suggested that the male was very much in need of civilizing too—perhaps much more than the wife. Shakespeare never wrote *A Taming of the Lout,* but more than one of his tragicomedies suggest that he considered the male brute very much in need of taming. Then, in the years of his mellowest maturity, he chose a greatly different, vastly more original, and much more civilized route to domestic tranquility, because he had learned how to create the humane and commanding woman who would not and could not stoop to farcical or violent methods.

The shrew's taming—even the humane part—is traditional enough. Patriarchy had often attempted or recommended it with different methods and mixed results. This play does not present its achievement as coming about by blandly traditional, pious, or orderly means, and the contrast between the conclusion and the bold and even subversive actions of the play itself suggests that what is achieved is rather a Blakean union of dynamic opposites and contrarieties than a Thomistic or Protestant, a Dantesque or Petrarchan or even Chapmanesque hierarchy. The movement of the plot insults or overturns expected and conventional values in a way that wins our laughing or generally approving acclaim. To begin with, Katherine is notably more interesting and high-spirited than her tame sister Bianca, whom the familial and social preference has made something of a meek oppressor. Katherine says to her father, "She [my sister] is your treasure, she must have a husband. / I must dance barefoot on her wedding day, / And for your love to her, lead apes in hell [that is, become an old maid]" (2.1). Katherine too wants marriage and competence, and her hard position elicits considerable sympathy. Next, in Petruccio she has met her match in directness, honesty, force of personality, and unconventional boldness; in this couple "two raging fires meet." Kate seems to sense this, for she, who herself has been called "stark mad or wonderful froward" (1.1) now calls her wooer a "half lunatic, / A madcap ruffian" (2.1). He is even more unconventional than she: appearing as a bridegroom even though outlandishly dressed, he curses, with a mighty cuff knocks down the priest with his book, calls for wine, downs a mighty draught, throws the sops in the sexton's face, and smacks his bride with a resounding kiss—and then reverts to a very old feudal tradition by calling her his "goods and chattels" (3.3). The two are so alike that, for all his cruelty, he is using homeopathic medicine: he "kills her in her own humour" (4.1), and artistlike, parodies her stormy violences. Finally, such compatibility will sooner or later lead to play and only slightly submerged banter, and this comes, clearly enough, on the way home when Kate complies with all her husband's assertions, however outrageous. If you call the sun the moon and then change your mind, indeed if you change your mind even as the moon does, I'll call the heavenly body anything you choose. The cure is over, the play is virtually finished, it remains only for him to add a sexual note to this now established play of personalities—to kiss her in public, to exchange bawdry with the other newly married couples, to give her a chance to demonstrate calm self-confidence and a total cure of her quondam childish insubordination. She does this last by a show of obedience now fully in character that can only be said to be playfully bold, given the expectations of the group; and the timid sister, still fully in character, remains too frightened to show anything now except puppetlike *dis*obedience.

Is it impertinent to ask of this comedy whether its two leading characters have attained friendship? Certainly on one level they have—the level Edmund Tilney is on when in his *Flower of Friendshippe* he defines it as the duty of wives to be merry in bed.[12] But deeper compatibility is not out of the question either, for, as we have seen, the couple turns out to be anything but *mal assorti.* Admittedly, there is more likelihood of friendship in the later, more civilized, more humane, less stylized, and less farcical comedies, which keep obedience as a wifely virtue but give to the delighted and technically submissive woman, along with her high intellectual and verbal gifts, a streak of sexual boldness that Kate apparently joins Petruccio in possessing. Perhaps the best way to regard this early play in relation to the comic masterpieces is to view it as we have the marriage of Theseus and those in the first historical tetralogy—as a form of pacification that Shakespeare so frequently finds lurking in the past of male-female relationships. The Amazonian Katherine is tamed into the wifely Kate but is not shriveled in the process. At the very least she will not have to lead apes in hell. The volatility inherent in the union of two such raging fires is given, necessarily perhaps, a setting of order. The matter of domestic government is traditionally resolved in the Judeo-Christian manner. This pact having been made, others can be also—more humane, more modern, more joyfully and overtly mutual ones. And the great gallery of Shakespearean comic women can now be created.[13]

Of that gallery much has been written, and we need not portray each heroine in full or describe the complete environment the dramatist provides for her. But each protagonist, remarkably mature however young and self-contained, can be used to illustrate important individual traits that form crucial elements in the composite portrait. I begin by emphasizing the trait of assertive sexual boldness, and give two examples, Portia of Belmont, and Rosalind of *As You Like It.* The rich, fair, intelligent, multitalented, and virtuous heroine of *The Merchant of Venice* is a woman deeply in love—her ecstasy is so compelling she must restrain herself in order to appear decently modest—but she possesses a firm philosophy of what are the implications of the married state. She is under no illusions that she will reign maritally, though she may in fact rule, and she bestows her considerable wealth on her husband to control and manage. She strongly believes in similitude in love. "There must be needs a like proportion / Of lineaments, of manners, and of spirit," and Bassanio, she says, possesses "the semblance of my soul" (3.4). And the choice of caskets to determine the proper husband, established by her father as a hurdle to jump, at least has this merit: it eliminates outsiders like Morocco and Aragon, who besides being examples of the unacceptable "other" in this rather closed and self-satisfied society are stupid, self-regarding, boastful, superficial—generally fatuous and foolish. Bassanio has the advantage of being a neighbor, and this outweighs the fact that adventurism seems to have flawed his character and that he is less interesting than his future wife, who is a keen-minded woman of legal knowledge and personal wit, acidulous of tongue, capable of spicy speech emanating from an ironical and playful mind and sometimes directed toward her husband, whom she is capable of teasing boldly and even sexually. Consider the precise and proud speech with which Portia taunts Bassanio for having given his wedding ring to the judge who saved the life of his dearest friend and whom he did not know to be his fiancée.

> Let not that doctor e'er come near my house.
> Since he hath got the jewel that I lov'd,
> And that which you did swear to keep for me,
> I will become as liberal as you.
> I'll not deny him any thing I have,
> No, not my body nor my husband's bed.
> Know him I shall, I am well sure of it.
> Lie not a night from home. Watch me like Argus,
> If you do not, if I be left alone
> Now by mine honour, which is yet mine own,
> I'll have that doctor for my bedfellow.
>
>   (5.1)

Here speaks the new secular woman. The old double standard that Adriana in *The Comedy of Errors* feared and deplored is gone, and the old purity and piety of traditional marital incorporation that that Christianized "Roman" wife invokes is also gone. The woman is man's equal not only intellectually but sexually as well, and in this new and freer ambience she threatens to use the traditional husbandly measures of wanton liberality to enforce her rights. This is verbal play, of course, but the serious matter in this jocosity reveals a new woman who may not be shrewish but knows her power and intends to use it.[14]

The most hymeneal of the comedies is *As You Like It,* which literally puts Hymen on the stage and consummates no fewer than four marriages of varying kinds (a number exceeded only by *A Midsummer Night's Dream*). That of the cynical Touchstone and the goatherd Audrey (clearly suggesting class difference in marriage) is sexual only and from it not much can be expected. That of Silvius and Phoebe usefully saves the hapless bride from marrying a female she had fallen in love with, Rosalind-Ganymede, and does what Rosalind's wit does better—satirize the conventional unions of outworn literary traditions like the pastoral. When the converted Oliver and Rosalind's closest friend, Celia (a person of worth in her own right though somewhat more conventional than her friend), marry, it is a union of a love-at-first-sight, "heart to heart" romantic pair; since Shakespeare believed Nature had a hand in such unions it bodes reasonably well for future happiness. But it does not reach the pinnacle, which is reserved for the marriage of the passionate and true minds of Orlando and Rosalind.[15]

Once more I wish to put emphasis on a comic heroine's assertive sexuality—here specifically Rosalind's bold wit about married wit (4.1), which she expresses to her future husband while still in her impenetrable disguise as Ganymede, a disguise which in the mind-opening Forest of Arden gives her the liberty of being more fully herself than the town aristocratic society would have permitted. Responding to a belief about men that was even then frosted with age—they are "April when they woo, December when they wed"—she registers her hearty unwillingness to accept passively such a chill upon marital affection. She concludes a series of determinedly volitional future-tense expressions by threatening to disturb her prospective husband's sleep: "I will laugh like a hyena, and that when thou art inclined to sleep." A spirited lady apparently is not going to allow slumber when she wishes the marital debt paid. Accepting Orlando's compliment that she is wise, she adds, "the wiser, the waywarder." The last word suggests that marital wit as Rosalind conceives it has more than a touch of the wanton which, as we saw in chapter 10, Bacon rejected but which Wordsworth incorporates in his household scene. As she continues, it becomes even clearer that wit stands for suppressed sexual desire: "Make [that is, shut] the doors upon a woman's wit, and it will out at the casement. Shut that, and 'twill out at the keyhole. Stop that, 'twill fly with the smoke out at the chimney." Had Freud known Shakespeare as well as he knew the Greeks, Rosalind might have become his emblem of the assertiveness and irrepressibility of the libido. She presses on, and now with great boldness and a heady sense of emancipation she even toys with what her own milieu and doubtless Shakespeare himself regarded as the deadly sin of adultery—only to excuse it if the provocation of the woman through sexual denial is sufficient. She sends her "wit" (by now a clear displacement for female sexual desire) a-packing to a "neighbour's bed." Orlando, by this time surely astonished and alarmed, asks: "And what wit could wit have to excuse that?" Rosalind keeps the sexual meaning but turns the charge against *him*: "Marry, to say she came to seek *you* there. You shall never take her without her answer unless you take her without her tongue" (emphasis added). With another allusion to January and May in Chaucer's *Merchant's Tale,* Rosalind returns to wit merely as wit and to woman's traditionally recognized role as its master.

In this highly textured passage, possessing a richness about love that Shakespeare seldom gives to a man, we hear a cry not only for the right to exercise verbal play and metaphorical intelligence but also for the right to recreative as well as procreative sex, the latter being invoked when Rosalind introduces the image of the nursing child at the end of her flight of proleptical fancy. Plato may have given little or no cognitive value to marriage, though he did to other forms of eros; Paul and Augustine hedged in marital sexuality with restrictions and warnings. Shakespeare does not—though he is sometimes acutely aware, as we have seen, of the need of orderly contexts for eros. Using the word *wit* (from *witan,* to know), he clearly invokes knowledge, as we do today in the phrase *carnal knowledge,* and as the Hebrews did when they used the verb *to know* for the heterosexual act (a usage surely transmitted to Shakespeare through the Geneva Bible, where for a man to "know" his wife usually meant only one thing).

The comedies we have just considered involve disguises and temporary transvestism by the heroines; this, plus the regular casting of boys for women's parts in the theater and the plot exigencies of mistaken identities in *Twelfth Night,* has made this play seem to influential critics one that strongly implies androgyny or homosexuality. Such suggestions do flicker here and there in the situation and the language, for Olivia and Orsino are simultaneously in love with Cesario-Viola, Cesario loves and indirectly courts "his" master, and the devotion of Antonio for Sebastian may not be entirely free of sexual passion. And certainly there are enough mysterious metamorphoses of character, even across sexual boundaries, and sufficient literalization of the old topos (that in love two become one spiritually and that one becomes two again sexually) to recall not only the mythological Ovid but also transcendent and mystical religious experience.[16]

But I suggest that the intellectual données of the play arise from a concept deep in Shakespeare's culture and psyche—that is, nature, a brief analysis of which will both disclose the energies of the art in *Twelfth Night* and place it in one of the millennial traditions already explored in the present study. Shakespearean nature seems ultimately beneficent: we learn from the *Winter's Tale* (4.4) to respect "great creating nature," whether with the middle-aged Polixenes we favor grafts to create new flowers, using nature itself to make the "mean" that "adds to nature," or with Perdita in her blaze of youthful beauty we refuse to set a spade in the earth to modify her ways. Still, nature was far from univocal in her promptings or workings. For, as we learn from Friar Laurence, there is within her as within man himself both "grace and rude will," and inside the rind of a flower "poison hath residence, and medicine power" (*Romeo and Juliet* 2.2). For Shakespeare, as for thinkers from antiquity on, nature besides being fruitful and fecund was a minister of both rational virtue and the alluring grace of personal beauty, and in this play Olivia concedes that the duke, whom she cannot love, is nevertheless "in dimension and the shape of nature / A gracious person" (1.5), and Antonio asserts that "In nature there's no blemish but the mind. / None can be call'd deformed but the unkind. / Virtue is beauty, . . ." (3.4). And in the denouement Sebastian says to Olivia, who had loved Cesario-Viola unnaturally (as was then thought) though blindly, that "nature in her bias drew [created an emblem] in that" (5.1). He means that the weight of nature, like the weight placed in a bowling ball, created a curve in the trajectory so that while it for a time aimed at the disguised girl, it in the end achieved its true target in a passionate attachment to a male. And so by indirection natural direction finally comes.

If nature can possess several, sometimes contradictory, meanings, it always invokes an outside force acting salvifically upon us from without our enclosed psyches, and in that role nature is here especially pertinent in inspiring a normal climax. The beleaguered and isolated figure of Malvolio in his dark room is especially in need of nature's external ministrations, as is the duke in his first state of narcissistic internality and self-enclosure, and as is Olivia in the prison of her unnaturally prolonged and isolating grief for her dead brother. Like Providence, whose almost comically confusing mediations we shall later confront in other plays, nature works in mysterious way its wonders to perform—and this explains the tergiversations of plot and identity in this whirligig of a comedy, at whose center, however, stands the worthy, poetic, loving, and mature Viola, one of Shakespeare's truly magnificent young women, whose life destiny is very much worth the natural effectuation it climactically receives. She herself pays tribute to "nature's own sweet and cunning hand," and her exquisite praise of Olivia can be applied to her:

> Lady, you are the cruell'st she alive
> If you will lead these graces to the grave
> And leave the world no copy.
>   (1.5)

It is in such plays as this that Shakespeare takes his place in a largely secularized version of the naturalistic tradition we have traced from antiquity through the Middle Ages and Chaucer up to the Renaissance. Considerable religious awe still attached to nature, and without that respect and the formal sanctions with which earlier naturalistic thought endowed the concept, Shakespeare might seem to encourage subjectivism, lawless individualism, and illusion. In *Twelfth Night* and elsewhere he portrays initial inclination, falling in love at first sight, the body throbbing underneath its disguises, and accidental encounter. And he endows all the foregoing with the considerable beneficent authority of nature, whose stoical and religious roots protect him not only from sentimentalism but also savagery or whimsicality. That physical nature could lead to these last qualities, his highly articulate bastards keep reminding us. Shakespeare must surely have known that nature comes to us profoundly acculturated: it often has an aristocratic bias, as when Perdita stands out from her rural surroundings and Belarius, observing the young princes' gentility, wonders that "an invisible instinct should frame them / To royalty unlearned, honour untaught" (*Cymbeline* 4.2.178–79). It is probably true that Shakespearean nature when used as a norm avoids the extremes of signalizing either bastardy or blood royal and had therefore best be conceived of as something equivalent to *la belle nature,* Pope's "Nature still, but Nature methodized," or even Blake's "Organized Innocence." We shall return to this concept later.

By presenting two powerfully contrasting love affairs (those of Claudio and Hero and of Benedick and Beatrice), each of which achieves its resolution in dramatically riveting ways, *Much Ado about Nothing* is a diptych structured by sharp intellectual and aesthetic antitheses, culturally satisfying in its related but alternative visions of amorous and erotic realities.[17] The friends Don Pedro and Claudio seem conventional at the beginning, with their talk of Hero's modesty and of love as consisting of "soft and delicate desires" (1.1). But then, at the first villainous mention of a possible dark past in the life of the lovely paragon ("Even she. Leonato's Hero, your Hero, every man's Hero," 3.2), they both seem obscenely eager to embrace the prospect of shaming and disgracing the girl at the ceremony. Are they, we wonder, no more than small-minded, convention-ridden egotists? Claudio's cruel and mischievously timed intervention and accompanying coolness in the ceremony, his heartless flippancies with Don Pedro after Hero's "death" and before her "resurrection" make us wonder of what woman either could possibly be worthy. Indeed, their prejudices of thought and action are so callously and inhumanly orthodox that there remains an unforgivable residue in them that witnesses either to the author's failure in managing the tone of his play or to his sharp disapproval of their actions and of their jejune moral inheritance from the past. Leonato, feeble, wavering, conventional, is not much better, and Hero as passive sufferer seems not to rise to the level of Shakespeare's admirable heroines.

Still, this plot—structurally and dramatically the central and causative intrigue of the entire action and skillfully linked to the other plot—cannot be dismissed out of hand as weak-visioned. For one thing, the author gives it notable dramatic energy. The church scene is a magnificent coup de théâtre that takes stunning advantage of the open opportunity for denunciation ritually provided but rarely responded to ("if either of you know any impediment, why ye may not be lawfully joined together in Matrimony, ye do now confess it"). And the death, burial, and resurrection of the bride has its own kind of solemn resonance, going back at least as far as Greek romance and invoking the central mysteries of the Christian faith. The decently if somewhat sentimentally conceived plan proposed by the friar to gain time is fundamentally based on his religiously disciplined instincts and has the seeds of salvation in it. In his own way, the cleric belongs with the good watch, God's fools, whose untutored utterance is wiser than the wisdom of this world and who ensure the good resolution. The resurrection plot suggests a real break with the past—separation from extreme female passivity and submissiveness, from jealous and orthodox cruelties, from conventional fears and conventional revenges. And father, bride, and bridegroom do seem to have made some advances in achieving personal force, integrity, and dignity.

Nevertheless, all this constitutes a Christian *device,* not a deep providential ordering: the old Hero was dead only as long as the slander lasted, and she rises again when it is revoked and when external evil has been dismissed. The truly interesting, impressive, and culturally emergent social and human values are instantiated in Benedick and Beatrice, who, in the event, are vastly more than converted love skeptics with their wit and intelligence totally intact even after Cupid's arrows have pricked them. They are true heroes, and there are few cleansing catharses in comic literature to match Beatrice's reaction to Claudio's trick of leading his bride on into the marital rite and then accusing her just when they had taken hands: "O God that I were a man! I would eat his heart in the market place" (4.1). Or her indignant injunction to her lover, "Kill Claudio." Or Benedick's crisp and steely challenge to his quondam friend, who has been so flippantly cruel in his suspicions: "You are a villain. I jest not. I will make it good how you dare, with what you dare, and when you dare" (5.1).

The wit and spirit of Benedick and Beatrice need not be further illustrated. They are modern secular youths, moving into a permanent relationship that is big with the promise of a friendship that embodies at least two of Aristotle's types, that of pleasure (consisting of wit or good sex), and that of virtue and the mutuality that arises between two good and compatible minds, possessing the same kind of goodness and force.[18] Indeed, Beatrice and Benedick seem to illustrate as well as any couple we have encountered anywhere the fourfold constituents of love outlined in the introductory taxonomy: libido, eros (they will know how to decorate love verbally in their own way), affection (they have both learned tenderness and displayed benevolence in sympathizing with and acting upon Hero's grief), and friendship. And so the play ends, not with another wedding—*one* of the kind Don John, Claudio, and Don Pedro interrupted is quite enough. Instead, we are given a conclusion ritually stripped down to a swirling, celebratory dance and a naughty penile allusion, as Benedick says to Don Pedro: "Prince, thou art sad; get thee a wife, get thee a wife! There is no staff more reverend than one tipped with horn." (It strikes me that to interpret the last word as a reference to cuckoldry is most inappropriately to hint at adultery in a relationship that has promised wit and sexuality, both of the recreative and procreative kind but also much more—intellectual rapport, for one thing. Moreover, the prospect of cuckoldry could scarcely be calculated to assuage the Duke's sadness, while enjoyable, licit libido just might.)

This is the place to ask what the uxorial climaxes that end all of Shakespeare's comedies imply. We paused earlier to note the naive charm that attends the concluding love masque of Xenophon's *Symposium,* when the male spectators, all rendered amorous, ride off home to their marital couches, while Socrates and a friend go out for a walk and further talk. There being no theater curtain on Shakespeare's stage, the sense of dramatic finality was perhaps considerably less pronounced in his day than in ours, and our earlier discussion of Renaissance eros has suggested that a such a Xenophontic denouement to a Shakespearean love comedy is not totally unthinkable.

In order for us to keep a sensible perspective on the matter of endings, the satirical wit and hilarious grotesquerie of David Lodge in *Small World* may not be inapposite: Angelica near the end of the novel reads a paper on endings to romances. She takes seriously the view of Barthes that the pleasure of a classical text is all foreplay. Narrative kills desire, tragedy and epic discharge it suddenly, explosively. For romance another model is necessary, and "Derrida," expectedly, supplies it: "invagination," the inward fold of the outside text, a pocket which, though empty and longed for, is impossible to possess. Romance therefore concludes in climax after climax, one mystery, one adventure after another, ending only with the author's exhaustion.[19]

Now we all know—and this is of course why the merry novelist chose to address the matter—that literary endings have received steady, intense, often sophisticated, and sometimes politically partisan attention in our day. Quite plainly considered, most of Shakespeare's comedies and romances seem to resolve at their close into some version of Hippolyta's "great constancy," which implies, I take it, both stability and growth. Or so one might have thought—until avant-garde criticism proclaimed other views. Peter Erickson believes that *As You Like It* affirms male control and renders woman threatless, the only alternatives for Rosalind at the end being lyrical inflation into an all-powerful woman or stereotypical reduction to powerless compliance. Clara Claiborne Park credits Shakespeare with having created a gallery of "brilliant and fascinating women" who are "a pleasure to watch, once we can be sure they will accept the control even of the Bassanios and the Orlandos of the world—at least this was so in Elizabethan England." Carol Thomas Neely perceptively studies Shakespeare's female identities created in defiance of Petrarchan stereotypes and permitted by him to defy fathers, choose their own marriage partners, woo them aggressively, and make full use of their verbal superiority. But then she concludes: "Shakespeare's maids are moving toward and necessitating [presumably by their own superior powers] their subordination as wives—their domestication by silence, by removal of disguise, and by giving themselves, their possessions, and their sexuality to their husbands."[20]

But before we allow the witty, articulate, emancipated, enterprising Rosalind to "dwindle into a wife" (Congreve), to live in the "suburbs of [her husband's] pleasure" (Brutus's Portia), or to shrivel into a stereotype when we take her home with us in our minds, we must consider the matter further. If we are indeed intended to feel, postdramatically, the chilling shades of the heroine's marital prison close around her, what is our reaction supposed to be to *that?* Has Shakespeare induced a mood of acquiescence or protest? Or, if we agree with Northrop Frye that a new society, crystallized in marriage, is born at the end of comedy, do we take this as a structure of permanent human desire, only fortuitously blazoned in the uxorial and perhaps never socially realized? Or do we find that the final action of comedy is Freudian (as stated by Frye): "the erotic pleasure principle explodes underneath the social anxieties sitting on top of it and blows them sky-high"?[21] Or what?

Poetic closure is of course a complex matter, and I certainly do not wish to pin a tail onto the action, an after-curtain appendage not unlike the girlhood of those same heroines that the hapless Victorian critic Mary Cowden Clarke pinned onto the front. I take to heart the warning of Darryl Gless that we should normally not ask probing questions about partners who marry at the end of romantic narratives, but I respect his right to speculate that the Angelo of *Measure for Measure* may become "a humane and loving husband." A leading authority on closure in our time, Barbara H. Smith, has suggested that these are the responses to arbitrary or successful closure: what follows is of "no significance," "completely predictable," "another story," or "another set of themes"—or, when the sense of closure is infirm, "indefinitely extensible." I should like to add one more: there remains an after-image of what we have witnessed, a lingering on in the mind of the very melody we have heard, with variations, of course, that can be fruitfully challenging and indeed can alter life itself.[22]

The very nature of the Elizabethan and early Jacobean plays requires such prospective contemplation. Rhetorical and moral in their origins, book and theater demand even in their sophisticated maturity the vigorous exercise of the ethical imagination. We respond correctly and historically when we weigh alternatives, suspend easy belief, and project the dynamics of a work of art into a future that reaches out to our own situation. Albertus Magnus, commenting on Aristotle, speaks of the dramatic production of wonder and adds that "the further effect of wonder is to excite inquiry."[23] Intelligent reading will not allow us the fantasies that Charles Lamb indulged for a dream-while in contemplating the wit of the Restoration stage, fantasies in which the effectual energy of the drama smokes away into airy nothingness. Nor will a proper response allow us to acquiesce in placing the great Shakespearean characters in an Elizabethan status quo that effectually deprives them of their humanity—all this because the Elizabethan social scene does not mirror the present postrevolutionary view of gender relations. Hans Robert Jauss has said, rightly, that "the horizon of expectations of literature is differentiated from the horizon of expectations of historical life by the fact that it not only preserves real experiences but also anticipates unrealized possibilities, widens the limited range of social behavior by new wishes, demands, and goals and thereby opens avenues for future experience."[24] Precisely. And I claim as much for what Shakespeare has done in his presentation of heterosexual relations leading up to and into marriage. Not *all* Shakespearean closures are coextensive with marital closures, but most comedic and some tragic ones are. In comedy we get a foretaste of what *could* follow, in tragedy of what *might* have been—without the tragic abortion. After witnessing either, the sensitively responding mind is allowed to play with life-altering possibilities.

Marriage under a Mysterious Providence

I have suggested that Shakespeare and his age, being deeply implicated in Christian belief, could not have rested content with nature, however solemnly conceived, as the only norm in sexual relationships. If the Protestant Reformation had dethroned marriage as a formal sacrament, it had not tried to eliminate divine grace or providential ordering from so important a liaison. And Shakespeare's language, even when he is portraying pagan, classical wives, can ennoble that liaison through anachronistic references to the sacramental doctrine of "one flesh." Thus Brutus's wife, Portia, appeals to "that great vow / Which did incorporate and make us one," and Adriana in *The Comedy of Errors* refers to herself as being an "undividable, incorporate" self with her husband. How should—indeed, how can—this condition be represented dramatically?

Only paradoxically, ironically, one would suppose. In Shakespeare's case, to the heading of "mysterious Providence" might also be added the adjectives *outrageous* or even *absurdist*. Divine design in initiating and then sacramentally sealing the intimacies, fluctuations, and sometimes insulting pettinesses of the domestic agenda must at times have seemed to a baptized but still skeptical intelligence as itself creaky, quirkish, whimsical. No wonder the dramatist sometimes preferred invoking Nature to God as the chief begetter of domesticity. Sex has of course been regarded throughout the centuries and in many diverse cultures as immitigably ridiculous, and it has seemed to come under the divine umbrella only awkwardly. Nowhere does the problem of uniting benevolent purpose with daily life become more potentially grotesque than in the problem comedies; no other dramatic form used by Shakespeare more strenuously requires for its appreciation a modern, absurdist sensibility. Perhaps, though the modern writer's extremes extend further than Shakespeare's, John Updike's narrative ability to combine traditional Protestant theology and ravenous and irregular sexual appetite provides a perspective on what we are discussing. One of his characters, Roger in *Roger's Version,* regards the "resurrection of the flesh" as "the most emphatic and intrinsic of orthodox doctrines," and his creator seems to agree that "what eventuates from these sighing cesspools of our being, our unconscionable sincere wishes" can be "cathedrals and children."[25] Shakespeare's unremitting realism and the essential dignity of his vision save him from the theological grotesquerie and sentimentality implicit in such language; but the machinery of the problem comedies and the tragicomedies often moves us, with creaking awkwardness, if not usually from sexual sewers to sonnets, at least from some grim and grimy problems to potentially satisfying if not utopian settlements.

Shakespeare's two uses of the ever-puzzling bed trick (in *All's Well That Ends Well* and *Measure for Measure*) will open this complex world for us. We must remember that bed substitution is a venerable literary practice, extending from at least as early as Genesis 29 through Terence, Tristan and Isolde, Middleton's *Changeling,* and Molière's *Amphytrion* at least as far as Yeats's "Three Bushes." That the Hebrews used the verb *know* for something so illusion-prone, so blinded and blinding, as copulation is itself paradoxical. And it would boggle the mind that the third of the founding patriarchs of Israel, Jacob, should labor seven years for the attractive bride of his choice, only to find when he awoke after his nuptial night that the plain older sister Leah had taken the place of Rachel—if we did not remember that custom had to be respected, that the eldest daughter had priority, and that, besides, Leah was the fruitful one and that the founding of a race was at stake. Yahweh could of course open wombs at will, but he did so somewhat whimsically for he saw that Leah was hated. Later on, the beautiful but barren Rachel contributed to the lineage at first by permitting her handmaiden to become fruitful in her place until the Lord finally blessed her with none other than the comely, historically great, and typologically significant Joseph. Such is the divine story Shakespeare and his culture inherited, and though it ultimately fulfills providential purpose, it does so surprisingly, suddenly, even swindlingly—though very humanly.[26]

What did the author of *All's Well That Ends Well* see in the Boccaccio story that was his source?[27] Surely an avant-garde tale directed toward marriage by a woman of wit and constancy, wonderfully capable of curing her handsome husband of his snobbery and class consciousness. But it is Shakespeare himself who heightens the contrasts between the couple and so gratuitously creates some of the improbabilities that disturb modern mentality. He exalts Helen at the same time that he depresses Bertram, who is dazzlingly handsome, courageous, and sexually vibrant, and who possesses the blue blood and status an ambitious Elizabethan girl of prowess and ambition would naturally covet. But at the same time he is immature and deceitful—and it is Shakespeare, not Boccaccio, who has put into his mouth the series of sordid lies he tells in the denouement (5.3).

It is Helen who is the agent of Providence in this play, which ends with the heroine pregnant on the stage. This puts the emphasis where it belongs. To return to my initial taxonomy, we cannot say there is time or room for friendship or companionship of any kind, or that Erōs poetizes the love that arises, as he does in *A Midsummer Night's Dream* or *As You Like It;* tender affection (benevolent love) seems to arise only when Helen thinks of Bertram on a battlefield in danger, and here the love may be rather more ambitious and interested (in lineage, for one thing) than disinterestedly self-rewarding. But libido is powerfully present—along with ambition for procreative sexuality—and it is this which chiefly drives our heroine. She early on reveals her interest in and her liberated frankness about sex. She is a healer, the daughter of a great physician, and she cures the king of his impotency homeopathically: with no suspicion that the untoward or irregular is being actualized, her own vibrancy restores him, and "banished sense" returns to his hand (2.3). Her "spoiled" and snobbish husband, given her as a reward for the royal cure, immediately longs for his military vocation; outraged at having had to lower his social status, he deserts his bride and their home ("the dark house and the detested wife," 2.3) for Florence. But nothing daunted, Helen disguises herself, goes in pursuit, takes the place of a virtuous girl he was about to seduce and becomes pregnant. By securing his wedding ring, she later convinces the court and everyone else that it was indeed the true wife to whom he had been "wondrous kind" (5.3) that dark night in Florence when he thought he was enjoying the virgin (*kind* can be a sexual word, and points to the fact that her marriage has at length been consummated and produced the child she now carries).

The bed trick emphasizes the libidinous base of the relationship, and Helen, reflecting on her deception of her husband, allows herself the following antimasculine outburst that does nothing if not strengthen the sexual foundation on which her ruse rests:

> But O, strange men,
> That can such sweet use make of what they hate,
> When saucy [lascivious] trusting of the cozened thoughts
> Defiles the pitchy night; so lust doth play
> With what it loathes, for that which is away.
>
> (4.4)

The situation does not bear close moral scrutiny: Helen recognizes that she is hated, that the "pitchy night" has been somewhat defiling, that the lust of the male is grotesquely misdirected at the innocent, mother-influenced virgin named Diana. But no matter. No matter that *lust* is often an ugly, corrupting word in Shakespeare. No matter either that the play moves too quickly to its destined resolution groaning with improbabilities, legalisms, and quibbles and is unredeemed by deep feeling or noteworthy expression. The casuistries that pile up do not obscure the hand of Providence working to establish a stable and sanctioned locus for the libido, male and female alike. God's ancient Hebrew purpose of fruitful multiplication has been served by the dangerous bed trick managed by his "spy," the heroic Helen—and perhaps even the Pauline belief has been instantiated, that the unworthiest of husbands can be sanctified in the wife (see 1 Corinthians 7:14). In any case libido and leadership are rewarded with security and stability. We must not forget that sexual fruit grows on a tree of knowledge, that creation and procreation have been traditionally considered cognitive and redemptive—an insight that cannot be plausibly rendered by a religiously sensitive but nevertheless skeptical intelligence without a considerable degree of absurdist invention and convention.

The same kind of reduction of marriage to its essential and defining sexuality survives, along with richer possibilities, from another confusingly ambiguous and teasingly paradoxical plot that must nevertheless be regarded as providentially regulated, though one concedes at once that the divine element should perhaps be called "providential improvisation." *Measure for Measure* also includes a bed trick, this one arranged by that character who comes closest to embodying heavenly values, the duke, who, though he leaves his office for a while in order to observe and improve the government of his sexually active state, is by no means a *deus absconditus*.[28] He becomes in fact a particularly mercurial and only partially concealed intervener in social affairs, and it is perhaps he more than any one else who makes the play absurdist and improbable without forfeiting either his earthly or spiritual overlordship. Serious definitions of love by earnest or reformatory people like Wordsworth and Havelock Ellis can sometimes come up with no better definition of love, even marital love, than lust plus friendship. If that view prevails here, one would have to say that it is lust, not friendship, that predominates—not so singly and strikingly as in *All's Well* but prominently enough to press hard against and to limit the widely acknowledged Christian ambience of the play. That Christian ambience is broad and diverse enough to include the steely, nunlike virtue of Isabella ("a thing enskied and sainted," 1.4), the low-life impertinence but essentially decent folk wisdom of the "fantastic" Lucio ("Why, what a ruthless thing is this [in the acting governor], for the rebellion of a codpiece to take away the life of a man!" 3.5), and the New Covenant spirit of forgiveness with which the final resolution is imbued.

The play, for all its wild improbabilities and grotesque juxtapositions, finally wins respect because it is socially and realistically situated. Isabella is a recognizable Protestant version of the Catholic nun. Claudio and Juliet's union is not a public marriage ("we do the denunciation lack / Of outward order," says Claudio, 1.2), but it is in fact what he calls it, a "fast" (1.2) marriage, since after a "true contract" (sponsalia per verba de futuro) there has followed consummation. Mariana of the moated grange had also been truly betrothed and awaited only consummation, which is provided by the bed trick. The disguised duke vouches for its legality: "He is your husband on a pre-contract. / . . . The justice of your title to him / Doth flourish the deceit" (4.1).

Moreover, the central paradox is, though volatile, essentially Christian, one that inevitably arises when, as in Shakespeare and the Christian naturalists who preceded him, there is an attempt to combine nature and heaven, the words being here used interchangeably (see 1.1). And it is not only Lucio who plays with the doubly intended word *sense,* meaning both sex and moral sentence, libido and ordered intelligence. The morally trained though hypocritical Angelo also puns on the same word, when he feels himself tempted by the insistently pure Isabella: "She speaks, and 'tis such sense / That my sense breed with it" (2.2). And it is out of Christian paradox that the bed trick grows, authoritatively planned and sanctioned as it is, in which the betrothed and still loving Mariana takes the virginal Isabella's place in the seduction by Angelo.

To a Voltairean, Shavian, Freudian, or Marxist intelligence, no possible good could come from any of this. But anyone who like Shakespeare clearly and historically *was* or who like many a modern *once was* inside the Christian system trying to make sense out of Providence in ordinary life can understand that ridiculous and implausible life complication and ultimate beneficent resolution are both well within a seemingly perceptual experience religiously structured. What love values emerge as this absurdist action works its paradoxical and whimsical will? They are not centered in the duke, who is important but not humanly involved. He is more plausible, to be sure, than a remote Providence surrogate could possibly be; he is rather more like a character from a comedy by the Christian T. S. Eliot, a divine spy moving about in society. He reveals considerable natural humanity all the way through the workings of his plot, though at times he is necessarily deceitful and even cruel in his machinations. Still, though he is not a *deus ex machina,* he can be said to be a kind of *machina ex deo,* and the dignity he possesses arises not just because the *deus* he represents is the generalized spirit of secular comedy but, more deeply, because he effectuates the venerable Judeo-Christian ideal of marriage stripped to its essentials of sexuality, procreation, and the creation of the personal and the human family.

He would, however, be Word only, without either natural or sophisticated Flesh, if it were not for Angelo, the most dramatic figure of the play, the one who arouses the strongest emotions, usually of hatred and dismay (the "enskied" Isabella could pluck his eyes out, 4.3), the one who most deeply embarrasses the providential structure. Why has Mariana loved him? "Take, O take those lips away" (4.1) shows, if nothing else does, that she continues to suffer the loss of him, pathetically, erotically. He must have been then what he is now, a man of suppressed but deep passion. His lust for Isabella is an intensification of what is deeply bred in the bone of Western culture, erotic arousal at the sight of the reluctant, virginal, modest woman, who unwittingly solicits temptation: our "cunning enemy" (Satan) "to catch a saint, / With saints doth bait [his] hook" (2.2). And as he is being tempted he is given a moment of deeply moral self-consciousness:

> Shall we desire to raze the sanctuary,
> And pitch our evils there? O, fie, fie, fie!
> What dost thou or what art thou, Angelo?
>   (2.2)

Like Puccini's Scarpia he commits a hideous crime in not countermanding the execution of one for whom Isabella has, as he thinks, paid the price of her body to him; but unlike Scarpia he has a moment of softening: "Would yet he [Isabella's brother] had lived!" (4.4). "Alack, when once our grace we have forgot, / Nothing goes right; we would, and we would not" (4.4), the last clause distantly echoing Paul: "For that which I do I allow not: for what I would that I do not; but what I hate, that I do" (Romans 7:15). And once that great coup de théâtre that disrobes the friar and reveals the duke has been delivered, Angelo humbly begs for the punishment of death.

Moderns will remain deeply offended that so calculating and inhuman a precisian should be rewarded in marriage by a woman who loves him, but this grotesquely Christian comedy does not primarily serve the ends of poetic justice. Basic Christian belief, which Shakespeare almost certainly shared, holds that any human being, however villainous, if his or her heart has been softened by true repentance, is a candidate for divine and human forgiveness.

How is the ideal of marriage served in all this? Only in the minimalist way of *All's Well.* Passion—not tender affection, not friendship, not eros (for there is little time for love fancies or amorous myths)—stands at the apex toward which all moves. But it is of course *marital* sexuality which prevails and which the workings of this strangely but attractively repellent plot serve. The play seems to invite this concluding reflection: Because it is better to honor sexuality of any kind than to ignore it or freeze it into the Puritan's rule book, fallible Vienna was not in as much need of reform as even the good duke had at first thought. But of course Angelo was.

Marriage under a Reparative Providence

If the problem plays we have dealt with are linked to the tragicomedies or romances we shall now consider by the imaginative, though sometimes only implicit, presence of Providence, what distinguishes the two categories? In the earlier plays absurdist paradoxes are more prominent, though they have by no means disappeared in the later. Comedic and problematical elements remain, still to be tested, still to be ultimately approved; sexuality, often of the aggressive, destructive kind, continues to work its quondam mischiefs, and the leaderly female usually commands our greatest respect though the often unworthy male proves in the end to be fully redeemable. Nature is more often directly invoked than Providence, but the latter has a hand in sanctifying the former. Who can tell whether ultimately beneficent sexual arousals, the production of invincible beauty and personal force, and restorative power come from the sky or the earth? It is easier to see that the plot action that moves from disease to health, from division to union is guided implicitly by the marital ideal of the post-Reformation world with its respect for freedom of choice, for sexual attraction and procreation, and for friendly esteem impregnated with eros. Indeed, *The Winter's Tale* provides almost all that an explorer of my theme could wish by way of summarizing climax, and it does not appear at the culmination of my study only because I wish to end with the more powerful emotions embodied in tragedy, especially in *Othello.*

The other romantic tragicomedies lack the expansive and mellow comprehensiveness of *The Winter's Tale,* but they are by no means negligible, despite weaknesses and lacunae, on the theme of long-term coupling. *Pericles,* which, set as it is in the ancient pagan world, throws our minds back to the Greek romances, lacks both the teasingly absurdist salt and the healing balm of Shakespeare's Christian Providence.[29] It can be crudely melodramatic, as when its innocent heroine, the girl Marina, exemplifies and also preaches virtue in the brothel in which she finds herself, even converting some of its customers. Or it can be crudely moralistic, as when Pericles becomes sexually inflamed by a young woman who continues to be engaged in a scarlet affair of father-daughter incest—apparently the cause of the storms and narrow escapes that torture both titular hero and subsequent plot.

But heavy moralizing, conscious "antiquing" of the scenes, awkward soliloquies and asides, stiff inflexible verse, and maddeningly missed opportunities for pathos, depth, and dignity cannot eclipse the glory of some scenes, especially the recognition between father and daughter. What values finally emerge? Not the wonderful combination of sex and sensibility that enriches the comedies. Not the emphasis upon family and fecundity we confronted in *All's Well,* for here the emphasis falls upon the preservation of virginity in a series of trials resembling early Christian and Greek-romantic adventures. But there is real uxorial devotion when Pericles says to his restored wife, "O come, be buried / A second time within these arms" (scene 22), and the reunited family, tested as few others have been, comes to rest in a world purged of evil and excess.

The Tempest, a highly aristocratic play, seems more concerned with authority than love. And even its treatment of love throws it back to earlier venues, largely transcended in the Renaissance, of innocence and fussily narrow paternal authority. True, Miranda, a fifteen-year-old innocent raised in isolation from real life, does quickly achieve the virtue of a human sympathy that includes delicate sexual arousal; but the play is for Shakespeare virtually sui generis in containing no censure of the almost totally arranged marriage Prospero imposes on his daughter and hedges in with his conservative fears of the "Other," of the animalistic, and even of the naturally, humanly eager. He threatens that the breaking of his daughter's "virgin-knot" before "*all* sanctimonious ceremonies" (emphasis added) take place will cause "barren hate, / Sour-eyed disdain and discord" to "bestrew" the marital bed with "weeds so loathly / That you shall hate it both" (4.1). Female beauty usually provides Shakespeare with an opportunity to decorate libido with his most alluring poetic effects, but here Ferdinand unambitiously reverts to the weary classical cliché of physical perfection as an eclectic, artificial composite of the various and separate perfections scattered among many other beauties. Still, nature not artifice is at work: love at first sight implies providential inspiration; Miranda's sexual sympathy broadens to a pan-human benevolism; and the love, far from ending in primitive isolation, will establish itself in a restored and improved society. The play might be regarded as a gloss on the Prayer Book, where marriage is an "estate, instituted of God in paradise, in the time of man's innocency"—a theological perspective eloquently present in much post-Reformation marital propaganda. But taken as a whole—and of course from my perspective—*The Tempest* does not put Shakespeare on the frontier of the emergent.

Cymbeline, like *The Winter's Tale*, like *Othello*, but like very little else in Shakespeare, is a portrait of a marriage already entered into.[30] Jealousy leads to emotions in Posthumus's breast almost as searing as those that tortured Othello's. But in the threatened, tested, and finally restored marriage, though there has been monumental wifely *fides* and there comes finally to be abundant esteem mutually felt, desire itself seems muted or absent. Why? Not surely because the play is set in ancient times when Christ was a contemporary of the dramatis personae, for, as we have seen often and everywhere, Christ sanctioned marital desire. Not because Imogen is leaderly, courageous, hardy, for she is also tender of heart and deeply devoted to a wildly erring husband; and quality of leadership in the great comic heroines never seemed to suppress the erotic. The husband uses the image of snow to symbolize his wife's supposed marital chastity—a wearily conventional trope. Nor does that snow melt even when everyone's emotional life is warmed as the plot moves toward a springlike restoration. Deep repentance overtakes the husband even before he is assured of Imogen's innocence, and no one can deny the sincerity of his *cri de coeur:* "O Imogen! / My queen, my life, my wife, O Imogen, Imogen, Imogen" (5.6). But the sexual reticence remains.

No such silence mutes the emotions of *The Winter's Tale*, where the madness of jealousy sears the husband less artificially than in *Cymbeline* and almost as humanly and deeply as in *Othello*.[31] In fact, almost everything that we have seen challenging or limiting the marital vision of the other romances and of the problem comedies is present here—but in the end overcome. No sexual disgust is finally allowed to remain. Esteem and desire separately and together constitute fields of considerable force, and this play, though not set in pagan times, reaches out to connect with precedents in antiquity—Penelope, Pygmalion, Alcestis, and even Ceres. It is noteworthy that Hermione, the greatest glory of this play, does not stand dramatically alone without the company of other women as do Cymbeline, Miranda, or even Marina (though she, as we have seen, is for a while surrounded by prostitutes). Hermione's daughter, Perdita, provides a contrast, inevitable because of the difference in age and place, for the girl, a rare "piece of beauty," a "most peerless piece of earth" (4.4), is raised close to nature and partakes of that universal mother's innocency and springlike, flowery freshness. She is a fit bride for her disguised Prince Charming and a lovely antithesis to what is frozen and hidebound in the older generation. Paulina, loyal, resolute, high-spirited, a friend who advises, protects, and spiritually nourishes Hermione during the period of her "death" and stages her "resurrection" at the close, is not allowed her wish to wing her solitary way to a bough as "an old turtle [-dove]" but is married to the good old man Camillo, a wise, practical, humane counselor (5.3).

Hermione at the outset is close to the multifaceted, witty, charming, articulate, and sexually liberated heroines of Shakespearean comedy. In fact, the great scene (2) of the first act in which Leontes falls into jealous madness shows vividly what might have happened to Portia or Rosalind or Viola or Beatrice if we had been permitted to see them in the married state. If we think about it, we will surely be awed at what the great creating Shakespeare must have thought as he decided to plunge still another major character into the coils of the green monster, for the creation of Othello and Posthumus must have cost him considerable expense of spirit. Not even the author of the present study could have dreamed that Shakespeare would, in setting this action in motion, summon up in relatively few lines but with intense purpose so many of the great Western concepts profoundly associated in one way or another with marriage— innocence, Eden, original sin, betrothal, marital sexuality, incorporation, grace, friendship.

This last word should give us pause, but not until we have noticed how the speeches of the two kings, childhood friends, recapitulate the history of the human race. As boys Polixenes and Leontes were in Eden together, "twinned lambs that did frisk i'th'sun," exchanging "innocence for innocence." Free, as Polixenes thought they were, of the original "imposition . . . hereditary," he interprets their sinlessness as sexual innocence, no more and no less. At this hint Hermione presses in to suggest, with high and free spirits, that they must then have fallen into sin "with us, and that with us / You did continue fault, and that you slipped not / With any but with us [your wives]." Superficially this is the old conservative sexual view of the meaning of the Fall and its entailment of carnal sin upon marriage, but the teasing, joking queen has changed the tone, so that one cannot seriously place her in the theological camp of Polixenes (who, by the way, turns out later to be a paternal tyrant). It is she who in the space of twenty-five lines repeats the word *grace* three times and finally applies it both to her marriage to Leontes and her successful importunity in getting Polixenes to stay longer.

> 'Tis grace indeed.
> Why lo you now; I have spoke to th' purpose twice.
> The one for ever earned a royal husband;
> Th' other, for some while a friend.
>
> (1.2)

The last word, *friend,* used in a compound sentence which sets it off against *husband,* plunges Leontes's mind into a fit of insane jealousy and the subsequent plot into death, tragedy, separation, and the waste of a generation. For this sudden spin off balance, Shakespeare has not prepared us (no supersubtle Iago here whirls the brain): all we know is that the word *friend* triggers the jealousy, for Leontes at once mutters in agitation, "Too hot, too hot!" How could deadly sexual suspicions be precipitated by a word which today we take so much for granted and use so glibly? Because, as we have seen in analyzing a pregnant comment in *Romeo and Juliet,* for Shakespeare it was a word at whose heart lay a deadly contrast; it was a volatile word in the process of important semantic change. It could allude to the friendship of virtuous and like minds, but it could also mean "paramour," with graduated senses in between. With seismographic sensitivity to an important historico-linguistic moment, Shakespeare shows us a woman fully capable of the highest signification of *friendship* suddenly degraded within a jealous mind to its lowest, and it requires a long and complex action of suffering and loss to effectuate a restoration that will fulfill the word's most exalted promise in marriage.

If I seem to have placed too much emphasis upon a mere word, however much in transition, however richly ambiguous, I suggest that Shakespeare was aware of its implications, for immediately after uttering "Too hot!" Leontes is made to say, "To mingle friendship farre is mingling bloods" (and "to mingle blood" was an Elizabethan way of referring to sexual intercourse). Shakespeare might well have been pardoned had he eliminated from *friend* its inflammable ingredients and concentrated his dramatic energies on building a solid foundation of virtuous friendship alone for the shattered marriage and for Florizel and Perdita's new marital edifice. But no, he seems to insist on adhering to the potentially volatile symbiosis that *combines* eros and esteem. Florizel, of the new generation, says he will respect reason in loving Perdita if it is obedient to his fancy, but if it is not, "my senses, better pleas'd with madness, / Do bid it welcome" (4.4). And when Paulina near the end says to Leontes contemplating the statue of his now beloved wife, about to be revealed as living flesh and blood, "My lord's almost so far transported that / He'll think anon it lives," he replies, "O sweet Paulina, / Make me to think so twenty years together. / No settled senses of the world can match / The pleasure of that madness. Let't alone" (5.3).

"Transport"! "Madness"! The language has injected passion into marriages on two generational levels. Among the young this is to be expected of Shakespeare. To have erotic transport survive among the middle-aged after a purgatory of trial and loss says much for the persistence of the erotic in what Shakespeare elsewhere calls "inflamed respect." But to expect here *all* the freshness of the comedies and of teenage love and hope is wrong and perversely to expect too much. It is also to miss heedlessly the wonderful hush of reverence that comes late in this very late play and that would make overstatement verge on sentimentality and invite a brisk stroke of the demystifying and deconstructing axe.

Thus friendship, the thought of which in its sensual meaning had torn the union apart in the first place, seems like virtually everything else also to be restored, it too in the lovely, muted, and slightly displaced way that is appropriate after pain. In a tender and fully repentant reminiscence Leontes urges his queen to "look upon my brother. Both your pardons, / That e'er I put between your holy looks / My ill suspicion" (5.3). Shakespeare here makes us think back to the original "triangle," which in the heated mind of the jealous king precipitated the almost tragic action. Why? Does he want us to be cynical or realistic about the future happiness? Surely not, for here, if anywhere, Shakespeare is invoking the graceful power of Christian forgiveness, and the play will end with greater lyric harmony if we think back on how far ethically and emotionally the participants have come since the first disastrous act. I am not able to imagine what this signifies if not that Shakespeare is restoring Leontes to himself and also endowing this tragically interrupted marriage with the ideal of intelligent companionship that he has envisioned through so many plays. That ideal, we now know on our pulses, cannot be divorced from either esteem or desire, except at the greatest peril to life and sanity.

Shakespeare's Love Paragone

Ancient and Renaissance critical commentary was characterized by a tendency to view various occupations, the five senses, and even ideas and philosophies as competitive; rhetorical and critical *paragoni* (contests) existed between Homer and Phidias, sculpture and painting, the ear and the eye, Florentine design and Venetian color, nature and art, and, most commonly of all perhaps, between poetry and painting. The penultimate rivalry of those I have mentioned is invoked in *The Winter's Tale,* when Giulio Romano's skill in out-naturing nature is praised, and the last rivalry is glanced at by Kyd, Lyly, Spenser, and Shakespeare (in *Timon of Athens* 3.12). I have several times in these pages confronted a much older *paragone* than the critical-aesthetic one: that which since antiquity had pitted one type of human love against another. I wish to suggest here that Shakespeare himself may be said to have responded with a set of comparative formulations which embody this tradition, though not overtly. Both society and art often demonstrate that love in competition with itself can be complexly quarrelsome and confusing, and our own small sampling of earlier comparisons seems to show that each culture requires its own kind of *paragone.*

Before confronting the rivalry between friendship and love, Shakespeare's and his age's most profound amorous antithesis, let us consider a few contrasts related to literary love. Shakespeare made much in his early plays of differences between artifice and nature, and his most formal play, *Love's Labour's Lost,* whose language is often structured in the sonnet form, counterposes real life and the king's "little Academe" (1.1; the witty Biron suspects it to be given over to "angel knowledge" [1.1] only and considers it "flat treason 'gainst the kingly state of youth," 4.3). Although wit and the "gibing spirit" are also in need of mellowing, it is academic programming and its "maggot ostentation" (5.2) that most of all must be exorcised, and after this early play the maturing Shakespeare made a bias toward life, nature, and reality his fundamental though not sole orientation in matters of the heart.[32]

Shakespeare also became fond, when juxtaposing men and women, of giving the palm for wit, resourcefulness, and even general intelligence to the female sex; but since his ultimate ideal of esteem and desire combined required balance, he was also capable of embarrassing the overly aggressive female. Thus he tamed his shrew with embarrassing and sometimes cruel gusto and was capable of responding negatively to the heritage of the lawless, power-hungry, and eros-ridden female from classical myth and drama. I take *Venus and Adonis* to be an example of just such a reaction: the *paragone* between the title characters is one that Shakespeare inherited from Ovid, but he intensified its dynamics by making the male more passive and the female more aggressive. The indifferent, resistant, ideally beautiful Adonis, who would seem to appeal to both sexes alike, may be more interestingly reincarnated in the "friend" of the sonnets, and it is the goddess of love who captures our attention here since to her Shakespeare applies a powerfully deflating rhetoric. I cannot do better in describing the "heroine" of Shakespeare's erotic

epyllion than to quote two learned and witty scholars of an earlier generation. Don Cameron Allen calls her "a forty-year-old countess with a taste
for Chapel Royal altos," and C. S. Lewis, who considers her an ill-
conceived temptress made over-large for her victim, exclaims: "And this
flushed, panting, perspiring, suffocating, loquacious creature is supposed to be the goddess of love herself, the golden Aphrodite. It will not
do."[33]

Such contrasts as those between nature and artifice and between
passive male and dominating and erotically hungry female are important
but not nearly so central or poetically fructifying as the *paragone* between
friendship and love. Shakespeare must have been at least partially aware
of his many varied precursors: the friendship of Achilles and Patroclus
(made homoerotic by later Greek culture, the eroticism not being obviously present in Homer but later imposed on his pair); Plutarch's claims
and counterclaims in the *Amatorius* for boy-love and girl-love; the
competition in Greek romance between all-male love and male-female
love; the medieval contestation between Helen and Ganymede, a Latin
dialogue in which Helen and heterosexual love win decisively; the
Ciceronian mind-set of Eumenides in Lyly's *Endimion* ("The love of men
to women is a thing common, and of course; the friendship of man to
man infinite and immortal," 3.4); and the many Neoplatonic tracts from
Florence that expressed the same idea. It should be noted that the vast
majority of Renaissance exaltations of friendship over love were—
perhaps inevitably because of both external and self-imposed censorship
and also the influence of Cicero's *De Amicitia*—fully chaste, as in
Montaigne's essays and in the Sidney who placed the nobly loving
Pyrocles and Musidorus in his *Arcadia*. Similarly, in Shakespeare's own
brushes with the tradition the friendship seems for the most part unas-
sailably above erotic suspicion. Consider Valentine and Proteus, Romeo
and Mercutio, Claudio and Benedick, Hamlet and Horatio, but notice
too that the suspicion of desire may perhaps legitimately fall on Bassanio
and Antonio, that in the same play Salerio and Solanio seem clearly to be
gay friends, and that Oberon's love for a boy complicates his relations
with Titania.

Before we conclude this section with an examination of the sonnets,
it might be useful to consider both Shakespeare's last play, written with
Fletcher, and, more briefly, one of his earliest, *The Two Gentlemen of
Verona*.[34] I shall not here follow the improbable turns and twists of the
early romantic comedy or try to draw out the implications of its juxtaposing friendship and love, except to say that when at the climax—Proteus's
much needed though lamentably late and improbably sudden

repentance—Valentine forgives him in a trice and hands over to him his beloved Sylvia whom he had loved so long and to whom he had shown the deepest loyalty, the author seems to have lost control. Whatever this means or demonstrates—perhaps lack of authorial skill more than anything else and possibly authorial dismay at how to resolve the conflicting claims of the two kinds of love being portrayed—the most interesting and sensible character of all, Julia, faints but awakens for the denouement. Her wisdom may be necessary if the lovers are to remain both lovers and friends and if competition between friendship and love is to cease.

The Two Noble Kinsmen, first performed in 1613 or early 1614, may not be a masterpiece, but it contains no such crudeness as mars the climax of the comedy of 1591, though it even more strenuously explores the competition between love and friendship that Shakespeare and Fletcher inherited from Chaucer's "Knight's Tale."[35] The paragone that inheres in the hieratic structure of the play embodies, I believe, six distinguishable kinds of love: (1) the mature, equally matched, and by now fully conventional love of Theseus and Hippolyta, their legendary former conflict having been completely subdued; (2) a mature, military type of friendship between Theseus and Pirithous; (3) the teen-aged affection between Emilia and Flavina; (4) the passionate love across class lines of a teen-aged girl (the jailer's daughter) for the handsome aristocratic Palamon; (5) the deep but platonic love of Palamon and Arcite, who are differentiated in subtle but unmistakable ways that make the friendship more than mere mirroring of like virtues; and (6) the intense erotic desire conceived by each friend for the lovely Emilia. To disclose the dynamics of love in the play, we must reduce these six to a basic duality, consisting of friendship and love sharply opposed, the one privileged, the other ultimately degraded.[36]

How is romantic love degraded? In part by lowering Theseus from the at least partial raisonneur's position where Chaucer had placed him to one that reveals considerable coarseness, cruelty, and superficiality; in deeper measure by skillfully exploring the jailer's daughter's blinding and hopeless passion and grief and dramatically suggesting its inappropriateness for her by allowing it to recall the madness of Ophelia and the stunned disbelief of the terminally suffering Desdemona. The dramatists also degrade romantic love by ignoring beauty and potential values in Venus and making both the love goddess and her devotee Palamon totally fatuous and even comic—he hailing her as "thou that from eleven to ninety reign'st" (5.2) and exemplifying her power by claiming that she had put such "life into dust" (that is, into an octogenarian married to a fourteen-year-old girl) that though club-footed, gouty of finger, and swollen of eye he had still produced a son, the lass swearing it was his (5.2). And by keeping the lovely Emilia an unrepentant devotee of Diana ("I am bride-habited," she says, "but maiden-hearted," longing for death rather than love, 5.3).

In the end it is Palamon (morally somewhat inferior to his friend Arcite) who wins the prize and then complains that "naught could / Buy dear love but loss of dear love!" (5.6). Theseus in concluding cries out, Lear-like: "O you heavenly charmers, / What things you make of us!" (5.6). The deepest friendship in the play is thus lost, but romantic love, by this time degraded into illusion, is not won either.

In the end the concept of friendship, exemplified in the different ways we have already noted, remains on a much higher plane, no doubt because it conspicuously lacks sexuality. The soldierly comradeship of Theseus and Pirithous (he stood *in loco patris* at his friend's wedding) is a relationship Theseus's wife, Hippolyta, respects deeply—there is no rivalry between different affections evident here:

> Their knot of love,
> Tied, weaved, entangled, with so true, so long,
> And with a finger of so deep a cunning,
> May be outworn, never undone.
>
> (1.3)

Emilia also admires this soldierly friendship and reaches a mature insight, that it was more "maturely seasoned" than the one she will describe since it met mutual needs: "The one of th'other may be said to water / Their intertangled roots of love" (1.3). Her own girlhood relationship with Flavina, however—both being eleven years of age when her friend died—had its own kind of innocent charm, expressed in exquisite Shakespearean verse:

> The flower that I would pluck
> And put between my breasts—O then but beginning
> To swell about the blossom—she would long
> Till she had such another, and commit it
> To the like innocent cradle, where, phoenix-like,
> They died in perfume.
>
> (1.3)

There is no reason to doubt that the friendship between the Theban cousins was deep and throve in part on the delicate differentiation that

Shakespeare and Fletcher discriminate between the two youths. But it too perishes, poisoned by heterosexual passion for Emilia, who really wants neither lover but who is civilized enough to lament grievously the inevitable loss of one in the decreed combat-at-arms.

Though friendships may be lost in this play, they are not degraded. But what Emilia calls "sex dividual" (that is, male-female attraction) is irretrievably compromised, and her belief that "the true love 'tween maid and maid may be / More than in sex dividual" (1.3) is not overturned by the subsequent action. Quite the contrary, the same putative superiority imbues *all* the nonsexual relationships, and Emilia the maiden is superior to Emilia the bride, while Arcite the friend and ultimate loser is superior to Venus's disciple Palamon, who wins the prize. It is thus that Shakespeare valorizes the competing elements in the latest love *paragone* that he was to produce. The final effect is quite unlike anything we have so far encountered. In direct contrast to what happens in the comedies and the romances, romantic love is degraded and the moral and physical unions of marriage made to seem irrelevant or second best. Only friendship— same-sex friendship without the (inevitable?) stain of the erotic—stands unsullied, though it too succumbs to change, loss, and death. One of Shakespeare's fullest taxonomies of love—a late work, a collaborative work—ends in frustration and compromised stability.

Also complex and ambiguous, though vastly more so, is the *paragone* implicit in the sonnets, and a scholar might wish that the date of their writing and the originals, if any, behind actors and speaker could be precisely determined.[37] To bring out the essential rivalry of loves in *The Two Noble Kinsmen* I reduced to two the six kinds of love portrayed or implied. In the sonnets I find four, and these too will have to be reduced to essential categories to make the basic *paragone* stand out clearly. But first I must define and illustrate each of the more comprehensive four.

1. The *marital-erotic* is frequently alluded to but rendered only in one sonnet, the admirable number 8, where the concord of a domestic trinity—sire, child, and happy mother—is symbolized by suitable imagery and by the stately, flexible verse.

2. The poems of *heterosexual love* are dominated by lust, which is portrayed in the wisest, the saddest, the most traditionally inspired, and the most trenchantly beautiful of the sonnets, "The expense of spirit" (129). Others in this vein may be more specifically dramatic than this distillation of the libidinous anodyne, but none so effectively demolishes the erotically frivolous or sentimental in love expressed from Ovid's *Amores* to Keats's "Bright Star."

3. This category I had thought at first of calling nature or beauty (closely related concepts, as we have seen). But I am now convinced that the love comparisons that underlie the sequence requires us to be gender-specific, and so I shall call this topic *the homoerotic.* The friend in the decisive number 20 is not androgynous—the male is so decisively male that he can and elsewhere does minister to "women's pleasure" who might also find "their treasure" in his "love's use" (procreation). He is as beautiful of face as a woman, a quality portrayed in many Florentine portraits (figs. 30, 31); he possesses female gentleness and constancy; but he is by no means a third sex, a Narcissus, a hermaphrodite, Blake's Female Will, or Freud's phallic woman. The teasing four-line fable about doting Nature's adding that member which is to the speaker's "purpose nothing" is witty myth making: its chief point is that the friend is indisputably masculine. The poet's abjuration of pleasure from that phallic addition may be taken seriously or playfully—either interpretation will do. But the love that he keeps ("Mine be thy love") here implies what other poems demonstrate, the presence of homoerotic sensibility though not necessarily of homosexual acts.

4. *Friendship* may of course also be implied in number 20 as well as attraction by male beauty, but the sonnets create considerable space for a category of a long-term, stable commitment between men that resembles marriage, and number 105 sacramentally adds to the love relationship a Trinity, albeit a physico-psycho-ethical one ("fair, kind, and true," the three words exactly repeated three times). This Trinity is described as "Three themes in one, which wondrous scope affords": separately each has often been embodied individually. But here the stress is on a unity that leaves out difference—except in the varied language in which the unity is expressed. Although the three qualities become one, this is not idolatry; it is friendship, assimilated to the nuptial state and exalted by the spirit of religion, metaphorically rendered, to the level of "the marriage of true minds," which "bears it out even to the edge of doom" (116). Both these nobly ethical sonnets are addressed to or inspired by the friend.

I now reduce the fourfold taxonomy just given to two, not because I deny the presence of a memorably expressed contrast between exalted friendship and heterosexual love degraded to the level of lust. This remains one of the powerful contrasts of the entire sequence, instinct with life and experience. But we have examined its elements before, and we shall confront it again in the tragedies—and it is traditional. Far more original—and perhaps on an artistic parity with Shakespeare's union of

FIGURE 30 Botticelli, *Portrait of a Youth*. (National Gallery of Art, Washington; Andrew W. Mellon Collection.)

FIGURE 31 Raphael, *Bindo Altoviti*. (National Gallery of Art, Washington; Samuel H. Kress Collection.)

marital love and esteem in the comedies and romances—is his *paragone* between homoerotic love and virtuous friendship, a rivalry that is an energetic and fruitful interaction out of which both intense emotion and high human value arise.

But before we look closely at this tension within same-gender love I must make it clear, briefly, why I have omitted the category of married love and procreative sex from the *paragone*. I do so partly because Shakespeare gives it very little separate attention, which is confined virtually to the sonnet we have referred to (8), and even here such sexual, familial affection is closely tied to the desirability of reproducing the beloved friend's beauty. Procreative sex within the family thematically relates many important and memorable sonnets, whose purpose is regularly not to commend marriage or the family per se, but to celebrate, conceitedly, indirectly, the beauty of the beloved friend, which must not be allowed to wither and die without a copy. When the theme of immortality through verse becomes more prominent, the insistence that the friend marry to produce a copy loses both its frequency and urgency. But the alternations between the homoerotic and the truly permanent in love remain organically related all through the sequence, and it is to that alternation that we devote climactic attention.

We do not need to dwell longer than Shakespeare does on the level of the ideal (sonnets 105, 116). The exalted is never so dramatic as failures to achieve it, and Shakespeare's artistic instincts do not allow him to remain utopian for very long. But he does occasionally embody and more often implies the sweet, delicate, satisfying, abiding, rewarding, mutual, and universal qualities of love better perhaps than anyone else in the Western tradition, making him unique and treasurable in the long annals of amorous verse. In the sonnets the greatest poetic richness and efficacy reside neither in a marital utopia nor in the hell of lust nor in the tensions between the two, though these are indeed fruitful themes, but rather in the psyche of one who has envisioned the heaven of same-sex, noble, exalted friendship and desires to combine it with an eros which resembles that of heterosexual courtship and which, as any realist knows, shares with intersexual eros a magnetic downward bias, a *nostalgie de la boue.*

The poet does not always succeed in linking esteem with homoerotic desire, since he does not seem to be relaxed enough, as he was in proclaiming noble, permanent friendship per se, to make his utterance brief. With excessive iteration he praises the male beauty of the friend. He does so with very little use of mythology, with very little philosophical sophistication, and with insufficient variation of physical detail. We can, to be sure, summarize the friend's features: brightness of glance, loveliness, strength, grace, femininity, and delicacy (again, for the kind of male beauty that may have flashed upon Shakespeare's inward eye, see the Botticelli portrait in figure 30 and the Raphael in figure 31). But in the poetic event these either remain almost as static as in my summary or, without losing their abstractness and generality, become constituents of witty language and highly condensed logical or metaphorical structures. Too little attains the allure or excitement of the bodily enumerations of Spenser's *Epithalamion* or the exciting geographical metaphors of Donne's songs, sonnets, or elegies.

But still the physical is present, even when we do not expect or immediately perceive it. In sonnets 57 and 58 (see also 71, 72) the word *slave* is used, and the posture of abjectness requesting forgiveness can become tiresome. But perhaps it will take on some sparkle if we consider it less Christian humility than erotic prostration before the beloved, the same-sex equivalent of Cupidinous object worship. If we were right in sensing erotic elements in the submission of Augustine as the (Pauline) *doulos,* or slave, of deity, we may perhaps be permitted to see libidinal subjection in this more secular context. The idea of the beloved friend is far from being so imposing and formidable an Other as Augustine's God. Yet, with the sanction of scriptural sensualism behind him, Augustine is sometimes freer and more relaxed in his Amor-filled expression than is the subtly self-conscious, self-censoring Shakespeare.

In any case, now that we understand, better than earlier generations, Shakespearean bawdry and double entendre, we know that troping which superficially looks innocent carries an erotic charge within. The dull flesh of the horse that bears the speaker to his friend, not keeping pace with the poet's desire (51); the "sweet up-lockèd treasure" that may be opened but when closed "blunt[s] the fine point of seldom pleasure" (52); the "substance" and the "bounty" that reside in "the spring and foison of the year" (with more than a suggestion of the age-old topos, going back to early antiquity, of married sexuality as a ploughing of the ground, 53); and truth itself, which when not an "ever fixèd mark / That looks on tempests and is never shaken," is the sweet sweat of roses dying under pressure to distill perfume from "beauteous and lovely youth" (54)—all these and many more may be either seminal allusions or more general invocations of physical touch and press. Some scholars will, on the basis of contemporary linguistic evidence, be even more sex-specific than I have been here; others, stressing displacement, will find sexual data more generally and distantly rendered. But that Shakespeare expresses a same-sex eros cannot, I believe, be denied, though his double entendres are less immediately penetrable than those of, say, his comic heroines.

The most resounding sexual intentions are audible when the poet invokes procreative sexuality in marriage—and so I come back in concluding this section to the category of marriage, which I earlier put to one side because Shakespeare gives it little separate attention for its own sake. But he does relate it again and again to the friend's reluctance to create copies of himself, and it is here that the language becomes unforgettably strong and suggestive. In my paraphrase of relevant portions of sonnets 1, 4, 6, 9, and 10 using mostly modern English, I attempt to distill out the anger I sense in the necessarily somewhat formal utterance, which though bold cannot of course completely violate propriety. The speaker addresses the beloved and beautiful friend and says in effect: you are narcissistic and masturbatory, wedded to your own beautiful eyes. The fires that burn in you are fed with the substantial fuel of your own self. You are burying within the very buds of your love, within your own nascent arousals, the seeds of your own being. You are also something of a glutton, a cannibalistic one at that, since you yourself—and ultimately the grave will follow your example—are eating up what others ought to admire and enjoy. You are "having traffic with" yourself alone: you are suicidal, killing your own beauty, consuming your very self. You deny pleasure to others, but your self-containment (or is it also self-enjoyment?) murders your own being as well as others. Double shame on you!

How shall we explain such a sustained diatribe against the beloved, a charge not only of selfish indifference to the pleasure of others but of self-directed and unproductive enjoyment? C. S. Lewis, who believes that in the series of sonnets I have been discussing the "language is too lover-like for that of ordinary male friendship," implies and asks some penetrating questions: "The incessant demand that the Man should marry and found a family would seem to be inconsistent . . . with a real homosexual passion. It is not even very obviously consistent with normal friendship. It is indeed hard to think of any real situation in which it would be natural. What man in the world, except a father or potential father-in-law, cares whether any other man gets married?"[38] The answer to all of Lewis's troubled questions can never be fully satisfactory, but it may lie in the following psycho-somatic-artistic ganglion: a linguistic genius, accustomed to metaphoric displacement and now using a lyrical form that admits both direct emotional expression and also disguise, insistently keeps urging upon his friend a procreative marriage, where there is fully sanctioned physical contact. There are, as we know, better ways of praising beauty than such lackluster and repetitive calls for producing a copy of oneself. But here the praise includes a denunciation that is by no means dull, and the very angry personal force of the language suggests that frustrated erotic energy is frothing and boiling beneath the formal surface.

The *paragone* of friendship vs. love we have confronted here and in the preceding section recalls the millennial juxtaposition of heterosexual and homosexual love—Helen vs. Ganymede, for example. Such comparisons usually pivoted on the differences between fruitful procreative love (usually exalted) and recreative love, unproductive of heir, family, dynasty, or nation. Inverting the values of this culturally central and potent rivalry, could the speaker of the sonnets (living when he lived, knowing what he knew, and writing what he himself wrote about marriage) have completely evaded inner conflict and guilt? Could the friend only secondarily be the unproductive, self-consuming, masturbatory, suicidal niggard? Is the imprecatory lyricism also self-directed? Is the friend, leading his graces to the grave and leaving the world no copy, the cruelest *he* alive because *he* forces upon the speaker a truly disturbing inward gaze? If so, Shakespeare has in a subtext provided a most startling and revolutionary contribution to the literature of friendship vs. love, one that vastly transcends in energy and resonance another mere repetition or indeed any conceivable recuperation of the by now stale Florentine Neoplatonism. Shakespeare's *paragone,* vibrant at least in its imprecations, deserves a place in our story because it wryly and ironically implicates traditional marital values.

Marriage under Ultimate Stress

If Hamlet is punning when he says to Ophelia, "Get thee to a nunnery" (3.1), he is suggesting radically different alternatives to love and marriage (religious vocation or prostitution) that have often competed with it or replaced it in Western culture. The play suggests still another alternative in the character of Horatio, and our most recent *paragone* has shown that noble friendship between intellectual and moral equals constituted not only one of the most venerable but also one of the most troubling and emotion-filled competitions conceivable. But tragedy, a form that decrees consummation in death or loss, is something vastly different from rivalry however intense between competing forms of affection, for it confronts us with ultimate stress and mortal issue. It leads us to ask a most basic question, which applies not only to the marital but to all ideals dramatically presented: Do they survive the final testing the genre provides? Or does tragedy deconstruct or demystify what comedy and romance keep intact and reward climactically?

I hope it will become clear that the greatest tragedies are marriage-haunted, family-haunted. But first let us consider some views of tragedy which should be regarded as largely though not entirely irrelevant to the power and dignity of the Shakespearean. Plato's in the *Gorgias* has been said to put the emphasis on intellectual universality: "If Being and knowledge are tragic, life will be tragic. The most universal form of art will be that which by means of 'deception' can give knowledge of the tragic element revealed by ontology and epistemology."[39] Such darkening of life itself and cognition would seem to envisage the blanketing descent of Pope's universal darkness at the end of the *Dunciad* and may indeed hold out the specter of total nihilism—a specter that haunts Shakespeare's bleakest play, *Timon of Athens,* which, as we have noted before, "demonstrates the horror of a world completely devoid of marital love."[40] Such a vision comes to us in contemplating the Holocaust, the killing fields of Cambodia, the careers of Hitler and Stalin, the colonialist slaughters in Mesoamerica—or perhaps after reading *Macbeth.* But not, I think, after reading *Lear, Hamlet,* or *Othello,* for, as Richard P. Wheeler has said perceptively, there yawns a great gulf between Lear's "never" and Macbeth's "nothing."[41]

Nor do I find the Platonic view expressed by George Lukács or related religious visions appropriate models for Shakespeare's greatest tragic effects: tragedy "shows that it is only when what is individual— . . . a particular living individual—is carried to its final limits and possibilities that it conforms to the Idea and begins really to exist."[42] Shakespeare does not overtly or customarily lead us after supreme testing into an ultimate philosophical vision of the One—of Beauty, Truth, and Goodness as unified essence—or indeed of any ideology. But *Troilus and Cressida,* a play that approaches nihilistic desperation, also provides, though not climactically, a coherent vision of order, nothing less than the Elizabethan world-picture. When everything threatens to become power, power to become will, will appetite, and appetite "an universal wolf" that "Must make perforce an universal prey / And last eat up himself"—then degree (or order or old gradation) can apparently preserve "the unity and married calm of states" in their "fixture" (1.3). Such ordering within a dramatic situation is exceptional.

Nor is Shakespeare inclined to give us the personal consolations of the Christian martyr's vision, when hope is rewarded with the promise of future bliss, nor even those of George Herbert's more modest conceiving, whose divine glass of blessing finally provides rest for the more ordinary and less heroic life-tossed soul:

> Let him be rich and weary, that at least,
> If goodness lead him not, yet weariness
> May toss him to my breast.
>
> ("The Pulley")

Shakespeare at his most humanly tragic (that is, at his most Aristotelian) is far from nihilistic, but he is not hopefully Platonic or Christian either, and generations of critics have speculated whether Christian tragedy is even possible. Shakespeare the tragedian may well imply Christian meanings, since he has used the religious paradigms of his society in more than one comedy, even—more accurately, especially—the ones we have called absurdist. And he is insistently individualistic, not corporate or social, in his visions of searing loss. It is true that the tragedy of Antony and Cleopatra, that finely excessive grand opera, is played on a world stage, but the dynamics of the play, as so often in the lyric theater, finally isolate the lovers in their own private world. The author goes out of his way not to be religiously anachronistic as he sometimes can be, but he does finally spread a marital mantle over his lovers ("Husband, I come. / Now to that name my courage prove my title," 5.2) and then consigns them to a vague immortality of continuing Keatsian blisses.

It is otherwise in the greatest tragedies, which are all recognizably domestic and intimate, however exalted the heroism becomes, however grandly Satanic the evil. I bring out both the grandeur and the intimacy of Shakespeare's tragic individualism by quoting two somewhat different critics. Northrop Frye says tragic heroes are "the highest points in their human landscape," "great trees more likely to be struck by lightning than a clump of grass." And the young girl known to Harold S. Wilson said in crying out to the actor playing Othello, "You fool! Can't you *see* she's innocent."[43] In other versions of the story, the "girl" is an eccentric old gentleman shaking his cane at the actor. For generations, readers of *Lear* have assumed the good, honest Cordelia to be the raisonneuse and have found her good sense, a quality that for so many and for so long has been thought to be especially welcome on the domestic scene, a healthy contrast to the mad, cruel, lustful world that ultimately destroys her. She is now beginning to have her critical detractors, though it is not for that reason that I add to her own the authoritative voice of her husband. For the king of France, more clearly than she, reintroduces the "Shakespeare" of the first section of this chapter when he says of arranged marriages: "Love's not love / When it is mingled with regards [practical ambitious considerations] that stands / Aloof from th'entire point" (that is, from essential love itself, 1.1). He is also religiously romantic about falling in love, calling the now "dowerless daughter" Cordelia "this un-prized precious maid," whom the gods have "thrown to my chance," and he anticipates our central theme when he says, "Gods, gods! 'Tis strange that from their cold'st neglect / My love should kindle to inflam'd re-spect" (1.1). Thus as chaos comes to the world of *Lear* it engulfs not only the filial family (admittedly traditionally patriarchal in its structure) but the romantic marital ideal as well. The almost unbearable tragic pity and fear of this play are therefore at the very least dually caused (by the tear-ing apart of *both* marital and filial bonds), and marital love is everywhere reduced to a lust as hideous as the intergenerational cruelty with which it is allied.

Similarly, *Hamlet* is both a family and a marital tragedy, its binding and bonding concept being the Christian sacramental doctrine of one flesh. It appears with bitter irony when Hamlet on his way to England says farewell to Claudius:

> HAM. Farewell, dear mother.
>
> KING Thy loving father, Hamlet.
>
> HAM. My mother: father and mother is man and wife, man and
>   wife is one flesh, and so my mother.
>
>   (4.3)

The marital relation thus conceived makes the marriage to the elder Hamlet's brother specifically incestuous (it would have been theologi-cally shadowed in any event since second marriages had traditionally been regarded as being lustful and as complicating life in the Resurrec-tion). Hamlet's theology, perhaps sharpened at Wittenberg, rested, we may presume, on his own deep love of both mother and father and an appropriation by his adult spirit of the protective intimacies of child-hood. Excessively sensitive perhaps, morbid no: there is no need to pos-tulate with Freud rivalry with his own father for the love of his mother or a deep and debilitating sexual envy of his stepfather. And certainly over the regnant marital orthodoxy of the play (perhaps too eagerly embraced by the hero) we should not valorize the superficial common sense of the royal murderer ("your father lost a father; / That father lost, lost his") and of his speedily wedded wife ("Thou know'st 'tis common; all that lives must die," 1.2). Before the ghostly commission is laid upon him,

Hamlet senses that a most precious heritage from his personal past has been rent asunder. After the encounter with his father's spirit, the tensions become unbearable to a sensitive youth who is reluctant to take up arms against a sea of general troubles, to say nothing of raising a murderous arm against his new family, however loathsome and guilty its present head now seems to be.

One sign that Hamlet in the family that produced and reared him was not morbidly affectionate is that he grew up to be the "glass of fashion and the mould of form," an attractive suitor deeply attentive to his own heart and to his obligations, his suit fully supported by his mother and eagerly welcomed by Ophelia. His early and strange farewell to her is not merely an illustration of his antic disposition or of an already alienated mind. It is the grief of a sufferer who had deeply wished conditions to be other than they are and who now takes a long farewell of love as it normally might have been had his first family remained intact or even had his second not been founded on fratricide and blood-guilt. Ophelia speaks in piercing dismay at her loss:

> He falls to such a perusal of my face
> As a would draw it. Long stay'd he so. . . .
> He raised a sigh so piteous and profound
> That it did seem to shatter all his bulk
> And end his being; . . .
> He seemed to find his way without his eyes,
> For out o'doors he went without their help,
> And to the last bended their light on me.
>
>   (2.1)

Hamlet is indeed ending "his being," the being he had known as a son of his father and mother and as a suitor of the fair Ophelia. Pity and fear arise because the hero has been violently precipitated out of his smallest and best society, one whose replication had been eagerly awaited. We may grieve sublimely at the overthrow of a gifted and sensitive mind, a quintessential poet, a stimulating friend, or a benevolent political leader; we grieve intimately at the loss of a son and lover. For like *Lear* this is also a family-haunted, marriage-haunted, courtship-haunted play.

Othello is the most intensely domestic tragedy in our language; since the domestic has been the subject of important philosophical and theological thought and played a crucial role in social history from at least the high Middle Ages to the late Renaissance, it is not amiss to ask what basic orientation here guides the marital portrayal. Stephen Greenblatt argues

that Othello fears sexuality as a devout Catholic might and tends to regard even marital sexuality as being inevitably adulterous. I concede that
Othello suffers from sexual fears as an older man, a black man from a
different culture, and an outsider in the super-subtle Venetian vene-
reality. I also concede that these fears—most ironically and in the issue
most tragically—may have been aroused by Desdemona's sexual warmth
and eagerness, from what Greenblatt strikingly isolates as the intense
and eroticizing nature of her very submission to him.[44] But I cannot believe that Othello acts under the compulsive conviction that original sin
lurks in the physical act, that he is impelled by traditional Catholic rigorism, that he has been even remotely influenced by Jerome, Augustine—
or, for that matter, the Cambridge Puritan, William Perkins. I have earlier tried to show that the monopoly of such orthodox views of marriage
was surely broken by the twelfth century and that Chaucer's assertions of
the right of the wife to loving sexual courtesy after marriage as well as
gentle devotion before was a widespread hope and ideal in the high
Middle Ages. And the Renaissance and Reformation, with some exceptions, deepened the companionate ideal. Far more relevant, therefore,
for a proper perspective is Mary Beth Rose's invocation of the post-
Reformation Protestant view that marriage is an adventure not without
risks, what William Whately called "this one and absolutely greatest action of a man's whole life"[45]—a view we have seen shared by some of
Shakespeare's characters, notably by Theseus in *The Two Noble Kinsmen,* who calls marriage "this grand act of our life, this daring deed / Of
faith in wedlock" (1.1). Superficially, the African Othello and the Venetian Desdemona are about as far from an English or northern Protestant
couple as one could easily imagine, but *Othello* is the one tragedy of
Shakespeare set entirely in contemporary life (though for the English audience not without some exotic coloration)—a fact which, along with
the intense domesticity of its focus, makes it probable that Shakespeare's
own mind is at this point very close to the emergent mentality of his own
time.

For the marriage of this play to be a high adventure its principals
must be people of superior character, and so they remain, despite persistent impulses to join Iago in dethroning them. I myself cannot escape
the phrase about Othello given me years ago by one of my own teachers,
that he possesses a "grave and noble charm," and I ally myself with those
modern critics who find Desdemona to belong fully in the pantheon of
Shakespeare's great women. The poetic art of this work devotes itself
from the beginning to presenting the courtship and elopement as high
romantic adventure undertaken by interesting, bold, and imaginative

people, and when Desdemona accompanies her husband on his military mission to Cyprus Shakespeare shows two high-spirited people achieving a new kind of extradomestic intimacy. What a contrast she is to the spiritless, stay-at-home wife of Coriolanus!

Other characteristics of the marriage besides its adventuresomeness place it fully within contemporary mentalité. It is a consensual marriage, giving to the young a full and free choice that outrages the powerful Venetian senator who is the bride's father. The senator who questions Othello about how his marriage came about beautifully epitomizes the idea operative here:

> Did you by indirect and forcèd courses
> Subdue and poison this young maid's affections,
> Or came it by request and such fair question
> As soul to soul affordeth?
>
>> (1.3)

Does the marriage promise or take into full account the matter of mutual sexual pleasing? This question has seemed to many today to require a highly ambiguous answer. But I find the drift of the plot, the poetry, and the rhetoric unmistakably toward the affirmative. Othello does, to be sure, refer to "the young affects / In me defunct" (1.3)—whatever that means. I do not think it means impotence or any degree of incapacity, a condition a bridegroom would scarcely wish to reveal publicly to the assembly of "most potent, grave, and reverend signors" (1.3). Besides, at the moment he is not denying but delicately affirming the pleasurable potential of his erotic palate, calling the "satisfaction" that awaits him "proper," although he does not want to make it the motive of his present request for the presence of his wife on his military undertaking. The third scene of Act 2 makes it fairly clear that the marriage is not yet consummated; it is in fact annoyingly, mischievously interrupted. Indeed, one of the deepest ironies of this play may be that it is only on Desdemona's deathbed that we are assured of a consummation, a terrible and irrevocable one as death and desire move from their union in a famous Renaissance trope to hideous actualization. But all this is nothing to the point of what the newly married pair themselves *desire* in marriage or would have been capable by themselves of achieving.

I have referred to the drift of plot and rhetoric implying strongly that Othello and Desdemona are as fully capable in body as in adventurous imagination. Othello would not have fallen into a sexual rage as he did without himself possessing powerful sexuality, and Desdemona's banter with Iago is so full of sexual nuance that it has made some of the linguistically judicious grieve. But the strongest implication that this couple is potentially well sorted physically is the powerful contrast to both of them that their tempter and destroyer provides. For against their sexual eagerness and imaginative élan, against their romantic modernity and daring spirits, he poses ancient cynicism—"a violent commencement" will lead to an "answerable sequestration," or rupture (1.3). And against their warmth and passionate imaginings he counterpoises his own "scale of reason"—his cold, stoical, traditional rationality, which defines love as "merely a lust of the blood and a permission of the will" (1.3). That rationalistic blindness will entrap the villain in the end and at that point release into our consciousness all the loving sexual potential that has been forfeited to Iago's cold brain and hot ego.

Does the marriage hold the promise of friendship? Only by implication since so much has been aborted. Under Iago's snaky charms Othello goes horn-mad and Desdemona loses her modernity, reverting to traditionally tame girlish submissiveness in her stunned and disbelieving grief. But there are hints here and there that friendship in the lofty meanings of Aristotle and Montaigne is envisaged. The very compatibility of spirit revealed in the wooing seems to promise that. Desdemona's common sense moderating marital expectations (she may be adventuresome but is not starry-eyed) suggests steadiness of mind: "Nay, we must think men are not gods, / Nor of them look for such observancy / As fits the bridal" (3.4), Desdemona being far less sentimental than Chaucer's Franklin in defining marital courtesy, a passage that may be a distant ancestor of the present speech. And Othello's final restoration to love and his total tragic awareness at the close reveal even at that awful moment a mind capable of imagining (even as he suffers from loving "too well") what it means to "love wisely," a capability that this man of initial decency and modesty must surely have possessed, at least potentially. (Shakespeare delineates these qualities in brief, subtle, but unmistakable ways. Othello, for example, will promulgate his own great status and heritage "when I know that boasting is an honour" [1.2].)

We remember, however, from our discussion of the opening of *The Winter's Tale* that the word *friend* possessed contradictory meanings (sexual love *and* platonic companionship) and was undergoing great change at this time. When Desdemona offers *friendship* to Cassio she is admirably modern and free-spirited but in the circumstances is being risky beyond belief. At least Shakespeare describing Leontes's sudden spin into jealousy at the use of *friend* must have thought so if he remembered what he had Desdemona vow to Cassio: "Assure thee, / If I do vow a friendship I'll perform it / To the last article" (3.3). At least *we,* remembering the later play, feel like crying out, "Too hot! Too hot!"

This point about the potential for friendship in marriage may persuade if we consider more deeply what is in fact lost as the play moves into lacerating tragedy. What is lost is what Western culture had been getting glimpses of for millennia and moving toward for three or four centuries preceding Shakespeare, a perception that in a stable erotic situation there is opportunity for man-woman love to grow in both intimate vitality and companionable maturity. I do not wish to emphasize here the *reasons* for Othello and Desdemona's loss—they have been treated monumentally—but rather the much less obscure or ambiguous *nature* of the loss. This is displayed early when the married couple are at the height of their anticipatory bliss. Othello says:

> If it were now to die
> 'Twere now to be most happy, for I fear
> My soul hath her content so absolute
> That not another comfort like to this
> Succeeds in unknown fate.
>
> (2.1)

Othello's emotions give to momentary rapture the status of an absolute. Are we being invited to feel that so intense a rapture is shadowed with death—a haunting anticipation of the tragic conclusion? Or is Shakespeare giving panegyrical panache to a moment of fine and high rapture? Or is he bringing us down to the domestic scene, to the moral and psychological interaction of the couple, by suggesting that Othello's perception of amorous experience as rapture followed by a desire for everlasting cessation is badly in need of adjustment? Which corrective Desdemona, rising now to the stature of one of Shakespeare's truly great women, provides at once: "The heavens forbid / But that our loves and comforts should increase / Even as our days do grow" (2.1). In contrast to Othello's present tense ("hath") and obsessive singulars ("soul," "content," "comfort," "fate"), Desdemona's plurals are relaxed, human, vital, quotidian ("heavens," "loves," "comforts," "days"). I read closely in order to isolate Shakespeare's realistic vision of marital reality and relate it to culture. If I am correct, what she really offers is the Renaissance and Reformation ideal expanding into new and perhaps untried opportunities for human union and mutual development. She offers *Liebesleben* or *Liebeskraft* for his *Liebestod.* Once more a husband is seen as being sanctified in the wife, and female leadership reveals itself as potentially redemptive. The passage, whatever its precise denotation, suggests creative complementarity of the rarest kind.

Tragedy is not tragedy in Aristotle's full sense unless we keep before us a lively sense of alternative endings. Given time and freedom from Iago's poison, the loving skill of Desdemona could have kept pure "the fountain from which [Othello's] current ran," could have preserved viable the seedplace where he "had garnered up [his] heart" and made him "live" rather than "bear no life" (4.2). When such values, made vivid for us by powerful language, are lost, we grieve—almost beyond human endurance—that the hero threw away "a pearl . . . richer than all his tribe" (5.2), the jewel being a person of course but also a relationship, one of "esteem enlivened by desire."

'Merry' and 'tragical'? 'Tedious' and 'brief'?—
That is, hot ice and wondrous strange black snow.
How shall we find the concord of this discord?
A Midsummer Night's Dream 5.1 (1594/95)

hakespeare would not have been an honest love poet had he not been paradoxical, and he would not be Shakespeare were he not elusive, a *deus absconditus,* hiding behind his characters, lurking furtively in his plots, and even concealing himself in lyrical verse. It does not make the critical task easier that, as C. L. Barber said, Shakespeare leaves "the judgment free to mock what the heart embraces."[1] Still, it is clear that the "Shakespeare" we adumbrated at the beginning of the last chapter did regularly give privilege to the slighted or undervalued member in many important Western antitheses related to love. He seems to have favored passion over reason, making a "Hamlet" in most contexts preferable to a "Horatio"; woman over man, as all the great comedies and romances testify; consensual over arranged marriage, consistently allowing youthful choice to thwart paternal planning; nature over nurture, the "great creating Nature" that allied him with the medieval School of Chartres and Chaucer and with important strains in antiquity as well.

I have concluded the body of this work—appropriately, I hope—with a discussion of *Othello,* a domestic tragedy. When we considered domestic comedy, I asked whether it was proper to think about life after closure and concluded strongly that it was, if we allowed the force of the work to live on in us imaginatively and did not place the dramatis personae solidly in their contemporary status quo. I believe the same point needs to be made about tragedy, and I have argued that we are invited to imagine alternatives to the persons and programs that frustrated or destroyed those we had come to love. "Such relations, properly considered," said Henry James, "end nowhere." John Bayley, who quotes James, makes my point for me: "thus it is as relevant to ask ourselves what was the nature of Othello's and Desdemona's love, and what were their chances of happiness, as it is to wonder whether Isabel, in *The Portrait of a Lady,* would ever have left her husband, or how Elizabeth and Darcy would have got on after marriage. These queries are relevant because the resonance of such situations can never be stilled."[2]

I wish now, however, to go beyond personal reflection on what we have read or seen after the book has been closed or the theater darkened to glance very briefly at literary-cultural trends that followed Shakespeare's vision. Such movements and directions are now receiving abundant and diverse scholarly attention, which it is not appropriate to analyze here. It will have to suffice to point to exemplary moments in the work of John Donne (born in 1571, seven years after Shakespeare) and of John Milton (born in 1608, when Shakespeare was at the height of his career). Donne, an almost exact contemporary, is further from the Shakespearean spirit than Milton, who wrote a couple of generations later in vastly different social, political, and religious conditions.

Donne, like Shakespeare, honored both the body and the soul, but his suggestive word *interinanimation* seems better to serve Shakespeare's than his own portrayals of the two great loci of human love. He writes in "Air and Angels":

> But since my soul, whose child love is,
> Takes limbs of flesh (and else could nothing do)
>   More subtile than the parent is,
> Love must not be but take a body too.

And that is exactly what the pure Platonically loving souls do in "The Ecstasy": they descend to the body, to affections and faculties apprehensible by sense, "Else a great prince in prison lies."[3] And yet in his songs, sonnets, and elegies Donne is "all body" in an intense and open way that the serious, unironic Shakespeare seldom is. Traditionally comparing the two kinds of love (the two ancient Venuses, as it were) to sky and earth, he finds that Cupid is an underground, infernal god.

> Although we see celestial bodies move
> Above the earth we till and love,
> So we her airs contemplate, words and heart
> And virtues, but we *love* the centric part.
>   (Elegy 18, "Love's Progress," lines 33–36)

Donne's lyric tilling of the sexual earth, his excited exploration of erotic geography have not lost their vigor; but when he celebrates marriage and the growth of stable affection, he seldom "interinanimates" earth and sky as obviously as Shakespeare does, and the terrestrial and the uranian Venuses are not often united.

In his sermons the orthodox dean of St. Paul's fully accepts the doctrine of the resurrection of the body, which we have seen could be erotically transmogrified even in homiletical, confessional, or devotional literature. Dean Donne admonishes us, "Never go about to separate the thoughts of the heart, from the colledge, from the fellowship of the body. All that the soul does, it does in, and with, and by the body"—the very doctrine of "Air and Angels" and of "The Ecstasy." But in his marriage sermons Donne usually misses an opportunity to do what our tradition would have insisted on: he does not stress the fruitful union of both the body and the soul. He is as reserved about the state of matrimony as he could decently be in the circumstances, coolly supporting its rights and rites but preferring virginity (let those who now abstain continue their vows "a little longer than they doe"); keeping the woman in her place as the weaker vessel (a woman is a helpmeet taken originally from man's side, "but she must be no more" than a helper, and she is not made "fitter or meeter" through "wit, learning, eloquence, memory, music, or ceremony"); warning of marital indulgence ("there is not a more uncomely, a poorer thing than to love a Wife like a Mistress").[4]

Jack Donne is a bold eroticist in a highly traditional pagan way, and Dean Donne is far from the cutting edge of reformed Christianity. What a contrast Milton provides in his defense of the passions in *The Areopagitica:* "Wherefore did [God] create passions within us, pleasures round about us, but that these rightly tempered are the very ingredients of virtue?"[5] Or in his defense of marital sexuality in the divorce tracts: love is "the sensitive pleasing of the body," and beside the pleasures of the "genial bed" it should provide "fitness of mind and disposition" in a higher friendship than that envisaged by Plato, Aristotle, or Augustine. Or in his belief that when compatibility and mutual pleasing disappear God disappears too and the union should be dissolved. Or in *Paradise Lost,* with its Cupidinous bower of marital bliss, where Adam and Eve are joyously impelled by what in prose he called "the intelligible flame, not in Paradise to be resisted."

There is no evidence, to be sure, that Shakespeare or any Christian author we have studied would have followed Milton in believing that marriage should be dissolved when there is "no correspondence of the mind," a condition in which the couple will in Milton's view become "two carcases chained unnaturally together."[6] But the dramatist's comic and romantic heroines strike one as being daughters of Milton's Eve avant la lettre, and although he was not the scholar that the epic poet was, I suggest that he would have had some sense that the portrait of marital initiation in Eden just before the reward of bodily union respected a long tradition that was ever changing as it was being shaped to fit the deepest human needs. The newly created Eve is endowed with the millennially celebrated virtues of grace, beauty, modesty, dignity, knowledge; the sleeping Adam even before he awakens and indeed while the divine operation is taking place feels a "new" sweetness until then unknown and also "the spirit of love and amorous delight" (*Paradise Lost* 8.475, 477). Then when he awakens after momentary darkness, "on she came," led by her invisible maker, guided by his voice, "nor uninformed / Of nuptial Sanctitie and marriage Rites" (8.485–86). Milton has made his Eve *innately* nubile: fresh from her creator's hand and her husband's side, she brings with her into life and consciousness an already formed idea of religious union. Still, she must be wooed and must give her consent, though under such auspices marital "arrangement" might be considered forgivable and indeed prove to be irresistible. Milton names her, thus establishing a hierarchical relationship, and invokes at once the marital doctrine of "one flesh":

> She heard me thus, and though divinely brought,
> Yet Innocence and Virgin Modestie,
> Her vertue and the conscience of her worth,
> That would be woo'd, and not unsought be won,
> Not obvious, not obtrusive, but retir'd,
> The more desirable, or to say all,
> Nature her self, though pure of sinful thought,
> Wrought in her so, that seeing me, she turn'd;
> I follow'd her, she what was Honour knew,
> And with obsequious Majestie approv'd
> My pleaded reason. To the Nuptial Bowre,
> I led her blushing like the Morn.
>   (8.500–511)

Having so much we long for more. What was her "turn" like? A turn toward what or whom? A pirouette, an embrace? How long does she lead and Adam follow before he takes over and escorts her into the bower? And what arguments or solicitations did Adam use in his "pleaded reason"? But enough! Milton must surely be allowed to remain free of the inquisitive scholar's questions, even though he provoked them by suggesting so much of the marital-erotic tradition, including the sanction of Nature herself.

Shakespeare, with Milton, stands in the liberalizing tradition that in the late seventeenth and eighteenth centuries formed the synthesis of what Lawrence Stone has called "affective individualism" and what I have called "sex and sensibility."[7] That bourgeois marital tradition, sentimentalized and romanticized by the early nineteenth century and expressed by Coleridge as strong, tender, graceful, soothing, and conciliatory sexual difference which at the same time remains "perfectly pure, perfectly spiritual,"[8] grew through the Victorian era and up to the sexual revolution of our own day and the entry of woman into the work force.

The effects of these long overdue and momentous contemporary events upon the viability of the tradition explored in this book remain to be seen. The temporally and culturally provincial will regard both my boundary authors, Homer and Shakespeare, as being locked into cultures that no longer speak to us. But I have myself learned to count no old thing old that possesses enough *wit* to keep it *sweet*. By *wit* I do not mean only the ability to say smart Oscar Wildean things at parties; I refer to that great term which derives from *to know* (witan) and which historically also embraces the imagination and the ethical reason. *Sweet* has the taste of Hollywood and Valentines about it, but in his *Dictionary* Samuel Johnson defines it as "pleasing to any sense" *and* "pleasing to the mind or spirit."

In concluding I ask the reader to remember my preliminary love categories, discussed in chapter 1. For each of them I feel a desire to cast a quick glance toward the future and express a hope. Whatever new forms *libido* will take, however different the *erōs* that poetizes it may become from what we have studied, however *benevolence,* long-term *affection,* and *agapē* may in the future be institutionalized, and whatever capitalism may ultimately do to what I have called the *ego context of love,* which I have often presented as both realistic and savory, I hope that some of the hard-won achievements of our heritage will be seriously confronted. Confident that libido is in no danger of being diminished, whatever new forms it may take, I trust that culture will be rich enough to continue exalting it into eros and that Venus and her son will not give up on producing couples to rhythmic accompaniment. Obviously more is needed than appetency or even richly decorated and complexly realized desire, and we may be permitted the fervent hope that whatever humanizes and moralizes collective life will be honored. I suspect that justice, benevolence, and philanthropy will be well served if in house and home esteem and desire can be brought together and challenged to achieve what Shakespeare called "something of great constancy." At the very least, the modern student needs to know that it would betray the dreams of more centuries and cultures than we have hitherto realized if life enhancement through friendly intimacy were to be dismissed as being remote from human nature and unavailable to imaginative and intellectual talent.

NOTES

Preface

1. For a brief summary of the Greek classification, see Northrop Frye, *The Secular Scripture: A Study of the Structure of Romance* (Cambridge, Mass.: Harvard University Press, 1976), p. 17. Wallace Stevens has suggestively provided a modern socio-psychological definition of imagination that is relevant to my emphasis upon imagination in this book. "It is a violence from within that protects us from a violence without. It is the imagination pressing back against the pressure of reality. It seems, in the last analysis, to have something to do with self-preservation; and that, no doubt, is why the expression of it, the sound of its words, helps us to live our lives." I quote Stevens from R. Jahan Ramazani, "Yeats: Tragic Joy and the Sublime," *Publications of Modern Language Association of America* 104/2 (March 1989): 163, where it stands as the epigraph, without documentation.

2. I quote from the translation of Donald M. Frame, *Montaigne, Complete Works*, 2nd printing (Stanford, Calif.: Stanford University Press, 1958), pp. 137, 138. Despite its value in alerting us to imaginative alternatives, Montaigne's view here is doubly mischievous: (1) it airily dismisses women from even the possibility of friendship, and (2) it suggests—wrongly, as I hope to show in this book—that antiquity always held the same dismissive view.

Chapter One

1. Foote is quoted by William C. Carter, "Seeking the Truth in Narrative: An Interview with Shelby Foote," *Georgia Review* 41/1 (Spring 1987): 164.

2. Friedrich Engels, *The Origin of the Family* (Boston: New England Free Press, n.d.), p. 58. See also ibid., p. 57 (monogamy is not the "fruit of individual sex-love, with which it has nothing whatever to do"), p. 74 (where Engels cannot predict what will happen if monogamy does not fit the altered revolutionary situation); Engels, *The Origin of the Family, Private Property and the State*, ed. Eleanor Burke Leacock (New York: International, 1973), where Engels's background is commented on and where his most famous comment on marriage appears on p. 121: "The overthrow of mother right was the *world historical defeat of the female sex*. The man took command in the home also; the woman was degraded and reduced to servitude; she became the slave of his lust and a mere instrument for the production of children." See also discussions of Engels and his feminist followers in Alison M. Jaggar, *Feminist Politics and Human Nature* (Totowa, N.J.: Rowman & Allanheld, 1983), pp. 65, 219, 229–41, 264, 279, 322–

23, 345; and in Michèle Barrett and Mary McIntosh, *The Antisocial Family* (London: Verso Editions/NLB, 1982), pp. 7–18, 21–26, 32–43, 55–60, 73–145.

3. Edmund Leach is quoted by Jonathan Dollimore, "The Challenge of Sexuality," in *Society and Literature: 1945–1970,* ed. Alan Sinfield (London: Methuen, 1983), p. 61.

4. Barthes is quoted by Joseph Allen Boone, *Tradition Counter Tradition: Love and the Form of Fiction* (Chicago: University of Chicago Press, 1987), p. 144.

5. The tone is muted, though dismay may persist in some reactions to marriage by men in recent American poetry. See the lovely verse in the concluding section (VI) of Anthony Hecht's "See Naples and Die," *American Scholar* 59/3 (Summer 1990): 395–96; and Helen Vendler's discussion of Stephen Dunn (she finds that such poems by men on marriage constitute a recent genre), *New York Review of Books,* 23 October 1986, p. 48.

6. Donald Barthelme, "Not-Knowing," *Georgia Review* 39/3 (Fall 1985): 521, 522.

7. See Irving Singer's three volumes, *The Nature of Love* (Chicago: University of Chicago Press, 1984–87). The discussion extends from Plato to Sartre and in concluding chapters analyzes "scientific intimations" and develops a "modern theory of love."

8. Ludwig Feuerbach, *Lectures on the Essence of Religion,* trans. Ralph Manheim (New York: Harper & Row, 1967), p. 17.

9. P. N. Medvedev and M. M. Bakhtin, *The Formal Method in Literary Scholarship* (Baltimore: Johns Hopkins University Press, 1978), p. 7.

10. Clifford Geertz, *The Interpretation of Cultures* (New York: Basic Books, 1973), chap. 1 ("Thick Description: Toward an Interpretive Theory of Culture").

11. Roberto Mangabeira Unger, *Passion: An Essay on Personality* (New York: The Free Press/Macmillan, 1984), pp. 9, 25–26, 48. E. H. Gombrich reacts to Hegel's assertion that historical periods and peoples differ from each other by saying, "We all know that," and by being grateful to Dilthey for stressing what I have been discussing, the universal particular, adding, "The humanist will always have to be interested in the individual and nonrepeatable fact" ("'They Were All Human Beings—So Much is Plain': Reflections on Cultural Relativism in the Humanities," *Critical Inquiry* 13/4 [Summer 1987]: 689).

12. Michel Foucault, "What is an Author?" in *Textual Strategies: Perspectives in Post-Structuralist Criticism,* ed. Josué V. Harari (Ithaca, N.Y.: Cornell University Press, 1979), pp. 156–57.

13. By saying that imagination is also inevitably present in the scholar-critic, I am uttering a recent truism, which should not be allowed to obscure another and older one: that the critic must continually *strive* for suprapersonal norms and both particulars and generalizations that are verifiable in one way or another. I should perhaps confess to the ambition that what I have defined in this chapter as a heritage and some of the art and literature I shall describe in the

chapters that follow will affect what is now called canon formation, a matter seriously and even ferociously debated. I take heart from a recent statement by Jerome McGann: "Equally important is the need to preserve the resources of our literary archive—that notorious 'canon' which has lately been taken to embody so many fearful and self-destructive values. We must of course continually judge and revise that body of work, but no one can afford to give it up" (*Social Values and Poetic Acts: The Historical Judgment of Literary Work* [Cambridge, Mass.: Harvard University Press, 1988], p. viii).

14. On Aristotle, see chapter 3. For *De L'Amour* (1st ed., 1822) of Marie-Henri Beyle (de Stendhal), see *On Love*, trans. "H.V.B." (New York: Liveright, 1947), pp. 1–2. Herbert Spencer is quoted by Havelock Ellis, *Studies in the Psychology of Sex* (Philadelphia: F. A. Davis, 1906–19), vol. 6: *Sex Relations in Society* (1919), p. 135. C. S. Lewis's book is entitled *The Four Loves* (New York: Harcourt, Brace & World, 1960). For a taxonomy of love by a distinguished psychologist, see Robert J. Sternberg, *The Triangle of Love: Intimacy, Passion, Commitment* (New York: Basic Books, 1987). See p. 152 of Sternberg for John Lee's typology of love, divided into six main kinds: (1) *eros*, (2) *ludus*, (3) *storge*, (4) *mania*, (5) *agape* (here secularly defined as altruistic love), and (6) *pragma*.

15. Robert Sternberg's opinion is quoted in the *New York Times*, 10 September 1985.

16. Rollo May, *Love and Will* (New York: W. W. Norton, 1969), p. 75. On stylized "foreplay" in eighteenth-century and Romantic culture, see Jean H. Hagstrum, *Sex and Sensibility* (Chicago: University of Chicago Press, 1980); and Hagstrum, *Eros and Vision* (Evanston: Northwestern University Press, 1989), s.v. Rousseau, Sterne, and Delicacy.

17. I quote Santayana from Irving Singer's excellent analysis in *The Nature of Love* (n. 7 above), 3:258, 259.

18. T. R. Hummer, "Bluegrass Wasteland," *Georgia Review* 41/1 (Spring 1987): 119. Irving Singer's distinction in sexuality between the "passionate" (craving, yearning, the violent need for cathexis) and the "sensuous" (enjoyable playfulness) may be relevant here (*The Nature of Love* [n. 7 above], 3:376). Before we leave the topic of libido, we should note what anthropology shows: that few societies confine all coitus to legitimate marriage partners and that there is always a variance between normative rules and statistical occurrences. William H. Davenport, "Sex in Cross-Cultural Perspective," in *Human Sexuality in Four Perspectives*, ed. Frank A. Beach (Baltimore: Johns Hopkins University Press, 1977), chap. 5.

19. See Willard Van Orman Quine's classic essay, "On What There Is," in *From a Logical Point of View* (Cambridge, Mass.: Harvard University Press, 1953), p. 3 n.1.

20. On Cicero, see Hallett Smith, who is quoted in Maurice Hunt, "Leontes' 'Affection' and Renaissance 'Intention': *Winter's Tale* I.ii.135–46," *University of Mississippi Studies in English*, n.s. 4 (1983): 50; and W. Thomas MacCary, *Friends and Lovers: The Phenomenology of Desire in Shakespearean*

Comedy (New York: Columbia University Press, 1985), pp. 196–97. See also below, chapter 4 and epilogue.

21. Theodor Reik, *Psychology of Sex Relations* (New York: Rinehart, 1945), pp. 22–23.

22. Thomas Hobbes, *Leviathan* 4.9.17.

23. David Hume, "Of the amorous passion, or love betwixt the sexes," in *A Treatise of Human Nature* 2.2.11.

24. Freud, *Beyond the Pleasure Principle,* trans. James Strachey (New York, Bantam Books, 1967), p. 89; R. V. Krafft-Ebing, *Psychopathia Sexualis,* trans. F. J. Rebman (New York: Physicians & Surgeons, 1926), p. 11.

25. Singer, *The Nature of Love* (n. 7 above), 3:93.

26. Lewis, *Four Loves* (n. 14 above), pp. 107, 115. See Denis de Rougemont's view that the Christian church has had more success regulating the sexual instinct than eroticism, even within marriage: *Love Declared: Essays on the Myths of Love,* trans. Richard Howard (New York: Pantheon, 1963), pp. 8–9.

How does my eros differ from the brilliantly argued modern view of *sexuality* as being a mostly if not entirely acculturated form of sex (= nature)? I find that I give considerably more scope to nature in both literary and generally cultural eros, examples of the latter being teaching, learning, and even reading. See Steven G. Kellman, "*Ut Coitus Lectio:* The Poet as Lovemaker," *Georgia Review* 34/2 (Summer 1980): 302–12. For discussions of sexuality as opposed to sex, see Arnold I. Davidson, "Sex and the Emergence of Sexuality," *Critical Inquiry* 14/1 (Autumn 1987): 16–48; David M. Halperin, *One Hundred Years of Homosexuality and Other Essays on Greek Love* (New York: Routledge, 1990); John J. Winkler, *The Constraints of Desire: The Anthropology of Sex and Gender in Ancient Greece* (New York: Routledge, 1990); David M. Halperin, John J. Winkler, and Froma I. Zeitlin, eds. *Before Sexuality: The Construction of Erotic Experience in the Ancient Greek World* (Princeton, N.J.: Princeton University Press, 1990). I take it that in Stuart Hampshire's *Innocence and Experience,* which is now being reviewed but which I have not seen, he accepts both nature and culture as being operative: "Sexual love seems the bedrock, biologically necessary, original case of the power of imagination," but "the cultivation and elaboration of sexual love in all its varieties is the work of culture as much as nature." See the review by Alan Ryan, *New York Review of Books,* 1 March 1990, p. 36. E. H. Gombrich desiderates a struggle of contrarieties: "No style of life is conceivable in which the tension between the urge for satisfaction and the pressure of cultural demands fails to find expression. Literature, above all, has frequently concerned itself with these tensions" ("They Were All Human Beings" [n. 11 above], p. 694.

27. The Latin *velle bene* (I do not know that erotic meaning was consciously attached to it) could mean "to like," as *velle male* could mean "to dislike." A study of the meanings of the phrase in both Latin and the Romance languages might prove to be culturally instructive.

28. On friendship I am indebted to Ronald A. Sharp, *Friendship and Literature: Spirit and Form* (Durham, N.C.: Duke University Press, 1986), a book valu-

able for its discussion of theory as well as its comments on literature, notably Thoreau and Shakespeare's *Merchant of Venice*. For a suggestive account of nineteenth-century visual equivalents of the more erotically focused *amitié amoureuse*, to which we shall recur often in subsequent pages, see Fred Licht, "Friendship," in *The Ape of Nature: Studies in Honor of H. W. Janson*, ed. Moshe Barasch and Lucy Freeman Sandler (New York: Harry N. Abrams, 1981), pp. 559–68; and Robert M. Polhemus, *Erotic Faith: Being in Love from Jane Austen to D. H. Lawrence* (Chicago: University of Chicago Press, 1990), chap. 1 and relevant plates.

29. Gene Ouka, quoting Paul Tillich, finds eros "the normal drive towards vital self-fulfillment": *Agape: An Ethical Analysis* (New Haven: Yale University Press, 1972; rpt. 1976), p. 287. I wish to separate myself from John C. Moore's view (widely accepted) that Christianity by commanding love of God and the unilaterally directed love displayed in charity has not encouraged interpersonal love with individuals. This is unnecessarily limited, true of only one strain in Christianity that was powerfully challenged in creative periods. See "The Origins of Western Ideas: Irving Singer's *The Nature of Love: Plato to Luther*," *Journal of the History of Ideas* 29/1 (January–March 1968): 141–51; and my discussion in chapter 9.

30. Amélie Oksenberg Rorty, "Characters, Persons, Selves, Individuals," in *Mind in Action: Essays in the Philosophy of Mind* (Boston: Beacon Press, 1983), pp. 78–98.

31. Singer, *The Nature of Love* (n. 7 above) 3: 433–34.

32. Broad is quoted and criticized in Lawrence A. Blum, *Friendship, Altruism and Morality* (London: Routledge & Kegan Paul, 1980), pp. 215–16 and n.14.

33. *Boswell's Life of Johnson*, ed. G. B. Hill and L. F. Powell, 6 vols. (Oxford: Clarendon Press, 1934), 2:461 and 3:3. Nietzsche said in the *Will to Power*, "Only the complete person can love . . . one must be firmly rooted in oneself." See Singer, *The Nature of Love* (n. 7 above), 3:89, and accompanying discussion. On instrumental love, in which we "seek to use each other as instruments" and to satisfy "the reciprocal need of gratification of lovers," see Richard Center, *Sexual Attraction and Love: An Instrumental Theory* (Springfield, Ill.: Charles C. Thomas, 1975), pp. vi, 3, and passim. For a more idealistic view, see Robert Brown, *Analyzing Love* (Cambridge: Cambridge University Press, 1987): "We have no adequate reason to believe that loving an object must always be an expression of self-love" and "it is not possible for one person to love another and yet never have good will toward the beloved" (pp. 20, 29). On the universality of romantic love (defined as extreme idealization along with strong sexual impulses), see Paul C. Rosenblatt, "Marital Residence and the Functions of Romantic Love," *Ethnology* 6 (1967): 471–80.

34. Immanuel Kant, *Fundamental Principles of the Metaphysics of Morals*, trans. Thomas K. Abbott (Indianapolis: Bobbs-Merrill, 1949), pp. 18, 42 and n.11, 71; *Lectures on Ethics*, trans. Louis Infield (New York: Harper & Row, 1963), pp. 157, 166–67, 169.

35. Benedictus de Spinoza, *The Ethics,* trans. George Eliot (New York: Joseph Simon, 1981), pp. 118 (3.11), 130 (3.30); Henry E. Allison, *Benedict de Spinoza: An Introduction* (New Haven: Yale University Press, 1987), p. 138.

36. Jean-Paul Sartre, *Being and Nothingness: An Essay on Phenomenological Ontology,* trans. Hazel E. Barnes (New York: Philosophical Library, 1956), pp. xli, 311, 326, 339, 351. For a particularly acute commentary, see Roger Scruton, *Sexual Desire: A Moral Philosophy of the Erotic* (New York: The Free Press/Macmillan, 1986), passim. See also Michael Theunissen, *The Other: Studies in the Social Ontology of Husserl, Heidegger, Sartre, and Buber,* trans. Christopher Macann (Cambridge, Mass.: MIT Press, 1977; rpt. 1984), pp. 199–240. John Updike seems to reflect Sartre's thought in part in his review of Denis de Rougemont's famous book, *Love in the Western World:* "Our fundamental anxiety is that we do not exist—or will cease to exist. Only in being loved do we find external corroboration of the supremely high valuation each ego secretly assigns itself" *(New Yorker,* 24 August 1963), pp. 90–104.

37. See Sartre, *Being and Nothingness* (n. 36 above), pp. 366, 370, 371–97; and Singer *The Nature of Love* (n. 7 above), 3:302–10.

38. See Martin Buber, *I and Thou,* trans. Walter Kaufmann (New York: Charles Scribner's Sons, 1970), p. 80.

39. John Ashbery, *A Wave* (New York: Viking Press, 1984), pp. 84–85. The immediate context of the lines is "an old film about two guys walking across the United States." On matters treated in this chapter there are illuminating comments in: Stanley Cavell, *The Claim of Reason* (Oxford: Clarendon Press, 1979), pp. 395, 399, 435, 439, 444; Martha Nussbaum, review of Scruton, *Sexual Desire, New York Review of Books,* 18 December 1986, p. 52; Galen Strawson, review of same, (London) *Times Literary Supplement,* 28 February 1986; Annette Baier, "Unsafe Loves" (a wise and thoughtful recommendation to take the risks after analyses of the "misamorous" views of Kant, Descartes, and Spinoza and of the naturalistic and biological views of Hume, Darwin, and some Freudians), in *The Philosophy of (Erotic) Love,* ed. Robert C. Solomon and Kathleen M. Higgins (Lawrence: University Press of Kansas, 1991); Thomas Nagel, *Mortal Questions* (Cambridge: Cambridge University Press, 1979), p. 52; the title essay of Beach, *Human Sexuality in Four Perspectives* (n. 18 above); Bernard I. Murstein, "A Theory of Marital Choice and Its Applicability to Marriage Adjustment" in Murstein, ed., *Theories of Attraction and Love* (New York: Springer, 1971), pp. 100–51 (with bibliography); Willard Gaylin and Ethel Person, eds., *Passionate Attachments: Thinking about Love* (New York: The Free Press/Macmillan, 1988), pp. 85–100.

Chapter Two

1. Ralph Linton, "The Natural History of the Family," in *The Family: Its Function and Destiny,* ed. Ruth Nanda Anshen (New York: Harper & Brothers,

1949, rev. ed. 1959), p. 31. For succinct definitions of terms relevant to this chapter (matrilocality, matrilinearity, matriarchy), see Paul Friedrich, *The Meaning of Aphrodite* (Chicago: University of Chicago Press, 1978), p. 212.

2. *Myth, Religion, and Mother Right: Selected Writings of J. J. Bachofen,* trans. Ralph Manheim, pref. George Boas, introd. Joseph Campbell (Princeton, N.J.: Princeton University Press, 1967), pp. 69, 79, 80, 86. For a discussion of *Mutterrecht* that includes Bachofen and Engels, see Pierre Vidal-Naquet, *The Black Hunter: Forms of Thought and Forms of Society in the Greek World,* trans. Andrew Szegedy-Maszak (Baltimore: Johns Hopkins University Press, 1986), pp. 129–34.

3. Karen Horney, "The Distrust Between the Sexes" (1930) in *Feminine Psychology,* ed. Harold Kelman (New York: W. W. Norton, 1967), p. 115.

4. Robert Briffault, *The Mothers: A Study of the Origins of Sentiments and Institutions,* 3 vols. (New York: Macmillan, 1927), 1:v. See also 1: 126, 143, 388; 3: 516.

5. Joan Bamberger, "The Myth of Matriarchy: Why Men Rule in Primitive Society," in *Woman, Culture, and Society,* ed. Michelle Zimbalist Rosaldo and Louise Lamphere (Stanford, Calif.: Stanford University Press, 1974), p. 280. Bamberger adds (ibid.): "To free [the woman], we need to destroy the myth."

6. Marilyn French, *Beyond Power: On Women, Men and Morals* (New York: Summit Books, 1985), p. 27, see also pp. 18, 25–39; Julia Kristeva, *About Chinese Women,* trans. Anita Barrows from *Des Chinoises* (1974) (London: Marion Boyars, 1977), pp. 45–60; Adrienne Rich, *Of Woman Born: Motherhood as Experience and Institution* (New York: W. W. Norton, 1976), pp. 11–14, 72, 93. Rich appeals to Briffault as an authority (p. 127).

7. The surviving structure known by this name, standing in Athens near the Agora, is in fact the temple of Hephaistos. The real Theseum mentioned by Pausanias has not been located.

8. Simon Pembroke, "Women in Charge: The Function of Alternatives in Early Greek Tradition and the Ancient Idea of Matriarchy," *Journal of the Warburg and Courtauld Institutes* 30 (1967): 35. See also Jeannie Carlier-Détienne, "Les Amazones font la guerre et l'amour," *L'Ethnographie* 76 (1980–81): 11–33; Mary R. Lefkowitz, *Women in Greek Myth* (Baltimore: Johns Hopkins University Press, 1986), pp. 19–24; Wm. Blake Tyrrell, *Amazons: A Study in Athenian Mythmaking* (Baltimore: Johns Hopkins University Press, 1984), p. xiii, where he states his belief that there is no way for modern historical methods to determine the existence of Amazons; Guy Cadogan Rothery, *The Amazons in Antiquity and Modern Times* (London: Francis Griffiths, 1910), still useful for literary and mythological references. For Bachofen's belief in the existence of Amazons and in their association with hetaerism (despite degeneration they represent an appreciable rise in human culture), see *Myth, Religion, and Mother Right* (n. 2 above), pp. 104–6. For Bellerophontes (or Bellerophon), see *Il.*6.155. For Penthesilea, see *Aethiopis* fr.1.

9. For Herodotus I have been greatly helped by the translation, introduc-

tion, commentary, and notes of *The History of Herodotus,* trans. David Grene (Chicago: University of Chicago Press, 1987). Grene emphasizes Herodotus's belief in the universal qualities of the human imagination (p. 11).

10. The scholar who has called my attention to Herodotus's use of opposition and polarity does not discuss the opposition of men and women: Henry R. Immerwahr, *Form and Thought in Herodotus* (Cleveland: Western Reserve University Press, 1966), pp. 49–50, 152–53, 182, 199, 307, 309, 321, 324. See also François Hartog, *The Mirror of Herodotus: The Representation of the Other in the Writing of History,* trans. Janet Lloyd (Berkeley: University of California Press, 1988), p. 224. For Diodorus Siculus, see Carlier-Détienne, "Les Amazones" (n. 8 above), p. 25.

11. In the complex story of Candaules, who is deeply in love with his own beautiful wife, the underling, who acts out his master's jealous voyeuristic desires even on his royal spouse, crisply and firmly states the antiquity of monogamy (Herodotus, *Histories* 1.8). Carolyn Dewald, "Women and Culture in Herodotus' *Histories,*" *Women's Studies* 8 (1981): 95–98, points out that Herodotus in general portrays many conflicts and tensions within marriage; still, it is women and not men who usually act, and such women are passionately devoted to family values.

12. G. W. Bowersock, who disagrees with Momigliano that Herodotus's reputation was generally bad in antiquity (he was regarded as both the father of history and a liar), defends his "childlike simplicity" as embodying "a sophisticated view of the world that is both more subtle and more open than the constipated inwardness of Thucydides" ("Herodotus, Alexander, and Rome," *The American Scholar* 58/3 [Summer 1989]: 414). See Dewald, "Women and Culture" (n. 11 above), pp. 93–127, especially pp. 102–3 (on Amazons and Scythians) and 107–12 (on Candaules and others), where the historian shows the ignored woman rising to assert her rights without becoming the wild woman of Greek tragedy.

13. Joseph Campbell, *The Masks of God: Occidental Mythology* (London: Secker & Warburg, 1965), p. 159.

14. For the considerable body of archaeological and other scholarly work on the theme of the Mother Goddess and related matters, see Marilyn French's documentation in *Beyond Power* (n. 6 above), pp. 43–47 and passim. Besides the works mentioned in my text, I have found the following helpful in guiding me in my own speculations: Walter Burkert, *Structure and History in Greek Mythology* (Berkeley: University of California Press, 1979), pp. 102–5; Burkert, *Greek Religion: Archaic and Classical,* trans. John Ráffan (Cambridge, Mass.: Harvard University Press, 1985), p. 46; Marija Gimbutas, *The Goddesses and Gods of Old Europe 6500 to 3500 B.C: Myths and Cultic Images* (Berkeley: University of California Press, 1982), pp. 152–69, 176, 195–200, 237–38; Jacquetta Hawkes, *The First Great Civilizations: Life in Mesopotamia, the Indus Valley, and Egypt* (New York: Alfred A. Knopf, 1973); E[dwin] O[liver] James, *Prehistoric Religion: A Study in Prehistoric Archaeology* (London: Thames & Hudson,

1957), chap. 6 ("The Mystery of Birth") and chap. 7 ("Fertility and the Food Supply"); James's general survey entering Christian times, *The Cult of the Mother-Goddess: An Archaeological and Documentary Study* (New York: Frederick A. Praeger, 1959), pp. 13, 22, 161, 164. Also André Leroi-Gourhan, *Les Religions de la Préhistoire,* 3rd ed. (Paris: Presses Universitaires de France, 1976), which studies sources under the following heads: "Le culte des ossements," "Pratiques mortueuses," "Objets et rites," "L'art religieux," and "La religion au Paléolithique." In the end, after examining the great cave paintings, Leroi-Gourhan concludes that a very important ingredient of the sophistication attained between 15,000 and 12,000 B.C. by the high Paleolithic was "un principe général de complémentarité de valeur sexuelle différente" (p. 155). Gertrude Rachel Levy, *The Gate of Horn: A Study of the Religious Conceptions of the Stone Age, and Their Influence upon European Thought* (London: Faber & Faber, 1948), surveys the cult of the Great Mother from Sumerian times to the mystery cults of Attic Greece and concludes that this goddess, once an earth divinity, came, through her avatars, to serve the unity of the most civilized cities (Plato in the *Laws* calls her "our own Kore that is in the midst of us," quoted on p. 275). A popularly oriented work, which includes a good bibliography, is Merlin Stone, *When God Was a Woman* (San Diego: Harcourt & Brace Jovanovich, 1976), pp. 246–57. Also a lavishly illustrated, widely learned, and passionately written work by Monica Sjöö and Barbara Mor, *The Great Cosmic Mother: Rediscovering the Religion of the Earth* (San Francisco: Harper & Row, 1987), its considerable bibliography appearing on pp. 477–89. The passion arises no doubt from the authors' commitment to the emergent Goddess religion in feminist thought; for these writers there is no doubt of the literal existence of the Amazons, who are treated as heroes in the lost struggle to maintain matriarchy (see p. 247).

Mary Lefkowitz has argued that the presence of female statues need not indicate the existence of a cult of a universal Mother Goddess any more than the abundance of icons of the Virgin Mary reveal "her superior authority in Christian cult." But that is precisely what Mary icons do reveal, though of course her authority, while certainly superior, was not supreme. It would also seem to reveal a continuing female or maternal orientation in the Mediterranean world, despite the undisputed domination of a male authority figure. Mary Lefkowitz, "Feminist Myths and Greek Mythology," (London) *Times Literary Supplement,* 22–28 July 1988.

15. Maarten J. Vermaseren, *Cybele and Attis,* trans. A. M. H. Lemmers (London: Thames & Hudson, 1977), pp. 7–19, 24, 32–35.

16. James Mellaart discovered this terracotta figure among many other things in his notable excavations: see his *Catal Hüyük: A Neolithic Town in Anatolia* (New York: McGraw-Hill, 1967), pl. IX, facing p. 156, and fig. 52 (frontal and side-view drawings, facing p. 183. For a discussion, see pp. 180–83. Vermaseren verbally describes the face, which his reproduction does indeed show (*Cybele and Attis* [n. 15 above], pp. 15–16, pl. 5, figs. 4, 5). But Mellaart's reproductions show arms and the face only in the drawings, obviously reconstructions,

doubtless based on heads and arms found elsewhere in the area. He concludes, generally, about the Great Goddess at this ancient place (c. 6500–5700 B.C.) that she was conceived in human form with supernatural powers, that she was symbolized by animals, that she provided game, that she was a goddess of both life and death. Still, the archaeological remains also indicate that the male role in life was indeed known, though many more statues and figures represent the female than the male (pp. 181, 183, 184). All this is relevant to my discussion of the Fall (chapter 6). For other discussions of the terracotta figurine, see Marija Gimbutas, *The Language of the Goddess* (San Francisco: Harper & Row, 1989), pp. 107–8; and Elinor W. Gadon, *The Once and Future Goddess: A Symbol for Our Time* (San Francisco: Harper & Row, 1989), pp. 29, 34. On female goddesses in the Linear B texts, see Emily Vermeule, *Greece in the Bronze Age* (Chicago: University of Chicago Press, 1964), pp. 291–97.

17. Sheila McNally, "The Maenad in Early Greek Art," in *Women in the Ancient World: The Arethusa Papers,* ed. John Peradotto and J. P. Sullivan (Albany: State University of New York Press, 1984), pp. 107–41.

18. On Aphrodite, see Burkert, *Greek Religion* (n. 14 above), pp. 152–56; Paul Friedrich, *The Meaning of Aphrodite* (n. 1 above), pp. 17, 84, 85–86; Geoffrey Grigson, *The Goddess of Love: The Birth, Triumph, Death and Return of Aphrodite* (London: Constable, 1976), a readable popular account with lovely illustrations; Jean Hatzfeld, *Histoire de la Grèce Ancienne* (Paris: Petite Bibliothèque Payot, n.d.), pp. 69–70; Deborah Dickmann Boedeker, *Aphrodite's Entry into Greek Epic* (Leiden: E. J. Brill, 1974), pp. 1, 2, 4–6, 11–17, 22, 24, 29, 47, and especially 54 (her association with desire in marriage); G. S. Kirk, *The Nature of Greek Myths* (London: Penguin, 1974), p. 258; Charles Seltman, *The Twelve Olympians* (London: Pan, 1961), pp. 78–91.

19. For the Homeric hymn, see *Aphrodite: The Homeric Hymn to Aphrodite and the Pervigilium Veneris,* trans. F. L. Lucas (Cambridge: Cambridge University Press, 1948); *Fifth Homeric Hymn: To Aphrodite,* in *The Homeric Hymns,* trans. Apostolos N. Athanassakis (Baltimore: Johns Hopkins University Press, 1976), pp. 47–55 and notes; Peter Smith, *Nursling of Mortality: A Study of the Homeric Hymn to Aphrodite* (Frankfurt a.M.: Verlag Peter D. Lang, 1981).

20. This dualism regarding sexuality has been perdurable, stark, and sometimes mischievous. The last two qualities can be illustrated as late as Baudelaire in one of his *Journaux Intimes:* "Il y a dans tout homme, à toute heure, deux postulations simultanées, l'une vers Dieu, l'autre vers Satan. . . celle de Satan, ou animalité, est une joie de descendre. C'est à cette dernière que doivent être rapportés des amours pour les femmes et les conversations intimes avec les animaux, chiens, chats, etc." (*Mon coeur mis à nu,* sec. 11).

21. On these goddesses, their festivals, and the Homeric hymn, see Burkert, *Greek Religion* (n. 14 above), pp. 159–61; Froma I. Zeitlin, "Cultic Models of the Female: Rites of Dionysus and Demeter," *Arethusa* 15/1–2 (Spring and Fall, 1982): 129–57; Kirk, *The Nature of Greek Myths* (n. 18 above), pp. 230, 249–52; Marylin Arthur, "Politics and Pomegranates: An Interpretation of the Homeric

Hymn to Demeter," *Arethusa* 10 (1977): 7–47; C. Kerenyi, *Eleusis: Archetypal Image of Mother and Daughter,* trans. Ralph Manheim (New York: Pantheon, 1967); *The Homeric Hymn to Demeter,* ed. N. J. Richardson (Oxford: Clarendon Press, 1974). Mary Lefkowitz's brief comments on the goddesses here discussed and her praise of Jane Harrison's understanding of their importance are well taken, as is her warning that there was never a time when male deities were without authority. Review of Sandra J. Peacock on Harrison in *The American Scholar* 58/3 (Summer 1989): 466. For field and furrow as metaphors of the female body, see Page duBois, *Sowing the Body: Psychoanalysis and Ancient Representations of Women* (Chicago: University of Chicago Press, 1988), pp. 39–85.

22. For a commentary on the Triptolemos relief (fig. 5), see George E. Mylonas, *Eleusis and the Eleusinian Mysteries* (Princeton, N.J.: Princeton University Press, 1961), pp. 192–93 (where the differences between the goddesses are emphasized).

23. Hera is discussed by Seltman, *Twelve Olympians* (n. 18 above), pp. 26–31, 38–40; Claude Calamé, *Les Choeurs de jeunes filles en Grèce Archaïque I: Morphologie, fonction religieuse et sociale* (Rome: Edizioni dell'Ateneo & Bizzarri, 1977), pp. 209–10; Hans Licht (pseudonym for Paul Brandt), *Sexual Life in Ancient Greece,* trans J. H. Freese, ed. Lawrence H. Dawson (New York: Barnes & Noble, 1952), pp. 184–85; C. Kerenyi, *Zeus and Hera: Archetypal Image of Father, Husband, and Wife,* trans. Christopher Holme (Princeton, N.J.: Princeton University Press, 1975), passim; Burkert, *Greek Religion* (n. 14 above), pp. 131–35.

24. Kerenyi, *Zeus* (n. 23 above), p. 128.

25. The uxorial Hera must be very closely related to the cult of Zeus Philios (the friendly Zeus), who is credited with the habit of dining out. See Jane E. Harrison's discussion of this cult in *Prolegomena to the Study of Greek Religion* (New York: Arno Press, 1975), pp. 355–58.

26. This relief of Hera between two lions is reproduced as the frontispiece to Vermaseren, *Cybele and Atthis* (n. 15 above). The story recounted earlier in the paragraph may be read in the *Homeric Hymn to Apollo,* trans. Athanassakis (n. 19 above), pp. 24–25.

27. I here rely on Kerenyi, *Zeus* (n. 23 above), pp. 178–79.

28. Marcel Détienne, *The Gardens of Adonis: Spices in Greek Mythology,* trans. Janet Lloyd, introd. J.-P. Vernant (Atlantic Highlands, N.J.: The Humanities Press, 1977).

29. Thorkild Jacobsen, *The Harps That Once—: Sumerian Poetry in Translation* (New Haven: Yale University Press, 1987), p. 93. On Inanna, see Gadon, *Once and Future Goddess* (n. 16 above), pp. 115–42.

30. *The Epic of Gilgamesh: An English Translation with an Introduction,* trans. and introd. N. K. Sandars (Harmondsworth, Eng.: Penguin, 1971). On Mesopotamia and the Hebrew Bible, consult Gerda Lerner, *The Creation of Patriarchy* (New York: Oxford University Press, 1986); on Semitic attitudes and the Sacred Marriage, Judith Ochshorn, *The Female Experience and the Nature of*

the Divine (Bloomington: Indiana University Press, 1981). I wish to thank Thorkild Jacobsen for letting me see proofs of *The Harps That Once* (n. 29 above) and for discussing with me many questions that interested me about the relation of his specialty to my study. Egypt provides interesting parallels and differences: for illustrations and erotic texts, plus bibliography, see Lise Manniche, *Sexual Life in Ancient Egypt* (London: KPI, 1987). For a general account of Mesopotamian and Egyptian myths, see S. H. Hooke, *Middle Eastern Mythology* (Harmondsworth, Eng.: Penguin, 1973), pp. 18–78.

31. The student of ancient love and marriage should not ignore studies of marital contracts and legalities; therefore consult, among many others, Diane Owen Hughes, "From Brideprice to Dowry in Mediterranean Europe," *Journal of Family History* 3/3 (Fall 1978): 262–96; Carole Pateman, *The Sexual Contract* (Oxford: Basil Blackwell, Polity Press, 1968); Louis Gernet, *The Anthropology of Ancient Greece,* trans. John Hamilton and Blaise Nagy (Baltimore: Johns Hopkins University Press, 1981). More broadly relevant is the erotic commerce of gift exchange: Lewis Hyde, *The Gift: Imagination and the Erotic Life of Property* (New York: Random House, 1979).

32. William Gass, "The Polemical Philosopher," *New York Review of Books,* 4 February 1988, p. 40.

33. For the Hesiodic texts I have used *Theogony,* ed. M. L. West (Oxford: Clarendon Press, 1966), ed. Friedrich Solmsen (Oxford: Clarendon Press, 1970), and translations and commentaries by Apostolos N. Athanassakis (Baltimore: Johns Hopkins University Press, 1983); *Works and Days,* trans. and ed. Richmond Lattimore (Ann Arbor: University of Michigan Press, 1959). Some glosses in *The Remains of Hesiod,* trans. Charles Abraham Elton (London, 1809), have been useful. Herbert Marcuse has interesting and revisionary things to say in *Eros and Civilization* (New York: Vintage, 1962); as do Norman O. Brown in his introduction to his translation of Hesiod's *Theogony* (Indianapolis: Bobbs-Merrill, 1953; rpt., 1975), and Hugh Lloyd-Jones, *Females of the Species: Semonides on Woman* (Park Ridge, N.J.: Noyes Press, 1975). See especially Marylin B. Arthur, "Early Greece: The Origins of the Western Attitude Toward Women," *Arethusa* 6 (1973); 7–58, Annie Bonnafé, *Eros et Eris: Mariages divins et mythe de succession chez Hésiode* (Lyon: Presses Universitaires de Lyon, 1985); Michael Gagarin, "The Ambiguity of *Eris* in the *Works and Days,*" in *Cabinet of the Muses . . . ,* ed. Mark Griffith and Donald J. Mastronarde (Atlanta: Scholars Press, 1990), pp. 173–83; Robert Lamberton, *Hesiod* (New Haven: Yale University Press, 1988), pp. 69–71 (on Erōs), pp. 112–15 (on Eris), and pp. 73–78 (on Kronos and Gaia).

34. Herbert Marcuse, *Eros and Civilization* (n. 33 above), p. 146, and Norman O. Brown in his introduction to *Theogony* (n. 33 above), pp. 42–45, include the Hesiodic story itself and its aftermath among the scourges visited upon mankind and have looked to Orpheus, Dionysos, and even Narcissus for humane alternatives to the freedom-denying repressiveness of the dominant Western tradition. More modestly and more historically, Marylin Arthur, "Early Greece" (n.

33 above), pp. 19–22, finds in Hesiod, the prosperous Boeotian farmer-poet of middle-class values, an aggressive competitiveness that absorbs the wife in the works and days of gaining wealth and comfort and that is totally intolerant of sexuality and even attractiveness as being mischievously diversionary from the practical tasks at hand.

35. Jean-Pierre Vernant, "One . . . Two . . . Three: *Erōs,*" in *Before Sexuality: The Construction of Erotic Experience in the Ancient Greek World,* ed. David M. Halperin, John J. Winkler, and Froma Zeitlin (Princeton, N.J.: Princeton University Press, 1990), p. 467. For Euripides, see *Hippolytus,* lines 525–64.

36. Bonnafé, *Eros et Eris* (n. 33 above), pp. 18–22. She sees *philotēs* as the middle term between *erōs* and *eris*. Catherine Osborne comments on this antithesis and others relevant to it in *Rethinking Early Greek Philosophy: Hippolytus of Rome and the Presocratics* (Ithaca, N.Y.: Cornell University Press, 1987), pp. 95, 110–13, 119, 124 and n. 159, 126.

37. John A. Symonds, *Studies of the Greek Poets* (London, 1873, 1893).

38. For Sappho I have consulted Edgar Lobel and Denys Page, *Poetarum Lesbiorum fragmenta* (Oxford: Clarendon Press, 1963), this edition providing the numbers that appear after each quoted fragment; the translation of Willis Barnstone (New York: New York University Press, 1965); the translation, bibliography, and notes of Edwin Marion Cox (London: Williams & Norgate, 1925); the translation and introduction of Guy Davenport (Ann Arbor: University of Michigan Press, 1965). For additional commentary, see Paul Friedrich, *The Meaning of Aphrodite* (n. 1 above), pp. 110–17; and on active lesbianism (or tribadism) and other matters, Hans Licht, *Sexual Life in Ancient Greece* (n. 23 above), pp. 316–39. For the view that *lesbian* applied to Sappho is an anachronistic term, see André Lardinois, "Lesbian Sappho and Sappho of Lesbos," in *From Sappho to De Sade: Moments in the History of Sexuality,* ed. Jan Bremmer (London: Routledge, 1989), pp. 15–35.

39. Anne Carson, *Eros the Bittersweet: An Essay* (Princeton, N.J.: Princeton University Press, 1986), pp. 12–25. I use her translation of fr. 31. The matter of erotic triangulation that Carson discusses and that I amplify presently from the *Phaedrus* to include a relevant and revelatory deity receives stunning illustration in a piece of red-figure pottery by the Peleus Painter, now in Ferrara, celebrating the marriage of Thetis and Peleus. She by the gesture of *anakalupsis* (unveiling) summons Erōs, who has arrived to crown her as she is deeply sunk in thought, while Peleus gazes intensely not toward Thetis but toward Aphrodite, and while Apollo, who receives the glance of neither bride nor groom, looks at Thetis. Such are the divine and semantic signs that can enrich amorous art. See Robert Franklin Sutton, Jr., "The Interaction Between Men and Women Portrayed in Attic Red-Figure Pottery" (Ph.D. dissertation, University of North Carolina, Chapel Hill, 1981), p. 175 and pl. 10.

40. Lawrence Lipking, *Abandoned Women and Poetic Tradition* (Chicago: University of Chicago Press, 1988), p. 61.

41. K. J. Dover, *Greek Homosexuality* (Cambridge, Mass.: Harvard Univer-

sity Press, 1978), pp. 177–79. To the interpretations discussed in the body of my text, I must now add the eye-opening analysis of John J. Winkler, *The Constraints of Desire: The Anthropology of Sex and Gender in Ancient Greece* (New York: Routledge, 1990), pp. 162–87. Winkler, who would find Dover's and my suggestions androcentric (see p. 179), not only accepts fully the lesbianism of the verse but gives the sexual meanings of such Sapphic words as *numphē* (bride or clitoris), *mēlon* (apple or fleshy fruit), *pteruges* (wings or labia), *matēmi* (ferret out), pp. 180–85.

42. Calamé, *Les Choeurs de jeunes filles* (n. 23 above), pp. 27, 403, 454, 456; Denys Page, *Sappho and Alcaeus: An Introduction to the Study of Ancient Lesbian Poetry* (Oxford: Clarendon Press, 1955), especially pp. 7, 16–18 (on the meanings of sparrows, *philotēs,* and *erōs*), pp. 70–73, 119–20 (on the hymeneal poetry); Judith P. Hallett, "Sappho and Her Social Context: Sense and Sensuality," *Signs: Journal of Women in Culture and Society* 4/3 (1979): 447–64, especially 456–60. See Eva Stehle Stigers's rejoinder to Hallett, *Signs* 4/3 (1979): 465–71; and her "Retreat from the Male: Catullus 62 and Sappho's Erotic Flowers," *Ramus* 6 (1977): 83–102, where she discusses Sappho in connection with Catullus and the Homeric Hymn to Demeter. Thomas McEvilley, "Sappho, Fragment Ninety-four," *Phoenix* 25 (1971): 1–11, is useful for suggesting dreams in this poetry of long-term relations. See also Hermann Fränkel, *Early Greek Poetry and Philosophy,* trans. Moses Hadas and James Willis (New York: Harcourt Brace Jovanovich, 1973), pp. 170–86. George Devereux, "The Nature of Sappho's Seizure in Fr 31 LP as Evidence of Her Inversion," *Classical Quarterly* n.s. 20 (1970): 17–31, offers a psychomedical analysis of the poet's symptoms, growing out of the "abnormality" of her love, contrasting it with the "gloriously normal and complete love" revealed in Andromache's lament.

43. French, *Beyond Power* (n. 6 above), pp. 274–78.

44. Arthur W. H. Adkins, " 'Friendship' and 'Self-sufficiency' in Homer and Aristotle," *Classical Quarterly* n.s. 13/1 (May 1963): 30–45; Walter Burkert, *Homo Necans: The Anthropology of Ancient Greek Sacrificial Ritual and Myth,* trans. Peter Bing (Berkeley: University of California Press, 1983), pp. 63 and n. 21, 75; Fränkel, *Early Greek Poetry and Philosophy* (n. 42 above), pp. 82–84; Peter Green, "Sex and Classical Literature," in *The Sexual Dimension in Literature,* ed. Alan Bold (New York: Barnes & Noble, 1982), pp. 19–48.

45. W. Deonna, "Le Groupe des Trois Graces nues et sa descendance," *Revue archéologique* 31 (1930): 274–332; Tyrrell, *Amazons* (n. 8 above), p. 80. In *Iliad* 11:243, *charis* is used of marital joy, which in this context has been denied a dying hero. There are many significant uses in the *Odyssey:* 2.12, 6.18–19, 8.364, for example.

46. James Redfield, "Notes on the Greek Wedding," *Arethusa* 15/1–2 (1982): 181–201; and Redfield, *Nature and Culture in the* Iliad: *The Tragedy of Hector* (Chicago: University of Chicago Press, 1975), pp. 122–25; Arthur, "Early Greece" (n. 33 above), pp. 11–12; and Arthur, "The Divided World of *Iliad* VI," *Women's Studies* 8(1981): 21–46. Winkler concludes his sympathetic discussion

of marital likemindedness in Homer by conceding that Odysseus and Penelope are exceptional ("the best wife for the best husband") and then adding: "But the focus of the poet's demonstration is that the excellence of being a husband and being a wife are in some sense the same" (*Constraints of Desire* [n. 41 above], p. 161). For a revisionary view of Penelope that makes her as divided and duplicitous as Helen and as ambiguously conceived—in both the *Odyssey* and the traditions that ensued—see Mihoko Suzuki, *Metamorphoses of Helen: Authority, Difference, and the Epic* (Ithaca, N.Y.: Cornell University Press, 1989), pp. 74–91.

47. The marital and familial magic of this place had not faded by the third century B.C., and it is invoked to grace an affair that would not precisely reassure a marriage counselor. Apollonius Rhodius in the *Argonautica* is surely aware that the love of the bland Jason and the chthonian Medea, presided over by Love the Destroyer (*oulos Erōs*), is in need of all the traditional beauty and sanction it can get. And so he has them visit Phaeacia, where they are splendidly married and sent on their way, blessed by the attractive husband and wife.

48. Many references to the material bed itself occur in the literature covered in this chapter and the next. It is interesting to note that among Antonia Fraser's abundant and attractive anecdotes of marital love from seventeenth-century life in *The Weaker Vessel* (New York: Random House, 1985), pp. 50–51, the firm Homeric symbol has not been weakened. Mary Evelyn refers in *Mundus muliebris* to the "sturdy oaken" matrimonial bedstead destined to "last one whole Century through," and when Henry Oxinden married the seventeen-year-old Kate Culling, he commissioned, Fraser tells us, the making of a "vast bed . . . , seven foot seven inches in breadth, six foot three inches long, with four posts at the corners one foot round."

49. Linda Lee Clader, *Helen: The Evolution from Divine to Heroic in Greek Epic Tradition* (Leiden: E. J. Brill, 1976), p. 54 and passim; Martin P. Nilsson, *The Mycenaean Origin of Greek Mythology* (Berkeley: University of California Press, 1972), pp. 74–76. See Page duBois, "Sappho and Helen," in *Women in the Ancient World,* ed. Peradotto and Sullivan (n. 17 above), pp. 95–105, for, among other things, a contrast between Homer's and Sappho's Helen. See also Robert Flacelière, *L'Amour en Grèce* (Paris: Hachette, 1960), pp. 26–32; Arthur, "Early Greece" (n. 33 above), p. 34; Mary R. Lefkowitz, "The Heroic Women of Greek Epic," *The American Scholar* 56/4 (Autumn 1987): 503–18. See also Theocritus's *Idyll 18* (on Helen), and Herodotus, *Histories* 2:112–20 (on Helen in Egypt). K. J. Reckford provides a luminous discussion in "Helen in the *Iliad*," *Greek, Roman, and Byzantine Studies* 5/1 (Spring 1964): 5–20, and says that "Helen is distinguished in the *Iliad* not for inspiring passion but for experiencing it," but in the *Odyssey* she is a loyal wife, not unlike Penelope.

50. Anne Amory, "The Reunion of Odysseus and Penelope," in *Essays on the* Odyssey: *Selected Modern Criticism,* ed. Charles H. Taylor, Jr. (Bloomington: Indiana University Press, 1969), pp. 100–21; Helene P. Foley, " 'Reverse Similes' and Sex Roles in the Odyssey," *Arethusa* 11 (1978): 7–26; Jean-Pierre

Vernant, *Mythe et société en Grèce ancienne* (Paris: François Maspero, 1981), pp. 66–69; Norman Austin, *Archery at the Dark of the Moon: Poetic Problems in Homer's* Odyssey (Berkeley: University of California Press, 1975), pp. 181, 188–89, 197, 203–4. Austin regards *homophrosunē* as a crucial term (p. 188) and says: "The ideal of harmony between two persons is the keystone of the poem, the *telos* to which it moves" (p. 181). See also W. K. Lacey, *The Family in Classical Greece* (London: Thames & Hudson, 1968; rpt., Ithaca, N.Y.: Cornell University Press, 1984), pp. 33–44; W. B. Stanford, "Personal Relationships," in Taylor, *Essays on the* Odyssey, pp. 11–35; Paolo Vivante, *Homer* (New Haven: Yale University Press, 1985), who is especially good on the psychological subtleties of the recognition and reunion of Odysseus and Penelope and on the growing depth of her character (pp. 128–33).

Chapter Three

1. A. W. Gomme, "The Position of Women in Athens in the Fifth and Fourth Centuries," *Classical Philology* 20/1 (January 1925): 1–25; Bernard Knox, "Invisible Women" (a review of Eva Keuls: see n. 2), *Atlantic Monthly* 256/1 (July 1985): 96–98; Marylin B. Arthur, "Women and the Family in Ancient Greece," *Yale Review* 71/4 (Summer 1982): 532–47; Philip E. Slater, "The Greek Family in History and Myth," *Arethusa* 7 (1974): 9–44; Michel Foucault, *The Use of Pleasure,* trans. Robert Hurley, vol. 2 of *The History of Sexuality* (New York: Pantheon Books, 1985), pp. 182–83; Roger Just, *Women in Athenian Law and Life* (London: Routledge, 1989); Anne Carson, "Putting Her in Her Place: Woman, Dirt, and Desire," in *Before Sexuality: The Construction of Erotic Experience in the Ancient Greek World,* ed. David M. Halperin, John J. Winkler, and Froma I. Zeitlin (Princeton, N.J.: Princeton University Press, 1990), pp. 160–64 (on the marriage ceremony as purifying, confining, sealing, limiting, and "civilizing" the bride).

I am aware that the Pythagorean table of opposites "places the female element on the side of the boundless, . . . the realm of the uncivilized, whereas the male embodies civilization. This opposition was preserved as long as the civilization of the city endured": Pierre Vidal-Naquet, *The Black Hunter: Forms of Thought and Forms of Society in the Greek World,* trans. Andrew Szegedy-Maszak (Baltimore: Johns Hopkins University Press, 1986), p. 5 and nn. 12, 13. See also pp. 140–41. No one can deny the presence of misogyny. But the very fact of such otherness as women represented, intellectually and socially, provides the writer with great opportunities, and this study emphasizes, not history, but imaginative creation. For a survey of opinions regarding the status of Greek women and an attack on the "seclusion thesis," see Donald C. Richter, "The Position of Women in Classical Athens," *Classical Journal* 67/1 (October–November 1971): 1–8.

2. Catherine Johns, *Sex or Symbol: Erotic Images of Greece and Rome* (Aus-

tin: University of Texas Press, 1982), figs. 81, 82; Eva C. Keuls, *The Reign of the Phallus: Sexual Politics in Ancient Athens* (New York: Harper & Row, 1985), p. 214.

3. Here I stress the revelatory, but I am also committed (though it is difficult to adjudicate the rival claims) to the culturally and imaginatively constitutive, the case for which David M. Halperin states with force in the first two essays of *One Hundred Years of Homosexuality and Other Essays on Greek Love* (New York: Routledge, 1990). For close and revealing analyses of two of the terms important in this chapter and the preceding and following ones, see these studies of *erōs* and *philos* in a poet who wrote between the heroic and the classical age: John M. Lewis, "Eros and the *Polis* in Theognis Book II," and Walter Donlan, "*Pistos Philos Hetairos,*" in *Theognis of Megara: Poetry and the Polis,* ed. Thomas J. Figueira and Gregory Nagy (Baltimore: Johns Hopkins University Press, 1985), pp. 199–222, 223–44.

4. Gareth Morgan, "Euphiletos' House: Lysias I," *Transactions of the American Philological Association* 112 (1982): 115–23; Bertha C. Rider, *The Greek House: Its History and Development from the Neolithic Period to the Hellenistic Age* (Cambridge: Cambridge University Press, 1916); David M. Robinson and J. Walter Graham, *Excavations at Olynthus,* part 8: *The Hellenistic House* (Baltimore: Johns Hopkins University Press, 1938), pp. 157–69, 175–85; Simon Goldhill, *Language, Sexuality and Narrative: the* Oresteia (Cambridge: Cambridge University Press, 1984), pp. 184–89 (on the *nostos* of Odysseus and its implications for the *oikos*); Marylin Arthur, " 'Liberated' Women: The Classical Era," in Renate Bridenthal and Claudia Koonz, eds., *Becoming Visible: Women in European History* (Boston: Houghton Mifflin, 1977), pp. 60–89 (on adultery and the *oikos*); Fustel de Coulanges, *The Ancient City: A Study of the Religion, Laws, and Institutions of Greece and Rome,* trans. Willard Small, 10th ed. (Boston, 1873), pp. 29–31, 53–75, 111, 115, 123, 128; Martin P. Nilsson, "Wedding Rites in Ancient Greece" and "Roman and Greek Domestic Cult," *Opuscula Selecta* 3 (1960): 243–50, 271–85; Robert Flacelière, *L'Amour en Grèce* (Paris: Hachette, 1960), pp. 113–16; Foucault, *The Use of Pleasure* (n. 1 above), pp. 70–71.

Oikos and its derivatives are rich in meaning and range: *oikeios,* for example, refers to things in or of the house but also means "proper, fitting, suitable, private, personal, conformable to." The adverb, *oikeiōs,* means all this and also (later, in Menander and Theocritus) "affectionately" and "dutifully," showing the important cultural change that we shall comment on later (see chapters 4 and 5). *Oikeiotēs* takes on the meaning "friendship" as well as "kindred, intimacy." One of the commonest terms for "to marry" incorporates the word: *sunoikein.*

5. Xenophon, *Oeconomicus* 7.1–43. See Foucault, *The Use of Pleasure* (n. 1 above), pp. 152–65.

6. *In Neaeram,* oration 59, in *Demosthenes,* 7 vols., trans. A. T. Murray (Cambridge, Mass.: "Loeb Classical Library," Harvard University Press, 1939, 1956), 6:445–47; W. K. Lacey, *The Family in Classical Greece* (London: Thames

& Hudson, 1968; rpt. Ithaca, N.Y.: Cornell University Press, 1984), pp. 110–13. I am grateful to Lacey for the insight that the qualities and functions are not necessarily separated but may all exist in the wife. See also Keuls, *Reign of the Phallus* (n. 2 above), pp. 156–58.

7. A. W. Price, *Love and Friendship in Plato and Aristotle* (Oxford: Clarendon Press, 1989), 1–14, concluding that the topic of the *Lysis* is *philia;* Hans Georg Gadamer, *Dialogue and Dialectic: Eight Hermeneutical Studies on Plato,* trans. P. Christopher Smith (New Haven: Yale University Press, 1980), pp. 1–20, on which I have relied heavily; David K. Glidden, "The *Lysis* on Loving One's Own," *Classical Quarterly* 31/1 (1981): 39–59.

8. On Cecrops and/or serpents, see *Oxford Classical Dictionary,* s.v.; H. J. Rose, *A Handbook of Greek Mythology* (New York: E. P. Dutton, 1959), pp. 281–82 and nn. 24, 25; Philip E. Slater, *The Glory of Hera* (Boston: Beacon Press, 1968), pp. 80–108; Carson, "Putting Her in Her Place" (n. 1 above), p. 161; Vidal-Naquet, *The Black Hunter* (n. 1 above), pp. 216–17.

9. I have relied on the text, introduction, notes, and glossary of *The Oresteia,* trans. Robert Fagles, ed. W. B. Stanford (New York: Bantam Books, 1977 [cited by page number]), and Eduard Fränkel's edition (3 vols., Oxford: Clarendon Press, 1952, 1962 [Greek text cited by line number]). See also Froma I. Zeitlin, "The Dynamics of Misogyny: Myth and Myth-Making in the *Oresteia,*" in *Women in the Ancient World: the Arethusa Papers,* ed. John Peradotto and J. P. Sullivan (Albany: State University of New York Press, 1984), pp. 159–91. For a luminous overview of the trilogy, see John Herington, *Aeschylus* (New Haven: Yale University Press, 1986), pp. 111–56, and especially pp. 115–16 (for the unseen but powerful presence of Helen) and pp. 148–49 (on Apollo as a representative of liberal avant-garde Athenian views). D. J. Conacher provides a balanced scholarly account, which analyzes important previous opinion and the meanings of central words, in *Aeschylus' Oresteia: A Literary Commentary* (Toronto: University of Toronto Press, 1987), especially appendix 3 (on the "male-female conflict").

10. *Iphigenia in Aulis,* trans. Charles R. Walker (Chicago: University of Chicago Press, 1958). It is clear from the play that Aphrodite's gifts must be received with *sōphrosunē,* that Erōs is regarded ambiguously (he shoots two kinds of arrows, only one of which brings happiness), that the Graces are associated with desire, that love in quietness is the desideratum, that there are close father-daughter ties, and that the family is suffused with *philia,* making its rupture deeply pathetic (see pp. 241, 242, 246, and lines 544, 549, 585–86, 652).

11. Aristophanes, *The Clouds,* trans. William Arrowsmith (Ann Arbor: University of Michigan Press, 1962), pp. 13–14.

12. K. J. Dover, "Classical Greek Attitudes to Sexual Behavior," in *Women in the Ancient World,* ed. Peradotto and Sullivan (n. 9 above), p. 155. See also Dover, *Aristophanic Comedy* (Berkeley: University of California Press, 1972), pp. 42–43, 150–59.

13. But see Arthur, "Women and the Family" (n. 1 above). I have relied on the following edition of Aristophanes: *Lysistrata, Thesmophoriazusae,* and *Eccle-*

siazusae, trans. Benjamin B. Rogers (Cambridge, Mass.: "Loeb Classical Library," Harvard University Press, 1979). See also Dover, *Aristophanic Comedy* (n. 12 above), passim; Froma Zeitlin, "Travesties of Gender and Genre in Aristophanes' *Thesmophoriazusae,*" in *Reflections of Women in Antiquity,* ed. Helene P. Foley (London: Gordon & Breach Science Publishers, 1981), pp. 169–217; and the edition and commentary of Jeffrey Henderson, *Aristophanes Lysistrata* (Oxford: Clarendon Press, 1987), among whose many virtues are analyses of sexual puns and of references to the sexual organs.

14. Gregory Vlastos, *Platonic Studies* (Princeton, N.J.: Princeton University Press, 1981), p. 4, n. 4; David M. Halperin, "Platonic *Erōs* and What Men Call Love," *Ancient Philosophy* 5 (1985): 162. For Plato on the emotions and desires present in procreative sex, see *Timaeus* 91 A–D, where *epithumia* is used for the lust generated in the self-willed male organs disobedient to reason (*logos*)—a striking anticipation of Augustine's view of man's postlapsarian penile condition (see chapter 7). When *epithumia* and *erōs* unite, then conception takes place. For additional important commentary on the *Symposium,* see Martha Nussbaum, "The Speech of Alcibiades: A Reading of Plato's *Symposium,*" *Philosophy and Literature* 3 (1979): 131–72; and chap. 6 of her *Fragility of Goodness: Luck and Ethics in Greek Tragedy and Philosophy* (Cambridge: Cambridge University Press, 1986); Price, *Love and Friendship in Plato and Aristotle* (n. 7 above), pp. 15–54, 207–14; Halperin, "Why Is Diotima a Woman?" in *One Hundred Years of Homosexuality* (n. 3 above), chap. 6. Plato's Socrates gives little or no cognitive value to marriage, but there was allegedly a pre-Platonic Socratic dialogue by Aeschines of Sphettus, treating marriage as a vehicle for attaining virtue. See Barbara Ehlers, *Eine vorplatonische Deutung der Sokratischen Eros: Der Dialog Aspasia des Sokratikers Aischines* (Munich: C. H. Beck'sche, 1966), pp. 85–90. For luminous discussions of Diotima and Alcibiades, see Stanley Rosen, *Plato's* Symposium, 2nd ed. (New Haven: Yale University Press, 1988).

15. On the *Phaedrus,* see David Halperin, "Plato and Erotic Reciprocity," *Classical Antiquity* 5 (1986): 60–80, where he separates Plato's views from those of his own culture; Nussbaum, *Fragility* (n. 14 above), chap. 7; Price, *Love and Friendship* (n. 7 above), pp. 55–102, 215–22; Anne Lebeck, "The Central Myth of Plato's *Phaedrus,*" in *Greek, Roman, Byzantine Studies* 13 (1972): 267–90.

16. Halperin, "Platonic *Erōs*" (n. 14 above), p. 182.

17. It will be apparent to many readers how much my qualifications of the values in Platonic love owe to Gregory Vlastos and Martha Nussbaum (see n. 14 above).

18. Harold Beaver, "Homosexual Signs," *Critical Inquiry* 8/1 (Autumn 1981): 99–119, especially p. 116.

19. I have been helped by Michael Gagarin, "Socrates' *Hybris* and Alcibiades' Failure," *Phoenix* 31/1 (1977): 22–37; and through many years by works too well known to document: those by J. N. Findley, Paul Friedländer, J. C. B. Gosling, G. M. A. Grube, Thomas Gould, Ronald B. Levinson, C. W. Taylor, and others.

20. See Robert Franklin Sutton, Jr., "The Interaction Between Men and

Women Portrayed in Attic Red-Figure Pottery" (Ph.D. dissertation, University of North Carolina, Chapel Hill, 1981), pp. 185-89, 219-22.

21. *Bacchae of Euripides,* trans. Donald Sutherland (Lincoln: University of Nebraska Press, 1972); Charles Segal, *Dionysiac Poetics and Euripides'* Bacchae (Princeton, N.J.: Princeton University Press, 1982); Thomas G. Rosenmeyer, "Tragedy and Religion in the *Bacchae,*" in *Euripides: A Collection of Critical Essays,* ed. Erich Segal (Englewood Cliffs, N.J.: Prentice-Hall, 1968), pp. 169-70. On Dionysos see Walter Burkert, *Homo Necans: The Anthropology of Ancient Greek Sacrificial Ritual and Myth,* trans. Peter Bing (Berkeley: University of California Press, 1983), 184-85 and notes; G. S. Kirk, *The Nature of Greek Myths* (Harmondsworth, Eng.: Penguin Books, 1974), p. 230; Jane E. Harrison, *Themis: A Study of the Social Origins of Greek Religion* (Cambridge: Cambridge University Press, 1912).

22. Euripides, *Hippolytos,* ed. W. S. Barrett (Oxford: Clarendon Press, 1964); *Hippolytus,* trans. David Grene (Chicago: University of Chicago Press, 1942); Froma I. Zeitlin, "The Power of Aphrodite: Eros and the Boundaries of the Self in the *Hippolytus,*" in *Directions in Euripidean Criticism,* ed. Peter Burian (Durham, N.C.: Duke University Press, 1985), pp. 52-111; Bernard M. W. Knox, "The *Hippolytus* of Euripides" in *Euripides: A Collection of Critical Essays,* ed. Segal (n. 21 above), pp. 90-114; Helen North, *Sophrosyne: Self-Knowledge and Self-Restraint in Greek Literature* (Ithaca, N.Y.: Cornell University Press, 1966).

23. Sophocles, *The Women of Trachis,* trans. C. K. Williams and Gregory W. Dickerson (New York: Oxford University Press, 1978). On Herakles, see Philip E. Slater, *The Glory of Hera* (Boston: Beacon Press, 1968), pp. 337-79. On deaths of women, see Eva Cantarella, "Dangling Virgins: Myth, Ritual, and the Place of Women in Ancient Greece," in *The Female Body in Western Culture,* ed. Susan R. Suleiman (Cambridge, Mass.: Harvard University Press, 1986), pp. 49-67; Nicole Loraux, *Tragic Ways of Killing a Woman,* trans. Anthony Forster (Cambridge, Mass.: Harvard University Press, 1987); and Bernard Knox's review of Loraux, with its corrective examples, in *New York Review of Books,* 28 April 1988, pp. 13-14.

24. On *charis* in general, see Claude Moussy, *Gratia et sa famille* (Paris: Presses Universitaires de France, 1966); Gerhard Friedrich, ed., *Theological Dictionary of the New Testament,* vol. 9 (Grand Rapids, Mich.: Wm. B. Eerdmans, 1974); Raul Miguel Rosado Fernandes, *O Tema da Graças na poesia clássico* (Lisbon, 1962); Walter Burkert, *Greek Religion: Archaic and Classical,* trans. John Ráffan (Oxford: Basil Blackwell, 1985), pp. 189, 216-17, 273.

25. *Charizaesthai* (to oblige by granting of sexual favors) is used of both homosexual and heterosexual love: K. J. Dover, *Greek Homosexuality* (Cambridge, Mass.: Harvard University Press, 1978), p. 45 (in Plato's *Symposium*); Foucault, *The Use of Pleasure* (n. 1 above), pp. 223-24 (to indicate the boy complied by granting his sexual favors); Jeffrey Henderson, *The Maculate Muse: Obscene Language in Attic Comedy* (New Haven: Yale University Press, 1975), p. 160

(*charis* being a high-toned expression, but often used in comedy for sexual charms or favors); Mark Golden, "Slavery and Homosexuality at Athens," *Phoenix* 38/4 (1984): 316–17. *Charis* is used frequently in Homer, sometimes to refer to one dear to the heart of another (*kecharismene, Od.* 4.71; *kecharisto,* 6.23). Socrates reformulates *charis* in Plato's *Euthyphro;* see Stephen Fineberg, "Plato's *Euthyphro* and the Myth of Proteus," *Transactions of the American Philological Association* 12 (1982): 65–70. A lively debate in Euripides's *Hecuba* pivots on *charis:* D. J. Conacher, "Euripides' *Hecuba,*" *American Journal of Philology* 82/1 (1961): 1–26. James H. Oliver also discusses the word in connection with civic personality and virtue: *Demokratia, the Gods, and the Free World* (Baltimore: Johns Hopkins University Press, 1960), pp. 96, 103–16.

26. *Odes of Pindar,* trans. Richmond Lattimore (Chicago: University of Chicago Press, 1947, 1959); *Works of Pindar,* ed. and trans. Lewis Richard Farnell (London: Macmillan, 1930). On the Graces in general and *Olympian* 14 in particular, see the illuminating comments of D. S. Carne-Ross, *Pindar* (New Haven: Yale University Press, 1985), pp. 59–66.

The most relevant odes are: *Ol.* 1, 2, 4, 7, 8, 9, 13; *Pyth.* 2, 3, 9 (where *peithō* is also important), 12; *Nem.* 8; *Isth.* 4, 8. See Carne-Ross, *Pindar,* pp. 91–101, on *Pyth.* 9, where the poet brings together sport, statecraft, *hieros gamos,* and human marriage. On the important association in this ode of shyness and sexuality (so attractive to Western culture both inside and outside marriage), see Leonard Woodbury, "Cyrene and the *Teleuta* of Marriage in Pindar's Ninth Pythian Ode," *Transactions of the American Philological Association* 112 (1982): 245–58.

27. Euripides in the *Ion* (646–47) brings the words *charis* and *chairein* together.

28. Numbers 27:4, 17; C. D. Yonge, ed., *Works of Philo Judaeus,* vol. 3 (London, 1855), pp. 123–25; Harry Austryn Wolfson, *Philo,* 2 vols. (Cambridge, Mass.: Harvard University Press, 1948), 2:218–19.

29. See *Il.* 18.382. But at *Od.* 8.266, Hephaistos's wife is Aphrodite. Victor Matthews pointed out to me in 1991 that "these two goddesses are often linked and it may not be too strange to find craftsmanship married to Grace or Beauty."

30. Marcel Détienne, *The Gardens of Adonis: Spices in Greek Mythology,* trans. Janet Lloyd, introd. J.-P. Vernant (Atlantic Highlands, N.J.: The Humanities Press, 1977).

31. James Redfield, "Notes on the Greek Wedding," *Arethusa* 15/1–2 (1982): 181–201, especially p. 196; and his discussion in *Nature and Culture in the* Iliad: *The Tragedy of Hector* (Chicago: University of Chicago Press, 1975), pp. 161–63.

32. *Laws* IV. 721B–C, trans. R. G. Bury, in *Plato,* 12 vols. (Cambridge, Mass.: "Loeb Classical Library," Harvard University Press, 1984), 10:311, 313.

33. Arthur W. H. Adkins, "'Friendship' and 'Self-sufficiency' in Homer and Aristotle," *Classical Quarterly* n.s. 13/1 (May 1963): 31–32, 34.

34. Vlastos, *Platonic Studies* (n. 14 above), p. 22 and n. 65; K. J. Dover,

Greek Popular Morality in the Time of Plato and Aristotle (Berkeley: University of California Press, 1974), p. 212.

35. Aristotle's essays on friendship make up Books 8 and 9 of the *Nicomachean Ethics* and Book 7 of the *Eudemian.*

36. "The neglect of friendship as a serious subject of inquiry in modern thought is itself a strange and wondrous thing; after millennia during which it was one of the major philosophical topics, the subject of thousands of books and tens of thousands of essays, it has now dwindled to the point that our encyclopedias do not even mention it, and our publishing lists reveal only a forlorn sociological study here, a study of male or homosexual friendship there" (Wayne Booth, " 'The Way I Loved George Eliot': Friendship with Books as a Neglected Critical Metaphor," *Kenyon Review* n.s. 2/2 [Spring 1980]: 6).

37. For commentary, see Nussbaum, *Fragility* (n. 14 above), pp. 354–71; Price, *Love* (n. 7 above), pp. 103–61, 172 (a discussion of Aristotle's enthusiasm for the married state and of his belief that love of man and wife constituted a friendship of virtue); John M. Cooper, "Aristotle on Friendship," in *Essays on Aristotle's Ethics,* ed. Amélie O. Rorty (Berkeley: University of California Press, 1980), pp. 301–40; Julia Annas, "Plato and Aristotle on Friendship and Altruism," *Mind* 86 (1977): 532–54; Seth L. Schein, *"Philia* in Euripides' *Medea,"* in *Cabinet of the Muses . . . ,* ed. Mark Griffith and Donald J. Mastronarde (Atlanta: Scholars Press, 1990), pp. 57–73.

38. Sophocles, *Electra,* trans. Francis Fergusson (1938), in *Greek Plays,* ed. Dudley Fitts (New York: Dial Press, 1947/1955), lines 1126, 1138, 1163; *Antigone,* trans. Robert Whitelaw, in *Ten Greek Plays,* trans. Gilbert Murray and others (New York: Oxford University Press, 1929), lines 73 and 81 (for *philos* words) and 781–801, where the Chorus invokes love as Erōs and Aphrodite. See Ivan M. Linforth, "Antigone and Creon," *University of California Publications in Classical Philology* 15/5 (1961): 183–259; Matthew S. Santirocco, "Justice in Sophocles' *Antigone,"* *Philosophy and Literature* 4/2 (Fall 1980): 180–98, especially pp. 190–93.

39. Euripides, *Andromache,* trans. Arthur S. Way, in *Euripides,* 4 vols. (Cambridge, Mass.: "Loeb Classical Library," Harvard University Press, 1965/1978), 2:416–513; and the edition of P. T. Stevens (Oxford: Clarendon Press, 1971). In the end Peleus is deified and deserves to be: he hails the *charis* that has sprung from his marital couch (line 1274). For commentary on Euripidean heroines and related matters, see Mary R. Lefkowitz, *Heroines and Hysterics* (New York: St. Martin's Press, 1981). For a discussion that stresses what Andromache stood for and Thetis supports (*philia* and *gamos*), see Herbert Golden, "The Mute Andromache," *Transactions of the American Philological Association* 113 (1983): 123–33.

40. For *Alcestis,* I have used the translation of Arthur Way in *Euripides,* vol. 4, "Loeb Classical Library" (1964; see n. 39 above); and that of William Arrowsmith (London: Oxford University Press, 1974); and the edition of A. M. Dale, who sees this play as the forerunner of Menander (Oxford: Clarendon

Press, 1954), p. xxiv and passim. Philippe Ariès, who praises and invokes this play as exemplary, stresses the importance of complementarity in marital unions and also of mutual confidence, attachment, and identification: "L'amour dans le mariage," *Communications* 35 (1982): 116–22. See also Philip Vellacott, *Ironic Drama: A Study of Euripides' Method and Meaning* (Cambridge: Cambridge University Press, 1975); and Anne Pippin Burnett, "The Virtues of Admetus" in *Euripides: A Collection of Critical Essays,* ed. Segal (n. 21 above), pp. 51–69. The following lines use variants of *philos* for the central relationship: 42, 60, 279, 331, 369, 474, 712, 722, 1037, 1054, 1103, 1106.

41. For *Helen* I have used the translation and edition of James Michie and Colin Leach in the series, *The Greek Tragedy in New Translations,* ed. William Arrowsmith (New York: Oxford University Press, 1981). For a learned, philosophical, and thorough interpretation of *Helen* that brilliantly stresses the often-neglected romance elements and that associates *charis* primarily with the heroine (pp. 601–4), see Charles Segal, "The Two Worlds of Euripides' *Helen,*" *Transactions and Proceedings of the American Philological Association* 102 (1971): 553–614.

Chapter Four

1. "Felices ter et amplius, / quod inrupta tenet copula nec malis / divulsus querimoniis, / suprema citius solvet amor die" (*Odes and Epodes of Horace,* trans. Joseph P. Clancy [Chicago: University of Chicago Press, 1960], p. 41). A striking contrast to the marital idealism of this ode and of other Horatian utterances to be quoted later appears in his *Sermones* 1.2. There he mocks the conventions of Roman love poetry and concludes that quick sex (either a girl or boy will do) is preferable to passion. See Barry Baldwin, "Horace on Sex," *American Journal of Philology* 91/9 (October 1970): 460–65.

2. Paul Veyne, "La Famille et l'amour sous le haut-empire romain," *Annales* 33 (1978): 35. Peter Garnsey and Richard Saller dispute Veyne's view that the early senatorial order invented and disseminated a proto-Christian view of affectionate marriage, but they concede that literary and epigraphic evidence from Rome gives no support to the idea of several nuclear families living together dominated by an elderly patriarch, and they stress the great importance accorded to relations within the single nuclear family (*The Roman Empire: Economy, Society and Culture* [Berkeley: University of California Press, 1987], pp. 129, 133).

3. Larissa Bonfante, "Etruscan Couples and Their Aristocratic Society," *Women's Studies* 8 (1981): 157–87; and Larissa Bonfante Warren, "The Women of Etruria," in *Women in the Ancient World: The Arethusa Papers,* ed. John Peradotto and J. P. Sullivan (Albany: State University of New York Press, 1984), pp. 229–39.

4. Anne E. Hanson, "The Medical Writers' Woman," in *Before Sexuality:*

The Construction of Erotic Experience in the Ancient Greek World, ed. David M. Halperin, John J. Winkler, and Froma I. Zeitlin (Princeton, N.J.: Princeton University Press, 1990), pp. 309–37 (full notes and bibliography; stresses need to consult gynecologies rather than philosophies and moral essays on sexual practices); E. D. Phillips, *Aspects of Greek Medicine* (Philadelphia: Charles Press, 1987)., s.v. *semen, sense organs, sex.*

5. J. M. Rist, *Stoic Philosophy* (Cambridge: Cambridge University Press, 1969), pp. 35, 61. Rist believes that for the Stoics virtue was not a mean dictated by reason but was, in relation to excellence, an extreme, a point of view that would make a place for sexuality and love in some Stoic thought (p. 19). Daniel Babut, "Les Stoïciens et l'amour," *Revue des études grecques* 76 (1963): 53–63, believes that in Stoic thought the family is the basis of the state but amorous passion is foreign to it. Therefore a quest for boys, which can lead to wisdom through friendship, is not inconsistent with obligations toward society, which marriage and procreation fulfill (pp. 62–63). If anything is clear to us today about the Stoics and related schools, it is that they were far from being univocal and far from later and still current stereotypes of their position on sex. See Marcia L. Colish, *The Stoic Tradition from Antiquity to the Early Middle Ages,* 2 vols. (Leiden: E. J. Brill, 1985). They asserted equality between the sexes (1:36–38) and were notable for sexual latitudinarianism. They censured adultery but permitted prostitution, incest, masturbation, homosexuality—a liberal position not shared by Musonius Rufus, for whom the only virtuous sex was for procreation (1:39). Marriage was not, for the Stoics, an impediment to the virtuous life (1:41).

6. Antipater is quoted from Stobaeus by E. Vernon Arnold, *Roman Stoicism* (Cambridge: Cambridge University Press, 1911), p. 319. See Stobaeus, *Florilegium* 67:25.

7. In the following discussion of Lucretia I rely almost entirely on Ian Donaldson, *The Rapes of Lucretia: A Myth and Its Transformations* (Oxford: Clarendon Press, 1982). For help in understanding Roman laws and customs, I am indebted to Judith P. Hallett, *Fathers and Daughters in Roman Society: Women and the Elite Family* (Princeton, N.J.: Princeton University Press, 1984).

8. For a full analysis of Apuleius's tale and its influence on sentimental and romantic cultures, see my "Eros and Psyche: Some Versions of Romantic Love and Delicacy," in *Eros and Vision: The Restoration to Romanticism* (Evanston, Ill.: Northwestern University Press, 1989), pp. 71–92. Erich Neumann, *Amor and Psyche,* trans. Ralph Manheim (New York: Pantheon Books, 1956), gives a Jungian interpretation of Psyche as the eternal feminine, born because man's relations to Aphrodite had radically changed (p. 59). For a different view that stresses the real and actual pattern provided by the myth for resolving tensions through marriage, see Phyllis B. Katz, "The Myth of Psyche: A Definition of the Nature of the Feminine?" *Arethusa* 9/1 (1976): 111–18. For general studies of Erōs in late antiquity, see John M. Rist, *Eros and Psyche: Studies in Plato,*

Plotinus, and Origen (Toronto: University of Toronto Press, 1964); and T. B. L. Webster, *Art and Literature in Fourth Century Athens* (London: Athlone Press, 1956).

9. Rist, *Eros and Psyche* (n. 8 above), p. 100.

10. I have used the Loeb edition of Plutarch, 11 vols. (Cambridge, Mass.: "Loeb Classical Library," Harvard University Press). The *Coniugalia praecepta* and *Lacaenarum apophthegmata* are contained in the *Moralia,* trans. Frank Cole Babbitt, vols. 2 (1928) and 3 (1931); the Lives of Pericles and Phocion, trans. Bernadotte Perrin, appear in vols. 3 (1916) and 8 (1919). For the *Amatorius* (or *Erōticos*), also a part of the *Moralia,* see vol. 9, trans. Edwin L. Minar, Jr., F. H. Sandbach, and W. C. Helmbold (1961). See also the French edition of Robert Flacelière (Paris: Société d'Edition Les Belles Lettres, 1952); and the edition of C. Hubert (Leipzig: B. G. Teubner, 1938). For commentary, see Lisette Goessler, *Plutarchs Gedanken über die Ehe* (Zurich: Buchdruckerei Berichthaus, 1962). I must disagree with John Boswell's conclusion that "it is rather difficult to tell where Plutarch's sympathies lie" as between the gay and nongay speakers: *Christianity, Social Tolerance, and Homosexuality* (Chicago: University of Chicago Press, 1980), p. 126, n. 17. The whole dynamic of the dialogue strikes me as favoring heterosexual, especially married, love, as my discussion is intended to show.

11. The clause comes from an eccentric but learned nineteenth-century work by E. F. M. Benecke, *Antimachus of Colophon and the Position of Women in Greek Poetry* (London, 1896; rpt., Groningen: Bouma's Boekhuis, 1970), p. 2, a work which argues that Antimachus was a younger contemporary of Plato who turned the tide from misogyny to a modern sentimental view of intersexual love, especially in his lost *Lyde*. Great claims have also been made for later antiquity ("one of the great turning-points in the history of civilization"): see Philippe Ariès, "The Indissoluble Marriage," in *Western Sexuality: Practice and Precept in Past and Present Times,* ed. Philippe Ariès and André Béjin, trans. Anthony Forster (Oxford: Basil Blackwell, 1985), p. 141. Sarah Pomeroy records, soberly and using much archaeological evidence, a major shift in Hellenistic Egypt in the attitude toward Aphrodite, who now presides over lawful marital sexuality (*Women in Hellenistic Egypt from Alexander to Cleopatra* [New York: Schocken Books, 1984], pp. 31–33).

12. For the *Idylls* of Theocritus, I have used the Loeb edition, trans. J. M. Edmond (Cambridge, Mass.: "Loeb Classical Library," Harvard University Press, 1960); the edition and translation of A. S. F. Gow, 2 vols. (Cambridge: Cambridge University Press, 1950, 1973); K. J. Dover, ed., *Theocritus: Select Poems* (London: Macmillan, 1971); and the translation by Daryl Hine (New York: Atheneum, 1982). For commentary, see these editions and also Charles Segal, *Poetry and Myth in Ancient Pastoral: Essays on Theocritus and Virgil* (Princeton, N.J.: Princeton University Press, 1981); Nicolas P. Gross, *Amatory Persuasion in Antiquity* (Newark: University of Delaware Press, 1985); David

Halperin, *Before Pastoral* (New Haven: Yale University Press, 1983); Lawrence Lipking, *Abandoned Women and Poetic Tradition* (Chicago: University of Chicago Press, 1988), pp. 62–63.

13. Gow, *Theocritus* (n. 12 above), 2:35.

14. For Callimachus, consult the Loeb editions, trans. A. W. Mair (Cambridge, Mass.: "Loeb Classical Library," Harvard University Press, 1921, 1960); and trans. C. A. Trypanis (Cambridge, Mass.: "Loeb Classical Library," Harvard University Press, 1958), containing the *Aetia.* For commentary, see Paul Veyne, *Roman Erotic Elegy: Love, Poetry, and the West,* trans. David Pellauer (Chicago: University of Chicago Press, 1988), pp. 14, 17–23; and G. O. Hutchinson, *Hellenistic Poetry* (Oxford: Clarendon Press, 1988), pp. 28–31, 153–60, and on the *Aetia,* pp. 40–48. Ovid refers to the Acontius story in *Remedia amoris* 381–82, and mentions Callimachus in *Amores* 2.4.19–20. See also, for erotic elements and relations to the visual arts, Barbara Hughes Fowler, *The Hellenistic Aesthetic* (Bristol, Eng.: Bristol Press, 1989), pp. 40–48, 156–60.

15. *The Plays of Menander,* ed. and trans. Lionel Casson (New York: New York University Press, 1971); *Samia,* ed. and trans. D. M. Brain (Warminster, Wilts., England: Aris & Phillips, 1983); *Dyskolos,* ed. E. W. Handley (Cambridge, Mass.: Harvard University Press, 1965); A. W. Gomme and F. H. Sandbach, *Menander: A Commentary* (Oxford: Clarendon Press: 1973); R. L. Hunter, *The New Comedy of Greece and Rome* (Cambridge: Cambridge University Press, 1985); T. B. L. Webster, *An Introduction to Menander* (Manchester: Manchester University Press, 1974); L. A. Post, "Woman's Place in Menander's Athens," *Transactions of the American Philological Association* 71 (1940): 420–59. For expectedly high praise of Menander and the New Comedy in antiquity, see Plutarch, *Symposium,* in *Moralia* (Loeb edition [n. 10 above], 9:83). For a persuasive, realistic, and learned investigation of the New Comedy considered as portraying real life, see Elaine Fantham, "Sex, Status, and Survival in Hellenistic Athens: A Study of Women in New Comedy," *Phoenix* 29/1 (Spring 1975): 44–74.

16. Graham Anderson's comment appears in *Ancient Fiction: The Novel in the Graeco Roman World* (Totawa, N.J.: Barnes & Noble, 1984), p. 119; *The Letters of Alciphron, Aelian and Philostratus,* trans. Allen Rogers Benner and Francis H. Fobes (Cambridge, Mass.: "Loeb Classical Library," Harvard University Press, 1962), book 4, letters 2, 18, 19, pp. 252–55, 314–39; *Alciphron: Letters from the Country and the Town,* trans. F. A. Wright (London: George Routledge & Sons, n.d.); Gilbert Norwood, *Greek Comedy* (London: Methuen, 1936), pp. 315–17.

17. Veyne, *Roman Erotic Elegy* (see n. 14), p. 23.

18. The questions I have raised were in part suggested to me by the rich study of Claude Vatin, *Recherches sur le mariage et la condition de la femme mariée a l'époque hellénistique* (Paris: E. de Boccard, 1970).

19. Paul Veyne, "The Roman Empire," in *A History of Private Life,* ed. Philippe Ariès and Georges Duby, vol. 1: *From Pagan Rome to Byzantium,* ed. Paul

Veyne, trans. Arthur Goldhammer (Cambridge, Mass.: Harvard University Press, 1987), pp. 6–233; *Roman Civilization,* 2 vols., ed. Naphtali Lewis and Meyer Reinhold (New York: Columbia University Press, 1951, 1955); Ronald Syme, *The Roman Revolution* (London: Oxford University Press, 1966); Pierre Grimal, *Love in Ancient Rome,* trans. Arthur Train, Jr. (Norman: University of Oklahoma Press, 1986); E. Royston Pike, *Love in Ancient Rome* (London: Frederick Muller, 1965); James A. Brundage, *Law, Sex, and Christian Society in Medieval Europe* (Chicago: University of Chicago Press, 1987), pp. 25–36.

20. Livy, "The Rape of the Sabine Women," *History of Rome* 1.9–13; Ovid, *Ars amatoria,* 116–17, quoted in Molly Myerowitz, *Ovid's Game of Love* (Detroit: Wayne State University Press, 1985), p. 63.

21. Robert M. Adams, *The Roman Stamp: Frame and Façade in Some Forms of Neo-Classicism* (Berkeley: University of California Press, 1974), p. 23. For text and commentary on the *Laudatio Turiae,* see Eric Wikstrand, *The So-Called Laudatio Turiae* (Lund, Sweden: Studia graeca et latina Gothoburgensia 34, Acta Universitatis Gothoburgensis, 1976); Horace, *Carmen Saeculare* 57–58.

22. Michel Foucault, *Histoire de la sexualité,* vol. 3: *Le Souci de soi* (Paris: Gallimard, 1984), p. 97; Pliny, *Letters and Panegyrics,* 2 vols., trans. Betty Radice (Cambridge, Mass.: "Loeb Classical Library," Harvard University Press, 1969); my references are to book number and letter number.

23. Veyne, *Roman Erotic Elegy* (n. 14 above), passim; Sara Lilja, *The Roman Elegists' Attitude to Women* (New York: Garland, 1978); R. O. A. M. Lyne, *The Latin Love-Poets: From Catullus to Horace* (Oxford: Clarendon Press, 1980); Judith P. Hallett, "The Role of Women in Roman Elegy: Counter-Cultural Feminism," *Arethusa* 6/1 (Spring 1973): 103–24; Georg Luck, *The Latin Love Elegy,* 2nd ed. (London: Methuen, 1969).

24. Beside the general studies listed in n. 23 above, see *Tibullus,* trans. J. P. Postgate (Cambridge, Mass.: "Loeb Classical Library," Harvard University Press, 1976); *Poems of Tibullus,* trans. Constance Carrier (Bloomington: Indiana University Press, 1968); Michael C. J. Putnam, *Tibullus: A Commentary* (Norman: University of Oklahoma Press, 1965). The poem I analyze is 1.1.

25. I discuss 2.15 and am greatly indebted to Veyne, *Roman Erotic Elegy* (n. 14 above), pp. 154–58. See also Archibald W. Allen, "Elegy and the Classical Attitude Toward Love: Propertius I,i," *Yale Classical Studies* (1950): 253–77. Hans-Peter Stahl, in a comprehensive, illuminating, and politically oriented analysis of 2.15, concludes that the poem portrays the achievement of "tragic happiness" in a "new dimension" (*Propertius: 'Love' and 'War': Individual and State under Augustus* (Berkeley: University of California Press, 1985), pp. 216–29, quotation on p. 226).

26. See *Ovid: The Erotic Poems,* trans. Peter Green (Harmondsworth, Eng.: Penguin Books, 1984), pp. 22–24. For the cultural context of the Ovidian love poems, see Myerowitz, *Ovid's Game of Love* (n. 20 above), passim.

27. I place Catullus among the elegists, while recognizing that he greatly transcends the genre. *The Poems of Catullus: A Bilingual Edition,* trans. Peter

Whigham (Berkeley: University of California Press, 1969); *Poems of Gaius Valerius Catullus,* trans. F. W. Cornish in the Loeb edition, which includes also Tibullus and the *Pervirgilium Veneris* (n. 24 above); Stuart G. P. Small, *Catullus: A Reader's Guide to the Poems* (Lanham, Md.: University Press of America, 1983), chap. 6 ("The Marriage Theme") and p. 98 ("Catullus praises and glorifies marriage to a greater extent than any other Latin poet"); Carl A. Rubino, "The Erotic World of Catullus," *The Classical World* 68 (February 1975): 289–98. On 62, Eva Stehle Stigers, "Retreat from the Male: Catullus 62 and Sappho's Erotic Flowers," *Ramus* 6 (1977): 83–102. On 64, Lawrence Lipking, *Abandoned Women* (n. 12 above), pp. 29–31, and see pp. 63–66. On 109, P. McGushin, "Catullus' *Sanctae foedus amicitiae,*" *Classical Philology* 62/2 (April 1967): 85–93. For very general but sound criticism, see John Atkins, *Sex in Literature,* vol. 2 of *The Classical Experience of Sexual Impulse* (London: Calder & Boyars, 1973), pp. 46, 54. See Linda Clader and Keith Harrison, trans., *Catullus # 64: At the Wedding of Peleus and Thetis* (Minneapolis: Black Willow Press, 1981, 1983), with introd. and notes.

28. Sarah Pomeroy, *Women in Hellenistic Egypt from Alexander to Cleopatra* (New York, Schocken Books, 1984), p. 67.

29. For a discussion of passages in classical literature with, surprisingly, no mention of the visual arts, see Mario Praz, *Conversation Pieces: A Survey of the Informal Group Portrait in Europe and America* (University Park: Pennsylvania State University Press, 1971), chap. 2 ("The Family Portrait in Antiquity"), especially pp. 40, 43. I believe that departures from an ideal are always best understood if the norm is kept clearly in mind, the Roman one being in part the possibility of a good marriage but more pervasively the importance of a healthy because disciplined, psychological autarchy. Thus Soranus in the first century A.D. could seriously discuss the value of female virginity or the nonmarriage of girls and could claim that abstinent men were taller and stronger than other men. See Aline Rousselle, *Porneia: On Desire and the Body in Antiquity,* trans. Felicia Pheasant (Oxford: Basil Blackwell, 1988), passim but especially pp. 12, 72.

Chapter Five

1. Hermann Fränkel, *Ovid: A Poet Between Two Worlds* (Berkeley: University of California Press, 1945), p. 25.

I do not believe Myerowitz is in fundamental disagreement, though her treatment is more nuanced and refined. She believes that woman's essential equality in love makes the erotic game challenging. But she does see the woman as being erotically passive (though she may manipulate her lovers), as being *materia,* or nature, for the man's cultivation. Woman, however, is still far from being primitive. This scholar sees woman's cultus as lying in *pudor* and in taming herself and handling herself decorously. Man may be less modest, to be sure, but it is his essentially Roman task no less than hers of achieving autarchy, which of course all chronic sensual dependency can threaten. Molly Myerowitz, *Ovid's Game of Love* (Detroit: Wayne State University Press), 1985, pp. 68–127.

2. It is course possible that here Ovid is being wickedly witty, malely chauvinistic, and doubly standardized: if Jupiter can be faithless and get by with it, why can't all men? *Ovid: The Erotic Poems,* trans. Peter Green (Harmondsworth, Eng.: Penguin Books, 1982, 1984), p. 186. I am deeply indebted to this lively translation (which I quote) and to the learned and witty commentary on the erotic poetry. I have also consulted John A. Barsby, ed., *Ovid: Amores Book One* (Oxford: Clarendon Press, 1973); *The Art of Love, and Other Poems,* trans. J. H. Mozley (Cambridge, Mass.: "Loeb Classical Library," Harvard University Press, 1969); A. S. Hollis, "The *Ars amatoria* and *Remedia amoris,*" in *Ovid,* ed. J. W. Binns (London: "Greek and Latin Studies," Routledge & Kegan Paul, 1973), pp. 84–115; and I. M. Le M. DuQuesnay, "The Amores," in ibid., pp. 1–48.

3. I do more than echo Auden, whose lines Peter Green wittily applied to Ovid: Auden refers to himself and his contemporaries as ". . . the tail, a sort of poor relation / To that debauched eccentric generation / That grew up with their fathers at the war / And made new glosses on the noun Amor." Green, *Ovid: The Erotic Poems* (n. 2 above), p. 18 (on Auden and Ovid) and pp. 403, 404 (on the *Remedia amoris*). For this last poem, which in one sense is an *anteros* poem, see a comprehensive discussion of that tradition: Robert V. Merrill, "Eros and Anteros," *Speculum* 19/3 (July 1944): 265–84.

4. For *Tristia* and *Ex Ponto* see the Loeb edition, trans. Arthur Leslie Wheeler (Cambridge, Mass.: "Loeb Classical Library," Harvard University Press, 1965). See, *Tristia:* 1.3 and 1.6.25; 3.3.27; 4.3.9, 17, 35; 4.10.1, 65–74; 5.5.45–50; 5.11.29–30; 5.14.13; see *Ex Ponto:* 1.4, 3.1.

5. The references to the *Metamorphoses* in this paragraph come from 1.2.69, 76, 136. I have used the Loeb edition for the Latin (2 vols. [Cambridge, Mass.: "Loeb Classical Library," Harvard University Press, 1976–77]) and consulted the translation of A. E. Watts (Berkeley: University of California Press, 1954) and the commentaries of Leonard Barkan, *The Gods Made Flesh* (New Haven: Yale University Press, 1986); Leo C. Curran, "Rape and Rape Victims in the *Metamorphoses,*" in *Women in the Ancient World: The Arethusa Papers,* ed. John Peradotto and J. P. Sullivan (Albany: State University of New York Press, 1984), pp. 263–86; and Joseph B. Solodow, *The World of Ovid's* Metamorphoses (Chapel Hill: University of North Carolina Press, 1988).

6. On the données of this story, see Green, *Ovid: The Erotic Poems* (n. 2 above), pp. 400–401. I disagree with Green on one matter: he believes that even in the *Metamorphoses* version of the story all the morally compromising episodes of earlier versions were kept in mind by the author and remembered by the reader, producing a "sharply malicious literary pleasure" that would enforce the male double standard. But surely the author of so many metamorphoses must be given the right himself to "metamorphose" his inherited materials and create a story that fits the hard but not hopelessly infertile soil of his masterwork. Green

does, however, concede that "allowance should be made for possible Hellenistic romanticizing" ("The Innocence of Procris: Ovid *A.A.* 3.687–746," *Classical Journal* 75/1 [October–November 1979]: 24). If Green is too cynical here, Brooks Otis may be too sentimental in his view that Cephalus is "a lover and a gentlemen" who wears his grief like a "romantic halo" and that the most important element of this and other episodes of the *Metamorphoses* is a "new conception of love" (*Ovid as an Epic Poet* [Cambridge: Cambridge University Press, 1966], pp. 176, 384). But see Sara Mack's subtle reading, which shows how undercurrents from other tellings of the story stir the waters of the text, the poem being not a pastiche, to be sure, but a kind of palimpsest (*Ovid* [New Haven: Yale University Press, 1988], pp. 131–34).

7. Xenophon, *Cyropaedia,* trans. Walter Miller, 2 vols. (Cambridge, Mass: "Loeb Classical Library," Harvard University Press, 1960). The Greek quoted appears at 6.4.6 (*philia*) and 6.4.5 (*etimēsen* from *timaō*).

8. *Petronius,* trans. Michael Hesseltine (Cambridge, Mass.: "Loeb Classical Library," Harvard University Press, 1939), pp. 170, 229–35, 284, 292. See chap. 12 of Graham Anderson, *Ancient Fiction: The Novel in the Graeco-Roman World* (Totowa, N.J.: Barnes & Noble, 1984); and chap. 7 of Tomas Hägg, *The Novel in Antiquity* (Berkeley: University of California Press, 1983).

9. I have consulted the French translation of and have quoted the Greek from the edition of Georges Molinié, *Chariton: Le Roman de Chairéas et Callirhoé* (Paris: Société d'Éditions "Les Belles Lettres," 1979). For general commentary on the ancient novel as well as on Chariton's, besides the works by Anderson and Hägg noted above (n. 8), see Graham Anderson, *Eros Sophistes: Ancient Novelists at Play* (Chico, Calif.: "American Philological Association, American Classical Studies," Scholars Press, 1982), pp. 13–15; Gareth L. Schmeling, *Chariton* (New York: Twayne, 1974); John J. Winkler, "The Invention of Romance," *Laetaberis: Journal of the California Classical Association Northern Section* 1 (n.d.): 1–24; Ben Edwin Perry, *The Ancient Romances: A Literary-Historical Account of Their Origins* (Berkeley: University of California Press, 1967); Erwin Rohde, *Der griechische Roman und seine Vorläufer* (Leipzig: Breitkopf und Härtel, 1900), pp. 156–71 (on *erōs* and related or contrasting terms like *hybris* or *sōphrosunē*). For an excellent brief introduction to Chariton's romance, see B. P. Reardon, "Theme, Structure and Narrative in Chariton," *Yale Classical Studies* 27 (1982): 1–27. For a brilliant discussion of time and space in the Greek novel that does not neglect love, passion, and marriage, see *The Dialogic Imagination: Four Essays by M. M. Bakhtin,* ed. Michael Holquist, trans. Caryl Emerson and Michael Holquist (Austin: University of Texas Press, 1981), pp. 86–129.

10. The Loeb edition, trans. George Thornley (1657), rev. J. M. Edmonds (London: Heinemann, 1916); *Three Greek Romances,* trans. Moses Hadas (Garden City, N.Y.: Doubleday, 1953); Froma I. Zeitlin, "The Poetics of *Erōs:* Nature, Art, and Imitation in Longus' *Daphnis and Chloe,*" in *Before Sexuality:*

The Construction of Erotic Experience in the Ancient Greek World, ed. David M. Halperin, John J. Winkler, and Froma I. Zeitlin (Princeton, N.J.: Princeton University Press, 1990), pp. 417–64.

11. This view is not held, however, by the eminent scholar, Erwin Rohde, who resented the lascivious experimentation of arousing but never fully gratifying desire, calling this an innocence that masks prurience—a "schwule schlupfertigkeit." I owe the Rohde reference to Froma Zeitlin, "The Poetics of *Erōs*" (n. 10 above). As we have seen (chapter 3) and shall see (chapter 7), variants of this erotic situation (taking many forms, not all suggestive or prurient) have been a recurrent feature of Western culture. A brilliant interpretation by John J. Winkler, "The Education of Chloe: Hidden Injuries of Sex," in *The Constraints of Desire: The Anthropology of Sex and Gender in Ancient Greece* (New York: Routledge, 1990), chap. 4, lays stress on the violence that always attends the dawning sexuality of this idyl and says that the hymeneal blood that Daphnis learns about from his seductress and that haunts him ever after, even on the nuptial night, signifies that he becomes in effect the unwilling slayer of his beloved. But it is characteristic of the novel to abort quickly and easily and then instantly forgive much of the violence that intrudes upon sex—and the work may therefore be open to the charge of romantic escapism. The blood of the wedding night sentimentally implies that a natural fulfillment leading to offspring and a maturer sexuality will exact its own kind of price, but one really not very high if we remember the much graver violence that has earlier lain in wait to threaten the happiness of the pair. Froma Zeitlin finds after a thorough and illuminating exposition of aesthetic contexts for and mimetic realizations within the text that it "seems to balance out the uneasy relation in erotic psychology between pain and pleasure, violence and love" (*Before Sexuality* [n. 10 above], p. 459). I continue to call this idyl a Song of Innocence, not to deny the surrounding realism, which Winkler compendiously displays, but to suggest that the final happiness embodies what Western man has immemorially and sentimentally dreamed of— somehow retaining natural innocence in sexual experience. What Erōs's experiment creates is a largely natural couple on whom culture (and it is sometimes presented grimly) intrudes ineffectually. The country ends up clearly superior to the lascivious town. Such a view seems to me to account for the enduring popularity of the work and to isolate one important aspect of its imaginative élan, and also of its relationship to the multifaceted but persistent naturalism that has attached itself to my theme.

12. Dionysophantes is virtuous in spite of having exposed his son at birth; apparently it was not considered criminal or even terribly improper to expose a child, a practice that had gone on for centuries in the Greek world and was to continue in the Middle Ages as a form of birth control. The rich father feels the need to say only this by way of excuse—that Daphnis was a fourth child and the family was already too large. Chloe's father had exposed her because he had been reduced to poverty, a condition in which he did not wish to raise her. See

John Boswell, *The Kindness of Strangers: The Abandonment of Children in Western Europe from Late Antiquity to the Renaissance* (London: Allen Lane, The Penguin Press, 1988).

13. Xenophon Ephesius, *Les Ephésiaques,* ed. and trans. Georges Dalmeyda (Paris: "Les Belles Lettres," Collections des Universités de France, 1962); Xenophon, *An Ephesian Tale,* trans. Hadas, in *Three Greek Romances* (n. 10 above). B. P. Reardon's literary judgments are sound: "For literary skill, . . . Xenophon substitutes simple-minded religiosity"; and witty: Chariton's gods have "a penchant for melodrama, as keen a sense of suspense as any writer of soap operas, and appalling taste" ("The Greek Novel," *Phoenix* 23/3 [Autumn 1969]: 298, 299).

14. In "Why Is Diotima a Woman?" in *Before Sexuality* (n. 10 above), pp. 273–74, David Halperin quotes at what he calls "obscene length, the remarks of the advocate of women from the forthcoming unexpurgated translation of Achilles Tatius by John J. Winkler." In his essay Halperin provides a large and important (Platonic) context for the debated contrasts between love of women and love of boys (pp. 271–75). I have used *Achilles Tatius,* trans. S. Gaselee (London: "The Loeb Classical Library," Heinemann, 1917). Besides the general references in nn. 8 and 9 above, see Shadi Bartsch, *Decoding the Ancient Novel: The Reader and the Role of Description in Heliodorus and Achilles Tatius* (Princeton, N.J.: Princeton University Press, 1989).

15. "Le principe de l'institution du mariage n'a pas été l'amour, auquel le mariage n'était nullement nécessaire" E. P. de Sénancour, *De l'Amour, selon les lois premières et selon les convenances des sociétés modernes,* 4th ed. enlarged, 2 vols. (Paris, 1854), 1:5.

16. See discussions by Winkler in *The Constraints of Desire* (n. 11 above), pp. 23–44 and 212–16; and Michel Foucault, *Histoire de la sexualité,* vol. 3: *Le Souci de soi* (Paris: Gallimard, 1984), pp. 28–48.

17. An Italian friend of mine, a practicing Catholic, many years ago shocked my nineteenth-century American sensibilities by arguing seriously that a special divine grace was accorded whores for their great help in relieving dangerous erotic symptoms and so preserving the virginity of nubile girls and the chastity of wives. He stood in a long line: see Lucretius in *De Rerum natura* 4.1071–74, and Athenaeus, *Deipnosophistai* 13.568e–570a.

18. Foucault, *Histoire de la sexualité* (n. 16 above), pp. 187–238, 254 and n. 3.

19. *Rambler* 99 (26 February 1751). Johnson apparently coalesces two remarks of Aristotle in *Historia animalium,* A.1.488a7, 26–27.

Chapter Six

1. Gen. 5:22–24, Exod. 3:14, Gen. 16:2, 21:1–2, 25:21, 1 Sam. 1:5–6.
2. W. F. Lofthouse, "Hen and Hesed in the Old Testament," *Zeitschrift für*

die altertestamentliche Wissenschaft 51 (1933): 29–35; James A. Montgomery, "Hebrew *Hesed* and Greek *Charis*," *Harvard Theological Review* 32/2 (April 1939): 97–102; C. H. Dodd, *The Bible and the Greeks* (London: Hodder & Stoughton, 1935), pp. 59–61, useful also on *oikos* words and *eleos* (pity, mercy).

3. Lev. 18:6–23. On the importance of procreation and related matters, and on changes in the historical periods of biblical Israel (c. 1200–200 B.C.), see Denise L. Carmody, "Judaism," in *Women in World Religions,* ed. Arvind Sharma (Albany: State University of New York Press, 1987), pp. 183–206.

4. On the important topic of romantic sexuality and the favored wife, consult Raphael Patai, *Sex and Family in the Bible and the Middle East* (Garden City, N.Y.: Doubleday, 1959); R. Gordon, "The Knowledge of Good and Evil in the Old Testament and the Qumran Scrolls," *Journal of Biblical Literature and Exegesis* 76 (1957): 123–38 (on the whole range of sexual experience); Judith Ochshorn, *The Female Experience and the Nature of the Divine* (Bloomington: Indiana University Press, 1981), pp. 200–202 (generally hostile to the tradition of the woman as wife: the Bible has contributed to a legacy that "has been destructive to the humanity of both sexes" [p. 243]). Up to this point I have been alluding mostly to prescriptive utterance; I shall now turn to stories that involve the imagination and literary graces. For an important statement on imagination in relation to the concept of deity, see Cynthia Ozick's comments in Elaine M. Kauvar, "An Interview with Cynthia Ozick," *Contemporary Literature* 26/4 (1985): 394–95.

5. I have quoted (as usual unless otherwise specified) the King James Version. The New English Bible has "a woman turned into a man" (Oxford: Clarendon Press, 1970); the New Jerusalem Bible (Garden City, N.Y.: Doubleday, 1985) reads, "the Woman sets out to find her Husband again," and the note allegorizes the situation into a resumption of love between Israel and Yahweh (p. 1349, n. *h*); J. M. Powis Smith (Chicago: University of Chicago Press, 1935) translates, "the woman woos the man"; John Bright in the Anchor Bible finds the literal meaning ("a female man") wholly obscure, with no help available from the Septuagint (*Jeremiah* [Garden City, N.Y.: Doubleday, 1965], p. 282).

6. Mieke Bal, *Lethal Love: Feminist Literary Readings of Biblical Love Stories* (Bloomington: Indiana University Press, 1987), pp. 49–50 (on Delilah).

7. Northrop Frye, *The Great Code: The Bible and Literature* (San Diego: Harcourt Brace Jovanovich, 1983), p. 35. Frye says the name invokes an analogy with the sun but we do not know certainly that the story derives from a solar myth.

8. On *beena, ba'al,* and levirate marriages and on customs relevant to the story of Samson, see Gerda Lerner, *The Creation of Patriarchy* (New York: Oxford University Press, 1986), p. 167; George Aaron Barton, *Semitic and Hamitic Origins: Social and Religious* (Philadelphia: University of Pennsylvania Press, 1934), pp. 101–2; Julian Morgenstern, *Rites of Birth, Marriage, Death and Kindred Occasions among the Semites* (Cincinnati: Hebrew Union College Press, 1966), pp. 64, 109–16, 181–92.

9. A heifer traditionally was a trope for virgin, recalling the days when animal sacrifice redeemed the bride from the evil spirits that attended her virginity. Bal, *Lethal Love* (n. 6 above), pp. 42–43; Morgenstern, *Rites of Birth* (n. 8 above), pp. 111–12.

10. The tradition of divine derision has continued on into Christian sensibility: Augustine at one point wonders (*Confessions* 1.6) if God does not laugh at him when he Platonically—and a little in the manner of Wordsworth—wonders what took place in his personal story before his stay in his mother's belly: "Was I anywhere? anybody?" (fuine alicubi aut aliquis?).

11. Edward F. Campbell, Jr., *Ruth: A New Translation with Introduction and Commentary* (Garden City, N.Y.: "The Anchor Bible," Doubleday, 1975); Jan Wojcik, "Improvising Rules in the Book of Ruth," *Publications of Modern Language Association of America* 100/2 (March 1985): 145–53 (example of woman's initiative, appeal to use of imagination against the law). Articles listed in n. 2 above discuss concepts relevant to understanding Boaz. Cynthia Ozick has written a lovely and moving personal essay on this book: *Congregation: Contemporary Writers Read the Jewish Bible* (San Diego: Harcourt Brace Jovanovich, 1987), pp. 361–82. See Bal, *Lethal Love* (n. 6 above), pp. 69–101.

12. See Genesis 38 for a patriarchal version of levirate marriage, which also tells the story of the aggressive widow, Tamar, who takes the unconventional route of posing as a prostitute and so conceives a child by Judah, a son of Jacob and also her father-in-law. The child, like Ruth's, stands in the line of Jesse and David, and God once more has used mysterious ways his wonders to perform. No one should miss Harold Bloom's vivid recreation of J's vividness in telling this fascinating story in *The Book of J*, trans. David Rosenberg, interpr. Harold Bloom (New York: Grove Weidenfeld, 1990), pp. 220–23. Thomas Mann in *The Young Joseph* is doubtless right in presenting Judah as sexually experienced in the shameless ways of Canaan during his youth, a love career marked by disorder and suffering.

13. Immanuel Kant, "Speculative Beginnings of Human History" (1786), in *Perpetual Peace and Other Essays on Politics, History, and Morals,* trans. Ted Humphrey (Indianapolis: Hackett, 1983), pp. 49–59.

14. *Genesis,* trans. with intro and notes, E. A. Speiser (Garden City, N.Y.: "The Anchor Bible," Doubleday, 1964); The New Jerusalem Bible (n. 5 above); *The Interpreter's Dictionary of the Bible,* suppl. vol., ed. Keith Crim (Nashville: Abingdon Press, 1976), s.v. *marriage* (especially under *Levirate*), *woman* (under *Ancient Near East, Old Testament, New Testament*). Robert Alter, *The Art of Biblical Narrative* (New York: Basic Books, 1981), pp. 20–31; Bal, *Lethal Love* (n. 6 above), pp. 104–26; and Bal, "Sexuality, Sin and Sorrow: The Emergence of Female Character (A Reading of Genesis 1–3)" in *The Female Body in Western Culture,* ed. Susan R. Suleiman (Cambridge, Mass.: Harvard University Press, 1986), pp. 317–38; Julian Morgenstern, *The Book of Genesis: A Jewish Interpretation* (New York: Schocken 1919, rpt., 1965), pp. 53–59; Katherine M. Rogers, *The Troublesome Helpmate: A History of Misogyny in Literature*

(Seattle: University of Washington Press, 1966), pp. ix, 3–7; Phyllis Trible, "Depatriarchalizing in Biblical Interpretation," *Journal of American Academy of Religion* 41/1 (March 1973): 30–48; and Trible, *God and the Rhetoric of Spirituality* (Philadelphia: Fortress Press, 1978), pp. 15–21 and all of chap. 4 on the Fall ("A Love Gone Awry"); Ochshorn, *The Female Experience* (n. 4 above), pp. 214–15 (contra Trible); Leonard Swidler, *Biblical Affirmations of Woman* (Philadelphia: Westminster Press, 1979), p. 77; James G. Turner, *One Flesh: Paradisal Marriage and Sexual Relations in the Age of Milton* (Oxford: Clarendon Press, 1987), pp. 11–13, 17–18, 22, 28.

Harold Bloom contrasts the two versions of creation: "P's sublime Creation is a cosmos; J's gentle irony is content with an oasis" (*The Book of J*, n. 12 above), p. 293. For Bloom's brilliant and eye-opening discussion, see pp. 175–87. For what it is worth, I have come around to Bloom's modestly stated view that "J" was in all likelihood a woman. The postulated ambience of the Solomonic and later courts makes that plausible.

For the enormous influence of Genesis 1–3 on Christian thought and practice, see Elaine Pagels, *Adam, Eve, and the Serpent* (New York: Random House, 1988), which argues that for the first 400 years or so after Christ, Christians regarded freedom, including self-mastery, and not bondage, as the legacy of the Eden story and that most early Christians rejected the radical Christians' claim that the sin of Adam and Eve was sexual (pp. xxiii, xxv, and chap. 1).

15. "And God said, Let us make *man* in our image after our likeness: and let *them* have dominion . . ." Gen. 1:26); "so God created *man* in his own image, in the image of God created he him; male and female created he *them*" (1:27). I have added emphasis to show that the word *man* is generic and inclusive, the plural pronouns *them* showing that both sexes alike received the divine image. The necessities of grammar and a linguistic temporal order do not indicate hierarchy.

16. It is difficult for me to pinpoint the source of my ideas concerning the myth of the Fall, since I have had a succession of them since childhood. Certainly the classic studies by Bronislaw Malinowski of the Trobrianders of New Guinea (*Sex and Repression in Savage Society* [1927] and *The Sexual Life of Savages in North-western Melanesia* [1929]) lie somewhere in the background. I have recently been impressed with what David Bakan says about Gen. 6:1–4 and about God's being gradually conceived of as a nonsexual being, and I have found important his general discussions of lingering remnants in Hebrew culture of alternatives to patriarchy: *And They Took Themselves Wives: The Emergence of Patriarchy in Western Civilization* (San Francisco: Harper & Row, 1979), pp. 2–5, 8–10, 14–15. Barton, *Semitic and Hamitic Origins* (n. 8 above) has been more directly influential (pp. 110–11, 141–46).

17. I have derived Cassuto's translation from Turner, *One Flesh* (n. 14 above), pp. 17–18. On Gen. 4:1, I have consulted the notes of E. A. Speiser in the Anchor Bible *Genesis* (n. 14 above), pp. 29–30, and the commentary in *Ramban (Nachmanides): Commentary on the Torah Genesis*, trans. Charles B. Chavel

(New York: Shilo, 1971), p. 87, where Rashi is quoted. A literal translation of Gen. 4:1 follows: "And the Adam knew Eve his wife and she became pregnant and bore Cain and she said I acquired [or bought, *qaniti*] a person with [*eth*] God." The language is commercial, transactional, and the verb is assonant with the name, Cain (from *kanah*, "acquisition"). I have been helped with the Hebrew, which I do not know, by Ya'aquov Ziso of the Northwestern University Library. For the Trobrianders, see n. 16 above.

18. See Trible, "Depatriarchalizing," and Trible, *God and the Rhetoric of Spirituality* (n. 14 above), pp. 144, 152–55, 161; John B. White, *A Study of the Language of Love in the Song of Songs and Ancient Egyptian Poetry* (Missoula, Mont.: "The Society of Biblical Literature," No. 38, Scholars Press, 1978); James Hastings, *Dictionary of the Bible,* rev. ed. (New York: Frederick Grant & H. H. Rowley, 1963), s.v. *Song of Songs;* Leonard Swidler, *Women in Judaism: The Status of Women in Formative Judaism* (Metuchen, N.J.: Scarecrow Press, 1976), pp. 30–31; Robert Alter, *The Art of Biblical Poetry* (New York: Basic Books, 1985), chap. 8 ("The Garden of Metaphor"); Francis Landy, "The Song of Songs," in *Literary Guide to the Bible,* ed. Robert Alter and Frank Kermode (Cambridge, Mass.: Harvard University Press, 1987), pp. 305–19; Julia Kristeva, *Tales of Love,* trans. Leon S. Rudiez (New York: Columbia University Press, 1987), pp. 2, 89–100. For a sensitive and subtle interpretation that emphasizes the pure poetry and also the inevitability of its allegorization, see Harold Fisch, *Poetry with a Purpose: Biblical Poetics and Interpretation* (Bloomington: Indiana University Press, 1990), pp. 80–103.

19. *Song of Songs,* trans., ed., and comm. Marvin H. Pope (Garden City, N.Y.: "The Anchor Bible," Doubleday, 1977), passim but especially pp. 18, 23, 89, 145, 298, 303, 308, 480, 518; New Jerusalem Bible (n. 5 above), pp. 1027–28; notes to the Scofield Reference Bible, the fundamentalist position (King James Version, ed. C. Scofield [New York: Oxford University Press, 1917]).

I recall hearing an amusing segment by Garrison Keillor on his radio program, "A Prairie Home Companion," shortly before his marriage: one night in a hotel room, alone and longing for his bride-to-be, he reaches for the Gideon Bible. Although he intends (he said slyly) to read a psalm, the Bible falls open of itself to one of the lusher passages of the Song of Solomon, a passage he and his audience later sang with great éclat to a popular melody.

20. Pope, *Song of Songs* (n. 19 above), pp. 593, 617–19, 636, defends his substitution of *vulva* for *nose and navel* in the original, and explains the meaning of *crater* and *punch.* The King James Version has "the smell of thy nose like apples" (7:8); "thy navel is like a rounded goblet, which wanteth not liquor" (7:2).

21. Kristeva, *Tales of Love* (n. 18 above), p. 97; Pope, *Song of Songs* (n. 19 above), p. 480, citing Graham.

22. My colleague, Barbara Newman, points out that there are "no stories about couples in the New Testament except for Mary and Joseph, where the whole point is their *non*coupling. Medieval theologians and canonists would often cite their example to prove that the ideal marriage is sexless. Also there are

no saints in either East or West canonized as married couples, although there are many mother-son and brother-sister pairs. Even the saints involved in the Orthodox wedding prayers are all from the Old Testament, except for Constantine and Helena" (1991).

23. On pagan grace (*charis*), see chapter 3. For Christian love and grace, consult *The New Schaff-Herzog Encyclopedia of Religious Knowledge*, ed. Samuel Macauley Jackson (Grand Rapids, Mich.: Baker Book House, 1963), s.v. *marriage;* the extension of *New Schaff-Herzog*, the *Twentieth-Century Encyclopedia of Religious Knowledge*, ed. Lefferts A. Loetscher, (Grand Rapids, Mich.: Baker Book House, 1967), s.v. *love, sex; Encyclopedia of Religion and Ethics*, ed. James Hastings (New York: Scribner's, 1926), s.v. *love, marriage.* On Christian grace, see James Moffatt, *Grace in the New Testament* (New York: Ray Long & Richard Smith, 1932); Thomas F. Torrance, *The Doctrine of Grace in the Apostolic Fathers* (Edinburgh: Oliver & Boyd, 1948); Gillis P. von Wetter, *Charis: Ein Beitrag zur Geschichte des ältesten Christentums* (Leipzig, 1913).

On Christian thought in general about love and sexuality, the following are illuminating: John Boswell, *Christianity, Social Tolerance, and Homosexuality: Gay People in Western Europe from the Beginning of the Christian Era to the Fourteenth Century* (Chicago: University of Chicago Press, 1980), pp. 106–17; Peter Brown, *The Body and Society: Men, Women, and Sexual Renunciation in Early Christianity* (New York: Columbia University Press, 1988), pp. 50–60; Eric Fuchs, *Sexual Desire and Love: Origins and History of the Christian Ethic of Sexuality and Marriage,* trans. Marsha Daigle (Cambridge: James Clark & Co., 1983); James B. Hurley, *Man and Woman in Biblical Perspective* (Grand Rapids, Mich.: Zondervan, 1981). Hurley's book is written from an evangelical Christian perspective; for a different Christian perspective, see Raymond J. Lawrence, Jr., *The Poisoning of Eros: Sexual Values in Conflict* (New York: Augustine Moore Press, 1989), which finds that Christianity, influenced by its "Platonic" Greco-Roman heritage, modified its Jewish legacy of sexuality (with notable exceptions like Luther and his twentieth-century followers) into ascetic restriction and fear. See also John T. Noonan, Jr., *Contraception: A History of Its Treatment by Catholic Theologians and Canonists* (Cambridge, Mass.: Harvard University Press, 1966), pp. 36–55; Eric Osborn, *Ethical Patterns in Early Christian Thought* (Cambridge: Cambridge University Press, 1976), pp. 11, 33, 74; Irving Singer, *The Nature of Love,* vol. 1: *Plato to Luther* (Chicago: University of Chicago Press, 1984, pp. 159–61.

24. On Ephesians, see Peter Brown, *The Body and Society* (n. 19 above), pp. 57–60; J. Paul Sampley, *"And the Two Shall Become One Flesh": A Study of Traditions in Ephesians 5:21–33* (Cambridge: Cambridge University Press, 1971). More generally, consult W. D. Davies, *Paul and Rabbinic Judaism: Some Rabbinic Elements in Pauline Theology* (London: Cambridge University Printer, 1948), pp. 53–57, 299–320; Robert H. Gundry, *Soma in Biblical Theology with Emphasis on Pauline Anthropology* (Cambridge: Cambridge University Press, 1976).

25. Brown, *The Body and Society* (n. 23 above), p. 135. We might say the same of any strongly Christian century.

26. And of course for much longer. Donne wrote: ". . . arise, arise, / From death, you numberless infinities of souls, and to your scatter'd bodies go" ("At the Round Earth's Imagin'd Corners"). Dryden later in the century is even more literal, referring to the "last assizes," "When rattling bones together fly / From the four corners of the sky" ("To the Pious Memory of the Accomplish'd Young Lady, Mrs. Anne Killigrew").

27. Trans. Edgar J. Goodspeed, *The Bible: An American Translation* (Chicago: University of Chicago Press, 1935).

Chapter Seven

1. It will be apparent to some readers that in this chapter I am deeply indebted to the distinguished scholarship of Peter Brown: "Bodies and Minds: Sexuality and Renunciation in Early Christianity," in *Before Sexuality: The Construction of Erotic Experience in the Ancient Greek World,* ed. David M. Halperin, John J. Winkler, and Froma I. Zeitlin (Princeton, N.J.: Princeton University Press, 1990), a brief but brilliant overview of the immense landscape of the early Christian church, covering some 400 years and based on the reading of at least five major languages, disclosing three important related attitudes toward sexuality (pp. 479–93 and especially pp. 491–92, whence the epigraph of this chapter is drawn); *The Body and Society: Men, Women and Sexual Renunciation in Early Christianity* (New York: Columbia University Press, 1988); "The Notion of Virginity in the Early Church," in *Christian Spirituality: Origins to the Twelfth Century,* ed. Bernard McGinn and John Meyendorff in collaboration with Jean Leclercq (New York: Crossroad, 1985), pp. 427–43; and "Late Antiquity," in *A History of Private Life: I. From Pagan Rome to Byzantium,* ed. Paul Veyne, trans. Arthur Goldhammer (Cambridge, Mass.: Harvard University Press, 1987), pp. 237–311.

See also Robin Lane Fox, *Pagans and Christians* (New York: Alfred A. Knopf, 1987); Frances and Joseph Gies, *Marriage and the Family in the Middle Ages* (New York: Harper & Row, 1987), pp. 36–38; Jo Ann McNamara, *A New Song: Celibate Women in the First Three Christian Centuries* (Binghamton, N.Y.: Haworth Press, 1983); James A. Brundage, *Law, Sex, and Christian Society in Medieval Europe* (Chicago: University of Chicago Press, 1987), pp. 59–73; Aline Rousselle, *Porneia: On Desire and the Body in Antiquity,* trans. Felicia Pheasant (Oxford: Basil Blackwell, 1988), pp. 64–198. See also the vivid descriptions of early ascetics and fathers in Morton M. Hunt, *The Natural History of Love* (New York: W. W. Norton, 1959), pp. 107–16; and relevant portions of Edward Gibbon, *The History of the Decline and Fall of the Roman Empire,* 3 vols. (New York: Heritage Press, 1946), 2:1475–80.

2. "And why did Simeon sit like that / Without a mantle, / Without a hat, /

In holy rage / For the world to see? / It puzzled the sage. / It puzzles me. / It puzzled many / A desert father, / And I think it puzzled the / Good Lord rather" (quoted by Kenneth Leech in Robert Llewelyn, ed., *Julian: Woman of Our Day* [London: Darton, Longman & Todd, 1985], pp. 89–90).

3. McNamara, *A New Song* (n. 1 above), pp. 1–2, 124. For other references in this paragraph, see Gibbon, *Decline and Fall* (n. 1 above), 2:1475; Brown, "Notion of Virginity" (n. 1 above), p. 427.

4. Brown, *Body and Society* (n. 1 above), p. 327.

5. Brown, *Body and Society* (n. 1 above), pp. 150–51, 205–8, 429, 442.

6. Clement of Alexandria, *Christ the Educator,* trans. Simon P. Wood (New York: Fathers of the Church, Inc., 1954); M. L. W. Laistner, *Christianity and Pagan Culture in the Later Roman Empire* (Ithaca: Cornell University Press, 1951), pp. 58–60; Brown, *Body and Society* (n. 1 above), pp. 123–38.

7. *The Shepherd of Hermas,* trans. Joseph M.-F. Marique, in *The Fathers of the Church: The Apostolic Fathers,* ed. Ludwig Schopp, vol. 1 (New York: Fordham University Press, 1946), pp. 223–52; and *The Shepherd of Hermas,* 2 vols., ed. C. Taylor (London: Society for Promotion of Christian Knowledge, 1903). For the Greek text, I have used *Hermae pastor graece,* ed. Rudolphus Anger (Leipzig, 1866); and Stanislas Giet, *Hermas et les pasteurs: Les Trois auteurs du Pastor d'Hermas* (Paris: Presses Universitaires de France, 1963). For commentary, see Fox, *Pagans and Christians* (n. 1 above), pp. 381–90 and relevant notes; Brown, *Body and Society* (n. 1 above), pp. 70–72; E. R. Dodds, *Pagan and Christian in an Age of Anxiety* (Cambridge: Cambridge University Press, 1965), pp. 58 and n. 2, 104; Henry Chadwick, *The Early Church* (Harmondsworth, Eng.: Penguin Books, 1967, 1973), pp. 43–44. John Cassian uses Hermas to illustrate his belief that there is a good and an evil angel in each man: "The Second Conference of Abbot Serenus," chap. 17 in *A Select Library of the Nicene and Post-Nicene Fathers,* ed. Philip Schaff and Henry Wace (New York: Christian Literature Co., 1894), 11 (2nd ser.): 382 and n. 2.

8. John Chrysostom, *On Marriage and Family Life,* trans. Catharine P. Roth and David Anderson (Crestwood, N.Y.: St. Vladimir's Seminary Press, 1986); Chrysostom, "Homilies on First Corinthians," in *A Select Library of the Nicene and Post-Nicene Fathers,* ed. Philip Schaff (New York: Christian Literature, 1889), 12 (1st ser.): 192–93, 252; Elizabeth A. Clark, *Jerome, Chrysostom, and Friends: Essays and Translations* (New York: Edwin Mellen Press, 1979), pp. v, 1, 9–34, 43, and passim; Brown, *Body and Society* (n. 1 above), pp. 304–20; John T. Noonan, Jr., *Contraception: A History of Its Treatment by the Catholic Theologians and Canonists* (Cambridge, Mass.: Harvard University Press, 1966), pp. 73–74, 78–79. For the view that classical *philia* posed no ethical problems for John and other Greek fathers, see Leokadia Matunowicz, "Le Problème de l'amitié chez Basile, Grégoire de Nazianze et Jean Chrysostome," *Studia patristica* 16/2 (1985): 412–17.

9. The following discuss the Subintroductae: Clark, *Jerome* (n. 8 above), pp. 158–92; and Fox, *Pagans and Christians* (n. 1 above), pp. 369–70.

10. For Augustine consult the previously mentioned works by Brown (n. 1 above), and his *Augustine of Hippo* (Berkeley: University of California Press, 1967; rpt, New York: Dorset Press, 1986). See also Christopher Kirwan, *Augustine* (New York: Routledge, 1989). For Augustine's milieu in Africa, see Yvon Thébert, "Private Life and Domestic Architecture in Roman Africa," in *A History of Private Life* (n. 1 above), pp. 313–409. For a view of Augustine that contrasts him with Chrysostom and finds his sexual pessimism largely responsible for the turn that Christianity took away from the heterolithic moral freedoms of approximately the first four centuries of Christian history and toward an established belief in a universally enslaving moral-sexual corruption, see Elaine Pagels, *Adam, Eve, and the Serpent* (New York: Random House, 1988).

11. Elizabeth A. Clark, *Women in the Early Church* (Wilmington, Del.: Michael Glazier, 1983), p. 18 and pp. 44–47 (on Augustine and the Gnostics).

12. John D. Zizioulas, "The Early Christian Community," pp. 23–43, and Robert M. Grant, "Gnostic Spirituality," pp. 44–60, in *Christian Spirituality* (n. 1 above); Noonan, *Contraception* (n. 8 above), chap. 4; Elaine H. Pagels, *The Gnostic Gospels* (New York: Random House, 1979).

13. Jesus had just uttered his austere stricture against divorce and remarriage as being adulterous, save in the case of fornication: "His disciples say unto him, If the case of the man be so with his wife, it is not good to marry. / But he said unto them, All men cannot receive this saying save they to whom it is given. / For there are some eunuchs, which were so born from their mother's womb: and there are some eunuchs, which were made eunuchs of men: and there be eunuchs, which have made themselves eunuchs for the kingdom of heaven's sake. He that is able to receive it, let him receive it" (Matthew 19:10–12).

14. Brown, *Body and Society* (n. 1 above), p. 168, discussing Origen.

15. *Confessions,* trans. William Watts (1631), 2 vols. (London: "Loeb Classical Library," William Heinemann, 1912); and many other editions and translations through the years.

16. *De Continentia,* trans. C. I. Cornish, sections 20–21, in *A Select Library of the Nicene and Post-Nicene Fathers of the Christian Church,* ed. Philip Schaff (Grand Rapids, Mich.: Eerdmans Publishing, 1956), 3 (1st ser.): 387.

17. *A Select Library of the Nicene and Post-Nicene Fathers,* ed. Edgar C. S. Gibson (New York: Christian Literature, 1894), 11 (2nd ser.): 161–641, especially pp. 450–55.

18. *Saint Jerome: Dogmatic and Polemical Works,* trans. John N. Hritzu (Washington, D.C.: Catholic University of America Press, 1965), pp. 11–17, 33, 39–43; Clark, *Jerome* (n. 8 above), passim.

19. Augustine, *City of God, Books I–VII,* trans. Demetrius B. Zema and Gerald G. Walsh (New York: Fathers of the Church, Inc., 1950), 8:48; Rousselle, *Porneia* (n. 1 above), p. 21. See earlier in this chapter on the *Subintroductae.* Readers may well wonder how a midwife delivering a baby could injure the hymeneal membrane, but they should recall that midwives ran from house to

house to determine whether the virgins in the houses kept by allegedly continent Christian couples were in fact unpenetrated. One of these examinations, vigorously, curiously, or angrily performed, might have done the kind of injury to the membrane Augustine refers to.

20. Elizabeth Clark, " 'Adam's Only Companion': Augustine and the Early Christian Debate on Marriage," *Recherches Augustiniennes* 21 (1986): 150–51. This article is ground-breaking and essential, and also useful in dating and discriminating the changes in the marital works and relating each change to the controversies in which Augustine was engaged.

21. *De Bono conjugali,* trans. C. I. Cornish, in *A Select Library of the Nicene and Post-Nicene Fathers* (n. 8 above), 3 (1st ser.): 399–413; *De Virginitate,* trans. Cornish, in ibid., 3:417–38; *De Nuptiis et concupiscientia,* trans. and rev. Peter Holmes, Robert E. Wallis, and Benjamin B. Warfield, in ibid., 5 (1887): 263–308.

22. For Augustine's brilliantly imaginative envisioning of the primitive human past and the Christian future, see *City of God, Books VIII–XVI,* trans. Gerald G. Walsh and Grace Monahan (New York: Fathers of the Church, Inc., 1952), 14:356–408; and the Loeb edition, trans. William M. Green (London: William Heinemann, 1972), vol. 7. The most important statement about Edenic marriage in this work (that it was "a faithful partnership based on true love between each other" [inter se coniugium fida ex honesto amore societas]) is regarded by Clark, " 'Adam's Only Companion' " (n. 20 above), as pointing to friendship in marriage. James G. Turner has interesting and useful comments on Augustine's Eden in *One Flesh: Paradisal Marriage and Sexual Relations in the Age of Milton* (Oxford: Clarendon Press, 1987), pp. 43–55, to which I am indebted for my present modification of the somewhat more traditional views about Augustine I expressed in *Sex and Sensibility.*

23. Jupiter elsewhere gets a fuller comeuppance. Attacking in the *Confessions* the lascivious fables about the chief god, Augustine asks when the great torrent of custom of fabling about this deity will ever run dry: "Did I not read in thee of Jupiter sometimes thundering and sometimes adulterating?" ("nonne ego in te [perhaps chiefly Homer] legi et tonantem Iovem et adulterantem," 1.16). So much for *Jupiter tonans* or the invader of innumerable earthly beds.

24. This suggestion will surely seem extreme to some, but I ask the skeptical reader to compare the boiling and agitated verbs cited earlier from *Confessions* 2.2 with the verbs Marcel Detienne uses of the spurting, leaping effervescence characteristic of his subject's ministrations, in *Dionysos at Large,* trans. Arthur Goldhammer (Cambridge, Mass.: Harvard University Press, 1989), pp. 53–55, 62–64. Augustine is of course orthodox in his final central thought, but he is scarcely ever, least of all in this emotional paean of love and praise, apollonian.

25. Having made so much of the Christian sensualism and naturalism that is embodied in Augustine's lyrical art, it may be asked why I have not made more of the conceivably physical in his relations to his mother and to the friend of his youth whose loss occasioned such emotional trauma (*Confessions* 4.4–5) and

why I have not regarded the "amor Dei," so sharply distinguished from the "amor carnis" in Augustine's conscious mind, as a monumental self-deception. I hope I have by this time made it clear that I cannot sharply separate flesh from spirit in Christian thought and life—indeed I find their union virtually obligatory, as in most effective art. But still, as a literary historian, I must ally myself with those who remain skittish about practicing psychoanalysis on the long dead and gone.

I do not wish to give the impression that Augustine's sensibility was unique in ancient Christianity, though his sustained intensity may be unrivaled. Lives of converted prostitutes and/or actresses provided opportunities not only to confess carnal temptations but to intensify amorous devotion to God. The virtually unknown Nonnus, a fifth-century bishop of Edessa, the central male figure in the equally unknown James the Deacon's "Life of St. Pelagia the Harlot," sees, along with fellow bishops, a gorgeous actress of Antioch pass by, her nakedness only partly hidden by costly jewels and stuffs. He asks "Did not the sight of her great beauty delight you?" The others remain silent. The sensually inspired Nonnus then draws a stunning comparison to the divine Bridegroom, saying: "What think you, beloved? How many hours hath this woman spent in her chamber, bathing and adorning herself with all solicitude . . . that she may be a joy to all men's eyes, nor disappoint those paltry lovers of hers who are but for a day and tomorrow are not? And we who have in heaven a Father Almighty, an immortal Lover, with the promise of riches eternal . . . but what need is there of further speech? With such a promise, the vision of the Bridegroom, that great and splendid and ineffable face, . . . we adorn not, we care not so much as to wash the filth from our miserable souls, but leave them lying in their squalor" (Helen Waddell, ed. and trans., *The Desert Fathers* [Ann Arbor: University of Michigan Press, 1966], pp. 178–79; see also pp. 173, 174–75). What we have here and often elsewhere is neither modern sublimation nor mystical transcendence of the flesh. In Augustine I have just called it displacement of erotic longing, trying to keep much of the original physicality intact in its new venue. We shall encounter other manifestations of this kind of sanctified naturalism, its roots deep in Scripture, as we have seen. Stern asceticism might conceal or divert but did not extinguish it. Consider again the epigraph of this chapter, from Peter Brown.

Chapter Eight

1. *Song of Songs,* trans., ed., and comm. Marvin H. Pope (Garden City, N.Y.: "The Anchor Bible," Doubleday, 1977), p. 325 and note.

2. See John C. Moore, *Love in Twelfth-Century France* (Philadelphia: University of Pennsylvania Press, 1972), p. 73 (emphasis mine).

3. For a discussion of this poem and the tradition, see earlier, chapters 4 and 5, and later, chapter 12. Helmut Birkhan gives the full Latin text and a French translation of the altercation between Helen and Ganymede known in seven

manuscripts: "Qu'est-ce qui est préférable de l'hétérosexualité ou de l'homosexualité? Le témoignage d'un poème latin," *Amour, mariage et transgressions au moyen âge,* ed. Danielle Buschinger and André Crépin (Göppingen: Kümmerle Verlag, 1984), pp. 25–45. For a discussion, see John Boswell, *Christianity, Social Tolerance, and Homosexuality: Gay People in Western Europe from the Beginning of the Christian Era to the Fourteenth Century* (Chicago: University of Chicago Press, 1980), pp. 255–60. It is interesting to note that this contest between competing forms of love apparently entered the medieval classroom, where poems about Pyramus and Thisbe illustrated the heterosexual: Robert Glendinning, "Pyramus and Thisbe in the Medieval Classroom," *Speculum* 61/1 (1986): 51–78, especially pp. 74–75.

In this section and all through this chapter I am indebted to the following: Caroline Walker Bynum, *Holy Feast and Holy Fast: The Religious Significance of Food to Medieval Women* (Berkeley: University of California Press, 1987); Bynum, *Jesus as Mother: Studies in the Spirituality of the High Middle Ages* (Berkeley: University of California Press, 1982); Maurice Keen, *Chivalry* (New Haven: Yale University Press, 1984); Benjamin Nelson, "*Eros, Logos, Nomos, Polis:* Their Changing Balances and the Vicissitudes of Communities and Civilizations," in *Changing Perspectives in the Scientific Study of Religion,* ed. Allan W. Eister (New York: John Wiley & Sons, 1974), pp. 85–111. For a discussion of both older and very recent scholarly texts concerned with medieval love and its contexts, see the introduction by Robert R. Edwards and Stephen Spector to the collection of essays by thirteen scholars: *The Olde Daunce: Love, Friendship, Sex and Marriage in the Medieval World* (Albany: State University of New York Press, 1991).

4. Christine de Pizan, *The Book of the City of Ladies,* trans. Earl J. Richards (New York: Persea, 1982); Christine de Pizan, *A Medieval Woman's Mirror of Honor: The Treasury of the City of Ladies,* trans. Charity Cannon Willard and ed. Madeleine Pelner Cosman (New York and Tenafly, N.J.: Bard Hall Press/Persea, 1989), with useful bibliography and glossary; Diane Bornstein, *The Lady in the Tower: Medieval Courtesy Literature for Women* (Hamden, Conn.: Archon, 1983), pp. 12, 27–28, 44; Shulamith Shahar, *The Fourth Estate: A History of Women in the Middle Ages,* trans. Chaya Galai (London: Methuen, 1983), p. 73.

5. The subtle gradations of expression and posture in the couples in figure 10 shows that pictorial expression could be as sophisticated as literary. Did real life share this sophistication? If so, this marvelous picture could serve as a good visual epigraph for the cultural background of medieval love. For an enlarged, two-page reproduction, see frontispiece of Philippe Ariès and Georges Duby, eds., *A History of Private Life: II. Revelations of the Medieval World,* trans. Arthur Goldhammer (Cambridge, Mass.: Harvard University Press, 1988).

6. For scholarly answers to recurrent questions (what was the social rank and the marital status of the Lady? was the love consummated?), consult William D. Paden, Jr., "The Troubadour's Lady: Her Marital Status and Social Rank," *Studies in Philology* 72/1 (January 1975): 28–50; and Paden, "*Utrum Copularen-*

tur: Of *Cors,* " *Esprit créateur* 19/4 (1979): 70–83; also his illuminating survey of matters relevant to the present study in his introduction to and the essays in *The Voice of the Trobairitz: Perspectives on the Women Troubadours,* ed. William D. Paden, Jr. (Philadelphia: University of Pennsylvania Press, 1989).

See also Roger Boase, *The Origin and Meaning of Courtly Love: A Critical Study of European Scholarship* (Manchester, Eng., and Totowa, N.J.: Manchester University Press, Rowman & Littlefield, 1977); Joan M. Ferrante, *Woman as Image in Medieval Literature from the Twelfth Century to Dante* (New York: Columbia University Press, 1975); Richard Firth Green, "The *Familia Regis* and the *Familia Cupidinis,*" in *English Court Culture in the Later Middle Ages,* ed. V. J. Scattergood and J. W. Sherborne (New York: St. Martin's Press, 1983), pp. 87–108; Elizabeth Salter, "Courts and Courtly Love," chap. 12 in David Daiches and Anthony Thorlby, *The Medieval World* (London: Aldus, 1973), pp. 407–44; Leslie T. Topsfield, "*Fin'Amors* in Marcabru, Bernart de Ventadorn and the *Lancelot* of Chrétien de Troyes," in *Love and Marriage in the Twelfth Century,* ed. Willy van Hoecke and Andries Welkenhuysen (Louvain: Leuven University Press, 1981); Topsfield, *Troubadours and Love* (Cambridge: Cambridge University Press, 1975).

7. Paul Zumthor, "From the Universal to the Particular in Medieval Poetry," *Modern Language Notes* 85 (1970): 815–23; Zumthor, "Autobiography in the Middle Ages," *Genre* 6 (1973): 29–48.

8. Peter Dronke, *Medieval Latin and the Rise of European Love-Lyric,* 2 vols. (Oxford: Clarendon Press, 1968); Dronke, *Women Writers of the Middle Ages: A Critical Study of Texts from Perpetua to Marguerite Porete* (Cambridge: Cambridge University Press, 1984).

9. Maurice J. Valency, *In Praise of Love: An Introduction to the Love-Poetry of the Renaissance* (New York: Macmillan, 1958), pp. 15–31; Moshé Lazar, *Amour courtois et 'fin'amors' dans la littérature du XIIe siècle* (Paris: Klincksieck, 1964).

10. E. William Monter, "The Pedestal and the Stake: Courtly Love and Witchcraft," in *Becoming Visible: Women in European History,* ed. Renate Bridenthal and Claudia Koonz (Boston: Houghton Mifflin, 1977), pp. 119–36.

11. Andreas Capellanus, *The Art of Courtly Love,* introd. and trans. John Jay Parry (New York: Frederick Ungar, 1964), p. 186 (2.8.29), pp. 106–7 (1.6.7); see also p. 171 (2.7.9) and p. 175 (2.7.17).

12. Michelle A. Freeman, "Marie de France's Poetics of Silence: The Implications for a Feminine *Translatio,*" *Publications of Modern Language Association of America* 99/5 (October 1984): 860–83; Emanuel J. Mickel, Jr., "A Reconsideration of the *Lais* of Marie de France," *Speculum* 46 (1971): 39–65; Mickel, *Marie de France* (New York: Twayne, 1974); R. W. Hanning, "Love and Power in the Twelfth Century, with Special Reference to Chrétien de Troyes and Marie de France," *The Old Daunce* (see n. 3 above), pp. 95–99.

13. Abelard was born in 1079, Heloise in 1101. He arrived in Paris in 1113. The relations with Heloise took place from 1118 to 1120. The castration was

arranged by Heloise's uncle, the canon Fulbert; two of its actual perpetrators were caught and were themselves castrated and blinded. *Letters of Abelard and Heloise,* trans. Betty Radice (New York: Penguin, 1974, 1983).

The following are indispensable but differing studies: Peter Dronke, *Abelard and Heloise in Medieval Testimonies* (Glasgow: University of Glasgow Press, 1976); Dronke, "Heloise and Marianne: Some Reconsiderations," *Romanische Forschungen* 72/3–4 (1960): 223–56; Etienne Gilson, *Heloise and Abelard* (Ann Arbor: University of Michigan Press, 1963); Paul Zumthor, "Héloise et Abélard," *Revue des sciences humaines* 91 (1968): 313–32. For summaries of views concerning authenticity, consult Piero Zerbi, "Abelardo ed Eloisa: Il Problema di un amore e di una corrispondenza," in *Love and Marriage in the Twelfth Century* (see n. 6 above), pp. 130–61, chaps. 4 and 5, and pp. 61, 89–92. See Christopher N. L. Brooke, *The Medieval Idea of Marriage* (New York: Oxford University Press, 1989), pp. 40, 128–29, 266 (also on original meaning of *affectio maritalis*). See also Linda Kauffman, *Discourses of Desire* (Ithaca: Cornell University Press, 1986), chap. 2; Peggy Kamuf, *Fictions of Feminine Desire: Disclosures of Heloise* (Lincoln, Neb.: University of Nebraska Press, 1982), pp. xi–xv, 12–15; Jean-Charles Payen, "La 'Mise en roman' du mariage dans la littérature française des XIIe et XIIIe siècles: De l'Evolution idéologique à la typologie des genres," in *Love and Marriage in the Twelfth Century* (n. 6 above); Aldo Scaglione, *Nature and Love in the Late Middle Ages* (Westport, Conn.: Greenwood Press, 1976), pp. 25–32; R. W. Southern, *Medieval Humanism and Other Studies* (Oxford: Basil Blackwell, 1970), chap. 6. I am indebted also to unpublished papers and discussions by John Benton and Barbara Newman.

14. *Eneas: A Twelfth-Century French Romance,* trans. John A. Yunck (New York: Columbia University Press, 1974), pp. 209–66; Alfred Adler, "Eneas and Lavine: *Puer et Puella Senes,*" *Romanische Forschungen* 71 (1959): 73–91; Helen C. R. Laurie, " 'Eneas' and the Doctrine of Courtly Love," *Modern Language Review* 64 (1969): 283–94. On the queen's denunciation to her love-smitten daughter of Eneas as a homosexual and its structural importance, see the learned and subtle analysis of this epic by Patricia Harris Stäblein, "Sexual Specularity . . . ," in *Poetics of Love in the Middle Ages,* ed. Moshé Lazar and Norris J. Lacy (Fairfax, Va.: George Mason University Press, 1989), pp. 217–21. On the related matter of the contest, or *paragone,* between hetero- and homosexual love, see chapters 4, 5, and 12.

15. Joseph Bédier's reconstruction (an archetypal version) remains useful and highly readable (*The Romance of Tristan and Iseult,* trans. H. Belloc, [Portland, Me.: Thomas B. Mosher, 1922]) but of course must be compared with other versions, including his own of Thomas (2 vols. [Paris; Société des Anciens Textes Français, 1902, 1905]). See also Gottfried von Strassburg, *Tristan und Isolde,* ed. Francis G. Gentry and trans. A. T. Hatto (New York: Continuum, 1988); for Béroul's version, A. Ewert, ed., *The Romance of Tristan* (Oxford: Basil Blackwell & Mott, 1939); and for Béroul's version in modern French, with a

tabular comparison with Eilhart, the edition and translation of Donald Stone, Jr. (Englewood Cliffs, N.J.: Prentice Hall, 1966); *Le Roman de Tristan en prose,* ed. Joël Blanchard (Paris: Klincksieck, 1976); *Tristan and the Round Table: A Translation of La Tavola Ritonda,* trans. and ed. Anne Shaver (Binghamton, N.Y.: Medieval & Renaissance Texts and Studies, 1983); *The Saga of Tristan and Isönd,* trans. Paul Schach (Lincoln: University of Nebraska Press, 1973).

For additional commentary, consult Renée L. Curtis, "Le Philtre mal préparé: Le Thème de la réciprocité dans l'amour de Tristan et Iseut," in *Mélanges de langue et de littérature du moyen âge et de la renaissance offerts à Jean Frappier,* 2 vols. (Geneva: Droz, 1970), pp. 195–206; John H. Fisher, "Tristan and Courtly Adultery," *Comparative Literature* 9/2 (Spring 1957): 150–64; Joan M. Ferrante, *The Conflict of Love and Honor: The Medieval Tristan Legend in France, Germany and Italy* (The Hague: Mouton, 1973); W. T. H. Jackson, *The Anatomy of Love: The* Tristan *of Gottfried von Strassburg* (New York: Columbia University Press, 1971); Lazar, *Amour courtois* (n. 9 above), pp. 151–73; Leslie W. Rabine, "The Establishment of Patriarchy in *Tristan and Isolde,"* *Women's Studies* 7 (1980): 19–38; Tony Tanner, *Adultery in the Novel: Contract and Transgression* (Baltimore: Johns Hopkins University Press, 1979).

16. *Passion and Society,* trans. Montgomery Belgion (London: Faber & Faber, 1956), pp. 8, 15, 17, 22–23 (the American title is more widely used: *Love in the Western World,* rev. ed. [New York: Pantheon, 1956]; originally published in French as *L'Amour et l'Occident).* For searching critiques, see John Updike's review, *New Yorker,* 24 August 1963, pp. 90–104; and Irving Singer, *The Nature of Love,* 3 vols. (Chicago: University of Chicago Press, 1984–87) 1:312; 2:x–xi, 298, 299.

17. *Works of Sir Thomas Malory,* ed. Eugène Vinaver, 3 vols. (Oxford: Clarendon Press, 1967) 1:434–35.

18. I quote Chaucer throughout from *The Works of Geoffrey Chaucer,* ed. F. N. Robinson (Boston: Houghton Mifflin, 1933, 1961). Le Goff is quoted by Maurice Keen in *New York Review of Books,* 18 May 1989, p. 48. Flandrin is quoted from James A. Brundage, *Law, Sex, and Christian Society in Medieval Europe* (Chicago: University of Chicago Press, 1987), p. 160, and his chart appears on p. 162, fig. 41. But see Jean-Louis Flandrin, "La Vie sexuelle des gens mariés dans l'ancienne société," *Communications* 35 (1982): 109; Flandrin, *Families in Former Times: Kinship, Household and Sexuality,* trans. Richard Southern (Cambridge: Cambridge University Press, 1979), pp. 162–66; and Flandrin, "Sex in Married Life in the Early Middle Ages: The Church's Teaching and Behavioural Reality," in *Western Sexuality: Practice and Precept in Past and Present Times,* ed. Philippe Ariès and André Béjin (Oxford: Basil Blackwell, 1985), pp. 114–29. *The Meaning of Courtly Love,* ed. F. X. Newman (Albany: State University of New York Press, 1973), contains (pp. 19–42) a useful and richly documented historical article by John F. Benton, "Clio and Venus: An Historical View of Medieval Love."

19. The figure of 3,000 comes from the fittingly logical essay of Michel-

Marie Dufeil, "Regard d'amour" in *Amour, mariage et transgressions au moyen âge* (n. 3 above), pp. 535–59. My discussion is based on the following passages from Aquinas: *Summa theologica* 1a-2ae, 29.3; 1a-2ae, 32.29.2; 1a-2ae, 130.2; 2a-2ae, 57.4; 2a-2ae, 153.2.2–3; 2a-2ae, 154.1–3; 2a-2ae, 151.3.2. See also *Opusc.* 14, exposition, *De Divinis nominibus* 4.11; disputations, *De Caritate, 3.3*; *Contra gentes,* 3.123. For commentary, see also John T. Noonan, Jr., *Contraception: A History of Its Treatment by Catholic Theologians and Canonists* (Cambridge, Mass.: Harvard University Press, 1966), p. 255; Timothy C. Potts, *Conscience in Medieval Philosophy* (Cambridge: Cambridge University Press, 1980), p. ix (calls Aquinas's views "rather untypical of medieval philosophy").

20. Scaglione, *Nature and Love* (n. 13 above), p. 88.

21. George D. Economou, "The Two Venuses and Courtly Love," in *In Pursuit of Perfection: Courtly Love in Medieval Literature,* ed. Joan M. Ferrante and Economou (Port Washington, N.Y.: National University Publications, Kennikat Press, 1975), pp. 17–50; Economou, *The Goddess Nature in Medieval Literature* (Cambridge, Mass.: Harvard University Press, 1972); John Gower, *Confessio amantis,* ed. Russell A. Peck (Toronto: University of Toronto Press, 1980); Patrick J. Gallacher, *Love, the Word, and Mercury: A Reading of John Gower's* Confessio Amantis (Albuquerque: University of New Mexico Press, 1975); Ernst Curtius, *European Literature and the Latin Middle Ages,* trans. Willard R. Trask (Princeton, N.J.: Princeton University Press, 1953; rpt., 1963, 1973), pp. 123–24; C. S. Lewis, *The Allegory of Love: A Study in Medieval Tradition* (New York: Oxford University Press, rpt., 1975), pp. 87–111; Alain de Lille, *Complaint of Nature,* trans. Douglas M. Moffat (New York: Henry Holt, 1908); Robert R. Edwards, *The Dream of Chaucer: Representation and Reflection in the Early Narratives* (Durham, N.C.: Duke University Press, 1989), pp. 137–41 (an admirable summary of medieval nature); Barbara Newman, *Sister of Wisdom: St. Hildegarde's Theology of the Feminine* (Berkeley: University of California Press, 1987), pp. 121–42; Brian Stock, *Myth and Science in the Twelfth Century: A Study of Bernard Sylvester* (Princeton, N.J.: Princeton University Press, 1972); Claude Thomasset, "La Présentation de la sexualité et de la génération dans la pensée scientifique médiévale," in *Love and Marriage in the Twelfth Century* (n. 6 above), pp. 1–17; Winthrop Weatherbee, *Platonism and Poetry in the Twelfth Century: The Literary Influence of the School of Chartres* (Princeton, N.J.: Princeton University Press, 1972).

22. Emily may indeed be too stereotypical to be alluring, but she did cause Palamon, Arcite, and the late E. Talbot Donaldson to fall desperately in love with her, showing the force of an idea if not of a personality. Professor Donaldson once wrote: "May, May, May, May; lily, stalk, flowers, garden, flowers, garland; green, rose, yellow, white, red; morning, day, sunrise: all the best of nature in the Spring, and all parts of Emily, or rather, through the poet's intricate craft, of these things is Emily all compact" (*Speaking of Chaucer* [New York: W. W. Norton, 1970], p. 49). At least this now dated comment does celebrate the naturalism I am trying to expound. But for David Aers, Emily, the enclosed garden, the

flowers reveal only a dehumanized, passive woman who "exists solely as an object in the male's gaze" (*Chaucer* [Atlantic Highlands, N.J.: Humanities Press International, 1986], p. 77).

23. The relevant Inquisition Register runs from 1318 to 1325. Emmanuel Le Roy Ladurie, *Montaillou: The Promised Land of Error*, trans. Barbara Bray (New York: George Braziller, 1978), pp. vii, 158–59. Some of the details I have mentioned appear only in the French original (Paris: Gallimard, 1975) and in discussion by Dronke, *Women Writers* (n. 8 above), pp. 201–9. For an important critique of Le Roy Ladurie, consult Leonard E. Boyle, O. P., "Montaillou Revisited: *Mentalité* and Methodology," in *Pathways to Medieval Peasants*, ed. J. A. Raftis (Toronto: Pontifical Institute of Medieval Studies, 1981), pp. 119–40. No mention is made here of Grazide Lizier, but on the treatment of the Cathars, see pp. 133–36. See also Frances and Joseph Gies, *Marriage and the Family in the Middle Ages* (New York: Harper & Row, 1987), pp. 198, 181, 184.

24. Boswell, *Christianity, Social Tolerance, and Homosexuality* (n. 3 above), pp. 189–95, 220–26. I owe the *Ovide moralisé* and Ridewall references to Leonard Barkan, *The Gods Made Flesh: Metamorphosis and the Pursuit of Paganism* (New Haven: Yale University Press, 1986), pp. 132–33.

25. Benton, "Clio and Venus" (n. 18 above), pp. 32–33. On the woman's orgasm as essential to procreation and its consequent theological and medical support, see Gies and Gies, *Marriage and the Family* (n. 23 above), pp. 303–4. On the presence of sentimental and tender affection in medieval marriage, see ibid., pp. 246, 297–98.

26. Denis de Rougemont, *Love Declared: Essays on the Myths of Love*, trans. Richard Howard (New York: Pantheon, 1963), p. vii.

27. The translations I have used are not always exact, but their exuberance is faithful to Hugh's spirit and to what I believe is central, the juxtaposing of the two loves: *Selected Spiritual Writings* (New York: Harper & Row, 1962), pp. 165, 187, 188, 190, and *The Divine Love* (London: A. R. Mowbray, 1956), pp. 14, 27, both trans. "A Religious of C.S.M.V." The original Latin appears in *Patrologiae cursus completus*, ed. J.-P. Migne (Turnhout, Belgium: Editores Pontificii, Publisher Brepolis, n.d.), vol. 176, cols. 15A–C, 16C. The passage on the two fountains reads: "Unus fons dilectionis intus saliens duos rivos effundit. Alter est amor mundi, cupiditas: alter est amor Dei, charitas. Medium quippe est cor hominis unde fons amoris erumpit" (col. 15C).

28. Saint Bernard is quoted from the Treatise *De Diligendo deo*, in *Opera omnia*, 2 vols. (Paris, 1615), vol. 1, col. 958. Virtually all of the Bourges Last Judgment is by the Michael Master, but heavy nineteenth-century restoration makes stylistic judgments difficult. Still, iconography and meaning surely remain intact. See Tania Bayard, *Bourges Cathedral: The West Portals* (New York: Garland, 1976), pp. iv, 136.

29. Noonan, *Contraception* (n. 19 above), pp. 284–86; and Shahar, *Fourth Estate* (n. 4 above), p. 70.

30. Bynum, *Holy Feast* (n. 3 above), pp. 20, 32, 59, 60, 247. On the mystical

marriage with Christ, see Julia Kristeva, "Stabat Mater," in *The Female Body in Western Culture: Contemporary Perspectives,* ed. Susan Rabin Suleiman (Cambridge, Mass.: Harvard University Press, 1986), pp. 99–118.

31. Peter is quoted from Brooke, *Medieval Idea of Marriage* (n. 13 above), p. 103 and n. 2. I have been influenced in this section by what Bynum says about the body in "Fast, Feast, and Flesh: The Religious Significance of Food to Medieval Women," *Representations* 11 (Summer 1985): 14.

32. On the Florentine *catasto,* see Philippe Contamine, "Peasant Hearth to Papal Palace," in *A History of Private Life: II* (n. 5 above), pp. 426–30; and below.

My social history depends mostly on the following: Philippe Ariès, "Le Mariage indissoluble," *Communications* 35 (1982): 123–37; Georges Duby, Dominique Barthélmy, and Charles de La Roncière, "Portraits," and Dominique Barthélmy and Philippe Contamine, "The Use of Private Space," in *A History of Private Life: II* (n. 5 above), pp. 33–309, 397–505; Karl-Heinz Bender, "Beauté, mariage, amour: La Genèse du premier roman courtois," in *Amour, mariage et transgressions au moyen âge* (n. 3 above), pp. 173–83; Philippe Braunstein, "Toward Intimacy," in *A History of Private Life: II* (n. 5 above), pp. 535–630; Brooke, *Medieval Idea of Marriage* (n. 13 above), pp. 11–19, 119–25, 157–62, 248–57; Georges Duby, *Medieval Marriage: Two Models from Twelfth-Century France,* trans. Elborg Forster (Baltimore: Johns Hopkins University Press, 1978); David Herlihy, *Medieval Households* (Cambridge, Mass.: Harvard University Press, 1985); Charles Duggan, "Equity and Compassion in Papal Marriage Decretals to England," in *Love and Marriage in the Twelfth Century* (n. 6 above), pp. 59–87; Jean-Louis Flandrin, *Le Sexe et l'Occident: Evolution des attitudes et des comportements* (Paris: Seuil, 1981); and Flandrin, "La Vie sexuelle" (n. 18 above), pp. 102–115; Jack Goody, *The Development of the Family and Marriage in Europe* (Cambridge: Cambridge University Press, 1983); Jean Leclercq, "L'Amour et le mariage vus par des clercs et des religieux, spécialment au XIIe siècle," in *Love and Marriage in the Twelfth Century* (n. 6 above), pp. 102–15; JoAnn McNamara and Suzanne F. Wemple, "Sanctity and Power: The Dual Pursuit of Medieval Women" in *Becoming Visible* (n. 10 above), pp. 90–118; Robert C. Palmer, "Contexts of Marriage in Medieval England: Evidence from the King's Court circa 1300," *Speculum* 59/1 (January 1984): 42–67; Michel Rouche, "The Early Middle Ages in the West," in *A History of Private Life: I. From Pagan Rome to Byzantium,* ed. Paul Veyne, trans. Arthur Goldhammer (Cambridge, Mass.: Harvard University Press, 1987), pp. 415–549; Michael M. Sheehan, "Choice of Marriage Partner in the Middle Ages," in *Studies in Medieval and Renaissance History,* ed. J. A. S. Evans (Vancouver: University of British Columbia Press, 1978), 1:1–33; Shahar, *Fourth Estate* (n. 4 above); Zacharia P. Thundy, "Clandestine Marriages in the Late Middle Ages," in *New Images of Medieval Women: Essays Toward a Cultural Anthropology,* ed. Edelgard E. DuBruch (Lewiston, Wales: E. Mellen Press, 1989), pp. 303–20; Pierre Toubert, "La Théorie du mariage chez les moralistes carolingiens," in *Il Matrimonio della società altomedioevale* (Spoleto, 1977), pp. 233–82.

33. See especially Brundage, *Law, Sex and Christian Society* (n. 18 above); and Duggan, "Equity and Compassion" (n. 32 above).

34. Rouche, "Early Middle Ages" (n. 32 above), p. 471. For the modest influence of the Carolingian church on Germanic marriage customs, see Gies and Gies, *Marriage and the Family* (n. 23 above), pp. 83-98.

35. For a comparison of medieval consent with the pagan Roman and Augustinian, see Elizabeth A. Clark, " 'Adam's Only Companion': Augustine and the Early Christian Debate on Marriage," in *The Olde Daunce* (n. 3), pp. 22-23, 29-31, and relevant notes. Michael Sheehan, "The Formation and Stability of Marriage in Fourteenth-Century England: Evidence of an Ely Register," *Medieval Studies* 33 (1971): 229. Stressing love between spouses as that between equals and partners, Sheehan concludes in a later article that the view of Kenelm Foster (and many others, incidentally) cannot be sustained that medieval marriage was "a purely institutional and judicial state which only engages the personality in a relatively superficial way": "*Maritalis Affectio* Revisited," in *The Olde Daunce* (n. 3 above), pp. 32-43. Gies and Gies, *Marriage and the Family* (n. 23 above), pp. 53-56, 135-41, 243-44 (on related matter of clandestine marriages).

36. Toubert, "Théorie du mariage" (n. 32 above), p. 261 and n. 80.

37. The phrase *maritalis affectio* originally and technically referred to the intention to get married, closely related to the *consensus,* one of the defining determinants of marriage. But *maritalis affectio* came by stages to invoke sentiment, feeling, and romance, even when used by celibate canonists and Pope Alexander III, who were deliberately redefining Latin legal terms under contemporary cultural pressures. See Christopher N. L. Brooke, *Medieval Idea of Marriage* (n. 13 above).

38. Sheehan, "Choice of Marriage Partner," (n. 32 above), p. 29 and n. 74.

39. "Portraits," in *History of Private Life: II,* pp. 143-44 (n. 5 above). For Ekbert von Schönau, see F. W. E. Roth, *Die Visionen der hl. Elisabeth und die Schriften der Aebte Ekbert und Emecho von Schönau* (Brünn, 1884), pp. 196-212 (on the abbot) and pp. 230-342 (his writings in Latin).

40. Brundage, *Law, Sex and Christian Society* (n. 18 above), p. 229, and (on Huguccio and his shifting emphases), pp. 262, 268, 273 and n. 74. For a comprehensive and important discussion of marriage and friendship, see Erik Kooper, "Loving the Unequal Equal: Medieval Theologians and Marital Affection," in *The Olde Daunce* (n. 3 above), pp. 44-56.

41. On the great white house, see *History of Private Life, II* (n. 5 above), pp. 35-38; and on castle splendor, ibid., p. 423. The context for the latter is King Arthur's visit to the splendid hall of his sister Morgan. On Naumburg Cathedral, see Hans Jantzen, *Deutsche Bildhauer des dreizehnter Jahrhundert* (Leipzig: Insel-Verlag, 1925), figs. 129, 130 and pp. 242-44.

42. Georges Duby, *The Knight, the Lady and the Priest: The Making of Modern Marriage in Medieval France,* trans. Barbara Bray (New York: Pantheon, 1983), p. 8.

Chapter Nine

1. Huizinga is cited by John Stevens, *Medieval Romances: Themes and Approaches* (London: Hutchinson University Library, 1973), p. 40.

2. Michael Sheehan, "The Formation and Stability of Marriage in Fourteenth-Century England: Evidence of an Ely Register," *Medieval Studies* 33 (1971): 230.

3. Robert W. Hanning, *The Individual in Twelfth-Century Romance* (New Haven: Yale University Press, 1977), pp. 53–54. For related cultural alternatives to love and power (namely, scholarship and imaginative works of art), see Hanning, "Love and Power in the Twelfth Century, with Special Reference to Chrétien de Troyes and Marie de France," in *The Olde Daunce: Love, Friendship, Sex and Marriage in the Medieval World,* ed. Robert R. Edwards and Stephen Spector (Albany: State University of New York Press, 1991), pp. 87–103.

4. On art in this period I am indebted to Danielle Régnier-Bohler, "Imagining the Self," in *A History of Private Life: II. Revelations of the Medieval World,* ed. Philippe Ariès and Georges Duby, trans. Arthur Goldhammer (Cambridge, Mass.: Harvard University Press, 1988), pp. 313–93; to Rebecca Martin's unpublished lectures, delivered in May 1987 at the North Carolina State Museum of Arts, and to her dissertation bibliography, "Wild Men and Moors in the Castle of Love: The Castle Siege Tapestries in Nuremberg, Vienna, and Boston" (University of North Carolina, Chapel Hill, 1983); and to Millard Meiss, *Painting in Florence and Siena after the Black Death* (Princeton, N.J.: Princeton University Press, 1951), pp. 61, 108–10.

5. *Erec and Enide,* ed. and trans. Carleton W. Carroll, introd. William W. Kibler (New York: Garland, 1987); Mario Roques, ed., *Les Romans de Chrétien de Troyes,* vol. 1, *Erec et Enide* (Paris: Champion, 1970); Jean Frappier, *Chrétien de Troyes: The Man and His Work,* trans. Raymond J. Cormier (Athens, Ohio: Ohio University Press, 1982); Moshé Lazar, *Amour courtois et 'fin'amors' dans la littérature du XIIe siècle* (Paris: Klincksieck, 1964), pp. 200–212; Claude Luttrell, *The Creation of the First Arthurian Romance: A Quest* (London: Edward Arnold, 1974); L. T. Topsfield, *Chrétien de Troyes: A Study of the Arthurian Romance* (Cambridge: Cambridge University Press, 1981). For a learned and wide-ranging discussion of war and love, see Eugene Vance, "Le Combat érotique chez Chrétien de Troyes: De la figure à la forme," *Poétique* 12 (1971): 544–71.

6. It is here that Hartmann von Aue, in his powerful poem, *Erec,* gives to Enite a speech that surpasses in pathos and independence of thought anything in the earlier poem by Chrétien. In her angry aria the German heroine even chides her inexorable God, calls on animals to come and take her, thinks seriously of suicide, speaks both erotically and scoldingly to death, and cries out piteously to her parents. It should be noted that in the German tradition, one going back for centuries even as far as Tacitus, marriage and woman were often highly respected. In Wolfram von Eschenbach's *Parzival,* for example, there are some

fourteen marriages (four of them very prominent), while in Chrétien's grail stories there are none (though if *Perceval* had been finished, the hero would perhaps have married Blancheflor). Hartmann von Aue, *Erec,* trans. Thomas L. Keller (New York: Garland, 1987); Christopher N. L. Brooke, *The Medieval Idea of Marriage* (New York: Oxford University Press, 1989), pp. 188, 191; Patrick M. McConeghy, "Women's Speech and Silence in Hartmann von Aue's *Erec,*" *Publications of Modern Language Association of America* 102/5 (October 1987): 772–83.

7. *Cligès,* trans. L. J. Gardner (London: Chatto & Windus, 1912); Frappier, *Chrétien de Troyes* (n. 5 above), p. 86 (on relation to Tristan legend); Topsfield, *Chrétien de Troyes* (n. 5 above), pp. 63–69, 102; Lazar, *Amour courtois* (n. 5 above), p. 213 ("*L'une décrit, l'autre polémize*" [emphasis Lazar's]).

8. *Yvain,* trans. Robert W. Ackerman and Frederick W. Locke (New York: Frederick Ungar, 1957); Frappier, *Chrétien de Troyes* (n. 5 above), pp. 110–25; J. P. Collas, "The Romantic Hero of the Twelfth Century," in *Medieval Miscellany Presented to Eugène Vinaver,* ed. F. Whitehead et al. (New York: Barnes & Noble, 1965), pp. 80–96; Joan M. Ferrante, "The Conflict of Lyric Conventions and Romance Form," in *In Pursuit of Perfection: Courtly Love in Medieval Literature,* ed. Ferrante and George D. Economou (Port Washington, N.Y.: Kennikat Press, 1975), pp. 156–58; Penny Schine Gold, *The Lady and the Virgin: Image, Attitude, and Experience in Twelfth-Century France* (Chicago: University of Chicago Press, 1985), pp. 18–42 (where the discussion broadens to include many related and important matters); Hanning, "Love and Power" (n. 3 above), pp. 90–95; Lazar, *Amour courtois* (n. 5 above), pp. 245–51.

9. Joan M. Ferrante, *Woman as Image in Medieval Literature from the Twelfth Century to Dante* (New York: Columbia University Press, 1975), p. 127. On the relevant Dante, see *La Vita nuova,* trans. Mark Musa (Bloomington: Indiana University Press, 1962), pp. 19–20, 33–35, 37, 66; Maurice J. Valency, *In Praise of Love: An Introduction to the Love-Poetry of the Renaissance* (New York: Macmillan, 1958), pp. 204–10; and John Charles Nelson, *Renaissance Theory of Love: The Context of Giordano Bruno's* Eroici furori (New York: Columbia University Press, 1958), pp. 16 and n. 4, 21, 30, 36. I have also been helped by Christopher Kleinhenz, "Dante as Reader and Critic of Courtly Literature," in *Courtly Literature: Culture and Context,* ed. Keith Busby and Erik Cooper (Philadelphia: John Benjamins, 1990), pp. 379–93. For a thoughtful and undogmatic consideration of the spiritual body and of the possible fusion of religion and sex in Dante, see Colin Hardie, "Dante and the Tradition of Courtly Love," in *Patterns of Love and Courtesy,* ed. John Lawlor (Evanston, Ill.: Northwestern University Press, 1966), pp. 26–44. On Paolo and Francesca, see Douglas Radcliff-Umstead, "Erotic Sin in the Divine Comedy," in *Human Sexuality in the Middle Ages and the Renaissance,* ed. Radcliff-Umstead (Pittsburgh: University of Pittsburgh Publications on the Middle Ages and the Renaissance 4, Center for Medieval and Renaissance Studies), pp. 50–54.

10. Renato Poggioli quotes De Sanctis in "Paolo and Francesca," in *Dante:*

A Collection of Critical Essays, ed. John Freccero (Englewood Cliffs, N.J.: Prentice Hall, 1965), pp. 72. Poggioli discusses the "idealizing and sublimating illusions which literature creates around the realities of sex and lust" (p. 65). On developing concepts of love in Dante, see Jerome Mazzaro, "From *Fin Amour* to Friendship: Dante's Transformation," in *The Olde Daunce* (n. 3 above), pp. 121–37, which argues within an orthodox framework and explores learnedly, persuasively, and originally the topos of friendship in the Dantean development and dialectic.

11. Aldo Scaglione, "Petrarca 1974: A Sketch for a Portrait," in *Francis Petrarch, Six Centuries Later: A Symposium,* ed. Scaglione (Durham: University of North Carolina, Chapel Hill, and Newberry Library, 1975), p. 5. Ernst Curtius uses a different metaphor: "To modulate an erotic theme through hundreds of sonnets was an only too attractive invention of Petrarch's, which spread almost like an epidemic disease and made the sixteenth century sonnet-mad" (*European Literature and the Latin Middle Ages,* trans. Willard Trask [Princeton, N.J.: Princeton University Press, 1973], p. 396). Dismay at Petrarch's kind of obsession began early: Giordano Bruno saw him under the tyranny of "una indegna, imbecile, stolta e sozza sporcaria" (strong words quoted in Nelson, *Renaissance Theory of Love* [n. 9 above], p. 172), and many northern and English writers stood in opposition to the Petrarchan vogue. Against all this (old or new) is the modern praise of the poet's analytical, psychological penetration of the fluctuating states of the human soul. Compare Francesco de Sanctis, who says Petrarch has created in Laura the most real literary being the Middle Ages could produce and that in reading him "siamo in piena luce nel tempio dell'umana coscienza," observing "la vicenda assidua de' fenomeni più delicati del cuore umano" (*Storia della letteratura italiana,* 2 vols. [Milan: Edizioni A. Barion, 1934], 1:212, 218, 219. I find Leonard Barkan's point persuasive (one also congenial to the literary filiations pursued in this book) that Laura and *l'aura* recall Ovid's story of Cephalus and Procris, with its confusion of identity between Aura and Aurora (*The Gods Made Flesh: Metamorphosis and the Pursuit of Paganism* [New Haven: Yale University Press, 1986], pp. 208–9). See chapter 5 above.

For a brilliant placement of Petrarch's love myth in a psychoanalytic and historical narrative, see Gordon Braden, "Love and Fame: The Petrarchan Career," in *Pragmatism's Freud: The Moral Disposition of Psychoanalysis,* ed. Joseph H. Smith and William Kerrigan (Baltimore: Johns Hopkins University Press, 1986), pp. 126–58.

I quote the poetry from, and follow the numeration of, *Petrarch's Lyric Poems: The* Rime Sparse *and Other Lyrics,* ed. and trans. Robert M. Durling (Cambridge, Mass.: Harvard University Press, 1976).

12. *Le Pèlerinage de Charlemagne,* ed. and trans. Glyn S. Burgess, introd. Anne Elizabeth Cobby (New York: Garland, 1988). I make references by stanza numbers.

13. Ibid., pp. 10, 85 (note to line 446). Relevant to *gaber* and to my entire discussion of the humorous, realistic, and satirical in the pages that follow is Si-

mon Gaunt, *Troubadours and Irony* (Cambridge: Cambridge University Press, 1989), pp. 19, 22, 31. Glending Olson is also relevant: *Literature as Recreation in the Later Middle Ages* (Ithaca: Cornell University Press, 1982).

14. *Aucassin et Nicolette,* ed. Anne Elizabeth Cobby, trans. and introd. Glyn S. Burgess (New York: Garland, 1988). I make reference by stanza and line. It is the author himself who calls his work a *cante-fable* (41.24).

15. "Vostre gens me tient por fole, / Quant mes dox amis m'acole, / Et il me sent grasse et mole, / Dont sui jou a tele escole. . ." (33.3–6).

16. Ingrid Strasser, "Mariage, amour et adultère dans les fabliaux," in *Amour, mariage et transgressions au moyen âge,* ed. Danielle Buschinger and André Crépin (Göppingen: Kümmerle Verlag, 1984), pp. 425–33.

17. Danièle Alexandre Bidon and Monique Closson, "L'Amour à l'épreuve du temps: Femmes battues, maris battus, amants battus à travers les manuscrits enluminés," in ibid., pp. 493–513.

18. John A. Nichols, "Female Nudity and Sexuality in Medieval Art," in *New Images of Medieval Women: Essays Toward a Cultural Anthropology,* ed. Edelgard E. DuBruch (Lewiston, Wales: E. Mellen Press, 1989), pp. 165–206.

19. San Bernardino is quoted from Brooke, *Medieval Idea of Marriage* (n. 6 above), p. 29. Fra Paolino is discussed by Charles de La Roncière, "Tuscan Notables on the Eve of the Renaissance," in *A History of Private Life II* (n. 4 above), pp. 157–309. The entire section by La Roncière, with its copious illustrations, is relevant to this and the ensuing chapters on the Renaissance.

20. I have relied heavily on and quoted A. J. Smith's vivid retelling of the story: *The Metaphysics of Love: Studies in Renaissance Love Poetry from Dante to Milton* (Cambridge: Cambridge University Press, 1985), pp. 29–30.

21. *Genealogia deorum gentilium* 14.7: "Poesis . . . est feruor quidam exquisite inueniendi atque dicendi seu scribendi quod inueneris." For the extra-*Decameron* literature, I have relied on: Robert Hollander, *Boccaccio's Two Venuses* (New York: Columbia University Press, 1977); Dario Rastelli, "L'Elegia di Fiametta: Il Mito mondano e la caratterizzazione psicologica della protagonista," *Studia Ghisleriana* 2/1 (1950): 153–73; Judith Powers Serafini-Sauli, *Giovanni Boccaccio* (Boston: Twayne, 1982); Robert Griffin, "Boccaccio's *Fiametta;* Pictures at an Exhibition," *Italian Quarterly* 18/72 (1975): 75–94.

22. De Sanctis, *Storia della letteratura italiana* (n. 11 above) 1:250; *The Decameron,* trans. and ed. Mark Musa and Peter A. Bondanella (New York: W. W. Norton, 1977), p. 224; Thomas Bergin, "An Introduction to Boccaccio," in ibid., p. 165; Marga Cottino-Jones, "Fabula vs. Figura: Another Interpretation of the Griselda Story," ibid., pp. 295–306 (Griselda represents love on the sacrificial level, a *figura Christi,* as Gualtieri is "the Divine Father").

23. Bergin, "Introduction" (n. 22 above), pp. 162–64. For quotations from the *Decameron,* see *Decameron,* trans. John Payne, rev. and annot. Charles S. Singleton, paginated continuously through 3 vols. (Berkeley: University of California Press, 1982), p. 854. I refer to the tales by "day" and number. Though I have acknowledged help in the notes that precede and follow, I have, in my analysis of the *Decameron,* pretty much navigated on my own—for better or worse.

24. Singleton, *Decameron* (n. 23 above), pp. 190, 290, 854. The ladies coming from a church wedding must have looked like a gaggle of geese. The Italian word is *papere,* which is more colloquial than *oca.*

The implication of the father's refusal is naughty. The Italian reads, "Tu non sai donde elle s'imbeccano." The verb *imbeccare* means to feed the goose through the beak: being voracious it always wants more. But it is thus that the delicacy, pâté de foie gras, is produced, by cramming food down the long neck. To be obvious about it, the neck stands for that part of the female body most willing to receive what is induced, what is hungered for; the scholars refer us to the story of the judge in Pisa, where it is said that "the ill hole will have no holidays."

25. Vittore Branca, *Boccaccio: The Man and His Works,* trans. Richard Monges, ed. Dennis J. McAuliffe, foreword Robert C. Clements (New York: New York University Press, 1976), p. 276.

26. Erich Auerbach, *Mimesis: The Representation of Reality in Western Literature* (Garden City, N.Y.: 1957), p. 198.

27. On the conflicts in Boccaccio between nature and social hypocrisy, consult Aldo Scaglione, *Nature and Love in the Late Middle Ages* (Westport, Conn.: Greenwood Press, 1976), pp. 95–96, 124.

28. See Sheehan, "Formation and Stability of Marriage" (n. 2 above), pp. 229–30.

29. F. R. H. DuBoulay, *An Age of Ambition: English Society in the Late Middle Ages* (New York: Viking Press, 1970), p. 83, chap. 5. I have referred in this paragraph to Eve's creation from man's side. What scholars call the "rib topos" has a wide range of theological meaning, not all of it demeaning to woman: Hugh of St. Victor, followed by Aelred, says that being produced from man's middle proves woman was made for equality of association. See Erik Kooper, "Loving the Unequal Equal: Medieval Theologians and Marital Affection," in *The Olde Daunce* (n. 3 above), pp. 48–49. Kooper analyzes many more meanings, paradoxes, and nuances than I have space to note.

30. The comment on the married woman's "unpassioned" love is made by Du Boulay, *An Age of Ambition* (n. 29 above), p. 107. On the Lisle family, consult *The Lisle Letters,* ed. Muriel St. Clare Byrne, 6 vols. (Chicago: University of Chicago Press, 1981). For the Pastons, see Ann S. Haskell, "The Paston Women on Marriage in Fifteenth-Century England," *Viator* 4 (1973): 459–71.

31. I have here relied on Susan Crane, *Insular Romance: Politics, Faith, and Culture in Anglo-Norman and Middle English Literature* (Berkeley: University of California Press, 1986), pp. 5, 12, 13–14, 76, 102, 141–57, 179. On Hue, see especially pp. 158–74.

32. I have quoted "The Punished Atheist" from *The Pepys Ballads,* ed. Hyder Edward Rollins, 8 vols. (Cambridge, Mass.: Harvard University Press, 1929–32), 3:183 (poem 128). See also Francis James Child, *The English and Scottish Popular Ballads,* 5 vols. in 4 (Boston: Houghton Mifflin, 1885) 1:15–20, 55; 3:500 (F); 4:433. This passage of course may recall the Song of Songs, and the "fair and virtuous bride" might well have been not the speaker's sister but his

young wife ("my sister, my spouse," as the biblical masterpiece has it), who is horrified not at potential incest but at the proposed locus of his penetration.

33. For an exemplary discussion of this poem, see Thomas C. Moser, Jr., " 'And I Mon Waxe Wod': The Middle English 'Foweles in the Frith'," *Publications of Modern Language Association of America* 102/3 (May 1987): 326–37.

34. Patricia Mary Vinje, *An Understanding of Love According to the Anchoress Julian of Norwich* (Salzburg, 1983), pp. 2, 5, 21, 106, 167, 208.

35. *The Book of Margery Kempe,* trans. B. A. Windeatt (Harmondsworth, Eng.: Penguin, 1987). I make page references to this work. For commentary, consult Richard Kieckhefer, *Unquiet Souls: Fourteenth-Century Saints and Their Religious Milieu* (Chicago: University of Chicago Press, 1984), pp. 182–90, 196–98; and John A. Erskine, "Margery Kempe and Her Models: The Role of the Authorial Voice," *Mystics Quarterly* 15 (1989): 75–85. See also the biography by Louise Collis, *Memoirs of a Medieval Woman: The Life and Times of Margery Kempe* (New York: Harper & Row, 1983); and Gail McMurray Gibson, *The Theater of Devotion* (Chicago: University of Chicago Press, 1989), chap. 3. Gibson argues that Kempe lives out spiritual exercises on the life of Christ but at the same time remains "her inimitable self" with her "own and unique imagination" (p. 49).

36. The narrative is an autobiography, but Margery always refers to herself in the third person, using instead of the autobiographical "I" the term, "this creature." Such a form of self-reference must in part be a sign of Christian humility. The baby Jesus, unbearably real and ravishing, also moved her to tears, but the most potent stimulus seems to be the young man. Seeing Jesus once in the choir of a church, his face turned upward toward her, she beholds "the handsomest man that ever might be seen or imagined" (249), and she weeps bitterly when she sees that lovely body stabbed with a spear. Her sobs often became screams and loud cries, and were understandably resented by neighbors, fellow communicants, and fellow travelers.

37. E. Talbot Donaldson, *Speaking of Chaucer* (New York: W. W. Norton, 1970), p. 26; and Alfred David, *The Strumpet Muse: Art and Morals in Chaucer's Poetry* (Bloomington: Indiana University Press, 1976), p. 97. I have used throughout *The Works of Geoffrey Chaucer,* ed. F. N. Robinson (Boston: Houghton Mifflin, 1933, 1961). I make line references to particular texts.

38. V. A. Kolve, *Chaucer and the Imagery of Narrative* (Stanford, Calif.: Stanford University Press, 1984), p. 149. My point of view on the "Knight's Tale" is close to that of Paul A. Olson, *The Canterbury Tales and the Good Society* (Princeton, N.J.: Princeton University Press, 1986), p. 69: Theseus as the *Rex Imago Christi* "makes the natural law of desire into positive law to benefit the community," he is wise enough to forgive, and he foresees joy for the couple, Athens, and Thebes if Palamon acts to transform "his Venus into a *marriage*" and Emily to transform her Diana into "a *chaste* marriage." I find this position more plausible than that of Terry Jones, *Chaucer's Knight* (Baton Rouge: Louisiana State University Press, 1980), pp. 146–48, 154–55, 176–77; and David Aers,

Chaucer (Atlantic Highlands, N.J.: Humanities Press International, 1986), pp. 24–25, 76–78.

39. I most regretfully give a very brief comment on this great poem, believing that it is not fully relevant to my main emphasis. But see n. 40 below. Within the voluminous and sharply divided commentary on the *Troilus,* I am attracted to the following: whatever his purpose, Chaucer in the poem "succeeds only in fixing our hearts more firmly on the imperfect human love" (David, *Strumpet Muse* [n. 37 above], p. 33).

40. I do not see evidence that Troilus and Criseyde were joined in holy wedlock, as has been asserted by Kelly; such a view obscures what I think Chaucer wishes us to feel strongly here—the beauty of the pagan erotic moment. But certainly the idea that their secret union possessed the force of the by now widely accepted canonical and theological view that validity could arise in clandestine unions of choice and sexual consummation should not be ruled out as operating dynamically in the background. Henry Ansgar Kelly, *Love and Marriage in the Age of Chaucer* (Ithaca: Cornell University Press, 1975), pp. 217–40. This work is groundbreaking, extremely valuable in establishing the claims for married affection in Chaucer and medieval literature. My disagreement about the advisability of insisting on the technicality of actual Christian marriage in the pagan setting should not obscure my admiration.

41. Delicacy and irony are perforce present in the bourgeois Chaucer's presentation of the royal Gaunt in love. See Earle Birney, *Essays on Chaucerian Irony,* ed., with an essay on irony, Beryl Rowland (Toronto: University of Toronto Press, 1985), pp. 60–61. On the *Duchess* and its relations to Chaucer's narrative beginnings, see Robert R. Edwards, *The Dream of Chaucer: Representation and Reflection in the Early Narratives* (Durham: Duke University Press, 1989), pp. 65–91.

42. I isolate the love elements, which should also be seen in the rich context of source revision and aesthetic-intellectual patterning analyzed by Edwards, *Dream of Chaucer* (n. 41 above), pp. 123–46; and Kurt Olsson, "Poetic Invention and Chaucer's *Parlement of Foules,*" *Modern Philology* 87/1 (August 1989): 13–35.

43. Donaldson, *Speaking of Chaucer* (n. 37 above), p. 53; David Aers, *Chaucer, Langland and the Creative Imagination* (London: Routledge & Kegan Paul, 1980), pp. 151–60 (relating this portrait of marriage to the fragmentation in Chaucer's culture). Robert R. Edwards, with very full documentation, presents the tale as a complex moral speculation that is not reduced to either misogyny or facile orthodoxy about marriage but that is enriched by a dialectical opposition between these polarities ("Narration and Doctrine in the Merchant's Tale" [unpublished]).

44. R. E. Kaske, "Chaucer's Marriage Group," in *Chaucer the Love Poet,* ed. Jerome Mitchell and William Provost (Athens: University of Georgia Press, 1973), p. 65. George L. Kittredge believed that the Franklin ("no cloistered rhetorician, but a ruddy, white-bearded vavasour, a great man in his neighborhood")

brings the marriage debate to a definitive conclusion by presenting marriage under "a perfect rule of faith and practice" (*Chaucer and His Poetry* [Cambridge, Mass.: Harvard University Press, 1936], pp. 209–10). Similar, though more nuanced, views are presented by: C. Hugh Holman, "Courtly Love in the Merchant's and the Franklin's Tales," *ELH: Journal of Literary History* 18/4 (December 1951): 241–52; Kathryn Jacobs, "The Marriage Contract of the *Franklin's Tale*: The Remaking of Society," *The Chaucer Review* 20/2 (1985): 132–43; Elizabeth Salter, "Courts and Courtly Love," chap. 12 in *The Medieval World*, ed. David Daiches and Anthony Thorlby (London: Aldus Books, 1973), p. 440. In opposition of varying kinds are: Alan T. Gaylord (Franklin's weak conception of *fides*), "The Promises in *The Franklin's Tale*," *ELH* 31/4 (December 1964): 331–65; Traugott Lawler (Franklin's peculiar morality and shallow optimism), *The One and the Many in the Canterbury Tales* (Hamden, Conn.: Archon Books, 1980), pp. 74, 77, 80; Edmund Reiss (the solution is "facile"), "Chaucer's Courtly Love," in *The Learned and the Lewd: Studies in Chaucer and Medieval Literature*, ed. Larry D. Benson (Cambridge, Mass.: Harvard University Press, 1974), p. 100; Derek Traversi (attractive but unrealistic and incomplete answer), *The Literary Imagination: Studies in Dante, Chaucer, and Shakespeare* (Newark: University of Delaware Press, 1982), p. 117. Kittredge appealed to the Franklin's character, appearance, and position, but see Donald R. Howard, *The Idea of the Canterbury Tales* (Berkeley: University of California Press, 1976), pp. 268–70 (the Franklin is only an ambitious though genial Epicurean); and Henrik Specht, *Chaucer's Franklin in the Canterbury Tales: The Social and Literary Background of a Chaucerian Character* (Copenhagen: Akademisk Forlag, 1981), pp. 171–74 (believes the knightly virtues of "Trouthe and honour, fredom and curteisie" characterize the Franklin and give his marital portrait authority).

Since writing this note I have read two excellent essays on the Franklin and his tale. One, a defense of the wisdom of its marital ideal, provides a rich context: James I. Wimsatt, "Reason, Machaut, and the Franklin," in *The Olde Daunce* (n. 3 above), pp. 201–10. The other, by Alan T. Gaylord, "From Dorigen to the Vavasour: Reading Backwards," in *The Olde Daunce* (n. 3 above), pp. 177–200, and especially p. 193, gives the Franklin his due in stating the ideal, but then "reads backwards" to reveal, with wit and learning, a contrary, more ironical view in which "gentleniceness" replaces *gentilesse.*

45. James Sledd, in a stimulating article, has found the tale not flatly bad but middling, and too straightforward. But in teaching it to young people of professorial rank in the Washington area a few years ago, I found its narrative powers were highly respected though it did bruise modern sensibilities. See James Sledd, "The *Clerk's Tale*: The Monsters and the Critics," in *Chaucer Criticism: The Canterbury Tales*, ed. Richard J. Schoeck and Jerome Taylor (Notre Dame, Ind.: University of Notre Dame Press, 1960), pp. 160–74. See also the commentary in *The Clerk's Prologue and Tale*, ed. James Winney (Cambridge: Cambridge University Press, 1966), pp. 1–3, 6. Cristelle L. Baskins, in an unpublished paper, has shown the enormous popularity of the Griselda theme in the visual arts, no-

tably on *cassoni*. I am grateful to her for giving me bibliography from her dissertation ("*Lunga Pittura:* Narrative Conventions in Tuscan Cassone Painting circa 1450–1500" [University of California, Berkeley, 1988]).

46. William Matthews, "The Wife of Bath and All Her Sect," *Viator* 5(1974): 413–43, especially 440–43. For La Vielle, see *The Romance of the Rose by Guillaume de Lorris and Jean de Meung,* trans. Charles Dahlberg (Princeton, N.J.: Princeton University Press, 1971), the passage beginning at line 12,820 and pp. 222–48. For an astute analysis of the "chappitre de Reson," broadly applicable to the present discussion and to much else in this volume, consult John V. Fleming, *Reason and the Lover* (Princeton, N.J.: Princeton University Press, 1984).

47. Aers, *Chaucer, Langland and the Creative Imagination* (n. 43 above), especially the comments on "al is for to selle" (p. 147). On the striking of Jankyn, see Barbara Gottfried, "Conflict and Relationship, Sovereignty and Survival: Parables of Power in the *Wife of Bath's Prologue,*" *The Chaucer Review* 19/3 (1985): 202–24.

48. Highly relevant is Donald C. Green, "The Semantics of Power: *Maistrie* and *Soveraynetee* in *The Canterbury Tales,*" *Modern Philology* 84/1 (August 1986): 18–23, concluding that the Wife is heretical in challenging the natural and divine order by confusing sovereignty and mastery and desiring both in marriage. If applied mechanically, this verbal analysis would destroy my argument. But I do not think, though he organized his ideas tightly, that a writer of Chaucer's imaginative power is bound by them, and his Wife in challenging verbal-intellectual structures is not thereby imaginatively undercut, though the strictly orthodox of his contemporary readers may have shuddered. Compare Susan Crane, "Alison's Incapacity and Poetic Instability in the Wife of Bath's Tale," *Publications of Modern Language Association of America* 102/1 (January 1987): 20–28. Crane concludes that though the Wife's redefinitions are provisional, her dilemmas unresolved, and her longing elusive, "her insatiable desire is more forceful and preoccupying than any of her illusory conclusions" (p. 27).

49. Britton J. Harwood, "The Wife of Bath and the Dream of Innocence," *Modern Language Quarterly* 33/3 (September 1972): 257–73, especially pp. 272–73.

50. Lee Patterson, "'For the Wyves love of Bathe': Feminine Rhetoric and Poetic Resolution in the *Roman de la Rose* and the *Canterbury Tales,*" *Speculum* 58/3 (1983): 656–95, especially 693. This important article concludes that though the tale seems to articulate a fundamental orthodoxy, it finally, in the Wife's curse (1258–64), subverts the entire male enterprise that has been set up in the prologue and tale (683)—a good antidote to sentimentality in interpretation that does not, however, in my view, negate or make despicable her longing for and vision of mutuality.

51. We shall better understand Chaucer here and elsewhere when he uses the Middle English word *parfit* (our *perfect*), if we remember the Latin word from which it comes, *perficere,* whose past participle *perfectus* means essentially

what Chaucer's word did: that which is not deficient; "in the state proper to anything when completed" (OED). In other words Chaucer does not say, sentimentally, that there is neither evil nor difficulty in marriage, but that it is capable of being brought to a state that will realize its purposes. And this ideal his and the immediately precedent culture had stated newly and clearly, as we have seen. It is not far from what our forefathers meant when they proposed the formation of a "more perfect union." The comparative "more perfect" would, in our own contemporary meaning of "perfect," constitute a grievous solecism.

52. Derek Brewer, "Gothic Chaucer," in *Geoffrey Chaucer,* ed. Brewer (Athens, Ohio: Ohio University Press, 1975), finds "Chaucer the most notably feminist author in English until Richardson, and [he] has had few rivals since"; he considers the Wife "triumphantly human and sympathetic, gloriously selfish and materialistic" (p. 18). Hope Phyllis Weissman, "Antifeminism and Chaucer's Characterization of Women," in *Geoffrey Chaucer: A Collection of Original Articles,* ed. George D. Economou (New York: McGraw-Hill, 1975), pp. 93–100, says that "the Wife of Bath is most truly feminist in her effort to dispense with images of women altogether," but in the end she instantiates the popular image of woman and so is after all the prisoner of antifeminism (p. 105). For D. W. Robertson, Jr., *A Preface to Chaucer: Studies in Medieval Perspectives* (Princeton, N.J.: Princeton University Press, 1962), the Wife is quite simply an evil being, *in* but not *of* the church, a scorner of the perfection of virginity despite Christ's chastity and a lover of the barley bread of the old dispensation (pp. 329–31). Paul A. Olson, *The* Canterbury Tales *and the Good Society* (n. 38 above), says that the Wife belongs, with the Friar, the Summoner, the Pardoner, the Merchant, and the Franklin, to an Epicurean sect, related to the excesses of Cockaigne and belonging to Dante's Inferno with the three-headed Satan of impotence, ignorance, and hate (chap. 9). Kenneth J. Oberembt finds that Dame Alice's misogyny, though heretical, redounds to her credit, since she uses it to criticize widely accepted sexual doctrines (he also usefully calls the long roll of the defenders of the Wife from Root and Lounsbury on): "Chaucer's Antimisogynist Wife of Bath," *The Chaucer Review* 10/4 (1976): 287–302. See also Robert Hanning, "From *Eva* and *Ave* to Eglentyne and Alisoun: Chaucer's Insight into the Roles Women Play," *Signs* 2/3(1977): 580–99 (finds some self-hate in the Wife's denunciations).

53. *Works of Sir Thomas Malory,* ed. Eugène Vinaver, 3 vols. (Oxford: Clarendon Press, 1967). I refer to this work by volume, page, and line number. *Malory: The Morte Darthur,* ed. D. S. Brewer, parts 7 and 8 only (Evanston, Ill.: Northwestern University Press, 1974); Larry D. Benson, *Malory's Morte Darthur* (Cambridge, Mass.: Harvard University Press, 1976); Hanning, *Individual in Twelfth-Century Romance* (n. 3 above), pp. 230–32; Beverly Kennedy, *Knighthood in the Morte Darthur* (Dover, N.H.: D. S. Brewer, 1985); R. T. Davies, "The Worshipful Way in Malory," in *Patterns of Love and Courtesy* (n. 9 above), pp. 157–77; Terence McCarthy, *Reading the Morte Darthur* (Cambridge: D. S. Brewer, 1988); Maureen Fries, "Indiscreet Objects of Desire: Malory's 'Tris-

tram' and the Necessity of Deceit," in *Studies in Malory,* ed. James W. Spisak (Kalamazoo, Mich.: Medieval Institute Publications, Western Michigan University, 1985).

54. *Malory: The Critical Heritage,* ed. Marylyn Jackson Parins (London: Routledge, 1988), pp. 56–57.

55. Smith, *Metaphysics of Love* (n. 20 above), p. 38.

56. Discussed learnedly, and movingly, by Christopher N. L. Brooke, who makes loyalty (*triuwe*) the pillar of Wolfram's conception of cultural order. (*Medieval Idea of Marriage* [n. 6 above], pp. 186–202).

57. Juan Ruiz, *The Book of Good Love,* trans. Elisha Kent Kane (Chapel Hill: University of North Carolina Press, 1968), stanzas 585, 587, 604; Gottfried von Strassburg, *Tristan,* trans. and introd. A. T. Hatto (Harmondsworth, Eng.: Penguin, 1975), p. 248; W. T. H. Jackson, *The Anatomy of Love: The Tristan of Gottfried von Strassburg* (New York: Columbia University Press, 1971), pp. 111–17; *The "Tristan and Isolde" of Gottfried von Strassburg,* trans. and ed. Edwin H. Zeydel (Princeton: Princeton University Press, 1948), pp. 149–55, 208; Blake, letter to George Cumberland, 12 April 1827, in *Complete Poetry and Prose of William Blake,* ed. David V. Erdman (Garden City, N.Y.: Anchor/Doubleday, 1982), p. 783.

Chapter Ten

1. David Rosand, "Venereal Hermeneutics: The Lady on the Couch," paper delivered at the National Humanities Center, Research Triangle Park, North Carolina, 1986. Rosand also invokes for this marriage picture the Neoplatonic context of Ficino and Pietro Bembo. Printed versions of Rosand's paper will appear in a forthcoming volume of the National Gallery's Studies in the History of Art ("So-and-So Reclining on Her Couch"), and in *Renaissance Society and Culture,* ed. John Montfasani and Ronald G. Musto (New York: Italica Press, 1991), pp. 335–56. For Venus paintings relevant to my present discussion, see Veronese, *Mars and Venus United by Love* (Metropolitan Museum of Art, New York); Botticelli, *Venus and Mars* (National Gallery, London); Piero di Cosimo, *Venere, Marte, e Amore* (Staatliche Museen, Berlin); Joseph Heintz, *Venus and Adonis* (Kunsthistorisches Museum, Vienna).

2. For an excellent two-page reproduction in color of *Venus and Her "Children"* with commentary, see Millard Meiss, *The Great Age of Fresco* (New York: George Braziller, 1970), pp. 164, 166–67.

3. I have here quoted and paraphrased the perceptive and witty analysis of John Berger, "Scenes from a Marriage: The Portrait as a Barren Landscape," *Harper's* (April 1985): 48–49.

4. Jonathan Goldberg, however, while conceding that a "subversive element is present" and that some intimacy exists in the glances, finds that a patriarchal theme dominates in an "absolutist model" ("Fatherly Authority: The

Politics of Stuart Family Images," in *Rewriting the Renaissance: The Discourses of Sexual Difference in Early Modern Europe,* ed. Margaret W. Ferguson, Maureen Quilligan, and Nancy J. Vickers [Chicago: University of Chicago Press, 1986], pp. 27–29).

5. Stokes is quoted by David Carrier in "The Presentness of Painting: Adrian Stokes as Aesthetician," *Critical Inquiry* 12/4 (Summer 1986): 755.

6. I refer the reader to my discussion of eros in the taxonomy of terms in chapter 1, where I define eros as decorated or stylized libido. Perhaps Greenblatt, in insisting that boy actors playing the parts of women make the Elizabethan and Jacobean stage transvestite (in the sexual sense), goes too far; and even his analysis which I have embraced should not be allowed to obscure the fact that love in the comedies generates much more than heat, as we shall see in chapter 12. Shakespeare's imagination also encompasses politeness, concern, love, friendship; and even wantonness of language can denote more than love dallying. It can also mean celerity of intellect and the sheer pleasure of linguistic troping for its own sake. Stephen Greenblatt, *Shakespearean Negotiations: The Circulation of Social Energy in Renaissance England* (Berkeley: University of California Press, 1988), pp. 88–89. Still relevant is Lawrence Babb's discussion of the association of blood and the erotic: "The Physiological Conception of Love in the Elizabethan and Early Stuart Drama," *Publications of Modern Language Association of America* 56 (1941): 1020–35.

7. Noted by Marjorie Garber, *Coming of Age in Shakespeare* (London: Methuen, 1981), p. 126; and by Lawrence Stone, who discusses the extensive presence of the concept and finds it also in Calvin: see *The Family, Sex and Marriage in England 1500–1800* (New York: Harper & Row, 1977), p. 136.

8. John Harington is quoted by Alfred Harbage, *Shakespeare and the Rival Traditions* (New York: Macmillan, 1952), p. 222.

9. Quoted by Louis B. Wright in *Middle-Class Culture in Elizabethan England* (Ithaca: Cornell University Press, 1958), p. 222.

10. "Lectures on Genesis Chapters 1–5," in *Luther's Works,* trans. George V. Schick, ed. Jaroslav Pelikan, 56 vols. (Saint Louis, Mo.: Concordia Publishing House, 1955–86), 1:6, 7, 63, 69, 82, 116–17, 140, 185. With tart realism Luther discusses fallen reason, and he can be pointedly Augustinian in referring to the "epileptic and apoplectic lust of present-day marriage" (p. 134).

11. Luther intensely disliked allegorical interpretations, reacting against his hermeneutic practices as a monk when "I allegorized everything." Luther on allegorizing is quoted by George L. Scheper, "Reformation Attitudes Toward Allegory and the Song of Songs," *Publications of Modern Language Association of America* 89 (May 1974): 551. This article usefully discusses material that may help distinguish the Renaissance use of the Song of Solomon from that of the high Middle Ages. See chapter 6 above.

12. This is not the place to rehabilitate Germany, if it ever needed a defense in matters uxorial. Tacitus in antiquity praised its women and its marriages, and Stendhal in 1822 asked, "What country in the world contains the largest number

of happy marriages?" and answered, "Unquestionably Protestant Germany." A modern scholar (Steven Ozment), who says that "it would defy experience to believe that an age [he refers primarily to Reformed Germany] that wrote and taught so much about companionable marriage . . . utterly failed to practice what it preached," shows that the Protestant achievement took place against sobering social conditions, even of crisis proportions—or perhaps *because* of these conditions as an alleviating propaganda. Defenses of marriage appeared when 40 percent of all women were single, 20 percent being spinsters, 10–20 percent widows. Women found new advocates in a period during which 80 percent of the 100,000 persons executed for witchcraft (between 1400 and 1700) were women, the vast majority of these spinsters and widows. Stendhal, *On Love,* trans. "H.V.B." (New York: Liveright, 1947), p. 246; Steven Ozment, *When Fathers Ruled: Family Life in Reformation Europe* (Cambridge, Mass.: Harvard University Press, 1983), p. 55, also pp. 1–8, 27–42.

13. Calvin, *Institutes of the Christian Religion* 2.8.41–44; 2.8.50. I have used the translation of John Allen (Philadelphia: Presbyterian Board of Christian Education, 1936). For "The Lausanne Articles," "A Draft of Ecclesiastical Ordinances," theological treatises, versions of his catechism, and "Of Marriage," I have used *Calvin: Theological Treatises,* trans., introd., and annot. J. K. S. Reid (Philadelphia: "Library of Christian Classics" 22, Westminster Press, 1954), pp. 36, 48, 67 and n. 61, 82, 117, 149, 212–14. For commentary consult James A. Brundage, *Law, Sex, and Christian Society in Medieval Europe* (Chicago: University of Chicago Press, 1987), pp. 551–54 (also on Luther); and Bonnie S. Anderson and Judith P. Zinsser, *A History of Their Own: Women in Europe from Prehistory to the Present,* 2 vols. (New York: Harper & Row, 1988), 1: 256–61.

14. *Colloquies of Erasmus,* trans. Craig R. Thompson (Chicago: University of Chicago Press, 1965), where I have consulted the following: "Courtship" ("Proci et puella"), "The Girl with No Interest in Marriage," "The Repentant Girl," "Marriage," "The Young Man and the Harlot," "A Marriage in Name Only, or The Unequal Match," "The Epithalamium of Peter Gilles," "The Lower House, or The Council of Women." I have also read Erasmus's *Ecomium matrimonii* of 1518. The following provide commentary: Johan Huizinga, *Erasmus* (New York: Scribner's, 1924), pp. 39, 54–55, 128, 132, 137, 198–200; Huizinga, *Erasmus and the Age of Reformation* (New York: Harper & Brothers, 1957), pp. 155, 231–39; Emile V. Telle, *Erasme de Rotterdam et le septième sacrement: Etude d' évangelisme matrimoniale au XVIe siècle et contribution à la biographie intellectuelle d'Erasme* (Geneva: Droz, 1954). See especially p. 464 of Telle, *Erasme:* Erasmus argued that marriage alone permitted man to satisfy fully the laws of nature, of works, and of faith and that it could lead to a full flowering of human nature so that man could become a true Christian knight.

15. *Wilson's Arte of Rhetorique* [1553], ed. G. H. Mair (Oxford: Clarendon Press, 1909), pp. 40, 53–54. For a sixteenth-century English rendition of the *Encomium matrimonii,* see Richard Taverner, trans., *In laude and Prayse of Matrimony* (printed by Robert Redman, 1530), fols. A8 verso to B1 recto: "Greate

(sayeth Paule) is the mystery of matrimony: in Christe and in the chyche [*sic*]. If ther had been any cople in erth more holy, if there had been any bonde of loue and concorde more religiously to be kept, than wedlocke / undoubtedly he had fetched his similytude from thens. What lyke thyng do ye euer read, in all scripture of bachelershyp: Honorable wedlocke and the immaculat bryde bed is spoken of. Bachelershypppe is nat ones named."

16. Norbert Elias, *The Civilizing Process: The History of Manners,* trans. Edmund Jephcott (New York: Urizen Books, 1978), p. 174.

17. Francesco Barbaro, "On Wifely Duties" (preface and book 2 of *De Re uxoria*), trans. and introd. Benjamin G. Kohl, in *The Earthly Republic: Italian Humanists on Government and Society,* ed. Kohl and Ronald G. Witt (Philadelphia: University of Pennsylvania Press, 1978), pp. 179–228, especially p. 198. For commentary see Margaret L. King, ed., *Venetian Humanism in an Age of Patrician Dominance* (Princeton, N.J.: Princeton University Press, 1986), pp. 92–97; Constance Jordan, *Renaissance Feminism: Literary Texts and Political Models* (Ithaca: Cornell University Press, 1990); Guido Ruggiero, *The Boundaries of Eros: Sex Crime and Sexuality in Renaissance Venice* (New York: Oxford University Press, 1985), p. 174, n. 55.

18. I have consulted the following translations: Thomas Hoby, 1577, 1603 (a volume with English, French, and Italian in parallel columns), and 1561 in ed. of Walter Raleigh (London: David Nutt, 1900). I give folio references to the 1577 translation in the old-spelling text and page references to the 1561 version in the modern edition. The following provide commentary: in *Castiglione: The Ideal and the Real in Renaissance Culture,* ed. Robert W. Hanning and David Rosand (New Haven: Yale University Press, 1983), the editors' preface; Thomas M. Greene, "The Choice of a Game," pp. 1–15; and Eduardo Saccone, "*Grazia, Sprezzatura, Affetazione* in the *Courtier,*" pp. 45–67. See also Frank Whigham, *Ambition and Privilege: The Social Tropes of Elizabethan Courtesy Theory* (Berkeley: University of California Press, 1984), pp. 93–95 (a persuasive modern view of *sprezzatura*); Joan Kelly-Gadol, "Did Women Have a Renaissance?" in *Becoming Visible: Women in European History,* ed. Renate Bridenthal and Claudia Koonz (Boston: Houghton Mifflin, 1977), pp. 137–64; Linda T. Fitz, " 'What Says the Married Woman?': Marriage Theory and Feminism in the English Renaissance," *Mosaic* 13/2 (Winter 1980): 1–22. The last two scholars regard the position of woman as suffering regression during the Renaissance after considerable improvement during the Middle Ages.

19. Leone Ebreo, *The Philosophy of Love* (*Dialoghi d'amore*), trans. F. Friedeberg-Seeley and Jean H. Barnes, introd. Cecil Roth (London: Sconcino Press, 1937), pp. 3, 17, 30, 45, 345–62. For discussions of Ebreo and also Bruno, Lorenzo de' Medici, Pico, Bembo, Mario Equicola, and Castiglione, see John Charles Nelson, *Renaissance Theory of Love: The Context of Giordano Bruno's Eroici Furori* (New York: Columbia University Press, 1958).

20. Cornelius Agrippa's work was published in 1542. I have in part used the 1670 edition, whose translator is "H.C." [Henry Care]. I refer to it by page num-

ber; what I have quoted appears on pp. 2, 16. I have also consulted David Clapham's translation of 1534, quotations from which come from fols. B i recto, B iii verso, B iiii recto, B v recto. In places Agrippa comes close to a modern view of equality with only minor and essential sexual differentiation: "one similitude and lykenes of the sowle, to both male and female, betwene whose sowles there is noo maner dyfference of kynde" with "equall libertie of dignities and worthynesse" (1542 ed., pp. A ii recto and verso). I take it that Agrippa regards the superiority of women to reside in the cultural and not the natural or religious realms.

21. I thought at first that Tasso had gone beyond even this large claim to the modern one, going back in some senses to Plato's *Lysis,* that in intimacy we come psychologically to know ourselves in transcending barriers between us and the domestic Other. But I have come to believe that what Tasso means by learning to know oneself within marriage and the family is really seeing what we look like physically and also observing how we act, so making us feel that we belong. The situation is not one of psychological and moral discovery but of assurance arising from blood-ties.

Dello ammogliarsi piacevole contesa fra i due moderni Tassi Hercole, cioè, & Torquato (Bergamo, 1595) appeared in English in London in 1599: *Of Mariage and Wiving. An Excellent, pleasant, and philosophicall Controversie, betweene the two famous Tassi now living, the one Hercules the Philosopher, the other, Torquato the Poet. Done into English, by R. T. Gentleman.* I refer to the English, passim, and quote from it at K3 recto and verso, L1 recto and verso, L2 recto. The English seems to me more piously and biblically phrased, and the praise of physical love is heartier.

22. [William Whately], *A Bride-Bush, or a Wedding Sermon: Compendiously describing the duties of Married Persons: By performing whereof Marriage shall be to them a great Helpe, which now finde it a little Hell* (London, 1617), p. 36. Earlier, I did not dwell on medieval sermons as such (important inquiries are only now being called for and begun), but one striking difference between the earlier and the later is the sexual exuberance present in the post-Reformation homiletical literature. The medieval sermon praises love, friendship, mutuality, but is reticent about sexual enjoyment, though stressing procreation. See articles and relevant annotations by Michael Sheehan and Erik Kooper in Robert R. Edwards and Stephen Spector, *The Olde Daunce: Love, Friendship, Sex and Marriage in the Medieval World* (Albany: State University of New York Press, 1991), pp. 41–42, 52–55.

23. Paul Elmen, "On Worshiping the Bride," *Anglican Theological Review* 68/3 (July 1986): 243. I owe the Daniel Rogers quotation to Edmund Leites, *The Puritan Conscience and Modern Sexuality* (New Haven: Yale University Press, 1986), p. 101. The transfer of enthusiasm for Eden to marriage (a most popular association in the tracts and sermons) is made by Thomas Becon, as quoted by William and Malleville Haller in "The Puritan Art of Love," *Huntington Library Quarterly* 5 (1941–42): 245. Becon's comments are based on an influential Con-

tinental work that was widely known in England: H. Bullinger, *The Christen State of Matrimonye,* No. 646 in *The English Experience,* published in facsimile from the 1541 printing by Walter Johnson (Norwood, N.J., 1974). On fol. C8 verso, Bullinger makes it fully clear that he adheres to the consensual marriage established in the Middle Ages.

24. Quoted by Alan Macfarlane in *Marriage and Love in England: Modes of Reproduction 1300–1840* (Oxford: Basil Blackwell, 1986), p. 179.

25. Haller and Haller, "Puritan Art of Love" (n. 23 above), p. 250. I owe the Prayer Book quotation to Garber, *Coming of Age* (n. 7 above), p. 198. Gouge is quoted from Haller and Haller, "Puritan Art of Love" (n. 23 above), p. 250. Kathleen M. Davies, "The Sacred Condition of Equality—How Original Were Puritan Doctrines of Marriage?" *Social History* 5 (May 1977): 563–80, answers those who think that Puritan ideals were different from and more elevated than pre-Reformation or early Protestant views and takes a starkly realistic view of actual practices. James T. Johnson, "The Covenant Idea and the Puritan View of Marriage," *Journal of the History of Ideas* 32/1 (January–March 1971): 107–18, finds that the Covenant ideal differs from both Anglican and Thomist ideas of matrimony—friendship being one of the three analogies for Puritan marriage (along with the state and the congregation). See also Roland M. Frye, "The Teachings of Classical Puritanism on Conjugal Love," in *On Milton's Poetry,* ed. Arnold Stein (Greenwich, Conn.: Fawcett, 1970), pp. 97–100, who asserts that his evidence conclusively demonstrates that sexual life in marriage was regarded as the "Crown of all our bliss" (p. 98). An important literary study that makes use of Protestant and Puritan materials is Mary Beth Rose, *The Expense of Spirit: Love and Sexuality in English Renaissance Drama* (Ithaca: Cornell University Press, 1988). See also Juliet Dusinberre, *Shakespeare and the Nature of Woman* (London: Macmillan, 1975).

26. On the *Ritratto di Famiglia* (fig. 26), see Maria Teresa Cantaro, *Lavinia Fontana bolognese "pittora singolare" 1552–1614* (Milan: Jandi Sapi Editori, 1989), 4 a.89 (for color reproduction and catalog details) and p. 196 (for the comment quoted and paraphrased).

27. Patricia H. Labalme, "Women's Roles in Early Modern Venice: An Exceptional Case," in *Beyond Their Sex: Learned Women of the European Past,* ed. Labalme (New York: New York University Press, 1980), pp. 129–52.

28. Lowie is quoted by Macfarlane, *Marriage and Love* (n. 24 above), p. 120, who is very clear about the continuity from the Middle Ages.

29. John R. Gillis, *For Better, for Worse: British Marriages, 1600 to the Present* (New York: Oxford University Press, 1985), p. 38. I am everywhere indebted to this fine study.

30. I refer to the historians mentioned in the immediately preceding notes and also to Stone, *Family* (n. 7 above), pp. 151–218; Ralph Houlbrooke, *Church Courts and the People During the English Reformation 1520–1570* (Oxford: Clarendon Press, 1979), chap 3; and Keith Wrightson, *English Society: 1580–1680* (New Brunswick, N.J.: Rutgers University Press, 1982), chaps. 3 and 4.

31. A good example of Aretino's and others' bold eroticism may be seen in *I Modi: The Sixteen Pleasures: An Erotic Album of the Italian Renaissance,* ed. and trans. Lynne Lawner (Evanston, Ill.: Northwestern University Press, 1988). For a Hogarthian series on late medieval marital and "related" life, surely relevant to popular life in our period, see Diane G. Scillia, "Israhel van Meckenem's Marriage à la Mode: The Alltagsleben," in *New Images of Medieval Women: Essays Toward a Cultural Anthropology,* ed. Edelgard E. DuBruch (Lewiston, Wales: E. Mellen Press, 1989), pp. 207–54. On Venice, consult Achillo Olivieri, "Eroticism and Social Groups in Sixteenth-Century Venice: The Courtesan," in *Western Sexuality: Practice and Precept in Past and Present Times,* ed. Philippe Ariès and André Béjin, trans. Anthony Forster (Oxford: Basil Blackwell, 1985), pp. 95–102; and Ruggiero, *Boundaries of Eros* (n. 17 above). For an entirely different level of Italian life, see Margaret L. King, "The Religious Retreat of Isotta Nogarola (1418–1466): Sexism and Its Consequences in the Fifteenth Century," *Signs* 3/4 (Summer 1978): 807–22.

For France the following will be helpful for different levels of life: Natalie Zemon Davis, *Society and Culture in Early Modern France* (Stanford, Calif.: Stanford University Press, 1975); Madeleine Jeay, "Sexuality and Family in Fifteenth-Century France: Are Literary Sources a Mask or a Mirror," *Journal of Family History* 4/4 (Winter 1979): 328–45; Lillian Faderman, *Surpassing the Love of Men: Romantic Friendship and Love Between Women from the Renaissance to the Present* (New York: William Morrow, 1981), pp. 23–51 (on the court of Henri II and on Pierre Brantôme's *Lives of Fair and Gallant Ladies* and subsequent Renaissance conditions); Jacques Rossiaud, "Prostitution, Sex, and Society in French Towns in the Fifteenth Century," in *Western Sexuality,* ed. Aries and Béjin, pp. 76–94. For an English aristocratic couple, consult Alice T. Friedman, "Portrait of a Marriage: The Willoughby Letters of 1585–1586," *Signs* 11/3 (Spring 1986): 542–55. For a detailed historical study of prostitution (repressed, tolerated, and/or institutionalized) that extends from the Middle Ages to the Renaissance, see Leah Lydia Otis, *Prostitution in Medieval Society: The History of a Western Institution in Languedoc* (Chicago: University of Chicago Press, 1985).

32. *The Prettiest Love Letters in the World: Letters Between Lucrezia Borgia and Pietro Bembo 1503 to 1519,* trans. and pref. Hugh Shankland (Boston: David R. Godine, 1987).

33. G. R. Quaife, *Wanton Wenches and Wayward Wives: Peasants and Illicit Sex in Early Seventeenth Century England* (New Brunswick, N.J.: Rutgers University Press, 1978), passim but especially pp. 38–39, 45, 115–42, 165, 169–75, 246. For a contrasting picture and the spreading of Lutheran doctrine reinforcing patriarchal controls over marriage in rural Germany, see Thomas Robisheaux, "Peasants and Pastors: Rural Youth Control and the Reformation in Hohenloe, 1540–1680," *Social History* 6 (1981): 281–300.

34. The OED entry for *missionary position* is interesting. In this position the woman lies underneath the man, the first use of the term being in 1969; the *Daily*

Telegraph so used it in its color supplement for 10 January 1971. Some refer to the same arrangement as the "Mamma-Papa position," and we learn that in six of the United States a woman may be awarded a divorce if the husband makes love to her in any other position.

35. Quaife, *Wanton Wenches* (n. 33 above), p. 13.

36. On the *catasto* see chapter 8 above; and David Herlihy and Christiane Klapisch-Zuber, *Tuscans and Their Families: A Study of the Florentine Catasto of 1427* (New Haven: Yale University Press, 1985), passim but especially pp. xxiii, 1–3, 202–18.

37. Stone, *Family* (n. 7 above), graph on p. 45. See also Nicholas Canny, *The Upstart Earl: A Study of the Social and Mental World of Richard Boyle, First Earl of Cork, 1566–1643* (Cambridge: Cambridge University Press, 1982), pp. 87–93, 119–20.

38. W. G. Hoskins, "The Rebuilding of Rural England, 1570–1640," *Past and Present* 4 (November 1953): 44–59; Orest Ranum, "The Refuges of Intimacy," in *A History of Private Life: III. Passions of the Renaissance,* ed. Roger Chartier, trans. Arthur Goldhammer (Cambridge, Mass.: Harvard University Press, 1989), pp. 207–63.

39. Jacob Burckhardt, *The Civilization of the Renaissance in Italy,* trans. S. G. C. Middlemore (London: Phaidon, 1965), p. 268.

40. I owe the information about Altieri to Christiane Klapisch-Zuber, *Women, Family, and Ritual in Renaissance Italy,* trans. Lydia Cochrane (Chicago: University of Chicago Press, 1985), pp. 181, 247–58.

Chapter Eleven

1. By referring back to my introductory taxonomy (chapter 1), readers will see both how the categories have remained recognizable and how they have altered with changes in culture. My first category here is related immediately to *agapē* but it is also a historical manifestation of eros, since certainly the reformers were dialectically and sometimes poetically "decorating" libido. My second category here, naturalism, has in the Renaissance and high Middle Ages, more than in some ancient writers, brought into the light the libido itself, as we shall see everywhere, notably in Shakespeare. And my third category for the Renaissance illustrates, more directly than in any previous period, the earlier topic of friendship and esteem in the context of marriage and long-term intimacy.

2. Alfred Harbage, *Shakespeare and the Rival Traditions* (New York: Macmillan, 1952), p. 188; Stephen Greenblatt, "Loudun and London," *Critical Inquiry* 12/2 (Winter 1986): 343.

3. Bacon is quoted by Michael Hall, who uses the term *ascetic* for the most common type of love, which Bacon's statement represents. Other types are the seductive, the epic, the Petrarchan, the emasculating, the etherealized. *The*

Structure of Love: Representational Patterns and Shakespeare's Love Tragedies (Charlottesville: University Press of Virginia, 1989), p. 4. See also pp. 9, 11, 19, 22, 30.

4. For Pernette du Guillet and Scève, I rely entirely on T. Anthony Perry's excellent analyses in *Erotic Spirituality: The Integrative Tradition from Leone Ebreo to John Donne* (University: University of Alabama Press, 1980), pp. 53–64.

5. See E. A. M. Colman, *The Dramatic Use of Bawdy in Shakespeare* (London: Longman, 1974); and, on Jacobean city comedy, Mary Beth Rose, *The Expense of Spirit: Love and Sexuality in English Renaissance Drama* (Ithaca: Cornell University Press, 1988), chap. 2.

6. Hooker is quoted by Jonathan Dollimore, "Subjectivity, Sexuality, and Transgression: The Jacobean Connection," *Renaissance Drama* n.s. 17 (1986): 55.

7. Harry Levin, *Christopher Marlowe: The Overreacher* (London: Faber & Faber, 1954), p. 116. Marlowe dared to suspect that the love of Jesus and John the Apostle was "an extraordinary loue" (ibid.).

8. I borrow Edward Pechter's phrasing of the cynical and sentimental clichés in his "New Historicism and Its Discontents: Politicizing Renaissance Drama," *Publications of Modern Language Association of America* 102/3 (May 1987): 301, an important article, which sharpened my thought about this influential critical movement, so prominent on the landscape of Renaissance criticism (pp. 292–303). I am also indebted to Jean E. Howard, "The New Historicism in Renaissance Studies," *English Literary Renaissance* 16/1 (Winter 1986): 13–43.

9. Roberto Unger has said, "If invention is not the same as love, still it brings many of love's gifts. . . . Love alone can correct [the] failure of the ability to imagine diversity and community" (*Passion: An Essay on Personality* [New York: The Free Press/Macmillan, 1984], p. 218).

10. Many examples of the new point of view could be cited, but see especially Arthur F. Marotti, "'Love Is Not Love': Elizabethan Sonnet Sequences and the Social Order," *ELH* 49/2 (Summer 1982): 396–428.

11. My citations come from *The Plays of John Lyly,* ed. Carter A. Daniel (Lewisburg, Pa.: Bucknell University Press, 1988). For commentary, consult G. K. Hunter, *John Lyly: The Humanist as Courtier* (London: Routledge & Kegan Paul, 1962); Joseph W. Houppert, *John Lyly* (Boston: Twayne, 1975); G. Wilson Knight, "Lyly," in *Elizabethan Drama: Modern Essays in Criticism,* ed. R. J. Kaufmann (New York: Oxford University Press, 1961). Knight's view can no longer be maintained, that Lyly's "faith in the naked impulse of sexual attraction is exceptionally pure and independent of all moralizings" (p. 51).

12. My judgment of the play arises of course from the point of view of this study. Others, from a broader, less interested perspective, may view it otherwise. C. S. Lewis, for example, reports that "when I saw *Endimion* the courtly scenes (not the weak foolery of Sir Thopas) held me delighted for five acts," and he regards Lyly the dramatist as "the first writer since the great medievals whose

taste we can trust: the first who can maintain a work of any length" (C. S. Lewis, *English Literature in the Sixteenth Century Excluding Drama* [Oxford: Clarendon Press, 1954], p. 316).

13. Thomas Hyde, *The Poetic Theology of Love: Cupid in Renaissance Literature* (Newark: University of Delaware Press, 1986), p. 175. Relevant to Britomart is James E. Phillips, Jr., "The Woman Ruler in Spenser's *Faerie Queene,*" *Huntington Library Quarterly* 5 (January 1942): 211–34. More broadly relevant is Constance Jordan, "Woman's Rule in Sixteenth-Century British Political Thought," *Renaissance Quarterly* 40 (1987): 421–51 (an excellent guide to the interesting and subtle arguments about women related to queens Mary and Elizabeth, including arguments about the challenge to Christian husbandly authority posed by a married queen).

14. I quote the *Faerie Queene* from *The Poetical Works of Edmund Spenser,* ed. J. C. Smith and E. De Selincourt (London: Oxford University Press, 1935), and the other poetry from *Edmund Spenser's Poetry,* ed. Hugh Maclean (New York: W. W. Norton, 1982). For commentary see: Douglas Anderson, " 'Vnto My Selfe Alone': Spenser's Plenary Epithalamion," *Spenser Studies* 5 (1985): 149–66; Reed Way Dasenbrock, "The Petrarchan Context of Spenser's *Amoretti,*" *Publications of Modern Language Association of America* 100/1 (January 1985): 38–50; Thomas M. Greene, "Spenser and the Epithalamic Covention," *Comparative Literature* 9/3 (Summer 1957): 215–28; William C. Johnson, *Spenser's* Amoretti: *Analogies of Love* (Lewisburg, Pa.: Bucknell University Press, 1990); Marotti, " 'Love Is Not Love' " (n. 10 above), pp. 416–18; Charlotte Thompson, "Love in an Orderly Universe: A Unification of Spenser's Amoretti, Anacreontics, and Epithalamion," *Viator* 16 (1985): 277–335 (a learned study of the religious meanings of Spenser's amorous verse, related to a unifying calendar for part of 1553); Virginia Tufte, *The Poetry of Marriage: The Epithalamium in Europe and Its Development in England* (Los Angeles: Tinnon-Brown, 1970). For a brief discussion of Book 3 of the *Faerie Queene* in relation to the marital, see my *Sex and Sensibility* (Chicago: University of Chicago Press, 1980), pp. 36, 38–39.

15. The boldness may well be aristocratic. It is attractive and humane here, but in other contexts Sidney's class bias can be shockingly barbaric. I am thinking of the treatment in the *New Arcadia* (2.25) of the tradesmen who invade the royal bower. Sidney had earlier treated the lower classes with contempt, but here the "mutinous multitude," an "unruly sort of clownes," a "madde multitude" get a brutal comeuppance, which cuts off a tailor's nose, cleaves the face of a drunken "butcherlie chuffe," leaving only the jaw where the tongue still wags, while a miller's head is penetrated by a sword from ear to ear and the hapless victim "vomits" out his soul in "wine and bloud." Enough! But it may be relevant to note that one man, dreaming of marriage, thought himself a couple, and an avenging courtier fulfills the man's dream by cutting him in two—a brutal parody of what the outraged Zeus did to mankind in Plato's *Symposium.*

16. See chapter 9 on the traditions of long-term extramarital affairs. I confess that my general comments on the Renaissance shorter lyrics are based on my

rereading of one of my graduate school bibles, *Poetry of the English Renaissance 1509–1660,* ed. J. William Hebel and Hoyt H. Hudson (New York: F. S. Crofts, 1934), with longer excursions into Sidney and other poets treated at greater length in these pages. See also J. B. Broadbent, *Poetic Love* (London: Chatto & Windus, 1964); Walter R. Davis, *A Map of Arcadia* (New Haven: Yale University Press, 1965); Dorothy Jones, "Sidney's Erotic Pen: An Interpretation of One of the *Arcadia* Poems," *Journal of English and Germanic Philology* 73 (January 1974): 32–47; David Kalstone, *Sidney's Poetry* (Cambridge, Mass.: Harvard University Press, 1965); William W. Kerrigan and Gordon Braden, "Petrarch Refracted: The Evolution of the English Love Lyric," in *The Idea of the Renaissance,* ed. Kerrigan and Braden (Baltimore: Johns Hopkins University Press, 1989), pp. 157–89; Mark Rose, "Sidney's Womanish Man," *Review of English Studies,* n.s. 15 (1964): 353–63; Mark Rose, *Heroic Love: Studies in Sidney and Spenser* (Cambridge, Mass.: Harvard University Press, 1968); Neil L. Rudenstine, *Sidney's Poetic Development* (Cambridge, Mass.: Harvard University Press, 1967), pp. 256–69; Patrick M. Scanlon, "Emblematic Narrative and the Argument of Love in Sidney's *New Arcadia,*" *Journal of Narrative Technique* 15/3 (Fall 1985): 219–33.

17. Ben Jonson, *Poems,* ed. Ian Donaldson (London: Oxford University Press, 1975), an edition to which I refer in the text by page number. For commentary see: Gordon Braden, *The Classics and English Renaissance Poetry: Three Case Studies* (New Haven: Yale University Press, 1978), chap. 3; Paul M. Cubeta, "'A Celebration of Charis': An Evaluation of Jonsonian Poetic Strategy," *ELH* 25 (1958): 163–80; Anne Ferry, *All in War with Time: Love Poetry of Shakespeare, Donne, Jonson, Marvell* (Cambridge, Mass.: Harvard University Press, 1975); D. J. Gordon, *The Renaissance Imagination,* ed. Stephen Orgel (Berkeley: University of California Press, 1975), pp. 157–93 (on *Hymenaei*); Richard S. Peterson, "Virtue Reconciled to Pleasure: Jonson's 'A Celebration of Charis'," *Studies in the Literary Imagination* 6 (1973): 219–68; Wesley Trimpi, *Ben Jonson's Poems: A Study of the Plain Style* (Stanford, Calif.: Stanford University Press, 1962).

18. Dryden and Wordsworth are quoted in the edition I have used: *The Divine Weeks and Works of Guillaume de Saluste Sieur du Bartas,* trans. Joshua Sylvester, ed. Susan Snyder, 2 vols. (Oxford: Clarendon Press, 1979), 1:72. For quotations from Dubartas, I give week–day–part (when necessary)–line references.

19. *The Works of Rabelais,* illus. Gustave Doré (n.p.: Bibliophilist Society, n.d.). Michael Bakhtin, *Rabelais and His World,* trans. Helene Iswolsky (Bloomington: Indiana University Press, 1984), pp. 135–39, censures the abbey and places it well below Rabelais's triumphs with the realistically earthy and even the repellently physical. For a considerably altered view of Thélème, see Bakhtin's essay, "Forms of Time and of the Chronotope in the Novel," in *The Dialogic Imagination: Four Essays by M. M. Bakhtin,* ed. Michael Holquist, trans. Caryl Emerson and Holquist (Austin: University of Texas Press, 1981), p. 178, where

Thélème is said to be a "harmonious world with its harmonious human beings." M. A. Screech, *The Rabelaisian Marriage: Aspects of Rabelais's Religion, Ethics and Comic Philosophy* (London, Edward Arnold, 1958), passim; and Screech's unpublished paper, "Rabelais and Montaigne on Marriage: Comedy and Humour," delivered at the National Humanities Center, 1986. Jerome Schwartz, *Irony and Ideology in Rabelais: Structures of Subversion* (Cambridge: Cambridge University Press, 1990), pp. 144–47 (on marriage) and especially pp. 82–89 on the Abbey of Thélème. I am especially grateful to Schwartz for his definition of *thelēma* and his explanation of the motto of the abbey. See Peter Brown, "Bodies and Minds," in *Before Sexuality: The Construction of Erotic Experience in the Ancient Greek World,* ed. David M. Halperin, John J. Winkler, and Froma I. Zeitlin (Princeton, N.J.: Princeton University Press, 1990), p. 481 (on the opaque Christian "heart").

20. The Thélème motto bears contradictory meanings and evokes enormous resonances. It brings in the Lord's Prayer, "Thy Will be done" (Matt. 6:10); Augustine's "Dilige, et quod vis fac"; Erasmus's unpersuasive revision of the Latin petition in the Vulgate Lord's Prayer from "fiat voluntas sua" to "fiat quod vis" as being more faithful to the Greek, "genetheto to thelēma sou"; and the entire faith-works debate. Both the name and the motto of the abbey suggest Aristotelian and Christian meanings: that a disciplined instinct can be trusted to enhance life. This may indeed be another form of Christian freedom, a very complex concept that could also include sexual renunciation. See, once more, n. 19 above.

21. We have several times confronted the preliminary, unconsummated condition of much love. For a fresh and stimulating view of postponed consummations and postcoital disappointments in this period, see Kerrigan and Braden, "Petrarch Refracted" (n. 16 above).

22. Text for Musaeus: *Musée, Héro et Léandre,* trans. and ed. Pierre Orsini (Paris: "Les Belles Lettres," Collection des Universités de France, 1968). I give line references for the Greek. Notice that in lines 1–7 *gamos* words predominate over *erōs* words. In line 146 marriage and the nuptial couch are associated in the traditional Greek way: "gamos kai lektra." In lines 146–47 are embedded linguistic allusions to the great Greek love words, *philos, agapē, erōs:* ". . . esti gamos kai lektra. Su d'ei phileeis Kuthereian, / thelxinoōn agapaze meliphrona thesmon erōtōn" ([If you wish to know Aphrodite's laws], there's always marriage and the marital couch. And if you cherish Cythera, love also the sweet law of enchanting loves).

23. Both Marlowe's and Chapman's versions appear in "The Haslewood Reprints" no. 2: *Hero and Leander 1598* (London: Pelican Press, 1924). Though I retain the old spelling of both renditions, I give line numbers from Hebel and Hudson, *Poetry* (n. 16 above) for Marlowe. For commentary see: Braden, *Classics* (n. 17 above), pp. 55–57, 81–116, 141–52 (argues that man is an erotic agent and contrasts other kinds of love); William Keach, *Elizabethan Erotic Narratives: Irony and Pathos in the Ovidian Poetry of Shakespeare, Marlowe, and*

Their Contemporaries (New Brunswick, N.J.: Rutgers University Press, 1977), chap. 4 (on *Hero and Leander,* stressing the ambiguous, disturbing, and ultimately the violent and turbulent in love). Louis L. Martz, in his introduction to the facsimile edition of the first edition of 1598 (Washington, D.C.: Folger Shakespeare Library, 1972), pp. 5, 10, 14, disengages Marlowe's spirit and tone from Chapman's, stressing the comic, the bathetic, the grotesque in the former.

24. Chapman's rendition begins with the fourth sestiad, though he supplied all the earlier Arguments. My quotations come from the following: fols. E3 verso, F1 recto and verso, F3 recto–F4 verso, H2 recto. The contrasts between the views of Emile Legouis and C. S. Lewis epitomize the considerable differences of earlier generations about Marlowe vs. Chapman: for Legouis the palm goes to Marlowe for true poetry and sincere passion and not to the "overlearned" Chapman, "the most unintelligible, the gloomiest and the foggiest of the Elizabethans" (*A History of English Literature: The Middle Ages and the Renaissance,* trans. Helen Douglas Irvine [New York: Macmillan, 1935], pp. 324–25). Lewis finds that in his continuation (but not in his Homer) Chapman accomplished the work he was born to do and achieved real wisdom, psychological insight, and grandeur of passion, while Marlowe, though fully successful in his special way, is nevertheless hard, brittle, materialistic—and preposterous in his hyperboles (*English Literature in the Sixteenth Century* [n. 12 above], pp. 486–88, 513–14). I admire Lewis's much needed view but demur when he finds the crown of all Chapman's poetry in the lyric epithalamion of his extension, which strikes me as crabbed and dense.

25. Anyone wishing to see how Chapman's marital ideal might activate society in its upper echelons should study *The Gentleman Usher* (printed 1606, written during Elizabeth's last years), where the author ends by creating an epithalamion to the young, the equal, the hopeful, the adventuresome—and the disciplined, who, however, are not too stoically self-contained to shun supernatural aid. The play, not the poem, shows decisively what Hero and Leander would have had to grow into in order to fulfill, for Chapman, the promise of their passion.

26. Jonathan Dollimore uses this quotation to illustrate what went on in courtly life, suggesting that lechery and courtesy were inextricably intertwined: *Radical Tragedy: Religion, Ideology and Power in the Drama of Shakespeare and His Contemporaries* (Chicago: University of Chicago Press, 1984), p. 25. It is G. P. V. Akrigg who suggests the tortuous ways of King James's loving: *Letters of King James VI and I,* ed. Akrigg (Berkeley: University of California Press, 1984), p. 19; and D. Harris Willson who comments on the king's inquisitiveness, in *King James VI and I* (London: Jonathan Cape, 1956), p. 339.

27. The text I use is that of Brian W. M. Scobie (London: A. & C. Black, 1985) with scene and line numbers but without acts.

28. T. S. Eliot, *Selected Essays* (London: Faber & Faber, 1951), p. 181. Eliot finds Heywood "eminent in the pathetic" (ibid.) and "sentimental, and never ethical" (p. 179), a writer whom it is misleading to call a "realist": better to say

"his sensibility is merely that of ordinary people in ordinary life" (p. 175). I find, rather, that there is something powerfully contrived and almost indecently exaggerated about the "forgiveness." For other commentary, see Barbara J. Baines, *Thomas Heywood* (Boston: Twayne, 1984), pp. 79–103; Leonora Leet Brodwin, *Elizabethan Love Tragedy 1587–1625* (New York: New York University Press, 1971), pp. 103–14; Laura G. Bromley, "Domestic Conduct in *A Woman Killed with Kindness*," *Studies in English Literature* 26/2 (Spring 1986): 259–76; Diana E. Henderson, "Many Mansions: Reconstructing *A Woman Killed with Kindness*," *Studies in English Literature* 26/2 (Spring 1986): 277–94; R. W. Van Fossen, introd., *The Revels Play* (London: Methuen, 1961).

29. Two other interpretations are possible but not, I think, likely. First, Heywood may have accepted the wife's view and considered her adultery so heinous a sin that though the sinner's soul may be saved, her body is forever profaned and life in the desecrated home forever poisoned. One consideration militates against such a view. Wendoll is also guilty of a heinous sin, betraying a close friend in his very home. But though the villain is tortured with guilt for a while, he in time recovers his savoir faire, goes on a grand tour, learns languages, and hopes for a place at court. This could be a flick by the playwright at the highest level of English life (it could accommodate any kind of villain), but it shows in the context of the domestic sin that at least *male* recovery is possible. Can we therefore believe that draconian measures like those of Frankford are anything but blind and cruel? Second, Heywood may himself be satirizing the husband's behavior: could he be a new kind of precisian, who wraps himself in the mantle of Christian forbearance but has no notion that his true obligation is to forgive seventy times seven? More clues than the text offers would be needed for such an enlightened reading, and one would have to demonstrate that the entire play breathes such an air of Christian rationality and good sense.

30. *The Tragedy of the Duchess of Malfi*, ed. Louis B. Wright and Virginia A. LaMar (New York: Washington Square Press, 1959); Gunnar Boklund, The Duchess of Malfi: *Sources, Themes, Characters* (Cambridge, Mass.: Harvard University Press, 1962), pp. 92–97; Dympna Callaghan, *Women and Gender in Renaissance Tragedy* (Atlantic Highlands, N.J.: Humanities Press International, 1989), pp. 169–70; Lisa Jardine, *Still Harping on Daughters: Women and Drama in the Age of Shakespeare* (Totowa, N.J.: Barnes & Noble, 1983), pp. 72–75; Clifford Leech, *John Webster: A Critical Study* (New York: Haskell House, 1970); Kathleen McLuskie, *Renaissance Dramatists* (Atlantic Highlands, N.J.: Humanities Press International, 1989), pp. 142–45; Rose, *Expense of Spirit* (n. 5 above), pp. 155–75; Roger Stilling, *Love and Death in Renaissance Tragedy* (Baton Rouge: Louisiana State University Press, 1976), pp. 236–46; Frank W. Wadsworth, "Webster's *Duchess of Malfi* in the Light of Some Contemporary Ideas on Marriage and Remarriage," *Philological Quarterly* 35 (October 1956): 394–407; Frank Whigham, "Sexual and Social Mobility in *The Duchess of Malfi*," *Publications of Modern Language Association of America* 100/2 (March 1985): 167–86.

31. In discussing this scene, I have virtually ventriloquized Clifford Leech, *John Webster* (n. 30 above), pp. 63–64.

32. See, for example, the historical account of the love and union between Lusanna and Giovanni across class lines in Renaissance Florence, which reveals the courage of the bride, the vociferous approbation of the community, and the support (for a time at least) of the church: Gene Brucker, *Giovanni and Lusanna: Love and Marriage in Renaissance Florence* (Berkeley: University of California Press, 1986). The extensive letters of the Paston family in late medieval England include a vivid account of the difficulties and even persecutions (much less horrendous than those inflicted upon the Duchess of Malfi) suffered by an heiress who married her steward. See *Paston Letters and Papers of the Fifteenth Century*, ed. Norman Davis, 2 vols. (Oxford: Clarendon Press, 1971), pp. xxxvii, xlvii, liv–lv, lxii, and letters 415, 416 (the famous Valentine letters). For a translation into modern English, see *The Paston Letters*, ed. John Fenn, re-ed. Mrs. Archer-Hind, 2 vols. (London: J. M. Dent, 1938), p. viii and letters 2, 5, 65, 147, 228 (on reading Ovid's love poetry), 265, 273, 277, 279 (an excellent fifteenth-century love letter), 378–386. I have made my references generous: they include not only the love story across class lines but will reveal such matters as husbandly-wifely salutations and farewells and forms of address within the family. See also H. S. Bennett, *The Pastons and Their England* (Cambridge: Cambridge University Press, 1922), pp. 30, 33, 42–50; and Frances Gies and Joseph Gies, *Marriage and the Family in the Middle Ages* (New York: Harper & Row, 1987), pp. 265–67.

33. Stilling, *Love and Death* (n. 30 above), p. 148.

34. Germaine Greer, *The Female Eunuch* (New York: McGraw-Hill, 1971), p. 204.

35. I have here relied on Julius S. Held, "Flora, Goddess and Courtesan," in Millard Meiss, ed., *Essays in Honor of Erwin Panofsky*, 2 vols. (New York: New York University Press, 1961), 1: 201–18. David Rosand, "Venereal Hermeneutics" (see chap. 10, n. 1 above) has also pointed out that Flora was both goddess and courtesan and that her name was one of those adopted when a Venetian courtesan entered her profession.

Chapter Twelve

1. See Richard Levin, "The Poetics and Politics of Bardicide," *Publications of Modern Language Association of America* 105/3 (May 1990): 491–504. Richard P. Wheeler has helped me in developing the concept of "Shakespeare"; see his *Shakespeare's Development and the Problem Comedies: Turn and Counter-Turn* (Berkeley: University of California Press, 1981), pp. 27, 29–31.

Shakespeare is quoted, with act and scene reference and with exceptions specifically noted, from Stanley Wells and Gary Taylor, eds., *The Complete Oxford Shakespeare*, 3 vols. (Oxford: Oxford University Press, 1987, 1988).

2. *A Preparatiue to Mariage: The summe whereof was spoken at a contract, and inlarged after. . . . By Henrie Smith. Imprinted at London . . . 1591*, p. 3; Margaret Loftus Ranald, " 'As Marriage Binds, and Blood Breaks': English Marriage and Shakespeare," *Shakespeare Quarterly* 30 (1979): 81. See also Ranald, *Shakespeare and His Social Context: Essays in Osmotic Knowledge and Literary Interpretation* (New York: AMS Press, 1987), a work that anyone interested in my book and the plays I discuss will wish to consult.

3. See Alfred Harbage, *Shakespeare and the Rival Traditions* (New York: Macmillan, 1952), p. 216: "The comedies are marriage plays, and the wanton jests anticipate wedding manners."

4. Napier reported on some 2,000 insane or disabled people. Michael Mac-Donald, *Mystical Bedlam: Madness, Anxiety, and Healing in Seventeenth-Century England* (Cambridge: Cambridge University Press, 1981), pp. 13, 75, 77–78, 88–111.

5. On *A Midsummer Night's Dream,* see the following: C. L. Barber, *Shakespeare's Festive Comedy: A Study of Dramatic Form and Its Relation to Social Custom* (Princeton, N.J.: Princeton University Press, 1959), p. 130, 132, 162 (relates the play to Spenser's *Epithalamion*); Harold F. Brooks, introd. to Arden edition of *A Midsummer Night's Dream* (London, Methuen, 1979) pp. cix, cxxxi–cxxxvii, cxliii (stresses hymeneal character of the play); James L. Calderwood, "*A Midsummer Night's Dream:* The Illusion of Drama," *Modern Language Quarterly* 26 (1965): 506–22; William C. Carroll, *The Metamorphoses of Shakespearean Comedy* (Princeton, N.J.: Princeton University Press, 1985, pp. 52–53, 147; E. A. M. Colman, *The Dramatic Use of Bawdy in Shakespeare* (London: Longman, 1974), pp. 27–31; R. W. Dent, "Imagination in *A Midsummer Night's Dream,"* *Shakespeare Quarterly* 15 (Spring 1964): 115–29 (denies view that love is irrational and that play ends with restoration of reason); Jan Kott, *Shakespeare Our Contemporary,* trans. Boleslaw Taborski (London: Methuen, 1967), pp. 171–90; Louis A. Montrose, " 'Shaping Fantasies': Figurations of Gender and Power in Elizabethan Culture," *Representations* 1/2 (Spring 1983): 61–94; Paul A. Olson, "*A Midsummer Night's Dream* and the Meaning of Court Marriage," *ELH* 24 (1957): 95–119; Joseph H. Summers, *Dreams of Love and Power: On Shakespeare's Plays* (Oxford: Clarendon Press, 1984), pp. 3–21; David P. Young, *Something of Great Constancy: The Art of "A Midsummer Night's Dream"* (New Haven: Yale University Press, 1966).

6. Arthur Brooke is quoted from Thomas Marc Parrott, ed., *Shakespeare: Twenty-Three Plays and the Sonnets* (New York: Scribner's, 1938), p. 164.

7. Brian Gibbons, introd. to Arden edition of *Romeo and Juliet* (London: Methuen, 1980), pp. 32, 43, 49, 52, 55–56, 76 and n.; Laurence Lerner, *Love and Marriage: Literature and Its Social Context* (London: Edward Arnold, 1979), pp. 6–7.

8. They are regarded by Sarup Singh as "the best comment we have in Shakespeare on contemporary 'forced' marriages" (*Family Relationships in Shakespeare and the Restoration Comedy of Manners* [Delhi: Oxford University Press, 1983], p. 47).

9. The wooing scene has been harshly judged. Samuel Johnson says that "not even Shakespeare can write well without a proper subject. It is a vain endeavour for the most skilful hand to cultivate barrenness or to paint upon vacuity" (Arthur Sherbo, ed., *Johnson on Shakespeare,* vol. 8 of *Yale Edition of the Works of Samuel Johnson* [New Haven: Yale University Press, 1968], p. 565). Moody Prior finds that Henry here becomes awkward and blunt, wooing Kate "with tedious courtesy" in some forty lines of "coy prose" (*The Drama of Power: Studies in Shakespeare's History Plays* [Evanston, Ill.: Northwestern University Press, 1973], pp. 271, 329).

10. Edward Hall's remarks appear in Andrew S. Cairncross, ed., Arden edition of *1 Henry VI* (London: Methuen, 1962), p. 160.

11. Sherbo, ed., *Johnson on Shakespeare* (see n. 9 above), p. 604. I have stressed the initiation of the marriage, which is indeed attractive, but Moody Prior is quite right in pointing out to me (1990) that in the event the union proved to be politically unwise. Prior gives a useful brief account of Edward IV in *Drama of Power* (n. 9 above), p. 102. Hall is quoted in Andrew S. Cairncross, ed., *2 Henry VI* (London: Methuen, 1957), p. lii and n. 1, and in Cairncross, ed., *3 Henry VI* (London: Methuen, 1964), p. 71. Samuel Daniel, *The Civil Wars,* ed. Laurence Michel (New Haven: Yale University Press, 1958), stanza 8, line 51. See Phyllis Rackin's perceptive article, "Anti-Historians: Women's Roles in Shakespeare's Histories," *Theatre Journal* 37/3 (October 1985): 329–44.

12. Tilney is quoted by Carroll Camden, *The Elizabethan Woman* (Houston: Elsevier Press, 1952), p. 126. On the *Taming of the Shrew,* consult the following: John C. Bean, "Comic Structure and the Humanizing of Kate in *The Taming of the Shrew,*" in *The Woman's Part: Feminist Criticism of Shakespeare,* ed. Carolyn Ruth Swift Lenz, Gayle Greene, and Carol Thomas Neely (Urbana: University of Illinois Press, 1980), pp. 65–78; William C. Carroll, *The Metamorphoses of Shakespearean Comedy* (Princeton, N.J.: Princeton University Press, 1985), pp. 41–59; George Cheatham, "Imagination, Madness, and Magic: *The Taming of the Shrew* as Romantic Comedy," *Iowa State Journal of Research* 59/3 (February 1985): 221–32; Carol F. Heffernan, "*The Taming of the Shrew:* The Bourgeoisie in Love," *Essays in Literature* 12/1 (Spring 1985): 3–14; Coppélia Kahn, *Man's Estate: Masculine Identity in Shakespeare* (Berkeley: University of California Press, 1981), pp. 111–18; Alexander Leggatt, *Shakespeare's Comedy of Love* (London: Methuen, 1974), pp. 46–53; Carol Thomas Neely, *Broken Nuptials in Shakespeare's Plays* (New Haven: Yale University Press, 1985), pp. 29–30; Karen Newman, "Renaissance Family Politics and Shakespeare's *The Taming of the Shrew,*" *English Literary Renaissance* 16/1 (Winter 1986): 86–100; Marianne Novy, *Love's Argument: Gender Relations in Shakespeare* (Chapel Hill: University of North Carolina Press, 1984), pp. 45–62; Maureen Quilligan, "*The Taming of the Shrew:* Shakespeare and the Question of Social History," paper delivered at National Humanities Center, 1986.

13. One of Harold Bloom's most striking collocations is to bring "J," the great Hebrew writer, and Shakespeare together on several occasions in his *Book of J* (1990). I am led to believe that behind Shakespeare's assertive women there

stand Sarai, Rebecca, Rachel, Tamar, Zipporah, and others. Bloom finds that these biblical women are characterized by a grand Yahweh-like hardness, or toughness. Shakespeare's women have some of that quality too, but, without losing their firmness of will, they are made of somewhat softer flesh. See Bloom, *Book of J,* trans. David Rosenberg, interpr. Harold Bloom (New York: Grove Weidenfeld, 1990), p. 312.

14. I refer to two discussions not directly related to my argument that should be considered in relation to it, perhaps to qualify it somewhat. Moody E. Prior says of the Belmont group, "Their happiness, fortunately for them, is virtually total. It is their humanity and understanding that we despair of." He insists that Shylock haunts the "summer idyll" ("Which Is the Jew That Shakespeare Drew? Shylock among the Critics," *American Scholar* [Autumn, 1981]: 488, 498). Ronald A. Sharp discusses latent antagonism between Portia and Antonio and quotes Nietzsche that "the best friend will probably get the best wife, because a good marriage is based on a talent for friendship" (*Friendship and Literature: Spirit and Form* [Durham, N.C.: Duke University Press, 1986], p. 128 [chap. 3 is devoted to this play]).

15. *As You Like It* might well be approached with W. Thomas MacCary's paradigm in mind: (1) male lovers love or seek out themselves; (2) they therefore love mirror images of themselves in twins or friends; (3) they then love those same images in transvestized young women; (4) they finally learn to love young women "in all their specific, unique, and complex virtues" (*Friends and Lovers: The Phenomenology of Desire in Shakespearean Comedy* [New York: Columbia University Press, 1985], p. 5 and then passim). See also Colman, *Dramatic Use of Bawdy* (n. 5 above), glossary under *hymen* ("not bawdy in Shakespeare"); Peter B. Erickson, "Sexual Politics and the Social Structure in *As You Like It*," *Massachusetts Review* (Spring 1982): 65–83; Erickson, *Patriarchal Structures in Shakespeare's Dramas* (Berkeley: University of California Press, 1985); Richard Knowles, ed., *As You Like It* (New York, "A New Variorum Edition," Modern Language Association, 1977). Commenting on 1.1.215, Knowles says *wit,* "a highly volatile word," is used some twenty-three times in this play. Elliot Krieger, *A Marxist Study of Shakespeare's Comedies* (New York: Barnes & Noble, 1979), maintains that Rosalind's disguise has a "homosexual bearing," the courtship is "homosexual," and in the end she extends her control, through Hymen, over all of society (pp. 82–83). Jan Kott, *Shakespeare Our Contemporary* (n. 5 above), pp. 221, 227, remarks that "every Rosalind is Ganymede and every Ganymede is Rosalind"; in his disgust with nature Shakespeare is a forerunner of Swift. Agnes Latham, introd. to Arden edition of *As You Like It* (London: Methuen, 1975); Leggatt, *Shakespeare's Comedy of Love* (n. 12 above), p. 195 (in the forest people become "more fully alive than before"), and see also pp. 187–212; Simon Shepherd, *Amazons and Warrior Women: Varieties of Feminism in Seventeenth-Century Drama* (New York: St. Martin's Press, 1981), pp. 187–217 (sees Rosalind as an Amazonian heroine); Kent Talbot Van Den Berg, "Theatrical Fiction and the Reality of Love in *As You Like It*," *Publications of Modern Language Association of America* 90 (October 1975): 885–93.

16. Compare Robert J. Stoller's careful diagnosis of transvestism and his five categories of transvestites. Though he is not concerned with Shakespeare, he strikes me as demonstrating how ill the women in comedic disguise fit the symptoms, though the term is constantly used in present-day literary criticism. See his *Observing the Erotic Imagination* (New Haven: Yale University Press, 1985), pp. 136–56. Much was then and is now made of boy actors' playing the role of girls and women—a situation that allegedly implied and implies homoeroticism, sexual ambiguity, narcissism, flagellation, sodomy, male marriage, father-son intimacy. Lisa Jardine has shown that the practice caused discomfort among contemporary divines: *Still Harping on Daughters: Women and Drama in the Age of Shakespeare* (Totowa, N.J.: Barnes & Noble, 1983), pp. 15–31. But illusion flickered in and out, the disguises were changed frequently, all sorts and conditions of femininity were represented, a boy played a girl who disguised herself as a boy and then returned to being a girl; and of course the clerical antitheatrical rhetoric was inflamed in any case. An extension of Johnsonian common sense may be welcome: if Elizabethan playgoers could assume that an apprentice boy of the lower classes could impersonate the great serpent of the Nile, their imagination could also leap a smaller gulf, that a boy could play a female role without the burden of overdetermined psychological meanings. And how much *trans* was really present in transvestism? Joel Fineman has well described Viola, "her femininity oozing out of her disguise" ("Fratricide and Cuckoldry: Shakespeare's Doubles," in *Representing Shakespeare,* ed. Murray M. Schwartz and Coppélia Kahn [Baltimore: Johns Hopkins University Press, 1980], p. 80). See Catherine Belsey's important article calling for fluidity, multiplicity, and plurality in the man-woman dichotomy, avoiding both "some third, unified, androgynous identity which eliminates all distinctions" and "a metaphysical sexual polarity" ("Disrupting Sexual Difference: Meaning and Gender in the Comedies," in *Alternative Shakespeares,* ed. John Drakakis [London: Methuen, 1985], pp. 188–90). Relevant to this theme and to *Twelfth Night* as a whole are: William C. Carroll, "The Ending of *Twelfth Night* and the Tradition of Metamorphosis," in *Shakespearean Comedy,* ed. Maurice Charney (New York: Library Forum, 1980), p. 60; Stephen Greenblatt, *Shakespearean Negotiations: The Circulation of Social Energy in Renaissance England* (Berkeley: University of California Press, 1988), chap. 3; Kott, *Shakespeare Our Contemporary* (n. 5 above), pp. 206–13; Leggatt, *Shakespeare's Comedy of Love* (n. 5 above), pp. 222–54; Phyllis Rackin, "Androgyny, Mimesis, and the marriage of the Boy Heroine on the English Renaissance Stage," *Publications of Modern Language Association of America* 102/1 (January 1987): 29–41; Elizabeth Sacks, *Shakespeare's Images of Pregnancy* (New York: St. Martin's Press, 1980), p. 43.

17. A. R. Humphreys, introd. to Arden edition of *Much Ado about Nothing* (London: Methuen, 1981); Richard A. Levin, *Love and Society in Shakespearean Comedy: A Study of Dramatic Form* (Newark: University of Delaware Press, 1985), pp. 87–114; Arthur Kirsch, *Shakespeare and the Experience of Love* (Cambridge: Cambridge University Press, 1981), chap. 3; Leggatt, *Shakespeare's Comedy of Love* (n. 12 above), pp. 151–82; David L. Stevenson, introd. to Signet

edition of *Much Ado* (New York: New American Library, 1964); Joseph West-lund, *Shakespeare's Reparative Comedies: A Psychoanalytical View of the Middle Plays* (Chicago: University of Chicago Press, 1984), chap. 3.

18. The sexuality that bubbles and now and then erupts in this relationship is well known. George Bernard Shaw censured Beatrice's wit as indelicate and Benedick's as coarse, indecent, lewd, obscene, even brutal; but then he was, for all his own wit, something of a puritan. Why did he not see how perfectly verbal sexual freedom fits the high spirits of this pair, who can surely be counted on to keep it in its place?

19. David Lodge, *Small World: An Academic Romance* (London: Secker & Warburg, 1984), pp. 322–23.

20. Erickson, *Patriarchal Structures* (n. 15 above), pp. 25–37; Clara Claiborne Park, "As We Like It: How a Girl Can Be Smart and Still Popular," in *The Woman's Part* (n. 12 above), p. 111; Neely, *Broken Nuptials* (n. 12 above), p. 6.

21. Northrop Frye, *A Natural Perspective: The Development of Shake-spearean Comedy and Romance* (New York: Columbia University Press, 1965), pp. 77–78, also pp. 2–3, 7–8, 12. Frye is of course the most penetrating and influential authority on comic closures in our day and has discussed the matter in many works. See, for example, *The Myth of Deliverance: Reflections on Shake-speare's Problem Comedies* (Toronto: University of Toronto Press, 1983), pp. 8–17, 53–54; and *Anatomy of Criticism* (New York: Atheneum, 1966), pp. 163–86 ("The Mythos of Spring: Comedy").

22. Mary Cowden Clarke, *The Girlhood of Shakespeare's Heroines,* 3 vols. (London, 1850–55); Darryl J. Gless, *Measure for Measure, the Law and the Con-vent* (Princeton, N.J.: Princeton University Press, 1979), p. 233 and n.; Barbara Herrnstein Smith, *Poetic Closure: A Study of How Poems End* (Chicago: Univer-sity of Chicago Press, 1970), p. 120.

23. Albertus Magnus is quoted by Joel B. Altman in *The Tudor Play of Mind: Rhetorical Inquiry and the Development of Elizabethan Drama* (Berkeley: University of California Press, 1978), p. 2. This seminal study of rhetoric in the Renaissance, to which I am greatly indebted, shows that the habit of arguing *in utramque partem,* which "permeated virtually all areas of intellectual life," is car-ried over into comedy and also tragedy, quoting Chapman that "material instruc-tion, elegant and sententious excitation to virtue and deflection from her contrary [are] the soul, limbs, and limits of an autentical tragedy" (pp. 5, 34, and passim).

24. Hans Robert Jauss, "Literary History as a Challenge to Literary The-ory," in *New Directions in Literary History,* ed. Ralph Cohen (Baltimore: Johns Hopkins University Press, 1974), p. 37. See also Robert C. Holub, *Reception Theory: A Critical Introduction* (London: Methuen, 1984).

25. John Updike, *Roger's Version* (New York: Knopf, 1986), p. 41.

26. Zvi Jagendorf, "Strangers in the Night: Sexual Encounters in Religious and Secular Texts," *University of Toronto Quarterly* 53/2 (Winter 1983–84):

135–48; Janet Adelman, "Bed Tricks: On Marriage as the End of Comedy in *All's Well That Ends Well* and *Measure for Measure*," in *Shakespeare's Personality*, ed. Norman H. Holland, Sidney Homan, and Bernard J. Paris (Berkeley: University of California Press, 1989), pp. 151–74.

27. G. K. Hunter, introd. to Arden edition of *All's Well That Ends Well* (London: Methuen, 1959); C. L. Barber, "The Family in Shakespeare's Development: Tragedy and Sacredness," in *Representing Shakespeare* (n. 5 above), pp. 188–220; Barbara Everett, introd., *All's Well*, in *New Pelican Shakespeare* (New York: Penguin, 1970); Kirsch, *Shakespeare and the Experience of Love* (n. 17 above), pp. 114–43; Joseph G. Price, *The Uncomfortable Comedy: A Study of All's Well That Ends Well and its Critics* (Toronto: University of Toronto Press, 1968); Sacks, *Shakespeare's Image of Pregnancy* (n. 16 above), pp. 51–53; Westlund, *Shakespeare's Reparative Comedies* (n. 17 above), chap. 6; Wheeler, *Shakespeare's Development* (n. 1 above), chap. 2.

28. Gless, *Measure for Measure, the Law and the Convent* (n. 22 above), passim; Hanns Sachs, *The Creative Unconscious* (Cambridge, Mass.: Sci-Art, 1942), chap. 3; David Sundelson *Shakespeare's Restorations of the Father* (New Brunswick, N.J.: Rutgers University Press, 1983), p. 93; Louise Schleiner, "Providential Improvisation in *Measure for Measure*," *Publications of Modern Language Association of America* 97/2 (March 1982): 227–36; David Lloyd Stevenson, *The Achievement of Shakespeare's* Measure for Measure (Ithaca: Cornell University Press, 1966). Perhaps my view of Isabella should be modified somewhat by Rupin W. Desai's penetrating Freudian analysis: "Freudian Undertones in the Isabella-Angelo Relationship of *Measure for Measure*," *The Psychoanalytic Review* 64/4 (Winter 1977): 487–94.

29. See introd. and notes to *Pericles Prince of Tyre*, ed. James G. McManaway, in *The Pelican Shakespeare* (New York: Penguin, 1967, rpt. 1979).

30. Kirsch, *Shakespeare and the Experience of Love* (n. 17 above), pp. 144–73; Geoffrey Bullough, ed., *Narrative and Dramatic Sources of Shakespeare*, vol. 8 (London: Routledge & Kegan Paul, 1975), pp. 7, 35–37. In the quotation from *Cymbeline* 5.6, for purely traditional reasons, I cannot get myself to follow the reading of the New Oxford Shakespeare from which I make my Shakespeare citations and have her husband cry out four times in two lines "O Innogen."

31. Charles Frey, *Shakespeare's Vast Romance: A Study of* The Winter's Tale (Columbia: University of Missouri Press, 1980); Peter Lindenbaum, "Time, Sexual Love, and the Uses of Pastoral in *The Winter's Tale*," *Modern Language Quarterly* 33/1 (March 1972): 3–22; Martin Mueller, "Hermione's Wrinkles, or, Ovid Transformed: An Essay on *The Winter's Tale*," *Comparative Drama* 5 (1971): 226–39; Neely, *Broken Nuptials* (n. 12 above), pp. 192–209; J. H. P. Pafford, introd. to Arden edition of *Winter's Tale* (London: Methuen, 1963).

32. See John Vyvyan, *Shakespeare and the Rose of Love: A Study of the Early Plays in Relation to the Medieval Philosophy of Love* (London: Chatto & Windus, 1960), pp. 49, 51, 54, 56, 67; Richard Cody, *The Landscape of the Mind: Pastoralism and Platonic Theory in Tasso's Aminta and Shakespeare's Early Comedies*

(Oxford: Clarendon Press, 1969), pp. 114–26; Leggatt, *Shakespeare's Comedy of Love* (n. 12 above), pp. 62–84; Kristian Smidt, *Unconformities in Shakespeare's Early Comedies* (New York: St. Martin's Press, 1986), pp. 100–18.

33. C. S. Lewis, *English Literature in the Sixteenth Century Excluding Drama* (Oxford: Clarendon Press, 1954), p. 499. Allen is quoted in William Keach, *Elizabethan Erotic Narratives: Irony and Pathos in the Ovidian Poetry of Shakespeare, Marlowe, and Their Contemporaries* (New Brunswick, N.J.: Rutgers University Press, 1977), p. 66, and see pp. 52–84.

34. René Girard, "Love Delights in Praises: A Reading of *The Two Gentlemen of Verona*," *Philosophy and Literature* 13 (October 1989): 231–47; Smidt, *Unconformities* (n. 32 above), pp. 40–45; Vyvyan, *Shakespeare and the Rose of Love* (n. 32 above), pp. 132–35.

35. I accept the allocation of authorship as given by Eugene Waith. Fletcher was a skillful plot-designer and no doubt fully shared responsibility for the play as a whole. The language of Shakespeare is regularly superior—he often rivals himself at his best. All the direct quotations that follow are now usually ascribed to Shakespeare. See Eugene M. Waith, ed., *The Two Noble Kinsmen by William Shakespeare and John Fletcher* (New York: Oxford University Press, 1989); E. Talbot Donaldson, *The Swan at the Well: Shakespeare Reading Chaucer* (New Haven: Yale University Press, 1985), pp. 50–73; Philip Edwards, "On the Design of 'The Two Noble Kinsmen,'" *Review of English Literature* 5/4 (October 1964): 89–105. Una Ellis-Fermor's comments on the play are in *Shakespeare the Dramatist and Other Papers,* ed. Kenneth Muir (London: Methuen, 1961), pp. 177–86. See also Mary Beth Rose, *The Expense of Spirit: Love and Sexuality in English Renaissance Drama* (Ithaca: Cornell University Press, 1988), pp. 212–28; Ann Thompson, *Shakespeare's Chaucer: A Study in Literary Origins* (Liverpool: Liverpool University Press, 1978), pp. 170, 176, 178, 188, 205, 207, 212–13. The comment of B. J. Pendlebury may fit the mood of this play: "in his later years, Shakespeare became embittered on the subject of marriage." Pendlebury finds it ironic that the best picture of true partnership in marriage that Shakespeare gives us is that of Macbeth and his lady, of a "butcher and his fiend-like queen." ("Happy Ever After: Some Aspects of Marriage in Shakespeare's Plays," *Contemporary Review* 227 [1975]: 328).

36. I have earlier cited the late Talbot Donaldson's lyrical praise of Chaucer's Emily. Perhaps one reason he regards *The Two Noble Kinsmen* as "that most distressing of plays," not good, not bad, but "very unpleasant," is that the romanticism has been degraded and the female paragon has become ineffectual (E. Talbot Donaldson, *Swan at the Well* [n. 35 above], p. 5).

37. Stephen Booth, *Shakespeare's Sonnets* (New Haven: Yale University Press, 1977), for the definitive edition and for close verbal analysis, sometimes pointing up the sexual meanings. See Joseph Pequigney, *Such is My Love: A Study of Shakespeare's Sonnets* (Chicago: University of Chicago Press, 1985), for a persuasive statement of the sexual orientation of the speaker. See also John Bayley, "Who Was the 'Man Right Fair' of the Sonnets?" (London) *Times Literary*

Supplement, 4 January 1974, p. 15; John Sparrow, "Viewpoint," *Times Literary Supplement,* 1 March 1974, p. 210, and related correspondence; Joel Fineman, *Shakespeare's Perjured Eye: The Invention of Poetic Subjectivity in the Sonnets* (Berkeley: University of California Press, 1986); Martin Green, *The Labyrinth of Shakespeare's Sonnets: An Examination of Sexual Elements in Shakespeare's Language* (London: Charles Skilton, 1974); Thomas M. Greene, "Pitiful Thrivers: Failed Husbandry in the Sonnets," in *Shakespeare and the Question of Theory,* ed. Patricia Parker and Geoffrey Hartman (New York: Methuen, 1985), pp. 230-44; Edward Hubler, *The Sense of Shakespeare's Sonnets* (New York: Hill & Wang, 1952); John Klause, "Shakespeare's *Sonnets:* Age in Love and the Goring of Thoughts," *Studies in Philology* 80/3 (Summer 1983): 300-324; Kott, *Shakespeare Our Contemporary* (n. 5 above), pp. 191-236; Adena Rosmarin, "Hermeneutics Versus Erotics: Shakespeare's *Sonnets* and Interpretive History," *Publications of Modern Language Association of America* 100/1 (January 1985): 20-36; Edward A. Snow, "Loves of Comfort and Despair: A Reading of Shakespeare's Sonnet 138," *ELH* 47 (1980): 462-83.

38. C. S. Lewis, *English Literature* (n. 33 above), p. 503. For the insistence that the beloved man marry and produce a child, see Katharine M. Wilson, *Shakespeare's Sugared Sonnets* (London: Allen & Unwin, 1974), pp. 146-54. Wilson adduces stereotypes from other sequences and illuminating parallels to Erasmus (via Wilson's English). But can Shakespeare be said to "parody" these? The relationship of speaker to beloved and to the tradition is much more complex. *Parody* (1) weakens the intensity of the speaker's homoerotic love and his desire for beauty, which does not mock or invert usual heterosexual lyricism but in redirecting it repeats or, if anything, intensifies it; and *parody* (2) does not do justice to the linguistic brilliance, strength, sincerity, and originality of the imprecations.

39. Mario Untersteiner, quoted by Stephen Greenblatt, *Renaissance Self-Fashioning: From More to Shakespeare* (Chicago: University of Chicago Press, 1980), p. 294 n. 38.

40. Ranald, " 'As Marriage Binds' " (n. 2 above), p. 81; and Ranald, *Shakespeare and his Social Context* (n. 2 above), pp. 215-31.

41. Wheeler, *Shakespeare's Development* (n. 1 above), p. 203. I have found helpful his division of the tragedies into two types, the merger group and the autonomy/isolation group (pp. 201-10).

42. Lukács is quoted by Greenblatt, *Renaissance Self-Fashioning* (n. 39 above), p. 295 n. 42.

43. Harold S. Wilson, *On the Design of Shakespearean Tragedy* (Toronto: University of Toronto Press, 1957), p. 52; Frye, *Anatomy* (n. 21 above), p. 207.

44. Greenblatt, *Renaissance Self-Fashioning* (n. 39 above), pp. 232-54, especially pp. 239, 243, altogether a most stimulating analysis. See also Stanley Cavell, *The Claim of Reason: Wittgenstein, Skepticism, Morality, and Tragedy* (New York: Oxford University Press, 1979), pp. 486-92; Lynda E. Boose, "Othello's Handkerchief: 'The Recognizance and Pledge of Love,' " *English Lit-*

erary Renaissance 5 (Autumn 1975): 360–74; Barbara Everett, *Young Hamlet: Essays on Shakespeare's Tragedies* (Oxford: Clarendon Press, 1989), pp. 37–54; William Kerrigan, "The Personal Shakespeare: Three Clues," in *Shakespeare's Personality* (n. 26 above), pp. 175–90 (stresses "incongruous attraction" and "radical exogamy" in Shakespearean marriages); Kirsch, *Shakespeare and the Experience of Love* (n. 17 above), chap. 2; Neely, *Broken Nuptials* (n. 12 above), pp. 105–34 (one of whose fine insights is that *Othello* profoundly recalls Shakespeare's comedies [p. 109]); Novy, *Love's Argument* (n. 12 above), pp. 125–45; Rose, *Expense of Spirit* (n. 35 above), pp. 131–55 and chap. 3 (on tragedy, stressing the heroics of marriage); Edward A. Snow, "Sexual Anxiety and the Male Order of Things in *Othello,*" *English Literary Renaissance* 10 (1980): 384–412; Roger Stilling, *Love and Death in Renaissance Tragedy* (Baton Rouge: Louisiana State University Press, 1976), pp. 145–68.

45. William Whately is quoted by Rose, *Expense of Spirit* (n. 35 above), p. 121.

Epilogue

1. C. L. Barber, *Shakespeare's Festive Comedy: A Study of Dramatic Form and Its Relation to Social Custom* (Princeton, N.J.: Princeton University Press, 1972), p. 223.

2. John Bayley, *The Characters of Love: A Study in the Literature of Personality* (London: Constable, 1962), p. 139.

3. Northrop Frye luminously extends the sexuality of this poem and of "The Canonization" to our present concerns in professing the humanities and, more broadly, to the unions of all readers with their texts. "In the sexual union two separate egos form a soul that is still not quite a body; in the reading process the object as book and the subject as reader merge into an identity equally fragile and temporary. But the reader belongs to a community of readers, the text to a family of texts, so that both text and reader have the support of an extending world of a kind that sexual experience, confined, as it is to two individuals, cannot provide" (Frye, "Literary and Linguistic Scholarship in a Postliterate World," *Publications of Modern Language Association of America* 99/5 [October 1984]: 994).

4. *The Sermons of John Donne,* ed. George R. Potter and Evelyn Simpson, 10 vols. (Berkeley: University of California Press, 1955). I give volume and page for sermons quoted: 2:339, 345, 346, 347; 4:358; 8:97–98, 106.

5. *The Student Milton,* ed. Frank Allen Patterson (New York: F. S. Crofts, 1934), p. 741. Milton is quoted from this edition of the complete poems and much of the prose.

6. These and related passages are quoted and discussed in my *Sex and Sensibility: Ideal and Erotic Love from Milton to Mozart* (Chicago: University of Chicago Press, 1980), pp. 26–34.

7. Lawrence Stone, *The Family, Sex and Marriage in England 1500–1800* (New York: Harper & Row, 1977), p. 4 and passim. On Milton, see William Kerrigan and Gordon Braden, "Milton's Coy Eve: *Paradise Lost* and Renaissance Love Poetry," *ELH* 53/1 (1986): 27–51; Kerrigan and Braden, *The Idea of the Renaissance* (Baltimore: Johns Hopkins University Press, 1989), pp. 191–218 (a brilliant discussion of postponements in love and of the love chase that complements my several discussions of modesty and lack of consummations; Kerrigan, *The Sacred Complex: On the Psychogenesis of* Paradise Lost (Cambridge, Mass.: Harvard University Press, 1983); Sandra M. Gilbert, "Patriarchal Poetry and Women Readers: Reflections on Milton's Bogey," *Publications of Modern Language Association of America* 93/3 (May 1978): 368–82.

8. *Coleridge on Shakespeare,* ed. R. A. Foakes (Charlottesville: University Press of Virginia, 1971), p. 93.

INDEX

Abbott, Thomas K., 415n.34
Ackerman, Robert W., 462n.8
Adam and Eve, 141, 150–56, 176,
  239, 258, 345, 408, 445n.14,
  446n.17. *See also* Bible, Hebrew
Adams, Robert M., 437n.21
Adelman, Janet, 491n.26
Adkins, Arthur W. H., 85, 424n.44,
  431n.33
Adler, Alfred, 455n.14
Adonis, 43, 44, 84
Adultery, 3, 161, 175, 205, 206, 208,
  254, 259, 364
Aelred of Rievaulx, 213
Aers, David, 457n.22, 466n.38,
  467n.43, 469n.45
Aeschines of Sphettus, 429n.14
Aeschylus, *Oresteia,* 67–70, 90
Affection, 11–12
Agape, 6, 15–16, 56, 107, 159–60,
  172, 182, 333, 482n.22. *See also*
  God
Agrippa, Henry Cornelius, 300–301,
  303, 474n.20
Akrigg, G. P. V., 483n.26
Albertus Magnus, 217, 371, 490n.23
Alciphron, 105–6
Alexander III, Pope, 219
Allan of Lille, 211–12, 231, 267, 323
Allen, Archibald W., 437n.25
Allen, Don Cameron, 385, 492n.33
Allen, John, 472n.13
Allison, Henry E., 416n.35
Alter, Robert, 444n.14, 446n.18
Altieri, Marco Antonio, *Li Nuptiali,*
  311
Altman, Joel B., 490n.23
Amazons, 26–30, 27 (fig. 1), 32–34,
  419n.14, 488n.15; in Shakespeare

(metaphorical), 359. *See also* Ma-
  triarchy; Theseus
Ambrose, Bishop of Milan, 157, 192,
  193
Amor, 96, 111, 142; in Aquinas, 211;
  Ovid, 120–21
Amor and Psyche, 96–98, 99 (fig. 8)
Amor de lonh, 201, 240, 241
Amory, Anne, 425n.50
Anderson, Bonnie S., 473n.13
Anderson, David, 449n.8
Anderson, Douglas, 480n.14
Anderson, Graham, 106, 436n.16,
  440nn. 8, 9
Andromache, 57, 87–88, 90, 122
Anger, Rudolphus, 449n.7
Anglican Church, 302, 306. *See also*
  Book of Common Prayer
Annas, Julia, 432n.37
Anshem, Ruth Nanda, 416n.1
Anthony, Saint, 163
Antimachus of Colophon, 108,
  435n.11
Aphrodite, 34–36, 37 (fig. 4), 50, 70,
  75–77, 80, 81, 83, 84, 88, 90,
  423n.39, 435n.11; in Homer, 56–59
Apollo, 42, 69–70
Apollonius Rhodius, 425n.47
Apuleius, *The Golden Ass,* 96
Aquinas, Thomas, 210–11
Archer-Hind, Laura, 485n.32
Architecture (and love), 57
Arcimboldo, Giuseppe, 319
Aretino, Pietro, 307, 477n.31
Ariès, Philippe, 89, 433n.40,
  435n.11, 436n.19, 453n.5,
  456n.18, 459n.32, 461n.4
Aristophanes, 70–73, 91; *The
  Clouds,* 428n.11